WISC–IV
CLINICAL USE
AND
INTERPRETATION

SCIENTIST-PRACTITIONER PERSPECTIVES

EDITED BY

AURELIO PRIFITERA
Harcourt Assessment, Inc.
San Antonio, Texas

DONALD H. SAKLOFSKE
Department of Educational Psychology
University of Saskatchewan
Saskatoon, Saskatchewan, Canada

LAWRENCE G. WEISS
Harcourt Assessment, Inc.
San Antonio, Texas

ELSEVIER
ACADEMIC
PRESS

AMSTERDAM • BOSTON • HEIDELBERG • LONDON
NEW YORK • OXFORD • PARIS • SAN DIEGO
SAN FRANCISCO • SINGAPORE • SYDNEY • TOKYO

Elsevier Academic Press
200 Wheeler Road, 6th Floor, Burlington, MA 01803, USA
525 B Street, Suite 1900, San Diego, California 92101-4495, USA
84 Theobald's Road, London WC1X 8RR, UK

This book is printed on acid-free paper. ∞

Library of Congress Cataloging-in-Publication Data
WISC-IV clinical use and interpretation : scientist-practitioner perspectives / edited by Aurelio Prifitera ... [et al.].– 1st ed.
p. cm.
Includes bibliographical references and index.
ISBN 0-12-564931-2 (alk. paper)
1. Wechsler Intelligence Scale for Children. I. Title: WISC-4 clinical use and interpretation. II. Title: WISC-four clinical use and interpretation. III. Prifitera, Aurelio, 1952-
BF432.5.W42W57 2004
153.9'3–dc22   2004014750

British Library Cataloguing-in-Publication Data
A catalogue record for this book is available from the British Library

For all information on all Elsevier publications
visit our Web site at www.elsevier.com

Printed in the United States of America
04 05 06 07 08 09   9 8 7 6 5 4 3 2 1

CONTENTS

PART I

WISC-IV: FOUNDATIONS OF CLINICAL INTERPRETATION

1

THE WISC-IV IN THE CLINICAL ASSESSMENT CONTEXT

AURELIO PRIFITERA, DONALD H. SAKLOFSKE,
LAWRENCE G. WEISS, AND ERIC ROLFHUS

2

CLINICAL INTERPRETATION OF THE WISC-IV FSIQ AND GAI

DONALD H. SAKLOFSKE, AURELIO PRIFITERA, LAWRENCE
G. WEISS, ERIC ROLFHUS, AND JIANJUN ZHU

3

INTERPRETING THE WISC-IV INDEX SCORES

LAWRENCE G. WEISS, DONALD H. SAKLOFSKE,
AND AURELIO PRIFITERA

4

THE WISC-IV INTEGRATED

GEORGE MCCLOSKEY AND ART MAERLENDER

5

INTEGRATED MULTILEVEL MODEL FOR BRANCHING ASSESSMENT, INSTRUCTIONAL ASSESSMENT, AND PROFILE ASSESSMENT

VIRGINIA W. BERNINGER, ALNITA DUNN, AND TED ALPER

PART II:

THE WISC-IV AND THE ASSESSMENT OF EXCEPTIONAL CHILDREN

6

RESEARCH-SUPPORTED DIFFERENTIAL DIAGNOSIS OF SPECIFIC LEARNING DISABILITIES

VIRGINIA W. BERNINGER AND LOUISE O'DONNELL

7

ASSESSMENT OF ATTENTION DEFICIT HYPERACTIVITY DISORDER WITH THE WISC-IV

VICKI L. SCHWEAN AND DONALD H. SAKLOFSKE

8

ASSESSEMENT OF CHILDREN WHO ARE GIFTED WITH THE WISC-IV

SARA S. SPARROW, STEVEN I. PFEIFFER, AND TINA M. NEWMAN

9

ASSESSMENT OF MENTAL RETARDATION
JEAN SPRUILL, TOM OAKLAND, AND PATTI HARRISON

10

LANGUAGE DISABILITIES
ELISABETH H. WIIG

11

HARD-OF-HEARING AND DEAF CLIENTS: USING THE WISC-IV WITH CHILDREN WHO ARE HARD-OF-HEARING OR DEAF
JEFFERY P. BRADEN

12

CULTURAL CONSIDERATIONS IN THE USE OF THE WECHSLER INTELLIGENCE SCALE FOR CHILDREN—FOURTH EDITION (WISC-IV)

JOSETTE G. HARRIS AND ANTOLIN M. LLORENTE

13

THE WISC-IV AND NEUROPSYCHOLOGICAL ASSESSMENT

KEITH OWEN YEATES AND JACOBUS DONDERS

14

ASSESSMENT OF TEST BEHAVIORS WITH THE WISC-IV

THOMAS OAKLAND, JOSEPH GLUTTING, AND MARLEY W. WATKINS

LIST OF CONTRIBUTORS

Numbers in parentheses indicate the pages on which the authors' contributions begin.

Ted Alper (151), Department of Educational Psychology, California State University at Hayward, Hayward, California 94542

Virginia W. Berninger (151, 189), University of Washington, Seattle, Washington 98195

Jeffery P. Braden (351), Department of Psychology, North Carolina State University, Raleigh, North Carolina 27695

Jacobus Donders (415), Mary Free Bed Rehabilitation Hospital, Grand Rapids, Michigan 49503

Alnita Dunn (151), Special Education Division/Psychological Services, Los Angeles Unified School District, Los Angeles, CA 90017

Joseph Glutting (435), School of Education, University of Delaware, Newark, Delaware 19716

Josette G. Harris (381), Departments of Psychiatry and Neurology, University of Colorado School of Medicine, Denver, Colorado 80262

Patti Harrison (299), Department of Educational Studies in Psychology, The University of Alabama, Tuscaloosa, Alabama 35487

Antolin M. Llorente (381), Department of Pediatrics, University of Maryland School of Medicine, Baltimore, Maryland 21201

R. Stewart Longman (66), Psychology Department, Foothills Hospital, Calgary, Alberta, Canada

Art Maerlender (101), Clinical School Services and Learning Disorders Program, Child and Adolescent Psychiatry, Dartmouth Medical School, Lebanon, New Hampshire 03755

George McCloskey (101), Psychology Department, Philadelphia College of Osteopathic Medicine, Philadelphia, Pennsylvania 19131

Tina M. Newman (281), Yale Child Study Center, Yale University PACE (Psychology of Abilities, Competencies, and Expertise) Center, New Haven, Connecticut 06520

Louise O'Donnell (189), Harcourt Assessment, Inc., San Antonio, Texas 78259

Thomas Oakland (299, 435), University of Florida Research Foundation Professor, University of Florida, Gainesville, Florida 32611

Steven I. Pfeiffer (281), Department of Educational Psychology and Learning Systems, Florida State University, Tallahassee, Florida 32306

Aurelio Prifitera (3, 33, 71), Harcourt Assessment, Inc., San Antonio, Texas 78259

Eric Rolfhus (3, 33), Harcourt Assessment, Inc., San Antonio, Texas 78259

Donald H. Saklofske (3, 33, 71, 235), Department of Educational Psychology and Special Education, University of Saskatchewan, Saskatoon, Saskatchewan, Canada S7N 0X1

Vicki L. Schwean (235), Department of Educational Psychology and Special Education, University of Saskatchewan, Saskatoon, Saskatchewan, Canada S7N 0X1

Sara S. Sparrow (281), Yale Child Study Center, Yale University PACE (Psychology of Abilities, Competencies, and Expertise) Center, New Haven, Connecticut 06520

Jean Spruill (299), Psychology Clinic, The University of Alabama, Tuscaloosa, Alabama 35487

Marley W. Watkins (435), Educational Psychology, Pennsylvania State University, University Park, Pennsylvania 16802

Lawrence G. Weiss (3, 33, 71), Harcourt Assessment, Inc., San Antonio, Texas 78259

Elisabeth H. Wiig (333), Knowledge Research Institute, Inc., Arlington, Texas 76016

Keith Owen Yeates (415), Columbus Children's Research Institute, Department of Pediatrics, The Ohio State University, Columbus, Ohio 43205

Jianjun Zhu (33), Harcourt Assessment, Inc., San Antonio, Texas 78259

PREFACE

Like its predecessors, the Wechsler Intelligence Scale for Children—Fourth Edition (WISC-IV) is expected to continue to be the most widely used measure for assessing the cognitive abilities of children by clinicians and researchers around the world. Because of the widespread use of Wechsler intelligence tests by school and child clinical psychologists, we earlier published *WISC-III Clinical Use and Interpretation* (Prifitera & Saklofske, 1998). That book originated from our perception that there is a need for books and information sources that focus more on the clinical use and interpretation of the Wechsler tests with exceptional children than on the psychometric descriptions of the test and test scores. The original edition of the book appeared 7 years after the publication of the test. In contrast, the chapters in this new edition were written only a year or so after publication of WISC-IV. As such, there is less material in the research literature for the chapter authors to use, although many studies and articles are in process and will soon be coming out in the literature. On the other hand, the depth of clinical experience found in our current team of authors and their familiarity with the WISC-III and WISC-IV suggested that this book could be published sooner as a current reference for practicing psychologists.

Because the WISC-IV is a revision of a well-known, well-researched, and rich clinical instrument, much of what we know about previous editions can be adapted to our understanding of the WISC-IV, especially its clinical use. The WISC-IV technical manual contains more validity data than other editions, which will certainly assist the clinician and researcher in using the scale and understanding its psychometric underpinnings. When some of the editors of this volume worked on the development of WISC-III, it became clear that more validity and psychometric information needed to be included with the test. Comparing the size and scope of the technical manuals of the WISC-R published in 1974 to the WISC-III published in 1991, and now to the WISC-IV published in 2003, attests to the increase in pages that present more validity studies, psychometric data, and interpretive information. Therefore, we know much more about the test at the time of publication than we did with previous editions. This trend has spread to other cognitive measures as well, in part because of the precedent work done on WISC-III, and because there is a much greater attention by test publishers and developers to best test practice as presented in the *Standards for Educational and Psychological Testing* (American Educational Research Association, American Psychological Association, and National Council on Measurement in Education, 1999).

While more WISC-IV psychometric data, research, and validation work are now available at time of publication in the test manuals, the chapters in this book are written primarily for the clinician who approaches practice from a scientist-practitioner model. The clinician often is confronted with unique situations that require clinical judgment and intuition that must be tethered by research and scientific data and discipline. While research, normative information, and data can help address many issues, the clinician often must combine and integrate such information with clinical history and judgment that makes each case somewhat different and often unique. This challenge gets at the distinction between psychological testing and assessment described by Matarazzo (1990) and others such as Kaufman (1994).

In this volume, we attempted to select topics that addressed some of the more common clinical diagnostic groups and interpretive issues. The first three chapters, authored by the editors, provide a general introduction and give a background on the WISC-IV as it relates to clinical and research use. We present some new data on the WISC-IV, not published elsewhere, with relevance for clinical interpretation but also because it will further serve as a general orientation to WISC-IV interpretation. Chapters 3 and 4 offer an extended description of the four index scores (Verbal Comprehension, Perceptual Reasoning, Working Memory, Processing Speed) but also discuss the relevance of the Full Scale IQ (and General Ability Index) in clinical assessment. We have included a chapter that describes the WISC-IV Integrated that provides a process-based approach to WISC-IV use and score interpretation.

The remaining chapters, while focused on the WISC-IV, are as much about how to assess individuals with specific disorders. Again, tests such as the WISC are part of an overall assessment and to discuss any one test outside of the clinical context is somewhat artificial. The chapters by Berninger and colleagues present some of the newest thinking and approaches on looking at diagnostic testing from a broader model, based on a long-term research program at the University of Washington. The WISC and other measures discussed are viewed in the context of these broader diagnostic issues. Other chapters by respective experts in their fields address more specific and special groups (e.g., ADHD, MR, etc.) and discuss what we know about the Wechsler scales and the WISC-IV in particular in the context of increasing our understanding of individuals with a particular background or disorder. In the end, it is an understanding of the individual that is the goal of any assessment, and the WISC-IV, like its predecessors, will be an essential tool in meeting that goal. Like any good psychological assessment tool, the WISC-IV needs to be used by an astute clinician. If we contribute to improving the use of this test by clinicians and researchers alike, we will consider this work a successful endeavor.

We wish to express our gratitude to the expert authors; it was their chapter contributions that made this book possible. They are exemplars of best practices in psychological assessment. Nikki Levy, our publisher at Elsevier, gave us the necessary support and showed us patience. We thank her for her belief in the book and its value for the professional community. We also appreciate the work of Elsevier staff Brandy Palacios, Barbara Makinster, Sheryl Avruch, and Trevor Daul to bring this book to completion. We acknowledge the support of the Harcourt Assessment (The Psychological Corporation) and the University of Saskatchewan. As always, a "special thanks" goes to our families for their support and willingness to give of themselves so that we can pursue our professional aspirations. Finally, we wish to thank the many children and their parents who allow us into their lives to conduct research and gain better clinical understanding. It is only through their involvement that our professional knowledge can grow.

PART I

WISC-IV: FOUNDATIONS OF CLINICAL INTERPRETATION

1

THE WISC-IV IN THE CLINICAL ASSESSMENT CONTEXT

AURELIO PRIFITERA

Harcourt Assessment, Inc.
San Antonio, Texas

DONALD H. SAKLOFSKE

Department of Educational Psychology
and Special Education,
University of Saskatchewan
Saskatoon, Saskatchewan, Canada

LAWRENCE G. WEISS

Harcourt Assessment, Inc.
San Antonio, Texas

ERIC ROLFHUS

Harcourt Assessment, Inc.
San Antonio, Texas

INTRODUCTION AND OVERVIEW OF THIS CHAPTER

The purpose of this book is to present information, research findings, and clinical thinking related to psychological and psychoeducational assessment issues in which the Wechsler Intelligence Scale for Children—Fourth Edition (WISC-IV) is part of the assessment battery. Each chapter contains both research and clinical findings pertaining to the use of WISC-IV that are related to assessment issues and/or clinical groups. This introductory chapter, like the introductory chapter to the last version of this book (WISC-III Clinical Use and Interpretation, Prifitera & Saklofske, 1998), is not intended to give an extensive overview and description of the WISC-IV. Because of the widespread use of the Wechsler scales by practitioners and researchers, properties of these scales are well known and full descriptions of the Wechsler scales can be found in other sources (e.g., Anastasi & Urbina, 1997; Kaufman, 1994; Sattler, 1988, 1992, 2001; Wechsler, 1991, 1997); and the WISC-IV in particular in Flanagan and Kaufman (in press), Sattler and Dumont (in press), and Wechsler (2003, 2004). However, because the changes in WISC-IV are more substantial than in previous revisions of the test, we will discuss the goals of the revision, describe some of the most important changes and new content in WISC-IV in addition to highlighting several critical elements that will be of benefit in the interpretation of the scale and understanding of what the scale is best suited for. Therefore, as in the previous version of this chapter on the WISC-III, topics addressed will be selective based on what the authors believe are issues that are often not well understood or neglected when using and interpreting the test, as well as selected topics that may not be readily available elsewhere.

To that end, we provide a brief description of the scale and rationale for its revision; we then discuss selected topics that we hope will assist practitioners and researchers when interpreting the results of the scale including the role of the WISC-IV *as part* of a psychological assessment rather than an end in itself, and its role in diagnosis. We also report data on group results of test scores with minority groups in the United States sample and discuss validity in other countries. Approaches to subtest and scale interpretation, which were included in Chapter 1 of the WISC-III edition of this book, are now included in Chapter 3 with expanded interpretation.

These topic areas were selected either because they have not been discussed in detail in the available literature (e.g., performance of minority groups on the WISC-IV) or to elaborate on the utility of intelligence tests in general and the WISC-IV in particular within the context of clinical assessment. All too often the assessment is viewed as synonymous with testing and diagnosis is viewed as synonymous with test scores, which, throughout the chapters that follow, we strongly propose are misguided assumptions in both our clinical work and research.

DESCRIPTION, RATIONALE, AND GOALS FOR THE REVISION

The WISC-IV (2003) is the latest revision of the scale, which has its roots in the Wechsler Bellevue Form II published in 1946 by Wechsler. Its predecessors, the WISC-III, WISC-R, and WISC, were published in 1991, 1974, and 1949, respectively. Until the publication of WISC-IV, the WISC-III, like its predecessor the WISC-R, continued to be the most widely used assessment of intellectual functioning of children (Reschly, 1997), and the expectation is that WISC-IV will continue in that role. A trend that is obvious from the publication dates is that revision cycles have become shorter. Shorter cycles have become important and necessary for a number of reasons including more rigorous standards (APA test standards) (American Educational Research Association, 1999), content becoming outdated more quickly than in the past, advances in the field of cognitive/ intellectual assessment, changing needs and requirements to meet certain government regulations such as IDEA in the United States, growing awareness of the presence of the Flynn effect (Flynn, 1987), the need to link to newer versions of achievement tests (e.g., WIAT-II, 2001), changing demographic patterns within the population, and the need to replace outdated norms. Kanaya, Scullin, & Ceci (2003) describe the issues of the potential adverse impact when age and test revision cycles are not taken into account.

As is evident by the chapters in this volume, the WISC-IV is used in a variety of ways and for a variety of purposes in research, clinical evaluations, and for other types of assessments and uses. Its strength has been its robustness and its ability to provide valuable information in a wide variety of assessments including neuropsychological assessments, a field that was in its infancy when Wechsler began developing his scales. The WISC-III as a Process Instrument (WISC-III PI) introduced a process based on this approach to assessment developed by Dr. Edith Kaplan and her coauthors (1999) and first introduced into the Wechsler Scales in 1991 (Kaplan et al., 1991). One of the major innovations for WISC-IV is the incorporation of the process approach into the WISC-IV from the beginning. The WISC-IV is published in two versions. The WISC-IV contains the revisions to the core of the test and is the major part of the revision to WISC-III. The WISC-IV Integrated (2004) incorporates and expands the process approach to assessment and clinical interpretation from the WISC-III PI and integrates this approach into one manual and record form and combined set of stimulus materials for those wishing to incorporate this approach into their assessment tools and technique. The chapter in this book by McCloskey and Maerlender (Chapter 4) is devoted to the process approach. This innovation expands the domains of psychological processes assessed by the WISC and provides a useful clinical tool for testing limits, improving clinical and diagnostic sensitivity, and developing intervention strategies. In addition, a quick screener for evaluating core processes, such as phonological processes for helping to evaluate and diagnose reading disorders, is now also available as part of the WISC offering (Early Reading Success Screener, 2004). This screening for evaluating key processes underlying reading in young children is consistent with much of the research and educational policy issues underlying the US Federal Reading First and No Child Left Behind legislative initiatives. These changes, additions of new subtests, and other improvements and innovations take WISC-IV far beyond most standard test revisions. In addition, the links to other scales, as discussed later and in the rest of the chapters in this volume, provide the clinician with a wealth of information for a comprehensive and integrated assessment.

NEED FOR NEW NORMS

One of the primary reasons for a revision is that scores become inflated over time and norms need to be reestablished. This phenomenon is well documented and has been referred to as the Flynn effect (Flynn, 1984). Therefore, one of the primary reasons for revising the WISC-IV was to develop current norms that would give more precise scores for individuals. Data from the WISC-IV manual suggests that WISC-IV composite scores are 2 to 4 points lower than the WISC-III, with performance subtests accounting for larger differences than verbal tasks. Therefore when comparing WISC-III and WISC-IV scores, expected differences between verbal and performance tasks should be taken into account in interpretation. Also, it must be remembered that these differences are averages across the standardization sample, and any one child will likely vary from these averages. Nonetheless, these averages are a relevant piece of information to take into account when interpreting changes. Other issues that may impact changes across time include developmental growth trajectories of that individual, impact of conditions such as learning disability, educational opportunities, and social-emotional factors.

In addition to changes in norms, test items become outdated and need to be revised to avoid bias and address other validity issues. Changes in test materials and items to make them more contemporary and appropriate to examinees was another reason for the revision. All items were reviewed for bias and either modified or replaced to address fairness. Exploratory and confirmatory factor analyses were conducted to clarify the factor structure of the scale and aid in interpretation. Ever since the original factor analyses of the Wechsler scales conducted by Cohen (1957, 1959), there has been debate regarding whether the WISC and other Wechsler Scales are best described in terms of one, two, or three factors. There has been much controversy about the third factor, which Cohen named "freedom from distractibility." It is now fairly well accepted that this traditional third factor is not a pure measure of distractibility or hyperactivity even though it has often been interpreted in that fashion (Kaufman, 1994; Wielkiewicz, 1990).

There has been some difference of opinion among both researchers and clinicians over the four-factor solution and the use of the four index scores as an alternative to the traditional Verbal IQ, Performance IQ, and Full Scale IQ scores. Sattler (1992), for example, initially suggested that a three-factor solution was more appropriate using the criterion of eigenvalues greater than 1 to determine the number of factors to interpret; more recently Sattler and Saklofske (2001) described support for the four-factor structure. Reynolds and Ford (1994) concluded that a three-factor solution is most consistent across the age range. Other analyses using both exploratory and confirmatory factor analyses (Wechsler, 1991; Roid, Prifitera, & Weiss 1993; Roid & Worrall, 1996, 1997) have found evidence for the four-factor solution in the original WISC-III standardization sample and have replicated it in countries outside the United States as well (e.g., Saklofske, Hildebrand, & Gorsuch, 2000). Also, Blaha and Wallbrown (1996) found support for the four-factor solution. Studies by Konold, Kush, & Canivez (1997) and Grice, Krohn, & Logerquist (1999) found support for the four-factor structure among learning disabled populations. However, other studies have found a three-factor solution more appropriate for children of Hispanic origin (Logerquist-Hansen & Barona, 1994). Still, the vast majority of studies with the WISC-III have consistently demonstrated a four-factor solution (Roid & Worrall, 1997; Grice, Krohn, & Logerquist, 1999; Blaha & Wallbrown, 1996; Konold, Kush, & Canivez, 1997). In addition, there is ample cross-cultural validation of the WISC-III factor structure (Georgas, Weiss, von de Vijver, & Saklofske, 2003). More to the point, the WISC-IV standardization data clearly support a four-factor solution (Wechsler, 2003).

One reason for the controversy over the factor structure of the WISC-III is the difference in using factor analysis as the sole-criterion for determining how many factors to interpret in contrast to using factor analysis as a tool to inform how best to interpret relationships among subtests and examine what latent underlying abilities groups of subtests may have in common. Analysis of the WISC-III subtests and factor structure has found that there are differences among clinical groups in their patterns of subtest and factor scores. For example, children with mental retardation show consistent scores across the first three index scores but have an elevated Processing Speed score on the WISC-III and WISC-IV. Children identified as gifted, however, show a relatively lower score on the WISC-IV Processing Speed and Working Memory Indexes compared to scores on the first two factors, which are about equal to each other (Wechsler, 2003). Looking at groups with learning disabilities and attention deficit disorders, Prifitera and Dersh (1993) found relatively lower WISC-III scores on the FD and PS index score compared to normal population and a high base rate of the ACID Profile. The same pattern with lower scores on the third and fourth factors compared to the first two were also found in the WISC-IV ADD group referenced in the manual, but the differences were not as pronounced as in the WISC-III. These results for learning disabled (LD) and attention deficit–hyperactivity disorder (ADHD) groups are similar to those reported in other research (Schwean, Saklofske, Yackulic, & Quinn 1993; Thomson, 1991; Wechsler, 1991).

More evidence for the validity of the four-factor structure is reported in a recently published study by Donders (1997) who found that the WISC-III Perceptual Organization and Processing Speed index scores are depressed in children with traumatic brain injury compared to the other scores. Also, depressed scores on these two indexes are relatively uncommon in the WISC-III standardization sample. Later in this chapter, analysis of minority group data also provides evidence for the use of these scores. These studies are cited to point out that by not including the four-factor structure, one would miss some very important information about these groups and individuals. So one must look at not only the various factor analytic criteria used to determine how many factors make sense but also at the psychological meaningfulness of the factors (Snook & Gorsuch, 1989), as well as clinical information. While the WISC-IV is too new to have additional published factor analytical criteria beyond those in the manual, the expectation is that the WISC-IV, like its predecessor, will demonstrate a robust factor structure.

One must not confuse the fact that a group has relatively lower scores on a test or group of subtests with the fact that any one individual will have low scores in the same areas. Knowledge of scores at the group level is useful in generating hypotheses about the individual case but does not confirm the hypothesis about an individual. Therefore patterns of performance of groups should inform interpretation by the clinician, but should not dictate it. This theme is the central point of this chapter and is discussed in more detail later and illustrated in several of the chapters that follow.

With WISC-IV, the primary scores are now derivatives of the four-factor-based index scores rather than the traditional Verbal and Performance scale of previous Wechsler tests. These are the Verbal Comprehension index (VCI), the Perceptual Reasoning index (PRI), the Working Memory index (WMI), and the Processing Speed index (PSI). The Full Scale IQ score continues to be the general composite score for the entire scale.

Figure 1.1 and Table 1.1 show the factor-based index structure and corresponding subtests with accompanying descriptions of each subtest. Also, Table 1.2 summarizes the subtests modifications made in the WISC-IV.

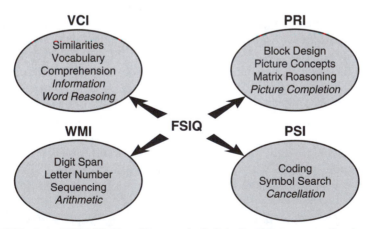

FIGURE 1.1 WISC-IV Test Framework Italicized subtests are optional subtests. From Wechsler *Intelligence Scale for Children—Fourth Edition*. Copyright © 2003 by The Psychological Corporation. Used by permission. All rights reserved.

TABLE 1.1 Abbreviations and Descriptions of Subtests.

Subtest	Abbreviation	Description
Block Design	BD	While viewing a constructed model or a picture in the Stimulus Book, the child uses red-and-white blocks to re-create the design within a specified time limit.
Similarities	SI	The child is presented with two words that represent common objects or concepts and describes how they are similar.
Digit Span	DS	For Digit Span Forward, the child repeats numbers in the same order as presented aloud by the examiner. For Digit Span Backward, the child repeats numbers in the reverse order of that presented aloud by the examiner.
Picture Concepts	PCn	The child is presented with two or three rows of pictures and chooses one picture from each row to form a group with a common characteristic.
Coding	CD	The child copies symbols that are paired with simple geometric shapes or numbers. Using a key, the child draws each symbol in its corresponding shape or box within a specified time limit.
Vocabulary	VC	For Picture Items, the child names pictures that are displayed in the Stimulus Book. For Verbal Items, the child gives definitions for words that the examiner reads aloud.
Letter–Number Sequencing	LN	The child is read a sequence of numbers and letters and recalls the numbers in ascending order and the letters in alphabetical order.
Matrix Reasoning	MR	The child looks at an incomplete matrix and selects the missing portion from five response options.
Comprehension	CO	The child answers questions based on his or her understanding of general principles and social situations.
Symbol Search	SS	The child scans a search group and indicates whether the target symbol(s) matches any of the symbols in the search group within a specified time limit.
Picture Completion	PCm	The child views a picture and then points to or names the important part missing within a specified time limit.
Cancellation	CA	The child scans both a random and a structured arrangement of pictures and marks target pictures within a specified time limit.
Information	IN	The child answers questions that address a broad range of general knowledge topics.
Arithmetic	AR	The child mentally solves a series of orally presented arithmetic problems within a specified time limit.
Word Reasoning	WR	The child identifies the common concept being described in a series of clues.

From Wechsler *Intelligence Scale for Children—Fourth Edition.* Copyright © 2003 by The Psychological Corporation. Used by permission. All rights reserved.

TABLE 1.2   WISC-IV Subtest Modifications.

	New Subtest	Administration	Recording & Scoring	New Items
Block Design		√	√	√
Similarities		√	√	√
Digit Span		√	√	√
Picture Concepts	√			
Coding		√	√	
Vocabulary		√	√	√
Letter–Number Sequencing	√			
Matrix Reasoning	√			
Comprehension		√	√	√
Symbol Search		√	√	√
Picture Completion		√	√	√
Cancellation	√			
Information			√	√
Arithmetic		√	√	√
Word Reasoning	√			

From *Wechsler Intelligence Scale for Children—Fourth Edition*. Copyright © 2003 by The Psychological Corporation. Used by permission. All rights reserved.

This configuration of subtests helps to accomplish several of the revision goals. First, the WISC-IV configuration of core subtests results in a quicker administration time. Some of the longer subtests such as Object Assembly and Picture Arrangement have been eliminated. Also, these tasks had lower reliabilities, and research did not support their utility in clinical assessment or diagnosis. For example, there was no compelling evidence that Picture Arrangement was a strong measure of social reasoning or sequencing ability as commonly thought. Elimination of these subtests also resulted in a drastic reduction of reliance on speed in the test scores, thus allowing ability to be measured separately from speed. Clinicians often found that the reliance on speed on some tasks unduly depressed scores for some children, which this change reduces.

Use of the VCI and PRI indexes as compared to the Verbal IQ/Performance IQ used in previous Wechsler versions provides purer measures of verbal comprehension and perceptual or nonverbal reasoning. The addition of several new subtests such as Matrix Reasoning, Picture Concepts, and Word Reasoning provides more measures of fluid reasoning and assesses the ability to reason with novel and less crystallized knowledge and information.

Some subtests that were formerly included on the Verbal and Performance scales, such as Digit Span, Arithmetic, Symbol Search, and Coding, are now calculated only as part of the WMI and PSI scores because of their factor loadings.

Adding the Letter–Number sequencing task along with Digit Span in the Working Memory Index provides a clearer picture of working memory and abandons the moniker "Freedom from Distractibility" for this factor. "Working Memory" is a more appropriate representation of the construct and avoids the ambiguity of the Freedom from Distraction Index (FDI) name, although the FDI in the WISC-III was described very much along the lines as being a working memory factor. This view of this factor is more in keeping with contemporary theories of cognition and working memory (Baddeley, 1997) and is discussed in Chapter 3. While Arithmetic can still be used as a supplemental subtest for this index, the working memory component of the Arithmetic task was confounded by arithmetical skills, which is now eliminated with use of the Letter–Number task. Arithmetic was kept in the battery because it is both a useful task that taps working memory (assuming the child had grade-appropriate numerical skills) and it is highly predictive of academic performance. In addition, the supplemental and testing-of-the-limits procedures in the WISC-IV integrated (see Chapter 4 in this volume) provide for rich clinical information for informing intervention and instructional strategies.

The fourth factor, Processing Speed, has not changed much from the WISC-III and includes the same two subtests. Coding and Symbol Search still make up this factor. However, another subtest, Cancellation, was included as a supplemental task. By giving prominence to the factor scores in WISC-IV compared to VIQ/PIQ, more focus is given to this construct, which has been related to mental capacity and reasoning through efficient use and conservation of cognitive resources.

The change to greater reliance on the index scores, coupled with changes in the composition of the subtests in WISC-IV, should be kept in mind when interpreting WISC-IV scores, especially in relationship to WISC-III scores. Including more subtests from the third and fourth factors, while having a theoretical rationale, does result in 40% as opposed to 20% of the subtest scores from these later indexes, contributing to the FSIQ in the newest version of the test. This may be one of the reasons that children identified as gifted have slightly lower FSIQ scores on the WISC-IV compared to the WISC-III. Gifted students tend to score lower on the third and fourth factors than on the first two, so a heavier weighting of these two factors probably contributes to a lower score. Also, the Arithmetic subtest on which gifted students scored high is now a supplemental test, thus further contributing to differences. Nonetheless, the increased information from the new subtests and structure on fluid reasoning, reduced reliance on speed, and working memory add significant new dimensions that compensate for the direct comparison differences that need to be taken into account. In addition, for those who want to base judgments on a purer measure of "g" or general intelligence, Chapter 3 of this volume contains information on the use of the GAI or General Ability index.

One of the most significant changes in the development of WISC-IV is the increased reliance on clinical data to make decisions on item and subtest retentions and overall interpretation. Numerous studies with clinical groups, described in the WISC-IV manual, were undertaken to provide assistance to the clinician when interpreting scores. In addition, like the WAIS-III, an oversample of low-ability children was included in the standardization sample to allow for proper scaling of scores in the lower ranges. IQ scores now range as low as 40, which allow for better measurement at this lower range than previous editions. In addition, more than 15 clinical and special studies were conducted as an aid to scale development and interpretation. While more research clearly is needed to confirm the result and utility of such studies, publishing such data in the manual provides useful information on such populations with the release of the test. Also a number of special studies were conducted to link or correlate the WISC-IV with other measures of constructs commonly assessed. These include achievement, adaptive behavior, giftedness, and memory. Other Wechsler intelligence scales are summarized and discussed in the WISC-IV technical manual.

The link to the WIAT-II allows for direct assessment of ability achievement discrepancies. This is useful for the evaluation of learning disabilities and other learning disorders. Having linking data on these two scales allows use of the regression approach to ability-achievement comparisons, which is the preferred methods for making such comparisons (Reynolds & Kaiser, 2003). Scoring software such as the WISC-IV Scoring Assistant and Writer facilitates such analyses. The topics of use, methodology, and interpretation of such discrepancies are discussed in the WISC-IV and WIAT-II manuals and not repeated here. However, the issue of using such differences in evaluating learning problems in light of pending changes in IDEA legislation is an important consideration that deserves some additional discussion here.

First, the pending IDEA legislation re-authorizing IDEA includes language to the effect that use of the ability-achievement discrepancy is not required to be used for diagnosis or for eligibility purposes. However, the language also states that the discrepancy can be used by the local education agency. Cautions against its use were introduced because of the lack of validity of the ability-achievement discrepancy for the diagnosis of a Specific Learning Disability (SLD), and in particular for reading disability. As an alternative, a response to intervention model (RTI) is recommended. However, the problem with the RTI model is that there are no validity studies cited to support its use or that demonstrate it as a more reliable and valid alternative. Hale, Naglieri, Kaufman, and Kavale (2003) provide a well-reasoned treatment of this issue. In that article they remind us that the diagnosis of a specific learning disability still requires an assessment of basic psychological processes, and caution should be taken not to rely on the RTI model, as it is scientifically unfounded to date. Rich clinical assessment that includes cognitive and intellectual assessment is needed as part of an assessment for LD regardless of the status of the ability-achievement discrepancy model as a basis for service eligibility. As they state: "even without the requirement of an ability-achievement discrepancy as part of the formal definition of SLD, the conceptual definition of SLD (based on old and new IDEA guidelines) implies a discrepancy between intact processes and those that are disordered. To measure these areas of integrity and deficit, we strongly believe that well-validated, reliable, stable, and well-normed cognitive tests need to be part of the assessment approach" (p. 11). Scruggs and Mastropieri (2002) provide similar cautions surrounding the abandonment of discrepancy models.

A recent study by Shaywitz *et al.* (2003) found IQ differences among persistently poor readers, improved readers, and nonimpaired readers both as children and adults. Discrepancies between IQ and achievement scores were found at first grade in the poor reader and the improved reader group but not in the nonimpaired group. The authors conclude that better cognitive ability may compensate for reading disabilities.

Most clinicians would agree that ability-achievement differences are important in understanding a child. Unexpected low achievement scores in light of high ability scores is certainly an area for the clinician to investigate even though such a discrepancy may not be the hallmark criterion for diagnosis of SLD. These issues are most thoroughly addressed by Berninger *et al.* in Chapter 6. In addition, intelligence tests are used for other types of assessments than SLD, many of which are discussed in this book.

BACK TO GORDON ALLPORT AND HENRY MURRAY: VIEWS ON WISC-III/WISC-IV AS A DIAGNOSTIC INSTRUMENT

This section of the chapter, which was in the WISC-III edition of this book, has been kept intact with minimal modification. It is the authors' belief that this section portrays a view of assessment that is consistent with Wechsler's clinical approach in which understanding of the individual is paramount and test scores are subservient to that end (see Tulsky, Saklofske, & Ricker, 2003; Tulsky, Saklofske, & Zhu, 2003). In all too many cases, there is overreliance on scores and not enough on the clinician and clinical judgment.

Allport and Murray were known as personologists. These two grand figures in the history of psychology provided theoretical and clinically rich descriptions of the person. As such they pursued both the nomothetic and the idiographic dimensions of personality, although Allport was probably more radical in his viewpoint on the uniqueness of the individual. In the nomothetic approach, one searches for general rules and laws that apply to all individuals. In the idiographic approach, strongly advocated by Allport, the best way to understand the person is to view the person as having unique characteristics or personal dispositions. The combinations and interactions of these unique characteristics allow nearly infinite variations of individuals. According to Allport, "each individual is an idiom unto himself, an apparent violation of the syntax of the species" (1955, p. 22). Note that in such a view of the person, issues like score scatter on subtest are viewed not as psychometric anomalies due to unfortunate vagaries and the confound of measurement error but rather as an expression of individuality that should be explored and understood. While it might be cleaner to have all scores line up as one would expect due to factor structure or other theoretical premises, it just may be the nature of the beast that people express abilities and subabilities in different ways that are not necessarily uniform. Furthermore Allport said "all the animals of the world are psychologically less distinct from one another than one man is from other men" (p. 23). This radical idiographic view underscores the notion in Allport's mind that generalizations are limited in helping us understand the uniqueness of the individual.

Murray, who first used the term *personology* in 1938, maintained that the unit of study should be the individual. However, he was not as radical a believer in the idiographic approach as Allport. Still, both are considered personologists whose primary interest is in the "complexity and *individuality* of human life" (Maddi, 1976, p. 7, authors, italics).

So what does all of this discussion of personology have to do with the Wechsler tests and intellectual assessment? Everything! Wechsler maintained that intelligence is part of the expression of the whole of personality. This is consistent with personology, which seeks to understand the whole person, which obviously included his or her intelligence. Also, Wechsler maintained that his tests measure only part of intelligence, the intellective aspects and that the nonintellective aspects were not measured well by his scales. Wechsler at heart was a personologist who was most interested in understanding the person in all his or her complexity. Matarazzo, in his preface to the WISC-III manual states that

> Wechsler was first and foremost a practicing clinician, with keenly honed skills and decades of experience in individual assessment. His many years of experience with children and adults impressed upon him that intelligence is more than what we are able to measure with tests of psychometric-cognitive performance. Rather, he early discerned that intelligence is a global capacity of the individual and that it is a product of both the individual's genetic makeup on one hand, and the individual's socio-educational experiences, drives, motivation, and personality predilections on the other. Because of the complex interplay of these multiple influences, Wechsler avoided the role of an intelligence-tester or psychometrist-technician. Rather, as did Alfred Binet before him, Wechsler became a practitioner skilled in the art of psychological assessment. Psychological assessment is a clinical activity that employs test scores, but only as one of the sources from which an astute clinician develops a well-integrated and comprehensive psychological portrait of the adult or child examined.

In his article, "Cognitive, Conative, and Non-Intellective Intelligence" written in 1950, Wechsler said

> factors other than intellectual contribute to achievement in areas whereas in the case of leaning, intellectual factors have until recently been considered uniquely determinate, and, second, that these other factors have to do with functions and abilities hitherto considered traits in personality. Among those partially identified so far are factors relating primarily to the conative functions like drive, persistence, will and perseveration, or in some instances, to aspects of temperament that pertain to interests and achievement.... that personality traits *enter into* the effectiveness of intelligent behavior, and hence, into any global concept of intelligence itself. (pp. 45–46)

The view that personality (as well as other variables) is related to intelligent behavior persists in practice as well as in the professional literature (Ackerman & Heggestad, 1997; Ackerman & Beier, 2003; Saklofske & Zeidner, 1995; Saklofske, Austin, Matthews, Zeidner, Schwean, & Groth-Marnat, 2003).

USE OF IQ TEST INFORMATION AS PART OF ASSESSMENT

So if Wechsler viewed himself as a personologist and clinician first and the test as a tool to understand the person, to what uses is it best to put intelligence tests and scores? First of all, regardless of the referral question, users of intelligence tests need to remember that tests yield information that is part of the diagnostic and decision-making process and they are not that process in and of themselves. In both psychology and education, it is rare that one test or score is in and of itself diagnostic of a specific disorder. The approaches to test interpretation and assessment advocated by Kaufman (1994), Kamphaus (1993), Matarazzo (1990), and others speak to the need to view test results as tools used by a clinician in the evaluation process whether for diagnosis, intervention planning, classification, description, etc. Test results need to be viewed in the context of other information and knowledge about the person. The clinician, then, based on knowledge of the patient, which includes a wide variety of sources only one of which is test information, looks across the information to confirm or disconfirm hypotheses of either an a priori or a posteriori nature.

Think of what happens when we go to a medical doctor complaining of headaches. The physician takes our temperature, blood pressure, medical history, and perform other aspects of a physical examination. Then let's say the result is that we have a high blood pressure reading. Is the diagnosis of hypertension given by the physician based on the results of the scores derived from the sphygmomanometer reading alone? Probably not because the physician may want to rule out many other factors before simply saying that an abnormally high blood pressure reading is definitive for a diagnosis of essential hypertension. Even then, various medical conditions can produce a short-lived or chronic elevation in blood pressure that will need to be investigated before the final diagnosis is made. In this scenario, note that the test instrument yielding a high blood pressure reading was giving an accurate result. Thus it may be highly accurate (or reliable) in describing the high level of blood pressure; but the high pressure reading may be due to essential hypertension or to numerous other conditions such as heart disease, toxemia, kidney dysfunction, or anxiety. Without other corroborative and/or exclusionary evidence, basing a diagnosis on one test score alone can lead to false conclusions. However, the physician does use his or her knowledge base about the relationship of high blood pressure reading and essential hypertension in the diagnostic activity even though this knowledge does not make the diagnosis in and of itself. Similarly, a relationship between low scores on WISC-IV PSI and WMI scores and attentional disorder is not in and of itself diagnostic of ADHD, but the knowledge of this relationship should be included when trying to understand the person who is the object of the assessment.

If one accepts the tenet that tests do not diagnose but clinicians do and that most psychological tests are not in and of themselves conclusive diagnostic indicators (true of tests in medicine as well), then the large number of articles in the literature that criticize tests such as the WISC for failing to properly diagnose a disorder with a high level of accuracy are misguided in their emphasis. Much of the criticism of intelligence testing surrounding the diagnosis of SLD and ability-achievement discrepancies discussed previously is based on such misconceptions of the role of tests in diagnosis. Perhaps these studies were needed to point out to practitioners that just looking at profiles of test scores (e.g., McDermott, Fantuzzo, & Glutting, 1990) leads to erroneous diagnostic decisions because subtest patterns in and of themselves are not conclusively diagnostic of a disorder. The thrust of these articles seems to admonish clinicians for even looking at and comparing scores. More balanced and critical clinical assessment such as the approach advocated by Hale *et al.* (2004) and Fiorello *et al.* (2001) yields richer and more useful test application results.

Would one want a physician, for example, not to look at patterns of test results just because they in and of themselves do not diagnose a disorder? Would you tell a physician not to take your blood pressure and heart rate and compare them because these two scores in and of themselves do not differentially diagnose kidney disease from heart disease?

The Kavale and Forness article (1984) is often cited as evidence that profile analysis of the Wechsler scores is not useful in the differential diagnosis of learning disorders. The value of this type of research has been helpful to put the brakes on cookbook, simplistic interpretations of test results devoid of the contextualism of the individual's unique life characteristics. However, the criticism of the practice of profile analysis as the sole piece of information used to make a diagnostic decision has often become a "straw man" argument and has been used to justify elimination of IQ and other psychoeducational tests, which is tantamount to the proverbial throwing out the baby with the bath water. What well-trained clinicians simply rely on test results or patterns as their sole source of information when performing an assessment? If clinicians do not practice in this simplistic way, then to say that a test is not useful because it does not accurately diagnose a disorder is a specious argument because it does not take into account the richness of other sources of information that the clinician is likely to use in arriving at a diagnosis. For example, if a child has a large VCI/PRI discrepancy with a lower VCI, and, based solely on this information, one concludes that left hemisphere functioning is impaired, this would most certainly be viewed as naïve and poor practice. Kaufman (1994) demonstrated many years ago, for example, that discrepancies between VIQ and PIQ are not uncommon in the normal population. However, there is a sufficient body of research supporting the notion that injuries to the left hemisphere result in lower VIQs compared to PIQs. Well, if we have additional information that our client recently suffered a head injury, that perhaps other areas of functioning related to verbal abilities are impaired, and that that previous functioning in relevant cognitive areas was higher, then the test results are certainly strong evidence that help corroborate a hypothesis of left hemisphere impairment that has resulted in cognitive impairment of certain types. It would appear that studies looking at the validity of test scores and profiles in the assessment process need to also look at the other variables that clinicians use in their assessment including the criterion and not just at test results. Also, studies that conclude that test results are not helpful in such assessments ignore the value of the descriptive nature of tests (e.g., this person has these types of strengths and weaknesses).

One of the chapters in this volume by Wiig on language deficits and intelligence scores illustrates the utility and value of looking at score discrepancies and comparisons in the assessment of children with these disorders, not only within but also across test batteries. In this case, the understanding gained of an individual is much richer and treatment implications much clearer by looking at patterns across tests of cognitive abilities and language functions. Unfortunately, psychologists and speech pathologists often practice within their own areas of specialties rather than look across the information and knowledge and understanding both disciples can bring. Looking at patterns of meaningful similarities and differences across a range of tests and other relevant information is the clinical model and use of testing Wechsler originally had in mind for assessment.

In most other chapters in this book the clear message is that good assessment involves looking at multiple sources of information in interpreting WISC scores. The chapter on the WISC-IV Integrated probably takes this approach furthest by looking at not only test scores achieved but also at errors and error patterns as clues to a deeper understanding and assessment of the child. Similarly, but from a different perspective, the two chapters by

Berninger and her colleagues point to using assessments in a way that is both theoretically informed and relevant to both diagnosis and instruction by looking not only at scores but score discrepancies, patterns, and variances from expectations that are based on sound empirical research.

Good practice in using tests should also include looking at test results in the context of multiple sources of information which include the WISC scores. The importance of taking into account test session behaviors on the WISC advocated by Oakland and Glutting and others in this text when interpreting scores also speaks to the fact that one cannot look at scores on any single test in isolation. Test session behaviors enable us to more accurately describe and evaluate a child's strengths and weakness. If we accept this type of notion as a necessary condition of sound clinical practice, then the idea of simply looking at patterns of test scores in isolation from other pieces of information, whether in clinical assessment or research, is limited and probably wrong in most cases. Truly multivariate thinking is needed, which is what the good clinician does.

USE OF THE WISC-III IN OTHER COUNTRIES AND WITH MINORITY POPULATIONS

The Wechsler scales are the most often used, individually administered, standardized tests for assessing the intelligence of children in the United States and have been frequently translated into other languages and used in other countries. This raises important questions. Is intelligence as defined and measured by the Wechsler scales a universal trait? How well do intelligence tests like the WISC-III "travel" across national, cultural, and linguistic boundaries?

There is general agreement about the universality of "g," or general intelligence, despite the debate regarding the various kinds of factors that are hypothesized to account for general mental ability or the extent of the item content required to provide an adequate sampling of "g." The robustness of "g" is also generally accepted in both theoretical and empirical descriptions of intelligence. Its clinical utility is evident in the widespread use of the Wechsler scales for assessing preschool, school-age, and adult intelligence.

However, the appropriateness or fairness of the item content in intelligence tests in general continues to be a focus of debate. This argument goes one step further to include the appropriateness of test norms for individuals and groups not represented in the standardization studies. It has been observed that particular groups of children may score differently on the same test for reasons varying from the item content issue to "real" differences that may exist outside of the test itself (i.e., motivation, test-taking behaviors, gender, and cultural differences). Although the WISC-III and WISC-IV were carefully standardized and normed on a representative sample of American children, the question most often asked is how well will the test "perform" when applied to culturally or linguistically different children, or children from different countries? The test should demonstrate its robustness across national and cultural boundaries, both in terms of its content and in the norms used to represent varying levels of performance.

A plethora of psychological literature exists on test bias (e.g., Reynolds, 1995), much of which has spilled over into the political and legal domains. There may be good reason to suspect that a particular test or some specific items may "work" less well with some children who are different from those on which the test was normed. For example, a child may not correctly answer an item only because he has never been exposed to that specific task or item content. In contrast, another child will perform poorly on an intelligence test because of low ability. Compared to chronometric measures of intelligence (e.g., reaction time), the WISC-III and other similar tests were intended to yield estimates primarily of crystallized ability, although fluid ability may also be tapped along with processing speed and working memory. We are reminded of Vernon's (1950) intelligence A, B, and C. Intelligence C is what the tests that we create actually measure in contrast to the more pure descriptions of intelligence A (genotypic intelligence) and intelligence B (phenotypic intelligence). Thus Intelligence C tests primarily tapping crystallized ability are also more open to concerns about item and score bias. The WISC-IV has successfully incorporated tasks that reflect fluid ability, so there is a greater balance in this instrument and the opportunity to observe score differences in subtests that pull more for fluid vs crystallized intelligence. As well, the integrity of the WM and PS factors has been more clearly operationalized and contribute even more to the calculation of the FSIQ.

These issues have been previously raised in Canada and other countries that employed the WISC-III for the assessment of children's intelligence. Considerable controversy had been heard earlier about the item content of the WISC-R, especially in relation to the Information subtest (see Beal, 1988). Some research also reported differences in scores earned by Canadian children, suggesting that the American norms were not applicable in the Canadian setting (e.g., Holmes, 1981). Studies comparing changes over time in the ability scores across different countries further indicated that American WISC-III norms may not accurately reflect the current ability distribution in other countries (see Flynn, 1984, 1987, 1998). While such major tests as the WISC-III are likely to be "imported" by other countries, the concerns that might result from this practice were summarized by Saklofske and Janzen (1990, p. 9):

> This situation can sometimes present rather major problems in the assessment process especially when norm-referenced tests are employed or the product being measured is tied to specific and unique experiences ... it is not always such a straightforward matter of simply using well-constructed American tests in Canada ... some American instruments that are brought into Canada may be renormed or modified after accumulation of data from research and clinical use.

THE WECHSLER TESTS IN OTHER COUNTRIES

As an historical note the WISC-R was translated into over 20 different languages and there are currently 20 translations of the WISC-III either in progress or completed, ranging from Japanese and Chinese to Greek and French. Based on the preceding debates about intelligence in general, and intelligence tests more specifically, there have been standardization studies of the WISC-III carried out in several English-speaking countries, including Australia, the United Kingdom, and Canada.

The UK version of the WISC-III (Wechsler, 1992) was published in 1992 and included a standardization sample of 824 children. As stated in the manual, "the majority of items in the final US selection work throughout Europe" (pp. 24–25). Some artwork changes were required, as were some minor scoring changes to reflect the specific UK setting. The Australian WISC-III study (Wechsler, 1995) was based on samples of students from five age groupings ($N = 468$). The manual (1995) states:

> The results indicated that the presentation order of some items should be modified in each of the Picture Completion, Information, Similarities, Picture Arrangement, Vocabulary, and Comprehension subtests. There was insufficient evidence to suggest the need to develop a full set of Australian norms. (p. 3)

The WISC-III Canadian Study (1996) evolved from a smaller study of the test performance of a representative sample of English-speaking Canadian children. When differences that were larger than could be accounted for by measurement error were found, a comprehensive standardization study was initiated that resulted in the publication of Canadian norms. Results showed that Canadian children scored 3.34 IQ points above the US normative sample, with differences ranging from 1.03 points for FD to 4.96 points for PIQ in favor of Canadian children. Further, significantly higher scores were earned by Canadian children on every subtest except Information and Arithmetic. Distribution differences were observed after adjustments were made for mean score differences and reported in the manual:

> The distributions of Full Scale IQ, Verbal Comprehension Index and Processing Speed Index differed significantly, and among the scaled scores the Coding, Digit Span, and Mazes subtests showed the most discrepancies ($p < .005$). The results across scales generally found the Canadians with more low-average IQs and scaled scores and with somewhat higher percentages in the high-average (100–119) and high categories (120–129) than in the U.S. sample. (p. 29)

The reliability and factor structure for the Canadian WISC-III data replicated the American results. Although no changes were made to any of the test items, guidelines were presented for scoring several of the items from each of the verbal subtests, with the exception of Similarities.

These three examples of WISC-III validity and standardization studies conducted outside of the United States suggest that while the psychometric

properties of the test are remarkably sound in their consistency and repli-
cability, there are score differences that need to be taken into account in the
measurement and assessment of intelligence when moving across national
and cultural boundaries. However these three standardization studies were
conducted in English speaking, industrialized countries; while there are
certainly cultural and experiential differences between the countries, there
are remarkable similarities. In contrast, a recently completed study by
Georgas, Weiss, van de Vijver, and Saklofske (2003) demonstrated that
while either a three- or four-factor structure was replicated in their study
of countries of North America, Europe, and southeast Asia, the number of
item changes increased as the language of the test changed from English to
French or Japanese. Further, variations across countries were observed on
the mean subtest, index, and IQ scores, suggesting that such factors as
country affluence and education are of relevance in the development, administration, scoring, and interpretation of ability test scores (Georgas, van de
Vijver, Weiss, & Saklofske, 2003). These findings point to the need for
careful standardization studies when a test is "imported" by another country. As was the case for the WISC-III, the WISC-IV is currently undergoing
standardization studies in a number of countries including Canada. These
data should be available at the time this book is published, and we encourage
readers to examine the findings from other countries. The data will be most
revealing regarding the factor structure of the WISC-IV, and the robustness
and portability of both test items and subtest, index, and FSIQ scores. To
date, preliminary indications are that the test does "travel well," especially in
English-speaking countries.

WISC-IV AND MINORITY POPULATIONS
IN THE UNITED STATES

Perhaps more relevant in the United States has been the literature on the
performance of minority groups on intelligence tests. The use of IQ tests
with minority students has been controversial because of concerns of test
bias. Despite many concerns over test bias, the vast majority of studies
investigating ethnic bias in IQ tests in general and in the Wechsler series
have not produced evidence of test bias (Reynolds & Kaiser, 2003). Still,
studies have consistently found that African Americans score on average 15
points lower than whites, and Hispanics score somewhere between these two
groups on IQ tests (Neisser, Boodoo, Bouchard, Boykin, Brody, Ceci,
Halpern, Loehlin, Perloff, Sternberg, & Urbina, 1996). It is therefore natural
to ask Does the WISC show evidence of test bias toward minorities?

In studies of prediction bias (Weiss, Prifitera, & Roid, 1993; Weiss &
Prifitera, 1995), the WISC-III predicted achievement scores equally well for
African American, Hispanic, and white children. Results of these studies are
similar to other studies using the WISC-R (Reynolds & Kaiser, 1990). Such

results are interpreted as evidence that the scales are not biased against minorities. In addition, item selection for both the WISC-III and WISC-IV was done in conjunction with item bias analyses and content bias reviewers (Wechsler, 1991, 2003). Results of the Canadian study discussed previously also demonstrated that the WISC-III was valid for the Canadian sample; the geographic proximity, linguistic, and other similarities between Canada and the United States make the comparison of intelligence test scores all the more relevant. Furthermore, there is ample evidence of cross-cultural validity of the Wechsler scales (Georgas *et al.*, 2003).

Wechsler was fully aware of the controversies regarding IQ testing with minority children (see Harris, Tulsky, & Schultheis, 2003). Wechsler, however, viewed the differences in mean scores not as indicators of lower intelligence among certain groups but as indicators of differences in our society and how variations in social, economic, political, and medical opportunities have an impact on intellectual abilities. In a 1971 article Wechsler discussed the fact that individuals from lower socioeconomic levels tended to score lower on intelligence tests. He viewed this fact as evidence for a call to change the social conditions that cause these differences rather than as an indictment of the IQ test. In discussing differences in IQ scores among socioeconomic groups, Wechsler stated, "The cause is elsewhere and the remedy not in denigrating or banishing the IQ but in attacking and removing the social causes that impair it" (Wechsler, 1971).

If differences in IQ scores among groups are attributable primarily to social and economic factors, then what implications do these have for the interpretation of IQ? First it is important to view the IQ score not as a fixed entity but as a reflection of an individual's current level of cognitive functioning. All too often in psychological reports one sees a phrase that states directly or strongly implies that the IQ reflects the individual's potential or inherited ability. There are many factors, however, including the socioeconomic, medical, temporary and transitory states of the organism, motivation, and inherent test unreliability, that all may impact the person's score. It is well accepted by the professional community that IQ is not a measure of genetic endowment (Neisser *et al.*, 1996) even though there is substantial evidence for genetic factors in intelligence. In our clinical practice, we need to ensure that we do not confuse or infuse a person's IQ score with genetic explanations. IQ scores are reflections of current level of functioning and expressed abilities, not an immutable number.

There is clear evidence from the WISC-IV standardization sample, as well as data from other IQ tests, of a substantial correlation between IQ and socioeconomic level. One of the reasons that test developers stratify their samples by socioeconomic status (SES) variables is to control for this effect. In the WISC-IV, the standardization sample was stratified by parental level of education because this variable is related to SES and considered a good measure of SES. Results show that children from homes whose parents have the highest level of education (college level or above) score considerably higher than all the other four levels of education groups (i.e., < 8th grade, 8–11 years of education, high school graduate, some postsecondary education or technical school). The mean FSIQ scores for the entire WISC-IV standardization sample for the five education levels from highest to lowest are 108.7, 102.2, 95.8, 88.1, and 88.7, respectively. This pattern is similar to that found in the WISC-III where the mean scores by education level were 110.7, 103.0, 97.9, 90.6, and 87.7, respectively. The impact of SES on IQ scores is another "truth" generally accepted among the professional community.

As mentioned previously, African American groups on average tend to score 15 points lower than white groups on IQ tests. Data from the National Assessment of Education Progress cited in Hale *et al.* (2004) also show that individuals from lower SES households score much lower than those in high SES households on reading and math tests. For example, in Iowa, 47% of the sample from low SES populations scored below basic proficiency on the NAEP reading test, while only 22% from high SES population scored below proficient. With regard to ethnicity, 66% of African Americans and 52% of Hispanics in Iowa scored below basic proficiency in reading, with only 26% of whites scoring below proficient. Similar discrepancies were found when looking at special education status and limited English proficiency status. Therefore, differences in SES and minority group scores are found in achievement tests as well.

Looking at groups at only this level conceals many issues and often leads to the erroneous conclusion that the intelligence of minority groups is lower than that of whites. This is erroneous because these overall group differences do not take into account other relevant variables such as SES. One issue that affects this outcome is that when developing IQ tests, developers stratify SES within racial/ethnic groups to obtain a representative sample. The effect of this practice is that minority groups tend to have a larger percentage of their sample as lower SES just because this reflects the population characteristics. Therefore, a simple comparison of means between minority groups and whites will yield scores that do not take into account the impact of socioeconomic and other demographic variables that might affect scores. Also, focusing on the overall IQ score alone misses other aspects of an individual's functioning. Remember what the IQ score represents: it tells us the score or standing of an individual relative to a reference group. Thus the individual's score must be interpreted in light of the reference group characteristics.

Group Differences

To investigate differences among different racial/ethnic groups, we examined the WISC-IV IQ and Index scores of African Americans, Hispanics, and whites in the WISC-IV standardization sample (see Table 1.3). In addition, rather than just looking at overall means, we compared samples that were matched on SES (level of education). Through matching we also

TABLE 1.3   Mean IQ and Index Scores by Race/Ethnicity for the WISC-IV
Standardization Sample

IQ or Index Score	African American	Hispanic	White
FSIQ	91.7	93.1	103.2
VCI	91.9	91.5	102.9
PRI	91.4	95.7	102.8
WMI	96.1	94.2	101.3
PSI	95.0	97.7	101.4

N = 2080. African American group, n = 343; Hispanic group, n = 335; white group, n = 1402. Data based on WISC-IV standardization sample. From *Wechsler Intelligence Scale for Children—Fourth Edition.* Copyright © 2003 by The Psychological Corporation. Used by permission. All rights reserved.

controlled for sex, age (in years), region of the country (Northeast, South, Midwest, and West), and number of parents living at home. Tables 1.4 and 1.5 present data for these matched samples.

When examining these data, several important points should be considered. First in Table 1.3, the mean FSIQ difference between the white and African American sample is *less than 1 standard deviation* (SD), which is also less (about one-third of an SD) than found in previous research on IQ tests (Neisser *et al.*, 1996) and on the WISC-R (Kaufman & Doppelt, 1976) and the WISC-III (Prifitera, Weiss, & Saklofske, 1998).

The difference between the white and Hispanic sample is smaller (approximately 10 points). The second point, however, is that there is considerable variation in the differences among African Americans, Hispanics, and whites among the other IQ and Index scores. For example, African Americans score only 5.2 and 5.4 points, respectively, below whites on WMI and FDI scores. Hispanics continue to show a relatively higher PRI score compared to their VCI scores, which is consistent with the previous literature. The difference in the PRI score between Hispanics and whites is 7.1 points. In addition, the Hispanic group's PSI score is 3.7 points below that of whites and there is only a 6.9 point difference between the groups on the WMI score. These results strongly suggest that simply looking at the FSIQ differences ignores relative strengths in the various domains of cognitive functioning among minority groups. It also strongly supports the practice of using the Index scores even though factor analyses may not always clearly support the four-factor structure as reported on the WISC-III for minority groups (e.g., Logerquist-Hansen & Barona, 1994).

SES and Group Differences

To further investigate the relationship of SES variables with IQ scores, we examined the data for matched samples of African Americans, Hispanics, and whites. Subjects were matched on age, region, sex, parental education level, and number of parents living in the household. Analyses of the WISC-IV standardization data found that children who live in a one-parent household have on average a FSIQ score that is 6.7 points lower than children living in a two-parent household. Therefore we matched on this variable as well. Results are provided in Tables 1.4 and 1.5.

The score differences between African Americans and whites are significantly reduced when one takes into account these gross SES and demographic variables. Also of interest is that contrary to what is often assumed, African Americans do in fact perform somewhat better on the verbal compared to the nonverbal performance tasks, which was also the case with WISC-III data. This is contrary to the usual assumption that African Americans perform more poorly on the verbal tasks because it is commonly assumed that verbal items are more culturally loaded and biased than nonverbal tasks. Also, the relatively lower score on performance measures cannot be attributed to the likelihood that minorities are disadvantaged on

TABLE 1.4 WISC-IV Scores of African Americans and Whites Based on a Sample Matched on Age, Parental Level of Education, Region, Sex, and Number of Parents Living in the Household

IQ or index score[a]	AfricanAmerican	Whites
FSIQ	91.5	100.3
VCI	91.9	100.4
PRI	91.1	100.0
WMI	96.4	100.1
PSI	94.5	98.8

[a]African American group, n = 257; white group, n = 257. From *Wechsler Intelligence Scale for Children—Fourth Edition*. Copyright © 2003 by The Psychological Corporation. Used by permission. All rights reserved.

TABLE 1.5 WISC-IV Scores of Hispanics and Whites Based on a Sample Matched on Age, Parental Level of Education, Region, Sex, and Number of Parents Living in the Household

IQ or index score	Hispanic N = 161	Whites N = 161
FSIQ	95.2	100.0
VCI	93.7	99.7
PRI	97.7	100.3
WMI	95.7	98.7
PSI	97.9	99.6

speeded tests because the smallest discrepancies for both minority groups are found on the PSI and WMI scores. What these data do suggest is that socioeconomic and demographic factors do have a strong impact on scores and again that there are considerable variations in scores among the cognitive components measured in the WISC-IV. This again underscores the value of using both the Index scores and IQ scores or else these patterns of relative strengths would be overlooked.

The score differences between Hispanics and whites are also significantly reduced when samples are matched on these demographic variables (see Table 1.5). All differences are less than 6 points. The relatively small differences on the PSI scores is of particular interest because it is sometimes assumed that Hispanics score lower on the IQ measure like the WISC because of the speeded nature of some of the tasks. The reasoning behind this is that speed and time are valued differently in Hispanic cultures, so on tasks requiring quick performance, Hispanics are likely to score lower. However, on the PSI, which is highly speeded, the Hispanic group scored only 1.7 points below the matched white sample.

Finally, we also looked for age trends in score differences between the African American, Hispanic, and white samples. Tables 1.6 and 1.7 present

TABLE 1.6   Difference Scores between Whites and African Americans on WISC-III IQ and Index Scores for a Matched Sample

IQ or index score	6- to 11-year-old group N = 143	12- to 16-year-old group N = 114
FSIQ	6	11.8
VCI	5.6	12.2
PRI	6.8	10.5
WMI	1.9	5.9
PSI	3.5	5.6

From *Wechsler Intelligence Scale for Children—Fourth Edition.* Copyright © 2003 by The Psychological Corporation. Used by permission. All rights reserved.

TABLE 1.7   Difference Scores between Whites and Hispanics on WISC-IV IQ and Index Scores for a Matched Sample

IQ or index score	6- to 11-year-old group N = 93	12- to 16-year-old group N = 68
FSIQ	1.3	8.0
VCI	3.7	8.5
PRI	−.2	3.9
WMI	2.4	5.5
PSI	−1.5	3.4

From *Wechsler Intelligence Scale for Children—Fourth Edition.* Copyright © 2003 by The Psychological Corporation. Used by permission. All rights reserved.

the different scores between groups by age bands. This is the same matched sample as in Tables 1.4 and 1.5 broken up into two age bands: 6- to 11-year-olds and 12- to 16-year-olds.

SES and Age Trends

The patterns in this table clearly illustrate that the differences between groups are even smaller among younger children. The differences across the various scores further argue for the importance of interpreting beyond the FSIQ scores. Of particular note is that PRI and PSI scores are slightly higher for the Hispanic compared to the white sample at the younger ages, and these two scores continue to be the highest scores in the older age group. It should also be remembered that these are not longitudinal but cohort data, so there are limitations on how to interpret such scores. The reasons for this age difference are unknown and are worthy of further research and investigation. However it does have implications for how we view scores and how and when we intervene. The impact of earlier intervention on outcomes of children, when score differences are smaller and very close to average or above, should be further investigated. These data also strongly suggest that research needs to look at more refined SES, cultural, linguistic, home environment, medical, and other variables that affect opportunity to learn and the development of cognitive abilities.

That IQ scores differ between younger African American and white children and Hispanic and white samples, with only gross matches on SES, are only one-half of a standard deviation or less and that the index scores are even smaller strongly suggest that the view that minorities have lower abilities is clearly wrong. One has to ask what the difference would have been if even more refined variables, such as household income, home environment variables such as parental time spent with children, per-pupil school spending, medical and nutritional history, exposure to toxins, etc. had been controlled for. It also strongly supports not interpreting IQ scores as indicators of some inherent or genetic endowment but rather as an indicator of current intellectual functioning.

It may be argued that the smaller group differences discussed previously do not support the notion of small IQ differences among groups because the FDI and PSI scores are less related to "g" or general intelligence. However, there is sufficient evidence that processing speed is in fact related to "g." For example, decision time and movement time are correlated with intelligence test scores (e.g., Deary, 2001). Moreover, the subtests (Arithmetic and Digit Span) that compose the WMI are good measures of working memory (Sternberg, 1993). Research in working memory suggests that working memory and reasoning (or general ability) are highly similar constructs that are highly correlated (Kyllonen & Christal, 1990).

A CONCLUDING COMMENT

This chapter has attempted to underscore that test scores in and of themselves are not sufficient for a proper psychological assessment. Scores should be interpreted in the context of other relevant information, all of which may not be clear and objective but relies in part on the integrative skills and professional expertise of the evaluator. This is one of the main themes in Matarazzo's 1990 APA presidential address in which he describes psychological assessment as an activity that:

> is not, even today, a totally objective, completely science-based activity. Rather, in common with much of medical diagnosis...the assessment of intelligence, personality, or type or level of impairment is a highly complex operation that involves extracting diagnostic meaning from an individual's personal history and objectively recorded test scores. Rather than being totally objective, assessment involves a subjective component. Specifically, it is the activity of a licensed professional, an artisan familiar with the accumulated findings of his or her young science, who in each instance uses tests, techniques, and a strategy, that, whereas also identifying possible deficits, maximizes the chances of discovering each client's full ability and true potential. (p. 1000)

The WISC-IV, then, like other key diagnostic and assessment instruments used by health professionals, should be viewed and used for what it is, a useful tool to help the clinician understand the child before them. The body of research on the Wechsler scale and the improvements and innovations made in the WISC-IV make it an especially useful tool because its psychometric and clinical properties are well known and have been scrutinized more than any other scales of their kind. Like other professionals who use tools as part of practicing their profession, clinicians need to understand how to use the scale, including its strengths and limitations. Above all, the clinician remains the ultimate clinical instrument who uses such tools as part of their clinical work. The remaining chapters in this volume emphasize the importance of both research and clinical acumen in the understanding of children with various disorders and strengths.

REFERENCES

Ackerman, P. L., & Beier, M. E. (2003). Intelligence, personality, and interests in the career choice process. *Journal of Career Assessment, 11,* 205–218.

Ackerman, P. L., & Heggestad, E. D. (1997). Intelligence, personality, and interests: Evidence for overlapping traits. *Psychological Bulletin, 121,* 219–245.

Allport, G. W. (1955). *Becoming: Basic considerations for a psychology of personality.* New Haven: Yale University Press.

American Educational Research Association. (1999) *Standards for educational and psychological testing.* Washington, DC: Author.

Anastasi, A., & Urbina, S. (1997). *Psychological testing*, 7th ed. Upper Saddle River, NJ: Prentice Hall.

Baddeley, A. (1997). *Human memory: Theory and practice*, rev. ed. Needham Heights, MA: Pearson Allyn & Bacon.

Beal, A. L. (1988). Canadian content in the WISC-R: Bias or jingoism. *Canadian Journal of Behavioral Science 20:* 154–166.

Blaha J., & Wallbrown, F. H. (1996). Hierarchical factor structure of the Wechsler Intelligence Scale for Children-III. *Psychological Assessment, 8,* 214–218.

Cohen, J. (1957). The factorial structure of the WAIS between early adulthood and old age. *Journal of Consulting Psychology, 21,* 283–290.

Cohen, J. (l959). The factorial structure of the WISC at ages 7–6, 10–6, and 13–6. *Journal of Consulting Psychology, 23,* 285–299.

Donders, J. (1997). Sensitivity of the WISC-III to head injury with children with traumatic brain injury. *Assessment, 4,* 107–109.

Early Reading Success Indicator (2004). *Manual for the Early Reading Success Indicator.* San Antonio: Harcourt Assessment Inc.

Fiorello, Catherine A., Hale, J. B., McGrath, Marie, Ryan, K., & Quinn, S. (2001). IQ interpretation for children with flat and variable test profiles. *Learning & Individual Differences, 13,* 115–125.

Flanagan, D. P., & Kaufman, A. S. (in press). *Essentials of WISC-IV assessment.* New York: Wiley.

Flynn, J. R. (1984). The mean IQ of Americans: Massive gains 1932–1978. *Psychological Bulletin, 95,* 29–51.

Flynn, J. R. (1987). Massive gains in 14 nations: What IQ tests really measure: *Psychological Bulletin, 101,* 171–191.

Flynn, J. R. (1998). IQ gains over time: Toward finding the causes. In U. Neisser (Ed.), The rising curve: Long-term gains in IQ and related measures (pp. 25–66). Washington, D.C.: American Psychological Association.

Georgas, J., Weiss, L., van de Vijver, F., & Saklofske, D. H. (2003). *Culture and children's intelligence: Cross-cultural analysis of the WISC-III.* San Diego: Academic Press.

Grice, J. W., Krohn, E. J., & Logerquist, S. (1999). Cross-validation of the WISC-III factor structure in two samples of children with learning disabilities. *Journal of Psychoeducational Assessment 17(3),* 236–248.

Hale, J. B., Naglieri, J. A., Kaufman, A. S., & Kavale, K. A. (2004). Specific learning disability classification in the new Individuals with Disabilities Education Act: The danger of good ideas. *The School Psychologist, Winter,* 6–13.

Harris, J. G., Tulsky, D. S., & Schultheis, M. T. (2003). Assessment of the non-native English speaker: Assimilating history and research findings to guide clinical practice. In D. S. Tulsky, D. H Saklofske, et al. (Eds.). *Clinical interpretation of the WAIS-III and WMS-III.* San Diego: Academic Press.

Holmes, B. J. (1981). *Individually administered intelligence tests: An application of anchor test norming and equating procedures in British Columbia.* Education Research Institute of British Columbia; Report No. 81: 11, Vancouver, B.C.

Kamphaus, R. W. (1993). *Clinical assessment of children's intelligence.* Needham Heights, MA: Allyn & Bacon.

Kanaya, T., Scullin, M. H., & Ceci, S. J. (2003). The Flynn effect and U.S. Policies: The impact of rising IQ scores on American society via mental retardation diagnoses. *American Psychologist, 58 (10),* 778–790.

Kaplan, E., Fein, D., Morris, R., & Delis, D. (1991). *Manual for WAIS-R as a neuropsychological instrument.* San Antonio, TX: The Psychological Corporation.

Kaplan, E., Fein, D., Kramer, J., Morris, R., & Delis, D. (1999). Manual for WISC-III as a neuropsychological instrument. San Antonio, TX: The Psychological Corporation.

Kaufman, A. S. (1976). Verbal-Performance IQ discrepancies on the WISC-R. *Journal of Consulting and Clinical Psychology, 44,* 739–744.

Kaufman, A. S. (1994). *Intelligent testing with the WISC-III.* New York: Wiley.

Kaufman, A. S., & Doppelt, J. E. (1976). Analysis of WISC-R standardization data in terms of stratification variables. *Child Development, 47,* 165–171.

Kavale, K. A., & Forness, S. R. (1984). A meta-analysis of the validity of Wechsler scale profiles and recategorizations: Patterns or parodies? *Learning Disability Quarterly, 7,* 136–156.

Konold, T. R., Kush, J. C., & Canivez, G. L. (1997) Factor replication of the WISC-III in three independent samples of children receiving special education. *Journal of Psychoeducational Assessment, 15,* 123–137.

Kyllonen, P. C., & Christal, R. E. (1990). Reasoning ability is (little more than) working memory capacity?! *Intelligence, 14,* 389–433.

Logerquist-Hansen, S., & Barona, A. (1994). Factor Structure of the Wechsler Intelligence Scale for Children-III for Hispanic and non-Hispanic white children with learning disabilities. Paper presented at the annual meeting of the American Psychological Association, Los Angeles.

Maddi, S. (1976). *Personality theories: A comparative analysis* (3rd ed.). Homewood, IL: The Dorsey Press.

Matarazzo, J. D. (1990). Psychological assessment versus psychological testing: Validation from Binet to the school, clinic, and courtroom. *American Psychologist, 45,* 999–1017.

Matthews, G., & Dorn, L. (1995). Cognitive and attentional processes in intelligence. In D. H. Saklofske & M. Zeidner (Eds.), *International handbook of personality and intelligence* (pp. 367–396). New York: Plenum Press.

McDermott, P. A., Fantuzzo, J. W., & Glutting. J. J. (1990). Just say no to subtest analysis: A critique on Wechsler theory and practice. *Journal of Psychoeducational Assessment, 8,* 290–302.

Neisser, U., Boodoo, G., Bouchard, T. J., Boykin, A. W., Brody, N., Ceci, S. J., Halpern, D. F. Loehlin, J. C., Perloff, R., Sternberg, R. J., & Urbina, S. (1996). Intelligence: Knowns and unknowns. *American Psychologist, 51,* 77–101.

Prifitera, A., Weiss, L. G., & Saklofske, D. H. (1998). The WISC-III in context. In A. Prifitera & D. H. Saklofske (Eds.), *WISC-III clinical use and interpretation: Scientist-practitioner perspectives.* San Diego: Academic Press.

Prifitera, A., & Dersh, J. (1993). Base rates of WISC-III diagnostic subtest patterns among normal, learning-disabled, and ADHD samples. *Journal of Psychological Assessment monograph series. Advances in psychological assessment: Wechsler Intelligence Scale for Children-Third Edition,* 43–55.

Reschly, D. J. (1997). Diagnostic and treatment utility of intelligence tests. In D. P. Flanagan, J. L. Genshaft, & P. L. Harrison (Eds.), *Contemporary intellectual assessment: Theories, tests, and issues* (pp. 437–456). New York: Guilford.

Reynolds, C. R. (1995). Test bias and the assessment of personality and intelligence. In D. H. Saklofske & M. Zeidner (Eds.), *International handbook of personality and intelligence* (pp. 545–573), New York: Plenum Press.

Reynolds, C. R., & Kaiser, S. M. (2003). Bias in the assessment of aptitude. In C. R. Reynolds & R.W. Kamphaus (Eds.), *Handbook of psychological and educational assessment of children* (2nd ed., pp. 519–562). New York: Wiley.

Reynolds, C. R., & Kaiser, S. M. (1990). Test bias in psychological assessment. In T. B. Gutkin & C. R. Reynolds (Eds.). *The handbook of school psychology* (2nd ed., pp. 487–525). New York: Wiley.

Reynolds, C. R., & Ford, L. (1994). Comparative three-factor solutions of the WISC-III and WISC-R at 11 age levels between 6 1/2, and 16 1/2, years. *Archives of Clinical Neuropsychology, 9,* 553–570.

Roid, G. H., & Worrall, W. (1996). Equivalence of factor structure in the U.S. and Canadian Editions of the WISC-III. Paper presented at the annual meeting of the American Psychological Association, Toronto.

Roid, G. H., & Worrall, W. (1997) Replication of the Wechsler Intelligence Scale for Children–Third Edition. Four-factor model in the Canadian normative sample. *Psychological Assessment, 9(4),* 512–515.

Roid, G. H., Prifitera, A., & Weiss, L. W. (1993). Replication of the WISC-III factor structure in an independent sample. *Journal of Psychoeducational Assessment,* WISC-III Monograph, 6–21.

Saklofske, D. H., & Janzen, H. L. (1990). School-based assessment research in Canada. *McGill Journal of Education, 25,* 1, 5–23.

Saklofske, D. H., & Zeider, M. (Eds.). (1995). *International handbook of personality and intelligence.* New York: Plenum Press.

Saklofske, D. H., Austin, E. J., Matthews, G., Zeidner, M., Schwean, V. L., & Groth-Marnat, G. (2003). Intelligence and personality. In L. E. Beutler & G. Groth-Marnat (Eds.). Integrative assessment of adult personality, (3rd ed., pp. 123–156). New York: Guilford Press.

Saklofske, H., Hildebrand, D. K., & Gorsuch, R. L. (2000). Replication of the factor structure of the Wechsler Adult Intelligence Scale—Third Edition with a Canadian Sample. *Psychological Assessment, 12,* 436–439.

Sattler, J. M., & Dumont, R. (in press). *Assessment of Children: WISC-IV and WPPSI-III Supplement.* San Diego: Jerome M. Sattler Publisher, Inc.

Sattler, J. M. (1988). *Assessment of children* (3rd ed.). San Diego: Jerome M. Sattler Publisher, Inc.

Sattler, J. M. (1992). *Assessment of children* (revised and updated, 3rd ed.). San Diego: Jerome M. Sattler Publisher, Inc.

Sattler, J. M. (2001). *Assessment of children: Cognitive applications* (4th ed.). San Diego: Jerome M. Sattler Publisher, Inc.

Sattler, J. M. & Saklofske, D. H. (2001). Wechsler Intelligence Scale for Children (WISC-III): Description. In J. M. Sattler, *Assessment of children: Cognitive applications* (4th ed.), (pp. 220–265). San Diego: Jerome M. Satler Publisher, Inc.

Schwean, V. L., Saklofske, D. H., Yackulic, R. A., & Quinn, D. (1993). WISC-III performance of ADHD children. *Journal of Psychoeducational Assessment monograph series. Advances in psychological assessment: Wechsler Intelligence Scale for Children-Third Edition.* 56–70.

Scruggs, T. E., & Mastropieri, M. A. (2002). On babies and bathwater: Addressing the problems of identification of learning disabilities. *Learning Disability Quarterly, 25,* 155–168.

Shaywitz, S. E., Shaywitz, B. A., Fulbright, R. K., Skudlarski, P., Mencl, W. E., Constable, R. T., Pugh, K. R., Holahan, J. M., Marchione, K. E., Fletcher, J. M., Lyson, G. R., & Gore, J. C. (2003). Neural systems for compensation and persistence: Young adult outcome of childhood reading disability. *Biological Psychiatry, 54,* 25–33.

Snook, S. C., & Gorsuch, R. L. (1989). Component analysis versus common factor analysis: A Monte Carlo study. *Psychological Bulletin, 106,* 148–154.

Sternberg, R. J. (1993). Rocky's back again: A review of the WISC-III. *Journal of Psychoeducational Assessment monograph series. Advances in psychological assessment: Wechsler Intelligence Scale for Children-Third Edition,* 161–164.

Thomson, B. (1991). Comparison of the WISC-R and WISC-III. Unpublished Masters Thesis. Trinity University, San Antonio, TX.

Tulsky, D. S., Saklofske, D. H., & Ricker, J. (2003). Historical overview of intelligence and memory: Factors influencing the Wechsler scales. In D. S. Tulsky, D. H. Saklofske, et al. (Eds.), *Clinical interpretation of the WAIS-III and WMS-III.* San Diego: Academic Press.

Tulsky, D. S., Saklofske, D. H., & Zhu, J. J. (2003). Revising a standard: An evaluation of the origin and development of the WAIS-III. In D. S. Tulsky, D. H. Saklofske, et al. (Eds.), *Clinical interpretation of the WAIS-III and WMS-III.* San Diego: Academic Press.

Vernon, P. E. (1950). *The structure of human abilities*. New York: Wiley.

Wechsler, D. (1950). Cognitive, conative, and non-intellective intelligence. *American Psychologist, 5*, 78–83.

Wechsler, D. (1971). Intelligence: Definition, theory, and the IQ. In R. Cancro (Ed.), *Intelligence: Genetic and environmental influences* (pp. 50–55). New York: Gruene and Stratton.

Wechsler, D. (1974). *Manual for the Wechsler Intelligence Scale for Children-Revised*. San Antonio: The Psychological Corporation.

Wechsler, D. (1991). *Manual for the Wechsler Intelligence Scale for Children-Third Edition*. San Antonio: The Psychological Corporation.

Wechsler, D. (1992). *Manual for the Wechsler Intelligence Scale for Children-Third Edition U.K. Edition*. Sidcup, Kent: The Psychological Corporation.

Wechsler, D. (1995). *Manual: Australian Supplement to the Wechsler Intelligence Scale for Children-Third Edition*. Sydney: The Psychological Corporation.

Wechsler, D. (1996). *Manual: Canadian Supplement to the Wechsler Intelligence Scale-Third Edition*. Toronto: The Psychological Corporation.

Wechsler, D. (1997). *Manual for the Wechsler Adult Intelligence Scale-Third Edition*. San Antonio: The Psychological Corporation.

Wechsler, D. (2003). *Manual for the Wechsler Adult Intelligence Scale-Fourth Edition*. San Antonio: The Psychological Corporation.

Wechsler, D. (2003b). *Wechsler Intelligence Scale for Children-Fourth Edition technical and interpretive manual*. San Antonio: The Psychological Corporation.

Wechsler, D. (2004). *Manual for the Wechsler Adult Intelligence Scale-IV Integrated*. San Antonio: The Psychological Corporation.

Weiss, L. G., & Prifitera, A. (1995). An evaluation of differential prediction of WIAT achievement scores from WISC-III FSIQ across ethnic and gender groups. *Journal of School Psychology, 33*, 297–304.

Weiss, L. G., Prifitera, A., & Roid, G. H. (1993). The WISC-III and fairness of predicting achievement across ethnic and gender groups. *Journal of Psychoeducational Assessment, monograph series, Advances in psychological assessment: Wechsler Intelligence Scale for Children-Third Edition* (pp. 35–42).

Wielkiewicz, R. Z. (1990). Interpreting low scores on the WISC-R third factor: It's more than distractibility. *Psychological Assessment: A Journal of Consulting and Clinical Psychology, 2*, 91–97.

2

CLINICAL INTERPRETATION OF THE WISC-IV FSIQ AND GAI

DONALD H. SAKLOFSKE

*Department of Educational Psychology
and Special Education
University of Saskatchewan
Saskatoon, Saskatchewan, Canada*

AURELIO PRIFITERA

*Harcourt Assessment, Inc.
San Antonio, Texas*

LAWRENCE G. WEISS

*Harcourt Assessment, Inc.
San Antonio, Texas*

ERIC ROLFHUS

*Harcourt Assessment, Inc.
San Antonio, Texas*

JIANJUN ZHU

*Harcourt Assessment, Inc.
San Antonio, Texas*

Each revision of the original 1939 Wechsler-Bellevue scale in relation to the assessment of children's intelligence (WISC, 1949; WISC-R, 1974; WISC-III, 1991; WISC-IV, 2003) has added to the Wechsler legacy and tradition. A number of significant improvements and modifications have been made to the Wechsler family of tests, driven by the demands of clinical practice but also reflecting advances in theory, research, and measurement sophistication. The Wechsler Intelligence Scale for Children–Fourth Edition (WISC-IV; Wechsler, 2003a) has rapidly found its way into the test batteries of many school and child clinical psychologists since its publication in 2003. There is every good reason to expect that the WISC-IV, like its predecessors, will continue to be among the most frequently used tests for assessing children's intelligence. The sound rationale for the revisions found in the WISC-IV and the excellent psychometric properties of the test reported in the Technical Manual and Chapter 1 of this book certainly support its continued use by psychologists for assessing children's intelligence. The Wechsler tests have also garnered an international reputation and now can be found in various translations in a number of different countries (see Georgas, Weiss, van de Vijver, & Saklofske, 2003). As we write this chapter, the WISC-IV is being standardized in Australia, Canada, England, and France and others will soon be under way.

Questions related to the anticipated "look" of the WISC-IV were frequently heard before publication. After all, the WISC-III was an established and often used test by school and clinical psychologists. Like its predecessors, the WISC-III formed the cornerstone of so many psychological and psychoeducational assessments of children. In spite of the criticisms that are invariably heard about any intelligence test, hundreds of research studies and a wealth of clinical information on the WISC-III resulted in the general view that:

> The WISC-III has been well received by those who use tests to evaluate children's and adolescents' intellectual ability. It has excellent standardization, reliability and concurrent and construct validity and useful administrative and scoring guidelines are provided. The manual is outstanding, and much thought and preparation have gone into the revision. The WISC-III will serve as a valuable instrument in the assessment of children's intelligence for many years to come. (Sattler & Saklofske, 2001a, p. 262)

Would the WISC-IV still look like a Wechsler test? Would it retain the IQ scores? Would there be more factors and new subtests? Foremost in the minds of psychologists was whether the WISC-IV would continue to meet the demanding assessment needs of psychologists in the twenty-first century? The Wechsler scales, in contrast to the Woodcock Johnson III Tests of Cognitive Abilities (WJ-III; Woodcock, McGrew, & Mather, 2001) or Stanford Binet Fifth Edition (SB-5; Roid, 2003) continue to be published as separate tests for younger children in the 2- to 7-year range (WPPSI-III, 2001), children 6 to 16 years (WISC-IV, 2003), and adults 16 to 89 years (WAIS-III, 1997). Until the publication of the WISC-IV, all three tests shared a common factor structure that included Verbal IQ (VIQ), Performance IQ (PIQ), and Full Scale IQ (FSIQ). While the WISC-III and WAIS-III increasingly directed the practitioner's attention to the factor analytically derived index scores (e.g., Verbal Comprehension [VC], Perceptual Organization [PO], Working Memory [WM], and Processing Speed [PS]), these tests, along with WPPSI-III, also retained the VIQ and PIQ found in all previous editions. The VIQ-PIQ components were considered by Wechsler to be a key contribution of his tests (Wechsler, 1944) and were synonymous with intellectual assessment and the Wechsler name for generations of psychologists. However, the newer Wechsler tests had created a dual system juxtaposing the core IQ and the alternate index scores. In a scientifically bold move, the developers of the WISC-IV abandoned the IQ score system by dropping the

VIQ and PIQ scores from the test. Both the VCI and renamed Perceptual Reasoning index (PRI) are argued to provide a purer measure of what was previously measured by VIQ and PIQ, in large part because the speed and memory components have more effectively been separated into the PSI and WMI, respectively. As discussed later in this chapter, it is the VCI and PRI that have been integrated to yield the General Ability Index (GAI) initially introduced for the WISC-III (Prifitera, Weiss, & Saklofske, 1998).

The focus of interpreting the WISC-IV now rests solidly on the four-factor, analytically based, and clinically meaningful index scores (see Weiss, Saklofske, & Prifitera, 2003; see also Chapter 3). Changes have been made to both the items and subtests comprising the VCI and the PRI, with just three subtests each required to calculate the index scores. The new subtests described in Chapter 1 (i.e., Picture Concepts, Matrix Reasoning) have enhanced the integrity of the factor structure, resulting in the name change from PO to PR. Furthermore, there has been an increased emphasis on what was previously referred to as "those small third and fourth factors," because of their potential utility in clinical and psychoeducational diagnosis. The factor previously labeled Freedom from Distractibility has also been retitled. The addition of Letter–Number Sequencing complements the Digit Span subtest as a measure of auditory working memory. The index scores and supplemental subtests have already been discussed in Chapter 1, and their clinical interpretation is addressed in Chapter 3.

Somewhat more controversial in certain professional circles, such as clinical neuropsychology, is the retention and relevance of the FSIQ. There is no question that a general mental ability factor is invariably found when a number of cognitively complex tasks are examined, whether this is based on tests such as the SB-5,WJ-III, or the Cognitive Assessment System (CAS; Naglieri & Das, 1997). Most convincing from a purely psychometric perspective are the findings from Carroll's (1993) factor analysis of more than 400 intelligence data sets. However, the question is whether a composite or summary estimate of intelligence reflected in an FSIQ has much clinical relevance and usefulness.

This chapter focuses mainly on the FSIQ and its complement, the GAI. Chapter 3 continues this discussion by reviewing the WISC-IV factor structure and the relevance of the four index scores in the assessment process. Both chapters also set the stage for the chapters to follow in this section and in the next section with their focus on the clinical use and interpretation of the WISC-IV in relation to various classifications of children with special needs. This chapter will more specifically:

- Review the role of the intelligence tests in psychological and psycho-educational assessment
- Revisit the relevance of the WISC-IV FSIQ in clinical assessment
- Present tables for calculating the General Ability Index (GAI), first described for the WISC-III (Prifitera, Weiss, & Saklofske, 1998)
- Provide tables that link the GAI with the WIAT-II.

INTELLIGENCE AND ISSUES OF
PSYCHOLOGICAL MEASUREMENT
AND ASSESSMENT

There is a general recognition and acceptance in psychology of the importance of intelligence in a description of human behavior and individual differences (see Deary, 2001). As well, there is every indication that the WISC-IV represents the best of current test measurement and assessment methodology. However, there continues to be a call from the professional side of psychology and from the public domain for the justification of continuing intelligence, ability, or aptitude test use in schools; in other settings such as the workplace and the military, intelligence tests are much more accepted and less controversial. Some of this is a carryover from the days of radical behaviorism, but much still relates both to court cases that hark back to the *Larry P. v. Riles* and other legal challenges, and anecdotal reports about instances of children being misdiagnosed, labeled, and inappropriately placed in less than optimal learning environments. While it might be hoped that these issues would by now be mainly of historical relevance, in actuality, the new Individuals with Disabilities Education Act (IDEA) is very much concerned about the overidentification of minority children as having special educational needs. Further, the more recent controversy surrounding ability-achievement assessment for the identification of children with learning disabilities would suggest these issues are anything but moot. The comprehensive training of school and child clinical psychologists in assessment, including the use of intelligence tests, the carefully crafted and clearly articulated practice standards and codes of ethics relating to psychological practice in general and assessment more specifically, together with the significant advances in the study of human intelligence and its measurement have done much to quell some of the IQ test controversy.

These changes are clearly reflected in how intelligence tests are used today in contrast to the early days of intelligence tests and testing (see Tulsky, Saklofske, & Ricker, 2003; Harris, Tulsky, & Schultheis, 2003). Further the philosophical and social context in which intelligence tests can provide relevant and important information has changed from one of simply measuring IQ and determining school placement to one that is cast within such far-reaching acts as IDEA and the philosophy of "no child left behind."

Meyer *et al.* (2001) concluded: "formal assessment is a vital element in psychology's professional heritage and a central part of professional practice today" (p. 155). A comprehensive psychological assessment includes the collection of information from different sources (e.g., parents, teachers, child) through the use of different methods (e.g., tests, observations, interviews) that reflect characteristics of the child (e.g., intelligence, personality, motivation) and the child's environment (e.g., home, school). The four pillars of assessment described by Sattler (2001) extends the methods by which children are assessed and provides even more potentially valuable information of relevance to most diagnostic decision needs, as well as for formulating prevention and intervention strategies. In the case of the WISC-IV, it is part of a much larger family of standardized measurement instruments ranging from other tests of intelligence (WPPSI-III, WAIS-III, WASI) and cognitive processes (WISC-IV Integrated), achievement (WIAT-II), and memory (CMS) to scales assessing giftedness (GRS-S), adaptive behavior (ABAS-II), and emotional intelligence (Bar-On EQ). These linking studies add important data beyond the single test and provide additional data that support and contribute to the convergent validity but also the incremental validity of two or more measures (see Hunsley, 2003). A case in point is the concurrent use of the WISC-IV and WISC-IV-Integrated to facilitate the understanding of how and why a child obtains particular scores on subtests such as Vocabulary (see Chapter 4).

While there is not a consensus on the relevance and need for intelligence tests in particular areas of diagnosis (e.g., see Siegel, 2003, for an introduction to the IQ-achievement discrepancy debate in the diagnosis of learning disability), empirical links together with improved diagnostic descriptions will certainly contribute to a fuller determination of the clinical relevance of intelligence tests such as the WISC-IV in the identification of and program prescription for children with special needs. There is still much that needs to be learned about intelligence, but there is also much that we know and can use in our descriptions and understanding of children (Deary, 2001; Neisser *et al.*, 1996; Saklofske, 1996). The practicing psychologist, like the physician or psychiatrist who must also diagnose complex conditions and prescribe treatments from a potentially large pool (e.g., the various pharmacological and psychotherapies for depression), must keep abreast of the current literature if they are to use the WISC-IV intelligently (Weiss, Saklofske, & Prifitera, 2003).

INTELLIGENCE AND THE WISC-IV

Much has been written on the history of the Wechsler tests and indeed about David Wechsler (see Boake, 2002; Tulsky *et al.*, 2003). It is indeed quite an accomplishment to know that the WISC-III and its predecessors, the WISC (Wechsler, 1949) and WISC-R (Wechsler, 1974), were among the most frequently used, individually administered, standardized intelligence tests in use during their time. There is every indication that the WISC-IV will live up to this high expectation. Yet, the question already posed by some is whether the Wechsler tests have outlived their usefulness for assessing children's intelligence in both the research but especially the clinical context. Thus we might expect that the most suspense preceding the publication of the WISC-IV was whether it was simply to be an update of the WISC-III or a radically different test. After all, new tests grounded in various theoretical models have appeared in recent years (e.g., CAS) and claim to have many advantages over a test that still follows a definition of intelligence as an aggregate or global capacity "of the individual to act purposefully, to think rationally, and to deal effectively with his environment" (Wechsler, 1944, p. 3).

The WISC-IV Technical and Interpretive Manual and Chapter 1 of this book have addressed the general issues relevant to the structure of intelligence, ecological validity of general intelligence, and limitations of a single test to tap the full range of intelligence. The most significant changes to the WISC-IV include the updating of norms, the addition of five new subtests, and the way that a child's cognitive abilities can now be represented. The FSIQ is retained because it is still so widely used in assessment and research, as discussed later. For this reason we have again suggested that the General Ability Index, composed of the 6 VCI and PRI subtests, may serve as a useful and representative indicator of general mental ability under particular conditions. At the same time, the emergence of the four-factor structure in the WISC-III was a major advancement in the Wechsler ability tests and in intelligence testing. While the factor scores were optional in contrast to the most often used VIQ and PIQ, practitioners and researchers alike have found considerable clinical utility in these scores over the past 12 years. Thus the WISC-IV has retained the FSIQ but dismantled the VIQ and PIQ and has elevated the four index scores to the primary level of interpretation (described in Chapter 3). The following section focuses on the FSIQ and the GAI.

WISC-IV FULL SCALE IQ

The calculation of a Full Scale IQ (FSIQ) continues to be important for several reasons. From a purely psychometric perspective, a general factor tends to emerge in studies of intelligence (Carroll, 1993) and is found in almost all intelligence tests that tap a cognitively complex array of abilities. The research literature has reported more studies on the relevance of general mental ability as a predictor of a vast array of other human behaviors than for any other major psychological concept or variable. Described in the WISC-IV Technical and Interpretive Manual is support for a general factor that has retained the label of FSIQ. The pattern of subtest correlations and the factor structure attest to this, as shown in Tables 5.1 and 5.3 through 5.6 of the manual. In fact, the correlations between the FSIQ and the 10 core subtests range from .46 to 72; the four index scores correlated between .70 and .86 with the FSIQ. This makes a psychometrically compelling case for the calculation of the FSIQ. But does it make a case for the clinical usefulness of the FSIQ?

More to the point, the key issue for psychologists is the relevance and meaning of the FSIQ in applied assessment practices. There is considerable ecological and criterion validity for the use of a measure of general intelligence (Gottfredson, 1997, 1998; Kuncel, Hezlett, & Ones, 2004). The FSIQ is central to defining and identifying children who are mentally retarded and intellectually gifted (see Chapters 8 and 9) as well as in aiding in the diagnosis of low achievers and learning disabilities as described in Chapter 6. It is a most useful summary score when there is little subtest or index score variability. For some time, the primary vehicle used by school psychologists for obtaining assistance for low achieving children has been to identify a significant discrepancy between the FSIQ and some standardized measure of achievement in such areas as reading and arithmetic. The ability-achievement discrepancy was written into federal law under the Individuals with Disabilities Education Act (IDEA: Public Law 101-476, 1990; IDEA '97, Public Law 105-17, 1997) and adopted by virtually all school districts in the United States; this "test data criteria" for identifying underachieving children was already commonplace in Canada and beyond. Now under review, it is likely that the ability-achievement discrepancy model will be only one method (e.g., documenting responsiveness to empirically supported classroom interventions; clinical evaluations of deficits in core cognitive processes that underlie specific disorders) for determining eligibility for special education services.

While there is convincing statistical evidence that the WISC-IV continues to adhere to Wechsler's broad definition of intelligence, another question facing the practitioner is how similar the FSIQ is from WISC-III to WISC-IV because of the change in items, subtest composition (e.g., addition of Matrix Reasoning, deletion of Object Assembly), and the differential contribution to the FSIQ from subtests that also align with the four factors (3 subtests for VC and PR, 2 WM, and 2 PS on the WISC-IV vs. 4 VC and PO, 2 WM and PS on the WISC-III). This is a critical point with respect to how much can be generalized from the clinical and research literature and professional experiences related to the WISC-III. Furthermore for children being reassessed using the WISC-IV, there is also the question of score differences. As expected from what is now commonly referred to as the Flynn Effect (e.g., Flynn, 1984, 1998), the WISC-III FSIQ will be higher than WISC-IV FSIQ. Based on the standardization data, the corrected correlation between WISC-III and WISC-IV FSIQ is .89, with a 2.5 higher score difference for WISC-III FSIQ.

In relation to other tests linked with the WISC-IV, the FSIQ in almost all instances shows the highest correlation with subtests tapping both achievement and memory. The FSIQ also correlates more highly with the GRS-S than do any of the index scores. In the final analysis, the psychologist must decide if the FSIQ is both accurate and relevant to describing the intelligence of the child being assessed, and in turn use this information to serve the best interests of the child.

While the structure of the WISC-IV, together with the suggested profile analyses outlined in the Technical and Interpretation Manual, might suggest essentially a top down approach to test score interpretation, beginning with the FSIQ, this is not strictly the case. If the 10 subtest scores or four index scores are not substantially different from each other, then the FSIQ can in all likelihood be considered a clinically useful and relevant estimate of overall ability. This is because the FSIQ incorporates not only verbal and nonverbal reasoning but also working memory and processing speed that are considered important to overall intelligence (see later).

It is quite possible, however, for a factor to "fracture" because the parts that comprise it break from the expected relationship amongst scores. When the psychologist discovers large differences between index scores or between some index scores and the FSIQ, then the FSIQ cannot and should not stand alone as the overall summary of a child's cognitive abilities. Rather, the interpretation of the FSIQ must also include a discussion of the differences in the various abilities of the child. Alternatively, the psychologist may elect not to report the FSIQ because it does not portray a clinically meaningful picture of the child's widely diverse abilities. In fact, reporting a FSIQ composed of subtest scores within and between factors that show considerable variability could lead to an inaccurate picture of the child's abilities. Thus, a child with VC and WM scores in the borderline and low average range, respectively, and PR and PS scores in the high average range is likely not to be well understood by the teacher in relation to his or her equally diverse achievement in the classroom if only an FSIQ of 98 is reported. To facilitate a clearer understanding of the child's WISC-IV results, a report might state:

> Maria's abilities cannot be accurately summarized by a single score. Her nonverbal reasoning abilities are much better developed than her verbal comprehension and reasoning abilities, and this is likely to be noticeable in the variability of her performance across classroom and other activities that tap these abilities.

Whether or not to calculate and report the FSIQ was a somewhat easier decision to make on the WISC-III because the VIQ and PIQ were summed together to yield the FSIQ. The WISC-IV FSIQ is a composite of the 10 subtests, although if the 10 core subtests are administered, this essentially yields the four index scores. Critical value and base rate tables for discrepancy comparisons contained in Appendix B.1 through B.6 of the WISC-IV Administration and Scoring Manual should be consulted to determine the appropriateness of combining subtests to yield both index scores and the FSIQ. These tables indicate when subtest and index scores differ significantly, as well as the base rate or frequency of various scaled score differences. At the end of this chapter is a table and description by Dr. S. Longman that permits a comparison of each index score to the mean of all four scores (see Appendix A). These tables should serve as guideposts for determining whether it is meaningful to proceed with the calculation and use of more summary or composite scores.

What size discrepancy invalidates the Full Scale score? Although an 11-point discrepancy, on average, is statistically significant at the $p < .05$ level for VCI-PRI discrepancies, differences of this size are not uncommon. In fact, 22% and almost 19% of the children in the WISC-IV standardization sample obtained VCI < PRI and VCI > PRI differences of 11 points or greater. This occurs because the formula for statistical significance takes into account the size of the sample (2200 children in the WISC-IV standardization sample). It should be remembered that "even the smallest relationship can become statistically significant if a large enough sample is used for the study" (Ives, 2003). Of even more relevance to psychologists is the "practicality" of results. While the difference between two or more WISC-IV index or subtest scores may be statistically significant, the results may not be of practical significance. Some psychologists may say that if the difference occurs in 10% of cases or less, then it is considered less common (or rare) and therefore potentially clinically meaningful, or at least it warrants further examination. As a general rule of thumb, we might suggest that a 20-point V-P discrepancy should raise red flags in the examiner's mind. A 20-point or greater VCI < PRI and VCI > PRI discrepancy was obtained by 6.1% and 6.7% of the sample, respectively. Of course this frequency varies depending on the index score comparisons being made, as well as the base rate for the population in which the individual is a member.

AN ALTERNATE APPROACH TO SUMMARIZING GENERAL INTELLECTUAL ABILITY: THE GENERAL ABILITY INDEX (GAI)

The Full Scale IQ score has been the only comprehensive method available within the Wechsler scales for summarizing overall or general cognitive ability. The model of intelligence proposed by David Wechsler as "an aggregate and global entity" continues through to the WISC-IV. As presented in Table 5.1 of the WISC-IV Technical and Interpretation Manual, correlations between the 10 core subtests of the WISC-IV are positive and low to moderately high (ranging from .10 to .75, with many falling in the .3 to .5 range), as are the correlations between each of the subtests with the FSIQ (ranging from .46 to .72). This lends support to the determination of a FSIQ. It would seem to make good sense for the FSIQ to broadly reflect the cognitive complexity of a test that measures VC, PR, WM, and PS. However, in the process of diagnosis, it may be most useful to determine how such important neurocognitive factors as WM and PS impact on the expression of intelligent behavior reflected in the broader FSIQ and the cognitively complex VC and PR factors.

As is so well known by teachers and psychologists, three children, all with a FSIQ of 100, may perform quite differently in the classroom and other real-world contexts. One child shows little variability on the WISC-IV subtests and index scores and is an average student. The second child has slightly more variable pattern of scores, is not motivated, has a poor academic self-concept, and is somewhat test anxious, all resulting in poor classroom achievement. The third child has high average scores on the PRI, average on the VCI and

WMI, but borderline scores on the PSI and an inconsistent pattern of achievement. Thus the FSIQ may at times be too gross a measure, since all three children with IQs of 100 would be predicted to manifest similar achievement results. The clear presence of WM and PS in the WISC-IV and their important role in describing the cognitive abilities of children also suggests there may be considerable clinical utility in determining or parsing out the effects of WM and/or PS on the expression of intelligent behavior

Concurrently, but from a different perspective, the search for a quick and accurate estimate of FSIQ has followed the publication of each of the more recent Wechsler tests. Sattler and Saklofske (2001a) describe the various short forms of the WISC-III. In general the best short forms have very good validity coefficients ranging from .81 to .86 for two subtests to .90 or higher for four and five subtests short forms. While "short forms save time and are useful screening devices, they have certain disadvantages" (Sattler & Saklofske, 2001a, p. 258).

Beginning with the WISC-III, which, like the WAIS-III, employed both VIQ and PIQ as well as index scores, we suggested that the FSIQ may not necessarily be the best or only way to summarize overall ability when the VCI and POI are better estimates of verbal and performance reasoning (Prifitera, Weiss, & Saklofske, 1998; Weiss, Saklofske, & Prifitera, 2003). The main issue here was the potential for confusion arising from the inclusion of the Arithmetic subtest on the VIQ but not on the VCI; rather, the Arithmetic subtest was placed on the WMI. The same argument was proposed in relation to PIQ vs POI because of the Coding subtest being part of both PIQ and PSI, but not POI. Further, if the intent of the assessment was to make full use of the IQ and index scores for interpretation, then having particular tests such as Arithmetic and Coding serve more than one purpose may confuse or confound this purpose. At a clinical level, those children who manifest problems in WM and/or PS will possibly earn lower scores on Arithmetic and Coding, which, in turn, can lower the FSIQ. For example, lower PS and WM scores are of note with some LD and Attention Deficit–Hyperactivity Disorder (AD/HD) children (see Schwean & Saklofske, 1998; Schwean & Saklofske, Chapter 7), and processing speed is a sensitive indicator of traumatic brain injury. As long as school districts continue to employ ability-achievement discrepancies as a major or even minor criterion for determining eligibility for special education services, the FSIQ may reduce this ability-achievement difference.

We previously suggested that psychologists using the WISC-III may prefer an alternative composite score derived from the subtests that enter the VCI and the POI. This composite score was termed the *General Ability Index* (GAI). On the WISC-III, the GAI is an eight subtest composite that excludes both Arithmetic and Coding, which load on the FD and PS factors, respectively. It is those subtests that load on the VCI and POI that also account for the most variance when estimating FSIQ. In fact, the Wechsler Abbreviated Scale of Intelligence (WASI; Wechsler, 1999) assesses FSIQ using either 2 or 4 subtests that would clearly be labeled as VC (Vocabulary and Similarities) and PR (Block Design and Matrix Reasoning). Here the correlations between the WASI 2 and 4 subtest FSIQ respectively and the WISC-IV FSIQ is .83 and .86; the WISC-IV Technical and Interpretive Manual reports correlations of .89 between the FSIQ scores of WISC-IV and WPPSI-III, WISC-III, and WAIS-III. Of relevance is that the GAI and FSIQ were found to correlate .98 in the Canadian WISC-III standardization sample (Weiss, Saklofske, Prifitera, Chen, & Hildebrand, 1999), suggesting that both measures provide an excellent estimate of general mental ability as reflected by the content of the WISC-III. This same procedure has recently been recommended for use with the WAIS-III, where the VCI and POI are composed of only 3 subtests each (Tulsky, Saklofske, Wilkins, & Weiss, 2001; Saklofske, Gorsuch, Weiss, Zhu & Patterson, in press). The GAI allows the examiner to estimate the child's general level of ability; the FSIQ might then, in comparison to the GAI, provide an indication of the effects of depressed (or elevated) WM and PS.

GAI NORM TABLES

GAI norms for the WISC-IV are presented in Table 2.1. GAI reliability coefficients for ages 6–16 years are as follows: .94, .95, .95, .96, .96, .96, .97, .96, .96, .96, and .96. These were calculated from the subtest reliabilities reported in the WISC-IV Manual using the formula for the reliability of a composite. The average GAI reliability, computed using Fisher's z transformations for ages 6 through 11, is $r = .95$, and for ages 12 through 16 is $r = .96$. The WISC–IV GAI and FSIQ correlate 96.

To use the WISC-IV GAI norms table, first calculate the general ability sum of scaled scores (SSS) by adding the scaled scores for the following six subtests: Vocabulary, Comprehension, Similarities, Block Design, Matrix Reasoning, and Picture Concepts. Find the resulting General Ability SSS in the column labeled Sum of Scaled Scores in Table 2.1 and read across the row to determine the GAI score, associated percentile rank, and confidence interval.

WHEN TO USE THE GAI

Estimates of overall intelligence calculated in this way should *always* be clearly identified as *General Ability Index* scores in psychological and psychoeducational reports. When the GAI is reported, it is because the psychologist has determined that it represents the best summary of the student's overall intelligence and, when clinically appropriate, should be given primary consideration in relevant psychological, educational, and vocational decisions. The GAI may be used to determine eligibility for services, and placement decisions in the same manner as the FSIQ is used only when it is deemed to provide the most accurate assessment of the child's general

TABLE 2.1   GAI Equivalents of Sums of Scaled Scores

Sum of Scaled Scores	GAI	Percentile Rank	Confidence Level		Sum of Scaled Scores	GAI	Percentile Rank	Confidence Level	
			90%	95%				90%	95%
6	40	<0.1	38–47	37–48	41	81	10	77–86	76–87
7	40	<0.1	38–47	37–48	42	82	12	78–87	77–88
8	40	<0.1	38–47	37–48	43	83	13	79–88	78–89
9	40	<0.1	38–47	37–48	44	84	14	80–89	79–90
10	40	<0.1	38–47	37–48	45	85	16	81–90	80–91
11	40	<0.1	38–47	37–48	46	86	18	82–91	81–92
12	41	<0.1	39–48	38–49	47	87	19	83–92	82–93
13	42	<0.1	40–49	39–50	48	88	21	84–93	83–94
14	43	<0.1	41–50	40–51	49	89	23	85–94	84–95
15	44	<0.1	42–51	41–52	50	90	25	86–95	85–96
16	45	<0.1	42–52	42–53	51	91	27	87–96	86–97
17	46	<0.1	43–53	43–54	52	92	30	88–97	87–98
18	47	<0.1	44–54	43–55	53	93	32	89–98	88–99
19	49	<0.1	46–56	45–57	54	94	34	90–99	89–100
20	51	0.1	48–58	47–59	55	95	37	90–100	90–101
21	52	0.1	49–59	48–60	56	96	39	91–101	91–102
22	53	0.1	50–60	49–61	57	97	42	92–102	91–103
23	55	0.1	52–62	51–62	58	98	45	93–103	92–104
24	57	0.2	54–63	53–64	59	99	47	94–104	93–105
25	58	0.3	55–64	54–65	60	100	50	95–105	94–106
26	59	0.3	56–65	55–66	61	101	53	96–106	95–107
27	61	0.5	58–67	57–68	62	102	55	97–107	96–108
28	63	1	60–69	59–70	63	103	58	98–108	97–109
29	64	1	61–70	60–71	64	104	61	99–109	98–109
30	65	1	62–71	61–72	65	105	63	100–110	99–110
31	67	1	64–73	63–74	66	106	66	101–110	100–111
32	69	2	66–75	65–76	67	107	68	102–111	101–112
33	70	2	66–76	66–77	68	108	70	103–112	102–113
34	71	3	67–77	67–78	69	110	75	105–114	104–115
35	73	4	69–79	68–80	70	111	77	106–115	105–116
36	74	4	70–80	69–81	71	112	79	107–116	106–117
37	75	5	71–81	70–82	72	113	81	108–117	107–118
38	77	6	73–83	72–84	73	115	84	110–119	109–120
39	78	7	74–84	73–85	74	116	86	111–120	110–121
40	79	8	75–85	74–85	75	117	87	112–121	111–122

(Continues)

TABLE 2.1 GAI Equivalents of Sums of Scaled Scores (*continued*)

Sum of Scaled Scores	GAI	Percentile Rank	Confidence Level		Sum of Scaled Scores	GAI	Percentile Rank	Confidence Level	
			90%	95%				90%	95%
76	119	90	114–123	113–124	95	143	99.8	137–146	136–147
77	120	91	114–124	114–125	96	144	99.8	138–147	137–148
78	121	92	115–125	115–126	97	146	99.9	139–149	139–150
79	122	93	116–126	115–127	98	147	99.9	140–150	139–151
80	123	94	117–127	116–128	99	148	99.9	141–151	140–152
81	124	95	118–128	117–129	100	150	>99.9	143–153	142–154
82	126	96	120–130	119–131	101	151	>99.9	144–154	143–155
83	127	96	121–131	120–132	102	153	>99.9	146–156	145–157
84	128	97	122–132	121–133	103	154	>99.9	147–157	146–157
85	129	97	123–133	122–133	104	155	>99.9	148–158	147–158
86	130	98	124–134	123–134	105	156	>99.9	149–158	148–159
87	132	98	126–135	125–136	106	157	>99.9	150–159	149–160
88	133	99	127–136	126–137	107	158	>99.9	151–160	150–161
89	135	99	129–138	128–139	108	159	>99.9	152–161	151–162
90	136	99	130–139	129–140	109	160	>99.9	153–162	152–163
91	138	99	132–141	131–142	110	160	>99.9	153–162	152–163
92	139	99.5	133–142	132–143	111	160	>99.9	153–162	152–163
93	140	99.6	134–143	133–144	112	160	>99.9	153–162	152–163
94	142	99.7	136–145	135–146	113	160	>99.9	153–162	152–163
					114	160	>99.9	153–162	152–163

mental ability. To assist the examiner, Table 2.2 shows the differences between GAI and FSIQ required for statistical significance.

What are the likely consequences of using the GAI in educational decisions? In some special education cases, the GAI will result in a slightly higher estimate of overall intellectual ability than the FSIQ. This occurs when either or both of the subtests comprising WM and PS, and in turn, the index scores, are significantly below both the VC and PR, as well as the FSIQ score. In determining eligibility to receive services for learning disabilities, this can increase the discrepancy between achievement and ability when estimated by the GAI, and in turn may increase the chances of receiving special assistance for some students. In placement decisions for entrance into gifted and talented programs, high functioning LD students may also have a better chance of being determined eligible based on the GAI score than on the FSIQ score. As before, several studies have reported that children with particular learning difficulties and ADHD tend to earn lower scores on both FD or WM and PS, suggesting that they would also tend to be more likely to have slightly higher GAI than FSIQ scores (see Schwean & Saklofske, 1998). Since there is also some evidence that children identified as gifted tend to score lower on both WM (M = 112.5) and PS (M = 110.6) in contrast to VC (M = 124.7) and PR (M = 120.4) (see Table 5.22 in the WISC-IV Technical and Interpretive Manual), the GAI score may also boost some children over their school district's preset cut-off score for entrance into gifted and talented programs. Of course, the situation can be different for any given student, especially when WM and PS are significantly higher than the FSIQ. For example, the standardization data suggest a tendency for African American and Hispanic children to score slightly higher on WM and PS than on VC and PR. The decision of which summary score to use should be based on these considerations and not on the desired outcome.

At the low end of the distribution, the situation is less clear. While the GAI score may tend to be higher than the FSIQ among certain special education populations, there is also some evidence that very low functioning children tend to score higher on Coding and Symbol Search than on other more cognitively challenging subtests (see Table 5.23, WISC-IV Technical and Interpretive Manual). This may be because these tasks are similar to the matching and copying drills used in many MR classrooms and are highly practiced skills. It should also be remembered that both of these subtests are cognitively very simple, as the aim was to measure processing speed. Thus, for some children in the intellectually deficient range (FSIQ < 70), the GAI score may tend to be lower than the FSIQ score. Of course, placement

TABLE 2.2   Difference Between GAI and FSIQ Scores Required for Statistical Significance (Critical Values) by Age Group and Overall Standardization Sample

Age Group	Level of Significance	Composite Pair GAI-FSIQ
6–11	.15	5.78
	.05	7.87
12–16	.15	6.31
	.05	8.59
All Ages	.15	5.90
	.05	8.03

Note. Differences required for statistical significance are based on the standard errors of measurement of each composite for each age group and calculated with the following formula:

$$\text{Critical Value of Difference Score} = Z\sqrt{SEM_a^2 + SEM_b^2}$$

where Z is the normal curve value associated with the desired two-tailed significance level and SEM^a and SEM^b are the standard errors of measurement for the two composites.

TABLE 2.3 Cumulative Percentages of GAI-FSIQ Discrepancies (Base Rates) by Clinical Group

| | Clinical Group | | | | | | |
| | Gifted (N = 59) | | MR-Mild (N = 56) | | MR-Moderate (N = 47) | | |
Amount of Discrepancy	GAI > FSIQ (−)	GAI < FSIQ (+)	GAI > FSIQ (−)	GAI < FSIQ (+)	GAI > FSIQ (−)	GAI < FSIQ (+)	Amount of Discrepancy
18	0	0	0	0	0	0	18
17	1.7	0	0	0	0	0	17
16	3.3	0	0	0	0	0	16
15	3.3	0	0	0	0	0	15
14	3.3	0	0	0	0	0	14
13	3.3	0	0	0	2.1	0	13
12	5	0	0	0	2.1	0	12
11	8.3	0	0	0	2.1	0	11
10	13.3	0	1.8	0	2.1	2.1	10
9	15	0	3.6	0	2.1	4.2	9
8	20	0	7.1	3.6	2.1	6.3	8
7	25	0	10.7	7.1	2.1	8.3	7
6	31.7	0	14.3	17.9	2.1	14.6	6
5	40	0	16.1	25	2.1	22.9	5
4	43.3	6.7	17.9	33.9	2.1	25	4
3	53.3	13.3	25	50	4.2	29.2	3
2	65	20	33.9	51.8	4.2	39.6	2
1	68.3	25	37.5	57.1	6.3	54.2	1
Mean	5.9	2.6	4.48	4.31	5.7	6.4	Mean
SD	3.9	1.1	2.8	1.93	3.8	2.7	SD

decisions for children with mental retardation should also be based on a comprehensive assessment that includes measures of adaptive functioning such as the Vineland Adaptive Behavior Scales (Sparrow, Balla, & Cicchetti, 1984) or the Adaptive Behavior Assessment Scales (Harrison & Oakland, 2003; Spruill, Oakland, & Harrison, Chapter 9 this book).

To guide the examiner, Table 2.3 presents GAI-FSIQ score differences for children in the standardization study who met criteria for gifted and mild and moderate retarded classifications. Readers are referred to Tables 5.22 to 5.37 in the WISC-IV Technical and Interpretive Manual, which present the index and FSIQ scores for various clinical groups. This information provides some indication of which groups are likely to earn lower or higher GAI than FSIQ scores based on the VC and PR vs WM and PS index score similarities and differences.

Finally, IQ and GAI (or index scores) that vary by only a few points will not have much differential impact on diagnostic accuracy. There is really nothing that is clinically significant or meaningfully useful about a FSIQ-GAI difference of two to three points, although this could affect a strictly statistical comparison of ability-achievement discrepancy. Even though cut-off scores are used for selection of placement purposes, there is clearly no statistical or clinically discernable difference between an IQ score of 130 that might be the minimum score required for selection into a gifted education program, and 129. There are many combinations of subtest scores that can yield either a FSIQ or GAI of 70, 100, 120, etc. Only at the extreme ends of the FSIQ or GAI range would one also expect all of the subtest scores to be either uniformly very high or very low. Again remember that 100 people all earning a FSIQ or GAI of 100 (50th percentile) may also vary in as many ways as there are individual differences variables. Every teacher can recall several or more children with average IQ scores but their paths of achievement and accomplishments varied: one who failed and dropped out of school, one who completed high school and works as a salesperson, another who went to a university and earned a degree and is now a teacher, and yet another who didn't complete high school but now is an internationally successful artist. This may be a good point to stress that tests do not make decisions (e.g., diagnostic, placement). That is our professional role and ethical responsibility as psychologists, and thus we must use tests such as the WISC-IV and the information gleaned from them to serve the best interests of children.

ABILITY–ACHIEVEMENT DISCREPANCIES: THE GAI AND WIAT-II

Most state departments of education continue to require evidence of a significant discrepancy between a student's ability and achievement in one or more content areas defined under the Individuals with Disabilities Education Act (IDEA: Public Law 101-476, 1990; IDEA '97, Public Law 105-17, 1997) in order to qualify the student for special educational services. To accomplish this comparison, some states use the simple difference method, while others use the predicted difference method (see Gridley & Roid, 1998; Konold, 1999).

In the WISC-IV Technical and Interpretive Manual are tables showing Wechsler Individual Achievement Test-Second Edition (WIAT-II, The Psychological Corporation, 2001) subtest and composite scores predicted from the WISC-IV FSIQ. The WIAT-II is a psychometrically sound achievement measure with extended diagnostic capabilities (Smith, 2001). Based on our suggestion that the GAI may, in many cases, be used in place of the FSIQ if the purpose is to mainly reflect general mental ability, the following tables have been created by the same statistical methods and using the same linking sample (n = 550) described in the WISC-IV technical manual for the prediction of scores on the WIAT-II from the WISC-IV GAI scores previously presented.

SIMPLE DIFFERENCE METHOD

The simple difference method involves subtracting the student's ability score, such as the WISC-IV FSIQ or GAI, from the child's score on a nationally standardized achievement test such as the WIAT-II. These two tests were examined together in a linking study during the standardization of the WISC-IV, which increases the likelihood that psychologists will use both tests when assessing intelligence and achievement.

For practitioners to most effectively utilize the simple difference method, it is also important to know the magnitude of the difference between ability and achievement required for statistical significance, as well as the frequency with which a difference of that magnitude occurs in the population. This information is already available in relation to the WISC-IV FSIQ but not for the GAI. Table 2.4 shows the differences between WISC-IV GAI scores and WIAT-II subtest and composite standard scores required for statistical significance for children in two age bands. For a 9-year-old child, a GAI score of 95 and a WIAT-II Word Reading standard score of 85 (a 10-point difference) would be considered a significant difference at the $p < .01$ level. Table 2.5 shows the differences between WISC-IV GAI scores and WIAT-II subtest and composite standard scores obtained by various percentages of children. As shown in this table, a 10-point difference between GAI and Word Reading was obtained by 14% of the children in the WISC-IV/WIAT-II linking sample.

PREDICTED DIFFERENCE METHOD

The ability score is used here to predict the students expected score on the achievement test (based on statistical regression equations, or their equivalents). This predicted achievement score is then compared to the student's actual achievement score, and the difference is evaluated for significance. This method is preferred on statistical grounds, but requires the use of ability and achievement tests that have been co-normed (and correlated) on the same national sample, which was done with the WIAT-II and WISC-IV. Thus, WISC-IV and WIAT-II discrepancy scores derived from the predicted difference method are based on ability and achievement scores that were obtained at the same point in time.

Tables for predicting WIAT-II achievement scores based on the WISC-IV GAI score are presented. Table 2.6 shows WIAT-II subtest and composite standard scores predicted from WISC-IV GAI scores for children ages 6 through 16 years old. The examiner looks up the student's obtained GAI score in this table, and then reads across the row to the predicted

TABLE 2.4   Differences Between WISC-IV GAI Scores and WIAT-II Subtest and Composite Scores Required for Statistical Significance (Critical Values): Simple-Difference and Predicted-Difference Methods by Age-Band

| | | Ages 6–11 | | Ages 12–16 | |
| | | Simple-Difference | Predicted-Difference | Simple-Difference | Predicted-Difference |
Subtest/Composite	Significance Level	GAI	GAI	GAI	GAI
Word Reading	.05	7.20	4.87	8.32	6.92
	.01	9.48	6.41	10.95	9.11
Numerical Operations	.05	13.15	12.01	9.75	8.59
	.01	17.31	15.81	12.84	11.31
Reading Comprehension	.05	8.32	6.52	8.82	7.52
	.01	10.95	8.59	11.61	9.90
Spelling	.05	9.75	8.24	9.75	8.38
	.01	12.84	10.85	12.84	11.03
Pseudoword Decoding	.05	7.78	5.42	7.78	5.91
	.01	10.24	7.14	10.24	7.78
Math Reasoning	.05	10.18	8.91	9.75	8.80
	.01	13.41	11.72	12.84	11.58
Written Expression	.05	12.47	11.18	12.47	11.59
	.01	16.42	14.72	16.42	15.25
Listening Comprehension	.05	13.79	12.77	14.10	13.41
	.01	18.15	16.81	18.56	17.65
Oral Expression	.05	11.76	10.21	12.82	11.73
	.01	15.48	13.44	16.87	15.44
Reading	.05	7.20	5.03	7.20	5.65
	.01	9.48	6.62	9.48	7.43
Math	.05	10.18	8.91	8.32	7.18
	.01	13.41	11.72	10.95	9.45
Written Language	.05	9.75	8.24	11.76	10.82
	.01	12.84	10.85	15.48	14.24
Oral Language	.05	11.00	9.66	9.75	8.72
	.01	14.48	12.72	12.84	11.48
Total	.05	7.78	6.25	7.20	5.93
	.01	10.24	8.23	9.48	7.81

TABLE 2.5   Differences Between Predicted and Obtained WIAT-II Subtest and Composite Scores for Various Percentages of the Theoretical Normal Distribution (Base Rates): Simple-Difference Method Using WISC-IV GAI

Subtest/Composite	Percentage of Theoretical Normal Distribution (Base Rates)								
	25	20	15	10	5	4	3	2	1
Word Reading	8	10	12	14	18	19	21	23	26
Numerical Operations	9	11	13	16	21	22	23	26	29
Reading Comprehension	8	9	11	14	18	19	20	22	25
Spelling	8	10	13	16	20	21	23	25	28
Pseudoword Decoding	10	12	14	18	23	24	26	28	32
Math Reasoning	8	9	11	14	18	19	20	22	25
Written Expression	9	11	13	16	21	22	24	26	29
Listening Comprehension	7	8	10	13	16	17	18	20	23
Oral Expression	10	12	15	19	24	25	27	29	33
Reading	7	9	11	14	17	18	20	21	24
Mathematics	8	9	11	14	18	19	20	22	25
Written Language	8	10	12	15	19	20	22	24	27
Oral Language	7	9	11	14	17	18	20	21	24
Total	6	7	9	11	14	15	16	17	20

Note: Percentages represent the proportions of the sample who obtained WIAT-II scores lower than their WISC-IV GAI scores by the specified amount or more.

achievement score. For example, according to this table, a child with a GAI score of 90 is predicted to have a Reading Comprehension (RC) standard score of 93. This is due to a statistical phenomenon known as *regression to the mean*. Let's say this child obtained an RC score of 79. The simple difference between her GAI (90) and RC (79) scores would be 11 points, but the difference between her predicted (93) and obtained (79) RC scores would be 14 points. Note, however, that for children with ability scores above 100, the regression to the mean phenomenon works in reverse so that the difference between predicted and obtained achievement scores would be smaller than the simple difference.

When using the predicted difference method, Table 2.4 also shows the differences between predicted and actual WIAT-II subtest and composite standard scores required for statistical significance in two age bands. Table 2.7 shows the differences between predicted and actual WIAT-II subtest and composite standard scores obtained by various percentages of children.

TABLE 2.6   WIAT-II Subtest and Composite Scores Predicted from WISC-IV GAI Scores

	WIAT-II														
	Subtest Scores									Composite Scores					
WISC-IV GAI	WR	NO	RC	SP	PD	MR	WE	LC	OE	RD	MA	WL	OL	TA	WISC-IV GAI
40	56	60	55	59	64	54	60	52	66	54	55	57	54	49	40
41	56	60	56	59	65	55	61	53	67	55	56	58	55	50	41
42	57	61	57	60	65	56	62	54	68	55	57	58	55	51	42
43	58	62	57	61	66	57	62	54	68	56	57	59	56	52	43
44	59	62	58	61	66	57	63	55	69	57	58	60	57	52	44
45	59	63	59	62	67	58	64	56	69	58	59	60	58	53	45
46	60	64	60	63	68	59	64	57	70	58	60	61	58	54	46
47	61	64	60	63	68	60	65	58	70	59	60	62	59	55	47
48	62	65	61	64	69	60	66	58	71	60	61	63	60	56	48
49	62	66	62	65	69	61	66	59	71	61	62	63	61	57	49
50	63	67	63	66	70	62	67	60	72	62	63	64	62	58	50
51	64	67	63	66	71	63	68	61	73	62	63	65	62	58	51
52	64	68	64	67	71	64	68	62	73	63	64	65	63	59	52
53	65	69	65	68	72	64	69	62	74	64	65	66	64	60	53
54	66	69	66	68	72	65	70	63	74	65	66	67	65	61	54
55	67	70	66	69	73	66	70	64	75	65	66	68	65	62	55
56	67	71	67	70	74	67	71	65	75	66	67	68	66	63	56
57	68	71	68	70	74	67	72	66	76	67	68	69	67	63	57
58	69	72	69	71	75	68	72	66	76	68	69	70	68	64	58
59	70	73	69	72	75	69	73	67	77	68	69	70	68	65	59
60	70	73	70	72	76	70	74	68	78	69	70	71	69	66	60
61	71	74	71	73	77	70	74	69	78	70	71	72	70	67	61
62	72	75	72	74	77	71	75	70	79	71	72	73	71	68	62
63	73	75	72	74	78	72	76	70	79	72	72	73	72	69	63
64	73	76	73	75	78	73	76	71	80	72	73	74	72	69	64
65	74	77	74	76	79	73	77	72	80	73	74	75	73	70	65
66	75	77	75	77	80	74	78	73	81	74	75	76	74	71	66
67	76	78	75	77	80	75	78	74	82	75	75	76	75	72	67
68	76	79	76	78	81	76	79	74	82	75	76	77	75	73	68
69	77	79	77	79	81	76	80	75	83	76	77	78	76	74	69
70	78	80	78	79	82	77	80	76	83	77	78	78	77	75	70

(Continues)

TABLE 2.6 (*Continued*)

| | WIAT-II | | | | | | | | | | | | | | |
| | Subtest Scores | | | | | | | | | Composite Scores | | | | | |
WISC-IV GAI	WR	NO	RC	SP	PD	MR	WE	LC	OE	RD	MA	WL	OL	TA	WISC-IV GAI
71	79	81	78	80	83	78	81	77	84	78	78	79	78	75	71
72	79	81	79	81	83	79	82	78	84	78	79	80	78	76	72
73	80	82	80	81	84	79	82	78	85	79	80	81	79	77	73
74	81	83	81	82	84	80	83	79	85	80	81	81	80	78	74
75	82	83	81	83	85	81	84	80	86	81	81	82	81	79	75
76	82	84	82	83	86	82	84	81	87	82	82	83	82	80	76
77	83	85	83	84	86	83	85	82	87	82	83	83	82	80	77
78	84	85	84	85	87	83	85	82	88	83	84	84	83	81	78
79	84	86	84	86	87	84	86	83	88	84	84	85	84	82	79
80	85	87	85	86	88	85	87	84	89	85	85	86	85	83	80
81	86	87	86	87	89	86	87	85	89	85	86	86	85	84	81
82	87	88	87	88	89	86	88	86	90	86	87	87	86	85	82
83	87	89	87	88	90	87	89	86	90	87	87	88	87	86	83
84	88	89	88	89	90	88	89	87	91	88	88	88	88	86	84
85	89	90	89	90	91	89	90	88	92	88	89	89	88	87	85
86	90	91	90	90	92	89	91	89	92	89	90	90	89	88	86
87	90	91	90	91	92	90	91	90	93	90	90	91	90	89	87
88	91	92	91	92	93	91	92	90	93	91	91	91	91	90	88
89	92	93	92	92	93	92	93	91	94	92	92	92	92	91	89
90	93	93	93	93	94	92	93	92	94	92	93	93	92	92	90
91	93	94	93	94	95	93	94	93	95	93	93	94	93	92	91
92	94	95	94	94	95	94	95	94	96	94	94	94	94	93	92
93	95	95	95	95	96	95	95	94	96	95	95	95	95	94	93
94	96	96	96	96	96	95	96	95	97	95	96	96	95	95	94
95	96	97	96	97	97	96	97	96	97	96	96	96	96	96	95
96	97	97	97	97	98	97	97	97	98	97	97	97	97	97	96
97	98	98	98	98	98	98	98	98	98	98	98	98	98	97	97
98	99	99	99	99	99	98	99	98	99	98	99	99	98	98	98
99	99	99	99	99	99	99	99	99	99	99	99	99	99	99	99
100	100	100	100	100	100	100	100	100	100	100	100	100	100	100	100
101	101	101	101	101	101	101	101	101	101	101	101	101	101	101	101
102	101	101	102	101	101	102	101	102	101	102	102	101	102	102	102
103	102	102	102	102	102	102	102	102	102	102	102	102	102	103	103

(*Continues*)

TABLE 2.6   (*Continued*)

	WIAT-II														
	Subtest Scores									Composite Scores					
WISC-IV GAI	WR	NO	RC	SP	PD	MR	WE	LC	OE	RD	MA	WL	OL	TA	WISC-IV GAI
104	103	103	103	103	102	103	103	103	102	103	103	103	103	103	104
105	104	103	104	103	103	104	103	104	103	104	104	104	104	104	105
106	104	104	105	104	104	105	104	105	103	105	105	104	105	105	106
107	105	105	105	105	104	105	105	106	104	105	105	105	105	106	107
108	106	105	106	106	105	106	105	106	104	106	106	106	106	107	108
109	107	106	107	106	105	107	106	107	105	107	107	106	107	108	109
110	107	107	108	107	106	108	107	108	106	108	108	107	108	109	110
111	108	107	108	108	107	108	107	109	106	108	108	108	108	109	111
112	109	108	109	108	107	109	108	110	107	109	109	109	109	110	112
113	110	109	110	109	108	110	109	110	107	110	110	109	110	111	113
114	110	109	111	110	108	111	109	111	108	111	111	110	111	112	114
115	111	110	111	110	109	111	110	112	108	112	111	111	112	113	115
116	112	111	112	111	110	112	111	113	109	112	112	112	112	114	116
117	113	111	113	112	110	113	111	114	110	113	113	112	113	114	117
118	113	112	114	112	111	114	112	114	110	114	114	113	114	115	118
119	114	113	114	113	111	114	113	115	111	115	114	114	115	116	119
120	115	113	115	114	112	115	113	116	111	115	115	114	115	117	120
121	116	114	116	114	113	116	114	117	112	116	116	115	116	118	121
122	116	115	117	115	113	117	115	118	112	117	117	116	117	119	122
123	117	115	117	116	114	117	115	118	113	118	117	117	118	120	123
124	118	116	118	117	114	118	116	119	113	118	118	117	118	120	124
125	119	117	119	117	115	119	117	120	114	119	119	118	119	121	125
126	119	117	120	118	116	120	117	121	115	120	120	119	120	122	126
127	120	118	120	119	116	121	118	122	115	121	120	119	121	123	127
128	121	119	121	119	117	121	118	122	116	122	121	120	122	124	128
129	121	119	122	120	117	122	119	123	116	122	122	121	122	125	129
130	122	120	123	121	118	123	120	124	117	123	123	122	123	126	130
131	123	121	123	121	119	124	120	125	117	124	123	122	124	126	131
132	124	121	124	122	119	124	121	126	118	125	124	123	125	127	132
133	124	122	125	123	120	125	122	126	118	125	125	124	125	128	133
134	125	123	126	123	120	126	122	127	119	126	126	124	126	129	134
135	126	123	126	124	121	127	123	128	120	127	126	125	127	130	135
136	127	124	127	125	122	127	124	129	120	128	127	126	128	131	136
137	127	125	128	126	122	128	124	130	121	128	128	127	128	131	137

(*Continues*)

TABLE 2.6   (*Continued*)

WISC-IV GAI	WIAT-II														WISC-IV GAI
	Subtest Scores									Composite Scores					
	WR	NO	RC	SP	PD	MR	WE	LC	OE	RD	MA	WL	OL	TA	
138	128	125	129	126	123	129	125	130	121	129	129	127	129	132	138
139	129	126	129	127	123	130	126	131	122	130	129	128	130	133	139
140	130	127	130	128	124	130	126	132	122	131	130	129	131	134	140
141	130	127	131	128	125	131	127	133	123	132	131	130	132	135	141
142	131	128	132	129	125	132	128	134	124	132	132	130	132	136	142
143	132	129	132	130	126	133	128	134	124	133	132	131	133	137	143
144	133	129	133	130	126	133	129	135	125	134	133	132	134	137	144
145	133	130	134	131	127	134	130	136	125	135	134	132	135	138	145
146	134	131	135	132	128	135	130	137	126	135	135	133	135	139	146
147	135	131	135	132	128	136	131	138	126	136	135	134	136	140	147
148	136	132	136	133	129	136	132	138	127	137	136	135	137	141	148
149	136	133	137	134	129	137	132	139	127	138	137	135	138	142	149
150	137	134	138	135	130	138	133	140	128	139	138	136	139	143	150
151	138	134	138	135	131	139	134	141	129	139	138	137	139	143	151
152	138	135	139	136	131	140	134	142	129	140	139	137	140	144	152
153	139	136	140	137	132	140	135	142	130	141	140	138	141	145	153
154	140	136	141	137	132	141	136	143	130	142	141	139	142	146	154
155	141	137	141	138	133	142	136	144	131	142	141	140	142	147	155
156	141	138	142	139	134	143	137	145	131	143	142	140	143	148	156
157	142	138	143	139	134	143	138	146	132	144	143	141	144	148	157
158	143	139	144	140	135	144	138	146	132	145	144	142	145	149	158
159	144	140	144	141	135	145	139	147	133	145	144	142	145	150	159
160	144	140	145	141	136	146	140	148	134	146	145	143	146	151	160

WR = Word Reading;   NO = Numerical Operations;   RC = Reading Comp;
SP = Spelling;   PD = Pseudoword Decoding;   MR = Mathematics Reasoning;
WE = Written Expression;   LC = Listening Comp;   OE = Oral Expression;
RD = Reading;   MA = Mathematics;   WL = Written Language;
OL = Oral Language;   TA = Total Achievement.

SOME CAUTIONS FOR USING THE GAI-WIAT-II TABLES

Although the methods described here to conduct ability (GAI)-achievement (WIAT-II) discrepancies are statistically sound and reflect current practice, some cautionary notes about this approach to special education assessment are in order. Practitioners must clearly understand that ability–

TABLE 2.7   Differences Between Predicted and Obtained WIAT-II Subtest and Composite Scores for Various Percentages of the Theoretical Normal Distribution (Base Rates): Predicted-Difference Method Using WISC-IV GAI

Subtest/Composite	Percentage of Theoretical Normal Distribution (Base Rates)								
	25	20	15	10	5	4	3	2	1
Word Reading	7	9	11	13	17	18	19	21	24
Numerical Operations	8	10	12	15	19	20	21	23	26
Reading Comprehension	7	9	11	13	17	18	19	21	24
Spelling	8	10	12	14	18	20	21	23	26
Pseudoword Decoding	9	11	13	16	20	22	23	25	28
Math Reasoning	7	9	11	13	17	18	19	21	23
Written Expression	8	10	12	15	19	20	22	24	27
Listening Comprehension	7	8	10	12	15	16	17	19	21
Oral Expression	9	11	13	16	21	22	24	26	29
Reading	7	9	10	13	16	17	19	20	23
Mathematics	7	9	11	13	17	18	19	21	24
Written Language	8	9	11	14	18	19	20	22	25
Oral Language	7	9	10	13	16	17	19	20	23
Total	6	7	9	11	13	14	15	17	19

Note: Percentages in Table 2.7 represent the proportions of the sample who obtained WIAT-II scores lower than their WISC-IV GAI scores by the specified amount or more.

achievement discrepancies are only one procedure that can be used to determine eligibility to receive special education services, and that determining eligibility based on this criterion may not always equate to a diagnosis of a learning disability, so clearly described in Chapter 6. A diagnosis of Learning Disability requires evidence of impairment in the core cognitive processes that underlie the academic skill in question. For example, we know that specific language impairments in preschoolers are often a precursor to learning disorders in school, and deficits in rapid automatized naming and pseudoword decoding are strong predictors of later reading disorders in early elementary school. The next frontier in school psychology will most certainly be the early identification of students with learning disabilities *before* the cumulative effects of the disability result in a discrepancy between their ability and achievement.

For some children with learning, attention, and other disabilities described in the later chapters of this book, the GAI partly removes the impact of disabilities in working memory and speed of processing on the estimate of intelligence. This may further increase the ability-achievement discrepancy when the latter is based only on measures of VC and PR. Thus, the GAI can be useful in evaluating the impact of the disability on intelligence, and the procedures described here are appropriate, as part of the larger assessment protocol, when determining eligibility for special education services. As discussed in Chapter 3, however, working memory and processing speed are essential to a more complete and integrated view of intelligence. Psychologists should not think that the GAI is a better or more valid estimate of overall intelligence for children presenting with various cognitive and achievement difficulties. As stated previously, the GAI may prove most useful for parsing out some of the cognitive issues for these children. A child with a GAI of 105 but a WMI and/or PSI of 80 will not be able to function in the classroom (or other settings such as employment) in the same way or as well as a child with an FSIQ of 105 who also earned similar scores on all four factors. This critical point certainly needs to be clearly heard and heeded. Finally, we would remind psychologists that the GAI, like the FSIQ, should be viewed as an "aggregate and global" measure of cognitive ability for the child being assessed. While we alluded to this in the previous pages, it is worth revisiting this critical point and drawing some firm conclusions. For each profile, the VC and PR scaled scores should be sufficiently similar (i.e., not statistically different with base rates suggesting infrequent occurrence) so that the GAI is clinically meaningful. Similarly, in the case of FSIQ, the four index or factor scores (and the subtests that compose them) should be similar enough, again guided by the use of both significance and base rate tables, if they are to be reported and used in a meaningful way. If the student's scores vary significantly on the subtests composing VC and PR, then the GAI is simply the average of two widely divergent sets of abilities and therefore not very meaningful as a summary of overall intelligence.

GENERAL INTERPRETATIVE STRATEGIES

It is has been common practice that reports of children's intellectual functioning begin with a discussion of the most global score and proceed in successive levels to less global, more specific scores (e.g., Kaufman, 1994). The Suggested Basic Profile Analysis described in the WISC-IV Technical and Interpretive Manual recommends beginning with the FSIQ; this is also recommended for the WISC-III (Kaufman, 1994; Sattler & Saklofske, 2001b). The approach outlined in the WISC-IV Technical and Interpretive Manual includes:

Step 1.   Report and describe the FSIQ
Step 2.   Report and describe the VCI
Step 3.   Report and describe the PRI
Step 4.   Report and describe the WMI

Step 5.   Report and describe the PSI
Step 6.   Evaluate index-level discrepancy comparisons
Step 7.   Evaluate strength and weaknesses
Step 8.   Evaluate subtest-level discrepancy comparisons
Step 9.   Evaluate the pattern of scores within subtests
Step 10.   Perform the process analysis

Is it best to begin one's prereport investigation of the child's WISC-IV profile at the Full Scale level (FSIQ or GAI) and then proceed with an analysis of the index and subtest scores in the same top-down manner? While rich and meaningful clinical information about an individual child may be gleaned at the subtest, index, and FSIQ levels, it is also necessary to ensure that the psychometric premises on which the WISC-IV is founded have not been compromised. To determine whether the FSIQ, GAI, and index scores are good summaries of performance, or which of these scores to focus interpretation on (e.g., FSIQ or the index scores), it is necessary to begin the investigation at a more detailed level and build up to the global interpretations. For example and as discussed previously, index score discrepancies of 20 or more points may render the FSIQ less meaningful as an overall description of intellectual ability. In this case, the FSIQ does not capture the child's general cognitive functioning, nor does it reflect the child's abilities based on either the 10 core subtests or 4 index scores. This is further supported by the fact that such differences may be both statistically significant and extremely rare; however, that does not negate the importance and clinical value of the discrepant finding. In fact, it is the large and uncommon discrepancy that may provide the most clinically interesting and useful information of relevance to the assessment protocol. For example, in cases of recent lateralized brain trauma, the presence of a large discrepancy between, for example, VC and PR may be very meaningful. However, the presence of large discrepancies makes interpretation of the child's overall intellectual functioning more difficult and complex, and quite possibly irrelevant, if not meaningless.

Similarly any factor-based score such as the PSI essentially "disintegrates" when, for example, a scaled score of 15 is obtained for Symbol Search vs 7 for Coding. Again this does not negate the potential clinical usefulness of the subtest findings and hypotheses that may be generated, assuming the test was properly administered and scored, the testing conditions were adequate, and the examinee was both motivated and seemed to understand the task demands. Graphomotor difficulties may underlie such discrepant scores, or the child may be meticulous when copying figures (at the expense of speed). Thus, it may be less than meaningful to combine subtest scores to yield either index scores or an FSIQ (or GAI) score if there are wide differences between them. Once the investigation is accomplished in this detailed, bottom-up manner, an integrated report may be written in the traditional top-down manner focusing on the most appropriate global scores when and where appropriate.

CLINICAL CONSIDERATIONS

Investigation of WISC-IV scores, at all levels, should be conducted within an ecological context. Interpretations of score patterns may vary depending on the sociocultural background (see Harris *et al.*, 2003, and Chapter 12), family values, pattern of academic strengths and weaknesses, motivation, psychiatric and medical history, or even compliance factors that occur and can be observed during the test session (Sattler, 2001; see also Chapter 14). A common mistake is to offer stock interpretations of score patterns that do not vary as a function of such mediating influences on the expression of intelligent behavior (Kamphaus, 1998). Thus while an FSIQ of 115 by itself suggests high average ability, an ADHD child with clearly observable hyperactivity and impulsivity and with a superior VCI and low average WMI, will certainly present differently in the classroom than a child with a flat profile of subtest and index scores. As well, all psychologists have had numerous opportunities to observe children perform contrary to expectations on the WISC-III and WISC-IV. Thus comments such as "He missed two of the more simple Similarities items but was successful on the more complex items" or "She completed the Block Design and Matrix Reasoning tasks quickly and efficiently, in contrast to teacher reports describing her disorganization and confusion with new tasks and her inability to form and use effective problem-solving strategies." Not only will interpretations differ in relation to the examinees' personal context and history, but the examiner's expectations of the likeliness of finding certain patterns will be influenced by the referral information (e.g., "Given his serious hearing impairment since an early age, I would hypothesize that his verbal test scores will likely be lower than his nonverbal scores").

The WISC-IV, alone and together with the WISC-IV Integrated, provides a comprehensive basis for assessing children's intelligence. It is grounded in a strong psychometric tradition but also provides a rich clinical context for supporting interpretations of the child's test scores. The top-down and bottom-up approach can be used in an iterative way to explore various clinical interpretations. Thus while the FSIQ can be a clinically meaningful summary of a child's overall cognitive functioning, an examination of the parts can also provide meaning and insight to the assessment process. For example, Arithmetic is now a supplemental test on the WMI, but it may be useful in assessing the effects or impact of more basic working memory difficulties. Both Digit Span Backwards and Letter–Number Sequencing are excellent measures of auditory working memory but are relatively artificial tasks. On the other hand, the Arithmetic subtest has an element of authentic assessment or ecological validity because it is one of the common essential learnings in elementary school and has everyday practical utility in the real world. Thus if a child has low scores on all three WM subtests, this may be further evidence that WM is a significant factor underlying his poor school performance rather than a specific arithmetic/mathematics disability. As Kamphaus (2001) points out, an anticipated or hypothesized pattern of strengths and weaknesses based on such factors and that are subsequently observed in the test data leads to a more meaningful and valid interpretation than the same pattern identified through a "buckshot" approach of comparing all possible test scores. This is amply demonstrated in the clinical chapters to follow in the next section.

SOME ADDITIONAL THOUGHTS: BEYOND THE FSIQ

One of the major advances of the WISC-IV is the operational definition and measurement of the four index scores labeled Verbal Comprehension, Perceptual Reasoning, Working Memory, and Processing Speed. Both VC and PR have a long history in both the theoretical and applied areas of intelligence and its assessment, whether viewed from the perspective of the original VIQ and PIQ or from models describing crystallized and fluid intelligence. The newer factors of WM and PS have emerged both in factor analytical studies of complex cognitive tasks (e.g., Carroll, 1993), as well as in the WISC-III and certainly in the WAIS-III. Both WM and PS appear to play an important role both in a description of intelligence and also in the clinical assessment of children.

We can be confident in the factor structure of the WISC-IV. Most factor analytic studies of the WISC-III have supported the four-factor structure (Konold, Kush, & Canivez, 1997; Blaha & Wallbrown, 1996; Roid, Prifitera, & Weiss, 1993; Roid & Worrall, 1997; Sattler & Saklofske, 2001a; Wechsler, 1991; Kush, Watkins, Ward, Ward, Canivez, & Worrell, 2001), although others have reported a three-factor structure (Logerquist-Hansen & Barona, 1994; Reynolds & Ford, 1994; Sattler, 1992). In a major cross-cultural study of the WISC-III factor structure across 15 nations, Georges, Weiss, van de Vivjer, and Saklofske (2003) concluded that the four-factor structure was generally supported. In those countries in which a three-factor structure emerged, Arithmetic loaded with the verbal comprehension subtests caused the working memory factor to collapse. This is another reason that Arithmetic was made supplemental in WISC-IV. A four-factor structure has also been replicated for the WAIS-III (Wechsler, 1997b; Sattler & Ryan, 2001). To date, factor analyses reported in the WISC-IV Technical Manual (Wechsler, 2003b), and replicated by Sattler and Dumont (2004), clearly support the four-factor structure. Thus we have strong evidence that VC,

PR, PS, and WM are not only robust cognitive constructs across the age span and across countries, but more to the point, they can be measured with psychometric integrity in the Wechsler tests. Of course, a general factor also emerges in all these studies.

Regardless of this strong empirical support for the factor structure of the WISC-IV (and WISC-III), factor analysis should not be the sole criterion to determine whether to use this test and how to summarize test performance. The critical question, given the psychometric strengths of the WISC-IV and the clinical history of its predecessors, is whether the psychologist can feel confident in using this test for the assessment of children's intelligence. While Dr. Wechsler most capably constructed a psychometrically sound test that has served as a prototype for generations of Wechsler tests, he was first and foremost a clinician (Tulsky, Saklofske, & Ricker, 2003). He would agree, that while the various Wechsler tests were in the first instance standardized, norm referenced, individually administered intelligence tests, the critical purpose of the test was to aid describing the cognitive abilities of the child in such a way that there was a greater understanding of the child and his or her needs. Wechsler clearly recognized the need to look beyond the question of "how much" to also meaningfully address the questions of "why, and what does this mean." Thus diagnosis and prescription are the foundational purposes of the Wechsler tests, and in this sense, the WISC-IV marks a further advancement.

The clinician's decision about which tests and subtests to administer to a given child, and how they inform us, cannot be governed exclusively by statistical taxonomies derived from correlation and factor patterns reported for the standardization samples. Psychologists must also be current in their knowledge of theory, research findings, and best practices as they all impact on children in general, and on the specific child referred for assessment. They should also be knowledgeable about the cognitive factors measured by the WISC-IV and its links with other tests such as the WIAT-II, CMS, GRS-S, and ABAS-II. The goal of the psychologist using the WISC-IV, or any other intelligence test for that matter, is to target the assessment to the specific cognitive processes underlying the clinical issue for which the child was referred (Prifitera & Saklofske, 1998). This requires an in-depth awareness of clinically meaningful test score patterns in the performance of diagnostic groups, as well as the careful observation and full case history of the child (Prifitera, Weiss, & Saklofske, 1998). Such decisions relevant to the goals of assessment are best made with the sound clinical knowledge of how meaningful patterns in performance may vary among diagnostically relevant groups. Chapter 3 will elaborate on the relevance of the WISC-IV, index, and subtest scores to important clinical issues. The chapters to follow in Section 2 examine the WISC-IV in the context of clinical assessment with those children most often referred for psychological testing and diagnosis.

REFERENCES

Blaha, J., & Wallbrown, F. H. (1996). Hierarchical factor structure of the Wechsler Intelligence Scale for Children–III. *Psychological Assessment, 8,* 214–218.

Boake, C. (2002). From the Binet-Simon to the Wechsler–Bellevue: Tracing the history of intelligence testing. *Journal of Clinical and Experimental Neuropsychology, 24,* 383–405.

Carroll, J. B., (1993). *Human cognitive abilities: A survey of factor-analytic studies.* New York: Cambridge University Press.

Daley, C. E., & Nagle, R. J. (1996). Relevance of WISC-III indicators for assessment of learning disabilities. *Journal of Psychoeducational Research, 14,* 320–333.

Davis, F. B. (1959). Interpretation of differences among averages and individual test scores. *Journal of Educational Psychology, 50,* 162–170.

Deary, I. J. (2001). *Intelligence: A very short introduction.* Oxford: Oxford University Press.

Donders, J. (1996). Cluster subtypes in the WISC-III standardization sample: Analysis of factor index scores. *Psychological Assessment, 8,* 312–318.

Donders, J. (1997). Sensitivity of the WISC-III to injury severity in children with traumatic head injury. *Assessment, 4,* 107–109.

Donders, J., Tulsky, D. S., & Zhu, J. (2001). Criterion validity of new WAIS-III subtest scores after traumatic brain injury. *Journal of the International Neuropsychological Society, 7,* 892–898.

Donders, J., Zhu, J., & Tulsky, D. (2001). Factor index score patterns in the WAIS-III standardization sample. *Assessment, 8,* 193–203.

Flannagan, D. P., & Kaufman, A. S. (in press). *Essentials of WISC-IV assessment.* New York: Wiley.

Flynn, J.R. (1984). The mean IQ of Americans: Massive gains 1932 to 1978. *Psychological Bulletin, 95,* 29–51.

Flynn, J. R. (1998). IQ gains over time: Toward finding the causes. In U. Neisser (Ed.), *The rising curve: Long-term gains in IQ and related measures* (pp. 25–66). Washington, D.C.: American Psychological Association.

Georgas, J., Weiss, L. G., van de Vijver, F., & Saklofske, D. H. (2003). *Culture and children's intelligence: A cross-cultural analysis of the WISC-III.* Amsterdam: Elsevier Science.

Gottfredson, L. S. (1997). Why g matters: The complexity of everyday life. *Intelligence, 24,* 79–132.

Gottfredson, L. S. (1998). The general intelligence factor. *Scientific American Presents, 9,* 24–29.

Gottfredson, L. S., & Deary, I. J. (2004). Intelligence predicts health and longevity, but why? *Current Directions in Psychological Science, 13,* 1–4.

Gridley, B. E., & Roid, G. H. (1998). The use of the WISC–III with achievement tests. In A. Prifitera & D. Saklofske (Eds.), *WISC-III clinical use and interpretation: Scientist-practitioner perspectives* (pp. 249–288). San Diego: Academic Press.

Harris, J. G., Tulsky, D. S., & Schultheis, M. T. (2003). Assessment of the non-native English speaker: Assimilating history and research findings to guide clinical practice. In Tulsky, D. S, *et al.* (Eds.), *Clinical interpretation of the WAIS-III and WMS-III.* (pp. 343–390). San Diego: Academic Press.

Harrison, P. L., & Oakland, T. (2003). *Adaptive behavior assessment system,* (2nd ed.). San Antonio, TX: The Psychological Corporation.

Hunsley, J. (2003). Introduction to the special section on incremental validity and utility in clinical assessment. *Psychological Assessment, 15,* 443–445.

Individuals with Disabilities Education Act Amendments of 1997, 20 U.S.C. 1400 *et seq.* (Fed. Reg. 64, 1999).

Individuals with Disabilities Education Act Amendments of 1991, Pub. L. No. 102–150, 105, Sta. 587 (1992).Itasca, IL, Riverside

Ives, B. (2003). Effect size use in studies of learning disabilities. *Journal of Learning Disabilities, 36,* 490–504.

Jöreskog, K., G. J. & Sörbom, D. (2002). *LISREL 8.54.* Lincolnwood, IL: Scientific Software.

Kamphaus, R. W. (1998). Intelligence Test Interpretation: Acting in the absence of evidence. In A. Prifitera & D. H Saklofske, (Eds.), *WISC-III: Clinical use and interpretation. Scientist-practitioner perspectives* (pp. 39–57). San Diego: Academic Press.

Kamphaus, R. W. (2001). *Clinical assessment of child and adolescent intelligence* (2nd ed). Needham Heights, MA: Allyn & Bacon.

Kaufman, A. S. (1994). *Intelligent testing with the WISC-III.* New York: Wiley.

Knight, R. G., & Godfrey, H. P. D. (1984). Assessing the significance of differences between subtests on the Wechsler Adult Intelligence Scale-Revised. *Journal of Clinical Psychology, 40,* 808–810.

Konold, T., Kush, J., & Canivez, G. L. (1997). Factor replication of the WISC-III in three independent samples of children receiving special education. *Journal of Psychoeducational Assessment, 15,* 123–137.

Konold, T. R., (1999). Evaluating discrepancy analysis with the WISC–III and WIAT. *Journal of Psychoeducational Assessment, 17,* 24–35.

Kuncel, N. R., Hezlett, S. A., & Ones, D.S. (2004). Academic performance, career potential, creativity, and job performance: Can one construct predict them all? *Journal of Personality and Social Psychology, 86,* 148–161. Kusch, J. C., Watkins, M. W., Ward, T. J., Ward S. B., Canivez, G. L., & Worrell F.C. (2001). Construct validity of the WISC-III for white and black students from the WISC-III standardization sample and for black students referred for psychological evaluation. *School Psychology Review,* 30(1), 70–88.

Logerquist-Hansen, S., & Barona, A. (1994). Factor structure of the Wechsler Intelligence Scale for Children-III for Hispanic and Non-Hispanic white children with learning disabilities. Paper presented at the meeting of the American Psychological Association, Los Angeles.

Meyer, G. J., Finn, S. E., Eyde, L. D., Kay, G. G., Moreland, K. L., Dies, R. R., Eisman, E. J., Kubiszyn, T. W., & Reed, G. M. (2001). Psychological testing and psychological assessment: A review of evidence and issues. *American Psychologist, 56,* 128–165.

Naglieri, J. A. (1993). Pairwise and ipsative comparisons of WISC-III IQ and index scores. *Psychological Assessment, 5,* 113–116.

Naglieri, J. A., & Das, J. P. (1997). *Cognitive assessment system.* Itasca, IL: Riverside.

Neisser, U., Boodoo, G., Bouchard, T. J., Jr., Boykin, A. W., Brody, N., Ceci, S. J., Halpern, D. F., Loehlin, J. C., Perloff, R., Sternberg, R. J., & Urbina, S. (1996). Intelligence: Knowns and unknowns. *American Psychologist, 51,* 77–101.

Payne, R. W., & Jones, G. (1957). Statistics for the investigation of individual cases. *Journal of Clinical Psychology, 13,* 115–121.

Price, L., Tulsky, D., Millis, S., & Weiss, L. (in review). Redefining the factor structure of the Wechsler Memory Scale-III: Confirmatory factor analysis with cross validation. *Journal of Clinical and Experimental Neuropsychology.*

Prifitera, A., & Saklofske, D. H. (1998). *WISC-III clinical use and interpretation: Scientist-practitioner perspectives.* San Diego: Academic Press.

Prifitera, A., Weiss, L. G., & Saklofske, D. H. (1998). The WISC-III in context. In A. Prifitera & D. H. Saklofske (Eds). *WISC-III clinical use and interpretation: Scientist-practitioner perspectives* (pp. 1–38). San Diego: Academic Press.

Pritchard, D. A., Livingston, R. B., Reynolds, C. R., & Moses, J. A. (2000). Modal profiles for the WISC-III. *School Psychology Quarterly, 15,* 400–418.

Reynolds, C. R., & Ford, L. (1994). Comparative three-factor solutions of the WISC-III and WISC-R at 11 age levels between $6\frac{1}{2}$ and $16\frac{1}{2}$ years. *Archives of Clinical Neuropsychology, 9,* 553–570.

Roid, G. H. (2003). *The Stanford Binet Intelligence Scales* (ed. 5). Itasca, IL: Riverside Publishing.

Roid, G. H., & Worrall, W. (1996). Equivalence of factor structure in the U.S. and Canada editions of the WISC- III. Paper presented at the annual meeting of the American Psychological Association, Toronto.

Roid, G. H., Prifitera, A., & Weiss, L. G. (1993). Replication of the WISC-III factor structure in an independent sample. *Journal of Psychoeducational Assessment WISC-III Monograph,* 6–21.

Saklofske, D. H., Gorsuch, R. L ,Weiss, L. G., Zhu, J. J., & Patterson, C. (in press). General ability index for the WAIS-III: Canadian norms. *Canadian Journal of Behavioural Science.*

Saklofske, D. H., Hildebrand, D. K., Reynolds, C. R., & Wilson, V. (1998). Substituting symbol search for coding on the WISC-III; Canadian normative tables for performance and full scale IQ scores. *Canadian Journal of Behavioral Science, 30,* 57–68.

Saklofske, D. H. (1996). *Using WISC-III Canadian study results in academic research. In D. Wechsler, WISC-III Manual Canadian Supplement* (pp. 5–13). Toronto, ON: The Psychological Corporation.

Sattler, J. M., & Dumont, R. (2004). *Assessment of children: WISC-IV and WPPSI-III Supplement.* San Diego: Author.

Sattler, J. M., & Ryan, J. J. (2001). Wechsler Adult Intelligence Scale-III (WAIS-III): Description. In Sattler, J.M., *Assessment of children: Cognitive applications* (4th ed.) (pp. 375–414). San Diego: Author.

Sattler, J. M., & Saklofske, D. H.(2001a). Wechsler Intelligence Scale for Children-III (WISC-III): Description. In J. M. Sattler, *Assessment of children: Cognitive applications* (4th ed.) (pp. 220–265) San Diego: Author.

Sattler, J. M., & Saklofske, D. H. (2001b). Interpreting the WISC-III. In J. M. Sattler, *Assessment of children: Cognitive applications* (4th ed.) (pp. 298–334). San Diego: Author.

Sattler, J. M. (2001). *Assessment of children: Cognitive applications* (4th ed.). San Diego: Author

Sattler, J. M. (1992). *Assessment of children* (revised and updated, 3rd ed.). San Diego: Author.

Schwean, V. L., & Saklofske, D. H. (1998). WISC-III assessment of children with Attention Deficit/Hyperactivity Disorder. In A. Prifitera & D. H. Saklofske (Eds.). *WISC-III clinical use and interpretation: Scientist–practitioner perspectives* (pp. 92–118). San Diego: Academic Press.

Siegel, L. S. (2003). IQ-discrepancy definitions and the diagnosis of LD: Introduction to the special issue. *Journal of Learning Disabilities, 31,* 2–3.

Smith, D. R. (2001). Wechsler Individual Achievement Test. In Andrews, J. W., Saklofske, D. H., & Janzen, H. L. (Eds.), *Handbook of psychoeducational assessment: Ability, behavior, and achievement in children* (pp. 169–193). San Diego: Academic Press.

Sparrow, S. S., Balla, D. A., & Cicchetti, D. A. (1984). *Vineland Adaptive Behavior Scales.* Circle Pines, MN: American Guidance Service.

The Psychological Corporation. (2001). *Manual for the Wechsler Individual Achievement Test* (2nd ed.). San Antonio: Author.

The Psychological Corporation. (1992). *Manual for the Wechsler Individual Achievement Test.* San Antonio: Author.

Tulsky, D. S., Saklofske, D. H., & Ricker, J. (2003). Historical overview of intelligence and memory: Factors influencing the Wechsler scales. In Tulsky, D. S., Saklofske, D. H. *et al,* (Eds). *Clincial interpretation of the WAIS-III and WMS-III.* San Diego: Academic Press.

Tulsky, D. S., Saklofske, D. H., Wilkins, C., & Weiss, L. G. (2001). Development of a General Ability Index for the WAIS-III. *Psychological Assessment, 13,* 566–571.

Wechsler, D. (2004). *WISC-IV Integrated Technical and Interpretation Manual.* San Antonio: The Psychological Corporation.

Wechsler, D. (2003a) *Manual for the Wechsler Intelligence Scale for Children* (4th ed.). San Antonio: The Psychological Corporation.

Wechsler, D. (2003b). *Wechsler Intelligence Scale for Children–IV: Technical and interpretive manual.* San Antonio: The Psychological Corporation.

Wechsler, D. (1999). *Manual for the Wechsler Intelligence Scale for Children as a process instrument.* San Antonio: The Psychological Corporation.

Wechsler, D. (1999) *Wechsler Abbreviated Scale of Intelligence.* San Antonio: The Psychological Corporation.

Wechsler, D. (1997a). *Manual for the Wechsler Adult Intelligence Scale* (ed. 3). San Antonio: The Psychological Corporation.

Wechsler, D. (1997b). *WAIS-III/WMS-III technical manual.* San Antonio: The Psychological Corporation.

Wechsler, D. (1991). *Wechsler Intelligence Scale for Children–Third Edition.* San Antonio: The Psychological Corporation.

Wechsler, D. (1974). *Manual for the Wechsler Intelligence Scale for Children–Revised.* San Antonio: The Psychological Corporation.

Wechsler, D. (1949). *Wechsler Intelligence Scale for Children.* New York: Psychological Corporation.

Wechsler, D. (1944). *The measurement of adult intelligence.* Baltimore: Williams & Wilkins.

Weiss, L. G., Prifitera, A., & Dersh, J. (1995). Base rates of WISC-III verbal-performance discrepancies in Hispanic and African American children. Unpublished manuscript.

Weiss, L. G., Saklofske, D. H., & Prifitera, A. (2003). Clinical interpretation of the WISC-III factor scores. In C. R. Reynolds & R. W Kamphaus (Eds.), *Handbook of psychological and educational assessment of children: Intelligence and achievement* (2nd ed.). New York: Guilford Press.

Weiss, L. G., Saklofske, D. H., Prifitera, A., Chen, H. Y., & Hildebrand, D. K. (1999). The calculation of the WISC-III General Ability Index using Canadian norms. *The Canadian Journal of School Psychology, 14(2),* 1–9.

Woodcock, R. W., McGrew, K. S., & Mather, N. (2001). *Woodcock-Johnson III Tests of Cognitive Abilities.* Itasca, IL: Riverside Publishing.

APPENDIX A

TABLES TO COMPARE WISC-IV INDEX SCORES AGAINST OVERALL MEANS

R. STEWART LONGMAN

Psychology Department, Foothills Hospital,
Calgary, Alberta, Canada

The WISC-IV provides guidelines and interpretative values to describe overall level of performance, as well as strategies to identify individual patterns of performance on the subtests and index scores (Wechsler, 2003b). Index scores are compared in pairwise fashion, VC to PR, VC to PS, etc., while subtest scores are generally compared against the overall mean. There are good statistical and practical reasons to compare index scores to their overall mean, instead of comparing pairs of scores.

Statistically, the six pairwise comparisons lead to an increased risk of falsely identifying differences between pairs of indexes (Knight & Godfrey, 1984). As a consequence, it is rare to find a WISC-IV profile without at least one significant difference between index scores. As well, some differences may be significant, while an equally large difference between another set of indexes may not be statistically significant. Comparing index scores against the overall mean allows us to make fewer comparisons, use appropriate corrections for overall comparisons, and identify a particular index as showing a relative strength, relative weakness, or no difference from the overall mean. These features all make use of overall comparisons easier to use and easier to communicate to other professionals and to the public (Naglieri, 1993).

Research with the WISC-III (Wechsler, 1991), WAIS-III (Wechsler, 1997a), and WISC-IV (Wechsler, 2003a) has shown several common profiles in the general population and in specific clinical groups (described here using the WISC-IV labels for the index scores). Research with the general population has found several common profiles, including no relative strengths or weakness, a single strength or weakness on the Processing Speed index (PS; Donders, 1996; Donders, Zhu, & Tulsky, 2001; Pritchard, Livingston, Reynolds, & Moses, 2000) or a relative imbalance between the Perceptual Reasoning index and the Working Memory index (PR & WM; Pritchard *et al.*, 2000), with one being relatively high and the other relatively low.

In clinical populations, specific patterns include a relative weakness in WM for individuals with learning disabilities (Daley & Nagle, 1996; Wechsler, 1997b), or a relative weakness in PS after traumatic brain injuries or in ADHD without other concerns (Donders, 1997; Donders, Tulsky, & Zhu, 2001; Wechsler, 2003b, pp. 88, 92–93). However, a specific index profile is not invariably found with a particular condition, and index profiles should be considered a shorthand description of general patterns of cognitive strengths and weaknesses, rather than providing a definitive diagnosis.

DERIVATION OF TABLES FOR STATISTICAL SIGNIFICANCE AND ABNORMALITY OF DIFFERENCES

The formula given by Davis (1959) was used to compare index scores to the overall mean of index scores for statistical significance. Because the reliabilities of the various indexes vary across age groups, the data were combined into three age groups with more homogeneous reliabilities: ages 6 and 7, ages 8 to 13, and ages 14 to 16. The average standard errors of measurement (SEMs) were calculated by averaging the sum of squared SEMs for each age and obtaining the square root of the results. The average SEMs and corresponding critical values for each index are presented in Table 2.8 using Bonferroni corrected values to correct for the multiple comparisons and keep overall significance levels of .15, .05 and .01.

To assess the relative infrequency of differences between a specific index and the overall mean, the cumulative percentages of differences were calculated using the WISC-IV standardization sample and reported in Table 2.9. Because data analysis revealed that the prevalence of the difference is not identical for an index score that is greater than the overall mean and for an index score that is less than the overall mean, the values are reported by the direction of the difference.

EXAMPLE

For example, consider a 9 year old referred for suspected learning disabilities, with the following index scores: VC of 97, PR of 105, WM of 84, and PS of 102. Her average index score is 97, and her relative strength on PR (at 8 points) is significant at the .15 level, while her relative weakness on WM

TABLE 2.8   Required Difference Between Index Scores and the Mean Index Score at Each Significance Level by Age Groups

Ages 6–7		Significance Level		
Index	Pooled S.E.M.	.15	.05	.01
Verbal Comprehension	4.37	8.25	9.92	11.98
Perceptual Reasoning	4.37	8.25	9.92	11.98
Working Memory	4.50	8.40	10.10	12.19
Processing Speed	6.36	10.69	12.85	15.52
Ages 18–13		Significance Level		
Index	Pooled S.E.M.	.15	.05	.01
Verbal Comprehension	3.77	7.10	8.53	10.31
Perceptual Reasoning	3.97	7.33	8.81	10.64
Working Memory	4.29	7.71	9.27	11.20
Processing Speed	4.93	8.50	10.21	12.34
Ages 14–16		Significance Level		
Index	Pooled S.E.M.	.15	.05	.01
Verbal Comprehension	3.35	6.58	7.91	9.55
Perceptual Reasoning	4.33	7.72	9.28	11.21
Working Memory	4.06	7.39	8.89	10.74
Processing Speed	4.89	8.41	10.11	12.21

(by 13 points) is significant at the .01 level. Inspection of Table 2.9 indicates that her strength on PR is commonly found because 18.3% of the standardization sample obtained PR scores that are 8 points or higher than their average index scores. On the other hand, her weakness on WM is relatively rare because only 8.8% of children show such a relative weakness. This profile can be described as showing a relative weakness on WM, with a possible strength on PR as compared to her overall functioning, a common pattern in children diagnosed with learning disabilities. Of course, to make any such diagnosis, academic achievement would need to be assessed and other possibilities evaluated, but the additional information from the WISC-IV may help select what areas require further evaluation.

TABLE 2.9 Abnormality of Differences between WISC-IV Index Scores and Overall Mean Index Score

Differ-ence				Cumulative Percentile				
	VCI < M[1]	VCI > M	PRI < M	PRI > M	WMI < M	WMI > M	PSI < M	PSI > M
30	0.0	0.1	0.0	0.0	0.2	0.2	0.2	0.0
29	0.0	0.1	0.0	0.0	0.2	0.2	0.3	0.2
28	0.1	0.1	0.0	0.0	0.3	0.3	0.4	0.3
27	0.2	0.1	0.1	0.0	0.4	0.4	0.4	0.4
26	0.3	0.1	0.1	0.0	0.5	0.4	0.6	0.5
25	0.3	0.2	0.1	0.1	0.6	0.5	0.7	0.6
24	0.4	0.2	0.1	0.3	0.7	0.7	0.9	0.9
23	0.6	0.3	0.2	0.4	1.0	1.0	1.1	1.3
22	0.9	0.5	0.3	0.5	1.5	1.3	1.5	1.6
21	1.2	0.9	0.4	0.8	2.0	1.6	2.1	2.0
20	1.5	1.2	0.7	1.0	2.4	2.0	2.7	2.7
19	1.9	1.6	1.2	1.4	2.8	2.5	3.1	3.6
18	2.2	2.1	1.5	2.0	3.6	3.1	4.0	4.5
17	2.8	2.8	2.2	2.5	4.3	3.5	5.2	5.8
16	3.8	3.5	2.9	3.1	5.0	4.4	6.1	7.0
15	5.2	4.1	3.5	4.2	6.0	5.0	7.7	8.0
14	6.3	4.9	4.6	5.4	7.7	6.1	9.1	9.2
13	7.7	6.0	5.7	6.8	8.8	7.4	10.7	11.3
12	9.3	8.0	7.5	8.4	10.8	9.5	12.5	13.4
11	11.7	9.7	9.1	10.3	12.5	11.0	14.6	16.3
10	14.6	12.3	11.5	13.0	15.4	13.4	17.2	19.0
9	17.2	15.0	13.9	15.2	18.0	15.8	19.6	21.8
8	20.0	18.0	17.0	18.3	21.0	18.5	22.1	24.0
7	23.6	21.1	20.5	21.8	25.5	21.9	25.4	27.0
6	27.7	24.9	24.7	26.4	29.3	25.6	28.4	30.1
5	31.7	28.1	29.4	30.2	33.2	29.2	31.0	33.5
4	36.0	31.1	33.2	34.5	37.0	33.6	35.2	37.0
3	40.2	35.0	37.5	39.0	40.7	37.6	39.6	40.0
2	44.7	39.5	42.0	44.0	45.3	41.5	44.1	43.7
1	50.5	44.0	46.8	48.4	49.7	46.1	47.9	47.5
Mean	7.2	7.2	6.8	7.0	7.8	7.5	8.3	8.7
SD	5.2	5.1	4.7	4.9	5.7	5.6	6.1	6.0
Median	6.0	6.0	6.0	6.0	7.0	6.0	7.0	8.0

[1]M stands for the overall mean of 4 WISC-IV index scores.

3

INTERPRETING
THE WISC-IV INDEX
SCORES

LAWRENCE G. WEISS

Harcourt Assessment, Inc.
San Antonio, Texas

AURELIO PRIFITERA

Harcourt Assessment, Inc.
San Antonio, Texas

DONALD H. SAKLOFSKE

Department of Educational Psychology
and Special Education,
University of Saskatchewan,
Saskatoon, Saskatchewan, Canada

The primary level of interpretation of the WISC-IV is at the index score level. While the Full Scale IQ (FSIQ) and General Ability Index (GAI) have strong explanatory power at the group level, as shown in Chapter 2, use of an overall summary score may mask individual differences among the various domains of general ability. At the same time, the overall level of cognitive ability provides a critical backdrop to interpretation of individual differences among the various domains of ability. The domains measured by the four indices are robust clinical constructs with strong psychometric properties. Thus, this chapter builds on the work presented in the previous chapters. The central tenant of this chapter is that individual differences among the factor-based index scores are clinically important and worthy of study. Interpretation of subtest scores is also noted, but considered secondary to qualitative analysis of the unique response patterns the child utilizes in approaching each task.

Interpretation begins with the psychologist comparing the index scores with each other to determine relative strengths and weaknesses. Practitioners may compare each index score to the mean of the index scores as shown in chapter 2, Appendix A. Alternatively, the minimum difference required for statistical significance between each pair of index scores is available in Table B.1 of the WISC-IV Administration and Scoring Manual, by age and overall. As a rule of thumb, these critical values are often near 12 points. Because strengths and weaknesses across cognitive domains are common among normally developing children, it is essential to determine the frequency with which such a difference is observed in the standardization sample. Table B.2 shows the base rates for the difference between each pair of index scores for the entire standardization sample, and by ability level, because analyses revealed that the frequency of various index score differences varies by ability level. For example, among the children whose FSIQ is 120 points or higher, about 13.7% obtained Verbal Comprehension Index (VCI) scores that are 15 or more points higher than their Perceptual Reasoning Index (PRI) scores. Among the children whose FSIQ is 79 points or less, about 10.2% obtained such a discrepancy. Base rates less than 10% or 15% may be interpretable, depending on the clinical presentation. In these cases, the specific indexes are discussed and interpreted as relative strengths or weaknesses in the child's profile of cognitive abilities.

To follow is a basic description focusing on the interpretation of the WISC-IV index scores. Since so much more has been written on the VCI and PRI (POI) beginning with WISC-III and WAIS-III (e.g., Weiss, Saklofske, & Prifitera, 2003; Sattler & Dumont, 2004) we give greater coverage to the Working Memory Index (WMI) and Processing Speed Index (PSI). We remind psychologists that while an understanding of the abilities being tapped by the index and subtests is fundamental to using this test, it is the chapters in Section 3 that will provide the child context and richness for sound clinical use and interpretation.

INTERPRETING THE WISC-IV VERBAL COMPREHENSION INDEX

"The VCI is composed of subtests measuring verbal abilities utilizing reasoning, comprehension, and conceptualization ... " (Wechsler, 2003, p. 6).

The composition of this index now involves less crystallized knowledge and more of an emphasis on reasoning and comprehension than the WISC-III. To determine if the VCI should be interpreted as a single index score or at the subtest level, the basic interpretive strategy is to compare each VCI subtest scaled score to the mean of the child's VCI subtest scaled scores, and evaluate the significance and frequency of any observed differences using Table B.5 in the WISC-IV Administration and Scoring Manual. Other authors have written extensively about interpretive issues with each of the verbal and perceptual subtests (Sattler & Dumont, 2004; Flanagan & Kaufman, 2004), and this will not be repeated here.

The Information (In) subtest, primarily a measure of crystallized knowledge, is now supplemental and a new subtest called Word Reasoning (WR) was created to assess reasoning with words. Intriguingly, however, reasoning with verbal material almost always involves some level of crystallized knowledge as a prerequisite. The Vocabulary (VC) subtest requires that the meaning of a word was learned, can be recalled, and expressed coherently. There is no apparent demand to reason in this subtest. At the same time, however, VC is one of the highest "g" loaded subtests, and one of the best predictors of overall intelligence, perhaps because higher-order thinking requires that more pieces of related information are chunked into a coherent whole for quicker processing. Individuals with larger vocabularies can chunk larger concepts into a single word. Individuals with larger vocabularies may have enjoyed a more enriched cognitive environment, but must also be able to apply their knowledge appropriately. Use of advanced vocabulary words in conversation requires the individual to accurately comprehend nuances of the situation. For example, do we say that the AIDS vaccine was *discovered* or *invented*? Consider that to use the word *obviate* appropriately in conversation, one must first perceive that some action will make another action unnecessary. And, finally, how intelligent does one need to be to tell the difference between *placating* and *appeasing* another person? In spite of these considerations, however, the conventional view is that a strong vocabulary is simply an indication of a high degree of crystallized knowledge. While word recognition and semantic understanding, memory, and retrieval, as well as expressive language skills are all involved, the Vocabulary and Information subtests primarily draw from the child's knowledge base.

Now, compare the underlying abilities required when the examiner asks the child to describe how "revenge and forgiveness" are alike on the Similarities (SM) subtest. A correct response requires prior knowledge of each of these words. More specifically, the concepts of revenge and forgiveness must have been acquired and stored in long-term memory. Further, the child must be able to access that knowledge from semantic memory on demand. Once these words are recalled, the child can begin the reasoning process to determine how they are similar. This reasoning process appears to take place within a transitory working memory space, and the ability to reason may be related to working memory capacity and the speed at which ideas are processed in working memory before the trace fades (see later section). Similar issues are at play with WR and Comprehension (CO).

The SM, CO, and WR subtests require a higher level of reasoning for successful performance than the Vocabulary and Information subtests. Thus it may be useful to examine IN and VC in tandem and compare these scores jointly to SM, CO, and WR. Children with deficits in crystallized knowledge and/or retrieval from long-term memory of previously acquired information may score higher on SM, CO, and WR than on VC and IN if they have adequate verbal reasoning ability. Conversely, children with an age-appropriate knowledge base that is readily accessible but with deficits in higher order categorization of abstract verbal concepts may show the reverse score pattern. In these cases, it may then also be instructive to compare performance on SM with Picture Concepts (PCn). Both subtests require categorization of abstract verbal concepts, but PCn relieves the child of the demand to verbally explain his or her thinking. Thus, children with good abstract reasoning skills but poor verbal expression may perform better on PCn than SM.

Before making an interpretation of low verbal ability, the psychologist should also ask: Was the knowledge encoded but cannot now be recalled (for several possible reasons), or was it never acquired in the first place? The methodology for addressing this issue is the "recognition paradigm." The VC subtests involve free recall, which is a much more difficult cognitive task then cued recognition. How many times have each of us been unable to recall an associate's name, but when others suggest a name we easily recognize if the suggestion was correct. This shows that the name was acquired and stored in long-term memory, but could not be accessed.

The WISC-IV Integrated, described in Chapter 4, is a useful assessment tool in such cases. It contains multiple-choice versions of the core WISC-IV Verbal Comprehension subtests. Children who answered incorrectly because they could not recall the information will more readily recognize the correct information in the multiple-choice paradigm. In this way, the examiner can explore if the incorrect responses were a function of lack of knowledge or lack of access to knowledge. Clearly, this makes a critical difference in interpretation. The second author clearly recalls a young girl who was referred because initial assessments and poor school performance suggested mental retardation (initial WISC-III FSIQ in the 50–60 range). On retesting, her VC score was 2, but on the Integrated, her Multiple Choice VC score was 8 and her Picture Vocabulary score was 12. Together with other clinical data, it became clear that mental retardation was not the basis for her poor classroom achievement.

INTERPRETING THE WISC-IV PERCEPTUAL REASONING INDEX

The PRI is "composed of subtests measuring perceptual reasoning and organization . . . the name change from POI in WISC-III to PRI in WISC-IV reflects the increased emphasis on fluid reasoning abilities in this index" (Wechsler, 2003, p. 6). By design, this composite has undergone the most extensive changes between WISC-III and WISC-IV. The construct measured by this composite has changed from primarily perceptual organization with some fluid reasoning in WISC-III to primarily fluid reasoning with some perceptual organization in WISC-IV. Primarily measures of visual–spatial ability, Picture Arrangement, and Object Assembly were reluctantly re-moved from the test due to the need to make room for the new, fluid reasoning subtests. Picture Completion (PCm) was removed from the core for similar reasons and made supplemental. Along with Block Design (BD), two new subtests were added, Matrix Reasoning (MR) and Picture Concepts (PCn), which primarily tap fluid reasoning. While all the core subtests in this domain are primarily measures of fluid reasoning, BD and MR also involve an element of perceptual organization, whereas PCm seems to require little perceptual organization. Overall, this composite invokes less visual spatial skills and more nonverbal fluid reasoning. Of course, PCn may invoke verbal mediation, but there is no demand for a verbal response. Thus, the name of the Perceptual Organization Index in WISC-III was changed to the Percep-tual Reasoning Index in WISC-IV.

Comparison of each PRI subtest to the child's mean subtest score can be accomplished with Table B.5 of the WISC-IV Administration and Scoring Manual. When neither the VCI nor PRI are significant strengths nor weak-nesses in the profile of index scores, the comparison of the VCI and PRI subtests should be against the mean of the 10 core subtests. If either VCI or PRI is significantly different from the mean of the four index scores, and the magnitude of the difference is rare, then the comparison of VCI and PRI subtests should be conducted with the relevant VCI and PRI means. Again, basic interpretations of individual PR subtests have been well documented elsewhere (Sattler & Dumont, 2004; Flanagan & Kaufman, 2004) and are not repeated here.

Concerns have been raised about the negative impact of time bonuses on performance subtests with gifted and talented students, and on various minority populations. The BD subtest may be scored with and without time bonuses. Only the score with time bonuses is used in the calculation of PRI and FSIQ. The impact of speed on the child's performance can be determined by comparing performance in these two conditions. Contrary to popular belief, there is very little difference in children's scaled scores on BD, with and without time bonuses. As shown in Table B.10 of the WISC-IV Administration and Scoring Manual, even a difference of two scaled score points between BD with and without time bonuses occurred in less than 10% of the standardization sample.

Again, the WISC-IV Integrated is likely to prove most useful to psych-ologists in their efforts to "understand" atypical WISC-IV scores. The Integrated includes a multiple-choice version of the BD subtest to help parse out those children whose low BD scores are due to the possible influ-ence of motor demands on the child's performance. For children with BD < BDMC discrepancies, it is possible that performance on Block Design was limited by the child's ability to construct the design, rather than difficulties with perceptual integration. Higher scores on Block Design than Block Design Multiple Choice (i.e., BD > BDMC) may occur for a number of reasons. Children with visual discrimination problems may fail to appreciate subtle differences among the distracters within the response options. There are no such competing visual stimuli in the Block Design subtest. Impulsive children may select a response without fully considering or scanning all response options.

This is an opportune spot to briefly mention the relationship of other cognitive functions on WISC-IV scores and again to link the WISC-IV and WISC-IV Integrated. Organization, planning, and other executive functions can impact performance on various WISC-IV subtests. Executive functions are a domain of cognitive skills that comprise many discrete abilities that influence higher order reasoning. As measured by Elithorn mazes (EM), executive functioning focuses narrowly on immediate planning, self-monitoring and ability to inhibit impulsive responding. Thus, full construct coverage of the domain of executive functioning is not represented by the EM subtest. However, EM allows a preliminary evaluation of some of these important influences and correlates highly with other measures of executive functioning.

The child's performance on MR and BDMC may be compared directly to EM. EM < MR suggests better developed visual discrimination and reasoning abilities than spatial planning. Difficulties with motor control and processing speed may also account for this difference and needs to be investigated directly. EM > MR suggests well-developed spatial planning abilities, visual-spatial sequencing, and execution; however, difficulties with detailed visual discrimination and reasoning may be present.

The BDMC–EM comparison enables clinicians to rule out deficits in basic visual identification and discrimination that may impact performance on EM. EM < BDMC may indicate that visual–perceptual processes do not account for poor performance on EM and may indicate that poor spatial planning is affecting performance. Visual scanning and processing speed may also account for this disparate performance and need to be evaluated further. EM > BDMC may indicate intact planning ability despite difficulties with visual discrimination and integration.

Apart from the scores and score differences, the child's approach to these tasks is equally important to informed interpretation. Various qualitative scores have been found to be useful with the EM subtest: motor planning, motor imprecision, and backward errors. For example, motor imprecision errors on EM reflect a rule violation in which the child significantly deviates from the maze pathway perhaps due to poor graphomotor control. Poor graphomotor control may be evident on other tasks such as coding and coding copy. If the child displays good graphomotor control elsewhere but many errors on EM, the errors likely reflect planning problems, difficulties negotiating the small tracks (motor precision problem), or inability to maintain the solution in working memory. Research into other process variables is ongoing, and further information about structured methods for evaluating the child's approach to various WISC-IV and WISC-IV Integrated tasks is presented in Chapter 4 and will be forthcoming in the research and clinical literature.

INTERPRETING THE WISC-IV WORKING MEMORY INDEX

The WMI is "composed of subtests measuring attention, concentration, and working memory" (Wechsler, 2003, p. 6). This composite was originally named Freedom from Distractibility (FDI) in research related to the WISC-R (Cohen, 1959), and the name was retained in the WISC-III for reasons of historical continuity. But, that label no longer fits with current neuropsychological research concerning the construct measured by these tasks. In the WISC-III, the FDI was composed of Digit Span and Arithmetic. Now called the Working Memory Index, this composite consists of Digit Span and Letter–Number Sequencing, with Arithmetic as supplemental. The change in nomenclature first took place with the introduction of the WAIS-III in 1997, in which the WMI consists of all three of these subtests.

Working memory is the ability to hold information in mind temporarily while performing some operation or manipulation with that information, or engaging in an interfering task, and then accurately reproducing the information or correctly acting on it. Working memory can be thought of as mental control involving reasonably higher order tasks (rather than rote tasks), and it presumes attention and concentration. Thus, this index measures the ability to sustain attention, concentrate, and exert mental control.

The work of Alan Baddeley is seminal in the area of working memory. He proposes a phonological loop and a visual-spatial sketchpad in which verbal and visual stimuli, respectively, are stored and refreshed, and a central executive that controls attention directed toward these sources. More recently, he proposed a fourth component of the model known as the *episodic buffer*. This buffer is assumed to be attentionally controlled by the central executive and to be accessible to conscious awareness. Baddeley regards the episodic buffer as a crucial feature of the capacity of working memory to act as a global workspace that is accessed by conscious awareness. According to this model, when working memory requires information from long-term storage, it may be "downloaded" into the episodic buffer rather than simply activated within long-term memory (Baddeley, 2003).

Models of working memory are still being actively researched and refined, and the associated terminology will continue to evolve for some time. For purposes of this chapter, however, we use the term *registration* to convey the process by which stimuli are taken in and maintained in immediate memory. Capacity for registering information in immediate memory can be measured by the length of the person's immediate forward span. We use the term *mental manipulation* to imply a transformation of information active in immediate memory and involving higher order cognitive resources. The precise point in this process at which working memory resources are invoked is debatable. These processes may be more of a continuum, as the point at which one moves from passive registration of auditory stimuli to active strategies for maintenance is not always clear, as we will see next.

Digit Span (DS) and Letter–Number Sequencing (LN) are excellent examples of tasks designed to tap working memory. As a case in point, Digit Span Forward (DSF) requires initial registration of the verbal stimuli—a prerequisite for mental manipulation of the stimuli. In some cases, DSF also requires auditory rehearsal to maintain the memory trace until the item presentation is concluded. To the extent that longer spans of digits require the application of a method for maintaining the trace, such as rehearsal or chunking, then some degree of mental manipulation of the stimuli is also involved. The point in the DSF item set at which this is required will vary as a function of age and ability level, and the response processes utilized by the examinee. In Digit Span Backward (DSB), the student must hold a string of numbers in short-term memory store while reversing the given sequence, and then correctly reproduce the numbers in the new order. This is a clear example of mental manipulation. Yet, shorter spans of digits may tax working memory resources only marginally in older or brighter children. Again, the point at which these children substantially invoke working memory resources on DSB will vary by age and ability. Tables B.7 and B.8 of the WISC-IV Administration and Scoring Manual provide base rate comparisons for DSF and DSB by age.

The Arithmetic (AR) subtest is a more ecologically valid working memory task than Digit Span backward. We are frequently called on to mentally calculate arithmetic problems in real life situations. Some examples include estimating driving time, halving a cake recipe, and changing U.S. to Canadian dollars. For students who have not learned grade level skills related to arithmetic calculation and mathematical operations, or students with a primary mathematical disability, the Arithmetic subtest may not be an accurate indication of working memory. The Arithmetic subtest assesses a complex set of cognitive skills and abilities, and a low score may have several appropriate interpretations depending on the clinical context.

It should also be remembered that all three of these subtests tap only verbal working memory, and not spatial or visual working memory. Working memory does not involve only numbers. Other examples include writing the main points of a teacher's lecture in a notebook while continuing to attend to the lecture, or keeping a three-part homework assignment in mind while recording the first two parts in an assignment pad, or keeping in mind the next points you want to make in a conversation while explaining your first point. Clearly, a serious deficit in working memory can have major implications in the academic life of a student, and create difficulties in daily life functioning, as well as in many vocational settings.

The WISC-IV Integrated also includes a Spatial Span subtest. This is a working memory task in the visual domain. It includes both registration (forward immediate span) and mental manipulation (backward span). Score differences between Spatial Span and Digit Span, Letter–Number Sequencing, or Arithmetic may reflect individual differences in visual versus auditory working memory abilities.

Children with learning or attentional disorders may be more likely to experience problems with working memory as suggested by significantly lower scores on this index (Wechsler, 1991, 2003). However, this must be demonstrated to be the case with each individual rather than being assumed to apply to all children with a particular diagnosis or being used as a diagnostic marker (see Kaufman, 1994). Children with serious deficits in working memory are academically challenged, but not necessarily because of lower intelligence. A weakness in working memory may make the processing of complex information more time consuming and tax the student's mental energies more quickly compared with other children of the same age, perhaps contributing to more frequent errors on a variety of learning tasks. Executive function system deficits in planning, organization, and the ability to shift cognitive sets should also be evaluated in these children. In addition, examiners should be alert to the social and behavioral consequences of these disorders and assess the level of parental support and emotional resiliency possessed by the child.

Of course, interpretation of the WMI, like all other WISC-IV index scores, presumes that it reflects an intact construct for the child being evaluated. If the Digit Span and Letter–Number Sequencing subtest scaled scores are very different from each other, then the WMI score can only represent the average of two widely divergent sets of abilities and would therefore have little intrinsic meaning. These two subtests load on the same factor in factor analyses of the WISC-IV, yet correlate only moderately (r = .49 across ages). Thus, divergent scores are certainly possible.

How large a difference is required before abandoning the WMI as an interpretable score? Table B.4 of the WISC-IV Administration and Scoring Manual shows percentages of the standardization sample obtaining various DS–LN discrepancies. As shown in the table, less than 10% of the sample obtained a 5-point difference or greater in either direction. Further, it would be clinically inappropriate to report that a child obtained a score in the average range on the WMI when the Digit Span and Letter–Number Sequencing subtest scaled scores are 7 and 12, respectively, a difference of 5 points. (Other examiners may consult this table and choose different guidelines depending on the context within which the profile is being interpreted.) When the Digit Span and Letter–Number Sequencing subtest scaled scores are 5 or more points apart, then these subtests should be interpreted independently. Differences between these subtests can be investigated in terms of differential encoding of the number line and alphabet.

Again it is relevant to mention that several WISC-IV Integrated Process Approach subtests and scores can assist the examiner in more in-depth interpretation of the child's performance. The WISC-IV Integrated Letter–Number Sequencing Processing Approach (LNPA) subtest is a variation of the core Letter–Number Sequencing subtest in which the scored trials contain embedded words in the presented sequence of letters and numbers. Unlike the core version of this subtest, the child is asked to repeat the letters first, and then the numbers. This difference is designed to cue the child to the presence of the embedded word. Children with well-developed executive control processes and adequate orthographic abilities are likely to perceive the embedded words and use this knowledge to focus additional working memory resources on the sorting and reordering of numbers and letters. Cognitively rigid children may experience difficulty disassociating the letters from the word, which is often required to properly reorder the letters. Low LNPA scores may be related to difficulties with auditory working memory, registration, discrimination, attention, sequencing, spelling ability, or material specific weaknesses in auditory encoding (numeric or alphabetic).

Other WISC-IV Integrated Process Approach subtests can assist the examiner in parsing out low performance in AR by systematically reducing the working memory load. In Arithmetic Process Approach Part A, the child is allowed to complete the items with the word problem remaining in view, and in Arithmetic Process Approach Part B, the child is also allowed to use a pencil and paper. Working memory demand is further reduced by examining performance on these process approach tasks with and without time bonuses. Finally, the child may be given a set of number (not word) problems to solve on paper and pencil to determine the extent of any deficits in numerical skills. Thus, the examiner has a range of observed behaviors from which to generate meaningful recommendations about teacher-generated modifications to lesson and test formats that may facilitate academic performance in the classroom.

INTERPRETING THE WISC-IV PROCESSING SPEED INDEX

The PSI is "composed of subtests measuring the speed of mental and graphomotor processing" (Wechsler, 2003, p. 6). On the surface, the Coding (CD), Symbol Search (SS), and Cancellation (CA) subtests are simple visual scanning and tracking tasks. A direct test of speed and accuracy, the CD subtest assesses ability in quickly and correctly scanning and sequencing simple visual information. Performance on this subtest also may be influenced by short-term visual memory, attention, or visual-motor coordination. The SS subtest requires the student to inspect several sets of symbols and indicate if special target symbols appeared in each set. It is also a direct test of speed and accuracy and assesses scanning speed and sequential tracking of simple visual information. Performance on this subtest may be influenced by visual discrimination and visual-motor coordination. New to the WISC-IV, the supplemental Cancellation subtest also requires these skills and a minor degree of decision making. Examinees must decide whether each stimulus is a member of the target class of stimuli (e.g., animals). While the decisions are generally simple, the psychologist must take care not to underestimate the cognitive load for the youngest children, especially those without preschool experience, or who are developmentally delayed.

Although the PSI subtests are easy visual scanning tasks for most children, it would be a mistake to think of the PSI as a measure of simple clerical functions that are not relevant or related to intelligence. Interestingly, while PSI is traditionally listed last in any representation of the WISC-III or WISC-IV factor structure, it actually emerges third in most factor analyses and accounts for greater variance in intelligence than does the working memory factor. Further, there is consistent evidence that both simple and choice reaction time correlate about .20 or slightly higher with scores from intelligence tests, while inspection time (hypothesized by some to be a measure of the rate that information is processed) correlates about .40 with intelligence test scores (see Deary, 2001; Deary & Stough, 1996).

Performance on the PSI is an indication of the rapidity with which a student can process simple or routine information without making errors. Many learning tasks involve a combination of routine information processing (such as reading) and complex information processing (such as reasoning). A weakness in the speed of processing routine information may make the task of comprehending novel information more time-consuming and difficult. A weakness in simple visual scanning and tracking may leave a child less time and mental energy for the complex task of understanding new material. This is the way in which these lower order processing abilities are related to higher order cognitive functioning.

The pattern of processing speed abilities being lower than reasoning abilities is more common among students who are experiencing academic difficulties in the classroom than among those who are not (Wechsler, 1991, 2003). Research studies with the WISC-III have also indicated that children with attention deficit–hyperactivity disorder (ADHD) earn their lowest scores on the PSI (Prifitera & Dersh, 1993; Schwean et al., 1993). Although little research exists on this topic, it can be hypothesized that children with processing speed deficits may learn less material in the same amount of time, or take longer to learn the same amount of material compared to those without processing speed deficits. These children may also mentally tire more easily because of the additional cognitive effort required to perform routine tasks. In turn, this could lead to more frequent errors, less time spent studying, and possible expressions of frustration. Conversely, a strength in the speed of processing information may facilitate the acquisition of new information.

If the CD and SS subtest scaled scores are very different from each other, the PSI score may have little intrinsic meaning and should not be interpreted as a unitary construct. That they correlate moderately (r = .53) suggests a shared processing speed component but also some unique variance. Table B.4 of the WISC-IV Administration and Scoring Manual shows percentages of the standardization sample obtaining various Coding–Symbol Search discrepancies. We recommend that a difference of 5 or more points between Coding and Symbol Search raise strong concerns about interpreting the PSI as a unitary construct. Actually, a difference between these two subtests of only 3.5 points is significant at the $p < .05$ level (see Table B.3 of the WISC-IV Administration and Scoring Manual). Only 11.2% of the sample obtained a 5-point difference or greater in either direction. If the difference between Coding and Symbol Search is 5 points or greater, then these two subtests are best interpreted separately.

Several WISC-IV Integrated Process Scores assist with more in-depth interpretation of the processing speed tasks. The Cancellation Random (CAR) and Cancellation Structured (CAS) process scores represent the child's ability to scan both a random and structured arrangement of visual stimuli for target objects (i.e., animals). Cancellation tasks have been extensively used in neuropsychological settings as measures of visual selective attention, visual neglect, response inhibition, and motor perseveration (Adair et al., 1998; Lezak, 1995; Na, Adair, Kang, Chung, Lee, & Heilman, 1999). Unlike some of the previous versions of this task that require the child to identify a simple visual-perceptual match, the Cancellation subtest requires the child to determine if visual stimuli belong to a target category (i.e., animals). Thus, the child may also employ visual-lexical associations to discriminate between target and distracter stimuli.

Children with high CAR and CAS process scores are likely to demonstrate rapid visual scanning ability, effective response inhibition, and organized visual search patterns. Low CAR and CAS process scores may be related to slow visual scanning or visual-motor abilities, poor response inhibition, disorganized search patterns, or difficulties with visual discrimination. In addition the child's visual-lexical associations (i.e., ability to correctly categorize objects) may be slow or incorrect.

For both the random and structured cancellation tasks, some children naturally invoke a search strategy to organize their visual scanning of the page. Presumably, an organized strategy allows for more efficient identification of target objects. The structured condition lends itself to an organized search strategy more readily than the random condition. Many children will follow the inherent structure of the rows to search for targets; however, some children will engage in a disorganized search despite the inherent task structure.

The CAR and CAS process scores are designed to assist the clinician in characterizing the child's search strategy. For each score, the clinician assigns a letter (i.e., A, B, C, or D) to describe and classify the child's search strategy into one of four categories. Search strategy A is characterized by a search pattern that remains organized throughout item administration. Search strategy B represents a pattern that began organized, but became disorganized as the child progressed. Conversely, a child that began the task using a disorganized search pattern and then adopted an organized pattern would be assigned a search strategy score of C. Visual search patterns that remain disorganized throughout item administration are assigned search strategy D. (Examples of each search strategy are provided in the scoring instructions for the Cancellation subtest in Chapter 3 of the Administration and Scoring Manual.) Table D.23 of the WISC-IV Integrated Administration and Scoring Manual provides base rate information from the standardization sample by age group. As data from this table indicate, the use of search strategy A (consistently organized search pattern) increases with age, whereas the use of search strategy D (consistently disorganized search pattern) decreases with age. It is important to recognize that a majority of children in most age groups have some degree of disorganization in their search pattern. The most common search pattern in the standardization sample was search strategy C (search pattern began disorganized but became organized).

Comparison of the CAR and CAS process scores provides information about how the child's performance on Cancellation varies with the arrangement of visual stimuli. A CAR < CAS discrepancy suggests that the child benefits from the structured presentation format. The child's search strategies could also be examined to provide additional information to confirm or refute hypotheses regarding the influence of structure on Cancellation performance.

Clinical studies reported in the WISC-IV Technical and Interpretive Manual suggest that subjects in the ADHD sample may have benefited from the introduction of structure in the CAS because they obtained higher scaled scores on CAS than on CAR. The sample of children with mental retardation may have been unable to benefit from the additional structure provided in CAS to the same degree as their peers, and therefore obtained lower scores on CAS than on CAR. The gifted sample scored essentially the same on CAR and CAS, suggesting that they may be able to apply an effective search strategy regardless of the condition.

The Coding Recall (CDR) subtest is designed to measure incidental learning that occurs during completion of the Coding subtest (Form B only). Some children may strategically attempt to learn the associations from Coding B, while others learn them without cognitive effort through repeated exposure. After standard administration of the battery, it may be useful to ask the child if he or she tried to remember the symbols on Coding. For those children with relatively good performance on Coding Recall and relatively poor performance on Coding B, a positive response to this question may suggest that the child lost time during performance of Coding B to learn the associations. Some children will do poorly on Coding Recall despite explicitly having tried to learn the associations, indicating the possible existence of deficits in multitrial learning and declarative memory.

Process scores are derived for each of the three Coding Recall items, Cued Symbol Recall, Free Symbol Recall, and Cued Digit Recall. The Cued Symbol Recall score represents the child's performance on a task requiring the child to recall symbols from the paired associates in Coding B. A child that performs well on this task has likely learned, without instruction, which symbol goes with which number. In performing the task, the child has learned both the content (symbol) and the association (the symbol and number pairing) included in the subtest task.

The Free Symbol Recall score represents the child's ability to recall the symbols from Coding B, with no regard to the associated number. Because this task requires only the recall of symbols, the clinician can determine if poor performance on Cued Symbol Recall is related to weaknesses in associative learning. The child may have known the symbols, but was unable to consistently link them with the proper number.

The Cued Digit Recall score represents the child's ability to recall the numbers from the paired associates in Coding B. Similar to Cued Symbol Recall, this task evaluates if the child has been able to encode the association between the symbol and the number. Despite the similar task demands, there are situations in which a child performs differently on Cued Symbol Recall and Cued Digit Recall. This occurrence may suggest that the child has difficulty maintaining consistent access to visualized representations of the associated information. In most cases, performance on Cued Digit Recall is better than performance on Cued Symbol Recall. Numbers are frequently automatized, and the child does not need to rely on encoding to recall the digits, whereas the symbols are novel and require significant effort to encode and recall.

The Time Interval Performance scores for Coding B and Coding Copy represent the child's performance on the respective task at 30-second time intervals. Thus, clinicians can evaluate the child's progress over time on these processing speed tasks, including problems with initiation (slow start), maintenance, or fatigue effects. Note that the child's performance during the last 30-second interval (i.e., 91 to 120 seconds) is not reported as a process score, because the number of items completed in this time interval is often dependent on the number of items remaining. Means and standard deviations for the standardization sample are reported in Tables D.24 and D.25 of the WISC-IV Integrated Administration and Scoring Manual for Coding B and Coding Copy, respectively. These data indicate that rate of production is fastest during the first 30 seconds and tapers off after that point, with younger children showing declines from time 2 to time 3 as well. This reduction in the average rate of performance over time may not be due to fatigue factors. The first rows of items are easier, as they involve only the lower numbers and thus fewer associations. Latter rows include all the items and are slightly more difficult. Nonetheless, performance that declines more rapidly over time than average may be meaningful.

THE DYNAMIC INTERPLAY OF WORKING MEMORY AND PROCESSING SPEED

The working memory and processing speed subtests generally have lower "g" loadings than the verbal comprehension and perceptual reasoning subtests. In considering this issue, keep in mind that "g" is more properly referred to as "psychometric g" because it can be assessed only in relation to the mix of tasks included in the analysis. The concept of pure "g" can never be assessed for a variety of technical reasons, but most important because intelligence and environment are inexorably linked. While the "g" loadings for these subtests are lower, they represent abilities that play a critical role in overall intellectual functioning including the acquisition of new learning and the ability to utilize encoded (crystallized) knowledge to solve new problems. Thus, working memory and processing speed may be central to Wechsler's definition of intelligence as the ability to learn and adapt to a changing environment. From the beginning, his tests have included tasks that tap these abilities (Digit Span, Coding, and Arithmetic), although the terminology has changed over time, as understanding of the underlying constructs continues to evolve.

The evidence in support of working memory and processing speed is increasingly convincing. There are large and obvious age-related trends in processing speed that are accompanied by age-related changes in the number of transient connections to the central nervous system and increases in myelination. Several investigators have found that measures of infant processing speed predict later IQ scores (e.g., Dougherty & Haith, 1997), and WISC-IV PSI scores have been shown to be potentially sensitive to neurological disorders such as epilepsy (Wechsler, 1991). In learning disabled and attention deficit samples, both PSI and WMI were found to be lower compared to their VCI and PRI scores, as well as compared with the normal population (Prifitera & Dersh, 1993; Schwean et al., 1993).

Of clinical relevance for school psychologists and specialists is the finding that the WMI contributes the second largest amount of variance, after VCI, to the prediction of reading, writing, and mathematics scores on the WIAT and other measures of achievement (Konold, 1999; Hale, Fiorello, Kavanagh, Hoeppner, & Gaither, 2001). High correlations between working memory and reading comprehension have been found and replicated numerous times (see Daneman & Merikle, 1996). Similar findings have been observed for a range of variables important to academic functioning in school, including spelling (Ormrod & Cochran, 1988), the acquisition of logic (Kyllonen & Stephens, 1990), note taking (Kiewra & Benton, 1988), and following directions (Engle, Carullo, & Collins, 1991). Generally, the magnitude of these correlations is near .50 (Baddeley, 2003), suggesting a moderate relationship between working memory and various academic outcomes. Kyllonen and Christal (1990) reported high correlations between these working memory research tasks and traditional measures of intelligence believed to tap reasoning ability. This study also found that high scores on these reasoning tasks were differentially sensitive to the extent of previous knowledge held by the subject, whereas successful performance on pure working memory tasks was more dependent on the person's ability to process information rapidly. The interrelatedness between working memory, reasoning, prior knowledge, and processing speed lead Kyllonen and Christal (1990) to conclude that reasoning ability is little more than working memory capacity. In this regard, Baddeley's (2003) proposal for an episodic buffer in which crystallized knowledge is downloaded from long-term storage for further manipulation is rather intriguing for the study of reasoning ability. At present, we do not know the extent to which these models will continue to evolve with future research. Nonetheless, this area of study is clearly central to the development of a more neuropsychologically informed understanding of the structure of intelligence.

With this background, it is not surprising that speed of information processing and immediate memory are included as components of most psychometric models of intelligence such as the Gf-Gc theory (Carroll, 1993). However, working memory should not be confused with many of the short-term memory measures included in the Gf-Gc model. Working memory is much more complex than the temporary storage and retrieval of auditory or visual information. Working memory involves the manipulation of information in temporary storage and, as such, is closely related to reasoning.

Some of the factor analytically derived models of intelligence suggest that each factor is a unique source of variance, contributing independently to general intelligence. However, this would not seem to be the case from two perspectives. First a "g" factor tends to emerge whenever a number of cognitively complex variables are factor analyzed (Carroll, 1993). The basis for the FSIQ (and GAI, see Chapter 2) on the WISC-IV are grounded in the fact that the four index scores, while tapping variance that is unique or exclusive to each, are all positively correlated. Further, the subtests are all more or less positively correlated (while also demonstrating subtest specificity), with those subtests defining a particular factor correlating even more highly.

Second, clinical research in developmental cognitive neuropsychology suggests a more dynamic picture, one that practicing psychologists attempt to construct in their every day clinical assessment practice. Fry and Hale

(1996) administered measures of processing speed, working memory, and fluid intelligence to children and adolescents between 7 and 19 years old. Age-related increases in speed of processing were associated with increases in working memory capacity, which, in turn, were associated with higher scores on measures of fluid reasoning. This study suggests that as children develop normally, more rapid processing of information results in more effective use of working memory space, which enhances performance on many reasoning tasks. Kail (2000) concluded that: "Processing speed is not simply one of many different independent factors that contribute to intelligence; instead processing speed is thought to be linked causally to other elements of intelligence."

This dynamic model of cognitive information processing suggests that language and reading impairments that interfere with the rapid processing of information may burden the working memory structures, and reduce the student's capacity for comprehension and new learning. This area is ripe for research.

COMMUNICATING THE INTERPRETATION

Once interpretation is accomplished, the psychologist must clearly and convincingly communicate the findings in writing. It is not adequate only to describe the pattern of scores, associated confidence intervals, and base rates of differences between various scores. This is because the most important reader is typically not another psychologist who understands the terminology and the implications of the scores, but a parent or teacher. Writing a clear report that is meaningful to parents and teachers is a skill that is separate from the ability to interpret profiles. Even the most competent of interpretation can be obscured by an overly technical writing style, which weakens the potential impact of the assessment results on the child's future. Parent, teachers, or other professionals who understand the report, and are convinced of its relevance, are more likely to follow the recommendations and to take actions that are in the best interest of the child.

Several software packages are available to assist the practitioner with report writing. The WISC-IV Writer is a software program that produces clear and concise narrative reports that follow the interpretive strategies recommended in this chapter. Automated reports should never be accepted uncritically. At best, these reports are aids, not substitutes for report writing. Appropriate use requires that the psychologist read and modify each report according to his or her professional opinion. The Writer report should be thought of as a first draft of the professional report. An automated first draft can be a valuable time saver that allows the psychologists to attend to customizing the final report in a way that best communicates meaning and relevance for the intended reader.

An example of a *WISC-IV Writer Interpretive Report* is shown in Appendix A for a 10-year-old boy with working memory and processing speed deficits. Notice that while scores and technical data are mentioned in the report, the emphasis is on a plain language summary of the important findings. For example, with regard to a significant but not rare VCI < PRI discrepancy, the report states, "He performed better on nonverbal than on verbal reasoning tasks. Such differences in performances, however, are not especially unusual among children in general." To communicate the relevance of a 30-point WMI < PRI discrepancy (which is both significant and rare), the report states the child's weakness in working memory may "... make the processing of complex information more time consuming for John, draining his mental energies more quickly as compared to other children his age, and perhaps result in more frequent errors on a variety of learning tasks."

Such plain language insights can have a profound impact on parents, teachers, and others who are trying to help the child because these insights reframe the observed academic and behavior problems in a new light. A well-written report can transform the reader's view of the child's behavior and motivate parents and teachers to carry out the recommended treatment plans. Let us not forget that this is the ultimate purpose of all of our assessment activities.

REFERENCES

Adair, J. C., Na, D. L., Schwartz, R. L., & Heilman, K. M. (1998). Analysis of primary and secondary influences on spatial neglect. *Brain and Cognition, 37(3)*, 351–367.

Baddeley, A. (2003). Working memory: Looking back and looking forward. *Nature Reviews/ Neuroscience, 4*, 829–839.

Carroll, J. B. (1993). *Human cognitive abilities: A survey of factor-analytic studies.* New York: Cambridge University Press.

Cohen, J. (1959). The factorial structure of the WISC at ages 7–6, 10–6, and 13–16. *Journal of Consulting Psychology, 23*, 285–299.

Daneman, M., & Merikle, M. (1996). Working memory and language comprehension: A meta-analysis. *Psychonomic Bulletin Review, 3*, 422–433.

Deary, I. J. (2001). *Intelligence: A very short introduction.* Oxford: Oxford University Press.

Deary, I. J., & Stough, C. (1996). Intelligence and inspection time: Achievements, prospects, and problems. *American Psychologist, 51*, 599–608.

Dougherty, T. M., & Haith, M. M. (1997). Infant expectations and reaction times as predictors of childhood speed of processing and IQ. *Developmental Psychology, 33(1)*, 146–155.

Engle, R. W., Carullo, J. J., & Collins, K. W. (1991). Individual differences in working memory for comprehension and following directions. *Journal of Educational Research, 84*, 253–262.

Flanagan, D. P., & Kaufman, A. S. (2004). *Essentials of WISC-IV assessment.* New York: Wiley.

Fry, A. F., & Hale, J. B. (1996). Processing speed, working memory, and fluid intelligence: Evidence for a developmental cascade. *Psychological Science, 7(4)*, 237–241.

Hale, J. B., Fiorello, C. A., Kavanagh, J. A., Hoeppner, J. B., & Gaither, R. A. (2001). WISC-III predictors of academic achievement for children with learning disabilities: Are global and factor scores comparable? *School Psychology Quarterly Special Issue, 16(1)*, 31–55.

Kail, R. (2000). Speed of information processing: Developmental change and links to intelligence. *Journal of Psychology Special Issue: Developmental Perspectives in Intelligence, 38(1)*, 51–61.

Kaufman, A. S. (1994). *Intelligent testing with the WISC-III*. New York: Wiley.

Kiewra, K. A., & Benton, S. L. (1988). The relationship between information processing ability and note taking. *Contemporary Educational Psychology, 13*, 3–44.

Konold, T. R. (1999). Evaluating discrepancy analysis with the WISC- III and WIAT. *Journal of Psychoeducational Assessment, 17*, 24–35.

Kyllonen, P. C., & Christal, R. E. (1990). Reasoning ability is (little more than) working memory capacity. *Intelligence, 14*, 389–433.

Kyllonen, P. C., & Stephens, D. L. (1990). Cognitive abilities as the determinant of success in acquiring logic skills. *Learning and Individual Differences, 2*, 129–160.

Lezak, M. D. (1995). *Neuropsychological assessment* (3rd ed.). New York: Oxford University Press.

Na, D. L., Adair, J. C., Kang, Y., Chung, C. S., Lee, K. H., & Heilmand, K. M. (1999). Motor perseverative behavior on a line cancellation task. *Neurology, 52(8)*, 1569–1576.

Ormrod, J. E., & Cochran, K. F. (1988). Relationship of verbal ability and working memory to spelling achievement and learning to spell. *Reading Research Instruction, 28*, 33–43.

Prifitera, A., & Dersh, J. (1993). Base rates of WISC-III diagnostic subtest patterns among normal, learning disabled, and ADHD samples. *Journal of Psychoeducational Assessment Monograph Series: Wechsler Intelligence Scale for Children* (ed. 3). Germantown, TN: The Psychological Corporation.

Sattler, J. M., & Dumont, R. (2004). *Assessment of children: WISC-IV and WPPSI-III Supplement*. San Diego: Author.

Schwean, V. L., Saklofske, D. H., Yackulic, R. A., & Quinn, D. (1993). WISC- III performance of ADHD boys: Cognitive, intellectual, and behavioral comparisons. *Journal of Psychoeducational Assessment, Special ADHD Issue Monograph*, 6–21.

Wechsler, D. (2003) *Manual for the Wechsler Intelligence Scale for Children* (ed. 4). San Antonio: The Psychological Corporation.

Wechsler, D. (1997). *Manual for the Wechsler Adult Intelligence Scale* (ed. 3). San Antonio: The Psychological Corporation.

Wechsler, D. (1991). *Wechsler Intelligence Scale for Children* (ed. 3). San Antonio: The Psychological Corporation.

Weiss, L. G., Saklofske, D. H., & Prifitera, A. (2003). Clinical interpretation of the WISC-III factor scores. In C. R. Reynolds & R. W. Kamphaus (Eds.), *Handbook of psychological and educational assessment of children: Intelligence and achievement* (2nd ed.). New York: Guilford Press.

CASE STUDY*

EXAMINEE:	John Smith	REPORT DATE:	5/5/2004
AGE:	10 years 1 month	GRADE:	5th
DATE OF BIRTH:	3/28/1994	ETHNICITY:	White not Hispanic origin
EXAMINEE ID:	Not Specified	EXAMINER:	Jim Jackson
GENDER:	Male		
Tests Administered:	WISC-IV	Age at Testing:	WISC-IV
	(4/30/2004)		(10 years 1 month)
Is this a retest?	No		

SCORES SUMMARY

WISC-IV COMPOSITE	SCORE
Verbal Comprehension Index (VCI)	95
Perceptual Reasoning Index (PRI)	104
Working Memory Index (WMI)	74
Processing Speed Index (PSI)	75
Full Scale IQ (FSIQ)	86

REASON FOR REFERRAL

John was referred for an evaluation by his counselor, Jane Brown. The reason for his referral is academic difficulties.

HOME

John is a 10-year-old child who lives with his parents. There are two children living in the home with John. His custodial arrangements have not changed in the last 3 years. John has been living in his present living arrangment since birth. John comes from an educated family. His mother completed 4 years of college. His father graduated from high school.

LANGUAGE

John's dominant language is English. He has been exposed to English since birth. He has been speaking English since talking. John's speech during testing was clear and intelligible and demonstrated English proficiency.

DEVELOPMENT

According to his mother, John was born with no apparent complications. John's mother also reports that he reached the following milestones within the expected age ranges: sitting alone, crawling, standing alone, walking alone, using toilet when awake, and staying dry at night. He reached the following milestones later than expected: speaking first words and speaking short sentences.

HEALTH

According to his mother, John's vision screen results revealed that he has a normal visual acuity. The results of his hearing screen revealed that he has a normal auditory acuity. John's mother reports that he has no sensory or motor difficulties. During testing, John had no apparent sensory or motor difficuties. John's mother reports that he has no major medical or psychiatric diagnoses. According to John's mother, he had no signs of neurological concerns in the past. Currently, he has no signs of neurological concerns. During the assessment, it was observed that John appeared to be in good health. According to John's mother, he has not used prescription medication. Currently, he is not taking any prescription medications. His mother also reports that he has no known substance abuse. During testing, John did not appear under the influence of any medication or substance.

SCHOOL

According to John's mother, his prekindergarten experience includes preschool program. His prefirst grade experience includes half-day kindergarten. John has been assigned to the same school since his initial enrollment. He currently attends regular education classes full-time. In the past, John had an excellent attendance record. Currently, he is maintaining good attendance. In the past, John had an exemplary conduct record. Currently, John has no disciplinary problems. In the past, John had some academic difficulties. Currently, John has many academic difficulties. His past performance was below average in the following areas: Reading, Math, and Language. Recently, his performance was below average in the following areas: Reading, Math, and Language.

BEHAVIOR OBSERVATION

John appeared alert and oriented. It was observed that John appeared to put forth best effort.

INTERPRETATION OF WISC-IV RESULTS

John was administered 11 subtests of the Wechsler Intelligence Scale for Children-Fourth Edition (WISC-IV) from which his composite scores are derived. The Full Scale IQ (FSIQ) is derived from a combination of 10 subtest scores and is considered the most representative estimate of global intellectual functioning. John's general cognitive ability is within the Low Average range of intellectual functioning, as measured by the FSIQ. His overall thinking and reasoning abilities exceed those of approximately 18% of children his age (FSIQ = 86; 90% confidence interval = 82–91). His ability to think with words is comparable to his ability to reason without the use of words. Both John's verbal and nonverbal reasoning abilities are in the Average range. He performed better on nonverbal than on verbal reasoning tasks. Such differences in performance, however, are not especially unusual among children in general.

John's verbal reasoning abilities as measured by the Verbal Comprehension Index are in the Average range and above those of approximately 37% of his peers (VCI = 95; 90% confidence interval = 90–101). The Verbal Comprehension Index is designed to measure verbal reasoning and concept formation. John performed comparably on the verbal subtests contributing to the VCI, suggesting that these verbal cognitive abilities are similarly developed. John performed much better on abstract categorical reasoning and concept formation tasks that did not require verbal expression (Picture Concepts = 12) than on abstract categorical reasoning and concept formation tasks that required verbal expression (Similarities = 8).

John's nonverbal reasoning abilities as measured by the Perceptual Reasoning Index are in the Average range and above those of approximately 61% of his peers (PRI = 104; 90% confidence interval = 97–110). The Perceptual Reasoning Index is designed to measure fluid reasoning in the perceptual domain with tasks that assess nonverbal concept formation, visual perception and organization, simultaneous processing, visual–motor coordination, learning, and the ability to separate figure and ground in visual stimuli. John performed comparably on the perceptual reasoning subtests contributing to the PRI, suggesting that his visual–spatial reasoning and perceptual–organizational skills are similarly developed.

John's ability to sustain attention, concentrate, and exert mental control is in the Borderline range. He performed better than approximately 4% of his age-mates in this area (Working Memory Index = 74; 90% confidence interval = 70–83). John's abilities to sustain attention, concentrate, and exert mental control are a weakness relative to his nonverbal and verbal reasoning abilities. A weakness in mental control may make the processing of complex information more time-consuming for John, draining his mental energies more quickly as compared to other children his age, and perhaps result in more frequent errors on a variety of learning tasks.

John's ability in processing simple or routine visual material without making errors is in the Borderline range when compared to his peers. He performed better than approximately 5% of his peers on the processing speed tasks (Processing Speed Index = 75; 90% confidence interval = 70–86). Processing visual material quickly is an ability that John performs poorly as compared to his verbal and nonverbal reasoning ability. Processing speed is an indication of the rapidity with which John can mentally process simple or routine information without making errors. Because learning often involves a combination of routine information processing (such as reading) and complex information processing (such as reasoning), a weakness in the speed of processing routine information may make the task of comprehending novel information more time-consuming and difficult for John. Thus, this weakness in simple visual scanning and tracking may leave him less time and mental energy for the complex task of understanding new material. The academic difficulties noticed by John's counselor may be related to this weakness in processing speed. The academic difficulties noticed by John's counselor may be related to his lower mental control and processing speed abilities. This pattern of mental control and visual processing speed abilities that are both less developed than the student's reasoning ability is more common among students with learning disabilities than among those without such disabilities. John has a history of academic difficulties in school and is experiencing many academic difficulties in his current classes. John's performance on the Cancellation subtests was significantly better when the stimulus objects were structured (Cancellation Structured = 9) rather than unstructured (Cancellation Random = 5). This difference is unusual among children his age, and suggests that John may have considerable difficulty structuring his own work without assistance, especially on tasks that require rapid scanning of visual information. This pattern is more common among children with attention and learning difficulties.

PERSONAL STRENGTHS AND WEAKNESS

John's performance was significantly better on the Picture Concepts subtest than his own mean score. On the Picture Concepts subtest, John was presented with two or three rows of easily identifiable pictures and asked to choose one picture from each row to form a group with a common characteristic. This subtest is designed to measure fluid reasoning and abstract categorical reasoning ability. The task invokes verbal concepts, but does not require verbal responses (Picture Concepts scaled score = 12).

SUMMARY

John is a 10-year-old child who completed the WISC-IV. He was referred by his counselor due to academic difficulties. His general cognitive ability, as estimated by the WISC-IV, is in the Low Average range. John's verbal comprehension and perceptual reasoning abilities were both in the Average range (VCI = 95, PRI = 104). John's general working memory and general processing speed abilities are both in the Borderline range (WMI = 74, PSI = 75). John's abilities to sustain attention, concentrate, and exert mental control are a weakness relative to his verbal comprehension and perceptual reasoning abilities. Furthermore, John's ability to process visual material quickly is also a weakness relative to his verbal comprehension and perceptual reasoning abilities. This overall pattern of scores is consistent with the academic difficulties noted by John's referral source.

COMPOSITE SCORES SUMMARY

Scale	Sum of Scaled Scores	Composite Score	Percentile Rank	Confidence Interval	Qualitative Description
Verbal Comprehension (VCI)	27	95	37	90-101	Average
Perceptual Reasoning (PRI)	32	104	61	97-110	Average
Working Memory (WMI)	11	74	4	70-83	Borderline
Processing Speed (PSI)	11	75	5	70-86	Borderline
Full Scale (FSIQ)	81	86	18	82-91	Low Average

WISC-IV Composite Scores

Composite Score Profile

	VCI	PRI	WMI	PSI	FSIQ	
155						155
150						150
145						145
140						140
135						135
130						130
125						125
120						120
115						115
110						110
105		+				105
100						100
95	+					95
90						90
85					+	85
80						80
75			+	+		75
70						70
65						65
60						60
55						55
50						50
45						45
	VCI	PRI	WMI	PSI	FSIQ	

FIGURE 3.1   WISC-IV Composite Scores. (Vertical Bar Represents the Standard Error of Measurement.)

Composite	Score	SEM	Composite	Score	SEM
VCI	95	3.67	PSI	75	4.74
PRI	104	3.97	FSIQ	86	2.6
WMI	74	4.24			

VERBAL COMPREHENSION SUBTEST SCORES SUMMARY

Subtests	Raw Score	Scaled Score	Test Age Equiv.	Percentile Rank
Similarities	16	8	8:10	25
Vocabulary	33	10	10:2	50
Comprehension	20	9	9:6	37

PERCEPTUAL REASONING SUBTEST SCORES SUMMARY

Subtests	Raw Score	Scaled Score	Test Age Equiv.	Percentile Rank
Block Design	34	10	10:10	50
Picture Concepts	20	12	14:10	75
Matrix Reasoning	20	10	9:10	50

WORKING MEMORY SUBTEST SCORES SUMMARY

Subtests	Raw Score	Scaled Score	Test Age Equiv.	Percentile Rank
Digit Span	11	6	6:2	9
Letter–Number Sequencing	10	5	6:10	5

PROCESSING SPEED SUBTEST SCORES SUMMARY

Subtests	Raw Score	Scaled Score	Test Age Equiv.	Percentile Rank
Coding	27	5	<8:2	5
Symbol Search	14	6	<8:2	9
(Cancellation)	51	6	6:6	9

WISC-IV Subtest Scaled Score Profile

	Verbal Comprehension				Perceptual Reasoning				Working Memory			Processing Speed		
	SI	VC	CO	IN	WR	BD	PCn	MR	PCm	DS	LN	AR	CD	SS	CA

```
19                                                                    19
18                                                                    18
17                                                                    17
16                                                                    16
14                                                                    14
15                                                                    15
13                                                                    13
12                              +                                     12
11                                                                    11
10       +            +     +                                         10
 9          +                                                          9
 8     +                                                               8
 7                                                                     7
 6                                      +              + +             6
 5                          +              +                           5
 4                                                                     4
 3                                                                     3
 2                                                                     2
 1                                                                     1

   SI  VC  CO  IN  WR  BD  PCn  MR  PCm  DS  LN  AR  CD  SS  CA
```

FIGURE 3.2 WISC-IV Subset Scaled Score Profile. (Vertical Bar Represents the Standard Error of Measurement.)

Subtest	Score	SEM	Subtest	Score	SEM
Similarities (SI)	8	1.12	Picture Completion (PCm)		
Vocabulary (VC)	10	0.95	Digit Span (DS)	6	0.99
Comprehension (CO)	9	1.34	Letter–Number Sequencing (LN)	5	0.99
Information (IN)			Arithmetic (AR)		
Word Reasoning (WR)			Coding (CD)	5	0.99
Block Design (BD)	10	1.2	Symbol Search (SS)	6	1.34
Picture Concepts (PCn)	12	1.2	Cancellation (CA)	6	1.2
Matrix Reasoning (MR)	10	0.99			

COMPOSITE SCORE DIFFERENCES

Discrepancy Comparisons	Scaled Score 1	Scaled Score 2	Diff.	Critical Value	Sig. Diff. Y/N	Base Rate
VCI-PRI	95	104	−9	7.79	Y	27%
VCI-WMI	95	74	21	8.08	Y	7.2%
VCI-PSI	95	75	20	8.63	Y	10.8%
PRI-WMI	104	74	30	8.36	Y	2.6%
PRI-PSI	104	75	29	8.9	Y	2.4%
WMI-PSI	74	75	−1	9.16	N	50.3%

Base Rate by Overall Sample.
Statistical Significance (Critical Values) at the .15 level.

SUBTEST SCORE DIFFERENCES

Discrepancy Comparisons	Scaled Score 1	Scaled Score 2	Diff.	Critical Value	Sig. Diff. Y/N	Base Rate
Digit Span-Letter–Number Sequencing	6	5	1	2.08	N	39.1%
Coding-Symbol Search	5	6	−1	2.61	N	44.8%
Similarities-Picture Concepts	8	12	−4	2.47	Y	13.2%
Coding-Cancellation	5	6	−1	2.63	N	44.8%
Symbol Search-Cancellation	6	6	0	2.79	N	

Statistical Significance (Critical Values) at the .15 level.

DIFFERENCES BETWEEN SUBTEST AND MEAN OF SUBTEST SCORES

Subtest	Subtest Scaled Score	Mean Scaled Score	Diff. from Mean	Critical Value	S/W	Base Rate
Block Design	10	8.1	1.90	2.60		>25%
Similarities	8	8.1	−0.10	2.60		>25%
Digit Span	6	8.1	−2.10	2.48		>25%
Picture Concepts	12	8.1	3.90	2.93	S	5–10%
Coding	5	8.1	−3.10	2.74	W	10–25%
Vocabulary	10	8.1	1.90	2.34		>25%
Letter–Number Sequencing	5	8.1	−3.10	2.28	W	10–25%
Matrix Reasoning	10	8.1	1.90	2.32		>25%
Comprehension	9	8.1	0.90	2.97		>25%
Symbol Search	6	8.1	−2.10	3.07		>25%

Overall: Mean = 8.1, Scatter = 7, Base Rate = 53.9%.
Statistical Significance (Critical Values) at the .15 level.

PROCESS SUMMARY AND DISCREPANCY ANALYSIS

Process Score	Raw Score	Scaled Score
Block Design No Time Bonus	34	11
Digit Span Forward	7	8
Digit Span Backward	4	5
Cancellation Random	17	5
Cancellation Structured	34	9

Process Score	Raw Score	Base Rate
Longest Digit Span Forward (LDSF)	8	9.0%
Longest Digit Span Backward (LDSB)	4	64.5%

PROCESS DISCREPANCY COMPARISONS

Process Score	Raw Score 1	Raw Score 2	Difference	Base Rate
LDSF-LDSB	8	4	4	11.3%

BASE RATE BY ALL AGES

Subtest/Process Score	Scaled Score 1	Scaled Score 2	Diff.	Critical Value	Sig. Diff. Y/N	Base Rate
Block Design-Block Design No Time Bonus	10	11	−1.00	2.39	N	24.3%
Digit Span Forward-Digit Span Backward	8	5	3.00	2.66	Y	21.8%
Cancellation Random-Structured	5	9	−4.00	3.23	Y	5.6%

Statistical Significance (Critical Values) at the .15 level.

WISC-IV TOTAL RAW SCORES

Subtest	Score Range	Raw Score
Block Design	0 to 68	34
Similarities	0 to 44	16
Digit Span	0 to 32	11
Picture Concepts	0 to 28	20
Coding	0 to 119	27
Vocabulary	0 to 68	33
Letter–Number Sequencing	0 to 30	10
Matrix Reasoning	0 to 35	20
Comprehension	0 to 42	20
Symbol Search	0 to 60	14
Picture Completion	0 to 38	
Cancellation	0 to 136	51
Information	0 to 33	
Arithmetic	0 to 34	
Word Reasoning	0 to 24	
Process Score	Score Range	Raw Score
Block Design No Time Bonus	0 to 50	34
Digit Span Forward	0 to 16	7
Digit Span Backward	0 to 16	4
Cancellation Random	0 to 68	17
Cancellation Structured	0 to 68	34
Longest Digit Span Forward	0,2 to 9	8
Longest Digit Span Backward	0,2 to 8	4

4

THE WISC-IV INTEGRATED

GEORGE MCCLOSKEY

Graduate Programs in Clinical and School Psychology
Philadelphia College of Osteopathic Medicine
Philadelphia Pennsylvania

ART MAERLENDER

Clinical School Services and Learning Disorders Program
Child and Adolescent Psychiatry
Dartmouth Medical School
Lebanon, New Hampshire

The WISC-IV Integrated (Wechsler with Kaplan et al., 2004) represents a combination of the revision and restandardization of the WISC-III contents with updated and restandardized process assessment tasks and procedures drawn from the WISC-III as a Process Instrument (the WISC-III PI; Kaplan *et al.*, 1999). The WISC-IV Integrated incorporates the core and supplemental subtests now published as the WISC-IV (Wechsler, 2003) along with 12 additional Process Approach Subtests and multiple process approach procedures for enhancing the collection of clinically relevant information from the performance of selected subtests. Combination of the WISC-III revision and WISC-III PI revision into the WISC-IV Integrated provides clinicians with a comprehensive set of flexible tools for characterizing in greater detail a child's cognitive strengths and weaknesses.

The conceptual basis for the WISC-IV Integrated grew out of the belief that the clinical utility of intellectual assessment procedures lies in their ability to accurately characterize the cognitive strengths and weaknesses of a child in order to better understand how to provide meaningful instruction

---

for that child. With plans for the revision of the WISC-III PI to progress in tandem with the revision of the WISC-IIII, the integration of the process approach components of the WISC-PI into the overall framework of the WISC-IV to form the WISC-IV Integrated was deemed the most sensible means of enhancing the clinical utility of the WISC-IV.

HISTORICAL PERSPECTIVE ON THE PROCESS APPROACH

The conceptual basis for the application of the process approach to the Wechsler Scales was derived from the work of Edith Kaplan and colleagues with what is known as the Boston Process Approach to neuropsychological assessment (Kaplan, 1983, 1988, 2000). Kaplan credits Heinz Werner's (1937) conception of the distinction between product and process in psychological assessment as the impetus for her work in developing the Boston Process Approach. Werner found that the analysis of errors was a meaningful device for understanding the ways in which the examinee's functional impairment could best be viewed and understood. In the 1990s Kaplan's long tradition of clinical assessment using the process approach was applied to the current editions of the adult and children's Wechsler Scales (Kaplan *et al.*, 1991, 1999) in the form of the WAIS-R as a Neuropsychological Instrument (WAIS-R NI) and the WISC-III as a Process Instrument (WISC-III PI). The WISC-III PI was composed of multiple choice versions of the WISC-III Information and Vocabulary Subtests; a motor-free multiple choice Block Design Subtest, and an alternative Block Design Subtest that could be used to further explore visuomotor performance; Letter Span and Spatial Span Subtests to supplement Digit Span in assessing registration and working memory processes; a process procedure for the Arithmetic Subtest to examine the contributions of working memory and calculation skills to task performance; a Coding Copy Subtest to examine graphomotor performance; an incidental recall companion task for the Coding Subtest; two measures of planning and executive control, the Sentence Arrangement Subtest and the Elithorn Mazes Subtest; and quantitative indicators of several qualitative process observations for various subtests. Other variables inherent in the test process were also calculated for the WAIS-R NI, such as the amount of intrasubtest scatter across items of a subtest.

The revision of the Process Approach components of the WISC-III PI—now included in the WISC-IV Integrated—added, deleted, and revised many of the original tasks and process scores, including the addition of multiple choice versions of the Similarities and Comprehension Subtests; revisions of the Information, Vocabulary, and Picture Vocabulary Subtests of the WISC-III PI; revision of the Block Design Multiple Choice Subtest; revision of the Letter Span Subtest and addition of a Visual Digit

Span and Letter–Number Sequencing Process Approach Subtest; a revision of the Arithmetic Subtest process approach procedures used to understand the contributions of working memory and calculation abilities; a revision of the Elithorn Mazes Subtest; deletion of the Sentence Arrangement Subtest, and addition of several process scores to better understand task performance. Through the combination of the updated WISC subtests; with the updated WISC PI subtests and process procedures and scores, the WISC-IV Integrated moves traditional intellectual assessment in the direction of cognitive assessment, capitalizing on the important findings and applications of clinical neuropsychology, cognitive psychology, and cognitive neuroscience to improve the depth and quality of information derived from the assessment of mental functions (Delis *et al.*, 1990).

THE PROCESS APPROACH
TO COGNITIVE ASSESSMENT

The process approach to the assessment of cognitive function represents a refined, highly integrated way of thinking about test content, assessment procedures, test session behavior, and test performance interpretation. The process approach is based on at least five interconnected principles for understanding what a cognitive assessment reveals about a child:

1. Complex, multifactorial tasks, such as those represented by the WISC-IV subtests, represent a complex interaction of many neuropsychological components. By attempting to identify the discrete processes that contribute to the final outcome, it is possible to locate the source of the difficulties and thus better establish a cognitive or brain-based explanation for the performance.

2. Variations in task performance parameters involving input, internal processing, and output demands can greatly affect the overall outcome of the task for any given child.

3. Careful, systematic observation of how a child engages a task is essential to understanding the outcome of task performance.

4. What a child did wrong when engaging a task is as important as what a child did right when engaging a task.

5. Specific observations can lead to enhanced hypothesis generation and confirmation (or refutation).

When applying the process approach, the scores that a child earns, whether on individual tasks (subtests) or combinations of tasks (Indexes), are interpreted contextually as outcomes of multiple sources of influence, including the specific kinds of materials and task formats a child is asked to engage, the cognitive processes and abilities utilized by a specific child, and the strategies chosen by the child to perform each item of a specific task. This approach helps to guide the examiner into a mode of observation and hypothesis generation that forms the core of a thorough assessment.

COMPARING THE PROCESS APPROACH TO OTHER FRAMEWORKS FOR TEST INTERPRETATION

The process approach can be considered one of many legitimate frameworks that can be applied to interpret intellectual functioning as reflected in test performance.

Frameworks for interpretation of test performance can be thought of in terms of successively more detailed levels of analysis. These levels start with a very broad, global approach that summarizes performance with a single score, moving to a somewhat more detailed multiple factors approach that summarizes performance with a set of composite scores, to a much more detailed subtest profile approach that summarizes performance with subtest scores and the score relationships among various subtests, and finally to a highly detailed process approach which incorporates subtest scores, the relationships among various subtest scores, and careful analysis of the manner in which subtest tasks are performed.

Proponents of the global interpretive approach often advance the claim that the most reasonable and most scientifically defensible interpretation of an assessment of intellectual functioning occurs at the level of the total score. In the case of the WISC-IV, this would be the Full Scale Standard Score referred to as FSIQ. From the global, or "g," perspective, the score produced by a good general measure of intelligence characterizes a child's general intellectual potential, and likelihood of success when engaging tasks requiring cognitive effort. Citing the extensive literature base that has established the relationship of global scores with multiple criteria, such as success in career pursuits, income, marital satisfaction, emotional health, and stability (Gottfredson, 1998; Kuncell, Hezlett, & Ones, 2004), proponents of "g" tout the predictive ability of a global score obtained from psychometrically sound measures of general intelligence. From a strict global perspective, scores below the total composite level have much less meaningful interpretive power because they fragment the overall picture and reduce the accuracy of prediction or strength of relationship that is embodied in the global composite score. Focusing interpretation only on the global score is thought to avoid the perceived difficulties that arise when subtest or Index scores fluctuate significantly from one administration of a test to the next because even in most situations where such fluctuation occurs, the global score tends not to vary significantly.

Psychologists who choose a multiple factors approach to interpretation utilize composites that group subtests together based on what is thought to be a common core cognitive capacity shared by the subtests. The multiple factors approach applied to the WISC-IV focuses interpretation on the four Index scores. Adherents to this position argue that the wide variations in Index scores demonstrated by many children reduces the descriptive and predictive power of the global FSIQ, and that a more refined picture of a child's cognitive abilities as represented in a description of the four separate Index scores is necessary to effectively characterize a child's intellectual capabilities. Many adherents of this approach, while uncomfortable with the "smoothing over" effect inherent in the interpretation of the all-encompassing global IQ, are equally uncomfortable with interpretation of the frequent "lumps" represented by significant differences among subtest scores that make up a single composite Index. The avoidance of subtest level score interpretation by proponents of a multiple factors approach typically stems from a perceived lack of psychometric adequacy of these more specific subtest scores in terms of reliability and validity.

Recognizing the cognitive diversity inherent in many of the clusters of subtests that comprise the separate Indexes of the Wechsler Scales, proponents of the subtest profile approach to interpretation make use of subtest level scores either as a supplement to, or a replacement for, interpretation of the global FSIQ and the multiple factors Index scores (Kaufman, 1994; Sattler, 2001). The techniques applied in the interpretation of Wechsler Scale subtest scores are varied. Identification of subtest strengths and weaknesses using deviation from the arithmetic mean of a group of subtests, theoretical and empirically-based reconfiguration of subtests into shared ability clusters, and interpretation of "unique variance" contributions of individual subtests are all techniques that have been applied in efforts to more accurately characterize individual children's cognitive strengths and weaknesses using subtest scores (Kaufman, 1994; Sattler, 2001).

Like the subtest profile approach to interpretation, the process approach posits that the exclusive use of the FSIQ or the four Index scores can gloss over individual variations in more specific areas of cognitive capacity, and that these variations often are at the heart of accurate characterizations of an individual child's test performance. The process approach makes use of clinical observation and description techniques that often involve even closer levels of scrutiny of task performance, requiring the psychologist to look beneath the level of scaled scores to the level of specific item performance. As noted in the basic tenets presented earlier, the process approach recognizes that even individual subtests are not "pure" measures of any specific cognitive process or ability, and therefore require the interplay of multiple processes and abilities for successful completion. The process approach also posits that whether the tasks are performed successfully or unsuccessfully, the clinician has the opportunity to observe what specific processes and abilities an individual attempts to employ, and how they attempt to employ them in their efforts to solve the task. Additionally, the process approach takes into account the empirically demonstrated fact that the processes and abilities used to attempt to solve a task can vary widely from child to child, and even from item to item within a single child's efforts at task completion, regardless of what processes or abilities the task is thought to be measuring (Kaplan *et al.*, 1981; Akshoomoff & Stiles, 1996; Kylonnen, Lohman, & Woltz, 1984; Lohman *et al.*, 1987; French, 1965). The process approach emphasizes the empirically derived fact that the same subtest score can be obtained in many different ways, and that each of those ways can represent substantially different applications of cognitive processes and abilities. To accurately characterize a child's performance on an individual subtest, the process approach often requires careful observation and analysis of the interaction between task components and the child's approach to task performance at the item level.

The task contents of the WISC-IV Integrated are grouped by four major cognitive domains: Verbal, Perceptual, Working Memory, and Processing Speed (see Figure 4.1). The task contents are also organized in a hierarchical structure that allows psychologists flexibility in interpretation. A selected subset of tasks from the verbal, perceptual, working memory, and processing speed domains is aggregated to produce an FSIQ for global score interpretation. Selected subsets of tasks within each major cognitive content domain are aggregated to produce four Index scores—Verbal Comprehension, Perceptual Reasoning, Working Memory, and Processing Speed—to allow for a major cognitive factors approach to interpretation. Within each cognitive content domain, the basic task contents of the WISC-IV Integrated are presented as a set of subtests and process approach procedures that are designed to facilitate subtest and process-oriented interpretation approaches.

THE PROCESS APPROACH APPLIED TO THE WISC-IV INTEGRATED

The process approach to interpretation of the WISC-IV Integrated is facilitated through various features of the content, structure, administration, and scoring of the test. These features include:

- Process approach subtests that can be used to refine hypotheses about cognitive abilities and processes.
- Process approach administration procedures that can be applied with selected WISC-IV Integrated core and supplemental subtests.
- Process scores derived from core, supplemental, and process approach tasks.
- Cumulative percentages for process approach coding of behavior observations obtained during task performance.

Table 4.1 provides a list of all of the WISC-IV Integrated features that facilitate error analysis and the process approach to interpretation. The

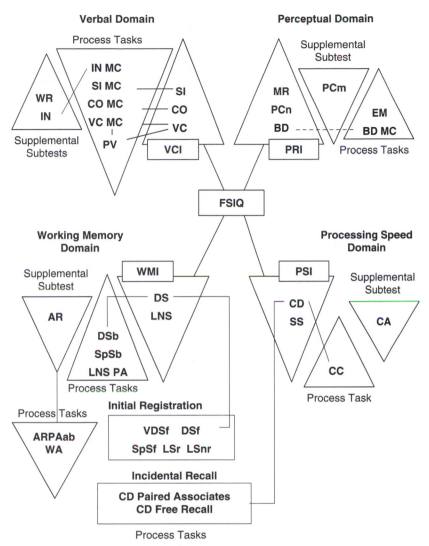

Verbal Domain

Process Tasks

IN MC
SI MC
CO MC
VC MC

WR
IN

Supplemental
Subtests

PV

SI
CO
VC

VCI

Perceptual Domain

Supplemental
Subtest

MR
PCn
BD

PCm

EM
BD MC

PRI

Process Tasks

FSIQ

**Working Memory
Domain**

Supplemental
Subtest

AR

WMI
DS
LNS

DSb
SpSb
LNS PA

Process Tasks

Process Tasks

ARPAab
WA

Initial Registration

VDSf   DSf
SpSf LSr LSnr

Incidental Recall

CD Paired Associates
CD Free Recall

Process Tasks

**Processing Speed
Domain**

PSI

CD
SS

Supplemental
Subtest

CA

CC

Process Task

FIGURE 4.1 WISC-IV integrated structure and content

number of interpretive enhancements enabled by the incorporation of process approach features in the WISC-IV Integrated is extensive. It is important for clinicians to keep in mind that the process approach features are intended for use on an as needed basis such that only the elements thought to provide necessary clarification of cognitive abilities and processes in specific instances are used during an assessment. In the majority of clinical situations, a need for the use of all of the features for a single case would be unlikely.

TABLE 4.1   WISC-IV Process Approach Features

Process Subtests and Procedures	Process Scaled Score Label	Norm-Referenced Coded Observations	Qualitative Observations
Verbal Domain			
Similarities Multiple Choice (SIMC)	SIMC		
Comprehension Multiple Choice (COMC)	COMC		
Vocabulary Multiple Choice (VCMC)	VCMC		
Picture Vocabulary Multiple Choice (PVMC)	PVMC		
Information Multiple Choice (INMC)	INMC		
Recording of Don't Know, Asks for Repetition, Prompting Required, and Self-Correction behaviors during verbal multiple choice subtest administrations		Total Sample Cumulative Frequencies	
Recording of item response times			Qualitative
Analysis of verbal responses to items			Qualitative
Error analysis for multiple choice subtest responses			Qualitative
Perceptual Domain			
Block Design Multiple Choice (BDMC)	BDMC		
Block Design Process Assessment A and B (BDPA)	BDPA-A BDPA-B		
Elithorn Mazes (EM)	EM		
Removing time bonus points from Block Design	BDn		
Removing time bonus points from Block Design MC	BDMCn		
Removing time bonus points from Elithorn Mazes (EMs)	EMn		
Recording latency time for EM		Total Sample Cumulative Frequencies by Item	
Recording motor planning for EM		Total Sample Cumulative Frequencies by Item	
Recording errors for EM		Total Sample Cumulative Frequencies by Item	

(Continues)

TABLE 4.1 *(Continued)*

Process Subtests and Procedures	Process Scaled Score Label	Norm-Referenced Coded Observations	Qualitative Observations
Analysis of errors for PCm			Qualitative
Recording item response times for MR, PCn, PCm			Qualitative
Working Memory Domain			
Visual Digit Span (VDS)	VDS		
Letter Span Rhyming (LSr)	LSr		
Letter Span Nonrhyming (LSnr)	LSnr		
Letter–Number Sequencing Process Assessment (LNSPA)	LNSPA		
Spatial Span Forward (SpSf)	SpSf		
Spatial Span Backward (SpSb)	SpSb		
Applying time bonus to Arithmetic (Art)	ARt		
Auditory/visual administration of Arithmetic (ARPA-A)	ARPA-A		
Applying time bonus to auditory/visual administration of Arithmetic (ARPA-At)	APRA-At		
Auditory/visual administration of Arithmetic with pencil and paper response option (ARPA-B)	ARPA-B		
Written calculation format administration of Arithmetic (WA)	WA		
Processing Speed Domain			
Coding Copy (CC)	CC		
Cancellation Random item score (CAR)	CAR		
Cancellation Structured item score (CAS)	CAS		
Recording performance in 30-second intervals for CD and CC		Means and Standard Deviations by Age	
Recording performance in 30-second intervals for SS			Qualitative
Recording response strategy type for Cancellation		Frequencies by Age	
Multiple Domains			
Recording of No Response behavior for various tasks		Total Sample Cumulative Frequencies	
Intrasubtest scatter score analysis			Qualitative

PROCESS APPROACH SUBTESTS

Process approach subtests are unique tasks whose content is independent of any of the WISC-IV core or supplemental subtests. Some of these subtests enable clinicians to better understand cognitive abilities or processes that are also involved in the performance of core and supplemental subtests (Block Design Multiple Choice, Block Design PA, Coding Copy), while others use different input modality and/or different item content to assess cognitive abilities and processes similar to those used by core or supplemental subtests (Elithorn Mazes, Visual Digit Span, Spatial Span, Letter Span, Letter–Number Sequencing Process Approach).

PROCESS APPROACH PROCEDURES

Process approach procedures involve the use of the same item content as core and supplemental subtests in a variety of ways. Some process approach procedures require administration of the same content as that used in administration of a core or supplemental subtest, but do so under altered conditions where the input format and/or input modality or response demands have been altered (e.g., Vocabulary Multiple Choice and Picture Vocabulary Multiple Choice). Other process approach procedures require the examiner to complete additional administration steps (e.g., Coding Incidental Recall), to complete additional recording procedures (e.g., Coding 30-second interval recording), to complete additional analyses of results (e.g., Picture Completion response error analysis), or to complete additional scoring procedures to obtain process scores (e.g., removing the time bonus points from Block Design). A complete list of process approach features available for use with the WISC-IV Integrated is provided in Table 4.1.

PROCESS SCORES

Process scores are derived from administration of the Process Approach subtests and from the application of process approach procedures to core and supplemental subtest content. The complete list of these scores is provided in Table 4.1. All scores listed in the table can be interpreted as norm-referenced scaled scores based on a mean of 10 and a standard deviation of 3. Process score standard scores were derived from analysis of the performance of a national standardization sample of 730 children and are tabled in the WISC-IV Integrated Administration and Scoring Manual as age-based scaled scores reported in 4-month age intervals.

PROCESS APPROACH BEHAVIOR OBSERVATION CODING

Some of the process approach procedures involve recording of behavior observations during the assessment. These observations can be quantified and translated into norm-referenced bases for interpretation involving either cumulative frequencies of the occurrence of behaviors (e.g., Requests for Repetitions with Arithmetic tasks), or means and standard deviations for performance by age group (e.g., 30-second interval performance recording for Coding).

CLINICAL APPLICATIONS OF THE PROCESS APPROACH TO THE WISC-IV INTEGRATED

Complete descriptions and clinical examples of the multiple applications of the process approach procedures with the content of the WISC-IV Integrated is beyond the scope of this chapter, so a brief summary is provided here by content domain.

Verbal Domain

The WISC-IV Integrated Verbal Domain includes three core subtests that make up the Verbal Comprehension Index—Similarities, Vocabulary, and Comprehension; two supplemental subtests—Information and Word Reasoning; and five Multiple Choice process approach subtests (procedures) that are identical in item stimulus content as their core and supplemental subtest counterparts, but alter presentation format, input processing demands, and response requirements—Similarities Multiple Choice, Vocabulary Multiple Choice, Picture Vocabulary Multiple Choice, Comprehension Multiple Choice, and Information Multiple Choice.

The Similarities, Vocabulary, Comprehension, Information, and Word Reasoning subtests all share some common elements required for successful performance, including attending to, processing, and comprehending the oral presentation of verbal stimulus items and a response format that demands verbal expression. Some of the subtests share an emphasis on the use of specific cognitive abilities more so than others. Vocabulary and Information both primarily require retrieval of information from long-term storage (i.e., those that draw on crystallized knowledge bases). While both of these subtests require a verbal response, the nature of the response demands is significantly different. The Vocabulary Subtest requires the ability to formulate and produce a verbal description that adequately represents the child's understanding of the meaning of the stimulus word. Activation of semantic networks during free response vocabulary tasks is thought to be extensive. In contrast, the Information Subtest requires much less in the way of amount of verbal production, but the expression must be more precise, as acceptable responses to each item are very limited and very specific. Although retrieval demands are more specific with the Information Subtest, less semantic access is required. A child who experiences difficulty with organizing and/or expressing the verbal knowledge he or she retrieves about the meaning of a word is more likely to experience difficulties with the response demands of the Vocabulary Subtest. Impairments in oral-motor function (dyspraxia) also limit the extended output required for Vocabulary Subtests responses. A child who is able to retrieve information related to the general topic of a factual information question, but cannot retrieve and/or express the exact word or words accepted as a correct response, is more likely to have difficulty responding with the required degree of precision to the items of the Information Subtest.

The Similarities and Comprehension Subtests both require the ability to organize and express thoughts in a manner similar to Vocabulary, but the internal processing demands of these two tasks emphasize generating novel verbal content much more than retrieval of stored information. Although both of these subtests differ from the Vocabulary Subtest in terms of internal processing demands, each one has its own unique requirements. Similarities requires the ability to generate different novel content for each item while maintaining the same context of an associative set for each item, thus requiring inductive analysis. Comprehension requires a greater diversity of idea generation, as each question provides a new context for problem-solving efforts. A child who has trouble organizing and expressing his or her understanding of how two things are alike is likely to have difficulties with the response demands of the Similarities Subtest. A child who has trouble organizing and expressing ideas he or she might generate for explaining verbally stated problems is likely to have difficulties with the Comprehension Subtest. In addition, several Comprehension items require a second response, thus activating working memory processes.

Multiple Choice Verbal Subtests

For children who experience difficulties with any of these four subtests, the clinician can administer the process approach Multiple Choice counterparts of those subtests to gain greater insight into the nature of the child's difficulties with these tasks. The four verbal process approach subtests—Similarities Multiple Choice, Vocabulary Multiple Choice, Comprehension Multiple Choice, and Information Multiple Choice—are all administered in the same manner. For each item of these subtests, the child is presented with the stimulus question and four or five response options printed in a stimulus booklet. The response options are read to the child as he or she views them, and the child must then choose the option the child believes to be the best answer to the question. As is the case with the free response format versions, each item of the Similarities, Vocabulary, and Comprehension Multiple Choice Subtests has one response option that is a more complete or more specific response that is awarded 2 points, one option that is a less precise or complete but relatively accurate response that is awarded 1 point. These correct responses are accompanied by two or three responses that are inaccurate statements that are scored 0. Consistent with its free response counterpart, the Information Multiple Choice Subtests only has one correct option that is awarded 1 point. The response choices for many multiple choice items, especially the Vocabulary Multiple Choice Subtest, include one incorrect response that has characteristics to "pull" the child to it, although it is clearly incorrect. For example, inclusion of the word *alfalfa* as a response choice for the Vocabulary word *alphabet* represents a phonological pull. An affirmative response to such an item could represent stimulus-bound behavior often associated with frontal lobe dysfunction.

The verbal multiple choice subtests offer children who struggle with the production of adequate verbal responses a chance to demonstrate their ability to accurately recognize a correct response. In these cases, a child with expressive language problems or retrieval difficulties might be able to perform substantially better than they did on the free response versions of the tasks because the recognition format either enables them to bypass expressive language difficulties or facilitates the retrieval of information that is known but inaccessible by means of free recall retrieval processes. An additional hypothesis that must always be considered when a child performs substantially better with the multiple choice format than with the standard free response format is the possibility that the child was able to use executive function-driven decision-making skills to work with the information provided in the response options, eliminate incorrect response options, and narrow selection down to the two correct responses. In such cases, the child is able to deduce the correct response through the application of good test-taking strategies rather than drawing from the stored knowledge base or selecting options that are consistent with their own thoughts on the subject. This hypothesis becomes a stronger possibility as the child's age increases and frequent exposure to multiple choice format examinations increases significantly.

It is extremely important to note that not all children with knowledge stores or reasoning abilities greater than they are able to show with a free response format will be able to demonstrate adequately the true extent of their knowledge and abilities with any or all of the multiple choice formats. Children who are poor readers sometimes have difficulty reading the four choices provided for each test question. These children will be able to demonstrate their knowledge store or reasoning ability only if they have well-developed listening skills and are able to retain in working memory the examiner's reading of each response option long enough to deliberate on and select an accurate response. When it is known that the child has a severe reading problem and the child is able to perform well on a multiple choice format task, it is reasonable to infer that the use of effective listening skills and effective working memory processes applied to orally presented information enabled the child to access their word knowledge store through the recognition recall format, or to effectively hold the orally presented information long enough to engage effective reasoning abilities or general test-taking strategies to deduce correct responses. A child who has poor reading skills and who also is not good at applying working memory processes to orally presented information, however, might not be able to demonstrate adequately his or her store of word knowledge or reasoning abilities using this multiple choice format.

The Vocabulary Subtest also has a Picture Vocabulary Multiple Choice counterpart. For Picture Vocabulary Multiple Choice, the same words as those used on the other versions of the Vocabulary subtest are presented in a multiple choice picture-identification format. For each item, the examiner shows the child a page with four pictures and says a word and the child points to the picture that he or she thinks is the best visual representation of the word. The Picture Vocabulary Multiple Choice format is the most likely format to enable a child with poor reading skills and/or a language impairment to demonstrate the full extent of their word knowledge store as it does not require reading or listening carefully to orally presented language. In some cases, the Picture Vocabulary Subtest will enable English Language Learners to demonstrate their receptive knowledge of words much more effectively than the Vocabulary Multiple Choice Subtest.

Children with severe language impairment also are more likely to find the Vocabulary Multiple Choice format as limiting as the free recall response format for reasons similar to those stated for children with reading problems, especially in light of the fact that most children with severe language impairments also experience reading difficulties. For children with reading problems and/or severe language impairments who also do poorly on the Vocabulary Multiple Choice format, the Picture Vocabulary Multiple Choice format is more likely to allow them to demonstrate their store of word knowledge.

In addition to the use of the multiple choice versions of verbal tasks, examiners using the process approach can develop skill in the analysis of the quality and quantity of verbal responses for subtests that use a free response format. Responses can sometimes reveal clinically significant patterns reflecting poor grasp of grammar and/or morphology, semantic confusions, word finding difficulties, poor pragmatic use of language, unusual speech prosody, or paraphasic responses that would indicate the need for a thorough speech/language evaluation.

Perceptual Domain

The WISC-IV Integrated Perceptual Domain includes three core subtests that involve working with visually presented nonverbal information—Block Design, Picture Concepts, and Matrix Reasoning—one supplemental subtest—Picture Completion—and two unique subtests incorporated from the WISC-III PI to enhance interpretation of visual task performance—Block Design Multiple Choice and Elithorn Mazes. Performance on the Block Design, Block Design Multiple Choice, and Elithorn Mazes Subtests can also be interpreted using process procedures that remove the effects of time bonuses for quick responses, yielding the Block Design No Time Bonus (BDn), Block Design Multiple Choice No Time Bonus (BDMCn), and Elithorn Mazes No Time Bonus (EMn) process scaled scores. For more in-depth exploration of a child's performance with visuomotor construction, a separate Block Design Process Approach procedure is available for administration.

The common bases for all of the tasks in this domain are visual perception, visual organization, and visual discrimination skills. This means that if a child's basic cognitive visual processes are compromised in some way, the deficit will impact performance on all tasks requiring visual perception, organization, and/or discrimination. When a child exhibits uneven performance with the tasks of the Perceptual Domain, it is untenable to posit a deficit in overall visual perceptual processes. In such cases, one or more of the other multiple processes and abilities that can be drawn on to complete these tasks is likely to be the source of the difficulties the child is having. When visual perception and discrimination difficulties do play a role in these cases of uneven performance on visual tasks, the problems are more likely to involve how the perceptions are being organized or encoded by the child for specific tasks rather than core deficits in the ability to visually perceive or the ability to make visual discriminations.

All of the tasks, with the possible exception of Block Design Multiple Choice, also require some degree of reasoning applied to novel problem solving to achieve success, at least on most of the more difficult items of each task. Working memory processes can play a large role in performance on Matrix Reasoning, Picture Concepts and Elithorn Mazes. Executive control processes involvement varies greatly across the tasks, with the greatest executive demands evidenced on Block Design and Elithorn Mazes. Block Design and Elithorn Mazes also require motoric responses by hand, whereas the other four tasks do not. Block Design, Block Design Multiple Choice, and Elithorn Mazes all award bonus points for speeded performance, although this factor is minimized greatly for younger children on Block Design. Picture Concepts and Picture Completion make use of concrete pictorial content, while Matrix Reasoning, Block Design, Block Design Multiple Choice, and Elithorn Mazes all make use of abstract geometric designs as visual input.

Block Design Subtests and Process Scores

A major focus of the process approach within the Perceptual Domain is on understanding the cognitive processes and abilities that underlie performance on Block Design. Block Design requires the child to produce designs that match models using two-color blocks. Effective performance requires understanding the nature of the task to be performed, accurately perceiving the stimulus pictures and blocks, analyzing the design into constituent parts (detail-processing), synthesizing the individual blocks into a whole that matches the model (pattern processing), engaging reasoning to aid problem-solving, manipulating the blocks by hand, self-monitoring for speed of performance and accuracy, self-correcting errors, and engaging executive control processes to coordinate all these cognitive and motor functions.

When a child performs poorly with Block Design, the Block Design Multiple Choice Subtest can be administered to take a closer look at the child's visual perception and discrimination abilities. If Block Design Multiple Choice performance is significantly better than Block Design performance, attention should be focused on sources other than visual perception and discrimination for the possible source of difficulties, especially when the Block Design Multiple Choice score is more commensurate with performance on other Perceptual Domain subtests such as Matrix Reasoning, Picture Completion, and Picture Concepts. For example, in the case of a 12-year-old child who earns a scaled score of 4 on Block Design, but scaled scores in the average range on Matrix Reasoning and Block Design Multiple Choice, a hypothesis that visual-motor output is defective might be considered rather than positing a generalized deficit in visual perception. Without the Multiple Choice Subtest, one is at a disadvantage for explaining the disparity in scores when Block Design performance is significantly lower than scores on other perceptual reasoning tasks. When visual perception difficulties are ruled out, other potential sources of difficulty include reasoning with visual information, executive control processes (including visual-motor output), motor dexterity, and psychomotor speed.

Processing speed and use of reasoning ability in Block Design performance can be separated out to some degree by calculating the BDn process score. This procedure is applicable for older students, as time bonuses have been eliminated for the first six items of the Block Design Subtest early trials. When the BDn process score is significantly better than the Block Design Subtest score, the child is likely to be demonstrating greater facility with problem-solving ability than might have been thought, but working at a relatively slow pace. For example, a 14-year-old child who receives no bonus points for speed but correctly completes all the block design items earns the same scaled score of 10 as a child who receives full bonus point credit for speed on four items but is unable to correctly complete the last two most difficult items. When the BDn scores are calculated for these two children, the child who correctly completed all of the items now earns a much higher BDn scaled score of 14, while the score of the child who could not complete the last two items earns a BDn scaled score of 10 consistent with the BD scaled score.

While the Block Design scaled score of 10 accurately communicates the overall level of performance with the entire task for both of these children, it does not relate the degree of effectiveness of the first child's problem-solving skill with the task. The BDN scaled score of 14, when considered in tandem with the Block Design score of 10, enables the clinician to more accurately characterize the true nature of this child's performance. Making the important distinction about the difference in performance for this child when a time factor is involved more thoroughly describes what transpired during the assessment and the resulting outcome and is likely to ring true with those who know the child well and who likely have frequently observed similar instances of the child not performing as well as expected when a quick work pace with similar kinds of tasks was required for success.

Executive control can be gauged through careful observation of the child's approach to design completion, as well as the impact of these efforts on the final outcome. One of the more frequently observed breakdowns in executive control involves correctly solving difficult items while failing to correct detail errors in easier items, thereby earning a score that really might not accurately characterize the true nature of the child's problem-solving capabilities. For example, consider the case of a 14-year-old child who correctly solves most of the Block Design items administered, including the two most difficult items, 13 and 14, but completes Items 8, 10, and 12 with detail errors (single blocks with the diagonals side rotated to an incorrect orientation) still present in the final designs. Although the Block Design scaled score of 8 that this child earns accurately describes the overall level of performance with the complete task, it fails to communicate the high degree of problem-solving capabilities demonstrated on the most difficult items, and the inconsistent attention to detail and/or failure to check final solutions for accuracy demonstrated on relatively easier items.

A process approach-oriented description of this child's performance would state that the child demonstrated superior problem-solving skills with difficult items, but was unable to consistently apply these superior problem-solving skills, with the result being errors on relatively easier items and a Block Design Subtest scaled score that reflects an overall level of performance in the lower end of the average range. Such a description honors the norm-referenced score that was legitimately assigned to describe overall level of performance, but qualifies this result in a manner that provides insight into the child's approach to task performance and gets to the heart of some cognitive inefficiencies that are likely to be sources of difficulty in the performance of certain kinds of academic tasks. This description also is more likely to be consistent with the observations and judgments of parents, teachers, and others who know the child well, and who would have difficulty believing that this child's ability to solve problems involving nonverbal visual material is only in the low end of the average range because what they observe instead is both the superior problem-solving abilities and the errors that result in incorrect performance of tasks that they believe the child is capable of performing accurately.

In addition to these types of performance inefficiencies, broken configurations produced en route to a correct final solution or offered as final solutions are indicative of breakdowns in executive control related to coordinating the integration of cognitive processes (neural networks involved with pattern processing and neural networks involved with detail processing) that must be used together effectively for successful task completion. Also indicative of executive control deficiencies or inefficiencies are production strategies that involve excessive rotation of individual blocks, dismantling of accurate partial solutions in an attempt to restart the problem-solving process, an overfocus on the details of individual blocks and the connections between individual blocks, an inability to disengage from pattern processing in order to shift to analysis of individual block details, and time-consuming overconcern with the precise alignment of individual blocks.

Configural errors reflect a perceptual bias towards local vs global judgments, suggesting an underlying visual processing tendency. Kramer, Kaplan, Share, and Huckeba (1999) noted that more than six breaks in the square configuration en route to a final product suggested impairment in visuospatial ability. More than one broken configuration as a final product is also indicative of difficulties. Breaking configuration was shown to be related to overall competence on BD and reflected a global response bias.

Careful observations of performance can also reveal difficulties with manual dexterity including such problems as dropping blocks, applying excessive pressure to individual blocks causing them to "pop" out of place, bumping of already placed blocks causing misalignments that require correction, and unusual grasping gestures or positioning of hands while working.

Poor performance on the Multiple Choice Block Design Subtest can also be examined to consider the effect of visual processing speed on performance by calculating the Block Design Multiple Choice No Time Bonus (BDMCn) score. When the BDMCn score is significantly better than the Block Design Multiple Choice Subtest score, the child is likely to be demonstrating better use of visual perception and discrimination processes than might have been thought, but unable to bring these to bear on item performance as quickly as peers the same age.

Occasionally, it is advantageous to use the Block Design Process Approach procedures to more thoroughly examine the nature of a child's performance with visual-motor construction tasks. These procedures involve additional block design items that require the child to make additional decisions about how many blocks will be required to complete a design as more blocks than are needed are provided for each item. A detailed description of the Block Design Process Approach procedures and their interpretation are included in a separate appendix of the WISC-IV Integrated Technical and Interpretive Manual (Wechsler, Kaplan, Fein, Morris, Kramer, Maerlender, & Delis, 2004).

Elithorn Mazes Subtest and Process Scores

Like Block Design, Elithorn Mazes is a cognitively complex, visually based task that requires multiple cognitive processes working in concert for effective performance. The basic visual processing demands of this task are fairly minimal, with the emphasis placed instead on inhibition of impulsive responding while directing the performance of careful visual planning before the engagement of a motor routine for drawing a desired path through a maze in a manner that connects a specified number of dots without backtracking along the selected route. The mazes are specifically designed to draw impulsive, stimulus-bound performers to incorrect routes through the mazes. Although good reasoning can assist with effective completion of the task, effective consideration of multiple alternatives to find the correct path is more heavily dependent on working memory skills. Many children supplement working memory processes by engaging in motor planning before drawing their path.

Elithorn Mazes performance can be interpreted using an overall Subtest scaled score and multiple process scores. Although success with the task is more likely when a latency period is observed before the drawing of a path, high scores are typically earned by children who can minimize the latency period and direct and complete their planning quickly and efficiently. Conversely, poor scores are most often earned by children who make no attempt to plan before engaging a motor response, or who plan quickly but inefficiently. For children who engage in efficient but more prolonged planning, the Elithorn Mazes No Time Bonus process scaled score can bring to the forefront their effective, though relatively slow planning and motor execution capabilities in a manner similar to what was illustrated with the BDn case example.

Cumulative percentages are offered to examine the time elapsed before motor engagement (Latency Time process score), frequency of motor planning during the latency period (Motor Planning process score), and frequency of errors while executing motor routines for drawing paths (Maze Errors process score). These additional process scores provide a quantitative means for more accurately characterizing how a child attempts to perform Elithorn Mazes.

Picture Completion Subtest

While the perceptual discrimination process base required for success with the Picture Completion Subtest items is acknowledged by most clinicians, the relatively heavy demands for retrieval of visual knowledge from long-term storage and the use of reasoning to "figure out" what might be missing for some of the more difficult items is often overlooked, with low scores being interpreted most frequently as indicative of a deficiency in visual perception and/or discrimination, or poor attention to visual details. Table 4.2 provides a content chart that divides the Picture Completion items into two broad categories, those that rely primarily on visual discrimination and have all the clues needed to discover the missing element embedded in the drawing itself, and those that rely on retrieval and possibly manipulation of visual images from a visual knowledge base or use of reasoning processes

TABLE 4.2   Picture Completion Items by Observational Category

Visual Discrimination Items	Prior Knowledge/Reasoning Items
1. Jacket	5. Bell
2. Fox	7. Mirror
3. Hand	8. Man's Watch
4. Cat	9. Door
6. Girl	13. Belt
10. Leaf	14. Clock
11. Ladder	16. Dice
12. Dresser	20. Tree
15. Face	21. Scissors
17. Light Bulb	22. Bridge
18. Shirt	23. Whistle
19. Bike Riders	25. Pig
24. Guitar	26. Bathtub
29. Orange	27. Bicycle
31. Trellis	28. Thermometer
32. Supermarket	30. Fish
34. Umbrella	33. Profile
37. Family Portrait	35. Water Skiing
38. Tennis Shoe	36. Shadow

to deduce what is missing from the picture. Use of the content chart can be helpful in identifying children who have difficulties predominantly with one or the other item category. A child who performs effectively with items that primarily involve visual discrimination while performing poorly with the items that require retrieval and manipulation of information from a visual knowledge base cannot be accurately described as demonstrating poor attention to visual details or poor visual discrimination abilities. If a child lacks the knowledge of what an object should look like, no amount of visual discrimination ability or attention to the visual details of the image on the page will find the missing element in a picture of that object. Conversely, children who focus their thinking on problem solving at a higher level and perform well with the items requiring prior knowledge and reasoning abilities sometimes have difficulty picking up on rather obvious missing details in common objects and perform less effectively with the basic visual discrimination items. It should be noted that items primarily involving only the use of visual discrimination abilities are not necessarily easier to perform than the items requiring additional reasoning or visual imaging abilities. Rather, the location of the visual detail information within the picture is the primary characteristic that determines the degree of difficulty of an item relying primarily on visual discrimination for success. Relatively easy items tend to require identification of missing details along the outer contours of objects while more difficult items require identification of missing elements deeply embedded in the images.

Working Memory Domain

The WISC-IV Integrated Working Memory Domain includes two core subtests that make up the Working Memory Index–Digit Span and Letter-Number Sequencing, one supplemental subtest Arithmetic, and multiple process approach subtests and procedures used to enhance the assessment of initial registration in short-term memory (Visual Digit Span Forward, Spatial Span Forward, Letter Span Rhyming and Nonrhyming), active manipulation in working memory (Spatial Span Backward, Letter–Number Sequencing Process Approach), and incidental recall (Coding Incidental Recall Paired Associates and Free Recall). This domain also includes several tasks that supplement the Arithmetic Subtest, including Arithmetic Process Approach A and B and Written Arithmetic.

Because of the complex nature of conceptions of memory, a process approach to interpretation is crucial to understanding the implications of the scores obtained from the Working Memory Domain measures. The Working Memory Index is derived from a combination of scores from the Digit Span and Letter–Number Sequencing Subtests. For the Letter–Number Sequencing Subtest the child is read a randomly ordered sequence of numbers and letters and is asked to respond by stating the numbers first in ascending order and the letters second in alphabetical order. The Digit Span Subtest is composed of two separate and cognitively independent tasks—Digit Span Forward and Digit Span Backward.

Letter–Number Sequencing is typically a strong measure of what is traditionally defined as a working memory process because it usually requires the active manipulation of initially registered information and formulation of a response before the delivery of the response (referred to as an Active Manipulation task). The Digit Span scaled score, on the other hand, is a combination of Digit Span Forward, a task that requires only initial registration of verbal information and passive holding of that information for immediate repetition, and Digit Span Backward, a task that requires active manipulation of the information after initial registration in order to formulate a response before delivery of the response (an Active Manipulation task). There is a rather extensive literature documenting the different neurological processes required for each. Working memory tasks are primarily frontally mediated, while short-term, span memory tasks are processed more posteriorly (in the left inferior parietal cortex, generally in the area of the inferior supramarginal and angular gyri, Vallar & Papagno, 1995).

Exactly what the Working Memory Index score is measuring can vary considerably for any given child because the contribution of initial registration and active manipulation of initially registered material can vary considerably relative to the child's age, ability level, and strategy for registering information. The Letter–Number Sequencing Subtest is typically a strong measure of active working memory for children ages 8 to 16 years, but for children ages 6 and 7 years and very low functioning older children, this task is much more likely to measure only initial registration, as the early items of the subtest require only initial registration for successful performance (i.e., responses that simply mimic the order of presentation of the stimulus series of numbers and letters is awarded full credit as a correct response).

Considering the composition of the Working Memory Index tasks and the item scoring system, it is imperative that the psychologist know what items were attempted by the child and how they performed on those items in order to know what the Working Memory Index score is reflecting in terms of memory processes. Consider the case of a 7-year-old child who only repeats what the examiner says for Letter–Number Sequencing items, but earns a raw score of 9, which converts to a scaled score of 9. This same child is able to repeat 5 digits forward consistently for a Forward Digit Span raw score of 8, but only reverses 2 digits consistently for a Backward Digit Span raw score of 4, providing a total Digit Span raw score of 12, which converts to a Digit Span Subtest scaled score of 10. Summing the Letter–Number Sequencing score of 9 and the Digit Span score of 10 yields a Working Memory Index Standard Score of 97, which suggests that this child has "working memory" capabilities solidly in the average range. When considering performance from a process approach perspective, however, it is clear that this child was much more effective in the use of initial registration than in the use of active manipulation of information after initial registration. This child performed effectively with the Digit Span Forward task (scaled score 12), was relatively much less effective with the Digit Span Backward task (scaled score 8), and performed the Letter–Number Sequencing Subtest strictly as an initial registration task.

The need for engaging a process approach to memory process assessment is further illustrated by the fact that a child has the freedom to use, or not use, any cognitive process or ability in an attempt to complete a task. The cognitive processes and abilities a specific child brings to bear on a specific task often can be revealed through careful clinical observation of how the child performs the task. In the case of memory assessment tasks, some children choose to reduce the difficulty of initial registration tasks by effectively engaging working memory processes to actively manipulate information that other children might choose to process only through relatively passive initial registration processes. This can be observed when the child, after the oral presentation of a series of numbers one at a time with no change in tone or inflection by the examiner (e.g., 8-1-4-9-2-6), reports the numbers with a distinct melodic intonation pattern (e.g., 814...926). In this case, the child has actively engaged the input and manipulated it using a chunking strategy before responding. For such a child, the Digit Span Forward task that is thought to be measuring initial registration is actually a measure of active manipulation.

To understand a child's memory functioning, it is important to distinguish between, and accurately characterize, a child's capabilities with various memory processes. To assist psychologists in doing this, the WISC-IV Integrated offers a number of process approach subtests and procedures and corresponding process scores. These process approach features provide a strong base for identifying a child's distinct capacities for initial registration and active manipulation, offer a means for understanding how a child does or does not use working memory effectively in arithmetic problem solving, and provide an indication of a child's incidental recall capabilities.

Initial Registration with Rote Repetition Tasks

As illustrated in the preceding case example, a separate process scaled score can be obtained for Digit Span Forward to characterize initial registration efforts with oral repetition after auditory presentation of verbal information. Because a child's initial registration capabilities can vary significantly with input, internal processing, and response format demands, it is often helpful to assess a child's initial registration processes with additional initial registration measures.

The Visual Digit Span Forward task is a visual analog to the Digit Span Forward task. For Visual Digit Span Forward, the child views a series of numbers for a brief interval of a few seconds and is required to orally repeat the numbers in order as they appeared on the page from left to right. This task provides a Visual Digit Span Forward process scaled score that can be contrasted with the Digit Span Forward score to better understand any differences in the child's initial registration capabilities with aurally presented and visually presented verbal/numerical information.

The Letter Span Rhyming and Letter Span Nonrhyming tasks require the child to repeat a series of letters in the same order as presented aloud by the examiner. The difference between the two is in the input content format and its effects on internal processing demands. The Nonrhyming task presents letters aloud as a series of easily distinguishable discrete phonemic units (e.g., X, F, L, T) while the Rhyming task presents letters aloud as a series of much less distinguishable phonemic units (e.g., V, D, Z, B, G).

The WISC-IV Integrated standardization data show that the Rhyming condition scores were consistently lower than the nonrhyming scores across all clinical and nonclinical groups. A trend demonstrating greater differences between rhyming and nonrhyming scores (within subjects) is found in language impaired groups relative to nonclinicals and an attention deficit–hyperactivity disorder (ADHD) sample (Maerlender & McCloskey, in preparation).

The Spatial Span Forward task uses a flat, rectangular white surface with 10 randomly located blue blocks attached to the surface. The examiner touches a series of blocks one at a time, and the child is then required to touch the blocks in the same order as they were touched by the examiner. This is a visually presented analog to the Digit Span and Visual Digit Span tasks and provides a Spatial Span Forward process scaled score that can be contrasted with these other scores to better understand any differences in the child's initial registration capabilities related to presentation format, internal processing demands, and response format.

Active Mental Manipulation Tasks

As illustrated in the preceding case example, a separate process scaled score can be obtained for Digit Span Backward to characterize efforts at active manipulation of orally presented verbal/numerical information after initial registration. Because a child's capacity for active manipulation can vary significantly with input, internal processing, and response format demands, it is often helpful to assess a child's working memory processes with additional active manipulation measures.

The Spatial Span Backward task uses a flat, rectangular white surface with 10 randomly located blue blocks attached to the surface. The examiner touches a series of blocks one at a time, and the child is then required to touch the blocks in the reverse of the order in which they were touched by the examiner. This is a visually presented analog to the Digit Span Backward task and provides a Spatial Span Backward process scaled score that can be contrasted with the Digit Span Backward score to better understand any differences in the child's active manipulation capabilities related to presentation format, internal processing demands, and response format.

The Letter–Number Sequencing Process Approach (LNSPA) task is administered in a manner identical to the core Letter–Number Sequencing Subtest. The difference is that rather than always presenting a random series of numbers and letters as input, the LNSPA task presents the letters of an actual word in correct order followed by random numbers (e.g., R-E-D-6-4; S-T-A-R-7-2-5-1) every first and third trial of each item. Data collected during the standardization of the WISC-IV Integrated indicated that a majority of nonclinical sample children alertly catch on to this alteration of presentation format and effectively use the embedded word to reduce the difficulty of the active manipulation task, resulting in higher raw scores on LNSPA than on LNS for items of comparable letter–number series length. When it is recognized that a real word is embedded in the presentation of the numbers and letters, the letters of the word are quickly chunked together and held while the numbers are organized in ascending order, then the word can be quickly accessed and manipulated to extract the correct alphabetical order of the letters. Throughout the process of reorganizing the letters, the whole word as a pattern containing the letters as details can be easily accessed as a guide for reordering the letters. As the data reveal, having such a mnemonic device available significantly reduces the amount of working memory effort needed to perform the task. For children who do not realize that the letters form words, the mnemonic device remains unused and LNSPA raw score performance is much more consistent with that obtained with LNS. However, because most children improve performance on LNSPA, a child who does not is likely to earn an LNSPA scaled score that is lower than the obtained LNS scaled score.

Results of validity studies with clinical samples and matched controls indicated that children identified as having learning problems are much less likely to catch on to the internal organization of the LNSPA presentation format than control group counterparts (Wechsler *et al.*, 2004). In addition, children who simply repeat the word's correct spelling without organizing it alphabetically (for example, saying "d-o-g" instead of saying "d-g-o") might be susceptible to "capture" responses. That is, these children become "captured" by the stimulus, lose the cognitive set of the task demand, and thus fail the task. Such responses are thought to reflect frontal or executive dysfunction.

Arithmetic Tasks and Process Scores

Although the Arithmetic subtest requires active mental manipulation of information for successful performance, the input and processing demands of the Arithmetic Subtest make it a very different task from the other active manipulation tasks in the Working Memory Domain. The major alterations in Arithmetic involve the contextual nature of the input-mathematics problems embedded in real-world situations, and the demand for engaging multiple cognitive processes beyond active manipulation, including retrieval from long-term storage of calculation algorithms and involvement of reasoning processes to set up the math problem in solvable terms before manipulation of the details using the retrieved calculation procedures dictated by the established problem setup conditions.

Because of its rich, multifactorial nature, the Arithmetic Subtest is an ideal starting point for engaging process approach procedures to better understand how a child uses, or does not use, various cognitive processes and abilities. After standard administration of the Arithmetic Subtest, the clinician can administer the Arithmetic Process Approach Part A (ARPA-A) procedure, which involves multimodal presentation of the same arithmetic word problems. For each item, the child is shown the mathematics problem in written form on a stimulus booklet page while the examiner states the arithmetic problem aloud. The child is then instructed to solve the math problem without the use of pencil and paper, but the written form of the problem remains in view of the child as long as the child is working on the problem or until 30 seconds has elapsed. The Arithmetic Subtest is administered in its entirety in this format starting with the suggested age start point and ending when the child incorrectly responds to four consecutive items.

In some cases, it is desirable to follow ARPA-A with ARPA Part B (ARPA-B). ARPA-B involves readministering each item answered incorrectly during the ARPA-A administration, including the four ceiling items. ARPA-B administration is identical to ARPA-A administration except that the child is given a pencil and paper and encouraged to use it to figure out the answer to each item that is presented.

An additional component of the process approach to Arithmetic is to have the child complete the Written Arithmetic task. The Written Arithmetic task consists of all of the problems from the Arithmetic Subtest setup as numerical calculation problems and printed in a workbook format. The child is given a pencil and asked to complete as many of the calculation problems as possible in 15 minutes.

By using these process approach procedures, a clinician can gauge the effects of visual presentation and the related significant reduction in working memory demands, the effects of visual presentation coupled with the opportunity for manual calculation using a pencil, and the effects of translating the aurally and visually presented word problems into basic numerical calculation problems.

Although it is intuitively appealing to think that the administration of the variations of the Arithmetic items progresses from most difficult to least difficult, this is not necessarily the case. Analysis of the data collected during standardization of the WISC-IV Integrated indicates that a significant number of children perform significantly better with the auditory-only presentation of the Arithmetic Subtest items than they do with the auditory/visual presentation of these same items. Additionally, a significant number of children perform better with the aurally presented Arithmetic items than they do with the Written Arithmetic numerical calculation form of these same problems.

Consider the following word problem similar to an item encountered on the Arithmetic Subtest: John sees a group of seven people outside a store. Three people leave. Two other people join the group. How many people is he watching now? It is not unusual for some 6-, 7-, and 8-year-olds to be able to solve this problem in the Arithmetic Subtest format of only hearing the examiner state the problem. Some of these children, when presented with the printed format of this problem during and after the time it is being orally presented, will find it difficult to listen carefully to the oral presentation and will focus instead on the printed version of the problem. If the child's word reading and/or reading comprehension skills are not sufficiently developed or if the child has difficulty grasping grammar and syntax or if the child is confused by the mixing of written numerals with numbers spelled out as words, then once the auditory trace is gone, the child is at risk of not being able to complete the setup and solution of the problem despite the fact that the child correctly solved the problem only a short time ago when it was only presented orally.

Similarly, children in this same age range might have no difficulty solving this problem in either the auditory only or the auditory/visual presentation formats, but be unable to perform the required calculation on the Written Arithmetic Subtest. This should not be surprising after considering the fact that the Written Arithmetic version of the sample problem looks like this: $(7 - 3) + 2 =$. A significant number of younger children, unfamiliar with mathematical syntax represented by the use of the parentheses, will provide "2" as the answer, ignoring the parentheses and working the problem from right to left, following a progression similar to the one taught when adding and subtracting numbers in columnar format (e.g., $3 + 2 = 5$; $7 - 5 = 2$).

This last finding is especially relevant to the mathematics instructional process in elementary schools, as it confirms the position of some curriculum specialists, that before exposure to the procedural rules and syntax necessary to perform calculations when presented in mathematics notation format, many children are able to grasp mathematics concepts and set up and solve complex mathematics problems when they are presented in real-life contexts. Using the process approach to examine performance with the Arithmetic items can be extremely useful in understanding the conditions under which a child is able to grasp and demonstrate mathematics proficiency.

The role of working memory in these tasks is clearly more important in the aural presentation mode. Children who request that items be repeated could be demonstrating weak auditory working memory processes. The number of requested repetitions is also tracked and calculated in combination with other subtests to provide a process score in the form of percentile ranking.

Integrated Interpretation of Memory Tasks

Although it is true that basic initial registration tasks require less mental energy and effort than active manipulation tasks, and that a more complex task such as Arithmetic requires more cognitive resources to perform than initial registration or less complex active manipulation tasks such as Letter–Number Sequencing or Digit Span Backward, clinicians also should not expect to find that the core and supplemental Working Memory Domain Subtests, when failing to produce roughly comparable results, will align in a hierarchical order of performance with Digit Span Forward better than Digit Span Backward better than Letter–Number Sequencing better than Arithmetic.

Some children perform much more effectively on the Arithmetic Subtest than they do on the Letter–Number Sequencing or Digit Span Subtests, as they find it much easier to manipulate and work with information that is posed in the context of a real-life problem than with information that is presented as a random series of numbers and letters that lack any context that might aid in initial registration and manipulation efforts. One hypothesis is that the semantic cues engage retrieval processes more effectively than do "sterile" numbers or letters. Additionally, the most important aspect of working with these random numbers and letters is the sequence in which they were presented. Some children experience great difficulty with accurate sequencing of individual details despite the fact that they might have well-developed working memory abilities when such decontextual sequencing is not required.

In fact, clinicians should be especially attuned to looking for sequence errors in the performance of working memory tasks, since so many of these tasks do involve the sequencing of relatively decontextual informational input (Digit Span, Visual Digit Span, Letter Span, Spatial Span, Letter–Number Sequencing, and Letter–Number Sequencing PA). Frequent sequencing errors impact test performance levels and can have similar unwanted effects on a child's learning and production efforts in the classroom. It is likely that frequent sequencing errors reflect organization deficits, while errors of omission and commission (i.e., adding or deleting numbers such that the length of the string is changed) are likely more representative of auditory difficulties (for the aural tasks). Children who make these errors do not appear to encode the temporal acoustic aspects (the "auditory envelope").

Incidental Recall Tasks and Process Scores

Included in the Working Memory Domain is a process approach procedure that can be used to assess a child's incidental learning of the number–symbol associations used to perform the Coding (CD) Subtest. This procedure must be used immediately after the administration of the Coding Subtest and involves asking the child to fill in the symbols for a series of numbers without the use of the code key as a guide (CD Paired Associates process score) and to reproduce as many of the symbols used in the coding process as they can recall (CD Free Recall process score). Successful recall requires that the child notices the associations, learns the pairings, and is able to access the encoded information in stored memory, either with or without clues.

Processing Speed Domain

The WISC-IV Integrated Processing Speed Domain includes two core subtests, Coding and Symbol Search; one supplemental subtest, Cancellation; and one process approach subtest, Coding Copy. Additional process approach procedures enable the clinician to look more closely at Cancellation Subtest performance with separate Cancellation Random and Cancellation Structured process scaled scores and a Search Strategy analysis, and 30-second interval coding procedures that can be applied to Coding, Coding Copy, and Symbol Search.

Although the core and supplemental subtests of the Processing Speed Domain all assess speed of performance of relatively simple visually based tasks, each one has unique cognitive processing and response demands, and significant differences in scores among the three tasks are not uncommon. Coding differs from Symbol Search and Cancellation in its demand for multitasking involving use (and possible learning) of number–symbol associations while engaging as quickly as possible in graphomotor coordination and production of symbol shapes. Symbol Search minimizes graphomotor demands, as the child must simply mark a box after completing each item, but increases the demand for extended visual discrimination comparisons. Whereas the Coding Subtest requires repetition of a single routine, each Symbol Search item must be approached independent of the others with careful attention to the visual discriminations being performed. While the visual discrimination requirements of the Cancellation Subtest are less demanding than those of the Symbol Search Subtest, the Cancellation subtest requires greater executive control of self-generation of a search strategy for the random item, and picking up on the organizational structure provided to improve efficiency on the structured task. When significant differences exist among the scores of these three tasks, application of process approach observation procedures and qualitative analysis of performance should be employed to understand the differences and their implications for the performance of academic tasks.

Coding Subtests, Process Procedures, and Process Scores

The Coding Copy Subtest can be used when a child performs relatively poorly on the Coding Subtest, and qualitative observations indicate that graphomotor ability deficiencies might be having a major impact on performance. Such qualitative observations include excessive pressure on the pencil resulting in thick, heavy lines and sometimes even pencil point breakage, immature pencil grasp, extremely poor formation of symbols or illegible symbol production, and excessive muscle tension. The Coding Copy Subtest simplifies the Coding task to a basic copying exercise by simply requiring the child to copy symbols into boxes as quickly as possible. If the child performs significantly better on the Coding Copy task, graphomotor difficulties usually can be ruled out as a likely source of poor Coding performance.

In the absence of basic graphomotor difficulties, poor performance on Coding is more likely to be the result of difficulties with executive control, including difficulties with sustaining effort for the full 2-minute work period, inability to adopt a consistent work strategy and pace, adoption of a consistent but extremely slow work pace, excessive attention to the neat formation of individual symbols, frequent loss of place while working, adoption of an excessively fast or impulsive work pace resulting in coding errors, an inability to confine symbol drawings to the space of a single box, and continuous use of the coding key for the production of every symbol drawn. These difficulties can be contrasted with the qualitative observations of executive control used to engage adaptive strategies that make the task easier to perform, including referring back to previously drawn symbols in the same row instead of looking back up to the coding key and marking symbols from memory after only a few exposures.

The 30-second interval recording process approach procedure can be applied to Coding and Coding Copy. The 30-second interval recording procedure requires the examiner to count the number of items a child completes in each 30-second interval of the 2-minute work period. The 30-second interval scores can be referenced to the mean and standard deviation of the 30-second interval declines in performance of same-age children in the standardization sample. Although a slight decline in performance was typical for many children in the standardization sample, a significant number of children improved their performance over time, while others maintained a very steady work pace. For many children, declines in performance during the second and third 30-second interval resulted from the fact that the first 30-second interval coding required only the use of a limited subset of the number–symbol associations, whereas the second and third intervals included the additional number–symbol associations. Children who became proficient with the limited set of associations and began committing them to memory during the first interval needed to shift coding strategy somewhat to deal with the additional number-symbol associations entering into the coding process, thereby frequently reducing speed and efficiency during these subsequent intervals. Data are not provided for the fourth 30-second interval because fourth interval coding totals were often confounded when children who completed the entire coding task in less time than the maximum allotment of 120 seconds earned very low fourth interval scores because they had completed so many more symbols during the first three intervals.

The 30-second interval coding procedure is not meant to detect subtle shifts in effort or gradual decline, but rather to help document large swings in production or extreme declines. For example, a clear drop-off in output could signal a loss of focus or motivation. On the other hand, a dramatically lower first interval score relative to subsequent interval scores suggests initiation problems consistent with frontal lobe pathology. Low scores on Coding and/or Symbol Search have been implicated in deficient attentional processing (Mirsky, 1991).

Consider the performance of a 12-year-old child diagnosed with ADHD but receiving no pharmacological intervention. After completing only nine symbols in the first 30 seconds (a pace that, if consistently maintained, would produce a scaled score of 5), the child's production jumped to 21 symbols completed in the second interval (a pace that would translate into a scaled score of 17 if maintained consistently), dropped off slightly to 18 in the third interval, but then declined to only six symbols coded in the final 30 seconds (a pace that would translate into a scaled score of 2 if consistently maintained). Although the total raw score of 54 earned by this child translated into a scaled score of 10, characterizing this score as average and concluding that performance was not adversely affected by attention difficulties would hardly be considered an accurate interpretation. A more accurate characterization of this child would be to note that despite the fact that an average score was obtained, the child's performance reflected an inability to sustain a consistent level of effort for a 2-minute period for a simple cognitive processing task. Not only does qualifying the obtained normative score with a data-based process approach description provide a more accurate characterization of what the child actually did during the assessment, it likely will ring true to the parents and teacher of this child who report seeing similar inconsistencies of effort on a daily basis.

Errors on Coding, Symbol Search, and Coding Copy were demonstrated very infrequently in the performance of the WISC-IV and WISC-IV Integrated standardization samples. When errors occur, they are important to note and often clinically significant when they occur more than once or twice within a single subtest. A high number of errors relative to correct responses suggests a haphazard approach to task performance, which would be cause for invalidating the results of a subtest administration. For example, a child obtained a scaled score of 4 on Symbol Search, and scaled scores of 9 on both Coding and Cancellation. Although the child appeared to be adequately engaged with the task during administration, it was discovered during scoring that 40% of the total symbols were marked in error. Her score of 4 was a reflection of not being fully engaged in the task despite overt appearances of effortful performance.

Cancellation Tasks, Process Procedures, and Process Scores

The Cancellation Subtest requires the child to scan an $11'' \times 17''$ array of pictures and for a period of 45 seconds mark all examples of a certain class of target pictures (animals) as quickly as possible. Cancellation tasks are widely used in neuropsychological assessments and have been shown to be sensitive to visual focusing, engaging, and disengaging in visual attentional processes (Bate, Mathias, & Crawford, 2001; Wojciulik, Husain, Clarke, & Driver, 2001). The Cancellation Subtest consists of two separate search items. For the Random search item, the pictures are scattered randomly across the entire array. For the Structured search item, the pictures are aligned in even rows across the entire sheet. For each item, the child is told to draw a line through each animal and work as quickly as possible without making any mistakes. Separate process scaled scores can be obtained for the Random item (CAR) and the Structured item (CAS).

Careful observation of the child's approach to the Cancellation items reveals a great deal about the child's use, or lack of use, of executive control processes to guide performance. For the Random item, having an organized search strategy that covers the area systematically without overlap is likely to produce a better score than a haphazard, inefficient search that covers the same areas multiple times. When a child demonstrates an organized search strategy, he or she is engaging greater use of executive control processes than a child who appears to have no set plan for searching the page. When presented with the Structured item, the child is given the same directions as those given for the Random item. Many children significantly increase the number of animals they mark on the Structured item because they engage executive control processes and pick up on the organization provided by the row-by-row format and begin their search in the upper left hand corner and proceed left to right across each row. Other children fail to appreciate how the row-by-row structure can help to improve performance, and these children usually do not increase the number of animals they find on the Structured item.

Slow but accurate responders are the more typical "slow processors." If a child is engaged in a systematic search strategy but proceeds slowly, it is logical to hypothesize difficulty with disengaging from the stimuli. Errors of commission are rare but should be noted, as they often reflect either poor visual discrimination or impulsive responding. Significant errors of omission primarily or exclusively toward the far edge of a single side of the search field might be reflecting hemifield inattention or neglect.

For the Cancellation tasks, a four-category checklist is provided for the purpose of summarizing observations about how the child organizes visual searches for task completion (starts organized, becomes disorganized; starts disorganized, becomes organized; starts disorganized, remains disorganized; starts organized, remains organized).

Multiple Domain Process Approach Procedures

Intrasubtest Scatter

Intrasubtest scatter refers to the amount of inconsistency displayed among responses to the items of a single subtest. Consideration of intrasubtest scatter is a process approach procedure that can be very helpful in characterizing the performance of a child who demonstrates substantial capability with many cognitive processes, but is erratic in their use. Although some degree of scatter is common in the performance of many children in both clinical and nonclinical groups, frequent errors committed with relatively easy items by a child who correctly responds to many very difficult items is much less common. As a case example, consider the performance of a 13-year-old child on the Matrix Reasoning Subtest (Table 4.3).

The subtest begins with item 11 for this child. She demonstrates a very rapid response rate with the first 10 items, usually providing responses to these items in less than 5 seconds. Seven of these responses are correct, but three responses to relatively easy items are incorrect. A review of the selected responses for these incorrect items revealed that the child appeared to grasp the concept underlying success with the items, but failed to make important distinctions between the correct responses and alternatives that were highly

TABLE 4.3 Matrix Reasoning Subtest Item Responses of a 13-Year-Old Child

Item	Score	Resp Time	Item	Score	Resp Time	Item	Score	Resp Time	Item	Score	Resp Time
11	1	4″	17	1	7″	23	1	11″	29	0	18″
12	0	3″	18	0	5″	24	1	7″	30	0	16″
13	1	3″	19	1	7″	25	0	14″	31	0	20″
14	1	3″	20	1	10″	26	1	7″	32	0	20″
15	0	4″	21	0	14″	27	0	16″	33	-	
16	1	5″	22	1	12″	28	1	12″	34	-	

similar to the correct responses except for subtle differences in a single detail. Item 21 was missed in a similar manner, although the response time was longer (14 seconds). The child's work pace slowed considerably for Items 22 through 32 (usually delivered in 11 to 20 seconds) with correct responses provided to many of these more difficult items. The total raw score for this child is 22, which converts to a Matrix Reasoning scaled score of 8. In this particular case, it could be argued that the child demonstrated visual discrimination and reasoning abilities at a level substantially better than what the scaled score reflects. Older children who successfully complete Items 22, 23, 24, 26, and 28 very infrequently respond incorrectly to Items 12, 15, and 18. This is not to say that the score the child obtained is not a valid or accurate descriptor of the level of performance. The point to be made in this case is that stating only the obtained score does not effectively characterize the true nature of this child's performance. In this situation, it would be more informative to state that the child's score accurately reflects level of overall performance, but that this level of performance resulted from inconsistent, often hasty application of visual discrimination and reasoning abilities resulting in errors on items that were much easier than many of the items the child was able to solve. This statement more thoroughly describes what transpired during the assessment, as well as the resulting outcome, and is likely to resonant more deeply with those who know the child well and who have frequently observed similar instances of subpar, inconsistent application of these kinds of abilities to similar types of tasks in everyday settings.

When intrasubtest scatter observations are applied judiciously and with adequate clinical acumen, they can be used extremely effectively to gain greater insight into how a child performs tasks and what can be done to help the child to improve performance.

Processing Speed and Item Response Timing

Although the Processing Speed Domain provides several good measures of basic processing speed, characterization of a child's cognitive processing speed should not rely solely on reporting of the information obtained from the Processing Speed Domain tasks and procedures. Clinicians should keep in mind that good performance on processing speed tasks does not guarantee that the child will perform more complex cognitive tasks with a similar degree of speed. Consideration of the contrasts between Block Design and Block Design No Time Bonus scores, Elithorn Mazes and Elithorn Mazes No Time Bonus scores, and Arithmetic and Arithmetic Time Bonus scores can be helpful in obtaining a more complete picture of the child's processing speed when complex tasks are performed. Additionally, it is helpful to time item performance on subtests such as Matrix Reasoning, Picture Concepts, Similarities, Comprehension, Vocabulary, Word Reasoning, and Information in order to consider the obtained results in a qualitative manner. Some children with exceptionally high Coding, Symbol Search, and Cancellation scores require an exceptionally long time to complete Matrix Reasoning and/or Picture Concepts items of moderate difficulty. Conversely, some children who perform very poorly on one or more of the processing speed subtests are able to consistently complete complex Matrix Reasoning and Picture Concepts items in a surprisingly brief time. When such discrepancies exist, it is important to report them and consider them carefully to more fully understand the conditions under which the child is likely to exhibit good or poor processing speed and the implications of such a finding on academic task performance.

Timing a child's responses to verbal items can help to characterize a child's speed of lexical access or rate of verbal fluency, which might stand in great contrast to the results obtained with processing speed measures. Some children who are exceptionally quick and precise with verbal responses struggle greatly with one or more of the processing speed subtests, and some children with good processing speed performance experience great difficulty accessing and expressing their thoughts when language processing is required. Even among the verbal tasks themselves, a child's speed of verbal production can vary greatly. Some children are adept at quickly "reasoning out loud" but find it difficult to access factual material with the same degree of speed. Some children who respond to Information Subtest questions and provide synonyms to Vocabulary Subtest words with game show-like speed struggle to organize and express their thoughts when faced with novel Comprehension or Similarities Subtest questions.

SUMMARY

Critics of the use of intellectual assessment instruments argue that the results of IQ tests typically offer limited information useful for informing classroom instruction (Boehm, 1985; Reschly, 1997). The process approach features of the WISC-IV Integrated represent a substantial set of clinical tools that can be used to characterize more effectively the cognitive capabilities of a child in a more applied manner to gain greater insight into how the child attempts to use these cognitive capabilities in performing challenging tasks. This approach supports the practice of hypothesis generation and testing, which is the key to good clinical practice. When shared with parents, teachers, and others who work with the child, the information obtained through the application of WISC-IV Integrated process approach elements can help guide efforts to provide the child with educational experiences and rehabilitative strategies that capitalize on the child's cognitive strengths and acknowledge and address the child's areas of need.

CASE STUDY

Jamal is a fourth-grade student at Oakwood Elementary School who was referred for a psychoeducational evaluation because of difficulties with reading. Jamal's fourth-grade classroom teacher indicates that Jamal has difficulty comprehending what he reads. She noted that Jamal does not appear to like reading very much and when asked to read aloud, he often acts as if he did not hear her request. When the request is repeated, Jamal reluctantly complies. When reading aloud, Jamal makes frequent word reading errors but very few self-corrections of these errors. Whether reading aloud or silently in class, Jamal has difficulty answering questions about the material he has just read. Jamal's teacher is not sure if Jamal has the "intellectual capacity" to grasp the concepts presented in the reading material, and she is unsure about how to help Jamal improve his understanding of what he reads. Jamal's teacher believes that Jamal is beginning to lose interest in school because of the difficulties he encounters with reading. She is noticing an increase in minor disruptive behaviors such as talking to his friends during classroom lessons.

A review of Jamal's educational history indicated that Jamal was identified in kindergarten as having some speech difficulties, but the nature of these difficulties was not specified in the records. He was referred for and received a speech evaluation early in the fall of his kindergarten school year and consequently received speech services for 30 minutes three times a week in a small group setting throughout the rest of the kindergarten school year. In first and second grade, Jamal's teachers did not indicate any problems with reading skill development.

In third grade, Jamal was referred to the district remedial reading program in late fall. Primary concerns focused on Jamal's lack of comprehension of what he read. He was provided remedial instruction using Reading Recovery, the district's standard remedial instruction program. At the end of the remedial instruction sequence, Jamal was judged to have made minimal gains, and he continued to struggle with reading activities in the regular classroom. It should be noted that reading instruction in all primary grades within the school district involves the use of a reading series that stresses whole language reading activities and instructional processes. Instruction in word decoding skills and structural analysis of words are not directly addressed in a systematic manner in the curricular materials that teachers are required to use for regular classroom reading instruction.

Jamal is right-handed with no familial left-handedness, is of average height and weight for his age, and does not have any obvious physical problems. Jamal is the oldest of three children. Jamal's 8-year-old sister is in second grade at the same elementary school, and Jamal's 4-year-old brother attends a preschool program three days a week. All members of Jamal's family are monolingual English speakers. Jamal's mother works part-time as a nurse's aide at a local hospital and Jamal's father is employed full-time as an automobile mechanic. No history of prenatal or early developmental difficulties or any hospitalizations or significant injuries were reported by Jamal's parents. Jamal's mother described Jamal as a good boy, but notes that he resists doing homework. Although she frequently reminds Jamal of the importance of a good education, she believes that Jamal is not as positively engaged with learning as she would like him to be. Jamal's father expressed an appreciation for the need for Jamal to complete his schooling, but he also noted that he did not graduate from high school but received a diploma by passing the GED exam a few years after leaving school to find work. Jamal's father indicated that he experienced problems with reading in school, but that he has done his best to learn to read well enough for his work. He describes himself as a person that learns best by watching how jobs are done instead of reading about how they are done.

When asked about his favorite activities, Jamal indicated that he enjoys playing with three very close friends who are in his fourth-grade class. At recess and during lunch and other activity times, Jamal can be seen almost exclusively with these three boys. Jamal indicates that he likes to ride bikes and play sports with his friends, especially basketball and football, but he does not participate on any school- or community-sponsored athletic teams. Indoor activities include watching television and playing cards with his friends. When discussing school, Jamal was less than enthusiastic. He indicated that school was hard work, especially reading, and that he doesn't like it when he has to do homework because his mother makes him do it before he can play with his friends. He indicated that his mother helps him with his homework when a lot of reading is required because reading is hard for him.

Based on the referral concerns, Jamal was administered the core and supplemental subtests of the WISC-IV Integrated, the reading and spelling subtests of the WIAT-II, and selected subtests from the NEPSY and the Process Assessment of the Learner. Test scores resulting from the administration of these tasks are listed in Table 4.4:

Based on the obtained test scores and the application of process approach procedures during the evaluation sessions and to test results, several

TABLE 4.4   Test Scores from Jamal's Assessment: Wechsler Intelligence Scale
for Children-Fourth Edition-Integrated (WISC-IV-Integrated)

Scales	Standard Score	Percentile
Full Scale	105	63
Indexes	**Standard Score**	**Percentile**
Verbal Comprehension	104	61
Perceptual Reasoning	115	84
Working Memory	80	9
Processing Speed	112	79
Verbal Comprehension Subtests	**Scaled Score**	**Percentile**
Similarities	12	75
Comprehension	13	84
Vocabulary	8	25
Information	8	25
Word Reasoning	11	63
Perceptual Organization Subtests	**Scaled Score**	**Percentile**
Picture Concepts	14	91
Matrix Reasoning	9	37
Block Design	14	91
Picture Completion	12	75
Working Memory Subtests	**Scaled Score**	**Percentile**
Letter–Number Sequencing	7	16
Digit Span	6	9
Arithmetic	6	9
Processing Speed Subtests	**Scaled Score**	**Percentile**
Coding	12	75
Symbol Search	12	75
Verbal Domain **Process Approach Subtests and Process Scores**	**Scaled Score**	**Percentile**
Vocabulary Multiple Choice	6	9
Picture Vocabulary Multiple Choice	7	16
Information Multiple Choice	7	16

(*Continues*)

TABLE 4.4   (*Continued*)

Scales	Standard Score	Percentile
Working Memory Domain		
Process Approach Subtests and Process Scores	**Scaled Score**	**Percentile**
Digit Span Forward	7	16
Digit Span Backward	5	5
Letter Span Nonrhyming	7	16
Letter Span Rhyming	6	9
Visual Digit Span	12	75
Arithmetic Process Approach Part A	10	50
Written Arithmetic	9	37

Wechsler Individual Achievement Test-Second Edition (WIAT-II) (selected subtests)

Subtests	Standard Score	Percentile
Reading Comprehension	102	55
Word Reading	80	9
Pseudoword Decoding	76	5
Spelling	89	23

NEPSY: A Developmental Neuropsychological Assessment (selected subtests)

Language Domain **Subtests**	Scaled Score	Percentile
Repetition of Nonsense Words	6	9
Phonological Processing	6	9
Speeded Naming	10	50

Process Assessment of the Learner (PAL) (selected subtests)

Rapid Automatic Naming **Task**	Decile
Letters	5
Words	5

WISC-IV Integrated Process Approach Subtests were selected for administration to help characterize more accurately Jamal's cognitive capacities. The scores obtained from these subtests are listed in Table 4.4.

In interpreting Jamal's performance on the WISC-IV Integrated, it is important to note that Jamal's obtained average range Full Scale Standard Score of 105 obscures some very important discrepancies among the four index scores that he earned. Jamal's average range Perceptual Reasoning Index Standard Score of 115 is significantly better than the average range Standard Score of 104 he earned on the Verbal Comprehension Index, and his Perceptual Reasoning, Verbal Comprehension, and Processing Speed Index Standard Scores are all significantly better than the low Standard Score of 80 he earned on the Working Memory Index.

Looking below the Index level of interpretation, Jamal exhibited significant discrepancies among the subtests that comprise the Verbal Comprehension Index (subtest scores ranging from low average to above average) and the Perceptual Reasoning Index (subtest scores ranging from average to superior), and these fluctuations deserve attention to more accurately characterize Jamal's performance. Examination of subtest performance from the process approach perspective also revealed much clinically relevant information about how Jamal attempted the tasks during the assessment. The administration of the additional process approach subtests of the WISC-IV Integrated further enhanced the accurate characterization of Jamal's cognitive strengths and weaknesses. Relevant WISC-IV Integrated findings at the subtest level and below are summarized here by content domain.

PERCEPTUAL DOMAIN

Jamal performed very effectively with most of the visually presented tasks that involved nonverbal visual materials. His responses were usually delivered with good speed and precision and reflected good use of reasoning abilities, as he earned high scores on three of the four subtests administered (Picture Concepts Scaled Score, 14; Block Design Scaled Score, 14; Picture Completion Scaled Score, 12). Jamal's relatively less effective performance with the Matrix Reasoning Subtest (Scaled Score, 9) was due more to a tendency to overlook important details on some of the easy and mid-range items than to a lack of reasoning with abstract visual material, as Jamal consistently responded correctly to many of the more difficult items of this subtest. In a similar manner, Jamal was unable to spot important missing details in three relatively easy Picture Completion items while accurately identifying the missing elements in several much more difficult items. Considering the pattern of errors demonstrated on the Matrix Reasoning and Picture Completion Subtests, it is reasonable to characterize Jamal's capacity for reasoning with visually presented nonverbal material is in the superior range, while noting that this capacity might not always be demonstrated because of occasional inconsistency in working with, or monitoring, important details in relatively easy problems.

PROCESSING SPEED DOMAIN

Jamal performed very effectively with basic visual and visuomotor tasks that required sustained attention and quick processing speed (Coding Subtest and Symbol Search Subtest Scaled Scores, 12). Use of 30-second interval coding procedures revealed a very steady work pace for both processing speed tasks. It is important to note that Jamal's efforts at self-directed adjustments to performance of the Coding task primarily involved looking back at his own work rather than accessing the number-symbol associations from working memory.

VERBAL DOMAIN

In an analysis of Jamal's performance with the Verbal Domain tasks, it is important to note that the Verbal Comprehension Index score of 104 obscures the fact that Jamal performed significantly better on tasks that required him to reason with verbal information and respond in a free response format (Similarities Scaled Score, 12; Comprehension Scaled Score, 13) and a task that required him to figure out a specific word from clues about the word's meaning (Word Reasoning Scaled Score, 11) than he did on tasks that required him to provide a free recall response based on what verbal knowledge he could retrieve from long-term storage (Vocabulary Scaled Score, 8; Information Scaled Score, 8).

When responding to orally presented questions that required a verbal response, Jamal demonstrated effective pragmatic language skills and appropriate use of grammar and other aspects of syntax. Jamal tended to respond with brief statements that seemed to effectively communicate his thoughts on a topic. When requests for clarification of a response to questions from the Similarities and Comprehension subtests were made, Jamal usually did not offer much in the way of additional information. When responding to questions from the Vocabulary and Information subtests, Jamal either quickly provided a response, or quickly stated "I don't know."

Correct word definitions were provided only for very commonly encountered words typically used in everyday language. Correct responses for the Information Subtest were also limited to questions about common knowledge topics. Jamal did not provide many accurate word definitions or factual responses for words and facts that are typically presented and learned in school settings in grades 3 and below. From Jamal's efforts and responses, it was not apparent whether he lacked knowledge required to respond accurately to the Vocabulary and Information questions or possessed the knowledge but was unable to access it effectively in order to respond accurately. To help clarify these issues, Jamal was administered the process approach Vocabulary Multiple Choice, Picture Vocabulary Multiple Choice, and Information Multiple Choice Subtests.

On the Vocabulary Multiple Choice (VCMC) Subtest, Jamal was able to recognize the correct definition of two additional words beyond those he could define using the free response format of the Vocabulary Subtest. Jamal's two-word improvement, however, is less than the average gain made by 9-year-old children in the standardization sample when a multiple choice format was provided. Consequently, despite Jamal's two-word improvement, his VCMC Scaled Score of 6 dropped below his Vocabulary Subtest score and reflected a relative inability to profit from the multiple choice recognition response format.

On the Picture Vocabulary Multiple Choice (PVMC) Subtest, Jamal was able to correctly identify the visual image that corresponded to a word for two additional words beyond those he defined with the free recall format of the Vocabulary Subtest. As was the case with the VCMC Subtest, Jamal's two-word improvement was less than the average gain made by 9-year-old children in the standardization sample when a pictorial multiple choice format was provided, and the resulting PVMC Scaled Score of 7 therefore reflected a relative inability to profit from the pictorial multiple choice recognition format.

A similar result was obtained for the Information Multiple Choice (INMC) Subtest, where Jamal provided correct responses for the same 14 items that he was able to answer correctly with the free recall format of the Information Subtest. This lack of ability to increase correct responses reflected a relative inability to profit from the multiple choice recognition response format, consequently earning Jamal an INMC Subtest Scale Score of 7.

Taken together, results of the multiple choice subtest administrations strongly suggest that Jamal's poorer performance on the Vocabulary and Information tasks relative to his performance on the Similarities and Comprehension tasks are a result of a lack of knowledge of the definitions of the words and the informational facts in question rather than an inability to effectively retrieve and/or articulate stored knowledge. Jamal's Vocabulary and Information Subtest scores at the lower end of the average range accurately reflect Jamal's store of knowledge of the items presented and indicate that his knowledge store sampled by these subtests is not commensurate with his above average reasoning abilities. Provided Jamal has been exposed to adequate instruction, these results strongly suggest that Jamal has not profited from that instruction as much as would be expected given his demonstrated capacity for reasoning.

WORKING MEMORY DOMAIN

Jamal experienced significant difficulties with the tasks of the Working Memory Domain, earning a low Letter–Number Sequencing Subtest Scaled Score of 7 and low Digit Span and Arithmetic Subtest Scaled Scores of 6. For the Letter–Number Sequencing Subtest, Jamal found it very difficult to manipulate the sequences to reorder the numbers and letters as required when three or more letter/numbers were presented. In these longer sequences, Jamal's successes came on items where simply moving the number before the two letters produced a correct response (for example, for B-5-F, Jamal correctly responded "5, B, F", but for 9-J-4, Jamal incorrectly responded "9, 4, J").

On the Digit Span Subtest, Jamal earned a low Subtest Scaled Score of 6 when scores from the initial registration task of repeating digits forward and the mental manipulation task of repeating digits backward were combined. Process scores were obtained to examine performance on these two tasks separately. Jamal was able to accurately repeat a series of 4 digits forward, yielding a low Digit Span Forward Scaled Score of 7. Jamal's performance on Digit Span Backward was even less effective as he was able to accurately reverse only a series of 2 digits yielding a low Digit Span Backward Subtest Scaled Score of 5. Both of Jamal's attempts to reverse a series of 3 digits resulted in sequencing errors where Jamal was able to retain the correct numbers, but could not manipulate them into the correct backward sequence (for 5-7-4, Jamal responded "4, 5, 7" and for 2-5-9, Jamal responded "9, 2, 5").

Jamal was able to listen carefully to single-step arithmetic problems involving addition and subtraction of two numbers and perform the required mental calculations without pencil and paper. Jamal was unable to provide correct answers for any of the problems that involved more than a single calculation step, resulting in a low Arithmetic Subtest Scaled Score of 6.

To better understand the effects of various types of memory demands on Jamal's ability to process information and respond effectively, five additional Process Approach Subtests were administered—Letter Span Nonrhyming, Letter Span Rhyming, Visual Digit Span, Arithmetic Process Approach Part A, and Written Arithmetic.

Jamal earned low scores on both Letter Span tasks (Letter Span Nonrhyming Scaled Score 7 and Letter Span Rhyming Scaled Score 6). Jamal was able to encode and repeat a series of 4 nonrhyming phonemes/letters (for example, F-H-N-Q), but this occurred only on the second attempt at a span this long. The rhyming nature of the Letter Span Rhyming items produced an interference effect as Jamal was only able to encode and repeat a series of 3 rhyming phonemes/letters (for example, D-C-T), but again, this was accomplished only on the second attempt at a span this long.

Relative to his performance on Digit Span Forward, Jamal performed significantly better when he was able to look at the number series for a few seconds before responding (Visual Digit Span Subtest Scaled Score, 12). With the visual presentation format, Jamal was able to increase his encoding and repetition of both 6-digit series.

The Arithmetic Process Approach Part A and Written Arithmetic Subtests were administered to Jamal specifically to explore the effect of working memory and word-problem format demands on Jamal's performance with basic arithmetic problem-solving and calculations and to determine if any mathematics deficiencies contributed to his low performance. The Arithmetic Process Approach Subtest provided a written form of each arithmetic item as it was being read to Jamal. The written form of the problem remained in view until Jamal provided a response or 30 seconds elapsed. After the presentation of each item, Jamal remained focused on the visual display of the problem, actively scanning the information presented until he was ready to provide a response. With the aid of the visual format and the substantial reduction in working memory process demands that accompanied this format, Jamal was able to solve an additional six problems that he was unable to correctly solve when only auditory presentation was involved. Jamal's increase in response accuracy earned him a significantly higher Arithmetic Process Approach Subtest Scaled Score of 10, indicating that the additional working memory demands of the auditory presentation format were the primary source of difficulty that led to the Scaled Score of 6 on the Arithmetic Subtest. When presented with written calculation items that reflected the mental calculations required to complete the same arithmetic problems as those presented on the Arithmetic and Arithmetic Process Approach Subtests, Jamal was able to complete all the calculations that involved basic addition, subtraction, and multiplication except those that used specialized mathematics notation (for example $(8 - 4) + 2$). Jamal's performance with basic calculations earned him a Written Arithmetic Subtest Scaled Score of 9.

In terms of initial registration and mental manipulation, Jamal performed best when the information was visually presented and working memory process demands were reduced, as was the case with the Visual Digit Span, Arithmetic Process Approach, and Written Arithmetic Subtests, as he obtained scores in the average range on these tasks (Scaled Scores 12, 10, and 9 respectively). When the identical type of information was presented in auditory format only, Jamal was less effective at initial registration (Digit Span Forward, 7; Letter Span Nonrhyming, 7; Letter Span Rhyming, 6). When additional demands of mental manipulation in working memory were added to the initial registration process, Jamal's performance was negatively affected (Letter–Number Sequencing, 7; Arithmetic, 6; and Digit Span Backward, 5).

ADDITIONAL COGNITIVE PROCESS
ASSESSMENT RESULTS

To gain greater insight into the cognitive processes most closely associated with word reading and word decoding skills, Jamal was administered the NEPSY Phonological Processing, Repetition of Nonsense Words, and Speeded Naming Subtests and the PAL Rapid Automatic Naming Letters and Words tasks.

Jamal struggled with both the Phonological Processing and Repetition of Nonsense Words Subtests of the NEPSY, earning Scaled Scores of 6 on both of these measures. On the Phonological Processing Subtest, Jamal was able to perform a few very simple deletions of initial phoneme items (for example saying "meat" without the /m/ sound [eat]), but was unable to do more complex deletions (for example, instead of saying "plod" without the /l/ sound [pod], Jamal responded with "odd") or substitutions (for example instead of changing the /p/ sound to the /z/ sound in hope [hose], Jamal responded with "zope"). Jamal's correct responses indicated a rudimentary understanding of sound segmentation, but Jamal was unable to maintain an accurate trace of the sequence of the sounds and manipulate that trace in various ways to produce recombinations of the sounds to form new words. The more sound units the words contained and/or the more mental manipulations Jamal had to perform to complete the task, the more deficient his performance became.

On the Repetition of Nonsense Words Subtest, Jamal usually was able to accurately repeat the first two sound units of nonsense words containing three and four sound units (for example, saying "in kews ent" for "in kews ment"), but was completely overwhelmed with the longer 5 sound unit items (for example, he did not even offer responses to items such as "plotiskenje-for").

In contrast to his performance on the NEPSY tasks that assess the ability to encode, process, and act on sound units, Jamal was able to perform in the average range on three tasks that assessed the ability to quickly access verbal labels for various types of stimuli including labels for size, color, and shape (NEPSY Speeded Naming Scaled Score, 10), letter names (PAL RAN Letters 5th Decile), and a short list of highly familiar words (PAL RAN Words 5th Decile). These results suggest that Jamal's ability to access, retrieve, and produce verbal labels when presented with visual cues is in the average range when compared to the performance of 9-year-old peers in the standardization samples of these tests.

READING AND SPELLING ACHIEVEMENT ASSESSMENT RESULTS

Jamal was administered the three reading subtests and the spelling subtest of the WIAT-II to assess his level of skill acquisition in these areas. Age-based standard scores were used to describe Jamal's performance in comparison to the WIAT-II standardization sample.

Jamal earned a Word Reading Subtest score in the low range (Standard Score, 80), as he was able to read only several high frequency words from a list. Jamal read these familiar sight words at a fairly rapid pace. When uncertain about a word, Jamal showed only a brief instant of hesitancy and typically did not pause long enough to attempt to sound out the word, but rather substituted quickly a familiar word that started with the same letter or letter cluster as the word to be read (for example "inside" for "instead"; "state" for "sight"; "crawl" for "crowd"; "fixable" for "flexible"). Jamal demonstrated a good sense that word reading should be quick and automatic, but the speed of his word reading was compromised by his lack of familiarity with many of the less frequently encountered words on the list.

The WIAT-II Pseudoword Decoding Subtest assessed Jamal's facility with the application of phonological rules to word level structural analysis. Because the Pseudoword Decoding Subtest uses letter patterns that form nonsense words, Jamal was unable to use stored sight word knowledge to perform the task and was instead required to demonstrate his knowledge of phoneme-grapheme relationships and phonologically-based word structural analysis rules. Jamal performed poorly on this task earning a Standard Score of 76. Jamal experienced some success with simple three letter words that followed a very basic consonant/vowel/consonant pattern (for example, "bim," "pon," "vun," "nad," "kip"). As the nonsense words began to involve letter clusters and more diverse consonant/vowel patterns, however, Jamal did not attempt to analyze each orthographic unit in each nonword and assign a corresponding phonemic sound unit based on the rules of synthetic phonics, but instead offered real words that began with the same consonant letter/sounds and shared many visual features with the nonsense words (for example, "drip" for "dreep"; "slick" for "sluck"; "sway" for "snay"; "ripe for "rith"; "flip" for "flid"; "than" for "thag"; "safe" for "shafe"; "yam" for "waim").

The WIAT-II Reading Comprehension Subtest required Jamal to read sentences (orally as required) and read paragraphs (read silently by Jamal's choice) and orally answer questions about what he read. The sentences of the reading comprehension passages are composed primarily of high frequency words and organized to aid the use of context clues for deriving meaning in order to emphasize assessment of comprehension of what was read rather than to assess the degree of facility with decoding difficult, lower frequency words.

Jamal's oral reading of the sentences was at a pace much slower than would be expected considering his average speed with the RAN tasks. Words were frequently misread and left uncorrected until the entire sentence was read. After reading each sentence, Jamal tended to reread the sentence silently in an apparent effort to grasp the meaning of what he had just read. During these rereadings, Jamal would sometimes call out a correction to a word he had misread orally. Jamal silently read the longer text passages at rates ranging from 2.7 to 3.2 words per second, a pace tending toward the lower end of the typical range for a 9-year-old child. When asked comprehension questions about these text passages, Jamal almost always had to look back at the passage to find the information that related to the question before providing a response. These look-backs frequently involved 15 to 30 seconds and were often followed by correct answers to questions involving recognizing stated or implied details, recognizing stated cause and effect, and drawing conclusions. Jamal was less effective at answering questions that dealt with recognizing implied cause and effect and using context to determine word meaning. In contrast to his difficulties with word reading, Jamal demonstrated an average capacity to grasp the meaning of the material he read when the words he was required to read were relatively simple, high frequency words (Reading Comprehension Standard Score, 102).

The WIAT-II Spelling Subtest required Jamal to write the spellings of words as they were dictated to him. Jamal produced correct spellings for many of the high frequency sight words, earning him a Spelling Subtests Standard Score in the lower end of the average range (89). Jamal's misspellings reflected little attempt to apply structural analysis and phoneme-grapheme correspondence knowledge, and were more representative of attempts to recall the visual pattern of letters in a word, but with sequencing errors or omissions ("jumpd" [jumped]; "carels" [careless]; "guss" [guess]; "cold't" [couldn't]; "rogh" [rough]).

SUMMARY

Jamal demonstrated well-developed reasoning abilities that he was able to apply with both verbal and nonverbal sources of information. Jamal also demonstrated effective oral and manual processing speed when working with visually presented verbal and nonverbal material. Expressive and receptive language skills were used effectively and executive control of language production was adequate for Jamal's age. Jamal also demonstrated average ability to encode and mentally manipulate visually presented verbal information including number series, arithmetic problems, and written text.

Jamal experienced many difficulties with tasks that required initial registration of aurally presented sequential verbal information such as letter and number series and nonsense words, and struggled greatly with tasks that required mental manipulation of aurally presented verbal information such as phonological processing tasks, reversing number series, and doing mental calculations to solve arithmetic problems.

In contrast to his well-developed ability to reason with verbal information, Jamal demonstrated a relative dearth of stored verbal knowledge related to word meanings and factual information of the type that is typically presented in formal school settings. Although Jamal's visual processing abilities are well developed and usually used effectively with reasoning tasks, Jamal displayed a tendency to overlook important visual details, resulting in a decrease in overall efficiency of processing and responding to some visually presented tasks.

Although Jamal demonstrated average ability to extract meaning from what he read, he required considerable additional time to process what he read as he relied more on the visual trace of the information to guide his efforts to derive meaning after his first reading rather than constructing meaning from mental manipulation of the information as he was reading it for the first time. Despite his demonstrated understanding of the reading process and less efficient but relatively effective strategies for grasping the meaning of what he read, Jamal struggled greatly with the reading of unfamiliar words. Jamal did not demonstrate more than a rudimentary understanding of phonology or rules that govern grapheme-phoneme associations in the English language. Jamal's encoding and mental manipulation process weaknesses with aurally presented sequentially ordered sound units such as phonemes and letter and number names made it unlikely that he would attempt to draw in any way on these processes to aid in his efforts to read words effectively. In addition, his relative lack of exposure to systematic instruction in the use of phonology or the rules underlying grapheme-phoneme associations made it difficult for him to know how to attempt to bypass his processing weaknesses in his efforts to read words. Jamal's efforts at spelling words were also affected by these difficulties, but he was able to compensate somewhat with his strong visual encoding and memory skills as he retrieved the visual images of many frequently encountered words, although his tendency to overlook visual details could be seen in many of the incorrect spellings he retrieved from memory. While spelling words, Jamal appeared to make no efforts to apply phonological or grapheme-phoneme association knowledge to his attempts to spell unfamiliar words.

Jamal's difficulties with encoding and mental manipulation of information presented in an auditory fashion, and his associated difficulties with word reading are likely to have substantially contributed to Jamal's ineffectiveness with holding on to and storing word meanings and factual information presented and discussed in school. As was the case with his fourth-grade teacher, when assessment of Jamal's intellectual capabilities focus on his store of factual information knowledge and word meanings, his ability to reason and profit from appropriate instruction are likely to be underestimated.

When instruction involves the use of regular textbooks that do not control for degree of familiarity of words and do not necessarily structure text for optimum use of context clues to derive meaning in the way that the WIAT-II Reading Comprehension Subtest did, Jamal's difficulties with word reading are likely to greatly interfere with his ability to accurately read and effectively grasp the meaning of what he reads. As a result, Jamal's primary reading problem will appear to be in the comprehension of what he reads while the reality of the situation is that Jamal lacks the word reading skill that would enable him to demonstrate his more adequately developed reading comprehension capabilities.

If Jamal is taught and effectively learns a rule base for how to decode words, the average reading comprehension capabilities and the average reading speed potential Jamal demonstrated in the assessment are more likely to be realized. This is not to say that Jamal does not face challenges in his efforts to comprehend what he reads. Jamal's overreliance on the visual trace of the words on the page due to his working memory deficiencies is likely to hold him back from developing reading comprehension skills commensurate with his above-average reasoning abilities unless he is taught and effectively learns ways to improve the effectiveness of his approach to comprehending text as he reads it.

In a discussion with school staff, the need to provide Jamal with word reading instruction using a synthetic phonics program that teaches the scope and sequence of word analysis rules and word decoding skills along with vocabulary development and spelling skill instruction was emphasized. As Jamal improves his word reading skills, instruction can begin to focus more on helping him develop strategies for active processing and comprehending of what he is reading as he is reading it. The crucial need to supplement oral presentation of material with visual supports was also discussed as a way to help Jamal bypass his difficulties with mental manipulation of orally presented verbal information in the classroom. Discussion with Jamal's classroom teacher focused on ways that she could engage Jamal in active learning exercises that emphasized the use of his effective reasoning abilities rather than his inability to draw information from long-term storage that, in fact, he does not possess.

ACKNOWLEDGMENTS

The authors wish to thank Edith Kaplan, Ph.D., Deborah Fein, Ph.D., and Larry Weiss, Ph.D., for their content reviews and thoughtful comments provided during the preparation of this manuscript.

REFERENCES

Akshoomoff, N. A., & Stiles, J. (1996). The influence of pattern type on children's block design performance. *Journal of the International Neuropsychological Society, 2(5)*, 392–402.

Bate, A. J., Mathias, J. L., & Crawford, J. R. (2001). Performance on tests of everyday attention and standard tests of attention following severe traumatic brain injury. *The Clinical Neuropsychologist, 15(3)*, 405–422.

Boehm, A. (1985). Educational applications of intelligence testing. In Wolman, B. B. (Ed.), *Handbook of intelligence: Theories, measurements and applications.* New York: Wiley.

Carroll, J. B. (1993). *Human cognitive abilities: A survey of factor-analytic studies.* Cambridge, England: Cambridge University Press.

Delis, D. C., Kramer, J. H., Fridlund, A. J., & Kaplan, E. (1990). A cognitive science approach to neuropsychological assessment. In P. McReynolds, J. C. Rosen, & G. J. Chelune (Eds.), *Advances in psychological assessment* (Vol. 7, pp. 101–132). New York: Plenum.

Kaufman, A. S. (1993). *Intelligent testing with the WISC-III.* New York: Wiley.

Kaplan, E. (1983). Process and achievement revisited. In S. Wagner & B. Kaplan (Eds.), *Toward a holistic developmental psychology* (pp. 143–156). Hillsdale, NJ: Erlbaum.

Kaplan, E. (1988). A process approach to neuropsychological assessment. In T. Boll and B. K. Bryant, (Eds.), *Clinical neuropsychology and brain function: Research, measurement, and practice* (pp. 125–167). Washington: American Psychological Association.

Kaplan, E. (2000). Serendipity in science: A personal account. In A. Y. Stringer, E. Cooley, & A. Christensen (Eds.), *Pathways to prominence: Reflections of 20th century neuropsychologists*. New York: Psychology Press.

Kaplan, E., Palmer, E. P., Weinstein, C., Baker, E., & Weintraub, S. (1981). Block design: A brain-behavior based analysis. Paper presented at the annual meeting of the International Neuropsychological Society, Bergen, Norway.

Kaplan, E., Fein, D., Morris, R., Kramer, J. H., & Delis, D. C. (1999). *The WISC-III as a processing instrument*. San Antonio, TX: The Psychological Corporation.

Kaplan, E., Fein, D., Morris, R., Kramer, J. H., & Delis, D. C. (1991). *The WAIS-R as a neuropsychological instrument*. San Antonio, TX: The Psychological Corporation.

Kramer, J. H., Kaplan, E., Share, L., & Huckeba, W. (1999). Configural errors on WISC-III Block Design. *Journal of the International Neuropsychological Society, 5*, 418–524.

Kyllonen, P. C., Lohman, D. F., & Woltz, D. J. (1984). Componential modeling of alternative strategies for performing spatial tasks. *Journal of Educational Psychology, 76*, 1325–1345.

Matarazzo, J. D., Daniel, M. H., Prifitera, A., & Herman, D. O. (1988). Intersubtest scatter in the WAIS-R standardization sample. *Journal of Clinical Psychology, 44*, 940–950.

Mearlender, A., & McCloskey, G. (In preparation). Rhyming and nonrhyming letter span differences among clinical and nonclinical groups. Mirsky, A. F., Anthony, B. J., Duncan, C. C., Ahern, M. B., Kellam, S. G. (1991). Analysis of the elements of attention: A neuropsychological approach. *Neuropsychological Review, 2*, 109–145.

Reschly, D. J. (1997). Diagnostic and treatment utility of intelligence tests. In Flanagan, D. P., Genshaft, J. L., & Harrison, P. L. (Eds.), *Contemporary intellectual assessment: Theories, tests and issues*. New York: Guilford.

Sattler, J. M. (2001). *Assessment of children: Cognitive applications* (4th ed.). San Diego: Author.

Vallar, G., & Papagno, C. (1995). Neuropsychological impairments of short-term memory. In A. D. Baddeley, B. A. Wilson, & F. N. Watts (Eds.), *Handbook of memory disorders*. New York: Wiley.

Wechsler, D., Kaplan, E., Fein, D., Morris, R., Kramer, J. H., Maerlender, A., & Delis, D. C. (2004). *The Wechsler Intelligence Scale for Children-Fourth Edition Integrated*. San Antonio, TX: The Psychological Corporation.

Werner, H. (1937). Process and achievement: A basic problem of education and developmental psychology. *Harvard Educational Review, 7*, 353–368.

Wesman, G. (1968). Intelligent testing. *American Psychologist, 23*, 267–274.

Wojciulik, E., Husain, M., Clarke, K., & Driver, J. (2001). Spatial working memory deficit in unilateral neglect. *Neuropsychologia, 39*, 390–396.

5

INTEGRATED MULTILEVEL MODEL FOR BRANCHING ASSESSMENT, INSTRUCTIONAL ASSESSMENT, AND PROFILE ASSESSMENT

VIRGINIA W. BERNINGER

University of Washington
Seattle, Washington

TED ALPER

Department of Educational Psychology
California State University at Hayward
Hayward, California

ALNITA DUNN

Los Angeles Unified School District and
American School London and
California State University at Hayward
Hayward, California

BACKGROUND

Over the past decade, a growing body of research is pointing to the shortcomings of relying *exclusively* on an IQ-achievement discrepancy definition for learning disability (e.g., Berninger, Hart, Abbott, & Karovsky, 1992; Berninger, Smith, & O'Donnell, 2004; Bradley, Danielson, & Hallahan, 2002; Fletcher, Francis, Morris, & Lyon, in press; Lyon, Fletcher, Shaywitz, Shaywitz, Torgesen, Wood, Schulte, & Olson, 2001; Steubing *et al.*, 2002; Vellutino, Fletcher, Snowling, & Scanlon, 2004; Vellutino, Scanlon, & Lyon, 2000). The major concerns are that (1) many students have to experience chronic failure until the discrepancy is large enough to qualify for services; (2) many students who obviously are struggling in learning to read do not score high enough on the IQ tests to meet the ability–achievement discrepancy as it is calculated in their state; (3) statistically significant discrepancies do not consistently predict response to early intervention and thus are probably not the best way to select children for early intervention; (4) children who come from low literacy homes may benefit from the same kinds of early intervention as children at risk for biologically based reading disabilities; and (5) children who are at risk both environmentally and biologically especially need early intervention. There is a consensus among researchers that the federal government and local educational districts should devote more effort to early intervention for all children regardless of whether they have an ability–achievement discrepancy early in their journey toward literacy.

Other concerns (Berninger, 1998a) are that (1) the system is not flexible enough to accommodate a wide range of specific learning disabilities and other instructional needs; (2) school practitioners and psychologists are confusing qualifying children for special education services under the category of learning disability with diagnosing specific learning disabilities—a child can have a research-based learning disability and still not qualify for services under the learning disability category (see Berninger & O'Donnell, this volume); and (3) some children benefit from research-supported differential diagnosis whether their educational needs are best met in general education (with curriculum modification and supplementary assistance) or special education (with specialized instruction). Many students' learning needs could be met within the general education program if teachers were more appropriately trained in preservice teacher training programs (Berninger & Richards, 2002; Berninger, Dunn, Lin, S., & Shimada, in press). Specifically, teachers would benefit from a clearer understanding of normal variation within students at the same grade level and how these normal learning differences are different from specific kinds of learning differences that fall outside the normal range. New approaches to diagnosis are needed that can inform teachers' understanding of individual differences among their students and that have implications for instructional practices. Many parents, especially those with a family history of learning problems, seek diagnosis to understand why their child struggles with academic learning. Current diagnostic practices by practitioners who focus only on qualification for special education services, with no discussion of the neurocognitive processes associated with a learning disability and the classroom instructional implications for the learning disability, are not providing the kind of explanatory and treatment information parents seek (see Berninger, 1998a; and Berninger & O'Donnell, this volume).

However, there are still some unresolved issues regarding the role of IQ and measures of processes related to reading (writing or math) in diagnosis of specific learning disabilities. For example, there is evidence that ability–

achievement discrepancy is associated with biologically based reading disability, whereas low achievement that is not discrepant from IQ is more likely to be environmentally based (Olson, Datta, Gayan, & DeFries, 1999). Also, although most beginning readers respond to explicit, systematic instruction in phonologically based alphabetic reading, not all do (Torgesen, Wagner, Rashotte, Rose et al., 1999). Measuring psychological processes in treatment nonresponders or slower responders may provide important instructional clues for transforming them into treatment responders (e.g., Berninger, 1998a, 1998b, 2001a, 2001b, 2004, in press-a, in press-b; Torgesen, 1979, 2002; Wagner, Torgesen, & Rashotte, 1999). Although ability–achievement discrepancy based on Verbal IQ or Full Scale IQ did not predict response to early intervention in first grade (Stage, Abbott, Jenkins, & Berninger, 2003; Vellutino et al., 2000), Verbal IQ and process measures reliably differentiated the faster and slower responders in a 2-year longitudinal study of first and second graders (Berninger et al., 2002). Clearly, there is need for further research to create research-supported diagnostic practices that meet the needs of all students in a school across the school-age years.

To investigate the role of neurocognitive processes related to the acquisition of reading and writing in school-age children, the assessment and instructional research at the University of Washington (UW) is organized around a three-tier model (Berninger, Stage, Smith, & Hildebrand, 2001). This research program has three specific aims regarding assessment: (1) identifying research-supported assessment for early identification of at-risk children and early intervention treatments (tier one); (2) developing instructionally based assessment procedures to monitor student response to modified or supplementary instruction and to identify why some students do not respond to such instruction (tier two); and (3) validating assessment measures for differential diagnosis of specific learning disabilities on the basis of *inclusionary criteria* (tier three). In this chapter we focus on research-supported assessment practices at tiers one and two (see the chapter by Berninger & O'Donnell in this volume for recent research on tier-three assessment). This three-tier model, which also emphasizes assessment–intervention links, was designed for delivery of optimal and efficient school psychology services. Another three-tier model (Denton & Mathes, 2003) is organized for delivery of instructional services in general and special education.

MULTILEVEL, INTEGRATED ASSESSMENT

In this section, we introduce the concept of multilevel, integrated assessment at tiers one and two. The levels are *stages of assessment* and *types of assessment* (achievement, process, and cognitive functioning). Assessment practices are more effective and efficient if these stages and types of assessment are integrated.

STAGES OF ASSESSMENT

Performing assessment in stages allows psychologists to use their precious time for assessment more efficiently. For example, it is not necessary to administer all measures in a standard battery that are used routinely to qualify a student for special education in order to acquire the information that leads to meaningful instructional intervention at tiers one and two. Tier one targets early intervention for at-risk students, and tier two involves curriculum modification for students who are not succeeding in specific aspects of the general education classroom or meeting state high-stakes standards. Initial testing is confined to skill(s) related to reason for referral. Within a test session, testing proceeds to other skills only if the initial results point to other skills being affected as well. Further assessment sessions are needed only if the initial assessment does not lead to positive change in the student's academic performance. Thus, the initial stage of assessment determines whether further assessment is needed and, if so, points to which other skills should be assessed. To illustrate this process, early in literacy or numeracy learning, brief screens for at-risk learners may be sufficient (tier one). At any stage of learning, however, if a student shows daily struggles, a more comprehensive assessment may be needed, with a focus on modifying the general education curriculum to meet the instructional needs identified through the assessment (tier two). In those cases, where the learning problems are chronic and persist despite curriculum modifications, differential diagnosis of specific learning disabilities may be warranted (tier three).

NATURE OF ASSESSMENT

The nature of the assessment performed at each stage may differ depending on the reason for performing it:

- To determine, using achievement measures, which children are low achievers in reading or writing and would benefit from extra help (supplementary instruction in regular general education program).
- To evaluate, using achievement and process measures, which of the low achievers are most at risk and will probably need intensive supplementary instruction to learn to read and write.
- To plan an instructional program, informed by measures of language and neuropsychological processes related to academic learning, for low achievers and monitor their progress (response to intervention) from the beginning to the end of the school year.
- To explain why a student is not responding well to the general education curriculum or the supplementary instruction, based on a more comprehensive assessment including measures of cognitive development (intellectual functioning related to school learning, that is, scholastic aptitude), achievement measures, and process measures that

research has shown are related to reading or writing acquisition. (See section on profile analysis in this chapter.)

THREE KINDS OF ASSESSMENT

In this chapter we discuss three kinds of assessment that are relevant at tiers one and two: branching assessment, instructional assessment, and profile assessment. The purpose of *branching assessment* is to give only the minimum number of achievement and process measures to identify those students who would likely benefit from supplementary instruction. Depending on the outcome of the initial assessment, a decision is made to continue assessment or postpone assessment, pending the outcome of response to instruction designed on the basis of that initial assessment.

The purpose of *instructional assessment* is to monitor the student's response to early intervention (tier one) or general education curriculum modification (tier two) to determine progress adequacy. A combination of achievement and process measures are used to assess response to instruction. If progress is inadequate, the assessment results are used to plan additional instructional interventions.

The purpose of *profile assessment* in the primary grades, a developmentally critical period in learning to read and write and do arithmetic (Berninger & Richards, 2002), is to describe the student's individual profile, on the basis of intellectual abilities, achievement in specific academic domains, and measures of processes related to learning in specific academic domains. The goal is to identify and explain the child's absolute and relative strengths and weaknesses in a way that is relevant to instructional planning in the general education program (or special education program if that is found to be appropriate).

OVERVIEW OF CHAPTER

In this chapter, research studies are presented that illustrate the application of three types of assessment (branching, instructional, and profile) with groups of children found in tiers one and two. Also included in the chapter are 15 case studies.

BRANCHING ASSESSMENT

We briefly summarize (in text and tables) the results of cross-sectional studies of nonreferred, normally developing children and discuss their application to clinical practice. The choice of measures depends on the curriculum area in which the student is having difficulty. Only a few measures are given—those that were the best predictors of a specific skill in research accounted for unique variance in multiple regression or structural equation modeling. Additional assessment may be conducted contingent on the initial assessment results (see Berninger & Whitaker, 1993).

INSTRUCTIONAL ASSESSMENT

We briefly describe a tier-one instructional intervention conducted by school psychologists and teachers in the Los Angeles Unified School District in low-achieving schools with many at-risk students (Dunn, in press). Tier-one assessment was used to screen classrooms and identify the lowest achievers who were most at risk. A few process measures (based on principles of branching assessment) were also given. At-risk students were then given supplementary, research-validated early intervention in reading and writing. Tier-one assessment was also used to evaluate which students were treatment responders and which were treatment nonresponders. Although most of the children who received supplementary instruction were treatment responders, some were not. Process assessment was used to determine why these students failed and to plan additional instructional interventions aimed at the instructional needs identified from process and achievement assessment.

PROFILE ASSESSMENT

This approach, which identifies strengths and weaknesses for purposes of curriculum modification, may be more appropriate than differential diagnosis of learning disabilities, especially early in literacy development. Although many parents fear a label or premature diagnosis of a learning disability in the early grades, there is value in conducting an in-depth assessment of those students who clearly are not succeeding in some aspect of the general education curriculum. Comprehensive assessment should not always be postponed until the upper grades. We make a case that comprehensive assessment (of specific cognitive factors, academic achievement, and processes related to literacy and numeracy) can yield instructionally relevant information that might not have been apparent had only low achievement and response to early, supplementary instruction been assessed. We make this case with results from a subsample of nonreferred second-grade children in a longitudinal study and in detailed case studies of referred primary grade children given the WISC-III (Wechsler, 1991), WIAT II (The Psychological Corporation, 2001), and PAL (Berninger, 2001b). In the case studies, the four cognitive indexes (Verbal Comprehension, Perceptual Organization, Freedom from Distractibility, and Processing Speed) of the WISC-III; the reading, writing, and math subtests of the WIAT-II; and subtests from the PAL were used. Because of the strong commonalities between the new WISC-IV (The Psychological Corporation, 2004) cognitive indices and the WISC-III cognitive indices, the WISC-IV can be confidently substituted for the WISC-III in comprehensive, multilevel assessment.

BRANCHING ASSESSMENT

Cross-sectional studies of 600 nonreferred children identified the best predictors of critical reading and writing skills in literacy development, that is, the measures that explained unique variance in reading and writing outcomes. Results of those studies are summarized in Table 5.1 for the primary grade sample (e.g., Berninger & Fuller, 1992; Berninger & Rutberg, 1992; Berninger, Yates, & Lester, 1991; Berninger, Yates, Cartwright, Rutberg, Remy, & Abbott, 1992) and intermediate grade sample (e.g., Abbott & Berninger, 1993; Berninger, Abbott, & Alsdorf, 1997; Berninger, Cartwright, Yates, Swanson, & Abbott, 1994; Graham, Berninger, Abbott, Abbott, & Whitaker, 1997). To interpret the results of Table 5.1, start with the skill(s) marked for the domain of difficulty (in reading or writing) for which the child was referred. The second and third columns contain the measures of the processes that were found to contribute uniquely to specific reading or writing skills in the primary grades and intermediate grades, respectively. For example, research showed that receptive orthographic coding of written word forms contributed uniquely to writing the alphabet from memory; PAL Receptive Coding and PAL Alphabet Writing, respectively, assess these processes.

To use the research-supported, clinical assessment rubric portrayed in Table 5.1, first assess achievement in the relevant reading or writing skill, and then administer the additional process measures empirically linked to achievement in that skill. If no problems are identified at the level of the initial reading or writing assessment, then no further assessment is probably needed. See Berninger and Whitaker (1993) for further discussion of branching assessment. To facilitate the translation of these research results into clinical practice, we include in Table 5.1 commercially available, nationally normed measures that are currently available to assess the same processes and reading or writing skills whose relationships were validated in research. We also included a few measures validated in more recent research with a referred population (e.g., subtests from the CTOPP, Wagner, Torgesen, & Rashotte, 1999; and TOWRE, Torgesen, Wagner, & Rashotte, 1999a) (see chapter by Berninger & O'Donnell, this volume). Criteria used to define a processing problem, and thus, to make decisions at branching points of the diagnostic process, depend on the goals of branching diagnosis—selecting at-risk students for tier-one intervention or progress monitoring for tier-two intervention. Processing problems can be defined on the basis of national norms and/or school-based norms for the population served.

TABLE 5.1   Research-Supported Branching Assessment of Reading and Writing in Elementary School Children[a,b]

Reading or Writing Skill (Achievement)	Process Skill Explaining Unique Variance	Process Skill Explaining Unique Variance
	Primary Grade Children (grades 1 to 3)	Intermediate Grade Children (grades 4 to 6)
Word Reading	PAL Receptive Coding	PAL Receptive and Expressive Coding
(WIAT II Word Reading)	PAL Syllables and Phonemes	PAL Syllables, Phonemes, and Rimes
	PAL RAN Letter and Word	PAL Word Choice
	WISC-IV Vocabulary subtest	PAL RAN Letter and Word
	TOWRE Sight Word Efficiency	WISC-IV Vocabulary subtest
		TOWRE Sight Word Efficiency
Phonological Decoding (WIAT II Pseudoword Reading)	PAL Receptive Coding	PAL Receptive Coding
	PAL Syllables and Phonemes	PAL Syllables, Phonemes, and Rimes
	PAL RAN Letter and Word	PAL RAN Letter and Word
	TOWRE Phonemic Reading	TOWRE Phonemic Reading
	CTOPP Nonword Repetition	CTOPP Nonword Repetition
Reading Comprehension[b] (WIAT II Reading Comprehension)	WISC-IV Verbal Comprehension Index	WISC-IV Verbal Comprehension Index
	PAL Sentence Sense	PAL Sentence Sense
	WIAT II Word Reading and Pseudoword Reading	PAL Verbal Working Memory
		WISC-IV Working Memory Index
		WIAT II Word Reading and Pseudoword Reading
Handwriting Automaticity (PAL Alphabet Writing)	PAL Receptive Coding	PAL Receptive and Expressive Coding
	PAL Finger Repetition and Finger Succession	PAL Finger Repetition and Finger Succession
Spelling (WIAT II Spelling)	WISC-IV Vocabulary subtest	WISC-IV Vocabulary subtest
	PAL Receptive Coding	PAL Word Choice
	CTOPP Nonword Repetition	PAL Expressive Coding
		CTOPP Nonword Repetition
	PAL Syllables, Phonemes	PAL Syllables, Phonemes, Rimes

(Continues)

TABLE 5.1   *(Continued)*

Reading or Writing Skill (Achievement)	Process Skill Explaining Unique Variance	Process Skill Explaining Unique Variance
	Primary Grade Children (grade 1 to 3)	Intermetiate Grade Children (grades 1 to 6)
Composition Fluency[b] (WIAT II Written Expression Word Fluency, Composition Prompts in PAL Test Manual, and/or WJ-III Writing Fluency)	PAL Alphabet Writing WIAT II Spelling	PAL Alphabet Writing WIAT II Spelling PAL Finger Succession WISC-IV Working Memory Index and Processing Speed Index
Composition Quality[b] (WIAT II Written Expression or WJ-III Writing Samples)	PAL Alphabet Writing WISC-IV Verbal Comprehension	PAL Alphabet Writing WISC-IV Verbal Comprehension Index and Working Memory Index

Notes: WIAT II = *Wechsler Individual Achievement Test* (The Psychological Corporation, 2001). PAL = *Process Assessment of the Learner Test for Reading and Writing* (Berninger, 2001b). WISC-IV = *Wechsler Individual Intelligence Test for Children, Fourth Edition* (The Psychological Corporation, 2003). TOWRE = *Test of Word Reading Efficiency* (Torgesen, Wagner, & Rashotte, 1999). CTOPP = *Comprehensive Test of Phonological Processing* (Wagner, Torgesen, & Rashotte (1999). WJ-III = *Woodcock Johnson, Third Edition* (Woodcock, MeGrew, & Mather, 2001).
[a]Based on the results of the research using measures available at the time the research was conducted, we recommend currently available, nationally normed tests that can be used to assess the same skill.
[b]Start with the skill(s) marked with this superscript for the domain of difficulty for which the child was referred (reading or writing). If the measures listed under process skill for that achievement skill identify a deficit in an academic skill that is also listed as a row heading (e.g., Word Reading, Pseudoword Reading, Alphabet Writing, etc.), then go to that row and also give the process measures that explain that skill. That is what is meant by branching diagnosis: the results at one level may determine which measures are given next, and if no problems are identified at the level where testing began, then further assessment is probably not needed.

INSTRUCTIONAL ASSESSMENT

During the 2002–2003 school year, an innovative partnership between school psychologists and teachers was launched in the Los Angeles Unified School District under the leadership of Dunn (2002, 2004). School psychologists serving the lowest achieving schools with many English-learning (EL) students from low-income families decided to redirect their focus from testing for special education eligibility to providing early intervention. These schools had adopted research-supported reading programs in general education (Open Court in all but one school that used Success for All) and thus had already put in place tier-one instruction according to the Denton and Mathes (2003) model. School psychologists decided to apply tier-one assessment of the Berninger *et al.* (2001) model for school psychologists and screen the classes for any students who were not responding to this code-oriented curriculum. They administered the WIAT II Word Reading and Pseudoword Reading subtests to entire first-grade classes and identified the lowest achievers at or below the 25th percentile. (Word Reading assesses real word reading; Pseudoword Reading assesses phonological decoding.) These children were randomly assigned to a treatment group or a control group within their own school. The school psychologists partnered with the general education teachers to provide tier-one early intervention to the treatment groups.

This early intervention was provided two or three times a week for about a half hour while control children did independent assignments in their regular reading program. The intervention began in winter and continued until spring. Instruction was provided in reading (24 lessons in PAL Lesson Set 1) and writing (24 lessons in PAL Lesson Set 3) (Berninger & Abbott, 2003). These lessons were based on previous randomized, controlled research with at-risk first graders for reading (alphabetic principle taught for transfer to real word reading and text reading) and writing (automatic handwriting, word writing, and composing) (see Berninger & Abbott, 2003). To evaluate the effectiveness of the early intervention, the school psychologists readministered WIAT II Word Reading and Pseudoword Reading at the end of the intervention. They also administered three process measures—PAL Receptive Coding, Phonemes, and Rapid Automatic Naming Letters—before and after the intervention to evaluate the effect of the intervention on three processes shown in previous research to be related to reading and spelling (Berninger, Abbott, Thomson, & Raskind, 2001). The ultimate goal of this partnership is to reduce the number of students who will eventually need special education by building a bridge between general education and special education (Dunn, 2002, in press).

The following section briefly summarizes some of the findings of the first year of this innovative partnership. Specifically, the focus is on (1) the effectiveness of the early intervention in helping students transfer knowledge of alphabet principle and phonological decoding to real words; and (2) the value of process measures in evaluating student response to early intervention and planning future instructional intervention. We also discuss how monitoring student response to instruction provides valuable diagnostic information and recommend that school psychologists add instructional assessment to their repertoire of assessment tools.

Time devoted to reading was equated across the control group (regular reading program + independent reading) and the treatment group (regular reading program + PAL Lessons). The way that the treatment group was taught alphabetic principle emphasized the one- and two-letter spelling units that corresponded to phonemes in pictured words. The way the

TABLE 5.2   Change in Achievement and Process Measures from Before to After Tier-One Instructional Intervention

	Time 1		Time 2	
	M	SD	M	SD
Significant Time × Treatment Interactions[a]				
WIAT II Word Reading[b]				
Treatment Group	81.4	1.3	83.9	2.2
Control Group	79.9	1.8	77.7	2.8
PAL Receptive Coding[c]				
Treatment Group	28.9	2.2	55.0	4.1
Control Group	36.0	3.8	50.0	4.1
Significant Time Effects				
WIAT II Pseudoword Reading[d]	86.0	8.2	91.9	12.7
WIAT II Spelling[e]	83.6	11.9	88.7	15.4
PAL Receptive Coding[f]	32.6	20.3	52.7	27.2
PAL Phonemes[g]	29.8	23.6	41.6	25.8
PAL RAN letters[h]	42.9	32.7	55.7	30.3

Note: WIAT II standard scores have mean $= 100$; standard deviation $= 15$. PAL scores are deciles.
[a]Directional hypothesis testing; one-tail statistical test.
[b]$F(1, 86) = 2.997, p = .0435$
[c]$F(1, 84) = 4.401, p = .0195$
[d]$F(1,85) = 14.47, p < .001$
[e]$F(1,61) = 6.438, p < .014$
[f]$F(1,84) = 48.412, p < .001$
[g]$F(1,84) = 27.707, p < .001$
[h]$F(1,84) = 13.763, p < .001$

treatment group learned to apply alphabetic principle to word decoding emphasized parsing the written word into these spelling units, which are then translated into phonemes (see Berninger & Abbott, 2003). Also the handwriting instruction called attention to a plan for sequential strokes needed to write letters. As a result, the lowest achievers seemed to benefit from this kind of training in developing their orthographic coding ability and their ability to apply alphabetic principle (correspondences between letters and phonemes) to real words. Not all children may require such explicit and intensive instruction but those most at risk may.

As shown in Table 5.2, children in the treatment group improved significantly more than did those in the control group on WIAT II Word Reading, a measure of real word reading. The children in the treatment group also improved significantly in comparison to the control group on PAL receptive coding, a measure of coding the orthographic word form into short-term memory and processing its constituent letters in working memory. Although both groups improved, the treatment group showed larger gains, on average, than did the control group. On average the treatment group moved from the lower limits of the 2nd quartile to above the mean in the 3rd quartile. Recent research shows that orthographic coding contributes uniquely to real word reading (e.g., Berninger *et al.*, 2001; Nagy, Berninger, Abbott, Vaughan, & Vermeulin, 2003). Both treatment and control groups improved significantly in phonological decoding, as expected, because both the regular reading program and the supplementary tier-one lessons emphasized phonological awareness and the alphabetic principle. Over the course of the intervention both groups also improved significantly, on average, in two other processes related to reading and spelling—phoneme skills and rapid automatic naming of letters. Individual subject analyses identified which children were treatment responders on real word reading and on pseudoword reading. The association between group and treatment responding was significant in chi-square analyses. For both real word reading and pseudoword reading, more treatment responders were likely to be in the treatment group than in the control group (Dunn, 2004).

Scores on receptive (orthographic) coding and phoneme skills before the intervention did not predict the size of the achievement gain in real word or pseudoword reading, but scores on receptive coding at the end of the intervention were significantly correlated with gains in real word reading, $r(84) = .238, p < .05$. Likewise, scores on phoneme skills at the end of the intervention were significantly correlated with gains in pseudoword reading, $r(83) = 405, p < .01$. Because receptive coding and phoneme skills had improved significantly over the course of the intervention, it appears that the improvement in processes related to learning to read may be related to the amount of improvement in reading.

The results also provide discriminant validity for the value of process assessment: Individual differences in receptive (orthographic) coding at the end of the intervention were associated with gains in real word reading, while individual differences in phoneme skills at the end of the intervention were associated with gains in phonological decoding. These results have practical educational significance. For those children identified as nonresponders in real word reading or in receptive coding, teachers can use or school psychologists can recommend Looking Games (Berninger, 1998a), which are best used with the real words in the reading program (see PAL Lesson Sets 11 and 12, Berninger & Abbott, 2003), to improve orthographic coding skills. For those children identified to be nonresponders in pseudoword reading or phoneme skills, teachers can use or school psychologists can recommend Sound Games (Berninger, 1998a), which can also be yoked to the specific words in a reading program (see PAL Lesson Sets 11, 12, and 15, Berninger & Abbott, 2003). Because most of the children in this study were

Spanish-speaking EL students, we also gave the teachers the Spanish phonological awareness lessons and progress monitoring instrument (Quiroga, Lemos-Britton, Mostafapour, Abbott, & Berninger, 2002) to use during second grade with Spanish-speaking EL children who had not grown in phoneme skills or phonological decoding during first grade. As shown in Table 5.2, phoneme skills were the first graders' weakest process skills, on average, at the end of the intervention.

A multimodal assessment approach that includes instructionally based assessment (IBA), curriculum based assessment (CBA), or curriculum based measurement (CBM), along with achievement and process assessment, is recommended (see Chapter 10, Berninger, 1998a). CBM is often equated with a fluency-metric (e.g., how many words can the child read orally in a minute, or how many math facts can the child answer correctly in writing in a minute). In the following section other CBM applications are offered, which illustrate its potential beyond a fluency-metric.

In Instructionally based assessment, children are assessed on the specific skills that were taught in a lesson. This approach, introduced by Stephen Peverley at Teachers' College at Columbia University (Peverley, 2004), links assessment to specific instructional goals. One of the unique features of the PAL Lessons is that progress-monitoring tools are provided for each lesson set, and all lesson sets have instructional goals. Because the instructional goals change for these lessons (five sets for each of the three tiers), so do the progress monitoring tools and the nature of the growth graph used to plot results. Table 5.3 illustrates this approach as the LAUSD school psychologists used it for PAL Lesson Set 1. Every six lessons children were tested by asking them to read orally the 48 words that are used in each lesson to model application of alphabet principle to word context. Near the end of the lesson set, children were asked on two occasions to read lists of transfer words constructed on the basis of the same correspondences between letters and phonemes but in different word contexts. As can be seen in Table 5.3, children differed in how many of these words they could pronounce after just 6 lessons and at the end of 24 lessons and had very different growth trajectories for the instructional goal. As expected, transfer always lagged behind learning the taught words but was higher for those who had steeper growth trajectories.

In Table 5.3 samples are shown of the progress monitoring data linked to the curriculum used in the regular reading program for both the treatment and control children. Open Court provides progress monitoring tests to give at specific times of the school year. These CBM measures show a similar picture to that of the IBA probes based on PAL Lessons—it is one of individual differences in where students are when instruction begins and in how they change over small time intervals in the instructional process. Results in Table 5.3 show that children were progressing better in reading than spelling. Based on these results, we recommended further supplementary instruction focused on spelling (e.g., PAL Lesson Set 2 for spelling for at-risk second-grade spellers). All

TABLE 5.3   Representative Instructionally Based Assessment (IBA) and Curriculum Based Measurement (CBM) for Tier-One Early Intervention (Treatment Group Only)

I. IBA[a]	List 2[b] (taught words)		List 3[b] (transfer words)		List 4[b] (transfer words)	
Lesson Student	6th	12th	18th	24th	18th	24th
1	20	26	29	38	31	31
2	5	19	23	28	21	24
3	na	30	38	45	16	23
4	1	1	1	2	2	2
5	12	24	25	36	25	24
6	7	19	21	35	8	18
7	0	2	7	19	6	7
8	5	8	13	23	4	4
9	7	19	21	35	8	18
10	12	30	28	45	29	27

II. CBM[c]

Week of Assessment Student	6th		12th		24th		30th	
	Read	Spell	Read	Spell	Read	Spell	Read	Spell
11	1	0					6	7
12	3	6					5	6
13	3	4	8	9				
14	3	6	8	8				
15	4	2	4	1	6	4	6	2
16	5	4	6	3	6	1	6	3
17	4	7	6	6	na	1	6	1
18	2	4	6	4	7	0	na	na
19	0	3	6	4	8	3	na	3
20	6	10	7	7	9	7	na	na

[a]PAL Lesson Set 1.
[b]48 words.
[c]CBM for Open Court; score of 6 meets expectations.

too often reading is emphasized to the exclusion of handwriting, spelling, and written composition for the students most at risk in literacy learning.

Although the children in the treatment group increased, on average, from the low average to the average range, the IBA and CBM results in Table 5.3 serve as a reminder that the journey to literacy is arduous for these students, their teachers, and psychologists and consists of many small steps. It takes explicit, systematic, and intensive instruction to achieve what the LAUSD partnership did—a demonstration that integrated multilevel assessment that incorporated supplementary instruction *and* progress monitoring (with achievement tests, process measures, IBA, and CBM) led to better literacy outcomes for many, if not all, students. This story is not finished yet, and LAUSD may find, as the University of Washington research program discovered, that some students just need a second year of explicit and systematic instruction to reach the average range in reading (Berninger, Abbott, Vermeulen, Ogier, Brooksher, Zook, & Lemos, 2002) or spelling (Berninger, Vaughan, Abbott, Brooks, Begay, Curtin, Byrd, & Graham, 2000). The school psychologists are also assessing which of the nonresponders would benefit from comprehensive assessment that includes a detailed developmental, medical, and family history. In the meantime, this study provides empirical evidence that supports the expanded role of the school psychologists. These psychologists, who represent the highest level of professionalism, not only test and diagnose but also get involved in (1) treatment to ameliorate academic learning problems, and (2) assessing response to instructional treatment. They do not diagnose and say adios.

PROFILE ASSESSMENT

One perspective is that screening children for low achievement and evaluating their response to instructional intervention may be sufficient (see Fletcher *et al.*, in press). Another perspective is that in some cases, children benefit from a more comprehensive evaluation as part of the tier-two progress monitoring. To evaluate the veracity of these perspectives, we first inspected results for a sample of nonreferred second graders in a longitudinal study (tested in the fall after completing a year of literacy instruction); and then we inspected the results for all students referred for evaluation of learning disabilities in a school over 2 years. The results of these preliminary studies are first presented followed by a discussion of the difference between profile assessment and differential assessment and the potential contribution of profile assessment to tier-two assessment and intervention in the delivery of school psychology services.

NONREFERRED SAMPLE IN LONGITUDINAL STUDY

Assessment results for 129 second graders in a longitudinal study of normal reading and writing development were reviewed to determine whether the test information was instructionally relevant. That is, from the perspective of teaching and clinical experience, would these test results suggest that the regular general education program in second grade should be modified, or was the program in place sufficient? Table 5.4 contains the results for 15.5% of the sample for which test results were thought to have

TABLE 5.4 Summary of Diagnostic Features[a] in Twenty Second Graders (15.5% of 129 Children in Unreferred Sample in Longitudinal Study)

Cases	1	2	3	4	5	6	7	8	9	10	11	12	13	14	15	16	17	18	19	20
VIQ[b]	125	98	116	77	64	107	96	100	130	133	120	116	114	107	116	87	89	95	85	100
Expressive Language[c]	9	5	6	9	3	8											10			
Receptive Language[c]	15	11	10	12	3	8											12			
Accuracy Word Reading[d]	105	77	97	91	80	86	82	90	99	107	99	101	93	87	96	90	106	78	109	90
Accuracy Decoding[d]	95	84	86	87	90	81	89	81	114	90	97	89	81	85	91	92	106	81	116	91
Word Rate[e]	103	75	97	80		83	78	85				103	87	86	94			67	114	91
Decoding Rate[e]	92	78	89	72		88	85	72				92	80	89	85			79	119	84
Oral Reading Accuracy[f]		5				5	6	7					6	7	7		8	5		6
Oral Reading Rate[f]		5				6	6	7				6	6	7	6			5		6
Reading Comprehension[d]					63				95		98				104	76	85	69	86	
Sentence Sense[g]		10		10					40	10	10		10	10	10		10	10		
Orthographic Coding[g]	10	30	10	10			20	30	30	20	10	60	10	10			10	20	60	10

Measure						
Orthographic Word Form[g]	10				10	
Phoneme[g]	20		20	10		60
RAN Letter[g]	10	30	20	80	10	70
RAN Word[g]		30		50	30	
RAS Words & Digits[g]	10	10			10	
Alphabet Writing[g]	10				10	
Spelling[d]	89					91
Written Expression[d]	76					79

---

[a]Scores in the profile that were diagnostically and instructionally relevant; the missing scores are not impaired or informative.

[b]WISC-III (Wechsler, 1991) Prorated Verbal IQ based on the four subtests of the Verbal Comprehension Factor; M = 100, SD = 15.

[c]CELF 3 (Semel, Secord, & Wiig, 1995) Sentence Formulation and Sentence Structure; M = 100, SD = 3.

[d]WIAT-II (The Psychological Corporation, 2001) Word Reading and Pseudoword Reading Accuracy, Spelling, Written Expression; M = 100, SD = 3.

[e]TOWRE (Torgesen, Wagner, & Rashotte, 1999) Sight Word Efficiency and Phonemic Reading Efficiency/Rate; M = 100, SD = 3.

[f]GORT3 (Wiederholt & Bryant, 1992) Oral Reading (Text) Accuracy and Rate; M = 100, SD = 3.

[g]PAL (Berninger, 2001b) Sentence Sense, Receptive (Orthographic) Coding, Word Choice, Phonemic Coding, Rapid Automatic Naming (RAN) and Switching (RAS), Alphabet Writing are reported in decile scores.

*educational significance for individual educational planning in the general education program.*For 84.5% of these children, there were no "flags" in their test results that would suggest the need for an instructional program different than the one that was already provided.

A brief synopsis of the 20 cases presented in Table 5.4 led to the following conclusions. Fourteen (75%) of these cases (1, 2, 3, 6, 7, 8, 9, 10, 11, 12, 13, 14, 15, 18, and 20) met the research criteria for dyslexia used in the University of Washington family genetics study of dyslexia (see Berninger, 2001a, and chapter by Berninger & O' Donnell in this volume). These children varied in how impaired they were (number of skills below the population mean, how many specific skills were one standard deviation or more below their WISC III Verbal IQ, and the number of associated processing deficits in phonological, orthographic, and rapid automatic naming skills). However, we are skeptical that cases 3 and 12 are really at risk for dyslexia because they have none of the associated processing deficits that characterize dyslexia. Instead there may be curriculum issues (missing components, see Berninger, 1998a) that explain their underachievement in second grade.

Nevertheless, these preliminary results raised two issues that require further research. First, if these children are not given appropriate early intervention and/or specialized instruction during the primary grades, will they be more impaired in the upper elementary grades than they are now? According to the questionnaires parents complete, few of these children were already receiving any kind of supplementary or specialized instruction. We recommended that the parent share the test report with the school and request some form of instructional intervention. These test results suggest that about 11.5% of second graders in general (three fourths of the 15.5 %) may benefit from explicit and systematic instruction in accuracy and rate of word reading and decoding and spelling to eliminate or prevent severity of future reading and writing problems. We would not have known who was most at risk without formal testing. Only as we follow these children over time, will we know the eventual educational outcome and the responsiveness of the schools to provide early intervention based on research-generated assessment information. We also wonder if those children with evidence of superior or very superior verbal abilities will receive programming for their intellectual talent, as well as their specific learning disabilities (see cases 1, 9, 10, and 11).

We are concerned about the other kinds of learning differences evident in these profiles. Case 4 has an unusual profile in that receptive and expressive language skills were better developed than Verbal IQ. Deficits were found in orthographic coding, rapid automatic naming, rapid automatic switching, and silent reading fluency. Cases 16, 17, and 19 have reading comprehension that is more than one standard deviation below their phonological decoding; they vary in which process skills are impaired. They would probably benefit from very explicit reading comprehension instruction at the word, sentence, and text level in the second-grade curriculum (Berninger, Vermeulen, Abbott, McCutchen, Cotton, Cude, Dorn, & Sharon, 2003). Case 5 has very impaired receptive and expressive language and Verbal IQ but oral word reading and decoding skills that fall within the normal range. These oral reading skills may mask a significant language disability that would benefit from more thorough assessment and intervention.

Further research is needed to establish criteria as to when low achievement criteria are sufficient and when more comprehensive assessment (including achievement, process, IBA and CBM, measures, and developmental and medical history information) is necessary to identify all the students who would benefit from tier-one or tier-two instructional intervention in the primary grades.

REFERRED CASES IN A SCHOOL SETTING

The third author has not only been a trainer of school psychologists for more than 30 years but has also maintained an active practice of school psychology over the years in school settings. He is currently providing psychological services in a school in London, which draws its student population from around the world. This population is diverse culturally and linguistically (many are English learners).

This school provides a number of early intervention (tier one) support services. However, despite these tier-one interventions, classroom teachers who see children struggle on a daily basis refer children for psychological evaluation for learning disabilities. Over 2 years he has received 18 such requests (17 in first, second, or third grade, and 1 in fifth grade for follow-up evaluation) for tier-two progress monitoring to explain why children struggle in the general education program. This referral rate is interesting because it shows that the school psychologist's assessment load need not be top heavy in the upper grades if a systematic program of tier-one and tier-two intervention is in place (Berninger *et al.*, 2001; Denton & Mathes, 2003). These assessments provide a unique data base because they include a complete multilevel assessment battery of cognitive (WISC-III IQ), achievement (WIAT II), and process (PAL) measures. The complete multilevel assessment model is the one originally envisioned and proposed by Aurelio Prifitera and Donna Smith in 1997 during an invited presentation at the Psychological Corporation of the University of Washington research program in progress since 1989.

In the next section, 3 evaluations are briefly discussed before focusing on 15 evaluations (see Table 5.5 for a summary of their multilevel results). These were all tier-two evaluations performed because the child was struggling with the general education curriculum after having received supplementary instruction through early intervention services in the school. Index scores are reported rather than Verbal, Performance, or Full Scale IQs (Prifitera, Weiss, & Saklofske, 1998). WIAT II subtest scores are reported

TABLE 5.5 Multilevel Assessment Results: Cognitive Factors, Reading, Math, and Writing Achievement, and Processes Related to Literacy and Numeracy

Cases	1	2	3	4	5	6	7	8	9	10	11	12	13	14	15
WISC-III Index															
Verbal Comprehension	107	102	136	136	93	113	127	139	130	92	108	130	125	95	110
Perceptual Organization	104	100	111	122	90	105	128	142	102	97	97	110	117	97	100
Freedom from Distractibility	81	101	112	109	87	104	90	121	124	115	96	131	121	93	98
Processing Speed	na	83	114	104	93	101	101	137	80	119	122	106	96	106	114
WIAT II Subtest															
Word Reading	96	83	86	103	89	91	98	108	102	111	104	112	93	104	100
Pseudoword Reading	114	93	97	99	87	85	82	104	99	122	100	109	94	101	112
Reading Comprehension	114	86	98	107	81	107	85	115	113	111	90	107	110	102	97
Numerical Operations	98	82	92	103	88	92	86	112	119	100	82	104	111	89	107
Math Reasoning	90	94	106	127	86	95	97	129	119	99	90	136	127	108	107
Spelling	106	91	93	98	88	96	96	91	106	96	96	93	87	101	97
Written Expression	106	90	95	95	89	103	96	94	83	88	102	106	98	109	110

Alphabet Writing	100	50	100	100	70	60	80	90	60	20	40	100	60	90	na
Copy A	100	30	100	30	10	20	na	30	60	30	90	90	40	80	
Copy B	100	30	100	70	30	10	80	40	80	50	100	100	40	90	
Receptive Coding	30	30	30	50	10	20	10	90	na	50	20	30	30	50	
Word Choice	50	10	10	80	na	20	na	100	30	70	70	40	20	40	
Syllable	100	70	100	40	100	80	80	100	na	20	50	100	80	30	
Phoneme	90	90	60	90	90	50	60	60	na	50	70	100	70	60	
Rime	70	80	80	80	70	20	60	20	na	40	70	80	50	40	
RAN Letters	60	40	80	90	40	20	30	50	na	80	40	50	40	80	
RAN Words	40	10	90	80	50	40	40	40	na	70	70	80	20	90	
RAN Digits	80	50	70	90	60	10	90	40	na	100	50	70	40	40	
RAS Words and Digits	70	30	na	100	30	20	10	40	na	90	30	80	20	40	
Finger Succession–Dominant	50	70	na	na	50	10	70	40	na	na	50	90	90	60	
Finger Succession–Nondominant	70	80	na	na	40	10	70	30	na	na	60	80	50	30	
Finger Recognition	40	100	na	na	100	10	100	100	na	na	100	100	10	100	
Finger Tip Writing	30	70	na	na	100	10	70	50	na	na	50	80	40	70	
Sentence Sense	40	20	20	20	40	na	10	10	10	10	40	10	10	60	

Note: WISC-III and WIAT-II have M = 100, SD = 15; PAL score is a decile.

because we find these more instructionally relevant for educational planning than the reading, math, and writing composites schools use for deciding whether children qualify for special education services. PAL scores are not reported in the order as in the test protocol but rather are organized so that tests of similar processes are grouped: handwriting (Alphabet Writing, Copy A, Copy B), orthographic coding (receptive coding, expressive coding, word choice), phonological coding (syllables, phonemes, and rimes), rapid naming (RAN) (letters, words, digits) and rapid switching (RAS) (words and double digits), finger sense (only finger succession, recognition, and finger tip writing are in Table 5.5), and sentence sense. Results of the parent interview regarding medical, developmental, and family history are mentioned only if relevant to the reason for referral. The PAL Lesson Sets that are recommended are from the University of Washington instructional research studies that have been translated into teacher-ready lessons (five lesson sets for each of the three tiers) (Berninger & Abbott, 2003).

THREE CASES USING BRANCHING ASSESSMENT AND RESULTS OF PRIOR ASSESSMENT

Case A

This child was referred for memory and written language problems. Achievement testing showed the child was overachieving in reading and was achieving at expected levels in math and written expression for previously assessed average reasoning ability. However, the child was significantly underachieving in math operations, which the referring classroom teacher had not noted. PAL Process measures identified processing deficits in both graphomotor planning (finger succession) and sensory-motor integration (finger recognition). Research has shown that these finger skills are related to paper and pencil math calculation problems (Shurtleff, Abbott, Berninger, & Townes, 1993) as well as written language (Berninger & Amtmann, 2003). Instructional recommendations were made for special help in using a pencil for writing letters and numbers and the visual notation system for numbers in performing paper and pencil calculations.

Case B

This third grader was referred for continuing difficulty with written assignments despite considerable private therapy in handwriting (as an isolated skill) and visual perceptual training. Prior assessment had showed significant cognitive strengths (WISC-III Verbal Comprehension, 133; Perceptual Organization, 120; Freedom from Distractibility, 104; and Processing Speed, 111). This assessment identified a relative weakness in spelling (WIAT-II spelling, 96). PAL Process assessment linked the spelling problem to a processing deficit in orthographic coding (decile score 20) and in copying letters (PAL Copy A) (decile score 20). Instead of either visual perceptual training, which is not a research-supported approach to remediating spelling problems, or handwriting training in isolation, which may not transfer to written language assignments in the classroom, PAL Lesson Sets 4 and 5 (for training spelling and its transfer to written composition) were recommended. When these lessons are completed, PAL Lesson Set 8 will be recommended for helping the student integrate handwriting, spelling, and composition processes at the critical transition between grades 3 and 4 when the writing requirements of the curriculum increase dramatically.

Case C

A fifth grader who had received four years of remediation and accommodation services was given follow-up testing. He had a previously documented strength in verbal reasoning (WISC-III Verbal Reasoning). His WIAT II results showed that he was achieving at expected level in reading comprehension (130) and math operations (122) and reasoning (126). He was well above the population mean (and no longer at risk) in word reading (118) and spelling (111) and was doing reasonably well in written expression (102) but far below his verbal reasoning ability. The only remaining disability was in phonological decoding on pseudoword reading (76). Not all PAL process measures were given, but a residual processing deficit was identified in silent reading comprehension fluency on a measure that requires close attention to word-level decoding and sentence syntax (sentence sense). This profile is highly typical of compensated dyslexics; all skills are developed to or above the population mean except pseudoword reading. Some, not all, dyslexics avoid reading, possibly because silent reading fluency problems may continue to make it difficult, and lack of reading practice can lead to further problems with reading speed. Instructional resources at the end of the PAL Intervention Guides (Berninger, 1998a) and PAL Lessons (Berninger & Abbott, 2003) under the sections on phonological decoding and reading fluency were recommended to the classroom teacher for a tier-two modification of the general education program. For example, materials developed by Marcia Henry can be used to teach decoding of long, complex words in intellectually engaging ways with older students. This child no longer needed pull-out services but does need a teacher-supervised daily reading program at the child's independent level to provide practice and develop fluency and a comfort level with reading throughout schooling and life.

MULTILEVEL ASSESSMENT OF FIRST GRADERS

Table 5.5 presents the results of 15 multilevel assessments.

Case 1

This child was referred for math problems in the classroom. In contrast to many first graders who have difficulty with paper and pencil calculation, this child had difficulty with math reasoning. Testing confirmed that the problems were specific to math. The only processing weakness identified was WISC-III Freedom from Distractibility, which is interpreted as evidence of working memory impairment. The new WISC-IV Working Memory Index and PAL Math Subtests (in progress) will permit a more complete process assessment of math problems. Concrete manipulatives were recommended to help the child understand place value and part-whole relationships. The teacher was also encouraged to teach math-specific vocabulary so that the child could understand the word problems used to teach and assess the child's math reasoning skills.

Case 2

An absolute and relative deficit in processing speed was identified in cognitive testing. TOWRE sight word efficiency (77) and phonemic reading efficiency (87) were also less well developed than accuracy of real word and pseudoword reading, respectively. Rapid naming of words lagged behind rapid naming of letters. Phonological skills were a relative strength but silent reading comprehension fluency was a relative weakness. The relative weakness in math operations may be due to an underlying problem in speed of math fact retrieval (which can be assessed with the PAL Math). Although this student does not yet show an ability–achievement discrepancy, the child is at risk for fluency problems across the curriculum. At follow-up, measures of writing fluency will also be given using the CBM measures the third author developed for the beginning and end of first through fifth grade to supplement the midyear norms for number of words and spelling accuracy in expository composition (in the PAL Test Battery Manual). Instructional recommendations included extra practice in learning sight words and math facts, using the selective reminding technique described in the PAL Intervention Guides (Berninger, 1998a).

Case 3

This child was referred for very slow response to supplementary reading instruction using Reading Recovery. The family has a history of dyslexia. Cognitive testing revealed strengths (very superior verbal reasoning and all the other cognitive indexes above average). All reading, math, and writing achievement fell in the average range except single-word reading, which fell in the low-average range. PAL process assessment identified weaknesses in orthographic skills (receptive coding and word choice) and in silent reading comprehension fluency (sentence sense). This student is achieving below verbal reasoning ability across the curriculum. PAL Lessons, which are designed to develop orthographic skills and reading fluency, were recommended for reading (Lesson Sets 11, 2, and 6, in that order) and for writing (Lesson Sets 4 and 5, in that order). The child is being monitored to evaluate whether further intervention for this child, who is at-risk on the basis of family history, will narrow the gap between verbal ability and achievement.

Case 4

This child was referred for failure to respond to supplementary instruction. Cognitive testing identified strengths (very superior and superior perceptual organization), but, with the exception of math reasoning, this child is underachieving for thinking ability across the curriculum. He is below the population mean in pseudoword reading, spelling, and written expression. He had processing deficits in copying letters (PAL Copy A) and silent reading comprehension fluency (PAL Sentence Sense). PAL Lesson Sets 2 and 6 were recommended for reading and PAL Lesson Sets 4 and 5 were recommended for writing. Annual progress monitoring was recommended until this student narrows the gap between ability and achievement.

Case 5

This child who was referred for problems across the curriculum has a history of slower speech and language development and notable problems in social–emotional self-regulation. He has received speech services but not language services. He may be a slow learner (see Berninger, 1998b, for criteria when this diagnosis is warranted); indeed his current achievement is not discrepant from his current intellectual functioning. However, process assessment identified weaknesses in copying letters (PAL Copy A) and in orthographic skills (PAL Receptive Coding). Also, he had a spark not captured in formal assessment. When succeeding on nonverbal problems, he announced "I like a challenge." Because his history has many indicators of language learning disability and thus he may not yet have learned to use decontextualized language to express his thinking (see chapter by Berninger & O'Donnell, this volume), a comprehensive evaluation of his language was recommended. Language (not speech) therapy may be indicated, if results of the language assessment warrant. Follow-up academic testing is also planned, but specific educational recommendations await the results of the language evaluation.

MULTILEVEL ASSESSMENT OF SECOND GRADERS

Case 6

This second grader was referred for slow response to supplementary reading instruction and struggles with arithmetic. Teachers described the child as eager to learn to read, as frequently trying to write, and as willing to work very hard. The child loves class discussions and science. Cognitive testing indicated average to above average skills. Academic testing indicated that word reading, especially pseudoword reading, math operations and reasoning, and spelling were below the population mean and below the child's above average verbal reasoning. In contrast to these weaknesses, the child had relative strengths in reading comprehension and written expression. These strengths were accompanied by the following processing weaknesses: in copying letters in a sentence (Copy A) or paragraph (Copy B), receptive (orthographic) coding, word choice, phonological analysis of rime units, rapid automatic letters or digits, rapid automatic switching between words and digits, finger succession (both hands), finger recognition, and finger-tip writing. Both testing and history are consistent with the diagnoses of developmental dyslexia, dysgraphia, and dyscalculia (see chapter by Berninger & O'Donnel and Berninger, this volume).

A challenging clinical dilemma is whether to make such a diagnosis or just focus on treating the academic problems at grade 2. The first instructional goal is to preserve the child's enthusiasm for learning and motivation for learning. PAL Lesson Sets 4, 5, and 8, in that order, were recommended to remediate processing deficits in the context of writing instruction designed to teach transcription skills (spelling or handwriting and spelling) and composition skills in an integrated fashion that transfers transcription skills to composition. PAL Lesson Sets 11, 2, and 6 were recommended, in that order, to remediate reading problems in a way that promotes transfer of alphabetic principle to decoding in word and story context. The math program could capitalize on the child's interest in discussion and encourage oral expression of mathematical thinking until the child has learned to use paper and pencil and the written symbol system to reliably express quantitative thinking in that mode. However, the child should also be taught strategies for using the paper and pencil and the visual notation system for numbers.

Case 7

This child was referred for very slow responding to phonological awareness, phonological decoding, and oral reading fluency training. Poor speech intelligibility interfered with social interaction. Cognitive testing revealed exceptional strengths in verbal reasoning and nonverbal reasoning and relative weaknesses in freedom from distractibility and processing speed. Achievement testing documented that achievement in reading, math, and writing was below the population mean and unexpected based on assessed reasoning abilities. PAL process assessment identified deficits in writing and naming letters under timed conditions, switching attention between word and digits, and silent reading comprehension fluency. This child appeared to have both specific learning disabilities affecting skills across the academic curriculum and a communication disability. A comprehensive language assessment was recommended to evaluate whether the communication problems are specific to speech (motoric output) or may also involve morphological and syntactic awareness and executive functions that support language. If those kinds of language processing problems are found, they may also be responsible for some of the child's academic learning problems.

Case 8

This child was referred because of more difficulty with phonological decoding than with automatic recognition of familiar words and because the child had difficulty with the sound sequencing and blends needed to spell words. Teachers reported a strength in verbalizing opinions on a range of topics. Cognitive testing yielded index scores that indicate the child is intellectually capable and likely to benefit from educational programming for the gifted. His lowest WISC-III cognitive index fell in the superior range; the rest fell in the very superior range. On academic achievement results, he meets research criteria for dysgraphia (Berninger, in press-a). Testing results show that he has been responsive to past supplementary instruction in phonological decoding but has remaining spelling difficulties related to underlying phonological but also other processes. Spelling (but not word-level reading measures for real words or pseudowords) falls below the population mean and is significantly discrepant from verbal reasoning. Moreover, associated processing deficits were identified in phonological analysis of rimes, silent reading fluency, and relative weaknesses in grapho-motor planning (finger succession), handwriting (copy tasks), RAN, and RAS tasks. This child has dual instructional needs. On the one hand, the child's superb reasoning skills needed to be nurtured through acceleration and/or enriched curriculum for the intellectually capable. On the other hand, the child required explicit, systematic instruction aimed at his handwriting, spelling, and composition in an integrated fashion. PAL Lesson Sets 4, 5, 7, and 8 may accomplish that.

Case 9

This second grader was referred for guidance as to the next goal in his supplementary reading instruction. Cognitive testing revealed an unusual range from very superior verbal reasoning and superior freedom from dis-tractibility to average nonverbal reasoning to barely average processing speed. Previous CTOPP results documented a deficit in phonological memory (standard score 82) and rapid automatic naming (standard score 88). Previous TOWRE results documented a deficit in rate/efficiency of real word reading (94) and phonemic reading (88). The PAL process assessment confirmed a deficiency in silent reading comprehension fluency as well. The word- and sentence-level reading rate problems were consistent with the WISC-III processing speed deficit, which might be related to the CTOPP result showing problems in rapid naming. PAL receptive coding was not administered, so its possible contribution to the rate problems cannot be evaluated. This child is a counterexample to the claim that processing speed is directly related to intelligence. This child's reasoning is superb, independ-ent of processing speed. Two kinds of instructional recommendations were made. First, the teacher should include fluency-promoting activities in the general education second-grade reading program. At the end of both the PAL Intervention Guides and the PAL Lessons are sections that contain commercially available instructional resources for developing reading rate and fluency. Second, the child should be given accommodations in the form of extra time to complete written assignments.

Case 10

This second grader was referred for problems in handwriting, immaturity, problems in self-control and emotional regulation, and attention/concentration. Mother reported problems during the pregnancy and labor. After birth, this child was more active than peers and needed less sleep than other children. He was very distractible during the testing. Cognitive testing yielded an unusual profile, especially given the many indicators of attentional problems. Freedom from distractibility fell in the superior range and processing speed fell in the high average range, while both verbal and nonverbal reasoning fell in the average range but below the population mean. Academic testing showed that reading was a strength (all skills above average to superior range), math skills were age-appropriate, and writing skills ranged from average (spelling) to low average (written expression). The child's writing problems were suggestive of dysgraphia but not unexpected due to verbal reasoning; they were unexpected relative to the child's reading skills. PAL process assessment identified problems in automatic letter retrieval, phonological analysis of syllables, and silent reading comprehension fluency.

Additional assessment supported a diagnosis of attention deficit/hyperactivity disorder, with both inattention and hyperactivity dimensions. Note that the WISC-III Freedom from Distractibility Index has been changed to the WISC-IV Working Memory Index to clarify that this factor is not measuring attention deficit. It is possible for a child to fall in the high average range on this index of working memory and also have attention deficit disorder. Writing problems and attention problems often co-occur in the same children. The child's greatest instructional needs were in (1) writing and (2) self-regulation of attention and related behaviors. PAL Lesson Sets 4 and 5 were recommended to develop spelling skills and transfer to composition. A behavioral plan was implemented to deal with attention and self-regulation behaviors.

MULTILEVEL ASSESSMENT OF THIRD GRADERS

Case 11

This child has received speech and language services and reading tutoring. The child repeated kindergarten because of "immaturity" (not delays in academic skills). Prior language evaluation documented average phonological, semantic, and speaking skills (at or near the mean), but impaired listening and syntax (outside the normal range; more than 2 standard deviations below the mean). Cognitive testing revealed unevenness, ranging from superior processing speed to average verbal reasoning (upper end of average range) to average perceptual organization and freedom from distractibility (lower end of average range). Reading comprehension and spelling were significantly below the child's verbal reasoning, word reading, and phonological decoding skills. Math operations were unexpectedly low for the child's verbal and nonverbal reasoning and word reading and phonological decoding skills. Math reasoning and reading comprehension were developed to comparable levels. Written expression was a relative strength. Taken together, results of the prior language assessment and the relative weakness in reading comprehension suggest that this child may have language learning disability (see chapter by Berninger & O'Donnell, this volume). If so, psychologists should help educators understand that language learning disability is best treated through direct language intervention services rather than repeating a grade such as kindergarten. PAL Lesson Set 6 was recommended to provide explicit reading comprehension instruction for words, sentences, and text. Math tutoring was also implemented.

Case 12

This child was referred for slow reading rate, limited written output, poor spelling, and awkward written sentence syntax. Cognitive testing revealed very superior verbal reasoning, high average nonverbal reasoning, and average processing speed. Reading, written expression, and math operations were above the population mean. Math reasoning was very superior, consistent with verbal reasoning as well as nonverbal reasoning. Only spelling, the most unexpectedly low skill, fell below the population mean. PAL processing assessment identified weaknesses in receptive coding, word choice, and silent reading comprehension fluency (which may explain why reading comprehension was lower than verbal reasoning). PAL Lesson Sets 5, 7, and 8 were recommended for development of spelling skills and their transfer to composition.

Case 13

This child was referred for slow oral reading rate (based on CBM measures), spelling problems, and reversals (b's and d's). His speech was delayed at 18 months and he has received speech services for many years and more recently occupational therapy services for dyspraxia (problems in planning, organizing, and executing motor responses). The family has a history of dyslexia on both sides. Cognitive testing revealed superior verbal reasoning and freedom from distractibility, above average perceptual organization, and average processing speed. His word reading, phonological decoding, spelling, and written expression were unexpectedly low for his verbal reasoning; but reading comprehension, math operations, and math reasoning were relative strengths. PAL process assessment identified weakness in receptive (orthographic) coding and deficits in word choice, RAN words, RAS, finger repetition, and sentence sense. Graphomotor planning (PAL finger succession) was a strength, possibly because of the recent occupational therapy for dyspraxia. Oral-motor dysgraphia, which might explain the slow oral reading, was not assessed but will be assessed in follow-up testing. The child met research criteria for dyslexia (see Berninger, 2001a, and chapter by Berninger & O'Donnell, this volume). PAL Lesson Sets 11 and 15 were recommended for treating the reading problems. PAL Lesson Sets 5, 7, 8, and 10 were recommended for treating the spelling and written composition problems.

Case 14

This child was referred for problems in processing information orally and in writing. Teachers reported that reading comprehension was poor, written composition was disconnected, and the child had a low tolerance for frustration. Cognitive abilities were consistently in the average range, with processing speed being the relative strength. Although achievement was lowest in math operations, achievement was not unexpectedly low on any of the achievement measures. PAL process assessment identified a strength in silent reading comprehension fluency (sentence sense). Other assessment instruments identified weaknesses in attention and concentration and possible depression. Additional assessment was scheduled to evaluate these possibilities further. Although there was no evidence of a specific learning disability, there might be social emotional issues related to school learning that are affecting school performance in a school setting with very high academic expectations.

Case 15

This child was referred to evaluate whether a specific learning disability explained the struggle with the general education curriculum. Cognitive testing revealed strengths in verbal reasoning and processing speed (above average range) and average perceptual organization and freedom from distractibility. Academic achievement was generally age appropriate; only spelling and reading comprehension fell slightly below the population mean. PAL process measures were not given, but CTOPP scaled scores all fell above the mean. However, other assessment instruments identified at-risk factors in attention and concentration and in anxiety, social stress, attitude toward school, school maladjustment, atypicality, clinical maladjustment, sense of inadequacy, and emotional problems. The role of social emotional variables in this child's school performance was further investigated through counseling sessions.

BENEFITS AND CHALLENGES
OF PROFILE ASSESSMENT

For tier-two assessment, comprehensive assessment based on cognitive, academic, and language/neuropsychological processes yields a profile of strengths and weaknesses that is relevant to educational planning in the current school year. Sometimes, for example in Case 6, the profile will yield a pattern of test findings consistent with the diagnosis of a specific learning disability. Whether the psychologist should use this information only in planning a tier-two modification of the general education program or should also discuss with parents the possibility of a tier-three diagnosis of a specific learning disability (see chapter by Berninger & O'Donnell, this volume) is a challenging issue. Some parents, especially if there is a family history for learning disability, welcome the diagnosis. Others prefer to forgo the label that they believe may stigmatize their child. Sometimes they change their mind later in their child's schooling as the curriculum requirements change and the underlying disability expresses itself in other ways. They come to realize that the label gets their child not only specialized instruction but also accommodations. In our experience, these issues have to be dealt with one case at a time and with great diplomacy and sensitivity.

Finally, not all referrals for learning disabilities assessment turn out to be learning disabilities. There are other reasons for children's struggles with school learning and behavioral regulation. Multilevel assessment should include tools for assessing attention, behavioral regulation, and social/emotion functioning as well as cognition, achievement, and related language and neuropsychological processes.

The PAL Lesson Plans (Berninger & Abbott, 2003) provide guidelines for choosing Lesson Sets based on results of process assessment and typical developmental sequence of reading and writing skills. In addition to instructional variables for specific reading and writing skills, interpersonal relationship variables need to be taken into account in educational intervention (Lerner, 2002). Self-esteem and motivation are developed through creating rapport, shared responsibility, structure, sincerity, success, and interest (Lerner, 2002).

CONCLUSIONS

In this chapter, we highlighted three kinds of assessment that can be applied by psychologists in assessing school-age children and recommend that psychologists use each of these as appropriate to the purpose of assessment: *Branching assessment* (time-efficient assessment linked to reason for referral and outcome of the assessment specific to that referring problem), *instructional assessment* (response to instructional intervention), and *profile assessment* (multilevel profiles of cognitive, academic, and language or neuropsychological processing strengths and weaknesses). While knowledge of the psychometric properties of test instruments is necessary, it is no longer sufficient. Psychologists also need to know *how to use those instruments in practice to perform a variety of assessment functions and link assessment more closely with prevention, educational treatments, and student progress monitoring.* The WISC-IV contributes to these changes in diagnostic practices by reducing the exclusive emphasis on the Full Scale IQ and by providing four cognitive indexes based on research. For the kinds of diagnoses discussed in this chapter and the related chapter (Berninger & O'Donnell), it is not always necessary to give all the subtests on the WISC-IV. Only those needed for the cognitive index most relevant to the reason for referral or response to supplementary instruction or general education curriculum may be necessary.

ACKNOWLEDGMENTS

Grants HD 25858-14 and P50 33812-09 from the National Institute of Child Health and Human Development (NICHD) supported the preparation of this chapter and some of the research that is discussed.

The authors thank the school psychologists in Los Angeles School District for the opportunity to tell their story about Tier-One Assessment-Intervention (Debby Barth Carrera, Rosalie Bell, Ph.D., Debbie Bloom, Patricia Burrows, Ruben Carranza, June Durr, Christina Harrell, Erin Holman, Chris Mealy-Ures, Nicole Mock, AnneMarie Serrano, Christine Toleson, Tiana Thorpe, Reymundo Verastigui, and Didi Watts) and the teachers at the participating schools (24th St. School, 96th St. School, 116th St. School, Fernangeles, Fletcher Dr., Hoover St., Hyde Park Blvd., Kittridge St., Los Angeles Elementary School, Murchison St., Pio Pico, Russell, Sierra Park, Westminster Ave., and Woodcrest). They also thank the teachers at the American School in London who referred students for Tier-Two Assessment. They acknowledge the contribution of Donna Smith, whose vision of multilevel assessment contributed to the model discussed in this chapter, and of Stephen Peverley, who introduced the concept of instructionally based assessment (IBA) used in this chapter.

REFERENCES

Abbott, R., & Berninger, V. (1993). Structural equation modeling of relationships among developmental skills and writing skills in primary and intermediate grade writers. *Journal of Educational Psychology, 85*(3), 478–508.

Berninger, V. (1998a). *Process assessment of the learner (PAL). Guides for intervention in reading and writing.* San Antonio, TX: The Psychological Corporation.

Berninger, V. (1998b). Assessment, prevention, and intervention for specific reading and writing disabilities in young children. In B. Wong (Ed.), *Learning disabilities* (2nd ed.) (pp. 529–555). New York: Academic Press.

Berninger, V. (2001a). Understanding the lexia in dyslexia. *Annals of Dyslexia, 51,* 23–48.

Berninger, V. (2001b). *Process assessment of the learner: Test battery for reading and writing.* San Antonio, TX: Psychological Corporation.

Berninger, V. (2004). Brain-based assessment and instructional intervention. In G. Reid and A. Fawcett (Eds.), *Dyslexia in context. Research, policy, and practice.* London and Philadelphia: Whur Publishers.

Berninger, V. (in press-a). Understanding the graphia in dysgraphia. In D. Dewey & D. Tupper (Eds.), *Developmental motor disorders: A neuropsychological perspective.* New York: Guilford.

Berninger, V. (in press-b). The reading brain in children and youth: A systems approach. To appear in B. Wong (Ed.), *Learning about Learning Disabilities* (ed. 3). San Diego: Academic Press (Elsevier Imprint).

Berninger, V., Abbott, R., & Alsdorf, B. (1997). Lexical- and sentence-level processes in comprehension of written sentences. *Reading and Writing: An Interdisciplinary Journal, 9,* 135–162.

Berninger, V., Abbott, R., Thomson, J., & Raskind, W. (2001). Language phenotype for reading and writing disability: A family approach. *Scientific Studies in Reading, 5,* 59–105.

Berninger, V., Abbott, R., Vermeulen, K., Ogier, S., Brooksher, R., Zook, D., & Lemos, Z. (2002). Comparison of faster and slower responders: Implications for the nature and duration of early reading intervention. *Learning Disability Quarterly, 25,* 59–76.

Berninger, V., & Abbott, S. (2003). *PAL Research-supported reading and writing lessons.* San Antonio, TX: The Psychological Corporation.

Berninger, V., & Amtmann, D. (2003). Preventing written expression disabilities through early and continuing assessment and intervention for handwriting and/or spelling problems: Research into practice. In H. L. Swanson, K. Harris, and S. Graham (Eds.), *Handbook of research on learning disabilities* (pp. 345–363). New York: Guilford.

Berninger, V., Cartwright, A., Yates, C., Swanson, H. L., & Abbott, R. (1994). Developmental skills related to writing and reading acquisition in the intermediate grades: Shared and unique variance. *Reading and Writing: An Interdisciplinary Journal, 6,* 161–196.

Berninger, V., Dunn, A., Lin, S., & Shimada, S. (in press). School evolution. Scientist-practitioner educators (SPEDs) creating optimal learning environments for ALL students. *Journal of Learning Disabilities.*

Berninger, V., & Fuller, F. (1992). Gender differences in orthographic, verbal, and compositional fluency: Implications for diagnosis of writing disabilities in primary grade children. *Journal of School Psychology, 30,* 363–382.

Berninger, V., Hart, T., Abbott, R., & Karovsky, P. (1992). Defining reading and writing disabilities with and without IQ: A flexible, developmental perspective. *Learning Disability Quarterly, 15,* 103–118.

Berninger, V., & O'Donnell, L. (2004). Research-supported differential diagnosis of specific learning disabilities. In A. Prifitera, D. Saklofske, L. Weiss, & E. Rolfhus (Eds.), *WISC-IV Clinical use and interpretation.* San Diego, CA: Academic Press.

Berninger, V., & Richards, T. (2002). *Brain literacy for educators and psychologists.* San Diego: Academic Press (Elsevier Imprint).

Berninger, V., & Rutberg, J. (1992). Relationship of finger function to beginning writing: Application to diagnosis of writing disabilities. *Developmental Medicine & Child Neurology, 34,* 155–172.

Berninger, V., Smith, D. , & O'Donnell, L. (2004, February). Research-supported assessment-intervention links and reading and writing intervention. *Communiqué.*

Berninger, V., Stage, S., Smith, D., & Hildebrand, D. (2001). Assessment for reading and writing intervention: A 3-tier model for prevention and intervention. In J. Andrews, H., D. Saklofske, & H. Janzen (Eds.). *Ability, achievement, and behavior assessment. A practical handbook* (pp. 195–223). New York: Academic Press.

Berninger, V., Vaughan, K., Abbott, R., Brooks, A., Begay, K., Curtin, G., Byrd, K., & Graham, S. (2000). Language-based spelling instruction: Teaching children to make multiple connections between spoken and written words. *Learning Disability Quarterly, 23,* 117–135.

Berninger, V., Vermeulen, K., Abbott, R., McCutchen, D., Cotton, S., Cude, J., Dorn, S., & Sharon, T. (2003). Comparison of three approaches to supplementary reading instruction for low achieving second grade readers. *Language, Speech, and Hearing Services in Schools, 34,* 101–115.

Berninger, V., & Whitaker, D. (1993). Theory-based, branching diagnosis of writing disabilities. *School Psychology Review, 22,* 623–642.

Berninger, V., Yates, C., Cartwright, A., Rutberg, J., Remy, E., & Abbott, R. (1992). Lower-level developmental skills in beginning writing. *Reading and Writing. An Interdisciplinary Journal, 4,* 257–280.

Berninger, V., Yates, C., & Lester, K. (1991). Multiple orthographic codes in acquisition of reading and writing skills. *Reading and Writing. An Interdisciplinary Journal, 3,* 115–149.

Bradley, R., Danielson, L., & Hallahan, D. (Eds.). (2002). *Identification of learning disabilities: Research to practice.* Mahweh, NJ: Lawrence Erlbaum.

Denton, C., & Mathes, P. (2003). In B. Foorman (Ed.), Interventions for struggling readers: Possibilities and challenges. *Preventing and remediating reading difficulties. Bringing science to scale* (pp. 229–251). Baltimore: York Press.

Dunn, A. (2002, Fall). Partnership and problem solving to promote early intervention in literacy: Using the PAL. *CASP Today.*

Dunn, A. (2004) Los Angeles Unified School District (LAUSD) School Psychology Project Bridging Special and General Education. *CASP Today, Spring.*

Fletcher, J., Francis, D., Morris, R., Lyon, G. R. (Ed.) (in press). Evidence-based assessment of learning disabilities in children and adolescents. *Journal of Clinical Child and Adolescent Psychology.*

Graham, S., Berninger, V., Abbott, R., Abbott, S., & Whitaker, D. (1997). The role of mechanics in composing of elementary school students: A new methodological approach. *Journal of Educational Psychology, 89(1),* 170–182.

Lerner, J. (2002). *Learning disabilities* (9th ed.), (pp. 127–131). Boston: Houghton Mifflin.

Lyon, G. R., Fletcher, J., Shaywitz, S., Shaywitz, B., Torgesen, J., Wood, F., Schulte, A., & Olson, R. (2001). Rethinking learning disabilities. In C. Finn, A. Rotherham, & C. Hokanson (Eds.), *Rethinking special education for a new century* (pp. 259–287). Washington, DC: The Fordham Foundation.

Nagy, W., Berninger, V., Abbott, R., Vaughan, K., & Vermeulin, K. (2003). Relationship of morphology and other language skills to literacy skills in at-risk second graders and at-risk fourth grade writers. *Journal of Educational Psychology, 95,* 730–742.

Olson, R., Datta, H., Gayan, J., & DeFries, J. (1999). A behavioral-genetic analysis of reading disabilities and component processes. In R. Klein & P. McMullen (Eds.), *Converging methods for understanding reading and dyslexia* (pp. 133–151). Cambridge, MA: MIT Press.

Peverley, S. (2004, August). *Teachers knowledge and student Achievement: Implications for curriculum based* assessment. In Symposium organized by Stephen Peverley, "Evolution of curriculum-based measurement (CBM) to instruction-based assessment (IBA): Rethinking identification and prevention of learning disability." American Psychological Association, Hawaii.

Prifitera, A., Weiss, L., & Saklofske, D. (1998). The WISC III in context. In A. Prifitera, L. Weiss, & D. Saklofske (Eds.), *WISC-III clinical use and interpretation: Scientist-practitioner perspectives* (pp. 1–38). San Diego: Academic Press.

Semel, E., Wiig, E.H., & Secord, W. A. (1995). *Clinical evaluation of language fundamentals* (3rd ed.). San Antonio, TX: The Psychological Corporation.

The Psychological Corporation. (2001). *Wechsler Individual Achievement Test* (2nd ed.). *WIAT II*. San Antonio, TX: The Psychological Corporation.

The Psychological Corporation. (2003). *Wechsler Individual Intelligence Test for Children* (4th ed.). San Antonio, TX: The Psychological Corporation.

Quiroga, T., Lemos-Britton, Z., Mostafapour, E., Abbott, R., & Berninger, V. (2002). Phonological awareness and beginning reading in Spanish-speaking, ESL first graders: Research into practice. *Journal of School Psychology, 40*, 85–111.

Shurtleff, H., Abbott, R., Berninger, V., & Townes, B. (1993). Luria's neurodevelopmental stages in relationship to intelligence and academic achievement in kindergarten and first grade. *Developmental Neuropsychology, 9*, 55–75.

Stage, S., Abbott, R., Jenkins, J., & Berninger, V. (2003). Predicting response to early reading intervention using Verbal IQ, reading-related language abilities, attention ratings, and Verbal IQ-word reading discrepancy. *Journal of Learning Disabilities, 36*, 24–33.

Steubing, K, Fletcher, J., LaDoux, J., Lyon, G.R., *et al.* (2002). Validity of IQ-achievement discrepancy classifications of reading disabilities: A meta-analysis. *American Educational Research Journal, 39*, 469–518.

Torgesen, J. (1979). What shall we do with psychological processes? *Journal of Learning Disabilities, 12(8)*, 16–23.

Torgesen, J. (2002). Empirical and theoretical support for direct diagnosis of learning disabilities by assessment of intrinsic processing weaknesses. In R. Bradley, L. Danielson, & D. Hallahan (Eds.), *Identification of learning disabilities. Research to practice* (pp. 565–613). Mahweh, NJ: Lawrence Erlbaum.

Torgesen, J., Wagner, R., & Rashotte, C. (1999). *Test of word reading efficiency (TOWRE)*. Austin, TX: PRO-ED.

Torgesen, J., Wagner, R., Rashotte, C., Rose, E., Lindamood, P., Conway, T., & Garwan, C. (1999). Preventing reading failure in young children with phonological processing disabilities: Group and individual responses to instruction. *Journal of Educational Psychology, 91*, 579–593.

Vellutino, F., Fletcher, J., Snowling, M., & Scanlon, D. (2004). Specific reading disability (dyslexia): What we have learned in the past four decades. *Journal of Child Psychology and Psychiatry, 45*, 2–40.

Vellutino, F., Scanlon, D., & Lyon, G. R. (2000). Differentiating between difficult-to-remediate and readily remediated poor readers: More evidence against IQ-achievement discrepancy definitions of reading disability. *Journal of Learning Disabilities, 33*, 223–238.

Wagner, R., Torgesen, J., & Rashotte, C. (1999). *Comprehensive Test of Phonological Processing (CTOPP)*. Austin, TX: PRO-ED.

Wechsler, D. (1991). *Wechsler Intelligence Scale for Children* (3rd ed.). San Antonio, TX: The Psychological Corporation.

Wiederholt, J., & Bryant, B. (1992). *Gray Oral Reading Test* (3rd ed.). Odessa, FL: Psychological Assessment Resources.

Woodcock, R., McGrew, K., & Mather, N. (2001). *Woodcock-Johnson III*. Itasca, IL: Riverside.

PART II

THE WISC-IV AND THE ASSESSMENT OF EXCEPTIONAL CHILDREN

6

RESEARCH-SUPPORTED DIFFERENTIAL DIAGNOSIS OF SPECIFIC LEARNING DISABILITIES

VIRGINIA W. BERNINGER

University of Washington
Seattle, Washington

LOUISE O'DONNELL

Harcourt assessment, Inc.
San autonio, Teyas

BACKGROUND

When, more than 25 years ago, federal legislation in the United States first mandated that children with learning disabilities receive a free, appropriate education, the government relied on current clinical practices, rather than research, to define learning disabilities. Because many children were known to be underachieving in reading relative to their IQ, the federal government adopted an ability–achievement discrepancy definition to identify children for special education services under the category of specific learning disabilities. However, not all states calculate ability–achievement discrepancy in the same way, and there is no consensus on how large the discrepancy should be or the best psychometric approach to use in calculating it (e.g., simple standard score difference or regression-based discrepancy measure) (Prifitera & Saklofske, 1998). The most curious shortcoming of the current federal definition in the United States for learning disability is that it is based on *exclusionary criteria*—what a learning disability is not—rather than on *inclusionary criteria*—what specific kinds of learning disabilities are. Although school practitioners, clinicians, and researchers are aware that learning disability is not a single, homogeneous learning disorder, current practices for identifying children for services under the category of learning disability do not specify inclusionary criteria for defining specific kinds of learning disabilities.

Limitations of the ability–achievement discrepancy approach are discussed in this volume (see chapter by Berninger, Dunn, & Alper). The three-tier assessment model provides an alternative for overcoming those limitations (Berninger, Stage, Smith, & Hildebrand, 2001): tier one screens for early intervention to prevent academic failure; tier two monitors progress and, if necessary, modifies curriculum; tier three diagnoses and treats chronic learning disabilities. The chapter by Berninger, Dunn, and Alpert focuses on tiers one and two, while this chapter focuses on tier three and examines differential diagnosis of specific learning disabilities.

One approach to address the limitation of ability–achievement discrepancy in qualifying children for individualized education is to reject IQ totally in assessment of specific learning disabilities. Another approach, which the University of Washington (UW) research program has adopted, is to question rigid use of ability–achievement discrepancy as the only approach to qualifying students for academic intervention (Berninger, Hart, Abbott, & Karovsky, 1992) and to include measurement of intellectual and other neurocognitive functions as integral components of assessment and intervention research. At tiers one and two, the UW research program uses cut-offs (e.g., a single subtest measuring ability to define words orally) to identify samples of children with at least low average intelligence (typically an estimated standard score of 80 and above). With this approach, results should generalize to the school-age population that is expected to achieve within the normal range in verbally oriented academic subjects.

At tier three, the UW research program on dyslexia uses an IQ factor that indexes verbal reasoning ability but also includes measures of other cognitive, language, and neuropsychological processes that research shows are related to learning to read, write, and think quantitatively. The UW research program does not use the Full Scale IQ for reasons discussed by Prifitera, Weiss, and Saklofske (1998). One of the compelling points made by Prifitera *et al.* is that the Full Scale IQ is based on intellectual abilities that are both spared and affected in children with specific learning disabilities and therefore is not a good single index against which expected level of academic achievement is compared. Because research available at the time the UW research on dyslexia commenced showed that Verbal IQ is the best predictor of reading achievement in referred (Greenblatt, Mattis, & Brad, 1990) and unreferred populations (Vellutino, Scanlon, & Tanzman, 1991), we used a prorated Verbal IQ based on the same subtests as the WISC-III Verbal Comprehension Index (information, similarities, vocabulary, and comprehension). Arithmetic was not used because it loads on the Freedom from Distractibility Factor on which many individuals with learning disabilities score very low because it taps processes related to their learning problems (Prifitera *et al.*, 1998).

OVERVIEW OF THE CHAPTER

First we provide a definition of dyslexia, followed by UW research findings relevant to operationalizing the diagnosis of dyslexia in children and affected adults using reliable and valid assessment instruments. We include both adults and children for two reasons. First, increasingly students are being assessed and reassessed for learning disabilities throughout schooling (K to graduate school) in order to qualify for special instructional services or accommodation. Second, the phenotype for dyslexia (behavioral expression) has some components that stay the same and other components that change over the course of development.

We discuss research-generated *inclusionary criteria* for defining dyslexia in children and adults. Key elements of the *inclusionary criteria include* (1) unexpectedly low achievement in specific reading and writing skills and (2) associated hallmark processing deficits. We discuss the differential diagnosis of dyslexia and language learning disability, with case studies to illustrate this distinction, because not all reading problems are dyslexia. We also discuss specific learning disabilities affecting writing or math because not all learning disabilities affect reading. Writing disabilities, in particular, are underdiagnosed and undertreated and may be an unrecognized contributor to academic failure and school drop-out rates.

For all these diagnoses of specific learning disabilities, we consider (1) how the WISC-IV can inform that differential diagnosis, and (2) how standardized measures of language and neuropsychological processes can be integrated with WISC-IV measures in the differential diagnosis of specific learning disabilities. The UW research program has used the *Wechsler Intelligence Scale for Children*, Third Edition (WISC-III) (Wechsler, 1991) in its research, which began before the recent WISC-IV (The Psychological Corporation, 2003) was available. Although the research-supported findings are based on WISC-III, we propose how the findings might be applied to practice using WISC-IV. For each of the specific learning disabilities discussed, we offer a summary of recommended diagnostic procedures, with special emphasis on how the WISC-IV could be used, along with other measures. We also propose how the WISC-IV might be used in future research, especially on reading, writing, and arithmetic fluency—a topic of cutting-edge research.

DYSLEXIA

DEFINITION OF DYSLEXIA

The International Dyslexia Association (IDA) defines dyslexia as a specific learning disability characterized by unexpected difficulty in accuracy and rate of decoding, word reading, and text reading and spelling (Lyon, Shaywitz, & Shaywitz, 2003). Dyslexia, which is conceptualized as only one of the many kinds of learning disabilities that may exist, is neurobiological in origin and is unexpected on the basis of other cognitive skills and instructional history. These unexpected difficulties are attributed to a phonological core deficit.

Inclusionary and exclusionary criteria in UW studies. The definition of dyslexia used in the University of Washington Family Genetics study for research purposes is essentially the same. For a child in grades 1 to 9 to qualify as a study participant and therefore qualify their nuclear and extended family members for participation, the child must meet these *inclusion criteria*: (1) unexpected difficulty in accuracy or rate of decoding, word reading, text reading, or spelling relative to prorated Verbal IQ[*] (at least one standard deviation below verbal reasoning based on the same subtests as the WISC-III Verbal Comprehension Factor) and age peers (below the population mean); and (2) prorated Verbal IQ[*] that is at or above the 25th percentile (a standard score of 90). This cut-off criterion was set because the prevalence of neurogenetic and other developmental disorders is higher, and the etiologies of reading problems may be more diverse in children whose verbal intelligence falls in the lowest quartile. Exclusionary criteria prevent confusion of dyslexia with reading problems having other biological causes. The exclusionary criteria employed in the UW studies include evidence of sensory deficit (auditory or visual), mental retardation, pervasive developmental disorder, autism, primary language disorder (specific language impairment or developmental aphasia), primary psychiatric disorder (severe social, emotional, or behavioral disturbance), brain trauma, injury, or disease, severe prematurity, or substance abuse (of mother during pregnancy or proband). Children are not excluded for attentional deficit disorder, but rarely meet the DSM-IV (American Psychiatric Association, 1994) diagnostic criteria for this disorder or conduct disorder. Thus, the reading and writing problems discussed in the research studies that follow are specific to children with cognitive, language, motor, social-emotional, and attention/executive function development falling generally within the normal range despite possible selective impairment in specific skills within those developmental domains (Berninger, 2001a). Often parents were first aware of a problem during kindergarten and first grade when their children had unusual difficulty learning to name letters and associate sounds with letters.

[*]Based on the WISC-III (Wechsler, 1991) information, similarities, vocabulary, and comprehension subtests (comparable to the Verbal Comprehension factor) in children and on five WAIS-R (Wechsler, 1981) subtests (same four as for children plus digit span per the WAIS-R test manual) in adults.

RESULTS OF THE UW PHENOTYPING STUDIES

Two phenotyping studies cross-validated the definition of dyslexia based on inclusion criteria described in the previous section. Phenotypes are the behavioral expression of underlying genotypes (inherited individual differences in DNA). Phenotypes are not related to genotypes in a simple one-to-one fashion because of differences in environmental experiences. The first study included 102 child probands and 122 affected parents (Berninger, Abbott, Thomson, & Raskind, 2001). The second phenotyping study included a new sample of 122 child probands and 200 affected parents (Berninger, Abbott, Thomson, Wagner, Swanson, & Raskind, submitted). In both samples the mean prorated Verbal IQ of the children and the adults fell at the upper limits of the average range (M = 109 in children and adults, Study 1) or border between the average and high average range (M = 110 in children and adults, Study 2).

In keeping with prior research (e.g., Bruck, 1990; Pennington, Van Orden, Smith, Green, & Haith, 1990; Scarborough, 1984; Shaywitz *et al.*, 2003) not all adults with dyslexia are fully compensated and indicators of dyslexia can still be identified through formal assessment. Many of the parents of probands (and other adult extended family members) met the same inclusion criteria as the children on specific reading or writing skills. Although children had to meet inclusion criteria on only one reading or writing skill to qualify for participation, most children in both studies were impaired in most reading and most writing skills assessed, despite special help for their reading problems in school and/or outside school. However, their parents tended to meet these inclusion criteria on fewer skills (on average one to two reading and one to two writing skills).

Although a discrepancy of only one standard deviation between verbal reasoning ability and achievement of age-peers was required, the child probands showed, on average, much larger discrepancies. In the first sample, child probands had decoding, word reading, and spelling skills that fell, on average, $1\frac{1}{3}$ standard deviations below the population mean and 2 standard deviations below their verbal reasoning abilities as measured by the WISC-III. In the second sample, child probands had decoding, word reading, and spelling skills that fell, on average, 1 standard deviation below the mean and $1\frac{1}{3}$ standard deviations below their verbal reasoning abilities.

To provide research evidence for an inclusionary definition of dyslexia in both phenotyping studies, the UW research team administered a large battery of measures, all of which had received some research support in the research literature, to the child probands and their family members. The second study included additional measures not available when the first study was begun. Table 6.1 summarizes most of the test battery given in the second study. Test measures are grouped according to the 11 construct areas assessed with multiple measures within each construct area.

TABLE 6.1   Test Battery Given to Child and Adult Dyslexics in UW Family Genetics Study[a]

Construct Assessed	Measure
Verbal Reasoning	• *Prorated Verbal IQ (WISC-III or WAIS-R)*. Long-term memory information retrieval; concept formation; vocabulary knowledge; practical understanding of the world
Reading	• *WRMT-R Word Identification*. Accuracy of word-specific mechanism (reading single words)
	• *WRMT-R Word Attack*. Accuracy of phonological decoding mechanism (reading single pseudowords)
	• *TOWRE Sight Word Efficiency*. Rate of word-specific mechanism (timed-reading of single real words)
	• *TOWRE Phonemic Decoding Efficiency*. Rate of phonological decoding (timed-reading of single pseudowords)
	• *GORT-3 Accuracy*. Accuracy of oral reading of connected text
	• *GORT-3 Rate*. Rate of oral reading of connected text
	• *GORT-3 Comprehension*. Oral reading comprehension
	• *WJ-R Passage Comprehension*. Cloze procedure for silent reading comprehension
Writing	• *PAL Alphabet Writing Task*. Automaticity (legibility in first 15 seconds)
	• *WRAT3 Spelling*. Spelling single words from dictation in writing
	• *WIAT-II Spelling*. Spelling single words from dictation in writing
	• *WIAT-II Written Expression*. Word fluency, sentence tasks, and paragraph composition
Phonology	• *CTOPP Elision*. Analyzing sound segments in phonological word form
	• *CTOPP Nonword Repetition*. Analyzing and reproducing sounds in phonological word form stored in phonological short-term/working memory (repetition of pseudowords)
	• *CTOPP Phoneme Reversal*. Analyzing sound segments in phonological word form in short-term/working memory
Orthography	• *PAL Receptive Coding*. Orthographic coding (short-term/working memory) without orthographic output
	• *PAL Expressive Coding*. Orthographic coding (short-term/working memory) with orthographic output
	• *PAL Word Choice*. Orthographic representations of word-specific spellings (long-term memory)
Syntactic	• *CELF-3 Formulated Sentences*. Plan and produce syntactic constructions
	• *SBIV Sentence Memory*. Analyze sentence syntax in short-term/working memory and reproduce sentence
Rapid Automatic Naming	• *Wolf RAN—Colors*. Rapid automatized naming of constant category
	• *Wolf RAN—Numerals*. Rapid automatized naming of constant category
	• *Wolf RAN—Letters*. Rapid automatized naming of constant category
Rapid Automatic Switching	• *Wolf RAS—Letters and Numerals*. Rapid automatized naming of switching categories
	• *Wolf RAS—Colors, Letters, and Numerals*. Rapid automatized naming of switching categories

(Continues)

TABLE 6.1   (*Continued*)

Construct Assessed	Measure
Fine Motor	• *PAL Finger Succession—Dominant Hand Nondominant Hand.* Graphomotor planning
	• *PaTaKa.* Oral-motor planning
Working Memory	• *WJ-R Numbers Reversed.* Phonological working memory
Executive Function	• *D-KEFS Verbal Fluency Letters.* Executive function that works with the phonological loop to find and create phonological word forms in long-term memory
	• *D-KEFS Color-Word Inhibition.* Executive function for suppressing irrelevant information—category constant
	• *D-KEFS Color-Word Inhibition/Switching.* Executive function for suppressing irrelevant information—category varies

[a]The complete battery contains additional measures. Some of these measures in Table 6.1 were not given when the family genetics project begin in 1995 and are only available since 2000.

Verbal Reasoning:
WISC-III = *Wechsler Intelligence Scale for Children, Third Edition* (Wechsler, 1991); WAIS-R = *Wechsler Adult Intelligence Scale Revised* (Wechsler, 1981);

Reading:
WRMT-R = *Woodcock Reading Mastery Test–Revised* (Woodcock, 1987); TOWRE = *Test of Word Reading Efficiency* (Torgesen, Wagner, & Rashotte, 1999); GORT-3 = *Gray Oral Reading Tests–Third Edition* (Wiederholt & Bryant, 1992); WJ-R = *Woodcock-Johnson Psycho-Educational Battery–Revised* (Woodcock & Johnson, 1990);

Writing:
PAL = *Process Assessment of the Learner Test Battery for Reading and Writing* (Berninger, 2001b) Alphabet Writing Task based on *UW Alphabetic Writing Task* (Berninger & Rutberg, 1992; WRAT-3 = *Wide Range Achievement Tests–Third Edition* (Wilkinson}, 1993); WIAT-II = *Wechsler Individual Achievement Test–Second Edition* (The Psychological Corporation 2001);

Phonology:
CTOPP = *Comprehensive Test of Phonological Processing* (Wagner, Torgesen, & Rashotte, 1999);

Orthography:
PAL = *Process Assessment of the Learner Test Battery for Reading and Writing* (Berninger, 2001b);

Syntactic:
CELF-3 = *Clinical Evaluation of Language Fundamentals-Third Edition* (Semel, Secord, & Wiig, 1995); SB-IV = *Stanford-Binet Intelligence Scale-Fourth Edition* (Thorndike, Hagen, & Sattler, 1986);

Rapid Automatic Naming:
WOLF RAN = *rapid automatic naming* (Wolf, Bally, & Morris, 1986; Wolf & Biddle, 1994;

Rapid Automatic Switching
RAS = *rapid automatic switching* (Wolf, 1986; Wolf & Biddle, 1994); also see Wolf & Denckla (2004);

Fine Motor:
PAL = *Process Assessment of the Learner Test Battery for Reading and Writing* (Berninger, 2001b; PATAKA = *Time-by-Count Test Measurement of Diadochokinetic Syllable Rate.* (Fletcher, 1978);.

Working Memory:
WJ-R = *Woodcock-Johnson Psycho-Educational Battery–Revised* (Woodcock & Johnson, 1990);

Executive Function:
D-KEFS = *Delis-Kaplan Executive Function System* (Delis, Kaplan, & Kramer, 2003).

The UW research team conducted confirmatory factor analyses to evaluate the measurement model based on latent traits underlying multiple indicators or measures of the same process. Then, the UW team conducted structural equation modeling to evaluate the structural relationships among predictor factors and reading and writing achievement outcomes. Then they documented different patterns of structural relationships from predictor process measures to reading and writing achievement outcomes for each of the reading and spelling skills in the definition based on inclusionary criteria (Berninger et al., 2001; and Berninger et al., submitted).

In the first study (Berninger et al., 2001), performance patterns were examined to determine if the sample evidenced the well-documented phonological core deficit (e.g., Morris et al., 1998; Olson, Forsberg, Wise, & Rack, 1994; Stanovich & Siegel, 1994; Wagner & Torgesen, 1987) and associated orthographic coding (Abbott & Berninger, 1993; Olson et al., 1994) and rapid naming (Wolf, Bally, & Morris, 1986; Wolf & Bowers, 1999) deficits. The more deficits children had in phonological, orthographic, or rapid automatic naming processes, the more impaired their reading and spelling achievement. The dyslexic children showed significant impairment in all reading skills involving word reading, phonological decoding, and oral text reading and in all their writing skills (handwriting, spelling, and written composition). Degree of impairment in reading comprehension depended on how impaired individuals were in word reading, decoding, and oral text reading; in general, comprehension was not as impaired as these other reading skills in either the children or adults in the family study. Many child dyslexics had relative strengths in math problem solving (providing additional evidence that the reading problem was specific and unexpected). However, some of the children had problems in paper and pencil arithmetic computations, indicating that they had both specific reading and specific arithmetic disabilities (but not necessarily disability in math concepts or math reasoning, see Busse, Berninger, Smith, & Hildebrand, 2001).

In the second study (Berninger et al., submitted), the finding of severe impairment in writing, as well as reading skills, replicated. As in many other studies (e.g., Shaywitz, Shaywitz, Fletcher, & Escobar, 1990) gender differences were not found in the reading of the child probands, but gender differences were found in the writing of child and adult probands; these gender differences, in which boys were more impaired, should be interpreted cautiously because they are also found in normally developing writers in unreferred samples (Berninger & Fuller, 1992). However, this finding does suggest that writing development should be carefully monitored in male dyslexics, and they may require more intensive writing treatment than female dyslexics. In addition, when the phenotyping battery had been expanded to include measures of oral language and executive functions, mild weaknesses in oral language and specific impairments in executive functions were also identified in the child dyslexics. On average, phonological, morphological, and syntactic abilities fell within the lower limits of the normal range but were discrepant from the children's verbal reasoning skills. Sentence formulation skills fell at the population average but were also discrepant from children's higher verbal reasoning skills.

Sometimes the same process(es) uniquely predicted a given reading or writing outcome in both child and adult dyslexics, but other times the unique predictors involved different processes (Table 6.2). The most significant impairments in both child and adult dyslexics, whether absolute criteria (low scores) or relative criteria (scores below the population mean that were also discrepant from Verbal IQ) were used, occurred in the following processes: precise storage and reproduction of novel phonological word forms; rate or efficiency of phonological decoding; rapid automatic naming of letters; rapid automatic writing of letters; rapid automatic attention switching (shifting mental sets); and inhibition (suppressing irrelevant information and focusing on relevant information on language tasks) (Berninger et al., submitted). *These are the hallmark processing deficits that, along with unexpectedly low reading and spelling achievement, serve as the inclusionary criteria for defining dyslexia.* (Table 6.3).

In keeping with the International Dyslexia Association definition of dyslexia that emphasizes its neurobiological origins, the neurobiological origin of the reading and spelling difficulties has been documented for child dyslexics acquired using the inclusion criteria described in this chapter. Differences between dyslexics and age- and Verbal IQ-matched controls have been found in imaging of neuroanatomical structures, chemical activation, and blood-oxygen-level-dependent brain activation; for reviews, see Berninger (in press-b, in press-c) and Berninger and Richards (2002). Also, genetic linkage for specific subphenotypes has been found (e.g., Chapman et al., in press).

INTRODUCING RESEARCH-SUPPORTED CLINICAL ASSESSMENT

Current school assessment practices focus on making educational decisions about whether children qualify for special education services rather than on making differential diagnoses (Berninger, 1998a, 1998b). Insufficient attention is given to etiology of reading problems, linking assessment to research-supported effective instruction, and prognosis for long-range outcomes. Given the time gap between research and translation of results into practice, many school and private practitioners do not have ready access to the latest research-supported approaches to differential diagnosis of specific learning disabilities. The purpose of this chapter is, therefore, to introduce a research-supported conceptual approach to differential diagnosis, which has implications for diagnosis and treatment of dyslexia and other specific learning disabilities.

Simply documenting low reading achievement is not sufficient. Children meeting the criteria for developmental disorders other than dyslexia typically

TABLE 6.2 Process Measures Validated for Specific Reading and Writing Achievement Outcomes

Reading or Writing Achievement Outcome Measure	Neurocognitive Process Measure									
	Phonological	Orthographic	Graphomotor	Oral-Motor	Automaticity	Switching Attention	Executive Function Inhibition	Executive Function Fluency	Cognitive	Expressive Language
Word Identification										
Child	CTOPP elision[a] CTOPP phoneme reversal	PAL word choice	none	none	WOLF RAN letter[a] WOLF RAN color	none	D-KEFS word reading	none	WISC-III vocabulary digit span[a] information	CELF-3 sentence formulation SBIV sentence memory[a]
Adult	CTOPP elision CTOPP phoneme reversal[a] CTOPP nonword repetition WJR numbers reversed	PAL word choice PAL receptive coding PAL expressive coding[a]	PAL finger succession non-dominant[c,d]	none	WOLF RAN letter	WOLF RAS number-letter	D-KEFS inhibition	D-KEFS verbal fluency letter	WISC-III vocabulary[a] digit span	CELF-3 sentence formulation SBIV sentence memory[a]

Measure	Group									
Word Attack	Child	CTOPP elision[a] CTOPP phoneme reversal[a]	PAL expressive coding[a] PAL word choice	none	WOLF RAN letter	WOLF RAS color number letter	D-KEFS color word reading	D-KEFS category switching correct[b]	WISC-III vocabulary digit span[a] information	CELF-3 sentence formulation SBIV sentence memory[a]
	Adult	CTOPP elision[c] CTOPP phoneme reversal[a]	PAL expressive coding[c] PAL receptive coding	PAL finger succession-non-dominant[c,d]	WOLF RAN letter	WOLF RAS number letter	D-KEFS inhibition	D-KEFS verbal fluency letter	WISC-III similarities vocabulary[a] digit span	CELF 3 sentence formulation[a] SBIV sentence memory
Sight Word Reading Efficiency	Child	CTOPP elision[c]	PAL word choice	none	WOLF RAN color[a] WOLF RAN number	WOLF RAS number letter[a] WOLF RAS color number letter[a]	D-KEFS word reading[a] D-KEFS color naming and reading	D-KEFS verbal fluency category	WISC-III information	none
	Adult	WJ-R numbers reversed	PAL receptive coding[a] PAL expressive coding	PA TA KA PAL finger succession non dominant[c,d,]	WOLF RAN color WOLF RAN letter[a]	WOLF RAS number letter[a] WOLF RAS color number letter	D-KEFS word reading[a] D-KEFS inhibition/ switching	D-KEFS verbal fluency letter	WISC-III digit span	CELF 3 sentence formulation[c]

(Continues)

TABLE 6.2 (Continued)

Reading or Writing Achievement Outcome Measure	Neurocognitive Process Measure									
	Phonological	Orthographic	Graphomotor	Oral-Motor	Automaticity	Switching Attention	Executive Function Inhibition	Executive Function Fluency	Cognitive	Expressive Language
Phonemic Reading Efficiency										
Child	CTOPP elision[a] CTOPP phoneme reversal	PAL expressive coding	none	none	WOLF RAN letter[a] WOLF RAN number	WOLF RAS color number letter	D-KEFS word reading	D-KEFS category switching correct	WISC-III vocabulary WISC-III digit span[a] information	SBIV sentence memory[c]
Adult	CTOPP elision CTOPP phoneme reversal[a] CTOPP nonword repetition	PAL expressive coding PAL receptive coding[a]	PAL finger succession non-dominant[c,d]	none	WOLF RAN letter	WOLF RAS color number letter WOLF RAS number letter[a]	D-KEFS inhibition/switching[b]	D-KEFS verbal fluency letter[a] D-KEFS category switching switches	WISC-III vocabulary[b]	SBIV sentence memory CELF 3 sentence formulation[a]
Oral Reading Accuracy										
Child	CTOPP elision	PAL word choice	none	none	WOLF RAN number	WOLF RAS color number letter	D-KEFS word reading[b]	D-KEFS category switching correct[c]	WISC-III vocabulary	SBIV sentence memory[c]
Adult	CTOPP elision[a] CTOPP nonword repetition CTOPP phoneme reversal WJR numbers reversed	PAL receptive coding PAL expressive coding[a]	PAL finger succession dominant[c,d]	none	WOLF RAN letter	WOLF RAS number letter	D-KEFS inhibition vs color naming[b]	D-KEFS verbal fluency letters[a] D-KEFS verbal fluency set loss errors	WISC-III vocabulary WISC-III similarities digit span	SBIV sentence memory CELF 3 sentence formulation[a]

Oral Reading Rate									
Child	CTOPP elision[a]	PAL word choice	none	WOLF color[a] WOLF number	WOLF RAS number letter[a] WOLF RAS color number letter	D-KEFS naming and reading	D-KEFS switching correct[b]	WISC-III information[a] vocabulary	none
Adult	CTOPP elision[a] WJR numbers reversed	PAL word choice PAL receptive coding PAL expressive coding[a]	PAL finger succession non-dominant[c,d]	WOLF color WOLF RAN letter[a]	WOLF RAS number letter[a] WOLF RAS color number letter	D-KEFS inhibition/switching[b]	D-KEFS fluency letter[a] D-KEFS fluency category switching switches	WISC-III vocabulary digit span[a]	CELF 3 sentence formulation[a] SBIV sentence memory
Comprehension (following oral reading)									
Child	CTOPP elision[c]	none	none	WOLF RAN color	WOLF RAS number letter[c]	none	D-KEFS category switching switches[c]	WISC-III information	none
Adult	CTOPP elision	PAL receptive coding[c]	none	none	WOLF RAS number letter	D-KEFS color naming[b]	none	WISC-III vocabulary	CELF 3 sentence formulation SBIV sentence memory[a]

(*Continues*)

TABLE 6.2 (*Continued*)

Reading or Writing Achievement Outcome Measure	Neurocognitive Process Measure									
	Phonological	Orthographic	Graphomotor	Oral-Motor	Automaticity	Switching Attention	Executive Function Inhibition	Executive Function Fluency	Cognitive	Expressive Language
Comprehension (following silent reading)										
Child	CTOPP elision[a]	PAL word choice[c]	none	none	none	WOLF RAS number letter	D-KEFS word reading[c]	D-KEFS category switching switches[c]	WISC-III vocabulary information[a] digit span	SBIV sentence memory[c]
Adult	CTOPP phoneme reversal WJR numbers reversed[a]	PAL receptive coding[a] PAL expressive coding	none	none	Wolf RAN letter[c]	WOLF RAS number letter	D-KEFS inhibition/switching[b]	D-KEFS category	WISC-III vocabulary	SBIV sentence memory[a] CELF 3 sentence formulation
Alphabet Writing 15 seconds										
Child	none	none	none	none	WOLF RAN letter	WOLF RAS color number letter	D-KEFS inhibition/switching	none	none	none
Adult	CTOPP elision[c]	PAL receptive coding PAL expressive coding[a]	none	none	WOLF RAN letter[c]	WOLF RAS number letter	D-KEFS inhibition/switching[b]	D-KEFS verbal fluency letter[a] D-KEFS category	WISC-III similarities[b]	sentence formulation[c]

WRAT 3 Spelling									
Child	CTOPP elision[a] CTOPP phoneme reversal	PAL expressive coding PAL word choice[b]	none	WOLF RAN letter[b]	WOLF RAS color number letter	D-KEFS word reading	D-KEFS category switching switches[c]	WISC-III vocabulary[a] information	CELF3 sentence formulation SBIV sentence memory[a]
Adult	CTOPP elision[a] CTOPP phoneme reversal WJR numbers reversed	PAL expressive coding[a] PAL word choice PAL receptive coding	PAL finger succession non-dominant[c,d]	WOLF RAN letter	WOLF RAS number letter	D-KEFS inhibition/switching[b]	D-KEFS verbal fluency letter	WISC-III vocabulary[a] similarities	none
WIAT II Spelling									
Child	CTOPP elision WJR numbers reversed[a]	PAL word choice	none	WOLF color	WOLF RAS number letter[b]	D-KEFS word reading	D-KEFS category switching switches[c]	WISC-III vocabulary[a]	none
Adult	CTOPP elision[a] CTOPP phoneme reversal WJR numbers reversed	PAL receptive coding PAL expressive coding[b]	PAL finger succession non dominant[c]	WOLF RAN letter	WOLF RAS number letter	D-KEFS word reading[b]	D-KEFS verbal fluency letter	WISC-III vocabulary	CELF3 sentence formulation[a] SBIV sentence memory

(*Continues*)

TABLE 6.2 (Continued)

Reading or Writing Achievement Outcome Measure	Neurocognitive Process Measure									
	Phonological	Orthographic	Graphomotor	Oral-Motor	Automaticity	Switching Attention	Executive Function Inhibition	Executive Function Fluency	Cognitive	Expressive Language
Written Expression										
Child	CTOPP elision[a] WJR numbers reversed	PAL expressive coding[a] PAL word choice	none	none	WOLF RAN letter[a] WOLF RAN color	WOLF RAS number letter	D-KEFS word reading	D-KEFS verbal fluency letter	WISC-III vocabulary digit span[a]	SBIV sentence memory[c]
Adult	CTOPP elision WJR numbers reversed[a]	PAL expressive coding	PAL finger succession non-dominant[c,d]	none	WOLF RAN letter	WOLF RAS number letter	D-KEFS inhibition[b]	D-KEFS verbal fluency letter	WISC-III vocabulary[b]	SBIV sentence memory CELF3 sentence formulation[a]

Key: No superscript means that only this measure (in the set of measures of the same process, see Table 6.1, that are correlated at $p < .001$ with the reading or writing skill) explains unique variance in the outcome.

[a] This measure explains the most variance of the unique predictors in a set of measures of the same process (see Table 6.1). Only measures that were correlated at $p < .001$ with the reading or writing outcome measures were entered into the multiple regressions to determine which measures within a process set were unique predictors.

[b] More than one measure of the same process (see Table 6.1) explains significant variance in the outcome but none is unique, but this one accounts for the most variance.

[c] Only this measure in the set was correlated with the outcome at $p \leq .001$. Bolding indicates that the same unique predictors are comparable across child dyslexics and adult dyslexics. However, even if a measure is not bolded, it was validated for use in assessment at the developmental listed at which it is listed (child or adult).

[d] The nondominant hand may be more predictive than the dominant hand because it is less practiced and automatic and thus may reflect the motor timing deficit Wolff and colleagues (e.g., Wolff, Cohen, & Drake, 1984) have reported and investigated for a number of years.

TABLE 6.3   Validated Hallmark Processing Deficits in Both Child and Adult Dyslexics

Impaired Processing Deficit	Validated Process Measure for Assessment
Storage of precise representations of complex phonological word forms in phonological short-term/ working memory	CTOPP (Wagner, Torgesen, & Rashotte, 1999) Nonword Repetition
Time-sensitive phonological loop function for accessing known words and learning new spoken and written words	TOWRE Phonemic Reading Efficiency (Torgesen, Wagner, & Rashotte, 1999) Rapid Automatic Naming of Letters (Wolf & Denckla, 2004) PAL Rapid Automatic Naming of Partially Decodable Words (Berninger, 2001b)[b] D-KEFS Verbal Fluency Letter[a] (Delis, Kaplan, & Kramer, 2001)
Executive functions for switching attention, inhibition, and automatic retrieval	Rapid Automatic Naming of Switching Stimuli (Wolf & Denckla, 2004) Rapid Automatic Naming of Alternating Words and Double-Digit Numbers (Berninger, 2001b)[b] D-KEFS Inhibition; Inhibition/Switching PAL Alphabet Writing (Berninger, (2001b)

[a]Initially serves phonological loop functions but becomes part of the executive function system.
[b]Not included in battery in Table 6.1 but measures the same process.

have low reading achievement, but for other reasons. Likewise, simply documenting a discrepancy between reading (or writing) and IQ is not sufficient; there could be many reasons for the underachievement. It is also necessary to assess the curriculum, assess response to instruction, and assess possible processing deficits to tease apart reasons for the underachievement (Berninger, 1998a). Underachievement is probably neurobiological in origin if (1) it persists despite appropriate, research-supported instruction; and (2) it is accompanied by neuropsychological impairments in processes research has shown are related to reading and writing. *Not all reading problems have the same etiology, respond to the same treatment, or have the same prognosis.* Differential diagnosis is necessary if professionals are to provide parents with (1) the explanatory evidence they seek for the children's struggles in academic learning, (2) the most effective interventions for their children, and (3) realistic educational goals to work toward (rather than false hope or overly pessimistic expectations). It is ironic that at this time in educational history, when there is a growing awareness and respect for research-supported instructional approaches, that there is not a comparable focus on research-supported differential diagnostic practices for students who do not respond to those instructional approaches.

In the next section findings from the UW family genetics study are presented for purposes of differential diagnosis of dyslexia and pinpointing the associated processing deficits. All measures utilized in the study are commercially available with demonstrated evidence of reliability and validity. Table 6.1 lists the specific measures used to assess the verbal reasoning, reading, and writing skills to determine whether dyslexics had unexpectedly low reading and/or spelling achievement. The UW research program used the WRMT-R (Woodcock, 1987) for assessing accuracy of reading real words or pseudowords, but the WIAT-II (The Psychological Corporation, 2001) and Woodcock Johnson Third Edition (Woodcock, McGrew, & Mather, 2001) also have measures that could be used for this purpose. As discussed previously, *the inclusionary criteria for diagnosing dyslexia are unexpectedly low achievement, relative to verbal reasoning and the population mean for age, in accuracy or rate of real word reading, accuracy or rate of pseudoword reading (phonological decoding), accuracy or rate of oral text reading, or accuracy of dictated spelling. The inclusionary definition of dyslexia also requires, in addition to unexpectedly low achievement in specific reading and writing skills, evidence of impairment in processing deficits.* Hale, Naglieri, Kaufman, and Kavale (2004) make a case for the importance of considering process measures in assessing specific learning disabilities.

In Table 6.2 the processes related to different brain systems that predicted specific reading and writing skills are listed. Only processes that had at least one best (statistically significant at $p < .001$) or unique predictor (in multiple regression) are reported. For example, the best orthographic predictor of word identification performance in children and adults was the PAL Word Choice subtest. However as shown in Table 6.2, it is not the only neurocognitive process involved in word identification performance. Cognitive, phonological, automatic, and expressive language processes also play a role. Assessment based on many brain systems yields an individual profile of phenotypic expression, which may provide both (1) insight into the etiology of the achievement problem and (2) important diagnostic clues for designing instructional programs or accommodation plans for students across schooling. For example, are the academic achievement problems related to problems in (1) automatic retrieval of language codes, (2) awareness of and coordinating the phonological, morphological, and/or orthographic word forms, and/or (3) executive functions needed for self-regulation of the learning process? (For case studies that illustrate this process approach to generating educational interventions, see chapter by Berninger, Dunn, & Alpert, this volume.)

Measures for assessing the hallmark, defining processing deficits in both child and adult dyslexics are summarized in Table 6.3. Of all the process constructs assessed in the UW research, these hallmark processing deficits (problems with storing precise representations of complex phonological word forms in phonological short-term/working memory; impaired time-sensitive phonological loop function; and impaired switching of attention, inhibition, and automatic retrieval) are at the heart of the *inclusionary criteria* for processing deficits in dyslexia. These processing deficits, which were found to be stable across development, can be used to explain processing constraints contributing to the etiology of dyslexia. However, an individual dyslexic may only have a subset of these hallmark features. Only if these processing deficits occur along with unexpectedly low achievement in reading and/or writing is the diagnosis of dyslexia necessary in children. In adults who have compensated for these processing limitations and learned to read and write, processing deficits signal the presence of biologically based risk factors that were overcome.

The hallmark indicators of dyslexia in Table 6.3 capture both (1) the *phonological core deficit in dyslexia* (preciseness of the phonological word form, the efficiency of phonological decoding, and executive functions for processing phonological information) and (2) the *verbal working memory deficit of dyslexia* (impaired storage in phonological short-term memory, impaired phonological loop function, and impaired supervisory attention system and inhibition during language processing) (Berninger *et al.*, submitted). Swanson and Siegel (2001) made a compelling case for a working memory deficit, as well as a phonological core deficit in reading disability.

Recent advances in modeling working memory emphasize (1) its multiple components and efficiency rather than span limitations (see Baddeley, 2002; Hitch, Towse, & Hutton, 2001); (2) the role of the phonological loop in learning new words as well as accessing stored familiar words (Baddeley, Gathercole, & Papagno, 1998); (3) the flexibility of working memory in adapting to different goals (see Crosson *et al.*, 1999; Engle *et al.*, 1999; Hutton & Towse, 2001; Martin & Romani, 1994; Ribaupierre, 2002); (4) the role of inhibition, processing speed, and executive schemes in the efficiency of working memory (Ribaupierre, 2002); (5) the relationship of working memory efficiency to higher-order thinking in reading, writing, and mathematics (Demetriou, Cristou, Spanoudis, & Platsidou, 2002); and (6) a reconceptualization of the central executive as a constellation of functions, rather than a single function (Towse, 1998; Towse, Hitch, & Hutton, 2000). The central executive includes the supervisory attentional system (Norman & Shallice, 1986) but also has critical mechanisms for inhibition (Gunter, Wagner, & Friederici, 2003). Miyake, Friedman, Emerson, Witzki, Howerter, and Wager (2000) identified three separable executive functions in working memory: mental set shifting, inhibition, and monitoring and updating. *Verbal* working memory is the most relevant for diagnosing reading and writing disability (Smith-Spark, Fisk, Fawcett, & Nicolson, 2003).

SUMMARY OF DIAGNOSTIC PROCEDURES
FOR DYSLEXIA

Table 6.4 outlines the sequential steps in differential diagnosis of developmental dyslexia from other developmental and learning disorders. The recommended diagnostic procedures are based on research-generated knowledge. While Table 6.3 is relevant to the inclusionary criteria for diagnosing dyslexia, Table 6.2 is relevant to generating the phenotypic profile to use in describing which of the various processes related to literacy learning are affected in an individual and thus relevant to individualized treatment planning. Because of nature-nurture interactions, many other processes may be affected other than those genetically constrained in a specific reading disorder such as dyslexia.

CASE STUDIES TO ILLUSTRATE THE DIFFERENTIAL DIAGNOSIS OF DYSLEXIA

The following case studies were selected because they illustrate how dyslexia, which is a genetic and brain-based disorder, may express itself differently across developmental stages. These case studies also highlight

TABLE 6.4   Differential Diagnostic Procedures for Dyslexia

1. First, based on developmental, medical, educational, and family history (and if necessary formal assessment), rule out all the other potential sources of difficulty using the exclusionary criteria in the UW study. (See the Inclusionary and Exclusionary Criteria in the UW phenotyping studies section of this chapter.)

   - If any of those exclusionary criteria are present and could explain the low reading achievement, then a diagnosis of dyslexia is inappropriate. Dyslexia is a genetically and neurologically based specific learning disability and not a reading problem due to problems more generalized across developmental domains (see Berninger, 2001a); it should not be equated with reading problems due to other genetic or neurological disorders.

   - If the exclusionary criteria are met, the practitioner still pursues appropriate diagnosis and treatment for the individual (but reading problems are not attributed to dyslexia and the prognosis may not be the same as for dyslexia).

2. Second, if none of the exclusionary criteria are met:

   - Use WISC-IV Verbal Comprehension Index to assess whether verbal reasoning ability falls in the average or higher range.

   - Administer measures of accuracy and rate (Lovett, 1987) of oral real word reading, phonological decoding (e.g., Torgesen *et al.*, 1999) and morphological decoding (e.g., Nagy, Berninger, Abbott, Vaughan, & Vermeulen, 2003), text reading, and written spelling to evaluate whether these reading and spelling skills are low (below the population mean). Morphological decoding refers to decoding long, complex words with constant bases and variant affixed morphemes.

   - See Table 6.2 for achievement measures. WIAT II Word Reading or WJ-III Letter and Word Identification can be used instead of WRMT-R Word Identification. WIAT II Pseudoword Reading or WJ III Word Attack can be used instead of WRMT-R Word Attack. WIAT II Reading Comprehension or WJ III Passage Comprehension can be used instead of WJ-R Passage Comprehension.

(Continues)

TABLE 6.4 *(Continued)*

3. Third, evaluate *whether inclusionary criteria* for dyslexia are present:

   - *(a) Unexpectedly low achievement in accuracy or rate of real word reading, phonological decoding, oral text reading, or spelling* (at least 1 standard deviation below WISC-IV Verbal Comprehension and below the population mean for age on achievement measures in Table 6.2);

   - *and* (b) *impairment in one or more of the hallmark processing deficits that are stable across the life span* (preciseness of phonological word form and its storage, phonological loop function for rapid naming of familiar orthographic symbols or words or of novel pseudowords, executive function for supervisory attention system—switching mental set, executive function for inhibition—suppressing irrelevant information so relevant information can be attended, or automatic retrieval of letter forms (see Table 6.3 for measures validated for this purpose based on both phonological core and working memory models).

   - If achievement is unexpectedly low but no research-supported processing deficits in Tables 6.2 or 6.3 are found, then seek reasons other than dyslexia for the reading or writing problems, especially the nature of the instructional program (see tier two of the three-tier model and Berninger, 1998a).

4. Fourth, evaluate the profile of individual phenotypic expression for processes related to the reading and writing phenotypes in dyslexia for clues to planning instructional treatment for the individual dyslexic.

   - Table 6.2 measures are validated within a model based on the relevant brain systems. Eleven processes were evaluated based on research reviewed in Berninger & Richards (2002), but results for morphological measures are not reported because they are not nationally normed; for each reading or writing outcome in Table 6.2, only processes that had at least one best or unique predictor are reported.

   - Both the bolded and nonbolded measures in Table 6.2 are research-validated for clinical assessment; use listed measures only at the age level (child or adult) where they appear in Table 6.2.

   - Those that are bolded indicate that the same measure was validated for both child and adult dyslexics. Some aspects of phenotypic expression stay constant across development and some express themselves at one stage but not another.

   - Valid assessment that leads to effective instructional intervention can be based on either the brain systems (Table 6.2) or working memory-system model (Table 6.3). See Berninger and Abbott (2003) for research-generated reading and writing lessons linked to these processes and designed to integrate different levels of language (subword, word, and text) taught close in time to create efficient working memory support for functional reading and writing systems.

   - Design a progress monitoring plan (see Chapter 10, Berninger, 1998, and end of lesson sets in Berninger & Abbott, 2003).

5. Evaluate whether the individual with dyslexia also has arithmetic or mathematical disability, attention deficit disorder, or depression or anxiety or self-concept problems due to chronic academic difficulty or other reasons. If so, address these issues in treatment planning. (See other chapters in this volume.)

the point that the age at which research-based intervention is implemented will affect educational outcome.

Case Study 1

A first grader participated in an early intervention study for children whose reading skills were behind at the end of first grade. This child, whose family had a history of dyslexia, already met research criteria for dyslexia at the end of first grade. After a year-long university-based intervention, which began during the summer between first and second grade and continued until the end of second grade, the child was reading on grade level (accuracy of decoding, real word reading, and reading comprehension). At the end of third grade, the child met criteria for another university-based study because reading rate was slow and oral reading was not fluent (smooth and coordinated). Mother reported that the child was a reluctant reader who avoided reading. After that summer intervention, the child's reading rate and fluency were grade-appropriate. Six years later the mother wrote the research director a thank-you note and explained the following. After a struggle throughout the primary grades, when the child hated school and faced daily challenges in keeping up with reading assignments, a transformation occurred in fourth grade and the change in attitude toward reading and the improved reading ability were maintained consistently after that. In ninth grade the child was an honor student, loved school, and had very high career aspirations. The mother was not only grateful but surprised that the family history had not repeated itself.

Case Study 2

A sixth grader, who had no special services previously because of parental fear of labeling, was a nonreader. During sixth grade, a special education teacher initiated specialized instruction using research-generated lessons (Reading Lessons in PAL Intervention Guides, Berninger, 1998a), which are similar to the PAL Lesson Set 11 (Berninger & Abbott, 2003). By eighth grade, the child was reading on grade level and the parents reported that their child now thought of himself as a reader. However, spelling problems persisted. Despite private tutoring, which commenced in high school, for spelling and writing (because the school did not provide special education services in school), problems in spelling persisted. The child attends college but needs accommodations because writing intervention was not initiated early enough and sustained sufficiently until the writing problems were overcome. To qualify for accommodation and special services geared to learning disabilities in college, this student will have to be repeatedly evaluated every 3 years. Just as research-based diagnostic procedures have not been available for dyslexia during childhood, likewise they have not been available for adolescents and young adults for whom diagnostic findings might inform instructional supports and accommodations after high-school.

LANGUAGE LEARNING DISABILITY

DEFINITION OF LANGUAGE LEARNING DISABILITY

The UW research program is taking a closer look at students who did not meet the state ability–achievement discrepancy criteria for learning disability or the UW research criteria for dyslexia, but who clearly have unusual difficulty in learning to read and write despite normal cognitive development. At issue is whether there is another specific learning disability affecting reading that can be distinguished from dyslexia on the basis of inclusionary criteria. The following discussion is based on close scrutiny of a number of case studies that pointed to a subtype who struggles a great deal in learning both oral language and written language.

This subtype is distinguishable from the slow learner who is consistently just within the lower limits of the normal range across all developmental and academic domains and learns in a fairly typical way but more slowly and needs more repetition and practice (Berninger, 1998b). The subtype in question is not as impaired in language as is the case for developmental aphasia, developmental language disorder, or primary language disorder in which a composite measure of receptive and/or expressive language falls more than two standard deviations below the mean. Complicating the diagnostic picture is ambiguity in application of terminology. It is not clear whether some use the term *specific language impairment* in the same way others use the term *language learning disability*. Children with language learning disability have selective language impairment and do not learn in a typical way when language is involved, but may learn in typical ways when language is not involved.

Unlike the dyslexics whose problems are first apparent in the school-age years, the problems associated with language learning disability (Butler & Silliman, 2002; Wallach & Butler, 1994; Wiig, 1991) are first apparent in the preschool years when affected children show difficulty in learning to understand and/or produce language. These children tend to be slower than siblings or age-peers in achieving language milestones, but eventually do so. They sometimes receive early intervention services in language and tend to respond faster to this intervention than children with more severe language impairment that meets criteria for primary language disorder. They typically are exited from language intervention services when they enter kindergarten or first grade because their receptive and expressive language at this developmental stage fall within the lower limits of the normal range or even higher, and they no longer meet the criteria for language services. See Catts (1993) for longitudinal evidence that some children with language problems in the preschool years no longer qualify as having a language problem in the school years. Yet these are some of the students who may continue to struggle, undetected, with subtle aspects of language function—metalinguistic morphological and syntactic awareness, executive regulation of language processes, and verbal mediation in cognitive learning.

During the school years, teachers and parents may think the child's language is normal because his language in conversation seems normal. However, language in conversation is contextualized and conversational partners provide many supports. The persisting language problems may be only apparent in formal testing when children are asked to perform tasks that require use of language outside the context of conversation, that is, decontextualized language. For example, using a word with the correct meaning in conversation shows contextualized language competence but defining a word correctly in a testing situation (e.g., WISC IV Vocabulary subtest) shows decontextualized language competence. Unless such decontextualized language tests are given to children early in the school-age years when literacy instruction is provided, educators may not realize that these children are having subtle problems in language processing, for example, in morphology (word parts that signal meaning and grammar), syntax (the structures that convey meaning by integrating strings of words), executive functions for planning and producing syntax, and/or verbal mediation (using language as a tool for thinking and for learning academic subjects). In the UW research, experimenter-designed measures of morphological and syntactic awareness were used based on the research literature. In the future there will be nationally normed tests for these metalinguistic aspects of language for psychologists to use in differential diagnosis of specific learning disabilities. Psychologists are also encouraged to keep abreast of the growing clinical (e.g., Silliman, Wilkinson, & Danzak, in press) and research literature (e..g., Bishop & Snowling, in press) on language learning disabilities in the field of child language and speech and communication sciences.

INSUFFICIENT RESEARCH-GENERATED KNOWLEDGE OF LANGUAGE LEARNING DISABILITY

Currently there are no diagnostic instruments for assessing how children use language during cognitive learning of academic subjects. What is observable is the immense struggle with learning to read and write. All too often the testing is not done to evaluate whether children have problems in learning written language that are related to subtle underlying problems in aural language (listening or receptive language) or oral language (speaking or expressive language) that involve morphology, syntax, executive functions, and verbal mediation. That is, children may have a specific learning disability in language learning (Butler & Silliman, 2002; Wiig, 1991; Silliman *et al.*, in press; Wallach & Butler, 1994), which differs from dyslexia in that its inclusionary criteria may include severe problems in morphology and syntax, executive supports for language, word retrieval, and use of language in abstract reasoning, despite otherwise normal cognitive development. Further research may identify other subtypes and inclusionary criteria.

Because these aural/oral language problems are not identified, they are not treated. However, effective treatment of language learning disability requires intensive aural/oral language therapy along with intensive reading and writing instruction in both word skills and sentence/text skills. For children with language learning disability, neither aural/oral nor written language learning is natural. All too often children with this specific kind of learning disability do not get the kind of treatment they need—both language therapy and literacy instruction. Their language problems are not severe enough to qualify for language services through the special education category of communication disabilities, and they do not meet the traditional ability–achievement discrepancy criteria for reading and writing services through the special education category of learning disabilities. More research is needed on the etiology, effective treatment, and prognosis of language learning disability.

SUMMARY OF DIAGNOSTIC PROCEDURES
FOR LANGUAGE LEARNING DISABILITY

Table 6.5 summarizes the sequential steps for differential diagnosis of language learning disabilities from other learning and developmental disabilities. The recommended practices are based on available clinical and research knowledge; much more research is needed on this specific learning disability.

CASE STUDIES TO ILLUSTRATE LANGUAGE
LEARNING DISABILITY

Some children with language learning disability grow up in supportive families who find services for them, and these children do not develop associated behavioral problems that may reflect low tolerance for frustration in coping with language learning disability. Others do not and may be labeled as having a behavioral disability and given special education services under that category; their language learning is often not assessed to identify possible disabilities in this domain and the relationship of possible language learning disabilities to the behavioral problems. Yet, treating the language impairment in language learning disabilities may be important in treating their behavioral disabilities.

By following case studies of children with language learning disability and dyslexia, we have discovered that their instructional needs are different. During the preschool years, those with language learning disabilities benefit

TABLE 6.5   Diagnostic Procedures for Language Learning Disability

1. Interview parent(s) or caregiver(s) and obtain a careful, detailed developmental history of language development and educational history including special services, with focus on preschool as well as school-age years, and medical and family history.

   - Evaluate whether the child meets DSM-IV criteria for attention deficit disorder (see chapter by Shewan & Saklofske, this volume), which also needs to be taken into account in treatment planning, or whether any attentional difficulties may be the result rather than the cause of language processing problems.

   - Make certain that none of the exclusionary criteria for dyslexia are present and could explain the language learning problems. If they are, proceed to do assessment relevant to those conditions.

   - Otherwise, *if inclusionary criteria for dyslexia are not found*, proceed with assessment specific to language learning disability.

2. Administer the WISC-IV to obtain Verbal Comprehension Index and Perceptual Reasoning Index.

   - If one or both of these measures of verbal or nonverbal reasoning falls in the low average range or higher, indicating that cognition is within the normal range, proceed to step 3.

3. Administer WISC-IV Working Memory Index and Processing Speed Index, the CELF-IV (Semel *et al.*, 2003), and other standardized measures of morphological and syntactic processing and awareness. Evaluate:

   - Whether verbal and nonverbal reasoning are significantly different from each other;

   - Whether either the Working Memory or Processing Speed indices are relative weaknesses; and

   - Whether receptive or expressive language is relatively better developed than the other.

   - Whether individual has significantly underdeveloped syntactic, morphological, word retrieval, or executive functions for language.

   - Taken together, these results are used to describe the individual's profile of aural/oral language learning skills. Although the Processing Speed Index is based on visual stimuli, it may inform how a general speed factor may influence language and/or academic learning in general.

4. Assess current achievement in reading and writing and related language and neuropsychological processes (see Table 7.1).

   - Use assessment results for literacy achievement and the aural/oral language learning profile to plan the instructional program (see Wallach & Butler, 1994; Butler & Silliman, 2002; Silliman *et al.*, in press).

   - Design a progress monitoring plan. (See Berninger, 1998a, Chapter 10; see end of each lesson set, Berninger & Abbott, 2003.)

---

from language therapy. In case 1, the child received speech but not language services during the preschool years, whereas the child in case 2 received both speech and language services. During the school-age years, children with language learning disabilities need explicit instruction in not only decoding, but also in real word reading and reading comprehension. In fact, they often respond more quickly to word decoding instruction than do dyslexics, but then struggle more with real word reading (possibly because of problems in word retrieval from long-term memory) much longer than do dyslexics. Children with language learning disability have more difficulty with reading comprehension than do dyslexics and require explicit reading comprehension instruction directed to all levels of language (vocabulary meaning, sentence understanding, and discourse structure) (see Berninger *et al.*, 2003). In contrast, dyslexics need explicit instruction in word decoding, and once that is brought up to grade level and they have sufficient practice in applying decoding to reading text, their reading comprehension proceeds normally. Dyslexics benefit from explicit instruction in reading comprehension, too, but they do not require language therapy (because of underlying problems in morphological and syntactic processing) or the intensity and degree of explicitness in reading comprehension instruction as the language learning disabled do. The child in case 1 received only multisensory phonics, whereas the child in case 2 initially received that approach and later, at our recommendation, received explicit comprehension instruction as well.

The differences in instructional needs between dyslexics and language learning disabled children may be related to severity of the language impairment, although impairments appear to be common (in phonology) and unique (in that severe morphological and syntactic processing deficits are more characteristic of the language learning disabled than dyslexics). Research should address the etiology (whether there are genetic and neurological differences that uniquely characterize these two specific learning disabilities), the most effective treatment, and the prognosis for both dyslexia and language learning disability. The two subtypes may differ in the long-term prognosis, with dyslexics more likely to become compensated readers if they receive appropriate reading instruction and the language learning disabled more likely to have lifelong language processing problems if they received only reading and not oral language instruction. There may also be a mixed subtype that has phenotypic markers and genotypic and neurological features of both specific learning disabilities and, as a consequence, a guarded adult outcome. The following case studies show that the language learning problems are the hallmark features; there may or may not be a discrepancy between a measure of nonverbal reasoning and reading or writing achievement or between verbal (lower) and nonverbal (higher) reasoning.

CASE STUDIES TO ILLUSTRATE LANGUAGE
LEARNING DISABILITY

Case 1

This boy was mildly delayed in saying his first words (slower than normal but just within the normal limits). During the preschool years he had difficulty focusing and was diagnosed by a medical professional as having an attention deficit disorder, but his parents decided not to use stimulant medication in treating the attentional problems because they noted that he had trouble focusing only when listening to oral language. The mother had heard a speech and language pathologist discuss a specific learning disability called language learning disability. However, during kindergarten and the primary grades, the school provided speech services for developmental articulation errors but not for language processing. Because he did not meet the state criterion for severe ability–achievement discrepancy, he was qualified for special education services under the category of attention deficit disorder (although he did not meet DSM-IV criteria for this attention deficit hyperactivity disorder or any of its subtypes). The special education instruction focused on multisensory phonics. Despite considerable help at school and home, he experienced a daily struggle with reading and writing. His spontaneous writing at home, which had interesting content, short sentences, immature handwriting, and phonologically based spelling errors, reflected his sadness at not being able to read and write like his peers.

When initially assessed by the UW research team when he was in third grade, his standard scores for accuracy of phonological decoding (98) and rate of phonological decoding (86) were higher than for accuracy of real word reading (86) and rate of real word reading (76). Typically with child and adult dyslexics, the reverse pattern is found: phonological decoding is less well developed than real word reading. The rate problem, which is shared by dyslexics and the language learning disabled, was found in oral reading of text as well (accuracy, 90; rate, 75). This boy had impaired orthographic, phonological, and rapid automatic naming, as is common in child dyslexics, but, unlike dyslexics, was significantly impaired in morphological processing.

He could not understand or perform decomposition or derivation (Carlisle, 2000), which requires breaking a complex word into its morphemes to fit a sentence context or adding a morpheme to make a base word fit a sentence context. On the UW Morphological Signals (deciding on the basis of suffixes which of four alternatives fits a specific sentence context) ($z = -3.11$) and Comes-From (deciding whether a second word with a true morpheme or morpheme foil is semantically related to the first word) ($z = -4.23$) tests (Berninger & Nagy, 2003; Nagy et al., 2003), he was also severely impaired in morphological processing. None of these morphological measures, which may explain his significant problems in reading comprehension, require decoding of written words because they are administered orally (but with visual words and sentences to inspect).

Both his reading comprehension and sentence formulation (planning and constructing syntax) fell at the lower limits of the low average range. Although he was not discrepant from his Verbal IQ in phonological decoding, he was in reading comprehension, morphological, and syntactic skills. His verbal and nonverbal reasoning on the WISC-III fell in the average range (near the population mean) but were not discrepant from each other. Like many other children with language learning disability, his attention problems were specific to his language processing problems. The UW research team recommended that the focus of the instructional program in special education and general education be redirected from an exclusive focus on multisensory phonics to a broader focus on automaticity of real word reading, fluency of text reading, and reading comprehension (reading vocabulary, sentence understanding, and paragraph comprehension). Although phonological decoding instruction is necessary for dyslexia and language learning disability, it is not sufficient for language learning disability.

Case 2

This boy's language learning problems surfaced when he was a toddler—when most children are learning to combine words, he still had less than 10 words and used gestures to communicate. He received intensive language therapy services during the preschool years, but was exited in kindergarten when he no longer met criteria for needing special education services focused on communication. He became very talkative, but wordy; careful analysis of his language production revealed occasional syntactic anomalies. His CELF-III profile was notable for better developed expressive than receptive language. Since first grade he has continuously received special education services for reading and writing. He received considerable training in multisensory phonics. Teachers have noted his problems in attentional focus, especially when language processing was involved. When tested at 6 and 8, his Verbal Comprehension Factor was slightly but not significantly higher than his Perceptual Organization Factor, but both increased over time from the lower limits of the average range to the upper limits of the average range. The Processing Speed Factor (21st percentile) was an area of relative weakness compared to his reasoning skills. Like the child in case 1, this child's phonological decoding skills (standard score of 100) were better developed than his word reading (standard score of 84) and reading comprehension (standard score less than 70); also, accuracy was better than rate of phonological decoding (standard score of 93) or real word reading (standard score of 81). Like the child in case 1, this boy was found to have a severe morphological processing problem ($z = -2.76$ on Carlisle, 2000, Decomposition; $= -2.15$ on Carlisle, 2000, Derivation; UW Morphological Signals $= -1.18$; UW Comes-From not available) and a severe syntactic processing problem (fifth percentile on a task requiring processing and reproduction of sentences of increasing syntactic complexity).

The UW research team recommended that the instructional program redirect its focus from exclusive focus on multisensory phonics to more focus on morphological and syntactic processing, oral word retrieval, and reading comprehension (reading vocabulary, sentence understanding, and paragraph comprehension). When tested a year later after daily instruction and reading practice at school, the same pattern of relative strength in word decoding (standard score 100) and relative weakness in reading real words (standard score 85) was found, but reading comprehension had improved to the average range (standard score of 95). This response to instruction illustrates that the language learning disabled have instructional needs in reading comprehension, as well as decoding. Further research is needed on effective instruction for improving the real word reading (accuracy and rate) of the language learning disabled.

DYSGRAPHIA

DEFINITION OF DYSGRAPHIA

Children with dyslexia and language learning disabilities invariably have spelling problems; they may or may not have handwriting problems. Some children have only writing problems: in handwriting only, spelling only, or both handwriting and spelling. (Berninger, in press-a). Some handwriting problems involve legibility. Other handwriting problems involve automaticity (ability to produce legible letters rapidly and effortlessly). Yet others involve orthographic coding or graphomotor planning problems. Some children have comorbid handwriting disability and attention deficit, both of which must be treated to improve writing ability.

Some spelling problems are related to imprecise representation of the phonological word form in short-term/working memory; children spell the words the way they perceive the sound features and often delete phonemes, add phonemes, or change the sequence of phonemes. Some spelling problems involve difficulty in learning alternative, acceptable correspondences for phonemes and one- or two-letter spelling units, and choosing which of these alternatives fits in a specific word context. Some spelling problems involve imprecise representations of orthographic word forms in long-term memory. Other spelling problems involve weak understanding of English morphology (word parts that convey meaning and grammar) and its rules for spelling long, complex words in which suffixes are affixed to stems. Handwriting and spelling (transcription) problems are a major cause of writing disabilities and are most treatable and preventable during the early elementary school years (Berninger & Amtmann, 2003).

As the curriculum requirements increase in the upper elementary and middle school grades, executive function impairments increasingly compromise writing, which depends greatly on ability to plan (e.g, envision goals, generate ideas, create organizational schemes, integrate working memory executive schemes and searches of long-term memory), self-monitor (review or update working memory), and revise (create plans to detect problems and to fix problems). Also, impairments in temporally coordinated working memory may interfere with writing as the task requirements increase. (For review of the brain basis, developmental changes, and instructional issues in writing and writing disabilities, see chapters 6 and 9 in Berninger & Richards (2002); for research-validated lessons for integrated handwriting and composition instruction, integrated spelling and composition instruction, and integrated handwriting, spelling, and composition instruction, see Berninger & Abbott (2003)).

SUMMARY OF PROCEDURES
FOR DIAGNOSING DYSGRAPHIA

Table 6.6 summarizes the sequential steps for differential diagnosis of dysgraphia from other learning and developmental disabilities. The recommended practices are based on research knowledge available to date, some of which was generated for children with dyslexia and dysgraphia and some of which was generated for children with dysgraphia only. Writing is critical for school and occupational success in the twenty-first century during which advances in technology have revolutionized the nature of writing and instructional practices in writing. More research is needed on biologically based writing disorders that require specialized instruction and accommodations to optimize the writing development of affected individuals.

CASE STUDIES TO ILLUSTRATE DYSGRAPHIA

Case Study 1

This third grader succeeded in all areas of the school curriculum except handwriting, which had been a problem for the child since kindergarten. PAL process assessment showed why reading was a strength, but handwriting was a problem. On the PAL Test all orthographic and phonological skills were relative strengths, falling in the 80th to 90th decile range. In contrast to copying letters or words, with a model present (in the 50th to 70th decile range), automatic retrieval of alphabet letters was relatively impaired (20th decile). Likewise, weaknesses were found in sensorimotor-symbol integration (Finger Tip Writing, 20th decile) and graphomotor planning for sequential finger movements on an imitation task (Finger Succession, 30th decile). This child's dysgraphia was specific to handwriting; spelling (WIAT II standard score of 117) was a strength. Consistent with UW research findings for writing (Berninger & Amtmann, 2003), this child's problem in handwriting automaticity impaired composing (standard score of 70 on WIAT II Written Expression, and of 38 on WJ-R Writing Fluency). PAL Handwriting Lessons (Berninger, 1998a) therefore were recommended to improve handwriting automaticity and transfer of automatic letter writing to composition (5-minute writing samples in response to prompts/composition starters).

TABLE 6.6   Diagnostic Procedures for Dysgraphia

1. As with dyslexia, begin by obtaining a developmental, medical, educational, and family history to rule out other developmental problems that might account for writing problems.
   - Determine if individual meets DSM-IV criteria for attention deficit disorder. Administer the WISC-IV to obtain Verbal Comprehension, Perceptual Reasoning, Processing Speed, and Working Memory Indices.
   - Evaluate whether verbal and/or nonverbal reasoning falls at least within the normal range.
   - If so, proceed to the next step in assessment and determine which writing component may be impaired.

2. For handwriting, use PAL Alphabet Writing and Copy subtests to assess legibility on tasks that do and do not require writing letters from memory, automaticity (timed production of letters from memory), and preciseness of letter forms (writing dictated letters from memory).
   - If low achievement in handwriting is found, use PAL Receptive and Expressive Coding and Finger Succession to evaluate whether orthographic coding in short-term/working memory and/or graphomotor planning may be contributing to the handwriting problems (see Berninger, in press-a, for more information).
   - Also, give the WISC-IV Processing Speed Factor, which is typically impaired in many students with handwriting disabilities.
   - Also, determine if the child has both attention deficit disorder and handwriting problems.

3. If low achievement in dictated spelling is found, evaluate:
   - Oral vocabulary knowledge (e.g., WISC-IV vocabulary or word reasoning)
   - Preciseness of phonological word form in short-term/working memory storage (e.g., CTOPP nonword repetition)
   - Efficiency of coding the orthographic word form in short-term/working memory (e.g., PAL receptive and expressive coding).

4. If low achievement in written composition is found:
   - Evaluate whether the WISC-IV Working Memory Index is a relative weakness compared to either verbal or nonverbal reasoning or compared to age-peers.
   - Also evaluate whether D-KEFS shows evidence of weakness in executive function (particularly inhibition or inhibition/switching on color-word form, or verbal fluency letters or repetitions) compared to age-peers.

5. See PAL Lesson Sets 3, 4, 5, 7, 8, 10, 13, and 14 for possible writing interventions and progress monitoring (Berninger & Abbott, 2003).

Case Study 2

This fifth grader was also a very strong reader (standard score of 119 on WIAT II Reading Composite). However, spelling was less well developed (standard score of 87 on WIAT II Spelling) than either reading or WISC III Verbal IQ (standard score of 115) or WISC III Full Scale IQ (standard score of 119). Weakness in spelling did not appear to impair quality of composition (standard score of 110 on WIAT II Written Expression) as much as handwriting automaticity had impaired written composition in case 1.

That pattern of results is consistent with what the UW research program has found for unreferred samples (Berninger & Amtmann, 2003) but not for dyslexic samples in which spelling impairs written composition (Berninger *et al.*, submitted). However, compositional fluency was a relative weakness (standard score of 91 on WJ-R Writing Fluency), although not as impaired as in Case 1.

The child did not qualify for learning disabilities services because the IQ-achievement discrepancy missed the cutoff by 1 point. Also, traditionally spelling disabilities have not been considered as important as reading disabilities, and school personnel were not concerned about the spelling problem even though the parents and affected child were. Had process assessment been taken into account, the child's need for specialized instruction would have been recognized. PAL assessment results revealed a strength in graphomotor skills on Finger Sense (all in the 90th to 100th decile range). Neither copying text nor handwriting automaticity (50th percentile) was impaired. Spelling impairment appeared to be related to deficits in receptive and expressive orthographic coding (10th decile) and phonological coding (10th decile) and knowledge of correspondences between orthographic and phonological codes as assessed by Pseudoword Reading (20th decile). RAS for Words and Digits (30th percentile) was also a relative weakness. Dr. Fry's Spelling Program (Fry, 1996) was recommended.

Case Study 3

This second grader had both dysgraphia and attention deficit hyperactivity disorder (ADHD). These developmental disorders co-occur in some but not all children with either dysgraphia or ADHD. This child was receiving special education services under the category of ADHD and was also taking medication under the supervision of a physician. The child's WISC-III Verbal IQ (104) fell in the average range, and WIAT II reading and PAL phonological skills were strong (range 61st to 79th percentile), but spelling (WIAT II standard score of 93) and rapid automatic naming (30th percentile) were relative weaknesses. The child's most significant impairment was in handwriting automaticity, that is, rapid automatic retrieval and production of alphabet letters (more than 1 standard deviation below the mean on PAL Alphabet Writing). The teacher recommended that the child repeat second grade. The research team identified instructional approaches for dealing with the child's weaknesses in attention and automaticity and proposed an alternative to retention: explicit, systematic, and integrated writing instruction aimed at all handwriting components in the third grade program (see PAL Lesson Set 8). The research team also identified the child's strengths in social interaction and the motivating influence of writing with other children; this social component is incorporated in many PAL lessons in which children share their compositions with one another.

SPECIFIC ARITHMETIC
AND MATH DISABILITIES

DEFINITION OF ARITHMETIC DISABILITY (AD)
AND MATHEMATICAL DISABILITY (MD)

Common problems include impaired automaticity in math fact retrieval and impaired execution of computational algorithms. Some children have strengths in quantitative problem solving in the internal working memory environment but have weaknesses in representing their quantitative knowledge externally using their graphomotor and/or sensory-motor integration system, pencil and pencil, and the written symbol system for representing quantitative knowledge. Other children have the opposite pattern of strengths and weaknesses and excel in performing paper and pencil arithmetic tasks in the external environment but have weaknesses in mental arithmetic. Some children have brain-based deficits related to the internal number line. Other children have brain-based deficits in the part-whole concept that impairs their ability to tell time with clock faces and grasp fractions, decimals, and measurement systems. Some children have difficulty with arithmetic but can think mathematically (see Hoffman, 1998), whereas other children excel at arithmetic but not at mathematical thinking. Visual-spatial and verbal reasoning may contribute, along with quantitative reasoning, to achievement in arithmetic and mathematics. For example, the WISC-IV Perceptual Organization Index and Verbal Comprehension Index can be used to tease apart factors contributing to low math achievement. Oral and written language abilities may also influence how children perform on math achievement tests, and it is important to tease apart whether low performance is really due to math disability alone or to language problems. (For review of the brain basis, developmental changes, and instructional issues in normal and disabled math learning, see chapters 7 and 10 in Berninger & Richards, 2002.)

SUMMARY OF DIAGNOSTIC PROCEDURES FOR
ARITHMETIC AND MATH DISABILITIES

Table 6.7 offers general guidelines for the differential diagnosis of arithmetic and math disabilities from each other and from other learning and developmental disorders. Differential diagnosis for this academic domain is a work in progress as the research on disorders in quantitative computation and reasoning continues to expand. The recommended practices are based on psychometric instruments for quantitative skills and research on normal and disabled quantitative learning (see Busse *et al.*, 2001), as well as more than 20 years of clinical assessment experience of each of the authors and teaching experience of the first author.

TABLE 6.7   Diagnostic Procedures for Arithmetic and Mathematics Disability

1. Take the same approach as for dyslexia to rule out other developmental problems that may also cause impaired math achievement but are not specific to math disabilities.

   • Obtain WISC-IV Verbal Comprehension, Perceptual Reasoning, Working Memory, and Processing Speed Indices.

   • Evaluate whether verbal reasoning and nonverbal reasoning (both visual-spatial and quantitative), all of which may contribute to achievement in arithmetic and mathematics, are at least in the normal range and if arithmetic or mathematical achievement is unexpectedly low for any of these kinds of reasoning.

   • If the individual does better on paper and pencil calculation than the orally administered WISC-IV Arithmetic subtest, evaluate whether the Working Memory Index is a relative weakness compared to indices of either verbal or nonverbal reasoning.

   • If students show problems in math fluency (Woodcock et al., 2001), evaluate whether the Processing Speed Index is a relative weakness compared to the other WISC-IV Indices.

2. A comprehensive assessment of visual-spatial, verbal, and quantitative abilities is needed because all of these abilities influence learning to do arithmetic and think mathematically.

   • For further recommendations for comprehensive assessment of specific arithmetic or mathematical disabilities, see Busse, Berninger, Smith, & Hildebrand (2001).

   • The PAL Math referred to in that chapter is under development (the second author is the project director) and additional recommendations for diagnosing specific disabilities involving quantitative skills will be available in the test manual for that instrument.

   • A major focus of those recommendations will be research-supported approaches to diagnosis of comorbid learning disabilities and their underlying processing deficits in reading and math; in reading and writing; in writing and math; and in reading, writing, and math.

   • Some students experience double or triple jeopardy—more than one specific learning disability—which provides challenges in developing effective treatment plans and judging prognosis for adult outcomes.

CASE STUDIES TO ILLUSTRATE ARITHMETIC AND MATHEMATICAL DISABILITY

Case 1

This third grader had extraordinary difficulty recalling math facts automatically. The child's teacher used a pedagogical approach called Minute Math to promote math fact retrieval automaticity. The child, who was significantly impaired in automaticity (PAL RAN for numbers at 10th decile), cried during Minute Math and could not complete more than a few items when asked to retrieve math facts on this timed paper and pencil activity. Assessment revealed that the child had a repertoire of clever strategies for figuring out the math facts, so the problem was in fact automatic production of answers, not in controlled, strategic deduction of the answers.

The clinician recommended (1) acknowledging the strength in strategy application, and (2) using alternatives to flash card number fact drill (e.g., selective reminding in which only missed items are practiced on subsequent trials; see Berninger (1998) and multisensory strategies in which children listen and write, listen and speak, read and write, and read and speak number facts to automatize all the numbers in the equation).

Case 2

Assessment showed that this second grader had automatic recall of grade-appropriate number facts, but made many errors during computation. Observation of the child performing multiplace subtraction (including problems involving regrouping) revealed that the child could not remember or verbalize the order of the steps in the algorithm. The clinician recommended teaching a strategy with verbal prompts for each step in the algorithm that the child could apply for self-regulated, independent computation.

Case 3

Assessment showed that this fourth grader, a sibling of the first child, also had automatic recall of grade-appropriate math facts, but made many errors during computation. Observation of the child performing multiplication of multiplace numbers and long division of multiplace divisors revealed that the child got lost in the process of continually switching direction in space—from top to bottom (mulipliers in one's place), bottom to top (to proceed to ten's place), and right to left (in contrast to reading most math proceeds from right to left) *during multiplication*; and from left to right (beginning with divisor), top to bottom (multiplying number at top with the divisor and placing the result below the appropriate digits), right to left (subtracting the product from the appropriate digits in the number being divided), and bottom to top (making sure that the difference is less than the divisor) *during long division*. The clinician recommended teaching a strategy with both verbal and visual prompts for each step in the algorithm that cued both the computational step and the direction of movement in applying the computational steps so that the child could apply the strategy for self-regulated, independent computation. When the mother of the children in cases 2 and 3 was asked if she understood the difference between the two recommended strategies, she readily responded that she did: one of her children was lost in time and the other was lost in space while computing. Application of arithmetic algorithms does require application of computational steps in time and space. Children may have requisite quantitative knowledge but have difficulty in negotiating the expression of this knowledge in the temporal and spatial dimensions of paper and pencil calculations.

Case 4

This fourth grader could retrieve math facts automatically and apply arithmetic algorithms reliably during paper and pencil calculations, but could not grasp the concepts of telling time, fractions, and decimals used in measurement. Part-whole relationships are difficult for some children to grasp. Unlike object permanence (objects stay constant despite irrelevant variations), objects also have relevant variance. They can be divided into a variable number of parts that are not always easily compared across objects (see Berninger & Richards, 2002). Without a grasp of the underlying part-whole relationships, errors will be made in telling time, fractions, decimals, and measurement. The clinician recommended that the conceptual understanding of part-whole relationships should be taught independent of paper and pencil activities that require application of part-whole relationships, for example, by using manipulatives to show the representation of different part-whole relationships.

Case 5

This second grade boy was referred for failure to complete paper and pencil arithmetic. Through administration of a number of visual spatial reasoning and mental quantitative reasoning tasks on several IQ test batteries, the clinician discovered that the child was thinking algebraically and had advanced understanding of geometry. This child was a budding mathematician, but the teacher did not recognize it, and the second grade curriculum was way behind where this child was in thinking mathematically. The clinician recommended that the child be given an accelerated program of math in an individual progress program for intellectually capable (gifted) children (see Busse *et al.*, 2001).

USE OF WISC-IV IN CLINICAL DIAGNOSIS AND FUTURE RESEARCH ON DYSLEXIA AND OTHER LEARNING DISABILITIES

DYSLEXIA, DYSGRAPHIA, AND SPECIFIC COMPREHENSION DISABILITY

Given the current interest among reading researchers in fluency problems in reading (Wolf, 2001) and other academic skills, the WISC-IV Processing Speed Index and Working Memory Index will be useful in teasing apart sources of fluency problems. Working memory efficiency may be the result of multiple factors: inhibition, processing speed, executive schemes (Ribaupierre, 2002), and working memory span (work space capacity). Both researchers and clinicians might use a battery with the D-KEFS (Inhibition and Inhibition/Switching), WISC-IV Processing Speed Index, WOLF and

Denckla and/or PAL Rapid Automatic Switching (RAS) measures, and WISC-IV Working Memory Index to tease apart the relative contribution of these various factors to working memory efficiency. D-KEFS provides a measure of inhibition. WISC-IV provides measures of both processing speed and working memory (defined on the basis of span). The RAS measures provide a measure of the supervisory attention system in the central executive and should not be confused with RAN measures that require naming of visual stimuli but do not require switching attention to the extent that RAS tasks do. Each of these contributing factors to working memory efficiency may differentially contribute to different aspects of reading fluency: word-level automaticity of real word reading and pseudoword decoding (TOWRE), smoothness and coordination of text-level oral reading fluency (GORT3), and silent reading fluency that requires coordination of word-level and text-level processes (PAL Sentence Sense, Berninger, 2001b). In prior research (Berninger, Abbott, Billingsley, & Nagy, 2001), child dyslexics had fluency impairments in specific reading or writing skills rather than generalized fluency problems across the board, suggesting that sometimes fluency problems are the result not the cause of a specific processing problem underlying reading or writing. It is important to differentiate general processing speed problems across all academic domains and fluency problems specific to certain reading, writing, or math skills.

Some children have a specific learning disability affecting comprehension only and not word decoding or word reading processes (e.g., Oakhill & Yuill, 1996). Further research is needed to determine whether this specific disability is the result of a working memory deficit, a processing speed deficit, and/or specific language impairments. The WISC-IV Working Memory Index and Processing Speed Index and the scales and subtests of the CELF-III (Semel *et al.*, 1995) or CELF-IV (Semel *et al.*, 2003) might be used in clinical assessment, as well as research, for that purpose.

Results reported in Table 6.2 show that sometimes individual subtests of the WISC-III uniquely predicted reading or writing achievement better than the Verbal IQ. Research is needed to evaluate which of the WISC-IV Verbal Scale subtests, some of which are new like Word Reasoning, most uniquely predict specific reading and writing skills. In keeping with the test construction of the WISC-IV, the Full Scale IQ is less likely to be useful or necessary for documenting unexpected difficulty. In fact, many of the severely impaired dyslexics in the UW research sample did not qualify for special education under the state's regression-based discrepancy model that uses only Full Scale IQ. The WISC-IV Verbal Comprehension Factor might be used along with the other inclusionary criteria discussed in this chapter to diagnose dyslexia.

LANGUAGE LEARNING DISABILITY

The WISC IV Perceptual Reasoning Index *or* the CELF-III or CELF-IV Receptive Language or Expressive Language Scale can be used to document unexpected difficulty in reading or writing for students with language learning disability. Factors in IQ tests like the WISC-IV may be useful in diagnosing language learning disability. Sometimes these children do not meet criteria for ability–achievement discrepancy because the Full Scale IQ masks a significant difference between the Verbal Comprehension Index and the Perceptual Reasoning Index, with the latter, a measure of nonverbal reasoning, higher than the former. The language learning disability may interfere with verbal reasoning, as measured on standardized tests. In such cases, the receptive language scale on the CELF III or CELF IV tends to be higher than the expressive language scale, and this pattern of receptive > expressive language is stable across development even when expressive language falls within the normal range. Occasionally the reverse pattern (expressive > receptive) occurs and is stable; however, nonverbal intelligence is not always higher than verbal intelligence in the language learning disabled. Cognitive assessment is needed to document that cognitive development (verbal and/or nonverbal) is in the normal range, so language problems cannot be attributed to abnormal cognitive development. However, the critical diagnostic inclusionary criteria for language learning disability, whether or not nonverbal and verbal intelligence are comparably developed or discrepant, are severe impairment in selected, specific language functions: morphology, syntax, executive functions for syntax, word retrieval, and/or use of language in cognitive tasks. Evidence from family observations (delayed oral language milestones, difficulties with verbally oriented curriculum early in schooling but excelling later in the schooling with curriculum oriented to nonverbal learning) suggest that Einstein had language learning disability rather than dyslexia (Overbye, 2000; Paterniti, 2001); thus, thinking ability may develop to high levels even if an individual has to cope with language learning disability.

ARITHMETIC AND MATHEMATICAL DISABILITIES

WISC IV Arithmetic subtest can be compared with WIAT II quantitative operations to evaluate relative strengths or weaknesses in mental arithmetic compared to paper and pencil arithmetic. Some children have strengths in the former and weaknesses in the latter or vice versa. Often assessment in the quantitative domain focuses only on the quantitative domain. It is equally important to assess the verbal and visual-spatial reasoning skills that have been shown to contribute to quantitative problem solving (Robinson, Abbott, Berninger, & Busse, 1996; Robinson, Abbott, Berninger, Busse, & Mukhopadhyay, 1997). Matrix Reasoning, a new subtest on the WISC IV, is a promising tool for assessing visual spatial reasoning to add to a growing tool box for assessing quantitative and nonquantitative variables influencing arithmetic and math learning (see Busse *et al.*, 2001).

INTELLIGENT TESTING
WITH INTELLIGENCE TESTS

The misapplication of intelligence tests in assessment of specific learning disabilities lies more in the inflexible policies for implementing federal special education law than in the intelligence tests themselves. All diagnoses of learning-related disabilities are informed by including measures of specific kinds of cognitive processes and other neuropsychological processes in the assessment battery. Current research-supported assessment practices seldom rely any more on a single index of cognitive ability, but current special education practices continue to rely on a single formula using a Full Scale IQ-achievement discrepancy, whether or not it is research supported for specific kinds of learning disabilities, to qualify students for services under the category of learning disabilities, as if one size can fit all to identify children for special help in learning at school.

That said, it is important not to lose sight of the role of intelligence assessment in the treatment of individuals affected with specific learning disabilities. Historically, it was a long, hard battle to gain recognition that individuals who struggle in learning to read and write are not mentally retarded. It is still a struggle to get services in schools for intellectually capable children (reasoning in superior to very superior ranges) who exhibit reading and writing achievement below the population mean and who have research-associated processing deficits. It is alarming that this group of students is underserved in many school settings because research-supported assessment can identify their specific learning disabilities (e.g., Yates, Berninger, & Abbott, 1994), and research-supported treatment can allow them to actualize their own potential and contribute to society despite the learning disabilities. An important aspect of clinical treatment of all individuals with a specific learning disability is convincing them that they are intelligent. Sometimes, using the results of an intelligence test to confirm that the individual is intelligent is part of the therapeutic process in demonstrating that learning problems are not simply a matter of lack of intelligence. Many affected individuals are fearful that they really are not smart; overcoming this fear often takes time, relationship-building with trusted professionals, and helping the affected person become successful in school learning (Shaywitz, 2003).

The solution is not to throw out the IQ tests. As Beverley Wolf, a leader in learning disabilities in Washington State, has pointed out, if professionals do not diagnose normal intelligence, the affected individuals self-diagnose that they are stupid. The solution is to use the IQ test results in more intelligent, flexible ways (Berninger *et al.*, 1992) and to rewrite the approach to qualifying children for special help in academic learning that is currently mandated by federal law in the United States so that it is more research-supported for specific kinds of learning disabilities and flexibly meets the needs of all children of normal intelligence who struggle in academic learning.

ACKNOWLEDGMENTS

Grants HD 25858-14 and P50 33812-09 from the National Institute of Child Health and Human Development (NICHD) supported the preparation of this chapter and some of the research that is discussed.

The authors thank Joan Waiss and Jennifer Thomson for assistance in scheduling families, and Allison Brooks, Rebecca Brooksher, Kate Eschen, Sarah Hellwege, Diana Hoffer, Stephanie King, and Dori Zook for administration of the phenotyping test battery to participants. They also thank Nancy Robinson and Aurelio Prifitera for helpful comments on an earlier version.

REFERENCES

Abbott, R., & Berninger, V. (1993). Structural equation modeling of relationships among developmental skills and writing skills in primary and intermediate grade writers. *Journal of Educational Psychology, 85(3),* 478–508.

American Psychiatric Association. (1994). *Diagnostic and statistical manual of mental disorders* (4th ed.). Washington, D.C.: Author.

Baddeley, A. (2002). Is working memory still working? *European Psychologist, 7,* 85-97.

Baddeley, A., Gathercole, S., & Papagno, C. (1998). The phonological loop as a language learning device. *Psychological Review, 105,* 158–173.

Berninger, V. (1998a). *Process assessment of the learner (PAL). Guides for intervention in reading and writing.* San Antonio, TX: The Psychological Corporation.

Berninger, V. (1998b). Assessment, prevention, and intervention for specific reading and writing disabilities in young children. In B. Wong (Ed.), *Learning disabilities* (2nd ed.) (pp. 529–555). New York: Academic Press.

Berninger, V. (2001a). Understanding the lexia in dyslexia. *Annals of Dyslexia, 51,* 23–48.

Berninger, V. (2001b). *Process assessment of the learner: Test battery for reading and writing.* San Antonio, TX: The Psychological Corporation.

Berninger, V. (in press-a). Understanding the graphia in dysgraphia. In D. Dewey & D. Tupper (Eds.), *Developmental motor disorders: A neuropsychological perspective.* New York: Guilford.

Berninger, V. (in press-b). The reading brain in children and youth: A systems approach. To appear in B. Wong (Ed.), *Learning about Learning Disabilities* (3rd ed.). San Diego: Academic Press (Elsevier Imprint).

Berninger, V. (in press-c). Brain-based assessment and instructional intervention. Chapter in book based on presentations at the annual meeting of the British Dyslexia Association. Editor Angela Fawcett and others.

Berninger, V., & Abbott, S. (2003). *PAL Research-supported reading and writing lessons.* San Antonio, TX: The Psychological Corporation.

Berninger, V., Abbott, R., & Alsdorf, B. (1997). Lexical- and sentence-level processes in comprehension of written sentences. *Reading and Writing: An Interdisciplinary Journal, 9,* 135–162.

Berninger, V., Abbott, R., Billingsley, F., & Nagy, W. (2001). Processes underlying timing and fluency: Efficiency, automaticity, coordination, and morphological awareness. In M. Wolf (Ed.), *Dyslexia, fluency, and the brain* (pp. 383–414). Extraordinary Brain Series. Baltimore: York Press.

Berninger, V., Abbott, R., Thomson, J., & Raskind, W. (2001). Language phenotype for reading and writing disability: A family approach. *Scientific Studies in Reading, 5,* 59–105.

Berninger, V., Abbott, R., Thomson, J., Wagner, R., Swanson, H. L., & Raskind, W. (submitted). *Modeling phenotypes for developmental dyslexia in children and adults: Evidence for phonological core and working memory deficits.*

Berninger, V., Abbott, R., Vermeulen, K., Ogier, S., Brooksher, R., Zook, D., & Lemos, Z. (2002). Comparison of faster and slower responders: Implications for the nature and duration of early reading intervention. *Learning Disability Quarterly, 25,* 59–76.

Berninger, V., & Amtmann, D. (2003). Preventing written expression disabilities through early and continuing assessment and intervention for handwriting and/or spelling problems: Research into practice. In H. L. Swanson, K. Harris, & S. Graham (Eds.), *Handbook of Research on Learning Disabilities* (pp. 345–363). New York: Guilford.

Berninger, V., & Fuller, F. (1992). Gender differences in orthographic, verbal, and compositional fluency: Implications for diagnosis of writing disabilities in primary grade children. *Journal of School Psychology, 30,* 363–382.

Berninger, V., Hart, T., Abbott, R., & Karovsky, R. (1992). Defining reading and writing disabilities with and without IQ: A flexible, developmental perspective. *Learning Disability Quarterly, 15,* 103–118.

Berninger, V., & Nagy, W. (2003). *Experimental Measures of Morphological Awareness and Decoding Used in University of Washington Writing Interventions Project and Multidisciplinary Learning Disability Center.*

Berninger, V., & Richards, T. (2002). *Brain literacy for educators and psychologists.* San Diego: Academic Press (Elsevier Imprint).

Berninger, V., & Rutberg, J. (1992). Relationship of finger function to beginning writing: Application to diagnosis of writing disabilities. *Developmental Medicine & Child Neurology, 34,* 155–172.

Berninger, V., Stage, S., Smith, D., & Hildebrand, D. (2001). Assessment for reading and writing intervention: A 3-tier model for prevention and intervention. In J. Andrews, H., D. Saklofske, & H. Janzen (Eds.), *Ability, achievement, and behavior assessment. A practical handbook* (pp. 195–223). New York: Academic Press.

Berninger, V., Vermeulen, K., Abbott, R., McCutchen, D., Cotton, S., Cude, J., Dorn, S., & Sharon, T. (2003). Comparison of three approaches to supplementary reading instruction for low achieving second grade readers. *Language, Speech, and Hearing Services in Schools, 34,* 101–115.

Bishop, D., & Snowling, M. (in press). Developmental dyslexia and specific language impairment: Same or different? *Psychological Bulletin.*

Bruck, M. (1990). Word recognition skills of adults with childhood diagnoses of dyslexia. *Developmental Psychology, 26,* 439–454.

Busse, J., Berninger, V., Smith, D., & Hildebrand, D. (2001). Assessment for math talent and disability: A developmental model. In J. Andrews, H., D. Saklofske, & H. Janzen (Eds.), *Ability, achievement, and behavior assessment. A practical handbook.* (pp. 225–253). New York: Academic Press.

Butler, K., & Silliman, E. (Eds.). (2002). *Speaking, reading, and writing in children with language learning disabilities.* Mahwah, NJ: Lawrence Erlbaum Associates.

Carlisle, J. (2000). Awareness of the structure and meaning of morphologically complex words: Impact on reading. *Reading and Writing: An Interdisciplinary Journal, 12,* 169–190.

Catts, H. (1993). The relationship between speech-language impairments and reading disabilities. *Journal of Speech & Hearing Research, 36*(5), 948–958.

Chapman, N., Igo, R., Thomson, J., Matsushita, M., Brkanac, Z., Hotzman, T., Berninger, V., Wijsman, E., & Raskind, W. (in press). Linkage analyses of four regions previously implicated in dyslexia: Confirmation of a locus on chromosome 15q. *Neuropsychiatric Genetics. A Section of the American Journal of Medical Genetics.*

Crosson, B., Rao, S., Woodley, S., Rosen, A., Bobholz, J., Mayer, A., Cunningham, J., Hammeke, T., Fuller, S., Binder, J., Cox, R., & Stein, E. (1999). Mapping of semantic, phonological, and orthographic verbal working memory in normal adults with functional magnetic resonance imaging. *Neuropsychology 13,* 171–187.

Delis, D. C., Kaplan, E., & Kramer, J. H. (2001). *Delis-Kaplan Executive Function System*. San Antonio, TX: The Psychological Corporation.

Demetriou, A., Cristou, C., Spanoudis, G., & Platsidou, M. (2002). The development of mental processing: Efficiency, working memory, and thinking. *Monographs of the Society for Research in Child Development, 67(268)*:1–167.

Engle, R., Kane, M., & Tuholski, S. (1999). Individual differences in working memory capacity and what they tell us about controlled attention, general fluid intelligence, and functions of the prefrontal cortex. In A. Miyake & P. Shah (Eds.), *Models of working memory: Models of active maintenance and executive control* (pp. 102–134). New York: Cambridge University Press.

Fletcher, S.G. (1978). *Time-by-Count Test Measurement of Diadochokinetic Syllable Rate*. Austin, TX: PRO-ED.

Fry, E. (1996). *Spelling book: Words most needed plus phonics for grades 1–6*. Now distributed as *Dr. Fry's Spelling Book* (available through Teacher Created Materials, 6421 Industry Way Westminster, CA 92683, 1-800-662-4321).

Greenblatt, E., Mattis, S., & Trad, P. (1990). Nature and prevalence of learning disabilities in a child psychiatric population. *Developmental Neuropsychology, 6*, 71–83.

Gunter, T., Wagner, S., & Friederici, A. (2003). Working memory and lexical ambiguity resolution as revealed by ERPS: A difficult case for activation theories. *Journal of Cognitive Neuroscience, 15*, 643–657.

Hale, J., Naglieri, J., Kaufman, A., & Kavale, K. (2004, Winter). Specific learning disability classification in the new individuals with disabilities education act: The danger of a good idea. *The School Psychologist, 58*, 6–13.

Hitch, G., Towse, J., & Hutton, U. (2001). What limits children's working memory span? Theoretical accounts and applications for scholastic development. *Journal of Experimental Psychology: General, 130*, 184–198.

Hoffman, P. (1998). *The man who loved only numbers. The story of Paul Erdös and the search for mathematical truth*. New York: Hyperion.

Hutton, U., & Towse, J. (2001). Short-term memory and working memory as indices of children's cognitive skills. *Memory, 9*, 383–394.

Liberman, A. (1999). The reading researcher and the reading teacher need the right theory of speech. *Scientific Studies of Reading, 3*, 95–111.

Lovett, M. (1987). A developmental approach to reading disability: Accuracy and speed criteria of normal and deficient reading skill. *Child Development, 58*, 234–260.

Lyon, G. R., Shaywitz, S., & Shaywitz, B. (2003). A definition of dyslexia. *Annals of Dyslexia, 53*, 1–14.

Martin, R., & Romani, C. (1994). Verbal working memory and sentence comprehension: A multiple components view. *Neuropsychology, 8*, 506–523.

Miyake, A., Friedman, N., Emerson, M., Witzki, A., Howerter, A., & Wager, T. (2000). The unity and diversity of executive functions and their contributions to complex "frontal lobe" tasks: A latent variable analysis. *Cognitive Psychology, 41*, 49–100.

Morris, R. Morris, R., Stuebing, K., Fletcher, J., Shaywitz, S., Lyon, G. R., Shakweiler, D., Katz, L., Francis, D., & Shaywitz, B. (1998). Subtypes of reading disability: Variability around a phonological core. *Journal of Educational Psychology, 90*, 347–373.

Nagy, W., Berninger, V., Abbott, R., Vaughan, K., & Vermeulin, K. (2003). Relationship of morphology and other language skills to literacy skills in at-risk second graders and at-risk fourth grade writers. *Journal of Educational Psychology, 95*, 730–742.

Norman, D. A., & Shallice, T. (1986). Attention to action. Willed and automatic control of behaviour. In R. Davidson, G. Schwarts, & D. Shapiro (Eds.), *Consciousness and self-regulation: Advances in research and theory* (Vol. 4, pp. 1–18). New York: Plenum.

Oakhill, J., & Yuill, N. (1996). Higher order factors in comprehension disability: Processes and remediation. In C. Cornoldi & J. Oakhill (Eds.), *Reading comprehension difficulties: Processes and intervention* (pp. 69–92). Mahweh, NJ: Lawrence Erlbaum Associates.

Olson, R., Forsberg, H., Wise, B., & Rack, J. (1994). Measurement of word recognition, orthographic, and phonological skills. In G. R. Lyon (Ed.), *Frames of reference for the assessment of learning disabilities* (pp. 243–277). Baltimore, Brooks.

Overbye, D. (2000). *Einstein in love. A scientific romance.* New York: Penguin Books.

Paterniti, M. (2001). *Driving Mr. Albert. A trip across American with Einstein's brain.* New York: Random House (Delta).

Pennington, B., Van Order, G., Smith, S., Green, P., & Haith, M. (1990). Phonological processing skills and deficits in adult dyslexics. *Child Development, 61,* 1753–1778.

Prifitera, A., Weiss, L., & Saklofske, D. (1998). The WISC-III in context. In A. Prifitera & D. Saklofske (Eds.), *WISC-III clinical use and interpretation: Scientist-practitioner perspectives* (pp. 1-38). San Diego: Academic Press.

The Psychological Corporation. (2001). *Wechsler Individual Achievement Test,* (2nd ed). *WIAT-II.* San Antonio, TX: The Psychological Corporation.

The Psychological Corporation. (2003). *Wechsler Individual Intelligence Test for Children* (4th ed.). *WISC-IV.* San Antonio, TX: The Psychological Corporation.

Ribaupierre, A. (2002). Working memory and attentional processes across the life span. In Graf, P., & N. Ohta (Eds.), *Lifespan development of human memory* (pp. 59–80). Cambridge, MA: The MIT Press.

Robinson, N., Abbott, R., Berninger, V., & Busse, J. (1996). Structure of precocious mathematical abilities: Gender similarities and differences. *Journal of Educational Psychology, 88,* 341–352.

Robinson, N., Abbott, R., Berninger, V., Busse, J., & Mukhopadhyay, S. (1997). Developmental changes in mathematically precocious young children: Longitudinal and gender effects. *Gifted Child Quarterly, 41,* 145–158.

Scarborough, H. (1984). Continuity between childhood dyslexia and adult reading. *British Journal of Psychology, 75,* 329–348,

Semel, E., Wiig, E. H., & Secord, W.A. (1995). *Clinical evaluation of language fundamentals* (ed. 3). San Antonio, TX: The Psychological Corporation.

Semel, E., Wiig, E. H., & Secord, W. A. (2003). *Clinical evaluation of language fundamentals* (ed. 4). San Antonio, TX: The Psychological Corporation.Shaywitz, S. (2003). *Overcoming dyslexia. A new and complete science-based program for reading problems at any level.* New York, Alfred A. Knopf.

Shaywitz, S., Shaywitz, B., Fletcher, J., & Escobar, M. (1990). Prevalence of reading disabilities in boys and girls. Results of the Connecticut longitudinal study. *Journal of the American Medical Association, 264,* 998–102.

Shaywitz, S., Shaywitz, B., Fulbright, R., Skudlarski, P., Mencl, W., Constable, R., Pugh, K. D., Holahan, J., Marchione, K., Fletcher, J., Lyon, G. R., & Gore, J. (2003). Neural systems for compensation and persistence: Young adult outcome of childhood reading disability. *Biological Psychiatry, 54,* 25–33.

Silliman, E., Wilkinson, L., & Danzak, R. (in press). Putting Humpty Dumpty together again: What's right with Betsy. In E. Silliman & L. C. Wilkinson (Eds.), *Language and literacy in schools.* New York: Guilford.

Smith-Spark, J., Fisk, J., Fawcett, A., & Nicolson, R. (2003). Investigating the central executive in adult dyslexics: Evidence from the phonological and visuospatial working memory performance. *European Journal of Cognitive Neuropsychology, 15,* 567–587.

Stage, S., Abbott, R., Jenkins, J., & Berninger, V. (2003). Predicting response to early reading intervention using Verbal IQ, reading-related language abilities, attention ratings, and Verbal IQ-word reading discrepancy. *Journal of Learning Disabilities, 36,* 24–33.

Stanovich, K. E., & Siegel, L. S. (1994). Phenotypic performance profile of children with reading disabilities: A regression-based test of the phonological-core variable-difference model. *Journal of Educational Psychology, 86,* 24–53.

Swanson, L., & Siegel, L. (2001). Learning disabilities as a working memory deficit. *Issues in Education, 7,* 1–48.

Thorndike, R. L., Hagen, E. P., Sattler, J. M. (1986). *Stanford-Binet Intelligence Scale* (ed. 4). Itasca, IL: Riverside Publishing.

Torgesen, J., Wagner, R., & Rashotte, C. (1999). *Test of Word Reading Efficiency (TOWRE)*. Austin, TX: PRO-ED.

Torgesen, J., Wagner, R., Rashotte, C., Rose, E., Lindamood, P., Conway, T., & Garwan, C. (1999). Preventing reading failure in young children with phonological processing disabilities: Group and individual responses to instruction. *Journal of Educational Psychology, 91*, 579–593.

Towse, J. (1998). On random generation and the central executive of working memory. *British Journal of Psychology, 89*, 77–101.

Towse, J., Hitch, G., & Hutton, U. (2000). A reevaluation of working memory capacity in children. *Journal of Memory and Language, 39*, 195–217.

Vellutino, F., Scanlon, D., & Tanzman, M. (1991). Bridging the gap between cognitive and neuropsychological conceptualizations of reading disabilities. *Learning and Individual Differences, 3*, 181–203.

Wagner, R., & Torgesen, J. (1987). The nature of phonological processing and its causal role in the acquisition of reading skills. *Psychological Bulletin, 101*, 192–212.

Wagner, R., Torgesen, J., & Rashotte, C. (1999). *Comprehensive Test of Phonological Processing (CTOPP)*. Austin, TX: PRO-ED.

Wallach, G., & Butler, K. (Eds.). (1994). *Language learning disabilities in school-age children and adolescents: Some principles and applications* (2nd ed.). New York: Maxwell Macmillan International.

Wechsler, D. (1981). *Wechsler Adult Intelligence Scale* (revised). San Antonio, TX: The Psychological Corporation.

Wechsler, D. (1991). *Wechsler Intelligence Scale for Children* (3rd ed.). San Antonio, TX: The Psychological Corporation.

Wiederholt, J., & Bryant, B. (1992). *Gray Oral Reading Test* (3rd ed.). Odessa, FL: Psychological Assessment Resources.

Wiig, E. (1991). Language-learning disabilities: Paradigms for the nineties. *Annals of Dyslexia, 41*, 3-22.

Wilkinson, G. (1993). *Wide Range Achievement Tests* (revised). Wilmington, DE: Wide Range, Inc.

Wolf, M. (1986). Rapid alternating stimulus naming in the developmental dyslexias. *Brain and Language, 27*, 360–379.

Wolf, M. (Ed.) (2001). *Dyslexia, fluency, and the brain*. Extraordinary Brain Series. Baltimore: York Press.

Wolf, M., Bally, H., & Morris, R. (1986). Automaticity, retrieval processes, and reading: A longitudinal study in average and impaired reading. *Child Development, 57*, 988–1000.

Wolf, M., & Biddle, K. (1994). [Unpublished norms for RAN and RAS tasks.]

Wolf, M., & Bowers, P. (1999). The double-deficit hypothesis for the developmental dyslexias. *Journal of Educational Psychology, 91*, 415–438.

Wolf, M., & Denckla, M. (2004). *Rapid Automatic Naming Tests*. Austin, TX: Pro-Ed.

Wolff, P., Cohen, C., & Drake, C. (1984). Impaired motor timing control in specific reading retardation. *Neuropsychologia, 22*, 587–600.

Woodcock, R. (1987). *Woodcock Reading Mastery Tests* (revised). Circle Pines, MN: American Guidance Service.

Woodcock, R., & Johnson, B. (1990). *Woodcock-Johnson Psycho-Educational Battery Revised Tests of Achievement*. Chicago: Riverside Publishing.

Woodcock, R., McGrew, K., & Mather, N. (2001). *Woodcock-Johnson III*. Itasca, IL: Riverside.

Yates, C., Berninger, V., & Abbott, R. (1994). Writing problems in intellectually gifted children. *Journal for the Education of the Gifted, 18*, 131–155.

7

ASSESSMENT OF ATTENTION DEFICIT HYPERACTIVITY DISORDER WITH THE WISC-IV

VICKI L. SCHWEAN

Department of Educational Psychology and Special Education
University of Saskatchewan
Saskatoon, Saskatchewan, Canada

DONALD H. SAKLOFSKE

Department of Educational Psychology and Special Education
University of Saskatchewan
Saskatoon, Saskatchewan, Canada

This chapter describes current theory and research that informs the psychologist who plays a central role in the initial diagnosis and subsequent assessments of children with attention deficit hyperactive disorder (ADHD). It is these theories and the published empirical findings that will guide psychologists in both deciding what to assess and how to interpret the findings relative to the arriving at a differential diagnosis. While intelligence tests such as the WISC-IV do not, and never were intended to, diagnose ADHD, they are of significant importance in the assessment of children with ADHD. Simply knowing the overall cognitive ability of a child with ADHD is of relevance in planning behavioral and educational programming. Current theories described in this chapter have, for example, also implicated the significance of working memory impairments in ADHD.

These clinical features and cognitive characteristics of ADHD can be effectively measured with today's intelligence tests. In this regard, the WISC-IV factor structure would appear most relevant to the assessment of ADHD. The WISC-IV also has considerable clinical value for monitoring cognitive changes of paramount importance in determining the efficacy of medical, psychological, and educational programs. An added advantage of the WISC-IV is that it is part of a larger family of linked and co-normed tests that are also so relevant to diagnosing and assessing children with ADHD.

In the main, it is the theories and research literature that psychologists must use to complement their clinical experience in guiding the interpretation of assessment data, including the WISC-IV. For this reason, considerable space is devoted to contemporary theory and research that have particular relevance for using and interpreting the WISC-IV when assessing children for ADHD. Without this framework to guide interpretation, the WISC-IV will be of limited value, and without the WISC-IV, there would not be the sound psychometric capability to assess these clinical guideposts.

DIAGNOSTIC CLASSIFICATION OF ADHD

ADHD is a relatively common neurobehavioral disorder, affecting approximately 9% of school-age boys and 3% of girls (Szatmari, 1992). While this population of children was recognized as early as 1902 with Still's reference to children exhibiting "defects in moral control," the condition was first introduced in the Diagnostic and Statistical Manual of Mental Disorder (DSM-II: American Psychiatric Association [APA], 1968) under the label of "Hyperkinetic Reaction of Childhood." As the label implies, defining criteria for this condition emphasized observable disruptive behavioral excesses. Reflecting scientific advancement in the field of ADHD, each subsequent edition of the DSM included a substantial revision in both nomenclature and nosology.

Advances in research findings demonstrating that subtle cognitive deficits in response inhibition and attention were more prominent and reliable diagnostic indicators than were motor excesses resulted in both a change in nomenclature to attention deficit disorder (ADD) in the 1980 revision of the DSM (DSM-III) and also in the recognition of subtypes differentiated only in the presence or absence of hyperactivity. In the 1987 edition (DSM-III-R), however, subtype differentiation was abandoned because of lack of empirical support and a new generic category, attention-deficit hyperactivity disorder (ADHD), characterized by developmentally inappropriate degrees of inattention, impulsivity, and hyperactivity, was created.

Keeping with factor analytic studies supporting the two-factor description of inattention and hyperactive-impulsive factors, together with studies documenting the external validity of subgroups differentiated on these factors

(Lahey *et al.*, 1994), the DSM-IV-TR (2000) now recognizes three subtypes of attention-deficit/hyperactivity disorder (ADHD): attention–deficit/hyperactivity disorder, combined type (ADHD/CT); attention–deficit/hyperactivity disorder, predominantly inattentive type (ADHD/IT); and attention–deficit/hyperactivity disorder, predominantly hyperactive-impulsive type (ADHD/HIT). The predominantly inattentive type is analogous to attention deficit disorder without hyperactivity and the combined subtype to attention deficit disorder with hyperactivity. The category of predominantly hyperactive-impulsive has no precedent in the DSM classification system (McBurnett *et al.*, 1993).

The DSM-IV criteria outline two clusters of symptoms, inattention and hyperactivity-impulsivity, each of which consist of nine behaviors. A child must present with six (or more) of the symptoms in either the inattentive or hyperactivity–impulsivity clusters or both to meet the diagnostic criteria for ADHD/IT, ADHD/HIT, or ADHD/CT, respectively. The symptoms must be developmentally inappropriate, have been present before the age of 7 years, cause impairment in at least two settings, and result in clinically significant impairment in social, academic, or occupational functioning. The DSM-IV-TR points out that associated features of ADHD vary depending on age and developmental stage and may include low frustration tolerance, temper outbursts, bossiness, stubbornness, excessive and frequent insistence that requests be met, mood lability, demoralization, dysphoria, rejection by peers, poor self-esteem, academic underachievement, and impairment in familial adjustment. Further, a substantial proportion of clinic-referred children with ADHD have oppositional defiant disorder or conduct disorder. Other associated disorders include mood disorders, anxiety disorders, and learning and communication disorders.

SUBGROUP ISSUES

No disorder in the history of childhood psychopathology has been subject to as many reconceptualizations, redefinitions, and renamings as ADD (Lahey *et al.*, 1988). At the heart of this activity is the simple fact that the disorder is characterized by considerable heterogeneity. Research findings underscore the diversity among children with attention disorders in etiology, cognitive, academic, psychological, and family correlates; clinical courses; outcomes; and intervention responses. This has led to calls for and efforts toward delineating more homogeneous, clinically meaningful subgroups. Particular controversy has focused on whether the IT vs the HIT and CT represent two subtypes of a single disorder or make up two distinct, separate disorders (Cantwell & Baker, 1992).

While internal validation studies would appear to support the hypothesis that the IT is a distinct syndrome from the other subtypes (Bauermeister *et al.*, 1992; Lahey & Carlson, 1992), external validation studies have yielded more contradictory results. Barkley (2001) contends that successful differentiation of these conditions rests on the need to recognize the multidimensional nature of attention and this can best be accomplished through studies using double-dissociation methods, as this methodology allows for the identification of the unique psychological domains affected by each condition.

CONCEPTUAL ACCOUNT OF ADHD

How best to conceptualize the underlying mechanisms of ADHD has been the subject of much debate over the years. The earliest attempts focused on excessive motor activity theoretically arising from minimum brain damage or dysfunction (Strauss & Lehtinen, 1947; Wender, 1971). However, in the 1970s, Douglas and colleagues argued for the primacy of constitutional impairments in attention, inhibitory control, arousal, and responses to reinforcement in ADHD (Douglas, 1972, 1976, 1980a, 1980b, 1983; Douglas & Peters, 1979). The research literature examining the cognitive weaknesses and pharmacological treatment responses of ADHD children suggested an underlying defect in self-regulation and that the impairments operative in ADHD exert a secondary and spiraling effect on the development of meta-cognitive abilities, effectance motivation, and cognitive schemata (Douglas, 1980a; Douglas & Peters, 1979).

Recent advancements in medical technology have led to refined causal explanatory hypotheses of ADHD. Research has implicated dysfunction in the prefrontal-striatal network and its interconnections with other brain regions that appear to subserve the executive functions and self-control (Barkley, 1998, p. 65). These findings have been incorporated into recent theories of ADHD including the working memory model postulated by Rapport and colleagues (Denny & Rapport, 2001; Rapport, 2002; Rapport *et al.*, 2000; Rapport *et al.*, 2001) and the disinhibition model of Barkley (1997a, 1997b).

WORKING MEMORY MODEL

Rapport *et al.* argue that working memory is the core deficit in ADHD. The impulsivity associated with ADHD is the result of deficiencies in working memory. Working memory includes those processes needed to construct, maintain, and manipulate incoming information; working memory is needed for problem solving and for the execution of an organized plan of action or behavioral sequence. Thus, working memory has a pivotal role in determining the individual's behavior. Following this conceptualization, the somewhat sporadic and inconsistent behavior (often ascribed to impulsivity) of individuals with ADHD results from the individual's inability to manipulate the incoming information and organize his or her own behavior. Similarly, the processes of working memory (e.g., the ability to maintain representations in memory) contribute to the stimulation-seeking behavior (distractibility) of individuals with ADHD and serve as a form of negative reinforcement in the face of high task demands. With the inclusion of the task demands as part of the conceptualization, Rapport's model provides an explanation of ADHD that incorporates the interaction of context characteristics and child characteristics consistent with diathesis-stress theory. Rapport *et al.* (2001) argue that disinhibition is a by-product of working memory process and, thus, impaired working memory causes disinhibition or mediates the influence of behavioral inhibition. That is, it is predicted that when working memory is controlled for, the relationship between disinhibition and ADHD symptoms should not exist or would be considerably reduced.

DISINHIBITION MODEL

Barkley (1997a, 1997b) links behavioral inhibition, including working memory, to the executive functions and self-regulation. Behavioral inhibition occupies a central point in relationship to the four other executive functions (i.e., nonverbal working memory, internalization of speech, self-regulation of affect/motivation/arousal, and reconstitution), which are dependent on it for their own effective execution. These four executive functions subserve self-regulation, bringing behavior (motor control/fluency, syntax) progressively more under the control of internally represented information, time, and the probable future, and wrestling it from control by the immediate context and the temporal now. Barkley (1997, 2000) stipulates that his model does not apply to those having ADHD-IT; indeed, he argues that this condition is qualitatively different from ADHD-HIT and ADHD-CT. Barkley maintains that the impairment in behavioral inhibition occurring in ADHD disrupts the efficient execution of the executive functions, thereby delimiting the capacity for self-regulation. The result is an impairment in the cross-temporal organization of behavior and in the guidance and control of behavior by internally represented information. This inevitably leads to a reduction in the maximization of long-term consequences for the individual.

Within Barkley's model, response inhibition is defined as the capacity (1) to delay prepotent responses (i.e., those for which immediate reinforcement, both positive and negative, is available or for which there is a strong history of reinforcement); (2) to interrupt ongoing responses given feedback about performance; and (3) to inhibit responding to sources of interference when engaged in tasks requiring self-regulation and goal-directed action. Response inhibition occupies a central point in relationship to the four other executive functions, which in turn, subserve self-regulation, bringing behavior (motor control/fluency/syntax) progressively more under the control of internally represented information, time, and the probable future) (Barkley, 1998).

Nonverbal working memory is defined as the ability to maintain mental information on-line that will be used subsequently to control a motor response. Within Barkley's framework, it is nonverbal working memory that facilitates hindsight or retrospective thinking, forethought or prospective thinking, and anticipatory set. Intact nonverbal working memory is essential to the cross-temporal organization of behavior (i.e., the linking of events, responses, and their eventual consequences, despite gaps among them in real time). Thus, self-regulation relative to time arises as a consequence of nonverbal working memory and the internally represented information it provides for the control and guidance of behavior over time (Barkley, 1998). The second executive function, internalization of speech or verbal working memory, arises out of progression in the development of behavioral inhibition, which permits language to become a means of reflection, as well as a means for controlling one's own behavior. In turn, this results in an increased capacity for self-control, planfulness, and goal-directed behavior. The third executive function, self-regulation of affect/motivation/arousal, sets the occasion for the inhibition of initial prepotent emotional and motivational responses, which subsequently facilitates self-directed actions that are required for the initiation and maintenance of goal-directed behavior. The delay in responding that behavioral inhibition permits also enhances a child's ability to engage in a process of synthesis or reconstitution, the fourth executive function. It is the reconstitution function that provides an individual with a means to synthesize novel speech and behavioral sequences in the service of problem-solving and goal-directed behavior. In concert, behavior inhibition and the executive functions it supports permit the construction and execution of increasingly lengthy, complex, hierarchically organized, and novel chains of goal-directed behavior (i.e., motor control/fluency/syntax). According to Barkley, this is achieved by generating internally represented information that serves to take over the control of behavior from the moment and immediate setting, and to direct behavior toward time and the probable or anticipated future.

APPLICATIONS OF BARKLEY'S THEORY TO ADHD

Barkley's theory leads to the prediction of specific deficits in response inhibition, the four executive functions, and in motor control/fluency/syntax. While Barkley's theory was initially informed by the empirical research, it has fostered considerable research designed to evaluate the nature of components in the model, the relationships between various components of the model, and the model as applied to ADHD. For the purposes of the current chapter, we examine a listing of impairments Barkley hypothesized to be evident in ADHD, along with a sampling of neuropsychological and cognitive studies investigating the application of the model to this population.

The impairment of behavioral inhibition occurring in ADHD is posited by Barkley to lead to disinhibited prepotent responses, perseveration of ongoing responses, and poor interference control. A number of studies, using a variety of tasks designed to assess differing aspects of response inhibition, have reported that ADHD children perform poorer than their normally developing peers (Cantrill, 2003; Epstein *et al.*, 2003; Houghton *et al.*, 1999; Kerns *et al.*, 2001; McInerney & Kerns, 2003; Meaux, 2002; Rubia *et al.*, 2001; Stevens *et al.*, 2002). However, other studies have reported no impairments for their ADHD samples on measures of inhibitory processes (Barkley *et al.*, 2001; Kirlin, 2003; Shallice *et al.*, 2002; West *et al.*, 1999; Wu *et al.*, 2002).

In terms of the executive functions, Barkley maintains that deficits in nonverbal working memory will express themselves through inability to hold events in mind, inability to manipulate or act on events, impaired imitation of complex sequences, defective hindsight, defective forethought, poor anticipatory set, limited self-awareness, diminished sense of time, deficient nonverbal rule-governed behavior, and delayed cross-temporal organization. Recent studies support Barkley's contention and show that ADHD children perform significantly poorer on various measurements of time (Barkley, 2001; Cantrill, 2003; Fleck, 2001; McInerney & Kerns, 2003; but see Risher, 2002). Keeping with Barkley's model, Cantrill (2003) and Meaux (2002) found that inhibition was a significant predictor of time sense and time perception. Research that has examined nonverbal working impairments has also demonstrated spatial working memory problems (e.g., Cornoldi *et al.*, 2001; Dietelin, 2001).

Deficits in the internalization of language are thought by Barkley to express themselves in reduced description and reflection; poor self-questioning/ problem solving, deficient rule-governed behavior, less effective generation of rules/meta-rules, impaired reading comprehension, and delayed moral reasoning. Studies examining the construct of verbal working memory itself have reported differing results. Differences between ADHD children and their normally developing peers are reported on a variety of verbal working memory tasks (e.g., digit span, reading span) (Cornoldi *et al.*, 2001; Dietelin, 2001; McInnes *et al.*, 2003; Sarkari, 2003; Stevens *et al.*, 2002). In contrast, other studies have not found auditory working memory deficits among their groups, although impairments in short-term memory were reported in several studies (e.g., Kerns *et al.*, 2001; Pallas, 2003; Vaughn, 1998). With respect to other predictions, Shallice *et al.* (2002) noted that strategy generation and use were severely affected in the ADHD group while McInnes *et al.* (2003) noted that ADHD children were poorer at comprehending inferences and monitoring comprehension of instruction.

Barkley posits that immature self-regulation of affect/motivation/arousal will be evident through limited self-regulation of affect, less objectivity and social perspective-taking, diminished self-regulation of motivation, and poor self-regulation of arousal in the service of goal-directed behavior. Relatively few neuropsychological studies have assessed this executive function. Stevens *et al.* (2002) examined the self-regulation of motivation in ADHD and normally developing children and reported that, contrary to prediction, the groups did not differ in their responsiveness to external reinforcement. However, several studies have reported that ADHD subjects are most influenced by the immediacy of reinforcement (Barkley, 2001; Neef, 2001). McInerney and Kerns (2003) administered two versions of a time reproduced paradigm (Regular and Enhanced) in which motivational level was manipulated by the addition of positive sham feedback and the prospect of earning a reward. Findings indicated that children with ADHD performed significantly better on the motivating Enhanced vs the Regular time reproduction paradigm, although they continued to perform significantly worse than controls on both tasks.

Barkley (1998) attributes limited analysis and synthesis of behavior, reduced verbal fluency/behavioral fluency, deficient rule creativity, less goal-directed behavioral creativity and diversity, less frequent use of behavioral simulations, and immature syntax of behavior to impaired reconstitution. The reconstitution function is evident in both the verbal domain (i.e., verbal analysis, fluency, and synthesis) and the nonverbal domain (i.e., design analysis, fluency, and synthesis) and can express itself in gross and fine motor behaviors such as dancing, handwriting, drawing, and so on. Law (2003) examined the differential pattern of motor deficits between subtypes of ADHD and the relationship between motor deficits and problems in attention, hyperactivity, behavioral inhibition, and executive functioning. Results showed a significant subtype effect on fine motor measures and parent ratings of gross motor skills, with the younger ADHD-CT group performing more poorly than the younger ADHD-IT group. Reduced motor performance in this study was correlated with problems on tasks measuring attention, vigilance, impulsivity, and working memory, but not with behavioral ratings of hyperactivity or disinhibition. Prout (2000) examined ADHD subtype differences on measures of response inhibition, processing speed, and visual-spatial skills. Findings suggested no differences between groups on a measure of response inhibition; however, when processing speed was examined, the ADHD-CT were more impaired than either the IT or control groups. Poor verbal fluency has also been noted in some studies (e.g., Shallice *et al.*, 2002; Wu *et al.*, 2002).

Goal-directed persistence or sustained attention is the product of the interaction of the components in the performance of self-regulation (Barkley, 1998). As Barkley noted, most measures of attention in neuropsychological research measure goal-directed persistence or sustained attention. Continuous performance tests are the most frequently used of such measures in research and practice (Riccio *et al.*, 2002). Studies using these measures, however, have yielded differential findings with respect to projected deficits or subgroup differences. Sustained attention deficits are reported in ADHD children (Chhabildas *et al.*, 2001; Collings, 2003; Epstein *et al.*, 2003; Jewell,

1998; Manly *et al.*, 2001; Westby, 1999; Wu *et al.*, 2002); however, in several studies, the tests failed to differentiate ADHD-CT from ADHD-IT or other comorbid disorders (see Axelrod, 2002; Kirlin, 2003; Westby, 1999; but see Chhabildas *et al.*, 2001; Collings, 2003; Lockwood *et al.*, 2001).

METHODOLOGICAL CONSIDERATIONS: CAUTIONARY NOTE

In the last 20 years, ADHD has become the most researched and best known of the childhood behavior disorders (Weiss & Hechtman, 1993). As in any burgeoning field of study, there is substantial variability among the research findings. Notable methodological criticisms include: (1) differential criteria used for subject selection, (2) small sample sizes, (3) failure to operationally define and label constructs according to the measurement scale or technique used, (4) measurement techniques that fail to capture the complex cognitive processes operative in ADHD, (5) failure to elucidate on operational criteria used with respect to exclusion, (6) inattention to medication status, (7) failure to take into account gender and developmental considerations, and (8) use of instruments that have questionable psycho-metric properties (Barkley, 1998; Shaywitz & Shaywitz, 1988). The reader is advised to remain cognizant of these methodological weaknesses, as they may prove explanatory when faced with inconsistent results.

CLASSIFICATION AND CONCEPTUAL ISSUES: THE ROLE OF ASSESSMENT AND INTELLIGENCE TESTING

While the debate about the merits of testing and labeling rages, we take the position that comprehensive assessment and diagnosis is both liberating and informing. Over the years, we have interacted with numerous children and adults who have self-labeled themselves as stupid, passive, unmotivated and so on, only to find that their difficulties are related to ADHD, a learning disability, or other disability. Positive outcomes from assessment of ADHD, though, are highly dependent on a clear stipulation and achievement of assessment goals. These include:

- Differential diagnosis of ADHD subtypes from other developmental conditions such as learning disabilities or various internalizing and externalizing disorders. Achievement of this goal rests on awareness of clinical classification criteria as well as the theoretical and empirical literature. In our work, we are informed by the DSM-IV and Barkley's unifying account of ADHD, as well as empirical and clinical accounts of other developmental disorders. The multisource, multimodal, and multi-method assessment battery we use, therefore, encompasses tasks assessing a broad range of neuropsychological, cognitive, psychosocial, behavioral, and educational strengths and weaknesses known to be characteristic of ADHD youngsters. This is in recognition that ADHD children show variable deficits on a variety of tests but that when multiple tests are used together, prediction of ADHD status improves. Moreover, we remain cognizant that ADHD may express itself differentially as a function of context and task demands and in response to varying informants (e.g., mother vs father; parent vs teacher).

- Assessment of co-occurring disorders such as language impairments, learning disabilities, conduct disorder, oppositional disorder, and so on. To accomplish this goal, we rely on our knowledge of the conceptual, clinical, and research literature as it applies to these varying conditions.
- Determination of previous and current intervention strategies and support resources.
- Identification of contextual protective and compensatory interventions that will foster resiliency in the child.

Intelligence testing plays an integral role in our assessment process. Intelligence tests like the Wechsler scales are not sufficiently sensitive to be used exclusively in making a diagnosis of ADHD or for discriminating among the various subtypes of ADHD (Schwean & Saklofske, 1998). They were never intended to do this, but they do provide us with information about the child's relative cognitive strengths and weaknesses that are relevant to both a priori and a posteriori hypothesis testing in assessment, information that is imperative to intervention planning. In some cases, these scales may also yield supporting data useful in differential diagnosis. In the following sections, we rely on research studies exploring the use of the WISC-III in ADHD assessment, but link these findings with what is known about the WISC-IV.

THE WISC-IV

Of relevance to the cognitive assessment and study of ADHD are the four index scores of the WISC-IV: the Verbal Comprehension (VC) index, the Perceptual Reasoning (PR) index, the Working Memory (WM) Index, and the Processing Speed (PS) index. The VC index is composed of subtests measuring verbal abilities utilizing reasoning, comprehension, and conceptualization; and the PR index is composed of subtests measuring perceptual reasoning and organization with a much stronger connection to fluid intelligence. The WM index subtests measure attention, concentration, and working memory; and the PS index subtests measure the speed of mental and graphomotor processing. While many of the subtests from the WISC-III remain unchanged in the WISC-IV, there are several new core and supplementary subtests and there are new subtests.

WISC-IV SAMPLE

The WISC-IV Technical Manual provides some preliminary evidence of clinical validity based on test-criterion relationships for groups of exceptional children, including those with ADHD and with Learning Disorder and ADHD (LD/ADHD). The various ADHD subtypes were combined into one sample. Approximately 64% of the children in the ADHD group were taking medication for ADHD symptomatology at the time of testing. The LD/ADHD group met DSM-IV-TR criteria for both a Learning Disorder and ADHD, and 65% of the children were on medication for ADHD symptomatology at the time of testing.

Medications such as methylphenidate (Ritalin) appear to temporarily redress the core symptoms of ADHD as well as secondary social and behavioral problems. A number of studies have shown direct short-term beneficial effects on various aspects of learning and memory (Barkley *et al.*, 1990a, 1991b; Douglas *et al.*, 1988; Lahey *et al.*, 1987; Whalen & Henker, 1991). Although methylphenidate's locus of action within the central nervous system remains a matter of some debate, growing evidence indicates that specific cognitive operations are enhanced by stimulant therapy. Saklofske and Schwean (1993) reported that a standard 10 mg dose of methylphenidate enhanced both efficiency and accuracy of performance on planning tasks dependent on the organization of selective attention and coding at the perceptual level. Also sensitive to methylphenidate was an attentional task conjointly dependent on focused and divided attention, and two simultaneous processing subtests in which improvements appeared to be related to an enhanced ability to inhibit particular behavior. No improvements were noted on three successive processing tasks as a function of medication. In contrast, studies that have examined the short-term effects of methylphenidate on the WISC-III have failed to reveal significant methylphenidate treatment effects for subtest, index, or VIQ and PIQ scores (Saklofske & Schwean, 1991; Schwean *et al.*, 1993). Given these results, it seems unlikely that the WISC-IV findings that were based on samples of ADHD children, which included a large percentage who were being treated with pharmacological agents, would have been affected by the medication. However, this is an issue for future research to address. Perhaps of greater concern is the failure to differentiate between subtypes of ADHD.

PSYCHOMETRIC PROPERTIES OF WECHSLER SCALES IN ADHD SAMPLES

To use a test with any degree of confidence requires that it is reproducible, stable (i.e., reliable), and meaningful (i.e., valid) (Sattler, 2001). The reliability and validity of a test may be sensitive to a neurobehavioral condition like

ADHD; therefore, its use among this population rests on data attesting to its psychometric soundness.

RELIABILITY

We are not aware of any studies examining the internal consistency reliabilities of either the WISC-III or WISC-IV for samples of ADHD children. However, several studies have examined the temporal stability of the WISC-III. Nyden *et al.* (2001) examined the stability of WISC-III Full Scale, Verbal, and Performance IQ scores obtained by ADHD children 1 to 2 years after initial assessments. Results showed that these scores remained stable, although subtest stability over time was slightly more variable. Schwean & Saklofske (1998) readministered the WISC-III to clinically referred ADHD children approximately 30 months after the initial evaluation. All test–retest correlations were statistically significant, although the PS index demonstrated the lowest correlation between testing due to an increase of almost 9 points. Future research designed to examine the internal consistency reliability and stability of the WISC-IV is necessary to use this test with confidence in assessing ADHD children.

The stability of test scores also need be considered when a new test such as the WISC-IV replaces an earlier version. We do know that WISC-IV index and FSIQ scores are lower in contrast to WISC-III scores, for the reasons described in chapters 1 and 2. As an example of previous research using the Wechsler tests, Horn-Alsberge (1999) examined the stability of the WISC-R and WISC-III IQs in clinical samples composed of children with learning disabilities, ADHD, and affective disorders. Among the ADHD sample, the WISC-III yielded an FSIQ approximately 6 points lower than its counterpart, the WISC-R. VIQ and PIQ on the WISC-III were also approximately 5 points lower than those obtained on the WISC-R. Mahone *et al.* (2003) also examined the differences between WISC-R and WISC-III performance among children with ADHD. Their findings revealed that ADHD children had significantly lower Performance IQ on the WISC-III compared to the WISC-R, with the Picture Arrangement subtest showing the most significant difference.

VALIDITY

Clinical and educational needs may require a reexamination of a child's ability in a short time span to confirm the first test results or to ensure an accurate diagnosis. As well, children may be reassessed to evaluate the effects of cognitive or neuropsychological interventions after a brief time interval. While the Wechsler Scales may be administered more than once to a child, it is often advisable to use a different test if the time interval between testing is fairly brief. Though this may reduce practice effects, it is necessary to "equate" the two tests to determine if they yield equivalent scores and information. If score differences occur, it is necessary to determine how much of this difference is due to "real" change and how much is due to the imperfect correlations between different tests.

Saklofske *et al.* (1994) compared the scores of 45 ADHD children on the short form of the Stanford-Binet Intelligence Scale-Fourth Edition (SB:FE; Thorndike *et al.*, 1986) administered at intake with the WISC-III given 4 weeks later. The mean WISC-III FSIQ was slightly lower than that obtained for the SB:FE Partial Composite. Of interest was that the FSIQ and Partial Composite scores varied from 1 to 29 points and that 33 of the 45 children obtained a lower score on the WISC-III. Although all mean scores fell in the average range, the highest scores were observed on the Perceptual Organization and Abstract Visual Reasoning while the Freedom from Distractibility and Short Term Memory Scores from the two tests were relatively lower. Correlation patterns between the IQ, Index, and Area Scores revealed that there was a fair amount of variance shared by the two tests. Lower correlations were observed between other Index–Area composites supporting, in part, the convergent–discriminant validity of these scales. We argued that these findings suggest that both tests may be employed in the assessment of general intellectual functioning in children with ADHD provided that examiners are aware that identical scores are not to be expected and will likely be slightly lower on the WISC-III. This will need to be determined for the *WISC-IV* and *Stanford Binet-Fifth Edition* that was published only a short time earlier.

Another aspect of test validity is reflected in the pattern of correlations between the parts of complex tests like the WISC-III and WISC-IV. As a measure of "g," it is expected that all subtests are positively correlated but that there will be a pattern that supports the measurement of verbal and performance IQs, four factors, and the meaningfulness of the various subtests themselves. Schwean *et al.* (1993) reported on a convergent–discriminant validity study with 45 clinically referred ADHD children. Children were administered the WISC-III and intercorrelations between subtests, index scores, and IQs examined. Findings revealed that the patterns of correlations for the ADHD sample were similar to those reported in the WISC-III standardization sample across parallel age groupings. It was our contention that these results indicate that the WISC-III is a highly robust measure that retains its psychometric characteristics when used in an examination of children with ADHD. Given that the WISC-IV generally maintains many of the same subtests and similar factor structure, we would suggest that, like its predecessor, it, too, will prove to be a psychometrically sound instrument applicable for use in assessing children with ADHD.

The predictive or discriminant validity of the WISC-III with respect to ADHD has been examined by several researchers. Assesmany *et al.* (2001) explored the ability of the WISC-III to discriminate between ADHD and a group of non-ADHD children, as well as to identify which combination of WISC-III subtests resulted in the highest level of correct classifications. A stepwise discriminant function analysis indicated that four WISC-III subtests contributed significantly to the prediction of group membership: Digit Span, Information, Vocabulary, and Picture Completion. An overall classification rate of approximately 39% was attained when the four WISC-III subtests were included in the equation. Approximately 90% of the children classified as ADHD and 17.5% of the non-ADHD children were correctly identified when using the four WISC-III subtests as predictors. Perugini (1999) examined the predictive power of combined neuropsychological measures for ADHD in children. Among other measures, Perugini administered the Arithmetic and Digit Span subtests of the WISC-III. Group differences were significant on the Digit Span and continuous performance tests only; however, while these two tests provided the strongest prediction, it was modest and offered limited diagnostic utility.

DIAGNOSTIC UTILITY OF THE WISC-IV FOR ADHD

COMPOSITE PROFILES

According to Barkley (1998), impairments that ADHD children experience in behavioral inhibition and the executive functions dependent on it could be expected to result in a small but significant and negative relationship between ADHD and IQ, particularly verbal IQ. "This is likely because the latter is likely to be related to working memory, internalized speech and the eventual development of verbal thought" (p. 98). Studies using earlier versions of the Wechsler scales have indeed found poor FSIQ performance relative to normal controls (Goldstein, 1987; Kostura, 2000; Loney, 1974; McGee et al., 1989; Palker & Stewart, 1972; Pineda et al., 2002; Tripp et al., 2002; Schaughency et al., 1989), although the differences are often not clinically meaningful. Studies that have controlled for the presence of coexisting disorders continue to point to lower intelligence scores in ADHD vs normal subjects (Barkley et al., 1990; Goldstein, 1987; McGee et al., 1984); however, lower intelligence is certainly not diagnostic of ADHD. Aside from children with mental retardation, other groups of children with exceptionalities (e.g., learning disabled) also attain lower mean IQ scores relative to normally developing children (Newby et al., 1993; Teeter & Smith, 1993).

The Technical and Interpretive Manual for the WISC-IV provides performance data on 89 children, ages 8 to 13 years, who were identified as having ADHD according to DSM-IV-TR diagnostic criteria. The ADHD group, composed of children representing the various ADHD subtypes (i.e., predominantly inattentive, predominantly hyperactive–impulsive, and combined), was collapsed and performance data are reported for this heterogenous group. Approximately 64% of the children were taking medication for ADHD symptomatology at the time of testing. Inspection of this data reveals that relative to the matched control group, children with ADHD achieved a slightly lower mean performance on the FSIQ. While the mean IQ for the ADHD group was 97.6 (SD = 14.0), the matched control group achieved a mean of 102.7 (SD = 12.5) (Table 7.1). These differences in FSIQ are statistically significant but the effect size is not large. The Technical Manual also provides data for children exhibiting comorbid ADHD and Learning Disorder relative to a matched control group. With a mean FSIQ of 88.1 and standard deviation of 13.0, this group scored significantly lower than the matched control group ($p < .01$).

Barkley's prediction is that children with ADHD are most likely to show differences with controls on the Verbal IQ. Prifitera and Dersh (1993) and Schwean et al. (1993) did find that ADHD children scored lower, albeit within the average range, on the Verbal IQ compared to the Performance IQ, as well as on the VC and PO factors. These results are less pronounced for the WISC-IV. As shown in Table 7.1, ADHD subjects obtained a lower mean on the Verbal Comprehension Index in comparison to a matched control group, although the difference was not significant or clinically meaningful. Only a 1-point scaled score difference between the WISC-IV VCI and PRI was observed. Kaufman (1994) has previously summarized that a PIQ > VIQ pattern has been found in numerous samples of exceptional children and reasons that it is related to the vulnerability of verbal tasks to children's learning difficulties. It is his recommendation that in many exceptional populations, PIQ and POI (and presumably PRI on the WISC-IV) may provide the best estimate of cognitive potential. Given this argument, it is interesting to note that in the LD/ADHD group, where, due to underlying language impairments, one might expect a more pronounced difference between the VCI and PRI, no differences were noted between the mean composite scores for these areas, although both were significantly lower than the scores observed in the matched control group.

WORKING MEMORY INDEX

The models of ADHD proposed by both Barkley and Rapport et al. argue that working memory plays a pivotal role in the expression of ADHD symptoms. A number of studies using a range of tasks have demonstrated verbal and nonverbal working memory impairments in ADHD children (see for example, Hill, 2000; Johnson, 2001; Kalff et al., 2002; McInnes et al., 2003; Muir-Broaddus et al., 2002). Several studies examining working memory in ADHD have looked at whether coexisting language–learning disabilities are explanatory in such deficits. While some of this research has demonstrated that coexisting language/learning disabilities account for the impairments in working memory (see McInnes, 2001; Swanson et al., 1999), other studies

TABLE 7.1   WISC-III and WISC-IV Scores for Children with ADHD

IQ	WISC-III Prifiteria & Dersh (1993) n = 65	WISC-III Schwean et al. (1993) n = 45	WISC-III Anastopoulos et al. (1994) n = 40	WISC-IV ADHD n = 89	WISC-IV ADHD+LD n = 45
Verbal IQ	99.5	95.5	101.9	n/a	n/a
Performance IQ	102.9	101.4	102.9	n/a	n/a
Full Scale IQ	101.0	98.0	102.4	97.6	88.1
Factor Index					
VCI	102.3	97.0	103.9	99.0	92.7
POI/PRI	106.8	105.1	103.3	100.1	92.7
FFD/Working Memory	94.6	93.0	96.0	96.1	88.7
PSI	93.2	92.6	n/a	93.4	88.2
Subtests					
Picture Completion	12.0	11.9	10.7	10.4	10.4
Information	9.8	8.7	10.4	9.7	9.7
Coding	7.8	7.9	10.0	8.3	8.3
Similarities	9.5	9.8	10.2	10.1	10.1
Picture Arrangement	9.6	8.9	10.2	–	–
Arithmetic	9.3	8.3	9.3	8.7	8.7
Block Design	11.1	11.4	10.6	9.9	9.5
Vocabulary	10.6	9.3	10.9	9.9	8.8
Object Assembly	11.3	10.6	10.0	–	–
Comprehension	10.2	9.8	10.4	9.3	8.9
Symbol Search	9.1	8.8	n/a	9.4	8.1
Digit Span	8.4	8.9	9.0	9.6	8.5
Mazes	10.1	11.0	n/a	–	–
Word Reasoning				10.1	9.4
Picture Concepts				10.5	8.4
Matrix Reasoning				9.7	8.5
Letter/Number Sequencing				9.3	7.7
Cancellation				9.1	8.5

have reported that the coexistence of the two conditions is predictive of the most significant working memory deficits (Lazar & Frank, 1998; Kirk, 2001; Roodenrys et al., 2001; Willcutt et al., 2001).

The WISC-III tasks subsumed under the Freedom From Distractibility (FFD) index have also been used by numerous researchers to evaluate auditory working memory processes in children with ADHD. Prifitera and Dersh (1993) reported that the FFD index appeared to differentiate both ADHD and Learning Disabled groups from the standardization sample, although the clinical groups performed similarly on this factor. Anastopoulos *et al.* (1994) reported that their ADHD sample scored significantly lower on the FFD index than on either the VC or PO index, with more children exhibiting significant PO-FFD differences than VC-FFD differences. When data were analyzed at an individual level, however, a significant percentage of children did not show any significant VC-FFD or PO-FFD differences. Factors such as gender, the presence of comorbid disorders, age, socioeconomic status, and behavioral ratings had little bearing on whether children displayed VC-FD or PO-FD factor score differences suggesting that the FFD has limited ability in the diagnosis of ADHD.

Albers (1998) evaluated four groups of children (ADHD, ADHD+LD, a clinical group with diagnoses other than ADHD or LD, and a control group) on the FFD factor score and Wechsler Individual Achievement Test. Only the FFD factor significantly distinguished between ADHD and non-ADHD students. Krishnamurthy (1999) investigated the utility of the FFD in the diagnosis of ADHD by comparing it to five psychological measures: anxiety, disinhibition, inattention, distractibility, and cognitive flexibility. The predictor variables predicted the FFD successfully, but accounted for only 40.5% of the variance. The greatest amount of variance in predicting the FFD was accounted for by both IQ and anxiety. The authors contend that the results of this study corroborate the findings of other researchers regarding the limitations in clinical utility of the FFD in the diagnosis of ADHD. They underscore that this factor should not be used independently in the diagnosis of ADHD.

Mayes *et al.* (1999) analyzed the WISC-III data in clinical samples of ADHD and normally developing children. The mean FSIQ exceeded the FFD at all ages in the ADHD group, but not in the non-ADHD group. Further, the discrepancy between FSIQ and FFD was significantly greater in the ADHD group. The four lowest mean subtest scores for the ADHD group were Digit Span, Arithmetic, Coding, and Symbol Search, which was not the case for the non-ADHD group. For significantly more children with ADHD (87%), the score for the FFD plus the Processing Speed index was less than the sum of the two remaining index scores. No children without ADHD had Digit Span and Arithmetic as two of their three lowest subtest scores, whereas this was found for 23% of the children with ADHD. An independent replication study involving 52 referred children with ADHD and 23 without supported these findings. Kostura (2000) administered a variety of measures, including the WISC-III, to 31 ADHD and 31 non-ADHD children. Results indicated that the ADHD children obtained significantly lower scores across the WISC Verbal and Full Scale IQs, as well as on the VC, the FFD, and PS index scores. While the FFD factor differentiated between the groups, significant correlations were not observed between FFD and the parent rating scales tapping hyperactivity–impulsivity and inattentiveness. The author concluded the FFD should not be used as a clinical indicator of ADHD. Krane and Tannock (2001) examined the WISC-III FFD factor in the diagnosis of ADHD and the contribution of behavioral, academic, and language variables to the factor. The WISC-III FDD subtests, along with subtests from the WRAT-3, the Woodcock Reading Mastery Test-Revised, and the Clinical Evaluation of Language Fundamentals, were given to 275 children with ADHD. Results from the study showed that a child's FFD score was not a valid diagnostic indicator of either ADHD or a subtype of ADHD. FFD scores were associated primarily with arithmetic and receptive language scores, implicating working memory. The researchers argue that low FFD scores may signal learning problems, particularly with arithmetic, language, and working memory, that may contribute to poor academic performance.

What the FFD is actually measuring in children with ADHD has been the topic of exploration in some studies. Support for the construct validity of the FFD on the WISC-III was obtained in a study reported by Anastopoulos et al. (1994). A sample of 40 clinic-referred children with ADHD were administered the WISC-III, and scores from the FFD index were correlated with parent and teacher ratings on the ADHD Rating Scale (DuPaul & Stoner, 1991), the Child Attention Problem Rating Scale (CAPRS; Edelbrock, 1991), and the Child Behavior Checklist (CBCL: Achenbach, 1991). None of the correlations between the FFD and mothers' ratings of inattention reached significance; however, significant correlations between FFD and teacher ratings on the Inattention Factors and Total Scores of the ADHD Rating Scale and the CAPRS were attained. Results of another validity study, however, led the authors to caution against using the FFD scores as a measurement of attention. In this two-part study, Lowman et al. (1996) asked undergraduate students in an introductory educational psychology class to label the factor represented by items like those on the Arithmetic and Digit Span subtests. In addition, a sample of 76 clinic-referred children on whom the Behavior Assessment System for Children-Teacher Rating Scale (BASC-TRS: Reynolds & Kamphaus, 1992) had been completed were administered the WISC-III. Correlations were then computed between the WISC-III FFD scores and the Hyperactivity, Attention Problems, and Learning Problems of the BASC-TRS. Results revealed that participants unfamiliar with the content of the FFD subtests did not choose labels that corresponded with attention; rather, they corresponded with terminology associated with problem solving, memory, and quantitative skills. Moreover, findings from the correlational analyses showed a significant relationship between FFD and teacher ratings of learning problems, but not attention and hyperactivity. Mayes and Calhoun (2002) explored the diagnostic agreement between the Gordon Diagnostic System and the FFD index. They reported a 70% agreement rate and suggested that the two measures tap both similar and unique traits. On the other hand, Reinecke *et al.* (1999) had ADHD subjects complete the WISC-III, Wide Range Achievement Test, and Test of Variables of Attention. The mean FFD scores were significantly lower than other WISC-III factor scores, but the vast majority of ADHD children did not show a significant relative weaknesses on this index. Further, correlational analyses failed to find significant relationship between the measure of sustained visual attention and the FFD index.

Despite the many research investigations designed to clarify the nature of the constructs that are being tapped by the FFD, the issue remains unresolved. One conclusion, however, remains incontrovertible; use of the FFD as a unitary measure of attention is fraught with problems and oversimplifies the complex processes underlying performance on this factor (Kamphaus, 1993; Kaufman, 1994).

In addition to a change in terminology (from Freedom from Distractibility to Working Memory), subtest differences are incorporated in the WISC-IV. Keeping with the *Wechsler Adult Intelligence Test: Third Edition*, the WISC-IV has added the Letter–Number Sequencing Task. Arithmetic, previously a core subtest, is now a supplemental one. As a result of these changes, it is difficult to know whether WISC-III findings can be generalized to the WISC-IV. While the Arithmetic subtests could be argued to add an "authentic" element to the WMI, it is a cognitively complex subtest that tends to load across several factors of the Wechsler scales. In contrast, the L-N subtest is a more direct measure of auditory working memory. Examination of the WISC-IV findings for ADHD and matched control groups as outlined in the Technical Manual do suggest that children with ADHD tend to score lower than their same-age peers on the Working Memory index. For example, the ADHD group attained a mean of 96.1 (SD = 15.5) on the Working Memory index compared to a mean of 101.7 (SD = 13.4) for the control group. The mean attained by the LD/ADHD group is even lower (i.e., mean of 88.7, SD = 13.7) than that of the matched control group (i.e., mean of 100.9). Keeping with previous findings for the WISC-III, the score obtained for the Arithmetic subtest was the lowest of the Working Memory tasks for the ADHD group. Among the LD/ADHD group, however, significantly depressed scores were noted on both Letter–Number Sequencing and Arithmetic subtests (mean of 7.7, SD = 3.5 and 7.7, SD = 2.3, respectively).

PROCESSING SPEED

Barkley's unified account of ADHD-HIT and CT predicts that youngsters with these conditions will demonstrate difficulties in motor control, dexterity, and sequencing. Further, children diagnosed with ADHD-IT will be challenged by tasks measuring selective attention. Some research with the WISC-III suggests that PS may tap these various functions. For example, Prifitera and Dersh (1993) and Schwean *et al.* (1993) found that their heterogeneous ADHD samples obtained scores on the FFD and PS factors that were within 2 points of each other, suggesting possible impairments in the abilities measured by both of these factors (Kaufman, 1994). Relative to their PO scores, scores on the FFD and PS indices were approximately 2/3 standard deviation lower. In examining subtest scores across the studies, it was apparent that subtests with the lowest mean scores were generally those that compose the FFD and PS factors (i.e., Coding, Arithmetic, Symbol Search, Digit Span). Both studies also reported that the lowest mean subtest score for the ADHD subjects was on the Coding subtest. Swanson (2002) also reported that LD, ADHD, and LD/ADHD subjects scored significantly lower than normally developing children on the PS factor but cautioned that results that imply a relationship between a low score on the PS factor should not be seen as diagnostic of either learning disability or ADHD. Rather, such test data should be viewed as helpful when trying to determine a child's strengths and weaknesses, especially for remedial planning. In examining the neuropsychological profiles of children with ADHD-IT and children with reading disability, Weiler *et al.* (2002) found that children in the former group were more likely to demonstrate poor performance on the Coding and Symbol Search task, whereas those with reading disability were distinguishable by their poor performance on written language measures. They later replicated these findings using other visual search tasks.

Burt *et al.* (unpublished manuscript) examined the predictive relationships between teacher- and mother-rated ADHD symptomatology (i.e., hyperactivity–impulsivity and inattention) and varied cognitive, intellectual, academic, and behavioral competencies in a sample of heterogeneously-defined ADHD children. While mother-rated symptomatology did not predict the factor scores of the WISC-III, teacher-rated symptoms of hyperactivity–impulsivity were predictive of lower scores on the PS index. The findings of Burt *et al.* underscore the importance of informant source in determining correlate patterns.

The PS tasks on the WISC-IV primarily tap an aspect of cognitive efficiency, reflecting the speed at which a child can make visual symbol discriminations. Keeping with findings from the WISC-III, ADHD children who were administered the WISC-IV obtained their lowest composite score on the Processing Speed index (Table 7.1). The Coding subtest proved to be the most difficult of all for these subjects. Interestingly, in the LD/ADHD group, while the Working Memory and Processing Speed Indices were the lowest, the difference between them and the VCI and PRI were not as great as that observed in the ADHD-alone group. Again, the lowest of all scores was on the Coding task. It will be particularly important for future studies to clarify what the Processing Speed factor is actually measuring and what role it may play in differential diagnosis.

OTHER PROFILES

Several other WISC-III profiles have been examined as a means for differentiating children with ADHD. The ACID profile, composed of a pattern of low scores on the Arithmetic, Coding, Information, and Digit Span subtests, was explored by Prifitera and Dersh (1993) in their study comparing the WISC-III standardization data to children with ADHD and LD. Their calculations indicated that while the full ACID pattern was quite rare in the standardization sample (1.1%), it was much more common in the LD (5.1%) and ADHD (12.3%) samples. Similar findings were reported when the same clinical groups were compared to the standardization sample on the Bannatyne profile (Spatial > Verbal Conceptualization > Sequential). However, results suggest that while the ACID and Bannatyne profiles may contribute to the identification of an exceptionality, they have limited utility for the differential diagnosis of ADHD. Similarly, Albers (1998) reported that the WISC-III Arithmetic, Coding, Information, and Digit Span (ACID) subtest mean scores were among the five lowest scores for both ADHD and ADHD+LD groups, there were no significant differences among them. A discriminant analysis further indicated that none of the ACID subtests contributed significantly to classification between ADHD and ADHD+LD.

Kaufman (1994) argued that because of the minimal contribution of the Information subtest to the ACID profile, it should be abandoned in favor of the SCAD profile (Symbol Search, Coding, Arithmetic, Digit Span). While Kaufman acknowledges that the SCAD has no greater utility than the ACID profile for differentially diagnosing ADHD, he reasons that the SCAD profile, being composed of subtests that largely measure process, is not as vulnerable to contamination of content as is the ACID profile, which includes the learning product-oriented information subtest. He further argues that in analyzing profile patterns, a discrepancy between the SCAD and PO subtests vs the SCAD and VC subtests is more meaningful given that performance on the VC subtests is likely to be degraded by learning or language impairments. Kaufman presented data to show that groups of LD and ADHD children differ significantly from normally developing peers in the magnitude of the discrepancy between PO and SCAD subtests and that large PO/SCAD differences are more likely to occur for abnormal than normal samples. Snow and Sapp (2000) compared ADHD children with two other groups of children described in the WISC-III manual (i.e., a sample with ADHD and the standardization sample) on the SCAD index and ACID profile. Comparisons of WISC-III scaled scores and subtest patterns for the samples with ADHD supported the congruence between them. Further, the cumulative percentages of children in the three samples who obtained differences between the SCAD index and the PO index were computed. Analysis indicated that 17 of the 35 subjects obtained differences of 9 points or greater. These findings were substantially different from the WISC-III standardization sample, but congruent with the WISC-III sample of children with ADHD. The researchers argue that their outcomes support the diagnostic utility of WISC-III subtest profile patterns for children with ADHD.

Another profile that has received some attention is the Deterioration index. Bowers *et al.* (1992) suggested that the Wechsler Deterioration index (WDI), an index of cognitive deterioration composed of the "hold" (Vocabulary, Information, Object Assembly, and Picture completion) vs "don't hold" (Digit Span, Similarities, Coding, and Block Design) tasks and is computed using the formula:

$$\text{WDI} = \frac{\text{hold} - \text{don't hold}}{\text{hold}}$$

may serve as a useful screening index of ADHD or support behavioral and observational indications of ADHD. On the basis of WISC-R results, Bower *et al.* compared the WDI of learning disabled, ADHD, and behaviorally disordered (but not ADHD) groups to nondisabled children. While the WDI did not predict LD status or severity, the WDI scores did significantly distinguish children with ADHD from non-ADHD samples. Hintz (2001) reported no statistically significant difference between the WDI overall mean scores of the ADHD group and Behavior Disordered/non-ADHD children. There was also no statistically significant difference among the three ADHD subtypes or between the ADHD subtypes and the Behavior Disordered/non-ADHD group.

SUBTYPES AND COEXISTING DISORDERS

Both Barkley's theoretical account of ADHD and the DSM-IV-TR posit neuropsychological differences between the varying subtypes of ADHD. Barkley (1997) maintained that the disorders are qualitatively different: while the ADHD IT is defined by sluggish cognitive tempo and selective attention problems, the other subtypes are defined by impairments consistent with his model (i.e., behavioral disinhibition and deficits in executive functioning). We have reviewed in previous sections some studies that have evaluated not only his theory but the usefulness of the Wechsler scales in differentiating between subtypes of ADHD. In addition to those studies, several others are reported in the literature. Schmitz *et al.* (2002) used the Digit Span task, among other neuropsychological measures, to evaluate the performance of various subtypes of ADHD adolescents. Results revealed that subjects with the IT and CT ADHD presented with significantly more impairments on the Digit Span task than did control subjects. In contrast, adolescents with the HIT did not differ from control subjects on this measure. Kinard (1999) assessed whether intrasubtest scatter on the verbal scales of the WISC-III occurs significantly more in LD and ADHD children than in normally developing children. A significant difference was found between the groups when compared on total scatter, with the ADHD and LD groups displaying significantly more scatter than the nonclinical group. Kinard cautioned that while the results indicated group differences, the magnitude of the difference was of little clinical utility. In a study investigating specific differences between the subtypes in terms of cognitive performance on verbal compared to visual and spatial tasks, Knigin-Calderon (2002) found that while some visual and spatial tasks differentiated the ADHD-IT, the visual subtests on the WISC-III did not.

Much research has documented the high comorbidity of ADHD with other psychiatric disorders (Barkley et al., 1991; Biederman et al., 1991; McGee et al., 1989). The presence of comorbid disorders in cognitive studies of children with ADHD presents a confound; intellectual deficits associated with the comorbid disorder may erroneously be attributed to ADHD (Caron & Rutter, 1991). Several studies that have attempted to clarify the neuro-psychological correlates of various childhood disorders have reported intellectual impairments specific to ADHD (Frick et al., 1991; Frost et al., 1989). However, this research remains in its infancy. For example, Faraone et al. (1993) administered the Vocabulary, Block Design, Arithmetic, Digit Span, and Coding subtests of the WISC-R to 140 children with ADHD and 120 normal control subjects. Results revealed that compared with control subjects, ADHD subjects had lower scores on all subtests, as well as on estimated FSIQ and the FFD factor. When linear regression models using the presence of comorbid conduct disorder, major depression, and anxiety disorders were used to predict WISC-R scores for the ADHD subjects, findings revealed a significant effect for the Block Design and Full Scale IQ. Interestingly, post hoc analyses indicated that for both scores, ADHD with depression predicted higher scores than ADHD alone, whereas conduct and anxiety disorders predicted lower scores. While the findings indicating that intellectual impairments were exacerbated by the presence of conduct and anxiety disorders, results indicating that depression predicted higher test scores were seen as enigmatic and suggest the need for further research.

ASSESSMENT

ADHD is one of the most common referrals to school psychologists and mental health providers (Barkley, 1998; Demaray et al., 2003). Hechtman (2000) points out that because ADHD is a condition with a broad extensive differential diagnosis, a high rate of comorbidity, and widespread significant impairment in academic, occupational, social, and emotional functioning, it is essential that psychological assessment be comprehensive and involve multiple domain informants, methods, and settings. In our clinical practice, a problem-solving process that is informed by both theoretical and clinical conceptualizations of ADHD is used.

While research indicates that most psychologists adhere to DSM-IV criteria when evaluating children for ADHD, there are inherent weaknesses in relying solely on a clinical classification system for making diagnostic decisions, including issues around the use of a fixed cut-off point (Handler, 2001), gender differences in the expression of ADHD symptomatology, duration and pervasiveness criteria, and employing potentially subjective guidelines for diagnosis (see Barkley, 1998). Moreover, because the DSM-IV criteria are clinically rather than theoretically derived, empirical findings with respect to causal explanatory factors are not probed. As previously noted, our clinical assessments are informed by both the DSM-IV criteria and theoretical conceptualizations such as Barkley's unified account of ADHD and Rapport and colleagues working memory model.

Our problem-solving process does not make a priori assumptions about the presence or absence of a specific condition; rather through a process of inductive and deductive analysis, it leads to documentation of presenting behaviors, as well as various hypotheses about underlying causal factors. This process is accomplished through the use of various assessment tools. Unfortunately, research indicates that not all psychologists (or even a majority) employ a comprehensive multimethod, multimodal, multisource assessment in the diagnosis of ADHD and this subsequently leads to a high prevalence of misdiagnosis (see, for example, Wilkin-Bloch, 2002). Handler (2001) found that only 15% of psychologists reported using multiple methods consistent with recommended standards of "best practice." In contrast, though, Demaray et al. (2003) found that most school psychologists are using multiple informants, methods, and settings for the assessment of ADHD, with rating scales, observations, and interviews the most common methods identified.

Our protocol for ADHD assessment includes the use of a clinical interview; rating scales; a range of cognitive and neuropsychological measures, including the WISC-III and now WISC-IV; and observation techniques. The clinical interview is the cornerstone of our assessment. It probes for a variety of information including presenting symptoms; a history of those symptoms; academic, social, and developmental history; current functioning in a variety of settings; current mental status; and the presence of other disorders that may be either the principal underlying disorder or a comorbid disorder that impacts the adaptive functioning of the child (Quinlan, 2000). Information is gathered not only from the child but from the parents and school as well.

Growing evidence points to the utility of behavioral rating scales in the identification of ADHD. For example, some research indicates that rating scales are more likely to predict group membership than are laboratory measures and intelligence test scores (see, for example, Pilling, 2000); however, it is important to note that variability may exist in ratings of a child as a function of the respondent. Findings indicating insignificant correlations between scores on behavioral rating scales and a range of performance measures further underscore that these diverse assessment measures may be capturing different and contextually sensitive cognitive and behavioral expressions of ADHD or, alternatively, that these expressions are discrete and not related to the same condition. Several recent articles have provided a critical analysis of behavioral rating scales commonly used in a best practice approach to a comprehensive assessment of ADHD (e.g., Angello *et al.*, 2003; Demaray *et al.*, 2003). These studies yield recommendations regarding the use of each scale with specific populations, as well as specific stages of assessment within a problem-solving process. The reader is encouraged to consult this literature to inform his or her choice of rating scales.

Other studies have examined the predictive power of neuropsychological assessment tools used in combination with other measures in classifying children with ADHD (e.g., intelligence tests, continuous performance tests, and so on) (e.g., see Purugini *et al.*, 2000). While findings point to the difficulty in identifying consistent mean differences on tests of frontal-executive functioning, there appears to be greater predictive validity when a number of tests are used in combination. By way of example, Doyle *et al.* (2003) used conditional probability and receiver operating characteristic analyses to examine the efficiency of test-based diagnostic discriminations in a large sample of referred boys with and without ADHD. In line with Purugini *et al.*, Doyle *et al.* (2003) reported that single neuropsychological tests had limited discriminating ability at various cut-off scores. However, when multiple tests were used together, prediction of ADHD status improved, but overall diagnostic efficiency remained limited. These authors concluded that children with ADHD show variable deficits on neuropsychological tests of attention and executive functioning. They further argue that while impairments on multiple neuropsychological tests may be predictive of ADHD, normal scores do not rule out the diagnosis.

Of all laboratory measures, perhaps the most commonly used are continuous performance (CP) tests, and several studies have documented the effectiveness of several CP measures in distinguishing between ADHD and non-ADHD children (see for example, Barkley *et al.*, 2001; Barringer, 2001; Epstein *et al.*, 2003). Other research has pointed to the weaknesses of CP tests in the differential diagnosis of ADHD (Kirlin, 2003; Manly *et al.*, 2001; McGee *et al.*, 2000; Westby, 1999). On another note, some evidence suggests that use of various versions of CP tests may lead to overdiagnosis. Schatz *et al.* (2001) reported, for example, that a continuous performance test vs an ADHD rating scale was more likely to identify control children as having ADHD. They caution that the use of computerized measures may run the risk of overdiagnosis and treatment of ADHD in normal children. Of interest also are findings that question the validity of CP test errors as specific measures of the core cognitive symptoms of ADHD (see, for example, Jewell, 1998). Riccio *et al.* (2002) comment that while CP measures demonstrate sensitivity to dysfunction of the attentional system, they are symptom-specific, not disorder-specific measures.

Observational analysis can provide integral information about the child's functioning in a variety of contexts; however, undertaking such an analysis can be both time and cost prohibitive. As a result, most psychologists gravitate toward the use of observations within the testing situations rather than during natural ones (Handler, 2001). There has been growing support for the use of functional observation as an integral element of a comprehensive assessment. Functional assessment is founded on the assumption that problem behaviors may be maintained through a relatively small number of functional relationships (Reitmen & Hupp, 2003).

WHY USE THE WISC-IV IN ADHD ASSESSMENT?

As previously referenced, Wechsler intelligence score patterns alone are not a valid diagnostic indicator of either ADHD or subtype of ADHD (see, Albers, 1998; Krane & Tannock, 2001) and should not be used independently in the diagnosis of ADHD (Krishnamurthy, 1999). Why then would a clinician routinely administer the WISC-IV in ADHD assessment? Barkley (1998, pp. 298–299) addresses this question:

- IQ and achievement data can contribute to establishing the ADHD diagnosis in more indirect ways because the determination hinges, in part, on documenting severity of impairment. A child's failure to acquire age-appropriate cognitive skills, particularly in areas known to be causal in ADHD (e.g., working memory), may be inferred from results of IQ evaluation.
- An intelligence test such as the WISC-IV can contribute to the diagnosis of ADHD by generating information that may help to rule in or out other possible explanations for presenting complain and/or aid in identifying coexisting disorders. For example, the attention and disinhibition problems that may be associated with mental retardation can be linked to that condition, in part, through intelligence testing. IQ results are also useful in establishing the presence of a learning disability that may either coexist with ADHD or be explanatory of specific attentional weaknesses.

- As part of a more comprehensive neuropsychological battery, intelligence test results on particular tasks and factors (e.g., working memory; processing speed) may identify patterns of weaknesses that, in concert with other assessment findings, are implicated in or explanatory of the ADHD symptomatology.
- Intelligence and cognitive evaluation can assist in identifying patterns of strengths and weaknesses that may inform intervention planning.

When using measures such as the WISC-IV in clinical settings, psychologists need to be particularly aware that the behavior of children with ADHD is highly sensitive to contextual conditions. Zentall and Javorsky (1993) argued that, for students with ADHD, behavior difficulties often arise or increase when: (1) the task is too difficult, unclear, or ambiguous; (2) the task or activity is too repetitive, nonengaging, or tedious; (3) there is little situational predictability or control; (4) there is little flexibility for movement or choice; (5) there is little supervision or proximity; (6) there are too few opportunities for active responding or social interaction; (7) there is an extended period of seatwork; (8) there are transition periods with little structure; and (9) there are frequent or long wait or delay times. Knowledge of the most enabling conditions to enhance the test-taking behaviors of children with ADHD, a high degree of clinical skills, and the adherence to best assessment practices are essential when evaluating the intelligence of ADHD children. While the clinician must ensure that departures from standard testing procedures do not preclude the use of standardized norms (Sattler, 2001), a wide range of modifications appears permissible. After many rewarding years of providing psychoeducational services to children and adults with ADHD, the authors have identified a number of testing adaptations that allow the child with ADHD to demonstrate his or her intellectual capabilities. Some of these are summarized in Table 7.2. We conclude also with a case study to illustrate the process of ADHD assessment and the relevance of the WISC-IV.

CASE STUDY — RYAN

Six-year-old Ryan was referred to our clinic by his teacher and parents because of learning problems related to a lack of task persistence, difficulty in focusing and sustaining attention, high activity level, low frustration tolerance, and difficulty listening to and following directions. Ryan's teacher noted that his behavior was particularly problematic during unstructured activities (e.g., recess) and transition periods. At these times, he engaged in highly impulsive behaviors that placed him and his peers at risk. Within the home environment, Ryan's parents were particularly challenged by their son's emotional outbursts, which were precipitated by relatively innocuous

TABLE 7.2   Adaptations for Assessing the IQ of Children with ADHD

- Administering a test such as the WISC-IV to a child who is extremely hyperactive and impulsive may tax the capabilities of even the most competent examiner. To ensure that the child stays on task, remains motivated, and exhibits behaviors that are conducive to test-taking necessitates the full attention of the examiner. As such, the examiner must be able to administer the test with relative automaticity so that he/she can remain vigilant to the child's behaviors.

- It is important that the examiner be fully prepared for the child by having all the test materials arranged before testing and out of the child's view and easy access.

- In most testing situations, the examiner elects to sit across from the child. We have found it helpful to situate ourselves next to the ADHD child. Being in close proximity to the child allows the examiner to more easily regulate the child's behavior and keep him/her on task. A simple act such as gently placing one's hand on the child's shoulder, for example, serves as an external reminder to the child to redirect his/her attention.

- Best assessment practices dictate that it is essential to establish rapport with the testee before testing. Our experience with ADHD children tells us that the nature of the tester/testee relationship must be a working one. Many children with ADHD experience significant difficulty with altering behavior to meet situational demands. If the examiner initially relates to the child in a "therapeutic" manner, it may be problematic for the child to adapt his behavior when performance demands change. To establish a working relationship, we ensure that before testing, we explain in developmentally sensitive language the purpose of our activity and our behavioral expectations. We clearly indicate to the child what he/she can do to enhance his/her performance (e.g., remain in the chair, feet on the ground). This is particularly important for younger children who are not sophisticated regarding appropriate test-taking behavior.

- Strategies that we have found helpful in keeping children with ADHD on task include: (1) verbally cuing the child that you are about to introduce an activity (e.g., "Ready"); (2) ensuring we have eye contact with the child before presenting a stimulus; (3) being particularly sensitive to the changes in the child's behavior and attention by legitimizing movement (e.g., directing the child to retrieve an object inconspicuously placed in the room) or through short breaks; and (4) removing all distractions from the testing room and keeping test materials out of the child's sight.

- Because of ADHD children's idiosyncratic responses to reinforcement, we have found it best to use social reinforcers on a continuous basis when administering an IQ test. It is our experience that when activity or tangible reinforcers are used on an intermittent basis, ADHD children tend to become more focused on the reinforcer than on what he/she has to do to earn the reinforcer. This lack of attention to the task may degrade performance.

- Subtyping research has shown that cognitive speed may be a differentiating variable between ADHD-Predominately Hyperactive/Impulsive and ADHD-Predominantly Inattentive, with the latter demonstrating a slower speed of processing auditory material. It is important that the examiner recognize these differences and alter both the tempo of the delivery of instructions and where appropriate, the time allowed for responses.

- Children with ADHD experience difficulties with transitions. An ADHD child who has been overstimulated before testing (or during a testing break) will experience difficulty adapting his behavior to fit new contextual demands. The examiner should take the child's preceding activities into account when scheduling IQ testing.

(Continues)

TABLE 7.2   *(Continued)*

- Cognitive impulsivity may interfere with test performance. The examiner should remain alert to the child's cognitive style and provide cues to encourage him/her to slow down (e.g., "take your time and think it through").

- Many ADHD children have low frustration tolerance, which is readily exhibited when tasks become cognitively complex. We have found it helpful to encourage the child through statements such as "this is getting tough, but give it a try anyway." If the frustration gets out of hand and is debilitating performance, the sensitive examiner should realize it's time for a break.

- While studies have not found group effects for psychostimulant medications on the intellectual performance of children with ADHD, there may be a great deal of variability among individuals within that group. Virtually every clinician who has experience in the assessment of children with ADHD will relate instances in which medication (or lack of) significantly altered the intellectual performance of a child with ADHD. Clinicians must remain aware of the potential confound of medication on test scores and ideally evaluate the child on alternate forms of the test under varying drug conditions. At minimum, the drug condition should be taken into account when interpreting the findings.

---

events and placed considerable strain on the family. His risk-taking behavior was also a source of considerable concern to the parents.

Structured interviews were held with Ryan, his parents, and classroom teacher. Interview data collected from the parents revealed that Ryan was the eldest of two children born to 31-year-old Pam and 34-year-old Mark. The couple also had a younger son, 4-year-old Ethan. Both parents were professionals and reported that their marriage was stable. Neither had a history of learning, medical, or psychological problems, although Pam noted that her brother presented with long-standing impairments in behavior and social relationships. Explorations of the pregnancy, labor, and delivery did not reveal any significant social or demographic, medical, or obstetric risk factors. Early infant temperament was described as difficult. Ryan was characterized by his mother as being an extremely active baby who was oversensitive to stimulation and reacted negatively to changes in his environment. She also recalled that Ryan displayed an irritable temperament and seemed to always be crying. While she initially attributed his negative mood to colic, this behavior continued throughout the preschool years. The parents found it extremely hard to manage Ryan's high levels of activity and noncompliance and were particularly concerned about his low tolerance for stress, temper outbursts, and impulsive tendencies. They commented that they lived in fear of him hurting himself or his brother. To illustrate, Ryan's mother related an occasion when she looked out the kitchen window and observed 5-year-old Ryan standing on the top of the family camper in preparation for a jump. Her immediate response was to grab Ryan and verbally chastise him for engaging in this risk-taking behavior. A few minutes later, she again found him in the same situation. Once more, she removed him from his dangerous precipice and this time, was very vocal in expressing her disapproval at his failure to comply with her request. She barely had time to reenter the house when she observed Ryan once again on top of the camper, but this time, he had his younger brother with him. "He just doesn't learn from his mistakes," she exclaimed.

According to Ryan's teacher, from his first day in kindergarten, Ryan was significantly challenged by the classroom demands for goal-directed persistence and attention. He was frequently observed to be out of his desk and disrupting his classmates. Impulsivity proved to be a significant impediment to Ryan's adjustment. He often and inappropriately spoke out, was unable to engage in turn-taking, and was frequently noted to engage in physically dangerous activities without considering the consequences. The latter was particularly problematic during recess times, when Ryan would jump from heights and place other children at physical risk because of his inability to "stop and think" before acting. These behaviors, together with Ryan's social immaturity, low frustration tolerance, and poor adaptability, caused him to be a social outcast among his peers. The teacher speculated that they were also causal in Ryan's reading problems. A teacher assistant was hired to support Ryan within the classroom and his teacher commented that without these services, Ryan could not be retained within the regular classroom.

How did Ryan feel about all this? During our interview with Ryan, he was reluctant to offer much information, although he was emphatic in his perception that he had lots of friends and other children liked him. He also felt that he was academically successful. When he was challenged with contrary information, he either recounted that others were responsible for problems he was experiencing (e.g., it was upon his brother's instigation that he took him to the top of the camper) or that there was no problem and our information was incorrect. Ryan did acknowledge that he enjoyed playing computer games and participating in a music program for young children.

Given this (and other) presenting information, the assessment team met to develop an assessment plan. This plan included a seminaturalistic observation, administration of a battery of neuropsychological tests including the WISC-IV, Children's Memory Test (CMT); selected domains from the Developmental Neuropsychological Assessment (NEPSY); and Woodcock Johnson Test of Cognitive and Academic Abilities, Third Edition (WJ-III); the Conners' Continuous Performance Test, Second Edition (CPT-II); Comprehensive Test of Phonological Processing (CTPP); Test of Developmental Language, Third Edition Primary (TOLD-III-P); and the Teacher and Parent Rating Scales from the Behavioral Assessment System for Children (BASC-TRS and PRS). A brief presentation of the results of this assessment are presented

For the observational analysis, the examiner arranged to observe Ryan while he participated in a structured group academic activity. She noted that Ryan was uncooperative if he did not understand the directions or if the tasks were difficult for him. On numerous occasions, the group leader found it necessary to verbally redirect Ryan back to the task and to again repeat the instructions. Because Ryan's off-task behavior was disruptive to the other group members, the group leader was observed to situate Ryan away from distracting materials and to use both verbal and nonverbal reminders to keep him seated. Near the end of the session, it was apparent that Ryan had "won." He no longer remained in his seat and appeared to be in command of the room. Upon leaving the room, the group leader explained to the examiner that "that kid is a handful!"

To assess Ryan's relative intellectual strengths and weaknesses, he was subsequently administered the WISC-IV. Tables 7.3, 7.4, and 7.5 present findings from this testing.

Analysis of Ryan's WISC-IV results reveals that while there is relative uniformity between his scores on the VCI and PRI, highly significant differences are apparent between the VCI and PRI vs the WMI and PSI, with Ryan demonstrating significantly stronger abilities on measures of verbal comprehension and perceptual reasoning than on tasks of working memory

TABLE 7.3   Ryan's WISC-IV Composite Scores

Composites	Standard Score	%	95% CI	Classification Range
Verbal Comprehension Index	99	47	92–106	Average
Perceptual Reasoning Index	102	55	94–109	Average
Working Memory Index	80	9	74–89	Low Average
Processing Speed Index	78	7	72–90	Borderline
Full Scale IQ	89	23	84–94	Low Average

TABLE 7.4   Ryan's WISC-IV Subtest Scores

Subtests	Standard Score	Percentile
Block Design	10	50
Similarities	11	63
Digit Span	6	9
Picture Concepts	10	50
Coding	5	5
Vocabulary	9	37
Letter–Number Sequencing	7	16
Matrix Reasoning	11	63
Comprehension	10	50
Symbol Search	7	16

TABLE 7.5   Ryan's Supplementary WISC-IV Subtest Scores

Supplementary Subtests	Standard Score	Percentile
Picture Completion	9	37
Cancellation	7	16
Information	7	16
Arithmetic	7	16
Word Reasoning	10	50

and processing speed. As noted throughout the preceding literature review, this Wechsler scale pattern is somewhat typical of children with ADHD, but also other exceptionalities (e.g., learning disabilities). Also consistent with the WISC-IV ADHD and ADHD/LD clinical studies (see Technical Manual), Ryan demonstrated his weakest skills on the Digit Span, Coding, Letter–Number Sequencing, Symbol Search, Information, and Arithmetic subtests. Closer inspection of his Digit Span performance indicated that Ryan obtained a lower standard score on the Digit Span Backward than the Digit Span Forward, a stronger indication of working memory deficits than is the Digit Span Forward measure. While these findings are certainly not diagnostic of any disorder, they do rule out particular exceptionalities such as mental retardation and help to narrow the search for other causal conditions (e.g., learning disability, ADHD). Perhaps most important, the WISC-IV results point to areas of strength (i.e., verbal comprehension and perceptual reasoning) that may be protective factors in remediation planning.

Subtests from another measure of cognitive abilities (i.e., the Woodcock Johnson Tests of Cognitive Abilities, Third Edition) that tapped weaknesses identified by the WISC-IV were given to Ryan. Findings were consistent with results obtained from the WISC-IV. Performance within the borderline to low average ranges were evident on domains assessing speed of automatized information processing, cognitive fluency, working memory, and broad attention. Several tasks were particularly problematic for Ryan, with scores suggesting abilities within the extremely low to borderline ranges. These tasks evaluated the speed at which Ryan could make visual symbol discriminations and recall verbal information from acquired knowledge, as well as his competencies at sustaining attention and interference control. In addition, an extremely low score was observed on a subtest measuring auditory selective attention. A neuropsychological inventory, the NEPSY, provided further information on Ryan's sensorimotor and attention/executive control competencies. Skills were well below the expected level in the broad areas measuring attention and executive function and sensorimotor functions. Noteworthy findings included highly depressed scores on subtests purporting to evaluate auditory vigilance and selective attention, visual attention (i.e., the speed and accuracy with which Ryan could scan an array and locate a target), and the executive functions of planning, monitoring, and self-regulation. In the sensorimotor area, Ryan was challenged by a task assessing finger dexterity, as well as visuomotor precision. Observational analysis suggested that Ryan's difficulties on the latter task stemmed from poor attention, lack of planning, and impulsivity.

On two separate occasions, Ryan was administered the Conners' Continuous Performance Test, Second Edition. This measure allowed us to further assess for the presence of sustained attention and arousal modulation problems, as well as impulsivity. On both testings, markedly atypical scores were noted on most measures, including errors of omission and commission. The CPT discriminant function on each administration indicated that the results better matched an ADHD clinical profile than nonclinical one (93.1% and 99.9%). The value of the confidence index indicated that the suggested classification was made with a high degree of certainty.

The relative weaknesses that were evident in working memory and on the Information subtest on the WISC-IV were further assessed through the use of the Children's Memory Scale, a scale designed to assess short- and long-term recall and recognition of auditory and visual stimuli, as well as working memory. On tasks of immediate and delayed verbal and visual recall, Ryan generally performed within ranges commensurate with his verbal and visual IQ. Inspection of subtest scores, however, revealed specific difficulties on a task evaluating the immediate and delayed recall of nonmeaningful verbal information. Interestingly, while children typically show stronger performance on tasks of recognition rather than recall, Ryan obtained a score at the first percentile on the delayed recognition composite. This is a finding we often see in children with ADHD, and it would appear that foils and distractors in the material interfere with their ability to focus on the material that stimulates recognition. Impulsive responding may also be a factor in poor performance on these tasks, which may be perceived by the child as very pedantic. Also in keeping with profiles characteristically observed in children with ADHD, Ryan showed extremely weak performance on the tasks assessing auditory working memory, with the composite score placing him within the borderline range.

While academic evaluation suggested low achievement in arithmetic areas, there was no evidence of a learning disability. Interestingly, relative to his age-peers, Ryan showed developmentally appropriate performance in areas of reading. A measure of phonological processing generated scores within average ranges on a domain evaluating phonological awareness; however, the Rapid Naming composite was within the borderline range. This finding was in keeping with results from an earlier cognitive measure. Further, a language assessment completed by a speech and language pathologist revealed age-appropriate speech and language skills but immaturity in verbal fluency. We interpreted these findings, along with those from previous cognitive and neuro-psychological testing that indicated sensorimotor and verbal fluency deficits, as possible indications of problems with reconstitution. Recall that Barkley maintains that one of the executive functions impaired in ADHD involves reconstitution (i.e., nonverbal and verbal analysis and synthesis), which can be manifested through impairments in verbal and behavioral fluency.

Relative concurrence was noted between respondents (i.e., mother, father, and teacher) evaluating Ryan's behavior on the BASC. T-scores within the clinically significant ranges were evident on scales measuring hyperactivity, attention, and atypicality. Ryan's parents' ratings also suggested extremely high levels of aggression, although this was not as evident in teacher ratings. All respondents also identified problems relating to adaptability and social skills. Again, this profile is consistent with that typically observed in children with ADHD (Combined Type).

In reaching a diagnostic decision, the team carefully considered all the data, eliminating conditions for which there was no substantive evidence (e.g., mental retardation, language impairment, learning disability). As the composite profile seemed to indicate the presence of ADHD (Combined Type), findings were compared to the DSM-IV criteria for this condition and to recent theoretical conceptualizations of this disorder. By way of example, we have graphically illustrated the measures that were considered in evaluating Ryan's assessment results relative to Barkley's model (Figure 7.1).

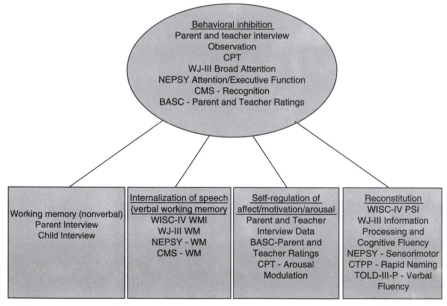

FIGURE 7.1 Application of Barkley's hybrid model of executive function to Ryan's assessment results.

Follow-up interviews were subsequently held with Ryan's parents and teacher to explain the assessment results and outline recommendations. At each of the interviews, assessment results were explained and recommendations for enhancing protective mechanisms and reducing risk factors were given (e.g., proactive behavioral management, pharmacological treatment, parent strategies, and adapting instruction). Of particular importance were several sessions that were held with Ryan. These sessions focused on empowering Ryan with knowledge about the nature of his condition and compensatory strategies that would foster resiliency. We are careful in our child interviews to present information in developmentally sensitive ways and to use age-appropriate books and other technological aids to ensure that it is a "resiliency enhancing" experience for the child.

REFERENCES

Achenbach, T. M. (1991). *Manual for the Child Behavior Checklist and Revised Child Behavior Profile*. Burlington, VT: Author.

Albers, N. C. (1998). Use of the Wechsler Intelligence Scale for Children-Third Edition and the Wechsler Individual Achievement Test in the diagnosis of learning in an attention deficit disorder referred population. *Dissertation Abstracts International: Section B: The Sciences and Engineering, 58(7-B)*, 3913.

American Psychiatric Association. (1968). *Diagnostic and statistical manual of mental disorders* (2nd ed.). Washington, DC: Author.

American Psychiatric Association. (1980). *Diagnostic and statistical manual of mental disorders* (3rd ed.). Washington, DC: Author.

American Psychiatric Association. (1987). *Diagnostic and statistical manual of mental disorders* (3rd ed., rev.). Washington, DC: Author.

American Psychiatric Association. (1994). *Diagnostic and statistical manual of mental disorders* (4th ed.). Washington, DC: Author.

American Psychiatric Association. (2000). *Diagnostic and statistical manual of mental disorders* (4th ed., text revision). Washington, DC: Author.

Anastopoulos, A. D., Spisto, M. A., & Maher, M. C. (1994). The WISC-III freedom from distractibility factor: Its utility in identifying children with attention deficit hyperactivity disorder. *Psychological Assessment, 6*, 368–371.

Angello, L. M., Volpe, R. J., DiPerna, J. C., Gureasko, M., Sammi, P., Gureasko-Moore, D. P., Hnebrig, M. R., & Ota, K. (2003). Assessment of attention-deficit/hyperactivity disorder: An evaluation of six published rating scales. *School Psychology Review, 32(2)*, 241–262.

Assesmany, A., McIntosh, D. E., Phelps, L., & Rizza, M. G. (2001). Discriminant validity of the WISC-III in children classified as ADHD. *Journal of Psychoeducational Assessment, 19(2)*, 137–147.

Axelrod, M. I. (2002). Signal detection, perceptual sensitivity, and response bias: Assessing attention and impulsivity in children with attention deficit hyperactivity disorder and children with anxiety using a continuous performance test. *Dissertation Abstracts International: Section B: The Sciences and Engineering, 63(5-B)*, 2572.

Bain, J. L. (2001). Language development in children with Attention Deficit Disorder. *Dissertation Abstracts International: Section B: The Sciences and Engineering, 61(10-B)*, 5593.

Barkley, R. A. (1997a). Behavioral inhibition, sustained attention, and executive functions: Constructing a unifying theory of ADHD. *Psychological Bulletin, 121*, 65–94.

Barkley, R. A. (1997b). *ADHD and the nature of self-control*. New York: Guilford Press.

Barkley, R. A. (1998). *Attention-deficit hyperactivity disorder: A handbook for diagnosis and treatment* (2nd ed.). New York: The Guilford Press.

Barkley, R. A. (1999). Response inhibition in attention-deficit hyperactivity disorder. *Mental Retardation and Developmental Disabilities-Research Reviews, 5(3)*, 177–184.

Barkley, R. A. (2000). Genetics of childhood disorders: XVII. ADHD, Part 1. The executive functions and ADHD. *Journal of the American Academy of Child and Adolescent Psychiatry, 39(8)*, 1064–1068.

Barkley, R. A. (2001). The inattentive type of ADHD as a distinct disorder: What remains to be done. *Clinical Psychology: Science and Practice, 8(4)*, 489–501.

Barkley, R. A., Anastopoulos, A. D., Guevremont, D. C., & Fletcher, K. E. (1991a). Adolescents with Attention Deficit Hyperactivity Disorder: Patterns of behavioural adjustment, academic functioning, and treatment utilization. *Journal of the American Academy of Child and Adolescent Psychiatry, 30*, 752–761.

Barkley, R. A., Cook, E. H., Dulcan, M., Campbell, S. *et al.* (2002). Consensus statement on ADHD. *European Child and Adolescent Psychiatry, 11(2)*, 96–98.

Barkley, R. A., DuPaul, G. J., & McMurray, M. B. (1991b). Attention deficit disorder with and without hyperactivity: Clinical response to three dose levels of methylphenidate. *Pediatrics, 87*, 519–531.

Barkley, R. A., Edwards, G., Laneri, M., Fletcher, K., & Metevia, L. (2001). Executive functioning, temporal discounting, and sense of time in adolescents with attention deficit hyperactivity disorder (ADHD) and oppositional defiant disorder (ODD). *Journal of Abnormal Child Psychology, 29(6)*, 541–556.

Barringer, M. S. (2001). Assessment of the ADHD-predominantly hyperactive/impulsive subtype using visual continuous performance, psychophysiological, and behavioral measures. *Dissertation Abstracts International: Section B: The Sciences and Engineering, 61(11–B)*, 6161.

Bauermeister, J. J., Alegria, M., Bird, H. R., Rubio-Stipec, M., & Canino, G. (1992). Are attentional-hyperactivity deficits unidimensional or multidimensional syndromes? Empirical findings from a community survey. *Journal of the American Academy of Child and Adolescent Psychiatry, 31*, 423–431.

Beebe, D. W., Pfiffner, L. J., & McBurnett, K. (2000). Evaluation of the validity of the Wechsler Intelligence Scale for Children-Third Edition. Comprehension and picture arrangement subtests as measures of social intelligence. *Psychological Assessment, 12(1)*, 97–101.

Bowers, T. G., Risser, M. G., Suchanec, J. F., Tinker, D. E., Ramer, J. C., & Domoto, M. (1992). A developmental index using the Wechsler Intelligence Scale for Children: Implications for the diagnosis and nature of ADHD. *Journal of Learning Disabilities, 25*, 179–185.

Boykin, C. L. (2001). A preliminary examination of Barkley's 1997 Hybrid Model of Attention Deficit Hyperactivity Disorder: A regression analysis utilizing a heterogeneous group of elementary school children. *Dissertation Abstracts International: Section B: The Sciences and Engineering, 61(9-B)*, 4964.

Cantrill, J. L. (2003). Inhibition, working memory, and time sense in children with attention deficit hyperactivity disorder. *Dissertation Abstracts International: Section B: The Sciences and Engineering, 63(7-B)*, 3466.

Cantwell, D. P., & Baker, L. (1992). Association between attention deficit-hyperactivity disorder and learning disorders. In S. E. Shaywitz & B. A. Shaywitz (Eds.), *Attention deficit disorder comes of age: Toward the twenty-first century* (pp. 145–164). Austin, TX: Pro-Ed.

Carella, S. E. (1998). The cognitive profiles of the inattentive and hyperactive-impulsive subtypes of attention-deficit/hyperactivity disorder. *Dissertation Abstracts International: Section B: The Sciences and Engineering, 58(11-B)*: 6229.

Caron, C., & Rutter, M. (1991). Comorbidity in child psychopathology: Concepts, issues and research strategies. *Journal of Child Psychology and Psychiatry, 32*, 1063–1080.

Carpenter, M. F. (2002). Predictive accuracy of the Gordon Diagnostic System and Wide Range Assessment of Memory and Learning in ADHD evaluation. *Dissertation Abstracts International: Section B: The Sciences and Engineering, 62(12-B)*, 5955.

Chae, P. K. (1999). Correlation study between WISC-III scores and TOVA performance. *Psychology in the Schools, 36(3)*, 179–185.

Chhabildas, N., Pennington, B. F., & Willcutt, E. G. (2001). A comparison of the neuropsychological profiles of the DSM-IV subtypes of ADHD. *Journal of Abnormal Child Psychology, 29(6)*, 529–540.

Cohen, N. J., Vallance, D. D., Barwick, M., Im, N., Menna, R., Horodezky, N. B., & Isaacson, L. (2000). The interface between ADHD and language impairment: An examination of language achievement, and cognitive processing. *Journal of Child Psychology and Psychiatry and Allied Disciplines, 41(3)*, 353–362.

Collings, R. D. (2003). Differences between ADHD Inattentive and Combined Types on the CPT. *Journal of Psychopathology and Behavioral Assessment, 25(3)*, 177–189.

Connor, D. E., Edwards, G., Fletcher, K. E., Baird, J., Barkley, R. A., & Steingard, R. J. (2003). Correlates of comorbid psychopathology in children with ADHD. *Journal of the American Academy of Child and Adolescent Psychiatry, 42(2)*, 193–200.

Cornoldi, C., Marzocchi, G. M., Belotti, M., Caroli, M. G., DeMeo, T., & Braga, C. H. (2001). Working memory interference control deficit in children referred by teachers by ADHD symptoms. *Child Neuropsychology, 7(4)*, 230–240.

Crawford, E. N. (2002). Profiles for exceptional samples on the cognitive assessment system using configural frequency analysis. *Dissertation Abstracts International: Section B: The Sciences and Engineering, 63(6-B)*, 3061.

Crundwell, R. M. A. (2002). The relations of regulation and emotionality in children with attention-deficit hyperactivity disorder: An initial investigation of Barkley's theoretical model of ADHD. Dissertation *Abstracts International: Section A: Humanities and Social Sciences, 62(12-A)*, 4054.

Davis, K. J. (2001). Comparison of the behavior assessment system for children and performance-based measures of attention. *Dissertation Abstracts International: Section B: The Sciences and Engineering, 61(9-B)*, 4977.

Demaray, M. K., Elting, J., & Schaefer, K. (2003). Assessment of attention-deficit/hyperactivity disorder (ADHD): A comparative evaluation of five, commonly used, published rating scales. *Psychology in the Schools, 40(4)*, 341–361.

Demaray, M. K., Schaefer, K., & Delong, L. K. (2003). Attention-deficit/hyperactivity disorder (ADHD): A national survey of training and current assessment practices in the schools. *Psychology in the Schools, 40(6)*, 583–597.

Denney, C. B., & Rapport, M. D. (2001). Cognitive pharmacology of stimulants in children with ADHD. In M. V. Solanto, A. F. Torrance *et al.* (Eds.), *Stimulant drugs and ADHD: Basic and clinical neuroscience* (pp. 283–302). London: Oxford University Press.

Deshazo, T. M. (2001). Executive functions in boys and girls with attention-deficit/hyperactivity disorder: Academic implications and potential benefits of stimulant medication. *Dissertation Abstracts International: Section B: The Sciences and Engineering, 61(9-B)*, 4978.

Dewey, D., Kaplan, B. J., Crawford, S. G., & Fisher, G. C. (2001). Predictive accuracy of the Wide Range Assessment of memory and Learning in children with attention deficit hyperactivity disorder and reading difficulties. *Developmental Neuropsychology, 19(2)*, 173–189.

Dietelin, N. R. (2001). Working memory and disinhibition in children with ADHD. *Dissertation Abstracts International: Section B: The Sciences and Engineering, 62(2-B)*, 1074.

Douglas, V. I. (1972). Stop, look and listen: the problem of sustained attention and impulse control in hyperactive and normal children. *Canadian Journal of Behavioural Science, 4*, 259–282.

Douglas, V. I. (1976). Perceptual and cognitive factors as determinants of learning disabilities: A review chapter with special emphasis on attentional factors. In R. M. Knights &

D. J. Bakker (Eds.), *The neuropsychology of learning disorders: Theoretical approaches* (pp. 413–421). Baltimore: University Park Press.

Douglas, V. I. (1980a). Higher mental processes in hyperactive children: Implications for training. In R. M. Knights & D. J. Bakker (Eds.), *Rehabilitation, treatment, and management of learning disorders* (pp. 65–92). Baltimore: University Park Press.

Douglas, V. I. (1980b). Treatment approaches: Establishing inner or outer control? In C. K. Whalen & B. Henker (Eds.), *Hyperactive children: The social ecology of identification and treatment*. New York: Academic Press.

Douglas, V. I. (1983). Attentional and cognitive problems. In M. Rutter (Ed.), *Developmental neuropsychiatry* (pp. 280–329). New York: The Guilford Press.

Douglas, V. I. (1988). Cognitive deficits in children with attention deficit disorder with hyperactivity. In L. M. Bloomingdale & J. A. Sergeant (Eds.), *Attention deficit disorder: Criteria, cognition, intervention* (pp. 65–82). London: Pergamon.

Douglas, V. I., Barr, R. G., Amin, K., O-Neill, M. E., & Britton, B. G. (1988). Dosage effects and individual responsivity to methylphenidate in attention deficit disorder. *Journal of Child Psychology and Psychiatry, 29*, 453–475.

Douglas, V. I., & Peters, K. G. (1979). Toward a clearer definition of the attentional deficit of hyperactive children. In G. A. Hale & M. Lewis (Eds.), *Attention and the development of cognitive skills* (pp. 173–247). New York: Plenum Press.

Doyle, A. E., Biederman, J., Seidman, L. J., Weber, W., & Faraone, S. V. (2003). Diagnostic efficiency of neuropsychological test scores for discriminating boys with and without attention deficit-hyperactivity disorder. In M. E. Hertzig & E. A. Farber (Eds.), *Annual progress in child psychiatry and child development: 2000–2001* (pp. 219–246). New York, NY: Brunner-Routledge.

Dunn, P. B. (2000). The application of signal detection theory to the assessment of ADHD. *Dissertation Abstracts International: Section B: The Sciences and Engineering, 60(7-B)*, 3560.

DuPaul, G.J., & Stoner, G. (1991). ADHD in the schools: Assessment and intervention strategies (2nd ed.). The Guilford school practitioner series. New York, NY: Guilford Press.

Edelbrock, C. (1991). Child Attention Problem Rating Scale. In R.A. Barkley (Ed.), *Attention deficit hyperactivity disorder: A clinical workbook* (pp. 49–51). New York: Guilford Press.

Epstein, J. N., Erkanli, A., Conners, C. K., Klaric, J., Costello, J. E., & Angold, A. (2003). Relations between continuous performance test performance measures and ADHD behaviors. *Journal of Abnormal Child Psychology, 31(5)*, 543–554.

Ewing, M. L. (1999). An analysis of the performance of a clinical sample of African-American, Caucasian, and Hispanic children on the WISC-III. *Dissertation Abstracts International: Section B: The Sciences and Engineering, 59(11-B)*, 6062.

Faraone, S. V., & Biederman, J. (1998). Neurobiology of attention-deficit hyperactivity disorder. *Biological Psychiatry, 44(10)*, 951–958.

Faraone, S. V., Biederman, J., Lehman, B. K., Spencer, T., Norman, D., Seidman, L.J., Kraus, I., Perrin, J., Chen, W. J., & Tsuang, M. T. (1993). Intellectual performance and school failure in children with attention deficit hyperactivity disorder and in their siblings. *Journal of Abnormal Psychology, 102(4)*, 616–623.

Fleck, S. L. (2001). Time perception in children with attention deficit hyperactivity disorder. *Dissertation Abstracts International: Section B: The Sciences and Engineering, 61(10-B)*, 5561.

Goldstein, H. S. (1987). Cognitive development in low attentive, hyperactive, and aggressive 6- through 11-year-old children. *Journal of the American Academy of Child and Adolescent Psychiatry, 26*, 214–218.

Frost, L. A., Moffitt, T. E., & McGee, R. (1989). Neuropsychological correlates of psychopathology in an unselected cohort of young adolescents. *Journal of Abnormal Psychology, 98*, 307–313.

Handler, M. W. (2001). Determining how psychologists assess children suspected of having attention deficit hyperactivity disorder: A survey of self-reported diagnostic practices. *Dissertation Abstracts International: Section B: The Sciences and Engineering, 61(7-B)*, 3845.

Hargung, C. M., Willcutt, E. G., Lahey, B. B., Pelham, W. E., Loney, J., Stein, M. A., & Keenan, K. (2002). Sex differences in young children who meet criteria for attention deficit hyperactivity disorder. *Journal of Clinical Child and Adolescent Psychology, 31(4)*, 453–464.

Hazell, P. L., Carr, V. J., Lewin, T. J., Dewis, S. A. M., Heathcote, D. M., & Brucki, B. M. (1999). Effortful and automatic information processing in boys with ADHD and specific learning disorders. *Journal of Child Psychology and Psychiatry and Allied Disciplines, 40(2)*, 275–286.

Hechtman, L. (2000). Assessment and diagnosis of attention-deficit/hyperactivity disorder. *Child and Adolescent Psychiatric Clinics of North American, 9(3)*, 481–498.

Heitzman, T. J. (2001). An investigation of children's timing abilities as a model for understanding the nature of ADHD deficits. *Dissertation Abstracts International: Section B: The Sciences and Engineering, 61(10-B)*, 5588.

Hill, D. E. (2000). An investigation into the memory abilities of children with attention deficit/hyperactivity disorder: A comparison of frontal lobe-mediated tasks and temporal lobe-mediated tasks using neuropsychological and neuroanatomical measurements. *Dissertation Abstracts International: Section B: The Sciences and Engineering, 60(8-B)*, 4225.

Hinds, P. L. (2000). Correlation of continuous performance test variables with teacher ratings of behavior among referred and nonreferred students. *Dissertation Abstracts International: Section A: Humanities and Social Sciences, 60(11-A)*, 3978.

Hintz, G. E. (2001). Assessing attention-deficit/hyperactivity disorder in children using the developmental index of the Wechsler Intelligence Scale for Children-Third Edition. *Dissertation Abstracts International: Section B: The Sciences and Engineering, 61(12-B)*, 6707.

Holifield, J. E. (1999). An examination of the memory performance of children with attention and learning deficits on the Wide Range Assessment of Memory and Learning. *Dissertation Abstracts International: Section B: The Sciences and Engineering, 60(5-B)*, 2343.

Horn-Alsberge, M. M. (1999). Stability of WISC-R and WISC-III IQs and subtest scores for a learning disabled sample. *Dissertation Abstracts International: Section B: The Sciences and Engineering, 60(5-B)*, 2344.

Houghton, S., Douglas, G., West, J., Whiting, K., Wall, M., Langsford, S., Powell, L., & Carroll, A. (1999). Differential patterns of executive function in children with attention-deficit hyperactivity disorder according to gender and subtype. *Journal of Child Neurology, 14(12)*, 801–805.

Huxford, B. L. (2001). Relationships between the California Verbal Learning Test Children's Version and the Wechsler Intelligence Test for Children-Third Edition. *Dissertation Abstracts International: Section B: The Sciences and Engineering, 61(10-B)*, 5589.

Jewell, L. A. (1998). Validity of continuous performance test errors as measures of impaired response inhibition in boys. *Dissertation Abstracts International: Section B: The Sciences and Engineering, 59(6-B)*, 3060.

Johnson, W. F. (2001). Working memory and ADHD: Can students with ADHD benefit from being taught strategies? *Dissertation Abstracts International: Section B: The Sciences and Engineering, 61(7-B)*, 3847.

Kalff, A. C., Hendriksen, J. G. M., Kroes, M., Vles, J. S. H., Steyaert, J., Feron, F. J., vanZeben, T. M. C. B., & Jolles, J. (2002). Neurocognitive performance of 5- and 6-year-old children who met criteria for attention deficit/hyperactivity disorder at 18 months follow-up: Results from a prospective population study. *Journal of Abnormal Child Psychology, 30(6)*, 589–598.

Kamphaus, R.W. (1993). *Clinical assessment of children's intelligence.* Boston, MA: Allyn and Bacon.

Kaplan, B. J., Crawford, S. G., Dewey, D. M., & Fisher, G. C. (2000). The IQs of children with ADHD are normally distributed. *Journal of Learning Disabilities, 33(5)*, 425–432.

Kaufman, A. S. (1994). *Intelligent testing with the WISC-III*. New York: John Wiley & Sons, Inc.

Kerns, K. A., McInerney, R. J., & Wilde, N. J. (2001). Time reproduction, working memory, and behavioral inhibition in children with ADHD. *Child Neuropsychology, 7(1)*, 21–31.

Kibby, M. Y., Cohen, M. J., & Hynd, G. W. (2002). Clock face drawing in children with attention-deficit/hyperactivity disorder. *Archives of Clinical Neuropsychology, 17(6)*; 531–546.

Kinard, L. R. (1999). Intrasubtest scatter on the Wechsler Intelligence scale for Children-Third Edition: A comparison of learning disabled, attention deficit hyperactivity disordered, and nonclinical 8- to 10-year olds. *Dissertation Abstracts International: Section A: Humanities and Social Sciences, 59(10-A)*, 3735.

Kirk, K. S. (2001). Relations between measures of attention and memory in the assessment of children with attentional difficulties. Dissertation Abstracts International: Section B: The Sciences and Engineering, 62(1-B): 553.

Kirlin, K. A. (2003). Inattentive and impulse profiles of the CPT-II and their relationship with DSM-IV ADHD subtypes. *Dissertation Abstracts International: Section B: The Sciences and Engineering, 63(8-B)*, 3922.

Klein, C., Raschke, A., & Brandenbusch, A. (2003). Development of pro-and antisaccades in children with attention-deficit hyperactivity disorder and healthy controls. *Psychophysiology, 40(1)*, 17–28.

Knigin-Calderon, O. (2002). Cognitive and learning style differences between subtypes of ADHD. *Dissertation Abstracts International: Section B: The Sciences and Engineering, 63(3B)*, 1565.

Korkman, M., Kirk, U., & Kemp, S. (1998). *NEPSY: A developmental neuropsychological assessment*. San Antonio: The Psychological Corporation.

Koschack, J., Kunert, H. J., Derichs, G., Weniger, G., & Irle, E. (2003). Impaired and enhanced attentional function in children with attention deficit/hyperactivity disorder. *Psychological Medicine, 33(3)*, 481–489.

Kostura, D. D. (2000). Identification of attention deficit/hyperactivity disorder, combined type. *Dissertation Abstracts International Section A: Humanities and Social Sciences, 61(3A)*, 880.

Krane, E., & Tannock, R. (2001). WISC-III third factor indexes learning problems but not attention deficit/hyperactivity disorder. *Journal of Attention Disorders, 5(2)*; 69–78.

Krishnamurthy, L. (1999). WISC-III third factor: Its relation to anxiety, attention, vigilance, distractibility, and cognitive flexibility. *Dissertation Abstracts International: Section A: Humanities and Social Sciences, 59(7-A)*, 2345.

Lahey, B. B., Applegate, B., McBurnett, K., Biederman, J., Greenhill, L., Hynd, G.W., Barkley, R. A., Newcorn, J., Jensen, P., Richters, J., Garfinkel, B., Kerdyk, L., Frick, P. J., Olldendick, T., Perez, D., Hart, E. L., Waldman, I., & Shaffer, D. (1994). DSM-IV field trials for attention deficit/hyperactivity disorder in children and adolescents. *American Journal of Psychiatry, 151*, 1673–1685.

Lahey, B. B., & Carlson, C. L. (1992). Validity of the diagnostic category of attention deficit disorder without hyperactivity: A review of the literature. In S. E. Shaywitz & B. Shaywitz (Eds.), *Attention deficit disorder comes of age: Toward the twenty-first century* (pp. 119–144). Austin, TX: Pro-Ed.

Lahey, B. B., Pelham, W. E., Schaughency, E. A., Atkins, M. S., Murphy, H. A., Hynd, G., Russo, M., Hartdagen, S., & Lorys-Vernon, A. (1988). Dimensions and types of attention deficit disorder. *Journal of the American Academy of Child and Adolescent Psychiatry, 27*, 330–335.

Lahey, B. B., Schaughency, E. A., Hynd, G. W., Carlson, C. L., & Nieves, N. (1987). Attention deficit disorder with and without hyperactivity: Comparison of behavioral characteristics of clinic-referred children. *Journal of the American Academy of Child and Adolescent Psychiatry, 26*, 718–723.

Law, R. T. (2003). Motor control and neuropsychological functions in ADHD subtypes. *Dissertation Abstracts International: Section B: The Sciences and Engineering, 63(7-B),* 3495.

Lawrence, V., Houghton, S., Tannock, R., Douglas, G., Durkin, K., & Whiting, K. (2002). ADHD outside the laboratory: Boys' executive function performance on tasks in videogame play and on a visit to the zoo. *Journal of Abnormal Child Psychology, 30(5),* 447–462.

Lazar, J. W., & Frank, Y. (1998). Frontal systems dysfunction in children with attention-deficit/ hyperactivity disorder and learning disabilities. *Journal of Neuropsychiatry and Clinical Neurosciences, 10(2),* 160–167.

Levy, F. (2002). Project for a scientific psychiatry in the 21st century. *Australian and New Zealand Journal of Psychiatry, 36(5),* 595–602.

Ligett, A. E. (2000). Piloting auditory selective and sustained attention tasks on ADHD subtypes and a comparison group. *Dissertation Abstracts International: Section A: Humanities and Social Sciences, 61(1-A),* 83.

Liu, Y., & Wang, Y. (2002). Gender difference of neuropsychological function in attention deficit hyperactivity disorder. *Chinese Mental Health Journal, 16(6),* 403–406.

Lockwood, K. A., Marcotte, A. C., & Stern, C. (2001). Differentiation of attention-deficit/ hyperactivity disorder subtypes: Application of neuropsychological model of attention. *Journal of Clinical and Experimental Neuropsychology, 23(3);* 317–330.

Loney, J. (1974). The intellectual functioning of hyperactive elementary school boys: A cross-sectional investigation. *American Journal of Orthopsychiatry, 44,* 754–762.

Lowman, M G., Schwanz, K. A., & Kamphaus, R.W. (1996). WISC-III third factor: Critical measurement issues. *Canadian Journal of School Psychology, 12,* 15–22.

Lufi, D. (2001). Double-coding Test: A new paper-and-pencil measure of eye-hand coordination. *Perceptual and Motor Skills, 92(3, Pt1),* 815–826.

Mahone, E. M., Hagelthorn, K. M., Cutting, L. E., Schuerholz, L. J., Pelletier, S. F., Rawlins, C., Singer, H. S., & Denckla, M. B. (2001). Effects of IQ on executive function measures in children with ADHD. *Child Neuropsychology, 8(1),* 52–65.

Mahone, E. M., Hagelthorn, K. M., Cutting, L. E., Schuerholz, L. J., Pelletier, S. F., Rawlins, C., Singer, H. S., & Denckla, M. B. (2001). Effects of IQ on executive function measures in children with ADHD. *Child Neuropsychology, 8(1),* 52–65.

Mahone, E. M., Miller, T. L., Koth, C. W., Mostofsky, S. H., Goldberg, M. C., & Denckla, M. B. (2003). Differences between WISC-R and WISC-III performance scale among children with ADHD. *Psychology in the Schools, 40(4),* 331–340.

Manly, T., Anderson, V., Nimmo-Smith, I., Turner, A., Watson, P., & Robertson, I. H. (2001). The differential assessment of children's attention: The Test of Everyday Attention for Children (TEA-Ch), normative sample and ADHD performance. *Journal of Child Psychology and Psychiatry and Allied Disciplines, 42(8),* 1065–1081.

Mather, N., & Woodcock, R. W. (2001). *Woodcock-Johnson III.* Itasca, IL: Riverside Publishing.

Mayes, S. D., & Calhoun, S.L. (2002). The Gordon Diagnostic System and WISC-III Freedom from Distractibility index: Validity in identifying clinic-referred children with and without ADHD. *Psychological Reports, 91(2),* 575–587.

Mayes, S. D., Calhoun, S. L., & Crowell, E. W. (1999). WISC-III Freedom from Distractibility as a measure of attention in children with and without attention deficit hyperactivity disorder. *Journal of Attention Disorders, 2(4),* 217–227.

McBurnett, K., Harris, S. M., Swanson, J. M., Pfiffner, L. J., Tamm, L., & Freeland, D. (1993). Neuropsychological and psychophysiological differentiation of inattention/ overactivity and aggression/defiance symptom groups. *Journal of Clinical Child Psychology, 22,* 165–171.

McGee, R. A., Clark, S. E., & Symons, D. K. (2000). Does the Conners' Continuous Performance Test aid in ADHD diagnosis? *Journal of Abnormal Child Psychology, 28(5),* 415–424.

McGee, R., Williams, S., Moffit, T., & Anderson, J. (1989). A comparison of 13-year-old boys with attention deficit and/or reading disorder on neuropsychological measures. *Journal of Abnormal Child Psychology, 17*, 37–53.

McGee, R., Williams, S., & Silva, P. A. (1984). Behavioral and developmental characteristics of aggressive, hyperactive and hyperactive-aggressive boys. *Journal of the American Academy of Child Psychiatry, 23*, 270–290.

McInerney, R. J., & Kerns, K. A. (2003). Time reproduction in children with ADHD: Motivation matters. *Child Neuropsychology, 9(2)*, 91–108.

McInnes, A. J. (2001). Listening comprehension abilities in children with attention deficit hyperactivity disorder and language impairment. *Dissertation Abstracts International: Section A: Humanities and Social Sciences, 62(4-A)*, 1325.

McInnes, A., Humphries, T., Hogg-Johnson, S., & Tannock, R. (2003). Listening comprehension and working memory are impaired in attention-deficit hyperactivity disorder irrespective of language impairment. *Journal of Abnormal Child Psychology, 31(4)*, 427–443.

Meaux, J. B. (2002). Time perception, behavioral inhibition, and ADHD. *Dissertation Abstracts International: Section B: The Sciences and Engineering, 62(8-B)*, 3556.

Muir-Broaddus, J. E., Rosenstein, L. D., Medina, D. E., & Soderberg, C. (2002). Neuropsychological test performance of children with ADHD relative to test norms and parent behavioral ratings. *Archives of Clinical Neuropsychology, 17(7)*, 671–689.

Naglieri, J. A., Goldstein, S., Iseman, J. S., & Schwebach, A. (2003). Performance of children with attention deficit hyperactivity disorder and anxiety/depression on the WISC-III and Cognitive Assessment System (CAS). *Journal of Psychoeducational Assessment, 21(1)*, 32–42.

Neef, N. A., Bicard, D. F., & Endo, S. (2001). Assessment of impulsivity and the development of self-control in students with attention deficit hyperactivity disorder. *Journal of Applied Behavior Analysis, 34(4)*, 397–408.

Newby, R. F., Recht, D. R., Caldwell, J., & Schaefer, J. (1993). Comparison of WISC-III and WISC-R IQ changes over a 2-year time span in a sample of children with dyslexia. *Journal of Psychoeducational Assessment, WISC-III Monograph Series*, pp. 87–93.

Norrelgen, F., Lacerda, F., & Forssberg, H. (1999). Speech discrimination and phonological working memory in children. *Developmental Medicine and Child Neurology, 41(5)*, 335–339.

Nguyen, M. T. (2002). A program design for ADHD students: Assessment and classroom intervention. *Dissertation Abstracts International: Section B: The Sciences and Engineering, 63(5-B)*, 2597.

Nyden, A., Billstedt, E., Hjelmquist, E., & Gilberg, C. (2001). Neurocognitive stability in Asperger syndrome, ADHD, and reading and writing disorder: A pilot study. *Developmental Medicine and Child Neurology, 43(3)*, 165–171.

Palkes, H., & Stewart, M. A. (1972). Intellectual ability and performance of hyperactive children. *American Journal of Orthopsychiatry, 42*, 35–39.

Pallas, D. M. (2003). A comparison of children with and without ADHD on verbal short-term and working memory tasks. *Dissertation Abstracts International: Section B: The Sciences and Engineering, 63(7-B)*, 3482.

Perugini, E. M. (1999). The predictive power of combined neuropsychological measures for attention deficit/hyperactivity disorder in children. *Dissertation Abstracts International: Section B: The Sciences and Engineering, 60(4-B)*, 1867.

Perugini, E. M., Harvey, E. A., Lovejoy, D. W., Sandstrom, K., Webb, A. H. (2000). The predictive power of combined neuropsychological measures for attention-deficit/hyperactivity disorder in children. *Child Neuropsychology, 6(2)*, 101–114.

Pilling, B. A. (2000). Teacher competency in identifying ADHD and other childhood mental health disorders: Some possible explanations for ADHD misdiagnosis. *Dissertation Abstracts International: Section B: The Sciences and Engineering, 61(5-B)*, 2777.

Pineda, D., Ardila, A., & Rosselli, M. (1999). Neuropsychological and behavioral assessment of ADHD in seven- to twelve-year-old children: A discriminant analysis. *Journal of Learning Disabilities, 32(2),* 159–173.

Pineda, D. A., Restrepo, A., Sarmiento, R. J., Gutierrez, J. E., Vargas, S. A., Quiroz, Y. T., & Hynd, G. W. (2002). Statistical analyses of structural magnetic resonance imaging of the head of the caudate nucleus in Colombian children with attention-deficit hyperactivity disorder. *Journal of Child Neurology, 17(2),* 97–105.

Power, T. J., Costigan, T. E., Leff., S. S., Eiraldi, R. B., & Landau, S. (2001). Assessing ADHD across settings: Contributions of behavioral assessment to categorical decision making. *Journal of Community Psychology, 30(3),* 399–412.

Prifitera, A., & Dersh, J. (1993). Base rates of WISC-III diagnostic subtest patterns among normal, learning-disabled, and ADHD samples. *Journal of Psychoeducational Assessment, WISC-III Monograph Series,* 43–55.

Prout, P. I. (2000). Subtype and gender differences in attention-deficit/hyperactivity disorder: An investigation of selected neuropsychological variables. *Dissertation Abstracts International: Section B: The Sciences and Engineering, 61(5-B),* 2777.

Quinlan, D. M. (2000). Assessment of attention-deficit/hyperactivity disorder and comorbidities. In T. E. Brown (Ed.), *Attention-deficit disorders and comorbidities in children, adolescents and adults* (pp. 455–507). Washington, DC: American Psychiatric Publishing, Inc.

Radonovich, K. J. (2002). Gender differences on executive function tasks in children with ADHD. *Dissertation Abstracts International: Section B: The Sciences and Engineering, 62(10-B),* 4801.

Rapport, M. D. (2001). Attention-deficit/hyperactivity disorder. In M. Hersen & V. B. Van Hasselt, *Advanced abnormal psychology (2nd ed)* (pp. 191–208). Dordrecht, Netherlands: Kluwer Academic Publishers.

Rapport, M. D., Chung, K. M., Shore, G., Denney, C. B., & Isaacs, P. (2000). Upgrading the science and technology of assessment and diagnosis: Laboratory and clinic-based assessment of children with ADHD. *Journal of Clinical Child Psychology, 29(4),* 555–568.

Rapport, M. D., Chung, K. M., Shore, G., & Isaacs, P. (2001). A conceptual model of child psychopathology: Implications for understanding attention deficit hyperactivity disorder and treatment efficacy. *Journal of Community Psychology, 30(1),* 48–58.

Reinecke, M. A., Beebe, D. W., & Stein, M. A. (1999). The third factor of the WISC-III: It's (probably) not Freedom From Distractibility. *Journal of the American Academy of Child and Adolescent Psychiatry, 38(3),* 322–328.

Reitman, D., & Hupp, S. D. A. (2003). Behavior problems in the school setting: Synthesizing structural and functional assessment. In M. L. Kelley & G. H. Noell (2003). Practitioner's guide to empirically based measures of school behavior. AABT clinical assessment series (pp. 23–36). New York, NY: Kluwer Academic/Plenum Publishers.

Reynolds, C. R., & Kamphaus, R. W. (1992). *Behavior assessment system for children.* Circle Pines, MN: American Guidance Service.

Riccio, C. A., Reynolds, C. R., Lowe, P., & Moore, J. J. (2002). The continuous performance test: A window on the neural substrates for attention? *Archives of Clinical Neuropsychology, 17(3),* 235–272.

Risher, E. A. (2002). Time perception in children diagnosed with attention deficit hyperactivity disorder. *Dissertation Abstracts International: Section B: The Sciences and Engineering, 63(4-B),* 2071.

Roodenrys, S., Koloski, N., & Grainger, J. (2001). Working memory function in attention deficit hyperactivity disordered and reading disabled children. *British Journal of Developmental Psychology, 19(3),* 325–337.

Rowland, H. E. W. (2000). Discriminating between attention deficit hyperactivity disorder and learning disabilities through the planning and placement team process. *Dissertation Abstracts International: Section A: Humanities and Social Sciences, 61(4-A),* 1310.

Rubia, K., Taylor, E., Smith, A. B., Oksannen, H., Overmeyer, S., & Newman, S. (2001). Neuropsychological analyses of impulsiveness in childhood hyperactivity. *British Journal of Psychiatry, 179,* 138–143.

Rucklidge, J. J., & Tannock, R. (2002). Neuropsychological profiles of adolescents with ADHD: Effects of reading difficulties and gender. *Journal of Child Psychology and Psychiatry and Allied Disciplines, 43(8),* 988–1003.

Saklofske, D. H. & Schwean, V. L. (1993). Standardized procedures for measuring the correlates of ADHD in children: A research program. *Canadian Journal of School Psychology, 9,* 28–36.

Saklofske, D. H., Schwean, V. L., & Ray, D. O. (1994). WISC-III and SB:FE performance of children with Attention Deficit Hyperactivity Disorder. *Canadian Journal of School Psychology, 10,* 167–171.

Sarkari, S. (2003). Do verbal working memory and reconstitution differentiate children with AD/HD hyperactive-impulsive/combined type from children with AD/HD-predominantly inattentive type and controls? *Dissertation Abstracts International: Section-B: The Sciences and Engineering, 63(7-B),* 3483.

Sattler, J. M. (2001). *Assessment of children: Cognitive Applications* (4th ed.). San Diego: Author.

Schatz, A. M., Ballantyne, A. O., & Trauner, D. A. (2001). Sensitivity and specificity of a computerized test of attention in the diagnosis of attention-deficit/hyperactivity disorder. *Assessment, 8(4),* 357–365.

Schaughency, E. A., Lahey, B. B., Hynd, G. W., Stone, P. A., Piacentini, J. C., & Frick, P. J. (1989). Neuropsychological test performance and the attention deficit disorders: Clinical utility of the Luria-Nebraska Neuropsychological Battery-Children's Revision. *Journal of Consulting and Clinical Psychology, 57,* 112–116.

Scheres, A., Oosterlaan, J., & Sergeant, J. A. (2001). Response execution and inhibition in children with AD/HD and other disruptive disorders: The role of behavioural activation. *Journal of Child Psychology and Psychiatry and Allied Disciplines, 42(3),* 347–357.

Schmitz, M., Cadore, L., Paczko, M., Kipper, L., Chaves, M., Rohde, L. A., Moura, C., & Knijnik, M. (2002). Neuropsychological performance in DSM-IV ADHD subtypes: An exploratory study with untreated adolescents. *Canadian Journal of Psychiatry, 47(9),* 863–869.

Schwean, V. L., & Saklofske, D. H. (1998). WISC-III assessment of children with Attention Deficit/Hyperactivity Disorder. In A. Prifitera & D. H. Saklofske (Eds.), *WISC-III clinical use and interpretation: Scientist-practitioner perspectives* (pp. 92–118). San Diego: Academic Press.

Schwean, V. L., Saklofske, D. H., Yackulic, R. A., & Quinn, D. (1993). WISC-III performance of ADHD children. *Journal of Psychoeducational Assessment, WISC-III Monograph,* 56–70.

Sengstock, S. K. (2001). The contribution of working memory and inhibition to the executive functioning of children with attention deficit hyperactivity disorder and children with reading disability. *Dissertation Abstracts International: Section B: The Sciences and Engineering, 61(11-B),* 6148.

Sergeant, J. A., Geurts, H., & Oosterlaan, J. (2002). How specific is a deficit of executive functioning for attention-deficit/hyperactivity disorder? *Behavioural Brain Research, 130(1–2),* 3–28.

Sergeant, J. A., Oosterlaan, J., & vanderMeere, J. (1999). Information processing and energetic factors in attention-deficit/hyperactivity disorder. In H. C. Quay & A. E. Hogan (Eds.), *Handbook of disruptive behavior disorders* (pp. 74–104). Dordrecht, Netherlands: Kluwer Academic Publishers.

Shallice, T., Marzocchi, G. M., Coser, S., DelSavio, M., Meuter, R. F., & Rumiati, R. I. (2002). Executive function profile of children with attention deficit hyperactivity disorder. *Developmental Neuropsychology, 21(1),* 43–71.

Shaywitz, S. E., & Shaywitz, B. A. (1988). Attention deficit disorder: Current perspectives. In J. F. Kavanagh & T. J. Truss, Jr. (Eds.), *Learning disabilities: Proceedings of the national conference* (pp. 369–546). Parkton, MD: York Press.

Shimizu, H. (2002). Visual-spatial selective attention in children with ADHD-combined type and ADHD-inattentive type using the Townsend task. *Dissertation Abstracts International: Section B: The Sciences and Engineering, 63(10-B)*, 4804.

Silverman, A. F. (2002). Disinhibition, memory, and attention deficit hyperactivity disorder. *Dissertation Abstract International: Section B: The Sciences and Engineering, 63(5-B)*, 2604.

Smith, A. L. (2000). School psychologists and attention-deficit/hyperactivity disorder: A survey of training, knowledge, practice, and attitude. *Dissertation Abstracts International: Section A: Humanities and Social Sciences, 60(11-A)*, 3906.

Snow, J. B., & Sapp, G. L. (2000). WISC-III subtest patterns of ADHD and normal samples. *Psychological Reports, 87(3, Pt1)*, 759–765.

Sonuga-Barke, E. J. S., Dalen, L., & Remington, B. (2003). Do executive deficits and delay aversion make independent contributions to preschool attention-deficit/hyperactivity disorders? *Journal of the American Academy of Child and Adolescent Psychiatry, 42(11)*, 1335–1342.

Spencer, T. J. (2002). Attention-deficit/hyperactivity disorder. *Archives of Neurology, 59(2)*, 314–316.

Steger, J., Imhof, K., Coutts, E., Gundelfinger, R., Steinhausen, H., & Brandeis, D. (2001). Attentional and neuromotor deficits in ADHD. *Developmental Medicine and Child Neurology, 43(3)*, 172–179.

Stevens, J. H. (2001). Behavioral inhibition, self-regulation of motivation, and working memory in children with and without attention deficit hyperactivity disorder (ADHD). *Dissertation Abstracts International: Section B: The Sciences and Engineering, 61(8-B)*, 4431.

Stevens, J., Quittner, A. L., Zuckerman, J. B., & Moore, S. (2002). Behavioral inhibition, self-regulation of motivation, and working memory in children with attention deficit hyperactivity disorder. *Developmental Neuropsychology, 21(2)*, 117–140.

Still, G. F. (1902). The Coulstonian lectures on some abnormal physical conditions in children. *Lancet, 1*, 1008–1012, 1077–1082, 1163–1168.

Strauss, A. Q. A., & Lehtinen, L. E. (1947). *Psychopathology and education of the brain-injured child.* New York: Grune & Stratton.

Swanson, C. H. (2002). WISC-III processing speed and freedom from distractibility factors in learning-disabled and ADHD populations. *Dissertation Abstracts International: Section A: Humanities and Social Sciences, 63(6-A)*, 2137.

Swanson, H. L., Mink, J., & Bocian, K. M. (1999). Cognitive processing deficits in poor readers with symptoms of reading disabilities and ADHD: More alike than different? *Journal of Educational Psychology, 91(2)*, 321–333.

Szatmari, P. (1992). The epidemiology of attention-deficit hyperactivity disorders. In G. Weiss (Ed.), *Child and adolescent psychiatry clinics of North America: Attention deficit disorder* (pp. 361–372). Philadelphia: W.B. Saunders.

Teeter, P. A., & Smith, P. L. (1993). WISC-III and WJ-R: Predictive and discriminant validity for students with severe emotional disturbance. *Journal of Psychoeducational Assessment, WISC-III Monograph Series*, 114–124.

Thorndike, R. L., Hagen, E., & Sattler, J. M. (1986). *Stanford-Binet Intelligence Scale: Fourth Edition.* Chicago: Riverside.

Tripp, G., Ryan, J., & Peace, K. (2002). Neuropsychological functioning in children with DSM-IV combined type attention deficit hyperactivity disorder. *Australian and New Zealand Journal of Psychiatry, 36(6)*, 771–779.

Uchigakiuchi, P. K. (2001). Attention deficits and scholastic achievement: A multisample analysis of gender differences in a community sample. *Dissertation Abstracts International: Section B: The Sciences and Engineering, 62(2-B)*, 1102.

Vaughn, M. L. (1998). Working memory deficits in children with attention deficit hyperactivity disorder: An examination of an executive function component in Barkley's unifying theory of ADHD. *Dissertation Abstracts International: Section B: The Sciences and Engineering, 58(12-B),* 6831.

Weiler, M. D., Bernstein, J. H., Bellinger, D., & Waber, D. P. (2002). Information processing deficits in children with attention-deficit/hyperactivity disorder, inattentive type and children with reading disability. *Journal of Learning Disabilities, 35(5),* 448-461.

Weiss, G., & Hechtman, L. (1993). *Hyperactive children grown up.* New York: Guilford Press.

Welsh, M. C. (2002). Developmental and clinical variations in executive functions. In D. L. Molfese & V. J. Molfese (Eds.), *Developmental variations in learning: Applications to social, executive function, language, and reading skills* (pp. 139–185). Mahwah, NJ, Lawrence Erlbaum Associates, Publishers.

Weller, M. D., Holmes-Bernstein, J., Bellinger, D. C., & Waber, D. P. (2000). Processing speed in children with attention deficit/hyperactivity disorder, inattentive type. *Child Neuropsychology, 6(3),* 218–234.

Wender, P. H. (1971). *Minimal brain dysfunction in children.* New York: Wiley.

West, J., Houghton, S., Douglas, G., & Whiting, K. (1999). Response inhibition, memory, and attention in boys with attention-deficit/hyperactivity disorder. *Educational Psychology, 22(5),* 533–551.

Westby, S. A. (1999). Test of Variables of Attention (TOVA) utility in differentiating attention deficit/hyperactivity disorder subtypes. *Dissertation Abstracts International: Section B: The Sciences and Engineering, 60(2-B),* 0846.

Whalen, C. K., & Henker, B. (1991). Social impact of stimulant treatment for hyperactive children. *Journal of Learning Disabilities, 24,* 231–241.

Wilkin-Bloch, S. (2002). The diagnosis of attention-deficit/hyperactivity disorder (ADHD) by psychologists, pediatricians, and general practitioners. *Dissertation Abstracts International: Section B: The Sciences and Engineering, 63(4-B),* 2081.

Willcutt, E. G., Pennington, B. F., Boada, R., Ogline, J. S., Tunick, R. A., Chhabildas, N. A., & Olson, R. K. (2001). A comparison of the cognitive deficits in reading disability and attention-deficit/hyperactivity disorder. *Journal of Abnormal Psychology, 110(1),* 157–172.

Williams, D., Stott, C. M., Goodyer, I. M., & Sahakian, B. J. (2000). Specific language impairment with or without hyperactivity: Neuropsychological evidence for frontostriatal dysfunction. *Developmental Medicine and Child Neurology, 42(6),* 368–375.

Wu, K. K., Anderson, V., & Castiello, U. (2002). Neuropsychological evaluation of deficits in executive functioning for ADHD children with or without learning disabilities. *Developmental Neuropsychology, 22(2),* 501–531.

Zentall, S. S., & Smith, Y. S. (1993). Mathematical performance and behaviour of children with hyperactivity with and without coexisting aggression. *Behavior Research and Therapy, 31,* 701–710.

Zayas-Bazan, M. M. (2001). An analysis of the applicability of WISC-III short forms with Black and Hispanic children diagnosed with ADHD. *Dissertation Abstracts International: Section B: The Sciences and Engineering, 62(4-B),* 2111.

8

ASSESSMENT OF CHILDREN WHO ARE GIFTED WITH THE WISC-IV

SARA S. SPARROW

Yale Child Study Center
Yale University PACE (Psychology of Abilities,
Competencies, and Expertise) Center
New Haven, Connecticnt

STEVEN I. PFEIFFER

Florida State University
Jallahassee, florida

TINA M. NEWMAN

Yale Child Study Center
Yale University PACE (Psychology of Abilities,
Competencies, and Expertise) Center
New Haven, Connecticnt

Ever since Terman published his seminal work on gifted children in 1925 (Terman, 1925), scientists, educators and parents have sought to better understand, identify, and provide for gifted children. Assessment and identification of gifted children and adolescents have been a major focus of studies undertaken in the interest of providing for the educational needs of these special children and adolescents.

This chapter addresses the assessment of gifted children using the WISC-IV. The Wechsler scales, in general, have been the most widely used instrument for this purpose, in part because they represent the most widely used intelligence tests in schools in the United States today, and because most school systems usually view the gifted child or adolescent as gifted either intellectually, academically, or both. Klausmeier, Mishra, and Maker (1987) conducted a national survey of assessment practices among school psychologists and found that the Wechsler scales had also become the overwhelming first choice for the assessment of gifted children. In addition to the WISC-IV, we also plan to discuss a new complementary instrument, the Gifted Rating Scales (GRS) (Pfeiffer & Jarosewich, 2003). This scale is designed to be completed by teachers who will assist in the identification of gifted children and adolescents.

Finally, we will make recommendations for how the WISC-IV and the GRS may be used to identify gifted children and adolescents.

DEFINITION OF GIFTEDNESS

One issue facing the gifted field is a lack of consensus on how to define giftedness. The federal definition has undergone a number of revisions, in 1972, 1978, 1988, and 1994. States have crafted their own definitions based on modifications of the different versions of the federal definition (Pfeiffer, 2002).

Most states are using a version of the 1978 modification of the 1972 federal definition, known as the Marland definition. The majority of states use the term *gifted and talented* in describing highly capable students, although 13 states restrict their definition to the term *gifted*. Almost all states include superior intelligence as a characteristic of giftedness. Specific academic ability is considered a type of giftedness by 33 states, creative ability a type of giftedness by 30, and leadership a type of giftedness by 18 states (Stephens & Karnes, 2000).

Experts in the gifted field do not agree on how to define giftedness (Pfeiffer, 2001, 2003). The lack of agreement among experts should come as no great surprise, since authorities in almost all applied fields, including education, psychology, and medicine, rarely reach consensus in defining social constructs of interest. The lack of professional consensus in how to define "giftedness," in conjunction with inconsistent state definitions, can make the identification of gifted students particularly challenging for the practitioner.

Exceptional general intelligence was once thought to be the hallmark of giftedness, but now is regarded by most authorities as only one manifestation of giftedness (Gardner, 1983; Pfeiffer & Jarosewich, 2003; Sternberg, 1997). New theories of giftedness emphasize the multidimensionality of outstanding abilities (Gagné, 1999; Gardner, 1983; Sternberg, 1997). For example, the Munich Model of Giftedness and Talent includes the following manifestations of talent: intelligence, creativity, social competence/leadership, and musical-artistic abilities (Zigler & Heller, 2000).

Gifted children can display many talents such as aesthetic, artistic, athletic, creative, dramatic, interpersonal, musical, and others. The number and types of gifts are limited only by what a given society recognizes and values as culturally important (Pfeiffer, 2002). Research suggests that different types of talents are moderately intercorrelated for many gifted children; however, there are many gifted children for whom this is not the case (Pfeiffer & Jarosewich, 2003).

Most, if not all, multidimensional conceptual definitions of giftedness include some reference to intelligence. Intelligence is viewed as goal-directed mental activity marked by efficient problem solving, critical thinking, and effective abstract reasoning (Pfeiffer, 2002).

This chapter restricts its discussion to the use of the WISC-IV in the assessment of one type of giftedness, intellectual. Robert Sternberg succinctly states that "intelligence comprises the mental abilities necessary for adaptation to, as well as shaping and selection of, environmental context" (1997, p. 1030). Intellectual giftedness includes cognitive abilities such as verbal and/or nonverbal abstract reasoning, effective and efficient problem solving, insight, mental speed, and memory (Pfeiffer & Jarosewich, 2003).

REVIEW OF THE LITERATURE

INTELLIGENCE AND GIFTEDNESS

Because the publication of the WISC-IV occurred only a few months before the preparation of this chapter, no research studies were available that investigated the use of the WISC-IV with gifted individuals except those carried out on the standardization sample and that were reported in the Technical and Interpretive Manual (Wechsler, 2003). Therefore, the most relevant literature concerning assessment of highly intelligent children with the Weschler Scales deals with the WISC-III. Since there are considerable differences between the WISC-III and the WISC-IV, in both content and structure, caution must be taken when comparing results from the WISC-III to the most recent revision. Data from the WISC-IV Technical and Interpretive Manual (Wechsler, 2003) are presented later in this chapter.

Quite aside from the use of the Wechsler scales to identify individuals who are gifted, there has also been debate over the use of *any* intelligence tests to identify gifted children. Tyerman (1986) argued that the cultural bias of intelligence tests unfairly places gifted children of "deprived or immigrant background(s)" at a disadvantage, even when conventional methods for reducing cultural bias are employed. He advocated instead the use of ability tests such as Raven's Progressive Matrices and Kohs' Block Design Test.

Others have not opposed the use of intelligence tests for the identification of gifted children, but have cautioned against the misapplication or misinterpretation of IQ scores. Harrington (1982), for example, cited a host of dangers in intelligence testing with gifted children. He pointed out that gifted children's IQ scores can be depressed by ceiling effects, the use of recently revised tests, or cultural bias. In addition, the use of arbitrary "cut-off scores" and the instability of IQ scores among preschool children can lead to misidentification of gifted children. Furthermore, intelligence tests can penalize gifted children by rewarding convergent-type responses, but granting no credit for divergent-type responses. Sparrow and Gurland (1998), in discussing the WISC-III and its use in identification of children and adolescents who are gifted, cautioned psychologists to be aware of ceiling effects and the emphasis of speed of performance that can penalize individuals with reflective cognitive styles.

Like Harrington, Sternberg (1982) identified widely used, but not necessarily sound practices in intelligence testing. Specifically, he questioned the premise that speed is an indication of intelligence, the claim that intelligence tests measure only intelligence and not achievement, the practice of administering intelligence tests in anxiety-provoking or stressful test-taking environments, and the tendency to treat a precise score as a necessarily valid score. In a similar vein, Barona and Pfeiffer (1992) cautioned that standard test administration procedures may compromise the maximal performance of students from culturally diverse backgrounds. Still other psychologists and educators have acknowledged the limitations of intelligence tests, but stress their value, when used properly, as a clinical tool for evaluating a child's intellectual abilities and as a predictor of future educational achievement. Robinson and Chamrad (1986), for example, took note of the valuable information yielded by intelligence tests, such as a child's scores, mental age estimates, predictions regarding the child's future academic achievement, and clinical observations made during the testing session. At the same time, they acknowledged that intelligence tests are not perfect and will not result in 100% accurate identification of gifted children, and that intelligence tests measure only intelligence and not other worthwhile characteristics of a child, such as creativity and other artistic talents.

Kaufman and Harrison (1986), too, acknowledged the limitations of intelligence tests, but argue convincingly in favor of their use for identifying gifted children. Intelligence tests, they argue, are very good predictors of academic achievement and academic success, and they have the most solid psychometric properties of all other kinds of tests used with gifted individuals. In addition, they pointed out that intelligence tests can identify as gifted, children who might otherwise go undetected because of behavior problems, learning disabilities, physical handicaps, or other attention-demanding characteristics that might cause educators or other professionals to overlook the child's intellectual abilities.

In addition, Kaufman and Harrison (1986) cautioned psychologists and educators to use intelligence tests responsibly. In particular, they cited the importance of using multiple criteria, not a single intelligence test score, in determining eligibility for gifted programs, and they stress that standard errors of measurement should always be taken into account. Further, they caution against making placement decisions in the absence of educational planning. That is, a child who is identified as gifted may be placed in a gifted program, but this placement should be made in the context of longer term educational planning for that child.

Despite the numerous cautions against misuse of, or overreliance on, intelligence tests for identification of gifted children, Kaufman and Harrison's (1986) point is well taken: currently no method has been demonstrated to be superior to intelligence tests for this purpose.

Pfeiffer (2002) echoed many of Kaufman and Harrison's (1986) suggestions in an article proposing best practices in identifying gifted students. The article included the following recommendations for psychologists and educators: gain familiarity with gifted children and their families, recognize the multiple manifestations of giftedness, appreciate the developmental nature of talent development and the developmental trajectories unique to the different domains of giftedness, and assess academic motivation when evaluating giftedness.

INTELLIGENCE AND THE WISC-III

Sevier, Bain, and Hildman (1994) investigated the relationship between the WISC-R and the WISC-III with gifted children by administering the WISC-III to 35 elementary school students in a gifted program who had previously been administered the WISC-R. They found the students' WISC-III global scores to be significantly lower than the WISC-R scores, such that 14 children (or 40%) in their sample would not have been placed in the local gifted program if the WISC-III had been used to determine eligibility. Sabatino, Spangler, and Vance (1995) conducted a similar investigation, employing a more robust methodology. They administered both tests in a counterbalanced design to 51 gifted children. They found very high agreement between the two tests, such that all 51 of their subjects who were found eligible for a gifted program with one test also would have been found eligible had the other test been used.

Without comparing it to other tests, Kaufman (1992) evaluated the psychometric strength of the WISC-III for gifted children. He found that the WISC-III places unduly high emphasis on the speed of the child's performance, and that low subtest stability can complicate an educator's or psychologist's efforts to interpret children's profiles. Overall, however, he stated that the WISC-III is quite useful for identifying gifted children in that it is a "carefully constructed, technically superior instrument with attractive materials, sensitive items (by gender and ethnicity), exceptional standardization(s), strong construct validity, reliable and stable IQ scores, and intelligently written manuals that facilitate test interpretation" (p. 158). Furthermore, he pointed out that the majority of subtests have ceilings ranging "from adequate to exceptional" (p.158).

Watkins and his colleagues (2002) recently conducted a factor analytic study of WISC-III performance of 505 gifted students. Results indicated a two-factor solution that approximated the Verbal Comprehension and Perceptual Reasoning indexes best demonstrated the strengths of the gifted students. Furthermore, Arithmetic, Coding and Picture Arrangement did not contribute to this solution. It is of interest that Arithmetic is no longer a part of the core battery and Picture Arrangement has been deleted from the WISC-IV.

WISC-IV STANDARDIZATION SAMPLE: PROFILES OF GIFTEDNESS

The changes from the WISC-III to the WISC-IV are substantial in both structure and content. Structurally, the WISC-IV has dropped the VIQ/PIQ designation to fully adopt the more valid four-factor model. The new model retains the previous factors Verbal Comprehension and Processing Speed, and adds in a reconceptualized Perceptual Reasoning factor. A new factor, Working Memory, completes the four-factor model. With respect to content, there are new subtests in the Core assessment including Perceptual Reasoning subtests—Matrix Reasoning and Picture Concepts, and a Working Memory subtest—Letter–Number Sequencing. The supplemental subtests have been reconfigured to include previous core subtests—Arithmetic, Picture Completion, and Information, with two new subtests—Cancellation and Word Reasoning. A full discussion of these changes appears earlier in this volume.

For the purposes of the WISC-IV standardization sample, giftedness was defined based on an existing score of 2 standard deviations above the mean on the WISC-III (60% of the gifted sample) or another standardized measure of cognitive abilities either individual (SB-IV, WJ-R/III, or KABC) (Thorndike, Hagen, & Sattler, 1986; Woodcock, & Johnson, 1989; Woodcock, McGrew, & Mather, 2001; and Kaufman, & Kaufman, 1983, respectively) or group administered (Otis, 19% of the sample; or CogAT, 10% of the gifted sample) (Otis & Lennon, 1997; and Lohman, & Hagen, 2001, respectively). In all, 63 children between 6 and 16 years old from the standardization sample were categorized as gifted, and their results in comparison to a matched control sample on the WISC-IV are summarized in the WISC-IV Technical and Interpretative Manual (Weschler, 2003, p. 77). In general, students in the gifted sample significantly outperformed students in the matched control sample on the WISC-IV subtests. However, on two subtests, the optional

Cancellation subtest and the required Coding subtest, the differences between the two groups were nonsignificant, indicating that these subtests did not distinguish students identified as gifted from the control sample. Both of these subtests fall under the Processing Speed factor and these nonsignificant findings are consistent with previous reports that suggest that processing speed is not a distinguishing characteristic of gifted individuals (Kaufman, 1993). In this regard, the new framework of the WISC-IV, with the lowered emphasis on processing speed in the verbal comprehension, perceptual reasoning, and working memory factors may actually assist psychologists in identifying gifted individuals whose gifts fall predominantly in the verbal or perceptual domains of intelligence. However, with the new factor structure, two measures of processing speed (Coding and Symbol Search) are included in the full scale IQ, as opposed to the WISC-III where only Coding (or optionally Symbol Search) contributed. This may be a disadvantage in identifying gifted individuals if a full-scale IQ is used.

Of note in the standardization sample is the large number of students previously identified as gifted who are not performing 2 standard deviations above the mean on any factor of the WISC-IV. It is unclear if this discrepancy is a product of the considerable changes to both the content and the structure from the WISC-III to the WISC-IV, or of there being a large number of students (29%) who are included in the WISC-IV gifted sample based solely on a group administered cognitive ability test that offers a less valid measure of abilities than an individually administered one. If we consider only the 34 students from the gifted sample who performed 2 standard deviations above the mean on a WISC-IV factor, the results in comparison to their matched controls indicate that, although the four factors still discriminate between the two groups, the subtests Cancellation (Randomized, Structured, and Total), Coding, Digit Span Backward, and Word Reasoning demonstrate no significant differences between gifted and matched controls (Table 8.1).

In addition, of the 34 students who scored greater than 130 on a factor of the WISC-IV, 27 achieved this score on the verbal comprehension factor, 4 additional (9 total) students achieved greater than 130 on the perceptual reasoning factor, and 1 additional student attained a score greater than 130 in each of the Working Memory, Processing Speed, and Full Scale Factors. For this sample, Verbal Comprehension was *the* important defining factor in determining giftedness, although we do not wish to discount other areas of giftedness that may be less prevalent, but are still important to success in school and beyond. The inability of Processing Speed subtests Coding and Cancellation to discriminate between the groups was expected based on previous findings and assertions that speed is not a defining characteristic of intelligence (Sternberg, 1982). It was surprising to note that the new Working Memory factor, often conceptualized as a higher level skill than Processing Speed, was not more influential in defining this gifted group and,

TABLE 8.1

Subtest	Mean Score for Students with at least 1 Index Score over 130	Mean Score for Matched Control Students	F	p-value
Arithmetic	14.83	11.42	23.974	.000
Block Design-no time	14.61	11.08	25.846	.000
Block Design	15.17	11.42	22.929	.000
Cancellation—randomized	10.50	10.63	.021	.886
Cancellationstructured	10.56	10.92	.205	.654
Cancellation–total	10.72	11.04	.127	.723
Coding	11.83	10.96	.727	.399
Comprehension	14.83	11.46	17.328	.000
Digit Span–bwd	11.78	11.04	.710	.405
Digit Span–fwd	12.56	10.25	6.127	.018
Digit Span—total	12.78	10.67	4.625	.038
Information	14.56	12.54	7.571	.009
Letter–Number	13.56	10.71	13.591	.001
Matrix Reasoning	14.89	11.33	23.312	.000
Picture Completion	13.72	11.17	12.161	.001
Picture Concepts	13.17	11.21	8.372	.006
Similarities	15.28	12.00	19.946	.000
Symbol Search	13.22	11.08	5.258	.029
Vocabulary	15.39	12.00	21.451	.000
Word Reasoning	12.56	12.17	1.556	.615

in addition, that the optional subtest Word Reasoning, from the Verbal Comprehension factor, did not discriminate between the two groups. The information regarding both the subtests and factor scores is important to consider in determining which subtests and/or factors to administer when assessing a child for giftedness.

HOW THE CHANGES TO THE WISC-IV IMPACT GIFTED IDENTIFICATION

Although the WISC-III also had an optional four-factor structure, the dropping of the VIQ/PIQ structure from the WISC-IV will result in the widespread use of the more descriptive and discriminating four-factor model. For gifted students, the new structure appears to provide a more discriminating means of identification for gifted programming. The greater weighting of the Verbal Comprehension and Perceptual Reasoning Factors (3 subtests each) into the Full Scale score is of benefit to students with strengths in these higher level cognitive areas. In addition, the separation of speed-based tasks into a separate factor allows students who have strengths in the higher level cognitive demands of the verbal comprehension and perceptual reasoning tasks to demonstrate their skills with time to reflect. It is interesting to note in the standardization sample that although these students did not perform significantly better than control subjects on the traditional processing speed tasks such as Coding and Cancellation, on the higher-level task, Block Design, which now offers options for scoring with and without time bonuses, the gifted students did not show any benefit from the no time bonus option. Still, the option of scoring Block Design without time bonuses will be important for students who demonstrate high ability on solving the problems, but who are more reflective in their approach to the task.

The four factors have all been changed to some degree. Verbal Comprehension has remained very similar to the WISC-III factor of the same name. For the gifted population, the skills required in the Verbal Comprehension factor are traditionally the strongest indicators of giftedness and this was found to be true with the standardization sample. The core subtests that make up this high-level, language-based factor are all familiar subtests from the WISC-III: Comprehension, Similarities, and Vocabulary. Two subtests are designated as supplemental in the Verbal Comprehension factor. Information is relegated from core status, and Word Reasoning was brought in as a new subtest. However, Word Reasoning, did not turn out to be a highly discriminating subtest with the above 130 gifted standardization sample, suggesting that this supplemental subtest should be used with caution in gifted identification.

Perceptual Reasoning has changed significantly from the old Perceptual Organization factor. It includes two new core reasoning subtests, Matrix Reasoning and Picture Concepts, in addition to Block Design. All of these subtests were found to discriminate between the gifted and control standardization samples. Although all the factors have undergone some degree of change, the only new factor is the Working Memory Factor. Before looking at the standardization sample, we hypothesized that Working Memory would be a better discriminating factor than Processing Speed for gifted students. Although both Processing Speed and Working Memory did discriminate between the Gifted and control samples, in both of these factors there were component tasks (Digit Span Backward, Cancellation, and Coding) for which there were no differences between the two groups. In addition, only one student would have been identified as gifted based solely on the Processing Speed or Working Memory factors.

Given the discrepancies often seen in gifted children between the stronger higher level verbal comprehension or perceptual reasoning tasks and the relatively weaker skills, especially in processing speed, it will be important to carefully consider which discrepancies may be clinically important. A superior Verbal Comprehension score and a high average Processing Speed score may create a significant discrepancy that bears little or no clinical relevance or validity for the child. Fortunately, the WISC-IV Manual offers tables indicating base rates of discrepancies for aiding in the interpretation of index differences.

CASE STUDY OF AMANDA

A case study of a gifted student highlights some of the resolved and unresolved issues in the WISC-IV. Amanda is currently a fifth-grade student who was assessed at the age of 6 years 4 months with the WISC-III and was determined to have very superior general ability. For the purposes of educational planning, Amanda was assessed again at the age of 10 years 2 months with the Woodcock-Johnson Tests of Cognitive Abilities. Two months later, at the age of 10 years 4 months, she was administered the WISC-IV for the purposes of providing information for this chapter. The WISC-III and WISC-IV scores presented here are very similar despite the significant changes that were made to the newer measure. Amanda's verbal comprehension performance remained virtually the same and although the perceptual tasks changed from having an emphasis on visualization to having an emphasis on reasoning, her scores remained highly similar. The Freedom from Distractibility index changed from the WISC-III to the WISC-IV to a purely Working Memory measure, and Amanda's performance decreased slightly with this new change. Interestingly, with the virtually identical Processing Speed index, Amanda's performance increased.

There are a number of issues to note in Amanda's WISC-IV performance. As with the standardization sample, Amanda performed best in the verbal comprehension domain and had a relatively weaker performance in processing speed, with the Coding subtest score only in the average range. Her performance also highlights the issue of statistical significance vs clinical significance. Although there is a significant difference between her higher verbal comprehension score and her lower processing speed score, it is clear that processing speed is not an area of deficit for Amanda. Her score is still within the superior range, indicating that this is not a difference of clinical importance. Finally, as with the WISC-III, ceiling effects continue to plague the WISC-IV. Amanda's performance on the Vocabulary measure in particular yielded a raw score of 61. However, any raw score between 55 and 68 yields a standard score of 19 for her age group. This ceiling effect is most significant at the younger ages, where raw score point spreads of up to 35 can

Amanda 6 years 4 months			Amanda 10 years 4 months		
WISC-III	**Factor Scores**	**Subtest Scores**	**WISC-IV**	**Factor Scores**	**Subtest Scores**
Full Scale	146		Full Scale	142	
Verbal Comprehension	143		Verbal Comprehension	144	
Information		19	Similarities		19
Similarities		19	Vocabulary		19
Vocabulary		19	Comprehension		14
Comprehension		13			
Perceptual Organization	124		Perceptual Reasoning	129	
Picture Completion		11	Block Design		16
Picture Arrangement		14	Picture Concepts		14
Block Design		14	Matrix Reasoning		14
Object Assembly		17			
Freedom From Distractibility	150		Working Memory	135	
Arithmetic		19	Digit Span		18
Digit Span		19	Letter–Number Sequencing		14
Processing Speed	114		Processing Speed	123	
Coding		8	Coding		12
Symbol Search		17	Symbol Search		16

yield the same score at the highest level. For children who are highly gifted, this can underestimate their true ability. On the WJ-III administered to Amanda 2 months before the WISC-IV, Amanda scored 170 on a measure of Verbal Ability (including verbal comprehension and general information subtests), indicating that the WISC-IV may be underestimating her verbal ability. Of course, in practical terms, both of these scores will allow Amanda access to most, if not all, special programs or resources serving the gifted. However, for students who demonstrate significant discrepancy in their profile, one or more subtest scores that underestimate their true potential may have a deleterious effect on their program eligibility.

USE OF WISC-IV AS PART OF GLOBAL ASSESSMENT OF CHILDREN WHO ARE GIFTED

As mentioned earlier, a number of authorities have recommended the use of multiple measures in the identification of giftedness (Kaufman & Harrison, 1986; Pfeiffer, 2001). A single test score should never be used alone in making a diagnostic or classificatory decision. Overall *predictive accuracy* (i.e., the overall probability that the result of an assessment procedure accurately identifies individuals as having a certain condition—in this instance, giftedness) is increased with the judicious use of technically meritorious, multiple measures, and clinical procedures (Pfeiffer, 2002).

THE GIFTED RATING SCALES (GRS): PART OF A COMPREHENSIVE GIFTED ASSESSMENT

Recognizing the value of a well-designed, teacher-completed rating scale to complement the WISC-IV (and WPPSI III) in the identification of gifted students, and as a stand-alone screening tool, *The Psychological Corporation* supported the development of the Gifted Rating Scales (GRS). Published in 2003, standardization of the GRS was linked with the standardization of the WISC-IV and WPPSI III. The following principles guided the development of the GRS:

- User-friendly. The GRS requires minimal training to administer, score, and interpret
- Scientifically sound. The GRS is reliable and accurate in identifying gifted students
- Simple interpretation. The GRS conceptualizes giftedness in a straightforward, direct, and conceptually meaningful way
- Flexible. The GRS can be used as a stand-alone screening instrument, with other diagnostic procedures such as auditions and portfolio samples, and with the WISC-IV as part of a comprehensive test battery

The GRS includes a School Form (GRS-S) and a Preschool/Kindergarten Form (GRS-P) to account for developmental differences in giftedness across the age range 4:0 years to 13:11 years. Although the two forms are similar in format, item overlap is only 29%.

Item development began with an exhaustive review and critique of existing rating scales (Jarosewich, Pfeiffer, & Morris, 2002). This was followed by a survey of experts in the gifted field (Pfeiffer, 2003) and a review of the talent development and gifted literatures. Experts in child development, education, school psychology, giftedness, and talent development were then invited to react to an initial pool of items, which subsequently went through a number of revisions as a result of a pilot test, field testing, and final item editing.

Since this chapter focuses on the assessment of gifted children with the WISC-IV, we discuss only the GRS-S, designed for children in elementary and middle school, grades 1 through 8, ages 6:0 through 13:11. (The reader interested in testing gifted preschool and kindergarten students is encouraged to read the GRS manual [Pfeiffer & Jarosewich, 2003]). The GRS-S consists of six scales. Each scale has 12 items. Each item is rated on a 9-point scale divided into three ranges: 1–3, Below Average; 4–6, Average; and 7–9, Above Average. This format permits the rater to determine first whether the student is below average, average, or above average for a specific behavior, compared to other students the same age. The teacher then determines, within the range, whether the child is at the bottom, middle, or top of the given range. Ratings of 1, 2, and 3 are part of the Below Average category; ratings of 4, 5, and 6 the Average category; and ratings of 7, 8, and 9 the Above Average category.

The six scales on the GRS represent five types of giftedness (intellectual ability, academic ability, creativity, artistic talent, and leadership ability) as well as motivation. Motivation refers to the student's drive or persistence, desire to succeed, tendency to enjoy challenging tasks, and ability to work well without encouragement. Motivation is not viewed as a type of giftedness but rather as a clinically useful and psychometrically reliable measure of how hard the student is working, whether or not he or she is gifted. The GRS-S yields five scale scores indicating the likelihood that a student is gifted in one or more of five areas of giftedness.

For each of the 72 items on the GRS-S, the teacher is asked to rate the student compared to other children of the same age. An illustrative item is provided for each of the six scales. These items are copyrighted and should not be reproduced or transmitted without written permission from the publisher.

- Intellectual Ability: *Learns difficult concepts easily*
- Academic Ability: *Completes academic work unassisted*
- Creativity: *Approaches the world "as a scientist" or explorer*
- Artistic Talent: *Performs or produces art marked by detail, complexity, sophistication, and/or richness*
- Leadership Ability: *Gets others to work together*
- Motivation: *Reacts to challenges enthusiastically*

GRS-S raw scores are converted to T-scores with a mean of 50 and a standard deviation of 10. The student's T-score on each of the gifted scales indicates the degree to which the student's ratings deviate from the standardization sample's average score. The T-scores were computed based on each age group and are age adjusted so that the ranges may be applied across age bands and GRS forms.

Standardization samples were collected across the United States. For the GRS-S, 600 children ages 6:0 to 13:11 years were rated by their teachers. This sample was stratified within eight 12-month age bands from 6:0 to 13:11. Samples were stratified to match the U.S. census by ethnicity and parent education level.

The GRS Manual (Pfeiffer & Jarosewich, 2003) includes detailed information on the reliability and validity of the test. We encourage the interested reader to review the manual. The manual reports that a sample of 406 students ages 6:0 to 13:11 years participated in a GRS-S:WISC-IV validity study. The average age was 9.9 years; 49.3% were female and 50.7% were male. Distribution by race/ethnicity was 67% white, 17% African-American, 10% Hispanic, 5% Asian, and 1% other. Distribution by parent level of education was 3%, 8 years or fewer; 8%, 9 to 11 years; 27%, 12 years; 33%, 13 to 15 years; 29%, 16 years or more.

The great majority of correlations between the GRS-S scale scores and WISC-IV full-scale and subscale scores were significant: In all, 44 of the 120 correlations were significant at the $p < .001$ level (36.6%) and 61 of the 120 correlations were significant at the $p < .01$ level (50.8%). As one might predict, the GRS-S Intellectual and Academic Ability Scales correlated most strongly with the WISC-IV subtest and composite scores. The GRS-S Intellectual Ability scale correlated .53 with WISC-IV Full Scale IQ, .45 with Verbal Comprehension Index (VCI), .42 with Perceptual Reasoning Index (PRI), .39 with Working Memory Index (WMI), and .32 with Processing Speed Index (PSI). All of these correlations are significant at $p < .001$ level.

Only 15 of the 120 GRS-S:WISC-IV correlations were not significant (12.5%). Nine of these 15 nonsignificant correlations were WISC-IV subtests not correlating significantly with the GRS-S leadership ability scale score.

The GRS-S can be easily used as a first-stage screening instrument to screen an entire class, school, or school district. The GRS-S also can be used as a second-stage screening device with a target subgroup of the school population who have already been identified using another method (e.g., students nominated by their last year teacher or scoring above a certain level on an end-of-year achievement test). Finally, the GRS-S can be used as part of a test battery in assessing giftedness. The GRS-S is designed to complement the WISC-IV in identifying intellectually and academically gifted students.

CASE STUDY OF KAYLEIGH

The GRS manual provides a case example illustrating the use of the GRS-S with the WISC-IV. Material from the case is provided here. Kayleigh was recommended for the school's gifted program by her principal. Kayleigh is a friendly, outgoing, and gregarious 12-year old described by her teachers as a leader. She obtained the scores, as part of her gifted evaluation:

Kayleigh's GRS-S scores indicate that her teacher perceives this solid B student as having a moderate probability of being intellectually gifted and a high probability of being academically gifted. However, her scores on the WISC-IV (and performance on curriculum-based assessment, classroom work and scores on the WIAT II) do not provide corroborating evidence in support of an intellectually or academically gifted classification.

GRS-S (MEAN = 50, SD = 10)

Domain	T-Score	Classification
Intellectual Ability	58	Moderate Probability Gifted
Academic Ability	60	High Probability Gifted
Creativity	50	Low Probability Gifted
Artistic Talent	50	Low Probability Gifted
Leadership	60	High Probability
Motivation	60	Above Average-to-High Motivation

WISC-IV (MEAN = 100, SD = 15)

Verbal Comprehension	121	Superior
Perceptual Reasoning	115	High Average
Working Memory	120	Superior
Processing Speed Score	112	High Average
Full Scale	120	Superior

Kayleigh's academic and cognitive skills are higher than many other students the same age and grade but not within the gifted range of ability. Although not necessarily a candidate for an academically accelerated gifted placement, Kayleigh might benefit from additional challenge in other ways such as after-school and weekend enrichment programs with enhanced opportunities for leadership. This example highlights the use of the GRS-S in concert with the WISC-IV when making a diagnostic decision or gifted classification.

DISCUSSION

This chapter discusses the changes in content and structure from the WISC-III to the WISC-IV that may impact the identification of gifted children. In addition, we have presented a recently developed rating scale for teachers (GRS) that can help in the process of identifying gifted students.

When deciding which tools to use in the identification of gifted students, many variables must be considered. The use of intelligence tests is a core tool, and justifiably so. In terms of reliability and validity, standardized intelligence tests are usually the most psychometrically sound instruments available. In addition, there is probably more consistency (reliability) among the many psychologists who administer these tests than any other tests developed for school-age children and adolescents. Because the goal of our public schools is to provide mainly for the academic education of our youth, it is understandable that the type of test most predictive of an individual's academic achievement would be one of the most appropriate selections for use in identifying students who are gifted.

The WISC-IV for many reasons is one of the most appropriate IQ tests to be used for this purpose. It is the most widely used IQ test in schools today and is well standardized. Issues of concern with the WISC-III are still evident in the WISC-IV, but probably to a lesser degree. Time bonuses have been cut back considerably, although ceiling effects are still an issue. There is no data yet on cultural bias. The new structure with the deletion of VIQ and PIQ may make it more difficult for some children to qualify for gifted programs. However, the new four indices model may make that less of an issue. Much depends on how states and school districts define "giftedness." At this time, some allow only an FSIQ at or above a certain point (e.g., 125 or 130). Others will accept VIQ or PIQ scores at this level. For the children in the WISC-IV standardization whom we categorized as gifted (IQ equal to or above 130 on any index or FIQ), the VC and PR were overwhelmingly the indexes where the gifted students scored at or above our required cut-off point, with the VC being the score most often elevated. Another problem with using the FIQ is that now two Processing Speed subtests are included (relatively the weakest index for students who are gifted), which will have a tendency to lower the height of the FIQ for students who are gifted.

Even on the strength of the many arguments in favor of using intelligence tests to identify gifted children, and even with all the appropriate cautions being taken, there are additional issues to consider when assessing potentially gifted children. Most often, intelligence testing is conducted with gifted children or children suspected of intellectual giftedness for purposes of educational planning and placement. The psychologist is charged with determining whether a given child is indeed academically gifted and with making recommendations about educational programs that would best suit the child's needs. Of course, many schools have no special services for children who are gifted. In many schools, psychologists will administer the WISC-IV to a group of children and then classify them as "gifted" or "not gifted," solely on the basis of an arbitrary Full Scale IQ, depending on local or state regulations and without regard to important issues regarding the interpretation of the score. Although this approach may be dictated by mandated regulations, the resulting placement decisions can relegate a child indefinitely to an inappropriate educational setting. It is our recommendation that from the WISC-IV, VC, PR, or FIQ be the scores used for determination of giftedness.

Finally, an IQ test alone should not be the sole criterion for classification of giftedness. Assessment with other instruments such as the GRS, academic achievement, review of academic work, and other factors, including creativity and leadership, should be part of the comprehensive assessment of giftedness.

REFERENCES

Barona, A., & Pfeiffer, S. I. (1992). Effects of test administration procedures and acculturation level on achievement test scores. *Journal of Psychoeducational Assessment, 10*, 124–132.

Gagné, F. (1993). Constructs and models pertaining to exceptional human abilities. In K. A. Heller, F. J. Mönks,, & A. H. Passow (Eds.), *International handbook of research and development of giftedness and talent* (pp. 69–87). New York: Pergamon.

Gardner, H. (1983). *Frames of mind: The theory of multiple intelligences*. New York: Basic Books.

Harrington, R. G. (1982). Caution: Standardized testing may be hazardous to the educational programs of intellectually gifted children. *Education. 103*, 112–117.

Jarosewich, T., Pfeiffer, S. I., & Morris, J. (2002). Identifying gifted students using teacher rating scales: A review of existing instruments. *Journal of Psychoeducational Assessment, 20*, 322–336.

Kaufman, A. S. (1992). Evaluation of the WISC-III and WPPSI-R for gifted children. *Roeper Review, 14*, 154–158.

Kaufman, A. S. (1993). King WISC the Third assumes the throne. *Journal of School Psychology, 31*, 345–354.

Kaufman, A. S. (1994). *Intelligent testing with the WISC-III*. New York: Wiley & Sons.

Kaufman, A. S., & Harrison, P. L. (1986). Intelligence tests and gifted assessment: What are the positives? Special Issue: The IQ controversy. *Roeper Review, 8*, 154–159.

Kaufman, A. S., & Kaufman, N. (1983). *Kaufman Assessment Battery for Children*. Circle Pines, MN: American Guidance Service.

Klausmeier, K. L., Mishra, S. P., & Maker, C. J. (1987). Identification of gifted learners: A national survey of assessment practices and training needs of school psychologists. *Gifted Child Quarterly, 31*, 135–137.

Lohman, D. F., & Hagen, E. (2001). *Cognitive Abilities Test (Form 6)*. Itasca, IL: Riverside Publishing.

Otis, A. S., & Lennon, R. T. (1997). *Otis-Lennon School Ability Test* (7th ed.). San Antonio, TX: The Psychological Corporation.

Pfeiffer, S. I. (2003). Challenges and opportunities for students who are gifted: What the experts say. *Gifted Child Quarterly, 47*, 161–169.

Pfeiffer, S. I. (2002). Identifying gifted and talented students: Recurring issues and promising solutions. *Journal of Applied School Psychology, 1*, 31–50.

Pfeiffer, S. I. (2001). Professional psychology and the gifted: Emerging practice opportunities. *Professional Psychology: Research & Practice, 32*, 175–180.

Pfeiffer, S. I., & Jarosewich, T. (2003). *Gifted Rating Scales Manual*. San Antonio, TX: The Psychological Corporation.

Prifitera, A., Weiss, L. G., and Saklofske, D. H. (1998). The WISC-III in context. In A. Prifitera & D. H. Saklofske (Eds.), *WISC-III: Clinical use and interpretation* (pp. 1–38). New York: Academic Press.

Robinson, N. M., & Chamrad, D. L. (1986). Appropriate uses of intelligence tests with gifted children. Special issue: The IQ controversy. *Roeper Review, 8*, 160–163.

Sabatino, D. A., Spangler, R. S., & Vance, H. B. (1995). The relationship between the Wechsler Intelligence Scale for Children–Revised and the Wechsler Intelligence Scale for Children-III scales and subtests with gifted children. *Psychology in the Schools, 32*, 18–23.

298

Sattler, J. M. (1992). *Assessment of children: Revised and updated third edition.* San Diego, CA: Author.

Seiver, R. C., Bain, S. K., & Hildman, L. K. (1994). Comparison of the WISC-R and WISC-III for gifted students. *Roeper Review, 17,* 39–42.

Sparrow, S. S., & Gurland, S. T. (1998). Assessment of gifted children with the WISC-III. In A. Prifitera & D. H. Saklofske (Eds.), *WISC-III: Clinical use and interpretation* (pp. 59–72). New York: Academic Press.

Stanley, J. C. (1997). Varieties of intellectual talent. *Journal of Creative Behavior, 31,* 93–119.

State Board of Education. (2000). Gifted education: Special education services and programs. *Pennsylvania Bulletin, 30,* 6330–6342.

Stephens, K. R., & Karnes, F. A. (2000). State definitions for the gifted and talented revisited. *Exceptional Children, 66,* 219–238.

Sternberg, R. J. (1982). Lies we live by: Misapplication of tests in identifying the gifted. *Gifted Child Quarterly, 26,* 157–161.

Sternberg, R. J. (1997). The concept of intelligence and its role in lifelong learning and success. *American Psychologist, 52,* 1030–1037.

Terman, L. M. (1925). *Mental and physical traits of a thousand gifted children.* Stanford. CA: Stanford University Press.

Thorndike, R. L., Hagen, E. P., & Sattler, J. M. (1986). *The Stanford-Binet Intelligence Scale* (4th ed.). Chicago, IL: Riverside Publishing.

Tyerman, M. J. (1986) Gifted children and their identification: Learning ability not intelligence. *Gifted Education International, 4,* 81–84.

Watkins, M. W., Greenawalt, C. G., & Marcell, C. M. (2002). Factor Structure of the Wechsler Intelligence Scale for Children-Third Edition Among Gifted Students. *Educational and Psychological Measurement, 62,* 164–172.

Wechsler, D. (2003). *Wechsler Intelligence Scale for Children-Fourth Edition: Technical and Interpretative Manual.* San Antonio, TX: The Psychological Corporation.

Weschler, D. (1991). *Weschler Intelligence Scale for Children–Third Edition.* San Antonio, TX: The Psychological Corporation.

Winner, E. (2000). The origins and ends of giftedness. *American Psychologist, 55,* 159–169.

Woodcock, R. W., & Johnson, M. B. (1989). *Woodcock Johnson Psycho-Educational Battery-Revised.* Allen, TX: DLM Teaching Resources.

Woodcock, R. W., McGrew, K. S., & Mather, N. (2001). *Woodcock-Johnson III.* Itasca, IL: Riverside Publishing.

Zigler, A., & Heller, K. (2000). Conceptions of giftedness from a meta-theoretical perspective. In K. A. Heller, F. J. Mönks, R. J. Sternberg, & R. F. Subotnik (Eds.), *International handbook of giftedness and talent* (2nd ed.) (pp. 3–21). Amsterdam: Elsevier.

9

ASSESSMENT OF MENTAL
RETARDATION

JEAN SPRUILL

Psychology Training Clinic
The University of Alabama
Tuscaloosa, Alabama

THOMAS OAKLAND

Department of Foundations Education
University of Florida
Gainesville, Florida

PATTI HARRISON

Department of Educational Studies in Psychology
The University of Alabama
Tuscaloosa, Alabama

The diagnosis of mental retardation can have a profound impact on a person's life. It can determine the types of public-supported services received by individuals, their access to jobs, the manner in which they are viewed by society, and other critical life-impacting events. Thus, considerable care must be displayed by professionals when assessing individuals who may have mental retardation.

Adequate assessment of mental retardation requires the careful review and interpretation of information that describes various traits displayed in different settings during the person's life. The information should be acquired from multiple sources using multiple assessment methods. Furthermore, accurate diagnoses and recommendations for interventions require clinicians to know the legal and professional definitions of mental retardation as well as possible etiologies and behaviors. Thus, assessment of mental retardation involves more than the use of a standardized test of intelligence.

This chapter provides a brief overview of definitions, possible etiologies, and behaviors associated with mental retardation. It then focuses on the WISC-IV (Wechsler, 2003b) as an assessment instrument useful in a comprehensive evaluation of an individual with mental retardation.

DEFINITIONS OF MENTAL RETARDATION

Definitions and classifications used to describe individuals with mental retardation differ with respect to behavior, degree of impairment, and etiology. Definitions from the American Association on Mental Retardation (AAMR), American Psychiatric Association, and the Individuals with Disabilities Education Act of 1997 are summarized below. These three definitions are used commonly when assessing mental retardation in children and youth.

AMERICAN ASSOCIATION ON MENTAL RETARDATION

The AAMR (2002) defines mental retardation as "...a disability characterized by significant limitations both in intellectual functioning and in adaptive behavior as expressed in conceptual, social, and practical adaptive skills. This disability originates before age 18" (p. 8). With regard to the intellectual criterion, a diagnosis of mental retardation, according to the AAMR (2002) manual, requires an IQ of approximately two or more standard deviations (SD) below the mean, or an IQ of 70 or below. For the adaptive behavior criterion, in its 2002 manual, the AAMR provides specific scores on adaptive behavior measures for a diagnosis of mental retardation. For mental retardation, the individual must have scores of at least two standard deviations below the mean on either (1) one of the following three types of adaptive behavior (i.e., conceptual, social, or practical), or (2) a total score on a standardized measure that includes an assessment of conceptual, social, and practical skills.

AMERICAN PSYCHIATRIC ASSOCIATION

The American Psychiatric Association's (2000) Diagnostic and Statistical Manual of Mental Disorders, Fourth Edition, Text Revision (DSM-IV-TR) defines mental retardation as "...significantly subaverage general intellectual functioning (Criterion A) that is accompanied by significant limitations in adaptive functioning in at least two of the following areas: communication, self-care, home living, social/interpersonal skills, use of community resources, self-direction, functional academic skills, work, leisure, health, and safety (Criterion B). The onset of mental retardation must occur before age 18 years" (p. 41). Like the AAMR definition, the criteria for significantly subaverage intellectual functioning generally is considered an IQ two or more standard deviations below the population mean, usually an IQ of 70 or below. However, an IQ of 75 or below may constitute the criterion in some settings.

INDIVIDUALS WITH DISABILITIES EDUCATION ACT OF 1997

The Individuals with Disabilities Education Act of 1997 (IDEA) defines mental retardation as "significantly subaverage general intellectual functioning, existing concurrently with deficits in adaptive behavior and manifested during the developmental period, that adversely affects a child's educational performance" (Individuals with Disabilities Education Act, 1999). In addition, IDEA provides guidelines for a diagnosis of developmental delay. Developmental delay refers to delays in physical development, cognitive development, communication development, social or emotional development, and/or adaptive development occurring in children between 3 and 9 years of age, and resulting in a need for special education and related services. There is new IDEA legislation pending which may have implications for administrators and school systems; however, changes are not available at the time of this writing.

LEVELS OF MENTAL RETARDATION

The DSM-IV-TR distinguishes four categories of mental retardation based on degrees of severity: mild mental retardation, moderate mental retardation, severe mental retardation, and profound mental retardation. The descriptions below represent a compilation of information from several sources (Weiss & Weisz, 1986; Sattler, 2001; Kamphaus, 2002). Whereas the IQs given are those specified by the deviations below the population mean, the DSM-IV-TR specifies IQ ranges for each of the four categories. The IQ ranges overlap somewhat, typically by 5 points. Thus, professional judgment is used when selecting the most appropriate category of mental retardation. The cut-off scores for each category may vary among various state and federal agencies, school systems, etc., and the clinician must be aware of the criteria required by the various agencies or states in which he or she works. Adaptive functioning (discussed later) consistent with the level of mental retardation also is important in the classification of the individual.

MILD MENTAL RETARDATION

Individuals in the mild category comprise approximately 85% of the persons diagnosed with mental retardation (American Psychiatric Association, 2000). Individuals with mild mental retardation have IQs that range between 50–55 to approximately 70, or between 2 and 3 SDs below the population mean. Additionally, there must be limitations in adaptive behavior. Although individuals who display mild mental retardation show some delay in the development of motor, speech, social, cognitive, and other abilities, their intellectual deficits typically are not identified as caused by mental retardation until they enter school. Individuals who display mild mental retardation generally learn to read and write, often to about the sixth grade level, by late adolescence. Although individuals at the high end of the mild mental retardation range usually are recognized as having mental retardation during their school years, they often blend into general society once they leave school, requiring assistance only during periods of severe personal or economic stress. They generally are capable of gainful employment, may become self-supporting, and may marry and raise a family. The prevalence of mental retardation is much higher for younger children than adults, lending support to the belief that adults with mild mental retardation often blend into society (Larson, Lakin, Anderson, Kwak, Lee, & Anderson, 2001).

MODERATE MENTAL RETARDATION

Those with Moderate Mental Retardation comprise approximately 10% of persons diagnosed with mental retardation (American Psychiatric Association, 2000). Individuals with moderate mental retardation have IQ scores that range between 35–40 and 50–55, or between 3 and 4 SDs below the mean. (Note: IQs on the WISC-IV only go down to 40.) They also display limitations in adaptive behavior. Individuals with Moderate Mental Retardation usually are identified during infancy or early childhood. They often display delays in attaining developmental milestones in motor, speech, social, or cognitive development. By late adolescence, they may acquire academic skills similar to a second- to fourth-grade student, provided they receive suitable special education services. Individuals with Moderate Mental Retardation typically require assistance and/or supervision in almost all aspects of daily living. With proper training, some may work at unskilled or semiskilled jobs.

SEVERE MENTAL RETARDATION

Those with Severe Mental Retardation comprise approximately 3 to 4% of persons diagnosed with mental retardation (American Psychiatric Association, 2000). Their IQs range between 20–25 and 35–40, or between 4 and 5 SDs below the mean. They also display limitations in adaptive behavior. Individuals with Severe Mental Retardation are identified in infancy, given their obvious delays in acquiring motor and language skills. In addition, they frequently display physical abnormalities. Although they may acquire some self-help skills, they are unable to function independently and will require close supervision throughout their life.

PROFOUND MENTAL RETARDATION

Individuals with Profound Mental Retardation comprise approximately 1 to 2% of persons diagnosed with mental retardation (American Psychiatric Association, 2000). Their IQs are below 20–25 or below 5 SDs below the mean. They also display marked deficits in adaptive behavior. Persons with Profound Mental Retardation often are identified at birth or shortly thereafter in light of their physical abnormalities. Delays in the development of skills during infancy and early childhood will be apparent. Physical abnormalities may preclude their being able to walk or talk. They are unable to assume responsibility for activities of daily living or care for their own needs. Thus, lifelong care is required.

ETIOLOGY OF MENTAL RETARDATION

There are many known causes of mental retardation. Ethological factors may be primarily psychosocial or primarily biological, or some combination of both (American Psychiatric Association, 2000). Among those with mental retardation, approximately 75 to 80% are thought to have psychosocial etiologies (formerly referred to as familial etiology) while 20 to 25% are thought to have biological etiologies (formerly referred to as organic etiology) (Grossman, 1983). Although the intellectual abilities of those with these etiologies overlap, specific etiologies are identified more often in individuals with Severe or Profound retardation. Those with psychosocial forms of mental retardation generally have IQs above 50. These children typically are from low socioeconomic groups, have one or more family members who display diminished functioning, particularly in school settings, and seldom have known neurological or obvious physical abnormalities. Most are diagnosed as having mental retardation during their elementary school years (Grossman, 1983).

Those with biological forms of mental retardation generally have IQs below 50. The socioeconomic status of their families ranges from high to low. Approximately 200 syndromes associated with mental retardation have been identified (Terdal, 1981). The three most common syndromes are Down syndrome, fragile X syndrome, and fetal alcohol syndrome. Most children with biological forms of mental retardation are diagnosed in infancy or early childhood, and frequently have physical abnormalities (Grossman, 1983; Jacobson & Mulick, 1996).

ADAPTIVE FUNCTIONING

The diagnosis of mental retardation requires documentation that an individual displays diminished levels of intelligence as well as significant deficits in adaptive behavior during the developmental period. Adaptive behavior generally refers to a person's ability to meet the standards of personal behavior and independence expected for their age peers within their culture. Measures of adaptive behavior typically ask respondents who know the person well to indicate whether the person displays important behaviors associated with a variety of adaptive behaviors.

The DSM-IV-TR (2000) identifies 10 specific skill areas that comprise adaptive behavior: communication, self-care, home living, social/interpersonal skills, use of community resources, self-direction, functional academic skills, work, health and safety, and leisure. The AAMR identifies three broad domains of adaptive behavior that include specific skill areas: conceptual (i.e., communication, functional academics, self-direction, health and safety), social (i.e., social skills, leisure), and practical (i.e., self-care, home living, community use, health and safety, and work).

Several standardized measures of adaptive behavior are available, including the Adaptive Behavior Assessment System-II (Harrison & Oakland, 2003), Vineland Adaptive Behavior Scales (Sparrow, Balla, & Cicchetti, 1984), AAMR Adaptive Behavior Scale-School, 2nd ed. (Nihira, Leland, & Lambert 1993a), AAMR Adaptive Behavior Scale-Residential and Community, 2nd ed. (Nihira, Leland & Lambert, 1993b), and the Scales of Independent Behavior-Revised (Bruininks, Woodcock, Weatherman, & Hill, 1996).

Individuals with mental retardation differ in their adaptive skill strengths and deficits and, except for those with severe and profound levels, are unlikely to show significant deficits in all areas of functioning. Measures of adaptive functioning and intelligence correlate moderately, typically between .20 and .50 (Platt, Kamphaus, Cole, & Smith, 1991; Keith, Fehrmann, Harrison, & Pottebaum, 1987). Thus, the constructs of intelligence and adaptive behavior overlap statistically yet differ sufficiently conceptually and in their content to warrant their joint use when assessing mental retardation.

INCIDENCE OF MENTAL RETARDATION IN THE POPULATION

Although definitions of mental retardation discussed earlier differ slightly, all use an IQ of 70 or below as an important criteria for a diagnosis of mental retardation. Approximately 2 percent of the population obtain IQs below 70 and *may* be classified as having mental retardation. Standards used to diagnose persons with mental retardation may vary between institutions, including school districts and possibly even schools within one district (Reschley & Ward, 1991). Part of the variation in diagnoses occurs because of the subjective nature of what is meant by "significant limitations in adaptive functioning." Some psychologists may use their judgment to decide if deficits in adaptive functioning are "significant" whereas others may use specific cut-off scores from standardized measures of adaptive functioning (Kanaya, Scullin, & Ceci, 2003).

State agencies were surveyed to determine their criteria for a diagnosis of mental retardation (Denning, Chamberlain, & Polloway, 2000). About 25%

of the states did not specify a cut-off score for the measure of intelligence and the remaining states typically required cut-off scores between 70 and 75. Although a total of 98% of states require consideration of adaptive behavior, only 27.5% listed specific practices for assessing adaptive behavior or criterion scores for deficits in adaptive behavior. However, as Robinson, Zigler and Gallagher wrote, "In the real world of educational placement however, such guidelines are often ignored or judged to be irrelevant" (2000, p. 1414). In practice, both standardized measures and clinical judgment are used when assessing adaptive behavior (Kamphaus, 2002; Sattler, 2001).

ASSESSING MENTAL RETARDATION USING THE WISC-IV

Measures of intelligence play a crucial role in the assessment of children with mental retardation. The WISC-III (Wechsler, 1991) frequently is used in the assessment of mental retardation in children and adolescents. The WISC-IV is expected to demonstrate the same degree of widespread use. It is a reliable and valid instrument for such assessments, particularly when assessing mild and moderate levels of mental retardation. The lowest Full Scale IQ obtainable on the WISC-IV is 40; thus, the WISC-IV cannot adequately measure IQs below 40. See comments above regarding WISC-IV ranges for different MR levels.

FACTOR STRUCTURE OF THE WISC-IV

The WISC-IV Technical and Interpretative Manual (Wechsler, 2003c) reports support for the following four factors through exploratory and confirmatory factor analyses. The Verbal Comprehension Index includes measures of children's acquired knowledge, verbal reasoning and comprehension, and attention to verbal stimuli. The Perceptual Reasoning Index includes measures of children's fluid reasoning, spatial processing, attentiveness to detail, and visual-motor integration. The Working Memory Index includes measures of children's short-term auditory memory and is an essential component of fluid reasoning. The Processing Speed Index includes measures of children's ability to quickly and correctly scan, sequence, and discriminate simple visual information. It also measures short-term visual memory, attention, and visual-motor coordination. The WISC-IV Technical and Interpretative Manual provides additional information about the Indexes (Wechsler, 2003c). Information about the factor structure of the WISC-IV currently is limited to that published in the Technical and Interpretative Manual. Based on research on the WISC-III, the WISC-IV, which retained 10 subtests from the WISC-III and added 5 new subtests designed to measure similar constructs, was predicted to measure 4 domains. The results of exploratory factor analysis, using both the 10 core subtests and another using all 15 subtests, confirmed the predicted factor structure of 4 domains. In addition, a cross-validation procedure similar to that used with the WISC-III confirmed the stability of the VCI, PRI, WMI, and PSI scores across samples. The procedure is described in detail in the Technical Manual (Wechsler, 2003c, p. 57). Confirmatory factor analyses also resulted in the four-factor model being the best fit for the standardization data.

The factor structure of the various editions of the WISC has been subject to considerable debate (Allen & Thorndike, 1995). Most WISC-III literature supports the four-factor structure: Verbal Comprehension, Perceptual Organization, Freedom from Distractibility and Processing Speed. The presence of the third factor, Freedom from Distractibility (renamed Working Memory in the WISC-IV) has received variable support. However, the robustness of the four-factor structure of the WISC in different countries using an adapted WISC-III has been amply demonstrated (Georgas, Weiss, van de Vijver & Saklofske, 2003).

Numerous studies support a four-factor structure for the WAIS-III: Verbal Comprehension, Perceptual Organization, Working Memory, and Processing Speed (Tulsky & Price, 2003; Kaufman, Lichtenberger, & McLean, 2001; Saklofske, Hildebrand, & Gorsuch, 2000). The WISC-IV's Working Memory Index is more similar to the WAIS-III's Working Memory Index than to the WISC-III's Freedom from Distractibility factor. Thus, it is highly likely that more support will be found for the WISC-IV's Working Memory Index than was found for the WISC-III's Freedom from Distractibility factor.

Scholars and practitioners have questioned whether the factor structure of the WISC-IV and other measures of intelligence are the same for children with various disabilities and disorders (e.g., mental retardation, learning disabilities) and those included in a test's norming sample. The four factors of the WISC-III, particularly the Verbal Comprehension Index, Perceptual Organization Index, Processing Speed Index, and, to a lesser extent, the Freedom from Distractibility factor, are robust across various clinical samples (e.g., Watkins & Canivez, 2001; Kush, 1996; Grice, Krohn, & Logerquist, 1997; Watkins & Kush, 2002). The four factors of the WAIS-III (Verbal Comprehension, Perceptual Organization, Working Memory, and Processing Speed) also have been shown to be robust across various clinical samples (e.g., Dickinson, Iannone, & Gold, 2002; van der Heijden & Donders, 2003). Given the research support for the four factors of the WISC-III and WAIS-III for clinical groups, we expect that the four factors of the WISC-IV also will be robust for various clinical samples.

WISC-IV AND WISC-III

Later editions of intelligence tests yield scores that are slightly lower than earlier editions of the test. Thus, the WISC-IV scores are slightly lower than comparable scores on the WISC-III. Comparison of WISC-IV and WISC-III, scores for approximately 240 children (N varied from 232 to 241 for the various index scores) are summarized in Table 9.1. The differences ranged from a high of 5.5 points for the Processing Speed index scores to 2.5 for the Full Scale IQ. The correlations between the scores for the two tests were high and follow the same pattern as the correlations for previous editions, i.e., Full Scale IQ and Verbal Comprehension Index correlate the highest and Processing Speed Index and Perceptual Reasoning Index/Perceptual Organization Index correlate the least. The scores from the WISC-IV are lower than the scores from the WISC-III. Table 9.1 also contains scores obtained from children in order to compare the WISC-III and WISC-R during the 1991 revision of the WISC-R (Wechsler, 1991). Differences between the WISC-III Verbal, Performance, and Full Scale IQ during the approximately 12-year time span show an increase in WISC-III scores, consistent with the Flynn effect (Flynn, 1987, 1998). The Flynn effect, named after James Flynn, a political scientist who first documented the phenomena, refers to a wide-spread, systematic, and pervasive rise in IQs, thus warranting a need to renorm IQ tests from time to time. In other words, "as time passes and IQ test norms get older, people perform better and better on the test, raising the mean IQ by several points within a matter of years" (Kanaya, Scullin, & Ceci, 2003, p. 778). WISC-III Full Scale IQs acquired in 1991 are 1.6 points lower than WISC-IV Full Scale IQs acquired in 2003, and 4.1 points lower than the WISC-III Full Scale IQs acquired in 2003.

TABLE 9.1   Comparisons of the WISC-III and WISC-IV

	2003 N = 244			1991 N = 206
	WISC-IV[a]	WISC-III	Correlation	WISC-III[b]
VIQ		105.4		101.5
PIQ		107.3		104.2
FSIQ	104.5	107.0	.89	102.9
VCI	102.9	106.0	.88	
PRI/PO	103.9	106.9	.72	
WMI (FD)	101.5	103.0	.72	
PSI	102.7	108.2	.81	

[a]Data for the 2003 WISC-IV and WISC-III are from WISC-IV Technical and Interpretative Manual (Wechsler, 2003a, p. 62).
[b]The WISC-III scores were reported in the WISC-III Manual (Wechsler, 1991, p. 198).
VIQ = Verbal IQ, PIQ = Performance IQ, VCI = Verbal Comprehension Index, PRI = Perceptual Reasoning Index, PO = Perceptual Organization index, WMI = Working Memory index, FD = Freedom from Distractibility Index, and PSI = Processing Speed Index, FSIQ = Full Scale Intelligence Quotient.

WISC-IV SCORES OF CHILDREN WITH MENTAL RETARDATION

Published research using the WISC-IV for children with mental retardation currently is available only for the study reported in the WISC-IV Technical and Interpretative Manual (Wechsler, 2003c). A total of 120 non-institutionalized children ages 6 through 16 with IQs ranging from 40 to 70 were administered the WISC-IV. Table 9.2 shows the WISC-IV scores of 63 children classified as in the mild range of mental retardation, 57 children classified as in the moderate range of mental retardation, and matched control groups of equal size. As expected, compared to their matched controls, mean scores for children with mental retardation were lower and standard deviations were smaller. These findings are in agreement with previous findings comparing persons who do and do not display mental retardation (e.g., Slate, 1995; Spruill, 1998). Mean scores from children with mild mental retardation were higher than those with a moderate level of mental retardation. These results are consistent with previous research on the WISC-III (e.g., Wechsler, 1991; Slate & Saarnio, 1995).

WISC-III scores for a clinical sample of 43 children diagnosed with mild mental retardation and tested during the WISC-IV standardization also are reported in Table 9.2. All WISC-III scores are numerically lower than the comparable WISC-IV scores. This pattern was unexpected because scores from older versions are likely to be higher than scores from newer versions of the same test. The unexpected lower WISC-III scores may be due to differences in the levels of mental retardation within the samples or differences in the core subtest composition of the respective index scores. For example, on the WISC-III, the Verbal Comprehension index consists of Information,

TABLE 9.2   WISC-IV Scores for Children with Mental Retardation

	Mild[a] N = 63 Mean (SD)	Matched[a] Control Group Mean (SD)	Moderate[a] N = 57 Mean (SD)	Matched[a] Control Group Mean (SD)	WISC-III[b] N = 43 Mean (SD)
VCI	67.1 (9.1)	98.7 (12.5)	52.3 (7.5)	97.2 (14.1)	61.3 (8.0)
PRI/PO	65.5 (10.3)	98.7 (15.2)	52.5 (9.2)	99.2 (15.2)	59.4 (9.2)
WMI	66.8 (11.1)	99.4 (13.8)	57.0 (9.5)	98.9 (14.6)	62.5 (10.9)
PSI	73.0 (11.6)	98.3 (13.4)	58.2 (11.0)	97.3 (12.3)	70.2 (11.1)
FSIQ	60.5 (9.2)	99.2 (13.6)	46.4 (8.5)	98.0 (14.5)	55.8 (7.8)

[a]Data from the WISC-IV Technical and Interpretative Manual (Wechsler, 2003a, p. 80–81).
[b]Sample with Mild Mental Retardation from WISC-III Manual (Wechsler, 1991, p. 210).
VCI = Verbal Comprehension index, PRI = Perceptual Reasoning index, PO = Perceptual Organization index, WMI = Working Memory index, PSI = Processing Speed index, and FSIQ = Full Scale Intelligence Quotient.

Similarities, Vocabulary, and Comprehension, whereas for the WISC-IV, the Verbal Comprehension index consists of Similarities, Vocabulary, and Comprehension. An alternative explanation, that scores of children with mental retardation may not show the same Flynn effect, seems unlikely. The Flynn effect occurs for children with mental retardation: they were more likely to display lower mean scores on the WISC-III than on the WISC-R (Kanaya, Scullin, & Ceci, 2003). Whether the same effect will occur for children tested on the WISC-III and retested on the WISC-IV remains to be determined.

WISC-IV AND WAIS-III FOR OLDER ADOLESCENTS WITH MENTAL RETARDATION

Comparisons between the WISC-IV and WAIS-III for samples of adolescents with mental retardation are not yet available. However, on the basis of the available data for comparisons of the WISC-IV and the WAIS-III, we can draw some conclusions that may be helpful to the clinician. Because the WISC-IV and WAIS-III overlap only at age 16 years, persons with mental retardation who were previously tested using the WAIS-III are not likely to be retested on the WISC-IV. However, the reverse may be true; children tested on the WISC-IV are quite likely to be retested with the WAIS-III. With the exception of the Working Memory index, mean WISC-IV scores for a non-clinical sample of 16-year-olds generally are 3 to 5 points lower than the corresponding scores on the WAIS-III (Table 9.3). The WISC-IV Technical and Interpretative Manual (Wechsler, 2003c, p. 67) reports predicted WAIS-III IQs for selected WISC-IV scores. For example, those who have a WISC-IV Full Scale IQ of 55 can be expected to have WAIS-III Full Scale IQs between 55 and 61. Similarly, those with WISC-IV Full Scale IQs of 70 can be expected to have WAIS-III Full Scale IQs between 71 and 75. These estimates are the predicted 95% confidence interval. When predicting WAIS-III scores from WISC-IV scores, the expected WAIS-III intervals are wider at the upper and lower ends of the distribution and narrower at the middle of the IQ distribution. Therefore, an individual whose WISC-IV IQs are close to 55 are likely to have WAIS-III IQs below the criterion score of 70 for a diagnosis of mental retardation. Conversely, an individual whose WISC-IV Full Scale IQ is close to 70 may score higher on the WAIS-III and no longer qualify for a diagnosis of mental retardation based solely on their IQs. These differences may result in individuals no longer qualifying for special education services, and the clinician should consider this factor in their interpretation of test results.

WISC-IV and WAIS-III scores from groups of individuals with mild and moderate mental retardation were compared (Table 9.4). For the groups of individuals in the mild range of mental retardation, the index scores and Full Scale IQs were higher on the WISC-IV except for the scores on the Perceptual Reasoning/Perceptual Organization index. This finding was also noted in the comparisons of the WISC-III and WISC-IV clinical samples. As can be seen in Table 9.2, the WISC-IV index and Full Scale IQs were higher than the comparable scores on the WISC-III except for the Perceptual Reasoning/Perceptual Organization index.

Samples of individuals classified as in the moderate range of mental retardation obtained scores 4 to 6 points higher on the WAIS-III than on

TABLE 9.3   Comparison of WISC-IV and WAIS-III for 16-Year-Olds

	WISC-IV[a] N = 198 Mean (SD)	WAIS-III[a] N = 198 Mean (SD)	WAIS-III (1997)[b] N = 192 Mean (SD)
VIQ		100.2 (14.3)	102.2 (15.1)
PIQ		102.3 (12.7)	103.5 (15.4)
FSIQ	98.5 (14.3)	101.6 (13.5)	102.9 (15.2)
VCI	97.3 (13.4)	100.8 (14.8)	101.9 (14.4)
PRI/PO	98.9 (13.3)	103.8 (14.5)	102.9 (14.8)
WMI	98.7 (14.8)	97.7 (15.1)	
PSI	99.5 (15.3)	102.8 (13.6)	101.7 (15.0)

[a]Data from the WISC-IV Technical and Interpretative Manual (Wechsler, 2003a, p. 66).
[b]Data from the WAIS-III WMS-III Technical Manual (The Psychological Corporation, 1997, p. 79).
VIQ = Verbal IQ, PIQ = Performance IQ, VCI = Verbal Comprehension Index, PRI = Perceptual Reasoning index, PO = Perceptual Organization index, WMI = Working Memory index, and PSI = Processing Speed index, FSIQ = Full Scale Intelligence Quotient.

TABLE 9.4   WISC-IV and WAIS-III Scores for Children with Mental Retardation

	WISC-IV[a] Mild N = 63 Mean (SD)	WAIS-III[b] Mild N = 46 Mean (SD)	WISC-IV[a] Moderate N = 57 Mean (SD)	WAIS-III[b] Moderate N = 62 Mean (SD)
VCI	67.1 (9.1)	63.4 (6.3)	52.3 (7.5)	56.8 (6.0)
PRI/PO	65.5 (10.3)	66.8 (5.6)	52.5 (9.2)	58.9 (5.4)
PSI	73.0 (11.6)	63.3 (4.0)	58.2 (11.0)	57.8 (3.8)
FSIQ	60.5 (9.2)	58.3 (4.8)	46.4 (8.5)	50.9 (4.1)

[a]Data from the WISC-IV Technical and Interpretative Manual (Wechsler, 2003a, p. 80–81).
[b]Clinical group of children with mild and moderate mental retardation reported in the WAIS-III WMS-III Technical Manual (Psychological Corporation, 1997, p. 169).
VCI = Verbal Comprehension index, PRI = Perceptual Reasoning index, PO = Perceptual Organization index, PSI = Processing Speed index, and FSIQ = Full Scale Intelligence Quotient.

the WISC-IV with the exception of the Processing Speed indexes, which were less than 1 point apart.

One reason for the results between the WAIS-III and WISC-IV samples of children with mental retardation may be the differences in the core subtests for the various index scores. For example, in both the WAIS-III and WISC-IV, the Verbal Comprehension Index consists of Vocabulary and Similarities with the third subtest being Information for the WAIS and Comprehension for the WISC. Similarly, although both the Perceptual Reasoning and Perceptual Organization indexes contain the Block Design and Matrix Reasoning, the WAIS-III also includes Picture Completion, whereas the WISC-IV includes Picture Concepts. Both Working Memory indexes include Digit Span and Letter–Number Sequencing; in addition, the WAIS-III includes Arithmetic. The subtests that compose the Processing Speed indexes are the same for both tests.

A second explanation may be due to the 6-year difference between the norming of the WAIS-III and WISC-IV. A 6-year period is shorter than the typical 10-year revision interval. Thus, the magnitude of the differences between scores from the WAIS-III and WISC-IV is expected to be smaller than the difference between the scores for WISC-III and WISC-IV.

Another possible explanation may be that the initial IQs that qualified the children for inclusion in the clinical groups were different. Further research to ascertain relationships between the WISC-IV and WAIS-III for children with mild mental retardation is needed.

WISC-IV AND WPPSI-III FOR YOUNGER CHILDREN WITH MENTAL RETARDATION

The WISC-IV (Wechsler, 2003b) and WPPSI-III (Wechsler, 2003a) were normed close together. As shown in Table 9.5, the scores for 182 6- and 7-year-olds are nearly identical, with less than 1 point difference between the corresponding index and FSIQs. Correlations between the two tests ranged from .65 for Processing Speed index/PSQ to .89 for Full Scale IQ. With the exception of the correlation between the two Processing Speed indexes, the correlations are similar to those found between mean scores from the WISC-IV and the WISC-III and between the WISC-IV and the WAIS-III. Although data comparing the WISC-IV and WPPSI-III for children with mental retardation are unavailable, the high correlations between the two tests, as well as the similarity in mean scores, suggest those first administered the WPPSI-III and found to have mental retardation will have similar scores and fall into the range of mental retardation when retested with the WISC-IV.

WISC-IV and WPPSI-III IQs for children with mild and moderate levels of mental retardation are reported in Table 9.6. Scores for children in the mild group are similar with the exception of Processing Speed index, which differs by almost 6 points. The magnitude of scores for children in the moderate

TABLE 9.5   Comparison of WISC-IV and WPPSI-III for 6- and 7-Year-Olds

	WISC-IV Mean (SD)	WPPSI-III Mean (SD)	Correlation
VCI/VIQ	100.5 (11.4)	100.2 (12.0)	.83
PRI/PIQ	102.6 (13.2)	102.0 (12.8)	.79
PSI/PSQ	103.1 (12.7)	104.4 (14.1)	.65
FSIQ	102.7 (13.1)	102.5 (12.4)	.89

Data from WISC-IV Technical and Interpretative Manual (Wechsler, 2003c, p. 64).
VCI = Verbal Comprehension index, VIQ = Verbal Intelligence Quotient, PRI = Perceptual Reasoning index, PIQ = Performance Intelligence Quotient, PSI = Processing Speed index, PSQ = Processing Speed Quotient, and FSIQ = Full Scale Intelligence Quotient.

TABLE 9.6   WISC-IV and WPPSI-III for Children with Mental Retardation

	WISC-IV Mild N = 63 Mean (SD)	WPPSI-III Mild N = 40 Mean (SD)	WISC-IV Moderate N = 57 Mean (SD)	WPPSI-III Moderate N = 19 Mean (SD)
VCI/VIQ	67.1 (9.1)	65.7 (9.7)	52.3 (7.5)	58.1 (7.9)
PRI/PIQ	65.5 (10.3)	65.6 (9.6)	52.5 (9.2)	57.1 (8.0)
PSI/PSQ	73.0 (11.6)	66.6 (13.4)	58.2 (11.0)	58.3 (8.9)
FSIQ	60.5 (9.2)	62.1 (10.8)	46.4 (8.5)	53.1 (7.5)

[a]Data from WISC-IV Technical and Interpretative Manual (Wechsler, 2003c, p. 80–81).
[b]Data from the WPPSI-III Technical and Interpretative Manual (Wechsler, 2003a, 109–110).
VCI = Verbal Comprehension index, VIQ = Verbal Intelligence Quotient, PRI = Perceptual Reasoning index, PIQ = Performance Intelligence Quotient, PSI = Processing Speed index, PSQ = Processing Speed Quotient, and FSIQ = Full Scale Intelligence Quotient.

group show greater differences. Except for Processing Speed index, mean scores on the WPPSI-III are higher than scores on the WISC-IV. These differences may be due to differences in sample size. The WPPSI-III sample was only 19. Alternatively, the differences may reflect differences that existed in the initial IQ scores of the groups (i.e., one group may have had more [or fewer] children with IQs at the lower end of Moderate Retardation). Children with mental retardation appear to score highest on the Processing Speed index on the WISC-III, the WISC-IV, and the WPPSI-III. However, the same is not true for adults with mental retardation.

The WPPSI-III and WISC-IV were normed during the same time. Thus, the Flynn effect is not expected to influence scores for children first tested on the WPPSI-III and retested on the WISC-IV. The probability of children first being tested on the WISC-IV and later being retested on the WPPSI-III is unlikely because overlap of the two tests is only 15 months.

The WISC-IV Technical and Interpretative Manual (Wechsler, 2003c, p. 65) reports predicted WISC-IV IQs for selected WPPSI-III scores. For example, children who have WPPSI-III Full Scale IQs of 55 are likely to obtain WISC-IV Full Scale IQs between 51 and 59. Similarly, those who have WPPSI-III Full Scale IQs of 70 are likely to obtain WISC-IV Full Scale IQs between 67 and 73. These estimates are at the 95% confidence interval. The expected WISC-IV scores are composed of intervals that are wider at the upper and lower ends of the IQ distribution and narrower at the middle of the distribution. Based on the predicted scores, children scoring in the range of mental retardation on the WPPSI-III can be expected to score in the range of mental retardation on the WISC-IV.

WISC-IV AND ADAPTIVE BEHAVIOR ASSESSMENT SYSTEM-II

Correlations between measures of intelligence and adaptive behavior generally are in the .20 to .60 range (Kamphaus, 2002). Some research suggests that correlations between IQs and measures of adaptive behavior are somewhat higher for teacher ratings than for parent ratings (Harrison & Oakland, 2003; Sparrow, Balla, & Cichetti, 1984, 1985). Scores from the WISC-IV were compared with those from the Adaptive Behavior Assessment System-II (ABAS-II; Harrison & Oakland, 2003) for both the Parent Form (N = 122) and the Teacher form (N = 145) using two separate samples of children ages 6 through 16 years. The mean scores were 99 and 100 on the ABAS-II Parent Form General Adaptive Composite and the WISC-IV Full Scale IQ, respectively. Correlations between scores from the two measures varied from .41 for the General Adaptive Composite and WISC-IV Full Scale IQ to .23 for the Processing Speed index. For ABAS-II Teacher Form, the General Adaptive Composite was 104.8. Higher correlations were observed between the teacher forms and the WISC-IV; General Adaptive Composite and WISC-IV Full Scale IQ correlated the highest, .58, while the General Adaptive Composite and Processing Speed index correlated the lowest, .34.

WHICH TEST? WISC-IV VS WPPSI-III AND WISC-IV VS WAIS-III

The WISC-IV overlaps with the WPPSI-III at ages 6:0 to 7:3 years and with the WAIS-III at ages 16 years 0 months through 16 years 11 months. If the examiner suspects a child between the ages of 6:0 and 7:3 years may have low or below average intellectual ability, we recommend the WPPSI-III be used instead of the WISC-IV. The WPPSI-III has a lower floor and may provide a more accurate assessment of the child's strengths and weaknesses. Similarly, for children who are 16 years old and who may have low or below average intellectual ability, we recommend the WISC-IV be used because it has a lower floor (i.e., will provide greater coverage of content) and thus may provide a more complete and accurate assessment of strengths and weaknesses. As indicated earlier, the WPPSI-III and WISC-IV were standardized at the same time; thus scores on the WPPSI-III and WISC-IV are virtually identical. Therefore, a child is likely to score the same on either test. However, because of the differences between the WISC-IV and WAIS-III, children ages 16 years old are likely to have different scores on the two tests. It is highly unlikely that a 16-year-old child will be tested for the first time because of concerns about his or her intellectual functioning. Therefore, the clinician needs to take the possible differences in the two tests into consideration when making the decision as to which test to use.

WHICH TEST? WISC-IV OR WISC-III?

The diagnosis of mental retardation depends heavily on the magnitude of scores obtained. The revision of intelligence tests, especially those that include an assessment of visual conceptual and fluid reasoning abilities, often results in establishing a higher standard and thus lower scores. Thus, as has been discussed previously, a child's score on the prior test is likely to be somewhat higher than the child's score on its recent revision.

The choice of using the older or newer edition may have far-reaching consequences for an individual. For example, changes in IQs for children who initially scored between 55 and 70 and were retested approximately 3 years later using the same or revised WISC tests were studied (Kanaya, Scullin, & Ceci, 2003). Full Scale IQs of 81 children first tested on the WISC-R and then retested on the WISC-R averaged changes of less than 1 point. Similarly, Full Scale IQs of 83 children first tested on the WISC-III and retested on the WISC-III also averaged changes of less than 1 point. However, Full Scale IQS of 53 children first were tested on the WISC-R (IQ = 64.2, SD = 4.9) and retested on the WISC-III (IQ = 58.9, SD = 7.9) averaged a 5.3 point decrease. Full Scale IQs for 206 children tested on both the WISC-R (Full Scale IQ = 108.2) and the WISC-III (Full Scale IQ = 102.9) also displayed a 5.3 decrease (Wechsler, 1991). Because the norming dates are closer between the WISC-III and WISC-IV, smaller differences would be expected between these two tests than would be true for the WISC-III and WISC-R.

There are no comparisons of individuals with mental retardation tested on the WISC-IV and WISC-III; Table 9.2 presents the scores of a sample of 43 children diagnosed with mild mental retardation who were tested on the WISC-III at the time of its renorming in 1991. Information presented in Table 9.2 indicated that WISC-III scores for a sample of children with Mild

Mental Retardation were lower than WISC-IV scores for children with Mild Mental Retardation. However, the need for caution exists, pending WISC-III and WISC-IV data from the same children. Scores reported in Table 9.2 were acquired from different groups of children, not the same children tested twice. Thus, whether WISC-IV scores for children with mental retardation will show the Flynn effect found for children tested on the WISC-R and then on the WISC-III is unclear at this time.

For the standardization population, mean scores on the WISC-IV were somewhat lower than mean scores on the WISC-III. If the same pattern holds true for children with mental retardation, then children originally diagnosed with mental retardation using the WISC-III IQs are likely to have scores that fall in the range of mental retardation on the WISC-IV. A study of the Flynn effect on children who had IQs between 71 and 75 on the WISC-R found a "nearly threefold increase in the percentage of children in this IQ range classified as MR on the WISC-III when compared to the percentage of children who scored in the equivalent range on the WISC-R" (Kanaya, Scullin, & Ceci, 2003, p. 785). Children with WISC-III Full Scale IQs of 55 and 70 are expected to obtain WISC-IV Full Scale IQs that fall within the ranges of 49 to 56 and 65 to 70, respectively, given a 95% confidence limit (Wechsler, 2003c, p. 63). Further research comparing the WISC-IV and WISC-III scores for children with mental retardation is needed to determine the accuracy of these predictions. Such research is particularly important because of the differences in norming dates. It was 20 years between the WISC-R and WISC-III and about 11 years between the WISC-III and WISC-IV.

DIAGNOSTIC AND CLINICAL ISSUES

The Full Scale IQ is the most reliable score obtained on the WISC-IV and is usually the first score to be considered when interpreting a child's score profile. However, unusual variability among the index scores that make up the Full Scale IQ suggests the Full Scale IQ does not summarize the child's intellectual abilities accurately. The term *unusual difference* refers to differences that are both statistically significant and that occur rarely in a population. A difference is determined to be *unusual* by examining the frequency of differences occurring in the standardization sample (Tables B.2 and B.6, Wechsler, 2003b). These differences are called base rates. As a rule of thumb, differences that are both statistically significant and that occur in 10% or less within the standardization sample are considered unusual (Sattler, 2001). Table B.2 provides base rates for differences among index scores for the standardization group as a whole and for various IQs. The base rates for those with IQs ≤ 79 differ from those from a normal population. It is recommended that the base rates for IQs ≤ 79 should be used for children with mental retardation. Full Scale IQs also will have an unusual amount of scatter when unusual differences exist among the index scores, thus reducing its validity as an accurate reflection of a child's intellectual abilities. Thus, when an unusual amount of scatter exists, WISC-IV interpretations should rely heavily on the index scores.

When the Full Scale IQ is not a unitary measure (Table B.6), there is no clear-cut answer as to which index score should be used in its place. The decision depends on a number of factors. The first consideration should be the classification of the various index scores. For example, if the Processing Speed index is in the Low Average or Borderline range and all other index scores are in the mentally retarded range, the child's intellectual ability is probably best represented by a classification of mental retardation. However, if the Verbal Comprehension index is 89 (Low Average), the Perceptual Reasoning index is 75 (Borderline), and the Working Memory index and Processing Speed index are 65 and 67, respectively, a diagnosis of mental retardation is less defensible.

Regulations and policies promulgated by most state departments of education and other regulatory agencies that govern diagnostic decisions do not consider changes in tests scores resulting from the renorming of tests or use of instruments that differ in reliability and validity. Therefore, psychologists and other clinicians who use data from recently renormed tests should be prepared to explain and justify the scores used to make diagnostic decision. The decision as to which score—the one from the previously normed test or the more recently normed test—may reflect a child's ability level more accurately may be assisted through the use of other information. For example, if the child's IQ has changed and this change is accompanied by corresponding changes in adaptive functioning, achievement test scores, and grades, then the score from the more recently revised test may be more accurate. If other scores have not changed, then the previously normed test score may be more accurate.

Differences in scores on tests that purport to measure the same construct occur for various reasons, including personal variables (e.g., motivation, rapport, health, distractions); other reasons are psychometric. Bracken (1988) provides an excellent discussion of the 10 most common psychometric reasons for discrepancies between test scores. One of the most common psychometric reasons is the differences in standardization or publication dates, an issue discussed previously.

REGRESSION TO THE MEAN

Another issue to consider in the diagnosis of mental retardation is the effect of regression to the mean on test scores. Over time, mean scores for persons with mental retardation have been shown to move toward the normative mean (i.e., regression toward the mean). For example, Spitz (1983) found the mean WISC-R Full Scale IQ for a group of children with mental retardation to be 55 at age 13 and 58 at age 15. Thus, when a clinician is evaluating a child using the WISC-IV and finds a current score somewhat higher (and outside the usual range of mental retardation) than his or her previous WISC-IV score, is the child still classified as having mental retardation? Suppose the current Full Scale IQ score is 71 and the previous Full Scale IQ score was 68. At present, except for the test-retest study reported in the WISC-IV manual, there are no studies comparing changes in WISC-IV IQs over time. The mean test-retest Full Scale IQs for children tested 23 days apart were 101.0 and 106.6, respectively. However, other research has shown that WISC-R and WISC-III scores have been remarkably stable over the typical 3-year retest interval. For example, Kanaya, Scullin, and Ceci (2003) report the mean WISC-R IQs of 64.1 (time 1) and 64.2 (time 2—approximately 3 years later) for a group of 81 children. The difference for a group of 83 children tested with the WISC-III 3 years apart also was small (63.5 at time 1 and 64.3 at time 2).

Knowledge of average expected changes for groups over time, however, is not much help in determining the causes of an individual's different scores over time. Knowing that regression to the mean does occur may alert the examiner to possible reasons for an individual's changes in IQs over time. Above all, professionals in school districts and other agencies that make decisions using test scores, especially decisions about special education placement that can change the course of children's lives, must take into account a variety of evaluation data and other factors. Need for and expected benefit from special services, and not test scores alone, should guide decisions. Professional judgments of the individuals making decisions are the primary factors in effective and valid decision making.

TESTING FOR MAXIMUM PERFORMANCE: CONSIDERATIONS WHEN TESTING CHILDREN WITH MENTAL RETARDATION

The testing process is guided by whether its goal is to describe a child's behaviors at his or her best or as the behaviors occur typically. When assessing achievement, intelligence, and perceptual qualities, clinicians generally attempt to create conditions that elicit children's best effort and work and thus to estimate their maximum abilities and capabilities, not their typical performance. In contrast, when assessing adaptive behavior, personality, and social qualities, clinicians generally attempt to create conditions that provide an understanding of a child's typical performance. Thus, the administration of tests of maximum performance, such as the WISC-IV, attempts to elicit a child's very best behaviors (Oakland & Glutting, 1998).

EIGHT QUALITIES THAT CAN AFFECT TEST PERFORMANCE

Various conditions can affect a child's test behaviors adversely and thus depress test scores artificially. Clinicians generally attend closely to the following eight qualities, knowing that problems in one or more may impact test performance negatively: testing room conditions (e.g., rooms should be free of distractions), health-related conditions (e.g., the child's performance should not be attenuated by pain, disease, or illness), rapport (e.g., interpersonal relationships between the examiner and child must be conducive to test performance), readiness for testing (e.g., self-confidence, willingness to be tested), temperament (e.g., children who are extroverted are more likely to express their ideas and to talk to themselves while being tested), language qualities (e.g., a child's receptive and expressive language skills must be sufficiently developed to serve as a reliable link between the examiner and child), motivation (e.g., to engage and sustain involvement in the testing activity), and severity of the child's handicapping condition (e.g., more modifications typically are needed when assessing a child with severe to profound mental and physical disabilities). Test behaviors displayed by older and more mature children generally are more suitable than those displayed by younger and less mature children. Thus, efforts to help ensure suitable test-taking behaviors are especially needed when assessing younger and less mature children.

Many children diagnosed as displaying mental retardation are inclined to display limited endurance, self-regulation, receptive or expressive language skills, attention span, and interest, and thus less motivation and involvement. These conditions are likely to affect their test behavior adversely, resulting in test scores that are depressed artificially, thus preventing the attainment of the goal to describe a child's best behaviors. In addition, children diagnosed with mental retardation may have one or more physical disabilities that must be considered and at times accommodated when attempting to obtain a clear and accurate assessment of their best abilities. The use of accommodations when testing children with mental retardation and other pervasive disorders should be documented (Pitoniak & Royer, 2001).

Three broad qualities known to influence children's test performance directly include avoidance (e.g., to avoid tasks and express fear), uncooperative mood (e.g., improper adjustment to testing, lack of cooperation, and need for praise and encouragement), and inattentiveness (e.g., lack of impulse-control and inattentiveness) (Oakland & Glutting, 1998).

The Guide to the Assessment of Test-Session Behavior (GATSB; Glutting & Oakland, 1993) provides the only nationally standardized norm-referenced measure of test-taking ability co-normed with the WISC-III and Wechsler Individual Achievement Test (WIAT). Correlations between GATSB Total Score and the WISC-III Full Scale IQs are substantial: −.36

for the total group, $-.28$ for whites, $-.37$ for African Americans, and $-.55$ for Hispanics. Thus, between 8 and 30% of the variance associated with Full Scale Scores may be attributable to children's test-taking behaviors. Among the three factors, avoidance accounts for the plurality of the variance. Children who display deficient test-taking behavior generally obtain WISC-III Full Scale IQs 7 to 10 points lower than those obtained by children with more suitable test-taking behaviors.

CONCLUSIONS

Mental retardation is a disability about which we are still learning. Mental retardation may exist concurrently with other developmental disabilities, mental and/or neurological disorders. A diagnosis of mental retardation can be made only after careful interpretation of the entire clinical data set: background information, history, intellectual and adaptive behavior measures, behavioral observations, academic achievement, and various other factors relevant to a particular individual.

CASE STUDY

Name: John Henry Jones
Parents: John and Mary Jones
Age: 8:03
Grade: 2

REASON FOR REFERRAL

John Henry's parents initiated this referral for a psychoeducational evaluation, given their concerns and those of his teachers about his slow educational progress. The purposes of this evaluation were to acquire information about John Henry's development; to determine if a diagnosis was warranted; and to discuss diagnostic, placement, and intervention issues with John Henry's parents and teachers, with the goal of furthering his development.

BACKGROUND INFORMATION

John Henry, an 8-year-old boy, is below average in height and weight. His stature resembles an average 6-year-old. He has dark brown hair and brown eyes. His parents came to the United States about 7 years ago from their native Belize, an English-speaking country contiguous with Mexico and Guatemala.

John Henry is an only child. He lives with his mother and father. Mr. Jones is unemployed due to a work-related accident. Ms. Jones is unemployed due to chronic health problems and has a limited life expectancy. John Henry experiences anxiety about her health problems and possible death.

Mr. and Mrs. Jones lived in Belize at the time of John Henry's birth. Ms. Jones had two prior miscarriages. She reports that she saw the doctor regularly and was in good general physical health throughout the pregnancy. John Henry was born during the seventh month of pregnancy. Ms. Jones does not recall complications associated with his premature birth or the C-section delivery.

John Henry's early development of gross motor and self-help skills generally was average. Toilet training was easy, he ate well, was calm and reasonably active, and was outgoing and sociable. Although his ability to follow simple commands matured early, his language developed slowly. For example, he was late in using single word sentences, used language difficult to understand, and displayed delays in learning basic concepts, including colors and numbers. He had frequent ear infections of a mild to acute nature from 6 months to age 7. Tubes were placed in his ears at age 2 years and amoxicillin was used. He also had chickenpox. His current health generally is good.

Ms. Jones reports no evidence of conditions that suggest possible neurological involvement. However, John Henry's history of problems associated with speech and language include difficulty speaking clearly, recalling the correct words to use, maintaining a focus to the content he is expressing, remaining on one topic, decoding other's speech, reading words, comprehending what is read, and spelling. These difficulties reflect possible "soft signs" of neuropsychological dysfunction.

Lack of concentration and attention has been apparent for some years, according to John Henry's mother. John Henry has a history of being distracted easily by sounds, sights, and physical sensations. He loses his train of thought easily and has difficulty concentrating. He initiates new activities without completing prior activities and does not listen attentively to others. His memory also has been problematic. For example, he forgets where he leaves items, recent events, tasks he is asked to perform, others' names, and school assignments.

John Henry was diagnosed with attention deficit–hyperactivity disorder (ADHD) last year. He takes Ritalin two times a day (i.e., 25 mg in the morning and 10 mg after lunch) to treat his ADHD-related symptoms. Although he is receiving Ritalin for ADHD, Ms. Jones reports that John Henry sometimes is fidgety, distractible, and experiences difficulty concentrating.

John Henry attended a Head Start program at age 4. He entered kindergarten at a parochial school serving children living in an inner city area and continues to be educated there. Although his grades were low, he was promoted from the first to the second grade. His favorite classes are physical education and art. He dislikes reading and math, and his grades in these two subjects are low.

Ms. Jones reports that John Henry makes friends easily and maintains good relationships with them at school and in the neighborhood. Most friends are younger. He enjoys going to the mall and watching cartoons. His teachers report that John Henry displays a pleasant disposition. However, he has few friends in class.

TEST BEHAVIORS

John Henry was dressed nicely and groomed neatly for all test sessions. He was pleasant and cooperative during the assessment process. Although initially quiet, he became more talkative through the course of the assessment. He appeared to be at ease with the examiner and comfortable with the testing procedures. However, John Henry became noticeably uncomfortable when performing tasks that relied heavily on memory or processing information quickly.

John Henry's test behaviors were assessed using the Guide to the Assessment of Test Session Behavior. His attentiveness, cooperation, and other responses to tests were in the average range on this measure (75th percentile). Thus, the data reported here are likely to be a valid reflection of his cognitive abilities.

TEST RESULTS

Intelligence

John Henry's intellectual abilities were assessed using the Wechsler Intelligence Scale for Children-Fourth Edition (WISC-IV). The WISC-IV provides a measure of general intellectual ability, Full Scale IQ, as well as four index scores (Table 9.7). With a chronological age of 8 years, 2 months, John Henry achieved a Verbal Comprehension index of 71, a Perceptual Reasoning index of 69, a Working Memory index of 59, a Processing Speed index of 56, and a Full Scale IQ of 57 on the WISC-IV. His overall performance is classified in the Extremely Low range and is ranked below the 1st percentile. The chances that the range of scores from 53 to 63 includes his true Full Scale IQ are about 95 out of 100. Subaverage general mental ability, such as that displayed by John Henry, is one of two criteria needed to make a diagnosis of mental retardation.

John Henry's Verbal Comprehension index of 71 is descriptively classified as Borderline and is at the 3rd percentile. The Verbal Comprehension index is composed of subtests measuring verbal abilities utilizing reasoning, comprehension, and conceptualization. There was little variability in the

TABLE 9.7   Wechsler Intelligence Scale for Children—Fourth Edition (WISC-IV)

	Standard Scores	Percentile Rank	Confidence Limits (95%)
Verbal Comprehension Index	71	3	66–80
Perceptual Reasoning Index	69	<1	52–70
Working Memory Index	59	<1	55–70
Processing Speed Index	56	2	64–79
Full Scale IQ	57	<1	53–63

Note: A scaled score of 100 is average, with most children scoring between 85 and 115.

WISC-IV Subtest Scale Scores:

Verbal Comprehension Subtests:		Perceptual Reasoning Subtests:	
Similarities	4	Block Design	6
Vocabulary	6	Picture Concepts	5
Comprehension	5	Matrix Reasoning	4
Working Memory Subtests:		**Processing Speed Subtests:**	
Digit Span	4	Coding	2
Letter–Number Sequencing	2	Symbol Search	2

Note: A scaled score of 10 is average, with most children scoring between 7 and 13.

scaled scores for the subtests comprising the Verbal Comprehension index indicating relatively even development of abilities within the index.

The Perceptual Reasoning index score of 69 is descriptively classified as Extremely Low and is at the 2nd percentile. The Perceptual Reasoning index is composed of subtests measuring perceptual and fluid reasoning, spatial processing, and visual-motor integration. His subtest scaled scores ranged from 4 to 6, indicating relatively even development of abilities within this index.

John Henry's Working Memory index of 59 is descriptively classified as Extremely Low and falls below the 1st percentile. Thus, his ability to sustain attention and concentrate and hold information in short-term memory while performing some operation or manipulation with it is extremely low. These weaknesses may make the processing of complex information more time-consuming for John Henry, drain his mental energies more quickly than to other children his age, and perhaps result in frequent errors on a variety of learning tasks.

Processing Speed is composed of subtests measuring a person's ability to process simple or routine visual information quickly and efficiently and to perform tasks rapidly based on that information. John Henry's score of 56 is in the Extremely Low range and falls below the 1st percentile. A weakness in processing speed may make the task of comprehending novel information more time-consuming and difficult for John Henry.

John Henry's Verbal Comprehension and his Perceptual Reasoning index scores are significantly higher than both his Working Memory and Processing index scores. However, the differences among John Henry's index scores are not clinically meaningful as they occurred in approximately 20 to 25% of the children in the standardization population. The difference between John Henry's Perceptual Reasoning index and his Processing Speed index likely reflect the effect of time demands on his visual-spatial reasoning and problem solving. With the exception of Block Design, Perceptual Reasoning subtests are not timed, whereas the Processing Speed subtests have a time limit. As mentioned earlier, John Henry became noticeably uncomfortable on tasks that relied heavily on memory or processing information quickly. Information on John Henry's processing skill and working memory deficits indicate a need to examine these abilities in detail, especially his memory abilities, given their importance to his retaining what he learns.

Memory

John Henry's memory abilities also were assessed using the Children's Memory Scale (Table 9.8). Data from this scale help confirm John Henry's general memory abilities are in the extremely low range. His score of 50 on General Memory is classified as Impaired and falls below the 1st percentile. General Memory is a global measure of memory function and consists of subtests measuring immediate and delayed recall of verbal and visual stimuli. His immediate recall of information presented visually (e.g., to place chips on a grid in places seen previously or to recognize faces he was shown) and verbally (e.g., to repeat word pairs heard previously or recall

TABLE 9.8   Children's Memory Scale

	Standard Scores	Percentile Rank	Confidence Limits (95%)
Visual Memory Immediate Index	72	3	59–86
Visual Memory Delayed Index	66	1	53–79
Verbal Immediate Index	78	7	67–89
Verbal Delayed Index	69	2	54–84
General Memory Index	60	<1	51–69
Attention/Concentration	50	<1	40–61
Learning	82	12	70–94
Delayed Recall	85	16	73–97

Note: A standard score of 100 is average, with most children scoring between 85 and 115.

information from stories) is classified as Borderline. His abilities to recall the same verbal and visual information after a period of delay are classified as Impaired. However, comparisons between his visual immediate and delayed memory scores and differences between his verbal immediate and delayed memory scores were not statistically significant, indicating relatively even development for both visual and verbal (immediate as well as delayed) memory. Thus, John Henry's abilities to encode/store newly learned material and his abilities to retrieve the material from delayed memory are evenly developed. His General Memory index is the best measure of his global memory; his score of 50 is reflective of generalized memory impairment. His attention and concentration as measured by the Attention/Concentration index of 50 is also classified as Impaired and falls below the 1st percentile. These scores are consistent with John Henry's equally low Working Memory Index and Processing Speed index on the WISC-IV.

Achievement

Reading

The Wechsler Individual Achievement Test-Second Edition (WIAT-II) was used to assess John Henry's achievement (Table 9.9). His Reading Composite score of 73 is descriptively classified as Borderline and is at the 3rd percentile. His word reading skills are Low Average (12th percentile),

TABLE 9.9   Wechsler Individual Achievement Test-Second Edition (WIAT-II)

	Standard Scores	Percentile Rank	Confidence Limits (95%)
Reading Composite	73	4	70–76
Word Reading	82		
Reading Comprehension	68		
Pseudoword Decoding	77		
Mathematics Composite	71	3	64–78
Numerical Operations	78		
Math Reasoning	69		
Written Language Composite	63	1	56–70
Spelling	68		
Written Expression	69		
Oral Language Composite	72	3	63–79
Listening Comprehension	73		
Oral Expression	78		
Total Composite	65	1	61–69

Note: *A standard score of 100 is average, with most children scoring between 85 and 115.*

whereas his reading comprehension skills are classified as Extremely Low (2nd percentile).

Mathematics

John Henry's skills in mathematics fall in the Borderline to Extremely Low range as measured by the WIAT-II. John Henry's math computation skills (Numerical Operations) are in the Borderline range (7th percentile), and his Math Reasoning skills are in the Extremely Low range (2nd percentile).

Written Language

John Henry's Spelling and Written Expression falls at the 2nd percentile and are classified as Extremely Low. His Written Language Composite of 63 is also classified as Extremely Low. His writing was messy and difficult to read. At one point he commented, "I learned that word yesterday, but I can't remember it."

Oral Language

John Henry's Composite Oral Language score of 73 falls at the 3rd percentile and is descriptively classified as Borderline, as are both of the subtests that compose the Oral Language Composite.

Although there was some variability among the subtests of the WIAT-II, the only Composite Score differences occurred between Reading and Written Language, with Reading being significantly higher than the Written Language. The Spelling subtest of the Written Language is heavily dependent on memory and, as previously indicated, memory is a weak ability for John Henry. John Henry's Composite scores on the WIAT-II are all in the Borderline or Extremely Low range and reflect the academic difficulties he reportedly is having in school.

Given John Henry's low reading skills, an assessment of his phonological processing skills was conducted using the Comprehensive Test of Phonological Processing (Table 9.10). Phonological processing refers to the ability to manipulate the phonological segments of words in various ways. John Henry's Phonological Memory Composite of 82 is descriptively classified as Below Average and is at the 12th percentile. Phonological memory skills refer to the ability to temporarily store and then retrieve phonological information in short-term or working memory. John Henry's phonological memory score suggests that he has difficulties in decoding unfamiliar words and comprehending what he reads or hears. John Henry's Rapid Naming Composite Score of 73 is descriptively classified as Poor and falls at the 3rd percentile. Rapid naming skills refer to the ability to efficiently retrieve phonological information from long-term memory. These deficits suggest that he is likely to experience problems in reading fluently.

TABLE 9.10   Comprehensive Test of Phonological Processing

	Standard Scores	Percentile	Classification
Phonological Awareness Composite	58	<1	Very Poor
Phonological Memory Composite	82	14	Below Average
Rapid Naming Composite	73	3	Poor
Alternate Rapid Naming Composite	58	<1	Very Poor
Alternate Phonological Awareness Composite	52	<1	Very Poor

John Henry's Phonological Awareness Composite of 58 is in the Very Poor range and is below the 1st percentile. Phonological awareness refers to an individual's understanding of and ability to use the phonological structures of oral language. His scores on both the Alternative Rapid Naming Composite (58) and Alternative Phonological Awareness Composite (52) also are classified as Very Poor and fall below the 1st percentile. John Henry's co-occurring deficits in rapid naming skills and phonological awareness are typical of those who are at the greatest risk for reading problems and may reflect diminished intellectual ability.

Adaptive Behavior and Skills

John Henry's adaptive behavior and skills were assessed using the Adaptive Behavior Assessment System-II (ABAS-II) parent and teacher forms (Table 9.11). Ms. Jones' responses on the ABAS-II parent form indicate that John Henry displays deficits in adaptive behavior. His overall General Adaptive Composite of 71 is within the Borderline range (3rd percentile). Abilities related to his Conceptual Composite (9th percentile) and Social Composite (14th percentile) are in the Below Average range. Abilities related to his Practical Composite (5th percentile) are in the Borderline range. His adaptive skills are within the Average range on leisure; are in the Below Average range on health and safety, self-direction, community use, home living, and functional academics; are in the Borderline range on communication and social; and are in the Extremely Low range on self-care.

Responses from John Henry's reading teacher on the ABAS-II teacher form also indicate deficits in adaptive behavior. Abilities related to his General Adaptive Composite, 68, are within the extremely low range (2nd percentile). Abilities related to his Social Composite (18th percentile) are in the Below Average range. Abilities related to his Practical Composite (2nd percentile) and Conceptual Composite (1st percentile) are in the Extremely Low range. His adaptive skills are in the average range on leisure; in the Below Average range on health and safety as well as social; in the Borderline

TABLE 9.11　Adaptive Behavior Assessment System—II

| | Standard Scores | | | | | |
	Standard Score Parent	Percentile Rank	CL 95%	Standard Score Teacher	Percentile Rank	CL 95%
General Adaptive Composite	71	3	68–74	68	2	65–71
Conceptual	80	9		65	1	
Social	84	14		86	18	
Practical	75	5		69	2	

Note: *A standard score of 100 is average, with most children scoring between 85 and 115.*

| | Subtest Scaled Scores | |
Adaptive Skill Areas	Parent	Teacher
Leisure	9	8
Health and Safety	7	7
Self-Direction	6	2
Community Use	6	5
Home/School Living	6	4
Functional Academics	6	2
Communication	4	5
Social	4	6
Self-Care	1	2

Note: *A standard score of 10 is average, with most children scoring between 7 and 13.*

range on community use, school living, and communication; and in the Extremely Low range on self-direction, functional academics, and self-care.

Social–Emotional Behaviors

Attitudes Toward Self and School

John Henry's self-concept was assessed using the Piers-Harris Self-Concept Scale. Questions were read to John Henry. His responses suggest that he possesses a favorable self-concept that generalizes across many areas of his life. However, he acknowledges difficulty with some behaviors. On occasion, he does bad things, is disobedient at home, and is difficult to get along with. He hopes he never does anything "really" bad. John Henry's attitudes toward school are favorable. Most teachers make him feel good and are fun, and he is happiest when he is in class. He also believes working hard in school is important.

Behavioral and Emotional Functioning

John Henry's behavioral and emotional functioning was assessed with the Behavioral Assessment System for Children, with separate scales completed by him and his mother. Again, questions were read to John Henry. His responses indicate normal social and emotional functioning. Ms. Jones' responses suggest John Henry is at risk to withdraw socially and for inattentiveness and distractibility. This report is consistent with John Henry's previous diagnosis of ADHD.

Attention Deficit-Hyperactivity Disorder

John Henry's ADHD was assessed further by the Attention Deficit Disorder Evaluation Scale, Home and School Versions Rating Forms. Responses from John Henry's teachers indicate his attention, together with his hyperactivity/impulsivity, is somewhat elevated, yet within the normal range. Ms. Jones' responses indicate normal levels of attention and slightly elevated levels of hyperactivity/impulsivity. Although John Henry may experience inattentiveness at times, medication may be aiding these behaviors.

DIAGNOSTIC IMPRESSIONS

John Henry exhibits mild mental retardation as defined by the Diagnostic and Statistical Manual of Mental Disorders (DSM-IV-TR). That is, he displays significantly subaverage intellectual functioning (e.g., IQ levels 50 to 55 to approximately 70) that is accompanied by significant limitations in adaptive functioning in at least two skill areas. Moreover, the onset of this disorder occurred before age 18. John Henry also meets eligibility criteria for special education services for students with mental retardation under the statutes and Board of Education rules applicable to the state in which he lives. Meetings with John Henry, Mr. and Mrs. Jones, and John Henry's teachers were held to discuss these findings and their implications, including diagnoses, placement options, and the nature of his curriculum and instructional arrangements.

REFERENCES

Allen, S. R., & Thorndike, R. L. (1995). Stability of WPPSI-R and factor structure using cross-validation of covariance structural models. *Journal of Psychoeducational Assessment, 13 (1),* 3-20.

American Association on Mental Retardation (2002). *Mental retardation: Definition, classification, and systems of supports* (10th ed.). Washington, DC: Author.

American Psychiatric Association (2000). *Diagnostic and statistical manual of mental disorders: Text revision (DSM-IV-TR)* (Eth ed.). Washington, DC: Author.

Bracken, B. (1988). Ten psychometric reasons why similar tests produce dissimilar results. *Journal of School Psychology, 26,* 155-166.

Bracken, B. A., McCallum, R. S., & Crain, R. M. (1993). Subtest composite reliabilities and specificities: Interpretive aids. *Journal of Psychoeducational Assessment, Monograph Series: Advances in Psychoeducational Assessment, 11* 22-34.

Bruininks R. H., Woodcock, R. W., Weatherman, R. F., & Hill, B. K. (1996). *Scales of independent behavior-revised.* Chicago, IL: Riverside.

Denning, C. B., Chamberlain, J. A., & Polloway, E. A. (2000). An evaluation of state guidelines for mental retardation: Focus on definition and classification. *Education and Training in Mental Retardation and Developmental Disabilities, 35,* 226-232.

Dickinson, D., Iannone, V. N., & Gold, J. M. (2002). Factor structure of the Wechsler Adult Intelligence Scale-III in schizophrenia. *Assessment, 9,* 171-180.

Flynn, J. R. (1987). Massive IQ gains in 14 nations: What IQ tests really measure. *Psychological Bulletin, 101.* 171-191.

Flynn, J. R. (1998). WAIS-III and WISC-III gains in the United States from 1972 to 1995: How to compensate for obsolete norms. *Perceptual and Motor Skills, 86,* 1231-1239.

Georgas, J., Weiss, L. G., van de Vijver, F. J. R., & Saklofske, D. H. (2003). *Culture and children's intelligence: Cross-cultural analysis of the WISC-III.* San Diego: Academic Press.

Glutting, J. J., Youngstrom, E. A., Ward, T., Ward, S., & Hale, R. L. (1997). Incremental efficacy of WISC-III factor scores in predicting achievement: What do they tell us? *Psychological Assessment, 9,* 295-301.

Glutting, J., & Oakland, T. (1993). *Guide to the Assessment of Test Session Behaviors for the WISC-III and WIAT.* San Antonio, TX: The Psychological Corporation.

Grice, J. W., Krohn, E. J., & Logerquist, S. (1997). Cross-validation of the WISC-III factor structure in two samples of children with learning disabilities. *Journal of Psychoeducational Assessment, 17,* 236-248.

Grossman, H. J. (1983). *Classification in mental retardation.* Washington, DC: American Association on Mental Deficiency.

Harrison, P. L. & Oakland, T. (2003). *Adaptive behavior assessment system,* (2nd ed.). San Antonio: Psychological Corporation.

Individuals with Disabilities Education Act, *48, Fed. Reg.* 12406-12672 (March 12, 1999).

Jacobson, J. W., & Mulick, J. A. (1996). *Manual of diagnosis and professional practice in mental retardation.* Washington, DC: American Psychological Association.

Kamphaus, R. W. (2002). *Clinical assessment of children's intelligence* (2nd Ed.). Boston: Allyn and Bacon.

Kamphaus, R. W., & Platt, L. O. (1992). Subtest specificities for the WISC-III. *Psychological Reports, 70,* 899-902.

Kanaya, T., Scullin, M. H., & Ceci, S. J. (2003). The Flynn effect and U.S. policies: The impact of rising IQ's on American society via mental retardation diagnoses. *American Psychologist, 58,* 778-790.

Kaufman, A. S. (1990). *Assessing adolescent and adult intelligence.* Needham, MA: Allyn and Bacon.

Kaufman, A. S., & Kaufman, N. L. (1983). *K-ABC: Kaufman Assessment Battery for Children: Administration and scoring manual.* Circle Pines, MN: American Guidance Service.

Kaufman, A. S., Lichtenberger, E. O., & McLean, J. E. (2001). Two- and three-factor solutions of the WAIS-III. *Assessment, 8,* 267-280.

Kaufman, A. S. (1993). King WISC the third assumes the throne. *Journal of School Psychology, 31,* 345-354.

Keith, T. Z., Fehrmann, P. G., Harrison, P. L., & Pottebaum, S. M. (1987). The relationship between adaptive behavior and intelligence: Testing alternative explanations. *Journal of School Psychology, 25,* 31-43.

Kush, J. C. (1996). Factor structure of the WISC-III for students with learning disabilities. *Journal of Psychoeducational Assessment, 14,* 32-40.

Larson, S. A., Lakin, K. C., Anderson, L., Kwak, N., Lee, J. H., & Anderson, D. (2001). Prevalence of mental retardation and developmental disabilities: Estimates from the 1994/1995 National Health Interview Survey Disability Supplements. *American Journal on Mental Retardation 106(3):* pp. 231–252.

Nihira, K., Leland, H., & Lambert, N. (1993a). *AAMR Adaptive Behavior Scale-Residential and Community* (2nd ed.). Austin, TX: Pro-Ed.

Nihira, K., Leland, H., & Lambert, N. (1993b). *AAMR Adaptive Behavior Scale-School* (2nd ed.). Austin, TX: Pro-Ed.

Oakland, T., & Glutting, J. (1998). Assessment of Test Behaviors with the WISC-III. In A. Prifitera, & D. Saklofske (Eds.), *WISC-III: A scientist-practitioner perspective.* New York: Academic Press.

Pitoniak, M. J., & Royer, J. M. (2001) Testing accommodations for examinees with disabilities: A review of psychometric, legal, and social policy issues. *Review of Educational Research, 71,* 53-104.

Platt, R. W., Kamphaus, R. W., Cole, R. W., & Smith, C. L. (1991). Relationship between adaptive behavior and intelligence: Additional evidence. *Psychological Reports, 68,* 139-145.

Reschley, D. J., & Ward, S. M. (1991). Use of adaptive behavior measures and overrepresentation of Black students in a program for students with mild mental retardation. *Journal of Mental Retardation, 96,* 257-268.

Robinson, N. M., Zigler, E., & Gallagher, J. J. (2000). Two tails of the normal curve: Similarities and differences in the study of mental retardation and giftedness. *American Psychologist, 55,* 1413-1424.

Saklofske, D. H., Hildebrand, D. K., & Gorsuch, R. L. (2000). Replication of the factor structure of the Wechsler Adult Intelligence Scale-Third Edition with a Canadian sample. *Psychological Assessment, 12,* 436-439.

Sattler, J. M. (2001). *Assessment of children: Cognitive applications* (4th ed.). San Diego, CA: Author.

Sattler, J. M. (2003). *Assessment of children: Behavioral and clinical applications* (4th ed.). San Diego, CA: Author.

Slate, J. R. (1995). Discrepancies between IQ and index scores for a clinical sample of students: Useful diagnostic indicators? *Psychology in the Schools, 32,* 103-108.

Slate, J., & Saarnio, D. A. (1995). Differences between WISC-III and WISC-R IQs: A preliminary investigation. *Journal of Psychoeducational Assessment, 13,* 340-346.

Sparrow, S. S., Balla, D. A., and Cicchetti, D. V. (1984). *Vineland adaptive behavior scales: Survey form.* Circle Pines MN: America Guidance Service.

Sparrow, S. S., Balla, D. A., & Cicchetti, D. V. (1985). *Vineland adaptive behavior scales: Classroom edition.* Circle Pines, MN: American Guidance Service.

Spitz, H. (1983). Intratest and intertest reliability and stability of the WISC, WISC-R and WAIS full scale IQs in a mentally retarded population. *Journal of Special Education, 17,* 69-80.

Spruill, J. (1998). Assessment of mental retardation with the WISC-III. In Prifitera, A., & Saklofske, D. (Eds.), *WISC-III Clinical use and interpretation: Scientist-practitioner perspectives.* (pp. 73-90). San Diego: Academic Press.

Terdal, L. G. (1981). Mental retardation. In J. E. Lindemann, *Psychological and behavioral aspects of physical disability* (pp. 179-216). New York: Plenum.

The Psychological Corporation (1997). *WAIS-III WMS-III Technical Manual.* San Antonio: Author.

Tulsky, D. S., & Price, L. R. (2003). The joint WAIS-III and the WIM-III factor structure development and cross-validation of a six-factor model of cognitive functioning. *Psychological Assessment, 15,* 149-162.

van der Heijden, P., & Donders, J. (2003). WAIS-III factor index score patterns after traumatic brain injury. *Assessment, 10*, 115-122.

Watkins, M. W. & Canivez, G. L. (2001). Longitudinal factor structure of the WISC-III among students with disabilities. *Psychology in the Schools, 38*, 291-298.

Watkins, M. W., & Kush, J. C. (2002). Confirmatory factor analysis of WISC-III for students with learning disabilities. *Journal of Psychoeducational Assessment, 20*, 4-19.

Wechsler, D. (1991). *WISC-III Manual.* San Antonio, TX: The Psychological Corporation.

Wechsler, D. (2003a). *WPPSI-III Technical and Interpretative Manual.* San Antonio, TX: The Psychological Corporation.

Wechsler, D. (2003b). *WISC-IV.* San Antonio, TX: The Psychological Corporation.

Wechsler, D. (2003c). *WISC-IV: Technical and Interpretative Manual.* San Antonio, TX: The Psychological Corporation.

Weiss, B., & Weisz, J. R. (1986). General cognitive deficits: Mental retardation. In R. T. Brown & C. R. Reynolds (Eds.), *Psychological perspectives on childhood exceptionality* (pp. 344-390). New York: Wiley.

10

LANGUAGE DISABILITIES

ELISABETH H. WIIG

Knowledge Research Institute, Inc.
Arlington, Texas

LANGUAGE DISABILITIES DEFINED

Children and adolescents with language disabilities form a large, heterogeneous group, accounting for from 10 to 20% of children (Tallal, 2003). This heterogeneity results from the fact that language and communication disorders can originate in a variety of etiologies, express themselves as different types, and be associated with different comorbidities. Furthermore, the nature of language and communication disorders changes with age as cognitive and linguistic demands associated with academic curricula, vocations and professions, and social interaction increase in complexity and diversity (Lord Larson & McKinley, 2003; Ratner & Harris, 1994). Language and communication disabilities are a part of genetic syndromes such as the Down, Fragile X, and Tourette Spectrum syndromes (Dornbush & Pruitt, 1995; Jung, 1989; Prestia, 2003). They also exist as comorbidities in developmental disorders such as autism, attention deficit–hyperactivity disorder (ADHD), and executive function disorders (EFD), or as a result of traumatic brain injury (TBI) (Barkeley, 1997, 1998; Brown, 2000; Culatta & Wiig, 2002; Ottinger, 2003; Wetherby, 2002).

DSM-IV (1994) defines language and communication disorders as being either of the Expressive or Mixed Receptive-Expressive type. Expressive language and communication disorders are identified by four criteria, three of which relate to inclusion and one of which specifies exclusion: (1) Expressive language development is significantly below receptive language development and nonverbal intellectual ability; (2) deficits interfere with academic, vocational, and professional achievement and/or social communication; (3) the language difficulties are in excess of those usually observed in cases with cognitive, sensory or motor deficits, or environmental deprivation; and (4) symptoms do not meet criteria for Mixed Receptive-Expressive language disorders or pervasive developmental disorders (DSM-IV, pp. 55–58). Mixed Receptive-Expressive disorders are defined against three diagnostic criteria, two or which are inclusive and one exclusionary: (1) Both receptive and expressive language development are significantly below measures of nonverbal intellectual ability; (2) deficits interfere with academic, vocational, and professional achievement and social communication; and (3) symptoms do not meet criteria for pervasive developmental disorders (DSM-IV, pp. 58–61).

Language disabilities can be the primary or secondary source of a student's exceptionality, and the impairments can involve different modalities (e.g., listening/receptive, speaking/expressive), modes (e.g., reading, writing), and dimensions of the language system (e.g., phonology, morphology and syntax, semantics, or pragmatics). Depending on which modalities and components of the language system are involved, the symptomatic manifestations, severity, and impact of a language disability on language learning, academic achievement, social competence, and emotional stability will vary (Bashir, Wiig & Abrams, 1987; Culatta & Wiig, 2002; Wetherby, 2002).

The term *specific language impairment* (SLI) is often used to label school-age children, adolescents, and young adults in whom language disability is of a primary nature and do not result from emotional disorders, cognitive delays, sensory impairments, or language differences (Leonard, 1991; NJCLD, 1994). Research has prompted the suggestion that there is a connection between SLI and verbal working memory (Montgomery, 2002). Furthermore, in these children and youth, other learning disabilities can be explained with reference to the nature of existing language impairments (Culatta & Wiig, 2002; Lord-Larson & McKinley, 2003; Ratner & Harris, 1994).

COGNITIVE REFERENCING
IN LANGUAGE DISABILITIES

There is an ongoing debate with regard to how to identify language disabilities and differentiate SLI and language differences, as well as whether cognitive referencing is essential or even relevant in the comprehensive assessment of children and adolescents for language disabilities (Paul, 2000). One point of view follows the DSM-IV diagnostic criteria and looks to identify discrepancies between language and nonverbal cognitive abilities on standardized measures. This position has been termed a *neutralist perspective*, as it does not account for ethnic, cultural, or social norms or expectations (Fey, 1986). The second depends on evaluating and observing how a child or youth performs in context with different demands and constraints (e.g., academic, family, community, and broader social). This perspective is referred to as the *normative position* (Fey, 1986; Merritt & Culatta, 1998; Nelson, 1998, 2000).

The controversy of whether to adopt a neutralist perspective or a normative position for the assessment and identification of language disabilities extends into all branches of special education. Thus, a normative position with Responsiveness-to-Intervention as the focus for identifying children with learning differences is being discussed and advocated by numerous professional organizations and concept papers abound (Fuchs, Mock, Morgan, & Young, 2003). The debates precede the upcoming reauthorization of the Education for All Handicapped Children Act (PL 94–142), and the outcomes will certainly affect the future of evaluating and identifying children with language disorders. The main issues center around whether norm-referenced testing, including assessment of intellectual abilities, has a place in the future of special education.

As a researcher and practitioner in the field of speech–language pathology, I acknowledge the validity of the discussion and the pros and cons of each position. In this context, I shall assume the stance that norm-referenced evaluations of language and cognitive abilities can contribute significantly in a multidimensional assessment and identification process. After decades of practice, I have seen many "babies thrown out with the dirty bath water," experienced cycles of fads and fancies in speech-language pathology and education, and seen reversals to previously vilified methods and procedures (e.g., phonological awareness testing and training). With this as a background, I will express my views of the relevance of cognitive test data in a comprehensive, multidimensional assessment of children with potential specific language impairments and/or disabilities.

First, using cognitive and intellectual referencing as an integral aspect of multidimensional language assessment does not contradict the current mandates of the Individuals with Disabilities Education Act (IDEA) (PL 94–142), which are to describe a student's strengths and weaknesses and relate these to potential for academic achievement and curriculum objectives which may be compromised.

As an example, if cognitive assessments indicate significant working memory or word finding (dysnomia) deficits and/or processing speed deficits, this knowledge can contribute to a broadened understanding of contributing factors to the student's language impairments (Berninger, 2001; McGregor, Newman, Reilly, & Capone, 2002; Montgomery, 2002; Semel, Wiig, & Secord, 2003; Weiler, Bernstein, Bellinger, & Waber, 2000). It can also explain how these deficits can influence performance on academic tasks such as note taking, literacy development, and oral and written presentations of narrative or dialogue and indicate needed classroom accommodations (Lord-Larson & McKinley, 2003; Montgomery, 2002; Ratner & Harris, 1994; Storkel & Morrisette, 2002).

Second, with exclusively normative or authentic assessment procedures and without cognitive referencing, the group of students identified to have language disabilities will be of high incidence and unmanageable heterogeneity. It would include children of any variety with language and communication problems that may not have underlying neuropsychological bases. This heterogeneous group cannot be expected to respond similarly to either standard educational or programmatic language intervention procedures. Furthermore, services that target the deficit areas and foster compensatory strategies may not be provided for students with specific neuropsychological deficits that interfere with language and communication in increasingly complex academic contexts as in, for example, the Tourette Spectrum syndrome (Dornbush & Pruitt, 1995; Prestia, 2003).

WISC-III AND LANGUAGE DISABILITIES

The third edition of the Wechsler Intelligence Scale for Children (WISC-III) (Wechsler, 1989) provided relevant data about intellectual and neuropsychological abilities in multidimensional assessments of students with language and communication difficulties. With cognitive and intellectual referencing, students with Mental Retardation or Pervasive Developmental Disorders (DSM-IV, 1994) were identified and comprehensive educational and psychoeducational supports, including language stimulation and/or intervention, were provided. Similarly, language impairments and learning disabilities with neuropsychological bases and comorbidities (e.g., ADHD, executive function disorders) could be differentiated from language disabilities related to deprivation, language differences, or interactions between language codes (e.g., English-Spanish bilingualism) (Langdon, 1992; Payne & Taylor, 2002).

Relationships between WISC-III measures of intellectual ability (Wechsler, 1991) and performances on norm-referenced receptive and expressive language tasks was explored during standardization of the Clinical Evaluation of Language Fundamentals–3rd Edition (*CELF-3*) (Semel, Wiig, & Secord, 1995). Correlations between the CELF-3 Total Language standard score and WISC-III Full Scale ($r = .75$), Verbal Scale ($r = .75$) and Performance Scale IQs ($r = .60$) were all significant ($p < .01$), but moderate in degree. The CELF-3 and WISC-II Verbal Scale relationships underscored that the measures shared a general language construct. However, the moderate size of the correlation indicated that the WISC-III Verbal Scale alone did not adequately identify aspects of the Expressive or Receptive-Expressive language syndromes described in DSM-IV.

WISC-IV AND LANGUAGE DISABILITIES

STUDIES OF CHILDREN WITH LANGUAGE DISABILITIES

The WISC-IV (Wechsler, 2003) and CELF-4 (Semel, Wiig, & Secord, 2002) were administered concurrently during standardization and the respective manuals report the results from different perspectives. The WISC-IV technical manual reports findings from a comparison of performances by 27 children between 6 and 16 years old with primarily expressive language disorders, as defined by DSM-IV-TR criteria, and 27 age-matched controls. The group mean differences between the WISC-IV Verbal Comprehension and Working Memory Index scores were highly significant ($p < .01$), indicating large negative effects of the expressive language disorder syndrome. There was also a significant, but moderate negative effect of expressive language disorders on WISC-IV Full Scale IQ. Among subtests, Comprehension and Information showed large negative effects for expressive language disorders ($p < .01$), and Vocabulary and Arithmetic showed significant but moderate effects.

Performances by a group of 41 children with Mixed Receptive-Expressive Language Disorders ranging in age from 6 to 16 years and identified according to DSM-IV-TR criteria and 41 age-matched controls were also compared. There were large and significant differences between groups for Verbal Comprehension, Perceptual Reasoning, Working Memory, and Processing Speed, as well as Full Scale IQ ($p < .01$). Group differences were substantial and significant for all Comprehension and Working Memory subtests, two Processing Speed subtests, and one Perceptual Reasoning subtest ($p < .01$). These findings support that children with Mixed Receptive-Expressive Language Disorders show global deficits in cognitive functioning, as well as in linguistic aspects of language and communication, working memory, and visual-verbal processing speed (e.g., rapid automatic naming) (Beitchman, Wilson, Brownlie, Walters, & Lance, 1996; Semel, Wiig, & Secord, 2002; Wiig, Zureich, & Chan, 2000; Wiig, Langdon, & Flores, 2001).

RELEVANCE AND APPROPRIATENESS

The statistical and clinical properties of WISC-IV and controlled studies of clinical populations support the relevance and appropriateness of its use for cognitive referencing in a multidimensional and multiperspective assessment of language disabilities. From the perspective of the clinical or educational diagnostician, the performance patterns on those subtests that contribute to the Verbal Comprehension and Working Memory index scores are of immediate relevance. Congruency in language test and WISC-IV

Verbal Comprehension measures can serve to validate a diagnosis of a language disorder. Working memory measures further serve to validate language test results, and identify a potentially critical component of a specific language impairment (Montgomery, 2002). Performance on subtests that contribute to the Perceptual Reasoning index are relevant and appropriate for assessing nonverbal cognitive and reasoning strengths and weaknesses to complete the diagnostic profile. These measures can identify strengths that can be employed in selecting language intervention strategies, such as conceptual mapping with cognitive mediation and determining the use of media to enhance language learning (Heyerle, 1996; Lord-Larson & McKinley, 2003; Wiig & Wilson, 2001).

Each of the subtests that form the Verbal Comprehension index can provide specific information relevant for identifying strengths and weaknesses and relating performances to social or academic learning content and tasks. Thus, the Similarities subtest probes verbal, semantic abilities that reflect concept formation and the development of semantic networks. Here the student is required to respond to two related words or concepts by referring to shared meaning features and semantic class membership. This task is often difficult for students with Mixed Receptive-Expressive language deficits and the spontaneous responses may indicate a focus on differences in meaning rather than on similarities. Responses may also focus on shared secondary, concrete characteristics (e.g., physical attributes) rather than essential abstract meanings (e.g., class membership). As examples of these response patterns, the student with a language disability may respond to the stimuli "cat" and "mouse" by saying either that they are not alike "because a cat eats a mouse" or that they are alike "because they are both brown, and have fur and a long tail." For the astute clinician, the nature of error responses is as important as the standard score earned on this subtest, as the error pattern points to objectives and procedures for intervention (e.g., developing semantic classification and superordinate naming).

The Picture Concepts subtest reveals information that is similar to that obtained from the Similarities subtest. It requires the student to identify one item from each of two or three rows of pictured stimuli to form a semantic group, and then to explain why the items go together. Students with primarily Expressive language disabilities generally perform well on the picture matching task, but may have problems expressing the reasons for their choices succinctly with, for example, superordinate names. Students with pervasive Receptive-Expressive language disabilities may show inadequate performance on both the nonverbal pointing and the verbal explanation tasks. Again the nature of the student's error patterns is relevant to the clinician by pointing out strengths and weaknesses and developing a focus and selecting strategies for intervention.

The Vocabulary Subtest uses two stimulus-response formats. In response to the picture items, the student is required to name the featured instance. In response to the verbal reasoning items, the student is required to formulate a definition by giving either a synonym, major use, primary feature, or category membership. Frequently, students with Mixed Receptive-Expressive Language Disabilities respond to the Verbal Reasoning items with circumlocutions, vague or terse responses, or concrete interpretations, thereby earning primarily part scores. Students with expressive language disabilities may exhibit word finding difficulties and substitute words. If the student self-monitors and corrects substitute responses, this should be noted as a positive. In all instances the clinician should be informed of error patterns so that appropriate follow-up evaluation of naming and word finding abilities can be provided (German, 1986, 1990, 1991).

The Comprehension subtest requires students to give reasons, state the importance and advantages or disadvantages of actions, characteristics or features, or social expectations for behavior. Students with Mixed Receptive-Expressive language disabilities generally have difficulties expressing cause-effect relationships and moral judgment. They typically earn part or no scores on this type of comprehension test, and it may be difficult to establish a ceiling. Their response and error patterns can indicate inadequacies in critical thinking, verbal reasoning, and moral judgment that are important for clinicians to be aware of. When these deficits are present, intervention procedures that develop critical thinking, abstract reasoning, and moral judgment through cognitive mapping and mediation, guided questioning, scaffolding, or other procedures are appropriate (Heyerle, 1996; Wiig & Wilson, 2001).

The Working Memory and Processing Speed index scores are also of importance and relevance to the understanding of language deficits and disorders. Naming speed deficits for highly familiar visual stimuli are prevalent among monolingual English and bilingual English-Spanish speaking students with Mixed Receptive-Expressive Language Disabilities, who earn language scores in the low-to-very low educational range (Wiig, Zureich, & Chan, 2000; Wiig,, Langdon, & Flores, 2001). These rapid naming speed deficits are indicative of inadequate processing speed, implicit working memory and verbal automaticity, validated by neuroimaging to be mediated by the temporal-parietal regions of the brain (Wiig, Nielsen, Minthon, & Warkentin, 2002). They are also predictors of dyslexia and difficulties in literacy acquisition (Wolf, Bowers, & Biddle, 2000). The WISC-IV Working Memory index provides important validation of the presence of verbal working memory and retrieval deficits for academically important materials (e.g., digits, letters, and other sequences). The Processing Speed index provides added information to determine whether or not a student's language disabilities and naming speed deficits are associated with processing speed deficits in the visual-perceptual and visual-motor domains. By integrating results from working memory and rapid automatic naming tests, featured in current, comprehensive language assessment tools (e.g., CELF–4), the results can assist in identifying underlying clinical behaviors that have negative effects on language and communication development and the attainment of mature competencies in language, communication, and literacy. Results can also serve to differentiate students with SLI from those with language differences. This differentiation will become increasingly important as funding for language intervention services and English as a Second Language services must be separated so that students can be assigned to appropriate services immediately after identification and differential diagnosis.

Last but not least, it is relevant for the clinician to have information about a student's strengths and/or weaknesses in nonverbal cognitive and reasoning abilities. The WISC-IV Perceptual Reasoning index provides this information. If a student shows relative strength in perceptual reasoning, this translates to potential success for using cognitive approaches to language intervention such as visual tools for conceptual mapping and cognitive meditation (e.g., Heyerle, 1996; Wiig & Wilson, 2001) to support development of concepts, linguistic rules, narrative structure, and other organizational strategies.

TESTING CONSIDERATIONS

Several aspects of WISC-IV administration and interpretation of results must be considered when testing students with probable language disabilities. First, the psychologist must satisfy that the test tasks and expectations for responding are understood by the student. This may mean asking direct questions about task characteristics and expected responses. Students with language disabilities of the Mixed Receptive-Expressive type often develop nonadaptive strategies for responding to tasks. They may guess what to do if directions were not understood, an approach that often leads to failure because the various scripts for spoken directions for tasks and tests may not be internalized or automatized.

Second, students with language disabilities often give error responses that can point directly to the underlying sources for difficulties in language learning and use. The psychologist should record inaccurate spontaneous responses for, for example, word definitions so that error patterns can be identified and interpreted either for or by a clinician. As an example, there is ample research of error associated with word-finding problems (dysnomia), a characteristic concomitant of language disabilities of the expressive type (German, 1986, 1990, 1991). It is especially important to identify circumlocutions, verbose descriptions, imprecise referencing with overuse of pronouns, word substitutions, and use of similar sounding words in context (e.g., television for telephone), all characteristics of word finding difficulties.

Third, the psychologist should relate the observed cognitive strengths and weaknesses to educational expectations, curriculum objectives, and classroom behaviors. A pragmatic interpretation of the WISC-IV results can then be compared to interpretations based on a student's performance on language tests. This can serve as validation or as a means of providing a more complete picture of the student. When cognitive deficits are observed that are commonly linked to language and communication disabilities, a referral to a clinician for in-depth language evaluation seems appropriate. It follows that the psychologist and speech pathologist should then collaborate to interpret and validate the WISC-IV results and the language measures that led to a diagnosis of a language disability of the Mixed Receptive-Expressive or predominantly Expressive type.

CLINICAL INTERPRETATIONS IN LANGUAGE DISABILITIES

CASE STUDIES

The following case studies describe language and cognitive test results for selected students with language disabilities. The three individuals were administered the CELF-4 and WISC-IV at the time of standardization. The clinical categories, from which the illustrative cases were selected, represent language disorders of the primarily Expressive type (Cases A and C), and Mixed Receptive-Expressive type (Case B). Each case study will follow a descriptive format in which the student's (1) background and prior diagnosis is described, (2) CEFL-4 norm-referenced index scores are presented and interpreted, (3) WISC-IV norm-referenced index scores and Full Scale IQ are reported, and (4) the combined findings are interpreted for clinical and educational implications.

CASE STUDY A. MALE, AGE 6:5

This study is of a 6-year 5-month-old boy with language disorders and learning disabilities. The student received speech and language intervention services at the time of the assessment. His language disorder was initially identified by administering the PLS (standard score 58), the PPVT (standard score 90), and the CELF-Preschool (Receptive 77; Expressive 65). The prior evaluations indicated performance on comprehensive language tests in the low to very low educational range for his age and determined eligibility for speech-language resources. The student's CELF-4 Core Language and Index scores are shown in Table 10.1 and WISC-IV Index scores and Full Scale IQ in Table 10.2.

This student's CELF-4 Core Language score (83) indicates performance in the marginal to average educational range and supports eligibility for continuation of language resource services. The Receptive index score (101) indicates performance within the average educational range, while the

TABLE 10.1   Overview of CELF-4 Core Language and Index Scores (age 6 years 5 months)

CELF-4 Index Scores	Standard Score	Confidence Interval (90%)	Percentile Rank	Educational Performance Range
Core Language	83	78–88	13	Marginal-Average
Receptive Index	101	93–109	53	Average
Expressive Index	83	77–89	13	Marginal-Average
Language Content	94	88–100	34	Average
Language Structure	88	82–94	21	Marginal-Average
Working Memory	80	71–89	9	Low-Marginal

TABLE 10.2   Overview of WISC-IV Index Scores and IQ (age 6 years 5 months)

WISC-IV Index Scores	Standard Score	Confidence Interval (90%)	Percentile Rank	Performance Range
Verbal Comprehension	95	90–101	37	Average Normal
Perceptual Reasoning	94	88–101	34	Average Normal
Working Memory	104	97–110	61	Average Normal
Processing Speed	97	90–105	42	Average Normal
Full-Scale IQ	96	92–100	39	Average Normal

Expressive index score (83) indicates performance in the marginal to average range. The Modality index scores (Receptive-Expressive) differ by 18 points and the discrepancy is significant ($p < .05$). In other words, this boy's language difficulties are primarily expressive in nature based on the modality index scores. The Language Content score (94) indicates performance within the average educational range, and the Language Structure score (88) indicates performance in the marginal to average educational range. The Content index scores (Language Content vs Language Structure) also did not differ significantly ($p > .05$). The Working Memory index score (80) falls within the low to marginal range, indicating that working memory presents an area of relative weakness. In other words, this student's primarily expressive language difficulties are associated with inadequate working memory ability, as measured by CELF-4.

This student's WISC-IV Full Scale IQ (96) and the Verbal Comprehension (95), Perceptual Reasoning (94), Working Memory (104), and Processing Speed (97) index scores are all within the average normal range. There are no significant differences between paired WISC-IV index scores, indicating no significant areas of cognitive strengths or weaknesses beyond the average normal range. Using the presence of a significant discrepancy between measures of language and cognition as a criterion for eligibility for special education resources may not have resulted in language services for this student. However, the persistence of an expressive language disability qualifies the student for continuation of already initiated resource services.

The implications of the combined WISC-IV and CELF-4 test results are that the student's relative cognitive strengths should be activated to facilitate internalization and automatization of verbal strategies for expression. Thus, language intervention approaches with a cognitive basis (e.g., visual tools for conceptual mapping, cognitive mediation, and mediated learning) should support activation and use of cognitive strengths such as verbal comprehension, perceptual reasoning, and visual and working memory.

CASE STUDY B. FEMALE, AGE 8:0

This study is of an 8-year 0-month-old girl with a diagnosed language disorder, who received language intervention and resource reading services at the time of testing. The language disorder was first identified with the TOLD-P3 at age 5. At the time of identification and determination of eligibility for service, Listening (standard score 94) was within the normal range, while Speaking (standard score 67) was significantly lower and indicated a severe expressive deficit. The student's CELF-4 Core Language and Index scores are presented in Table 10.3 and WISC-IV index scores and IQ are shown in Table 10.4.

The girl's CELF-4 Core Language score of 56 places her performance within the very low educational range and supports eligibility and continuing needs for speech and language resource services. The Receptive index score (53) falls within the very low educational range, as does the Expressive

TABLE 10.3   Overview of CELF-4 Core Language and Index Scores (age 8 years 0 months)

CELF-4 Index Scores	Standard Score	Confidence Interval (90%)	Percentile Rank	Educational Performance Range
Core Language	56	51–62	0.2	Very Low
Receptive Index	53	46–60	0.1	Very Low
Expressive Index	59	53–65	0.3	Very Low
Language Content	60	54–66	0.4	Very Low
Language Structure	58	51–65	0.3	Very Low
Working Memory	72	64–80	3	Low-Marginal

TABLE 10.4   Overview of WISC-IV IQ and Index Scores (age 8 years 0 months)

WISC-IV Index Scores	Standard Score	Confidence Interval (90%)	Percentile Rank	Performance Range
Verbal Comprehension	89	84–95	23	Average Normal
Perceptual Reasoning	106	99–112	66	Average Normal
Working Memory	88	83–95	21	Average Normal
Processing Speed	65	62–77	1	Very Low
Full-Scale IQ	85	81–90	16	Average-Marginal

index score (59), indicating a severe language disorder of the Mixed Receptive-Expressive type. The Language Content score (60) falls within the very low educational range, as does the Language Structure score (58). Neither the Modality index (Receptive vs Expressive) nor the Content index (Language Content vs Language Structure) scores differ significantly ($p > .05$). The Working Memory index (72) is in the low to marginal educational range, and while it represents an area of relative strength, it appears inadequate for successful compensation. In other words, the student's language and communication difficulties can be related to inadequate acquisition of content and structural linguistic rules in the presence of low to marginal working memory abilities.

The student's WISC-IV Full Scale IQ (85) is within the marginal to normal range, but this measure does not describe the student's cognitive strengths, weaknesses, or potential for learning. The student's Perceptual Reasoning (106) is significantly higher than Verbal Comprehension (89), indicating nonverbal reasoning abilities that may assist in building language and communication competence and developing adaptive compensatory strategies. The differences between the index scores for Verbal Comprehension and Processing Speed (24 points), Perceptual Reasoning and Processing Speed (41 points), Perceptual Reasoning and Working Memory (16 points), and Processing Speed and Working Memory (23 points) were all significant ($p < .05$). In other words, this student presents a complex picture of cognitive strengths and weaknesses. The very low Processing Speed index (65) suggests a need for extensive classroom accommodations in the form of use of basic technology (e.g., audio taping, word processing) and added time for completing tests and projects. This student would meet discrepancy criteria between Perceptual Reasoning and language abilities for continuing language resource services. In relation to language intervention, the student's relative strengths in perceptual reasoning should be activated for developing concepts, structural linguistic, and pragmatic rules for communicating in context. The nonverbal reasoning strengths should also be activated to develop executive functions (e.g., planning and organization) and compensatory strategies for communication. Visual supports in the form of conceptual maps, diagrams and other organizational structures, and cognitive approaches, such as mediated learning, conceptual mapping, and cognitive mediation, should also be used to strengthen the integration and internalization of new knowledge. The very low performance on measures of processing speed, including visual memory, visual discrimination, and visual-motor integration, suggests that the student may benefit from accommodations such as extended time for tests and tasks and introduction to basic technology in preparation for producing written products at the higher grades.

CASE STUDY C. FEMALE AGE 12:9

This study is of a 12-year 9-month-old girl with diagnosed language disorders and learning disabilities. The student was administered the TOLD-I 3 at age 9 and obtained a Listening standard score of 94, Speaking standard score of 68, and Total standard score of 79. Her test scores on the WISC-III indicated a significant discrepancy between Verbal (92) and Performance IQ (126). The student received special education services with emphasis on reading and writing at the time of testing. The CELF-4 Core Language and Index scores are presented in Table 10.5 and the WISC-IV index scores in Table 10.6.

This student's CELF-4 Core Language score (87) places her performance in the marginal to average educational range and supports her eligibility for continuing language intervention. The Receptive index (93) indicates performance within the average educational range, while the Expressive index (77) places her performance in the low to marginal educational range. The Language Content index (78) also places the student's performance in the low to marginal range. In contrast, the Language and Memory index (92)

TABLE 10.5 Overview of CELF-4 Core Language and Index Scores (age 12 years 9 months)

CELF-4 Index Scores	Standard Score	Confidence Interval (90%)	Percentile Rank	Educational Performance Range
Core Language	87	81–93	19	Marginal-Average
Receptive Index	93	86–100	32	Average
Expressive Index	77	70–84	6	Low-Marginal
Language Content	78	71–85	7	Low-Marginal
Language Memory	92	85–99	30	Average
Working Memory	97	87–107	32	Average

TABLE 10.6   Overview of WISC-IV IQ and Index Scores (age 12 years 9 months)

WISC-IV Index Scores	Standard Score	Confidence Interval (90%)	Percentile Rank	Performance Range
Verbal Comprehension	87	82–93	19	Average-Marginal
Perceptual Reasoning	102	95–108	55	Average Normal
Working Memory	110	103–116	75	High Average
Processing Speed	97	90–105	42	Average Normal
Full-Scale IQ	98	94–102	45	Average Normal

places her performance within the average range. The Modality (Receptive vs Expressive) and Content index scores (Language Content vs Language and Memory) both differ significantly ($p < .05$). In other words, there are obvious modality- and content-related strengths and weaknesses. Thus, receptive language skills are superior to expressive language skills and memory for spoken language is superior to language content acquisition. The student's Working Memory index (97) is within the average range and explains why receptive and language and memory abilities are areas of relative strengths for this student.

The student's WISC-IV Full Scale IQ (87) places her performance within the average to below average range. The profile of index scores, however, points to specific strengths and weaknesses among cognitive abilities. Notably, the differences between Perceptual Reasoning (102) and Verbal Comprehension (87), Working Memory (110) and Verbal Comprehension (87), and Working Memory (110) and Processing Speed (97) are all significant ($p < .05$). The student, therefore, shows strengths in nonverbal reasoning and working memory that may support further development of expressive language skills and language content. The CELF-4 Core Language and WISC-IV Verbal Comprehension scores are in agreement, validating the persistence of language disabilities in this student. Application of discrepancy criteria between language abilities and WISC-IV Verbal Comprehension and Perceptual Reasoning measures of cognition support the continuation of resource services for this student. The areas of weakness in oral language abilities suggest that resources should be expanded to include individualized language intervention in addition to continuation of reading and writing resource services. In language intervention, the perceptual reasoning and working memory strengths of the student should be activated in structured, cognitive approaches, especially to accelerate concept formation and understanding and use of language content.

CONCLUSIONS

The strength of the WISC-IV as a tool for broadening the assessment and understanding of students with language disabilities resides in the new model for categorizing and interpreting performances. This model stresses the use and interpretation of index scores, validated by factor analysis, rather than using the traditional Verbal vs Performance IQ categorization. From the perspective of the clinician, this model is attuned to current trends in assessment and differentiation of language disabilities (i.e., specific language impairment vs language difference) and responds to the IDEA mandates for language resources. The new model, which identifies strengths and weaknesses in Verbal Comprehension, Perceptual Reasoning, Working Memory and Processing Speed, avoids the tendency for static interpretations of IQ, supports the value of using language vs cognition discrepancy measures for determining eligibility for language resources, and points to targets for intervention, developing compensatory strategies, and providing classroom accommodations for access to content and curriculum. Without in-depth assessment of the student's cognitive strengths and weaknesses, as provided by WISC-IV administration, as well as of language and communication strengths and weaknesses, inappropriate placement, statements of individualized educational plan objectives, selection of intervention approaches, and stipulations of expected educational objectives may result. WISC-IV appears to provide assessments and measures of cognition that can be shared with clinicians in educational and clinical settings to foster interdisciplinary and transdisciplinary collaboration and sharing of responsibilities for intervention across the continuum of special needs.

REFERENCES

Barkley, R. A. (1997). *ADHD and the nature of self-control.* New York: Guilford Press.

Barkley, R. A. (1998). Attention-deficit hyperactivity disorder. *Scientific American, September,* 66–71.

Bashir, A. S., Wiig, E. H., & Abrams, J. C. (1987). Language disorders in childhood and adolescence: Implications for learning and socialization. *Pediatric Annals, 16,* 145–158.

Beitchman, J. H., Wilson, B., Brownlie, E. B., Walters, H., & Lancee, W. (1996). Long-term consistency in speech/language profiles: I. Developmental and academic outcomes. *Journal of the American Academy of Child and Adolescent Psychiatry, 35*(6), 804–814.

Berninger, V. (2001). *The Process Assessment of the Learner—Test Battery for Reading and Writing.* San Antonio, TX: The Psychological Corporation.

Brown, T. R. (2000). *Attention-deficit disorders and comorbidities in children, adolescents, and adults.* Washington, DC: American Psychiatric Press.

Culatta, B., & Wiig, E. H. (2002) Language disabilities in school-age children and youth. In G. H. Shames & N. B. Anderson (Eds.), *Human communication disorders* (6th ed.) (pp. 218–257). Boston, MA: Allyn & Bacon.

Dornbush, M. P., & Pruitt, S. K. (1995). *Teaching the tiger: A handbook for individuals in the education of students with attention deficit disorders, Tourette syndrome, or obsessive-compulsive disorders*. Duarte, CA: Hope Press.

Fey, M. (1986). *Language intervention with young children*. Austin, TX: ProEd.

Fuchs, D., Mock, D., Morgan, P. L., & Young, C. L. (2003). Responsiveness-to-Education: Definitions, evidence and implications for the learning disabilities construct. *Learning Disabilities Research & Practice, 18*, 157–171.

German, D. J. (1986). *National College of Education test of word finding*. Austin, TX: Pro-Ed.

German, D. J. (1990). *National College of Education test of adolescent/adult word finding*. Austin, TX: Pro-Ed.

German, D. J. (1991). *Test of word finding in discourse*. Austin, TX: Pro-Ed.

Hyerle, D. (1996). *Visual tools for constructing knowledge*. Alexandria, VA: Association for Supervision and Curriculum Development.

Jung, J. H. (1989). *Genetic syndromes in communication disorders*. Boston, MA: College Hill Press.

Langdon, H. W. (1992). *Hispanic children and adults with communication disorders: Assessment and intervention*. Gaithersburg, MD: Aspen Publishers.

Leonard, L. B. (1991). Specific language impairment as a clinical category. *Language, Speech, and Hearing Services in Schools, 22*, 66–68.

Lord-Larson, V., & McKinley, N. L. (2003) *Communication solutions for older students: Assessment and intervention strategies*. Eau Claire, WI: Thinking Publications.

McGregor, K. K., Newman, R. M., Reilly, R. M., & Capone, N. C. (2002). Semantic representation and naming in children with specific language impairment. *Journal of Speech, Language, and Hearing Research, 45*, 998–1014.

Merritt, D. D., & Culatta, B. (1998). *Language intervention in the classroom*. San Diego, CA: Singular Publishing Group.

Montgomery, J. W. (2002). Understanding the language difficulties of children with specific language impairments: Does verbal working memory matter? *American Journal of Speech-Language Pathology, 11*, 77–91.

National Joint Committee on Learning Disabilities (NJCLD) (1994). Position paper. Reprinted in *Topics in Language Disorders, 16* (1996), 69–73.

Nelson, N. W. (1998) *Childhood language disorders in context: Infancy through adolescence*. Boston, MA: Allyn & Bacon.

Nelson, N. W. (2000). Basing eligibility on discrepancy criteria: A bad idea whose time has passed. *ASHA Special Interest Division I, Language, Learning and Education, 7*(1), 8.

Ottinger, B. (2033). *Dictionary: A reference guide to the world of Tourette syndrome, Asperger syndrome, attention deficit hyperactivity disorders and obsessive compulsive disorder for parents and professionals*. Shawnee Mission, KS: Autism Asperger Publishing Co.

Paul, R. (2000) Language disorders from infancy through adolescence. (2nd ed.). St. Louis, MO: Mosby.

Payne, K. T., & Taylor, O. L. (2002). Multicultural influences on human communication. In G. H. Shames & N. B. Anderson (Eds.), *Human communication disorders: An introduction* (pp. 106–140). Boston, MA: Allyn & Bacon.

Prestia, K. (2003). Tourette's syndrome: Characteristics and interventions. *Intervention in Schools and Clinic, 39*, 67–71.

Ratner, V., & Harris, L. (1994). *Understanding language disorders: The impact on learning*. Eau Claire, WI: Thinking Publications.

Semel, E. M., Wiig, E. H., & Secord, W. A. (1995). *Clinical evaluation of language fundamentals 3*. San Antonio, TX: The Psychological Corporation.

Semel, E. M., Wiig, E. H., & Secord, W. A. (2003). *Clinical evaluation of language fundamentals 4*. San Antonio, TX: The Psychological Corporation.

Storkel, H. L., & Morrisette, M. L. (2002). The lexicon and phonology: Interactions in language acquisition. *Language, Speech, and Hearing Services in Schools, 33,* 24–37.

Tallal, P. (2003). Language disabilities: Integrating research approaches. *Current Directions iin Psychological Science, 12,* 206–211.

Wechsler, D. (1991). *Wechsler Intelligence Scale for Children* (3rd ed.). San Antonio, TX: The Psychological Corporation.

Weiler, M. D., Bernstein, J. H., Bellinger, D. C., & Waber, D. P. (2000). Processing speed in children with attention deficit/hyperactivity disorder, inattentive type. *Child Neuropsychology, 6(3),* 218–234.

Wetherby, A. M. (2002). Communication and language disorders in infants, toddlers, and preschool children. In G. H. Shames & N. B. Anderson (Eds.), *Human communication disorders* (6th ed.) (pp. 186–217). Boston, MA: Allyn & Bacon.

Wiig, E. H., Langdon, H. W., & Flores, N. (2001). Nominación rápida y automática en niños hispanohablantes bilingües y monolingües. *Revista de Logopedia, Foniatria y Audiologia, 21 (3),* 106–117.

Wiig, E. H., Nielsen, N. P., Minthon, L., & Warkentin, S. (2002). *Alzheimer's quick test: Assessment of parietal function.* San Antonio, TX: The Psychological Corporation.

Wiig, E. H., & Wilson, C. C. (2001). *Map it out! Visual tools for thinking, organizing and communicating.* Eau Claire, WI: Thinking Publications.

Wiig, E. H., Zureich, P., & Chan, H. N. (2000). A clinical rational for assessing rapid, automatic naming in children with language disorders. *Journal of Learning Disabilities, 33,* 369–374.

Wolf, M., Bowers, P. G., & Biddle, K. (2000). Naming-speed processes, timing, and reading: A conceptual review. *Journal of Learning Disability, 33,* 387–407.

11

HARD-OF-HEARING AND DEAF CLIENTS: USING THE WISC-IV WITH CLIENTS WHO ARE HARD-OF-HEARING OR DEAF

JEFFERY P. BRADEN

Department of Psychology
North Carolina State University
Raleigh, North Carolina

Intellectual assessment of clients who are hard-of-hearing or who are deaf is difficult, yet essential. Hearing loss has many psychological consequences beyond difficulties perceiving sound (Braden, 2000). Hearing loss affects children's development of language, attachment to and relationships with their parents, acquisition of literacy and general knowledge, and social identity. Although auditory amplification helps many children to better perceive sound, and in so doing, gain access to family, school, and society, many children continue to have difficulty perceiving sound even with consistent, state-of-the art technologies to boost sound perception. Those children are deaf or hard-of-hearing, and accurate appraisal of their intellectual abilities is an essential component for planning educational, social, vocational, and even medical interventions. This chapter is intended to help clinicians understand the unique issues that arise when they use the WISC-IV with deaf or hard-of-hearing children.[*]

The chapter is divided into five major parts. First, issues related to the intellectual assessment of deaf and hard-of-hearing children are presented and discussed. Second, recent developments relating to the assessment of individuals with disabilities, and to the development and structure of the WISC-IV, are reviewed. Third, prior research using the Wechsler Scales with deaf and hard-of-hearing examinees is presented to identify testing recommendations and concerns. Fourth, issues and recommendations for using the WISC-IV with deaf and hard-of-hearing children are presented. Five, a case study illustrates the ways in which the WISC-IV and the recommendations in this chapter might facilitate intellectual assessment of a deaf examinee. The chapter closes with some conclusions and recommendations for future research.

ISSUES FOR ASSESSING DEAF
AND HARD-OF-HEARING CHILDREN

The primary concern confronting examiners who are charged with assessing the intelligence of deaf and hard-of-hearing children is differentially diagnosing intellectual deficits from experiential deficits. Because more than 90% of deaf and hard-of-hearing children are raised in households where the native, and often exclusive, language is spoken (Gallaudet Research Institute, 2002), these children are denied early, consistent access to language. Additionally, language difficulties and delays create additional barriers to development, such as eroding communication and relationships between parents and children, reducing opportunities for accessing and exploring community and culture, and providing an impoverished knowledge base for acquiring information.

Consequently, deaf and hard-of-hearing children often share many of the symptoms associated with intellectual deficits. They talk later or not at all, and their speech typically ranges from immature to inarticulate compared to similar age peers. They may make unusual noises, resort to less linguistically

---

[*]Although style guides generally recommend first-person usage to describe individuals with disabilities, people with severe hearing impairments prefer to describe themselves as hard-of-hearing or deaf. I honor that tradition in this chapter. Furthermore, the term *deaf* is used for two related but distinct meanings. The first meaning indicates severe to profound hearing impairment and implies that a person who is deaf has significant difficulty understanding and using spoken communication. The second meaning indicates cultural identity, or membership in the Deaf community. People who are Deaf use sign language as their primary means of communication and share linguistic, cultural, and historical identities, but need not have a severe to profound hearing impairment. In this sense, most deaf people are also Deaf, but some deaf people are not, preferring instead to identify with the normal-hearing or hard-of-hearing communities.

mature forms of behavior to negotiate conflicts (e.g., tantrums), and often demonstrate deficits in adaptive behavior associated with communication (e.g., use of telephone, knowing their address). Although other behaviors (e.g., curiosity, motor development) differ markedly from peers who have significant intellectual delays or deficits, these behaviors may be over-shadowed by symptoms most commonly associated with deficits in intelligence. Therefore, effective assessment must differentiate whether a deaf or hard-of-hearing child's developmental problems are a function of a hearing impairment, an intellectual impairment, or both.

A second issue guiding assessment is that of communication. Examiners must establish the child's primary means of communication and ensure that the assessment is conducted within those means. Deaf and hard-of-hearing children vary substantially in their means of communication. Slightly more than half (54.9%) of the deaf and hard-of-hearing students in U.S. schools receive instruction using formal sign systems, and slightly less than half (44.5%) are taught exclusively via speech (Gallaudet Research Institute, 2002). However, students using speech as their primary means of communication often supplement their communication with formal or informal supports. Formal supplements include a variety of assistive technologies, such as real-time transcriptions, visual representation of sounds using a monitor worn on glasses, and closed loop hearing aid systems. Additionally, speech-dependent children often rely on speakers to accommodate their hearing impairment by ensuring direct eye contact, appropriate lighting and positioning of the speaker, clear and accent-free enunciation of words, and reduced background noise, limited facial hair, and elimination of other distractions that impair visual or auditory comprehension of speech. Informal supplements include gestures, writing, or "home signs" (i.e., gestures that convey meaning but are idiosyncratic). Examiners must identify relevant communication needs and ensure they accommodate those needs when communicating with and assessing deaf or hard-of-hearing children who rely primarily or exclusively on spoken communication.

Most deaf and hard-of-hearing children use formal sign systems as their primary means of communication, and are more likely to abandon speech and adopt signs as they become older. Therefore, examiners must ensure assessments are conducted using the sign system most familiar to the signing examinee. Sign systems vary along a continuum from exact representation of spoken English via signs (e.g., Gustason & Zawolkow, 1993) to American Sign Language (ASL). ASL is used by members of the Deaf community, and has a grammar and structure independent of spoken English (Liddell, 2003). Most deaf or hard-of-hearing children do not use only English signs, or only ASL. Instead, they use sign pidgins (Stewart & Luetke-Stahlman, 1998), which mix ASL grammar and English sign vocabulary. Determining the child's primary sign system is further complicated by dialectical sign variations, which may be unique to particular schools or areas of the country.

Therefore, examiners must identify the sign system children use as their primary mode of communication, use that sign system to conduct their assessment, and ensure that any translations of test content into that system retain validity across linguistic translations.

A third issue that emerges is consideration of shared and reciprocal influences between hearing loss and intelligence. Many forms of hearing loss co-occur with cognitive deficits, either via syndromic genetic conditions (e.g., Treacher Collins syndrome) or shared neurological damage (e.g., meningitis is a cause of deafness and brain damage). Also, hearing loss is likely to influence at least some aspects of intellectual development. Acquisition and use of language-dependent cognitive processes (e.g., verbal comprehension and reasoning) and those dependent on audition (e.g., auditory processing) are likely to be affected by hearing loss. Additionally, adapting assessments to accommodate hearing loss may alter the nature of the assessment. For example, providing a string of digits and letters via hand gestures instead of via speech may affect the cognitive strategies the examinee employs to complete the task (e.g., subvocal repetition of the digit/letter string is less likely for visually presented and encoded materials). Therefore, examiners must recognize and consider a myriad of variables that influence what they assess, how they assess it, and how they interpret the results.

Given the complexity of these issues, examiners should consider carefully whether they have the competence for assessing deaf and hard-of-hearing children. Ethical codes governing psychologists (e.g., American Psychological Association, 2002) direct psychologists to "provide services, teach, and conduct research with populations and in areas only within the boundaries of their competence, based on their education, training, supervised experience, consultation, study, or professional experience" (Standard 2.01). Examiners must have appropriate tools, skills, and knowledge to assess intelligence in deaf and hard-of-hearing children. Although the bulk of this chapter is devoted to discussing the tools and skills needed for assessment, examiners must also have substantial knowledge of deafness. Typically, this background knowledge would include formal study of hearing loss, psychological development in deaf and hard-of-hearing children, and supervised practice.

Unfortunately, few psychologists have the skills and knowledge needed to serve deaf and hard-of-hearing children, in part because it is difficult to acquire adequate background knowledge without substantial effort, and in part because deafness occurs rarely. Only 1.3% of the children currently receiving special education are deaf or hard-of-hearing (US Department of Education, 2002); less than 1 in 1000 children in the United States are deaf in both ears (National Center for Health and Statistics, 1994). Therefore, examiners who do not have prerequisite background knowledge should consider carefully whether they should assess deaf and hard-of-hearing clients. Resources for identifying and referring children to appropriate experts are discussed later in the chapter.

RECENT ADVANCES IN ASSESSMENT ACCOMMODATIONS AND THE WECHSLER SCALES

Although clinicians have long been sensitive to the need to accommodate examinees with disabilities in intellectual assessments, most prior research has been driven by clinical experience, intuition, and research with small clinical samples. Recent changes in civil rights laws (e.g., the Americans with Disabilities Act), litigation (Phillips, 1996), and advances in theory and research relating to assessment accommodations suggest examiners should adopt more deliberate and evidence-based strategies to guide assessment accommodations (Braden, 2003).

Fortunately, the most recent edition of the *Standards for Educational and Psychological Testing* (American Education Research Association, American Psychological Association, National Council on Measurement in Education, 1999) and other sources (e.g., Braden & Elliott, 2003; Elliott, Braden, & White, 2001; Office of Civil Rights, 2000) provide a framework for guiding assessment accommodations. These sources concur in suggesting six features that examiners could change in educational or psychological assessments to accommodate individuals with disabilities: (1) presentation format, (2) response format, (3) timing, (4) test setting, (5) using portions of a test, and (6) using substitute or alternate assessments.

Although all six options are available to examiners, some options are less controversial than others. The first four attributes involve changes in test conditions and are generally acceptable to a variety of researchers and writers. In contrast, the latter two options change test content, which many authors (e.g., Elliott, Braden, & White, 2001; Phillips, 1993; Thurlow, Elliott, & Ysseldyke, 1998) view as invalidating the assessment. The key principle guiding assessment accommodations is that accommodations should change features of the assessment that are related to an individual's disability, but that do not change the construct measured by the test. Such changes are acceptable from legal (Phillips, 1996) and conceptual (Braden & Elliott, 2003) perspectives. For example, altering a reading comprehension test by increasing the print size changes an aspect of the test related to an individual's visual disability (e.g., limitations in visual acuity) but unrelated to the construct of interest (e.g., font size is irrelevant to reading comprehension). In contrast, reading the test aloud to an examinee might alter a feature related to the examinee's visual disability (by allowing the examinee to hear the test content), but would also change the construct measured by the test (i.e., the test becomes an assessment of listening comprehension rather than reading). The distinction between access skills (i.e., those attributes of an assessment that are required but unrelated to the construct of interest) and target skills (i.e., the construct that an assessment intends to measure) can guide accommodation decisions so that assessments retain validity while concurrently avoiding construct-irrelevant variance (Braden, 2003; Messick, 1995; Phillips, 1993).

In contrast, changes to test content, either by eliminating portions of the test, or by using a different test, usually change the construct that the examiner assesses. For example, deleting Verbal Scale subtests from a Wechsler battery could help an examiner avoid confounding a deaf child's English language abilities with the child's intellectual abilities, but it would also restrict the range of abilities that contribute to estimating the child's general intelligence. Verbal Scale scores are better predictors of achievement than Performance Scale scores in deaf and hard-of-hearing children, in part because verbal scores sample language knowledge and hearing loss (Kelly & Braden, 1990). Substituting alternate tests, such as nonverbal tests, for broader batteries may narrow the range of abilities that examiners use to estimate general intellectual abilities (Braden & Athanasiou, in press). Examiners must therefore consider the degree to which eliminating portions of tests, or substituting alternate tests, alters the constructs assessed. Historically, the issue of construct representation in assessment has received little attention (Braden, 2003), particularly in regard to assessment of deaf and hard-of-hearing examinees (Brauer, Braden, Pollard, & Hardy-Braz, 1998).

Recent advances in the science and assessment of cognitive abilities have also influenced test development, and in particular, the structure and content of the WISC-IV. Although changes and their justification are reviewed in detail in other chapters in this book, it is important to consider how these changes may influence the assessment of deaf and hard-of-hearing examinees.

First, changes alter the composition and meaning of intellectual ability composite scores. Previous editions of the Wechsler provided a Performance IQ composite, which tapped fluid reasoning, visualization, manual dexterity, and processing speed abilities. The newer version eliminates the Performance (and Verbal) IQ, instead recommending the use of the Perceptual Reasoning index (PRI) as the composite score that best reflects fluid reasoning. The subtests that contribute to the PRI are also quite different than those that produced the PIQ; two subtests (Picture Arrangement and Object Assembly) were eliminated entirely. One subtest (Picture Completion) was relegated to supplemental status, one subtest (Coding) was reassigned to a different index (Processing Speed), and the one subtest remaining from the previous version that contributes to PRI (Block Design) was modified to decrease the influence of time bonuses. Two new subtests (Picture Concepts and Matrix Reasoning) combine with the new version of Block Design to produce the PRI. This composite is likely to be a more saturated measure of fluid reasoning and is less influenced by visualization, manual dexterity, and processing speed abilities. Whether these changes will lead to a better estimate of intelligence in deaf and hard-of-hearing children is not known at this time.

Other changes in the WISC-IV (e.g., the creation of Working Memory and Processing Speed composites) are also likely to influence score interpretations for deaf and hard-of-hearing children.

The second concern caused by changes from previous versions of the Wechsler is the ability to generalize prior research to the current edition. The Wechsler Scales and, in particular, the Performance Scales are the most popular and widely researched instruments for assessing intelligence in deaf and hard-of-hearing children (Braden, 1994; Spragins & Blennerhasset, 1998). Whereas prior updates (e.g., the WISC-R, WISC-III) involved minor changes in items and their appearance, the WISC-IV Perceptual Reasoning index is a radical departure from previous versions in content and structure. Consequently, the ability to draw on prior research in guiding the use of the new version is limited, speculative, and subject to confirmation with research using the WISC-IV with deaf and hard-of-hearing children.

PREVIOUS RESEARCH AND RECOMMENDATIONS

There is a substantial body of research regarding using previous versions of the Wechsler Scales to assess deaf and hard-of-hearing examinees. This literature has been summarized to help examiners apply the Wechsler Scales to deaf and hard-of-hearing children (Braden & Hannah, 1998; Jenkinson, 1989; Sattler & Hardy-Braz, 2002) to disabled adults in general (Braden, 2003) and to deaf adults in particular (Leutzinger, 2002). These resources concur in suggesting a number of accommodations that examiners should consider when assessing deaf and hard-of-hearing examinees. Table 11.1 organizes these recommendations according to the six features of assessment identified in contemporary standards (AERA, APA, NCME, 1999) that should guide assessment accommodations.

Although different recommendations have been presented in the literature, not all are supported by available research, and some may even be contraindicated. Some of the critical issues are: (1) use of Verbal Scale (or, on the WISC-IV, Verbal Comprehension) subtests, (2) translation of directions and item content into ASL, (3) desirability of deaf norms, (4) demographic differences within deaf and hard-of-hearing samples, (5) the distinction between performance and other nonverbal tests, and (6) the utility of profile analysis. Each of these is briefly discussed and considered in light of how previous research might guide use of the WISC-IV.

VERBAL SCALE/COMPREHENSION SUBTESTS

Many sources (e.g., Hunt, 1998; Leutzinger, 2002; Sattler & Hardy-Braz, 2002; Spragins & Blennerhasset, 1998) suggest—sometimes very strongly—

TABLE 11.1   Assessment Accommodations Recommended for Deaf and Hard-of-Hearing Examinees

Aspect of Assessment to Alter	Recommended Accommodations
Presentation Format Alternate the medium used to present test directions and items.	Additional examples; Administer using clear, deliberate speech, finger spelling, gestures, signs, and/or written materials; Avoid examiner's nonverbal cues.
Response Format Change the way in which examinees respond to test items or directions.	Allow gestured, pointed, signed, or written responses.
Modifying Timing Alter the interval in which tests are usually given.	Eliminate time limits; Provide extra time.
Test Setting Alter the setting in which assessment is administered.	Clear lighting; Reduced visual–auditory distractions; Use interpreters.
Use Portions of a Test Select portions of a test based on the individuals' disability.	Eliminate language-loaded, time-limited, and speeded tests; Remove "extra" items to reduce fatigue.
Using Substitute Tests or Alternate Assessments Replacing a standardized test with a test or alternate assessment specifically designed for individuals with disabilities	Provide additional examples and practice items; Use nonverbal tests; Use tests with norms based on deaf/hard-of-hearing clients.

Note: This table is an expanded and adapted version of the information in Braden (2000).

that examiners should not administer the verbal subtests on the Wechsler Scales to deaf and hard-of-hearing examinees. This recommendation is usually justified by noting that deaf and hard-of-hearing children consistently demonstrate lower scores on verbal subtests and composites in comparison to nonverbal or performance subtests and composites. More recent criticisms also cite analyses of differential item functioning, which show that verbal subtest items function differently for deaf and hard-of-hearing examinees (Maller, 1997, 2003). The differences between scores based on verbal vs nonverbal or performance subtests are large and clinically meaningful— usually about 15 points, or 1 standard deviation in magnitude (Braden, 1994; Hunt, 1998; Sullivan & Montoya, 1997). Furthermore, substantial differences between verbal and performance subtests and composites are found in international studies of deaf and hard-of-hearing examinees, including research in China (Meng & Gong, 1995), Nigeria (Alade, 1992), and Russia (Saraev & Kozlov, 1991).

Because most deaf people have substantially lower verbal scores than nonverbal scores, the use of language-loaded (verbal) estimates of intelligence may bias estimates of deaf and hard-of-hearing children's intellectual ability. Vernon and Andrews (1990, p. 203) provide a compelling example of misdiagnosis, in which a young deaf woman was initially assumed to have mental retardation on the basis of a low IQ. The examiner used language-loaded and speeded manipulation subtests, which interacted with the examinee's deafness and mild cerebral palsy to produce a low IQ. Later, the woman was reevaluated with motor- and language-reduced measures, and achieved an above-average IQ. Given the woman's postschool experiences (she earned undergraduate and graduate degrees, and was a career professional), the lower IQ was clearly an invalid estimate of her intellectual abilities.

Despite the potential for invalid estimation of intelligence, some recommend administering verbal subtests to deaf and hard-of-hearing examinees. Those who recommend this practice (e.g., Braden, 2000; Sullivan & Montoya, 1997) stress that verbal test scores are best interpreted as an index of prior incidental learning and language acquisition, rather than intelligence. Reasons for this recommendation include evidence that verbal scores are better predictors of academic achievement and occupational success in deaf and hard-of-hearing clients than language-reduced tests (e.g., Kelly & Braden, 1990) and therefore provide a better clinical index for estimating performance in educational, vocational, and social contexts. Additionally, Miller (1984) suggested alterations to verbal subtest administration that result in higher scores on verbal subtests for deaf and hard-of-hearing examinees, although it is not clear that the scores produced under this procedure are necessarily more valid than the lower scores produced under procedures more closely resembling standardized administration. Examiners must consider carefully whether the risk of misrepresentation of an examinee's intellectual ability justifies the additional information one might obtain from verbal subtests.

TRANSLATION OF ITEMS INTO ASL

Professional ethics (AERA, APA, NCME, 1999) and federal law (e.g., Individuals with Disabilities Education Act) require examiners to assess children in the child's primary mode of communication. For many deaf and hard-of-hearing children, the primary mode of communication is ASL or a pidgin combining elements of signed English and ASL. Although some examiners are fluent in sign systems, and it is increasingly possible for examiners to secure the services of certified sign language interpreters (see Registry of Interpreters for the Deaf, 2002), simply providing signed administration is not sufficient to ensure a valid and accurate test translation. Rather, interpretation of a test from a source language (e.g., English) to a target language (e.g., ASL) requires an extensive validation process. The steps in this process are the following:

1. Translate items from the source to the target language.
2. Use bilingual speakers "blind" to the original items to back-translate items from the target to the source language.
3. Validate the accuracy of blind back-translations by comparing source and translated versions; repeat steps 1 and 2 until all items are validated via blind back-translation.
4. Administer translated test to a small group of examinees whose native language is the target language (i.e., pilot study) to examine the psychometric properties of the translated test. If psychometric properties (e.g., reliability, validity estimates) are appropriate, proceed to the final step; if not, repeat steps 1–4 until pilot study data provide evidence of successful translation.
5. Conduct large-scale normative study and additional analyses to validate test use with individuals who are fluent in the target language.

Unfortunately, there are no translations of cognitive tests that have successfully implemented all five of the steps to produce a fully validated ASL translation. Fortunately, researchers have successfully completed steps 1 through 4 for ASL translations of the WISC-III (Maller, 1997; Maller & Braden, 1993) and the WAIS-III (Kostrubala & Braden, 1998). As of this writing, there are no currently validated ASL translations of the WISC-IV, although previous research on the Wechsler Scales suggests the Performance Scale subtests are fairly robust across a variety of translation variations (Braden, 1994; Spragins & Blennerhasset, 1998).

DEAF NORMS

Many experts (e.g., Vernon & Andrews, 1990) consider the availability of norms based on deaf and hard-of-hearing examinees to be ideal, and the inclusion of such examinees in the norm group to be necessary for validating a test for use with such examinees. Therefore, many examiners who work with deaf and hard-of-hearing clients welcomed the availability of norms for the WISC-R (Anderson & Sisco, 1977) and lament the lack of such norms for more recent versions of the Wechsler Scales (and other contemporary tests of intelligence).

However appealing the argument might appear, inclusion of deaf and hard-of-hearing examinees in normative samples, and the availability of deaf norms, are irrelevant to test validity. The validity of a test for a particular group rests not on norms or inclusion in the norm sample, but rather on evidence that the test has similar reliability and validity characteristics when used with a particular group (Maller, 2003). In fact, previous examinations of data available from deaf norms (Braden, 1985b) suggest use of such special norms is generally irrelevant (i.e., it produces trivial differences in scores relative to general norms), and may even attenuate clinically relevant data (Braden, 1985b, 1990). The lack of special norms for more recent versions of the Wechsler Scales renders this issue moot, but examiners should recall that the issue of inclusion in norm groups and availability of special norms cannot substitute for direct evidence of a test's reliability and validity in deaf and hard-of-hearing examinees.

DEMOGRAPHIC DIFFERENCES

Research on tests of intelligence using deaf and hard-of-hearing examinees yields a number of findings that examiners should consider when interpreting test scores. First, verbal subtest and composite scores are strongly correlated with the degree of hearing loss, whereas performance subtest and composite scores are not (Braden, 1994). Some researchers (e.g., Akamatsu, Musselman, & Zwiebel, 2000) believe the lack of relationship between degree of hearing loss and language-reduced IQs supports the argument that language-reduced IQs are more equitable, or fair, for representing intelligence in hearing-impaired examinees. Second, children attending residential schools tend to exhibit lower scores than those in mainstream or nonresidential school settings, although these differences are almost certainly due to selection bias rather than school setting effects on intelligence (Braden, Maller, & Paquin, 1993). Third, IQs vary by status of deaf relatives. Deaf children of deaf parents, and deaf children with at least one deaf sibling, have higher IQs than other deaf children—and may have higher IQs than normal-hearing peers (Akamatsu, Musselman, & Zwiebel, 2000; Braden, 1987, 1994). Finally, there are some studies of gender and ethnic group differences within deaf and hard-of-hearing samples. This research generally replicates findings in normal-hearing populations by showing small gender differences (Braden, 1994; Phelps & Ensor, 1987, 1989), although some small sample studies (e.g., Slate & Fawcett, 1996) show large gender differences. Because few studies using deaf and hard-of-hearing samples report IQ by ethnic group status, there are sufficient data only for comparisons between African-American and white groups. These comparisons are consistent with comparisons in the normal-hearing population; viz., children who are deaf or hard-of-hearing and African American exhibit nonverbal or Performance IQs approximately 1 standard deviation below white peers (Braden, 1994). Taken together, these findings suggest that demographic group differences (and similarities) found for normal-hearing populations are likely to be found in deaf or hard-of-hearing populations, but two unique demographic factors (i.e., degree of hearing loss and immediate family members who are also deaf or hard-of-hearing) emerge within studies of deaf and hard-of-hearing populations.

PERFORMANCE VS OTHER NONVERBAL TESTS

The available research suggests that deaf and hard-of-hearing children exhibit lower scores on nonverbal tests that reduce or eliminate manual dexterity than they exhibit on tests where motor manipulation is an important aspect of the test (Braden, 1994). For example, tests of figural matrices do not tap manual dexterity, because examinees can say or sign their response. In contrast, the Block Design subtest places significant demands on manual dexterity, because examinees must manipulate blocks to match the item stimulus. The limited evidence on this topic suggests that deaf and hard-of-hearing examinees score higher on tests emphasizing manual dexterity than on identical tests that eliminate manual dexterity (Braden, Kostrubala, & Reed, 1994), and the motor speed benefit is approximately 5 points, or 0.33 standard deviation units. The new tests (i.e., Picture Concepts and Matrix Reasoning) on the WISC-IV's Perceptual Reasoning Scale reduce or eliminate manual dexterity, and the changes in Block Design reduce the influence of speeded motor manipulation on the subtest score. Therefore, it is likely that deaf and hard-of-hearing children will have somewhat lower scores on the Perceptual Reasoning index than their historical average Performance IQs, although this speculation must be tested with evidence from samples of hard-of-hearing and deaf children.

UTILITY OF PROFILE ANALYSIS

The use of subtest scores and composites (i.e., profile analysis) to identify cognitive strengths and weaknesses within examinees has a long and well-researched tradition in the Wechsler Scales (e.g., Lichtenberger & Kaufman, 2004; Kaufman & Lichtenberger, 2000; Sattler, 2002). The new WISC-IV provides substantial guidance to help examinees identify reliable and unusual differences among WISC-IV composites and scores, and suggests that these differences reveal cognitive strengths and weaknesses, which in turn are useful for guiding educational and psychological interventions. However, profile interpretation has also been strongly criticized, in part because there is no direct evidence that the practice improves the selection, implementation, or outcome of interventions (e.g., Braden & Kratochwill, 1997; Reschly & Grimes, 2002).

Direct evidence of the utility of profile analysis for deaf or hard-of-hearing examinees is simply nonexistent, as is true for normal-hearing examinees. However, two forms of evidence suggest score differences within deaf or hard-of-hearing examinees may have meaning similar to score differences found in normal-hearing examinees. First, factor analytic research using previous versions of the Wechsler Performance Scales with deaf and hard-of-hearing examinees generally replicates the factor structure found in normal-hearing examinees (Braden, 1985a; Leutzinger, 2002; Maller & Ferron, 1997; Slate &

Fawcett, 1995; Sullivan & Montoya, 1997; Sullivan & Schulte, 1992). Furthermore, research on the WISC-III typically replicates the distinction between the Perceptual Organization and Processing Speed indexes, which the WISC-IV has now formally adopted as the recommended interpretive structure.

Second, studies of deaf or hard-of-hearing individuals who have learning problems show that those individuals often exhibit lower scores on the Coding subtest than on other Performance Scale subtests (Braden, 1990; Rush, 1989). Studies that do not specifically select examinees for learning problems show that deaf or hard-of-hearing examinees are likely to have lower scores on Processing Speed index subtests (i.e., Coding and Symbol Search) than other Performance Scale subtests (Leutzinger, 2002; Maller & Ferron, 1997), which is often explained as an outcome of the relatively higher proportion of deaf and hard-of-hearing examinees who have additional disabilities. Furthermore, Processing Speed subtest scores are related to measures of academic and social performance in deaf and hard-of-hearing examinees (Braden, 1990; Kelly & Braden, 1990; Stewart, 1981). Therefore, it is reasonable to expect that depressed scores on Processing Speed subtests for deaf or hard-of-hearing examinees may indicate relative cognitive weaknesses that influence academic and social performance, and therefore have some diagnostic utility.

USING THE WISC-IV WITH DEAF AND HARD-OF-HEARING EXAMINEES

The WISC-IV administration manual provides extensive information and recommendations to guide examiners who want to assess deaf or hard-of-hearing children with the WISC-IV (Hardy-Braz, 2003 in Wechsler, 2003, pp. 12–18). These suggestions are far more specific than those appearing in previous versions of the Wechsler Scales and include conditional recommendations for administering (or not administering) subtests and scales based on the examinee's preferred mode of communication. However, there are no data available in the WISC-IV materials (i.e., the administration manual, technical manual, or technical reports) providing information on reliability or validity of the WISC-IV with deaf or hard-of-hearing examinees. Consequently, recommendations in this chapter focus on those practices that have been found useful and have been supported by research on tests other than the WISC-IV. Examiners must recognize that all recommendations regarding the WISC-IV made in this chapter, and in the WISC-IV administration manual, are based on logical and subjective analyses, and not on direct evidence.

Figure 11.1 provides an overview of recommended steps for using the WISC-IV with deaf or hard-of-hearing examinees. Each of these recommendations is also elaborated in the following text.

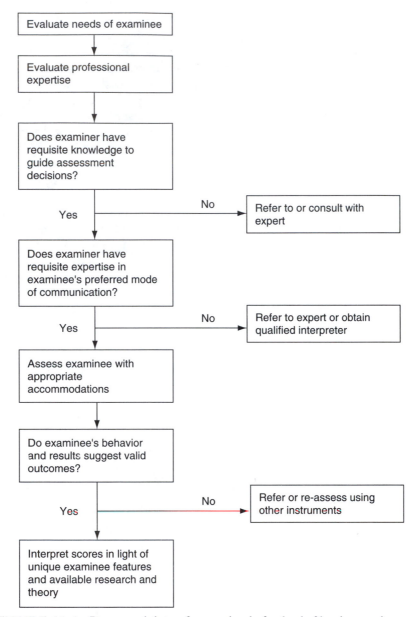

FIGURE 11.1   Recommended steps for assessing deaf or hard-of-hearing examinees.

STEP 1: EVALUATE THE NEEDS OF THE EXAMINEE

Examiners must fully understand the nature of the referral problem or question and the unique needs and characteristics of the examinee. Approximately one-third of children who are deaf or hard-of-hearing have add-itional disabilities (Gallaudet Research Institute, 2002), so examiners must thoroughly examine the child's available records, interview knowledgeable adults (e.g., teacher, parent), and consult other professionals with knowledge of the child's medical, audiological, and communication/language history to fully understand the child's needs before initiating psychological assessment.

STEP 2: EVALUATE PROFESSIONAL EXPERTISE

Ethical principles and recognized best practices in assessment dictate that the needs of the examinee, not the examiner's abilities and resources, deter-mine assessment procedures. Therefore, examiners must be candid, object-ive, and professional when appraising their knowledge and skills. As Kamphaus (2001) has argued, one may have technical expertise to adminis-ter assessments, but lack the in-depth knowledge needed to guide assessment decisions and interpretation of results. Examiners should have graduate study, supervised clinical practice, and consistent and ongoing familiarity with research on deaf and hard-of-hearing populations before assuming appropriate expertise.

STEP 3: DOES THE EXAMINER HAVE THE NECESSARY EXPERTISE?

Although there may be substantial pressure for an examiner to conduct an assessment, it is imperative that examiners make the decision about expertise based on the needs of the client and not on other considerations (e.g., needs of the referring agency). When examiners decide they do not have the necessary expertise, the best option for proceeding is to refer the client to an examiner with appropriate expertise. Resources serving deaf and hard-of-hearing children are listed annually in the April edition of the *American Annals of the Deaf*, and most states have experts within the state departments of education or vocational rehabilitation, and/or in residential schools serving deaf children who can be enlisted as resources. When pay-ment for services is an issue, examiners should explore exchange of services (e.g., asking a psychologist with expertise in a nearby school district to conduct the assessment in exchange for accepting one of their referrals), so that resource availability does not constrain appropriate assessment. Table 11.2 lists some on-line resources that examiners can use to obtain relevant research, information, and resources relevant to the needs of deaf and hard-of-hearing clients.

Examiners who have expertise, or who solicit expert consultation, should use their knowledge to plan the assessment. Examiners should not adopt a standard assessment routine or battery of tests; rather, examiners must select assessments based on the needs of the particular client and referral problem.

TABLE 11.2   On-line Resources Related to Deaf and Hard-of-Hearing Children

Resource	URL
Alexander Graham Bell Association (organization supporting oral/aural communication)	*http://www.agbell.org/*
American Annals of the Deaf	*http://gupress.gallaudet.edu/annals/*
American Deafness and Rehabilitation Association (ADARA; organization of professional mental health workers serving deaf and hard-of-hearing adults)	*http://www.adara.org/*
American Psychological Association Division 22: Rehabilitation Psychology	*http://www.apa.org/divisions/div22/*
American Society for Deaf Children (organization to support parents of deaf and hard-of-hearing children)	*http://www.deafchildren.org/*
Cochlear Implant Association (information about cochlear implants)	*http://www.cici.org/*
CODA International (support organization for children of deaf adults)	*http://www.coda-international.org/*
Council of American Instructors of the Deaf (educational organization embracing a range of communication modalities)	*http://www.caid.org*
Directory of National Organizations of and for Deaf and Hard of Hearing People (from the Laurent Clerc Center at Gallaudet University)	*http://clerccenter.gallaudet.edu/infotogo/ 184.html*
Gallaudet Research Institute (Research & publications on deaf and hard-of-hearing people in the United States)	*http://gri.gallaudet.edu/*
Gallaudet University (world's only liberal arts university for deaf people)	*http://www.gallaudet.edu/*
Journal of Deaf Studies	*http://deafed.oupjournals.org/*
National Association of School Psychologists Special Interest Group on Deafness (open only to NASP members)	*http://www.naspweb.org/ Members_Only_Test/deaf.asp*
National Association of the Deaf (social and fraternal organization representing Deaf people in North America)	*http://www.nad.org*
National Cued Speech Association (information and advocacy for cued speech)	*http://www.cuedspeech.org/*
National Technical Institute for the Deaf	*http://www.ntid.rit.edu/*

(Continues)

TABLE 11.2 *(Continued)*

NTID Research Projects	*http://www.rit.edu/~468www/ projectbytopic.php3*
Registry of Interpreters for the Deaf (interpreter resources, on-line directory)	*http://www.rid.org*
SHHH (Self Help for Hard of Hearing People; information and advocacy group)	*http://www.shhh.org/*
Standards of Care for the Delivery of Mental Health Services to Deaf and Hard of Hearing Persons	*http://deafness.dfmc.org/resources/ MHStandards/*
Volta Review	*http://www.agbell.org/periodicals.cfm*

In many cases, estimates of intellectual ability are unnecessary (e.g., routine triennial reevaluations, explorations of appropriate placement or setting, evaluating response to instruction or placement). When examiners decide that intellectual assessment is appropriate, they must then consider which domains or cognitive processes they want to assess. Historically, most clinicians have not carefully considered which cognitive processes should be included in the assessment, in part because the field did not clearly define the nature and structure of cognitive abilities, and in part because general intellectual ability is sufficiently robust to be estimated with reasonable accuracy despite substantial variations in test content (Braden, 2003).

Recent scientific advances, however, now provide examiners with substantially more direction and consensus regarding the nature and structure of cognitive abilities. Experts (e.g., Carroll, 1993; McGrew & Flanagan, 1998) generally agree on a hierarchical model of cognitive abilities organized according to three strata (i.e., general intelligence, second-order abilities, and narrow, specific abilities). Developers of the WISC-IV used this hierarchical model of abilities to guide revisions in the WISC-IV. Full Scale IQ is intended to reflect general intellectual ability, and the four WISC-IV Indexes are intended to reflect second-order abilities consistent with the hierarchical model. Therefore, examiners must consider which abilities they wish to include in the assessment and how to interpret scores intended to reflect those abilities, prior to initiating the assessment. Examiners must have strong working knowledge of contemporary research and theories regarding intellectual abilities and assessments, familiarity with a wide variety of nonverbal assessment approaches (e.g., McCallum, 2003; McCallum, Bracken, & Wasserman, 2001), and the ability to combine nonverbal tools to assess diverse cognitive abilities (Wilhoit & McCallum, 2003).

Based on available research and practice, most examiners will decide to administer Perceptual Reasoning subtests to deaf and hard-of-hearing examinees, and use the index (PRI) to reflect general intellectual ability. When examiners know that a child may have impaired motor coordination, they should decide in advance of the assessment to substitute Picture Completion for Block Design in calculation of the PRI. Additionally, examiners should consider administering Working Memory and Processing Speed scale subtests, and use indexes from these scales to reflect cognitive abilities that may be relevant to academic and social performance.

Except in situations where the examiner feels that the examinee has had adequate opportunity to acquire English knowledge and language, examiners should not use Verbal Comprehension subtests to estimate intelligence, either alone or in combination to produce Full Scale IQs. However, examiners may decide to administer Verbal Comprehension subtests as estimates of prior learning and performance on English-language tasks. Examiners may do so only if they determine that the benefits of this information outweigh the potential for misunderstanding and misdiagnosis. Examiners should also consult the recommendations in the WISC-IV administration manual (pp. 12-18) to guide subtest selection, administration, and interpretation. Examiners should decide which portions of the WISC-IV to administer (and delete) in advance of the assessment, and their decisions should be based on their general knowledge of deafness, psychology, and assessment, as well as their specific knowledge of the examinee's unique characteristics and context.

STEP 4: DOES THE EXAMINER HAVE THE NECESSARY COMMUNICATION SKILLS?

Whenever possible, the examiner should have the expertise to communicate directly with the examinee, rather than rely on an interpreter (Myers, 1995; National Association of the Deaf, 2003). Again, examiners who lack sufficient fluency for reliable and clear communication with deaf or hard-of-hearing examinees should refer to examiners who have such expertise. However, when examiners have sufficient knowledge, but do not have the requisite communication fluency, they may obtain interpreters. It is widely assumed that careful use of interpreters preserves the validity of psychological assessments (Freeman, 1989; Kluwin, 1994). Research addressing the issue is limited, but the available data support the validity of Wechsler Scale test administration conducted via signing interpreters (Sullivan, 1982). However, examiners must have sufficient background knowledge to guide the assessment; interpreters do not have the knowledge needed to guide assessment decisions, the assessment process, or the interpretation of results. Rather, their expertise is technical, and limited to facilitating communication between the examinee and the examiner.

Examiners must also be extremely vigilant to ensure that the interpreter has adequate skills for interpreting psychological assessments. More than half of all individuals employed by public schools as classroom interpreters perform below even minimally adequate levels (Kluwin, 1994; Schick,

Williams, & Bolster, 1999). Interpreters should hold a Comprehensive Skills Certificate from the Registry of Interpreters for the Deaf (see Table 11.2 for information on how to locate a certified sign language interpreter). Even expert interpreters must meet with the examiner before the assessment session so that the examiner can explain the nature and content of the test, the importance of adhering to standardized administration, and identify any potential problems in the assessment (Kostrubala, 1996 in Ford & Braden, 1996).

STEP 5: ASSESS EXAMINEE WITH APPROPRIATE ACCOMMODATIONS

Once examiners have determined what they want to assess and how they want to assess it, and have secured effective communication with the examinee, they must select and execute the assessment using appropriate accommodations. Careful consideration should be given to the range of accommodations in Table 11.1, throughout this chapter, and in other resources (e.g., Braden, 2000, 2003; Brauer, Braden, Pollard, & Hardy-Braz, 1998; Hardy-Braz & Sattler, 2002). Examiners should carefully distinguish between access skills, which are necessary for the assessment but irrelevant to the construct assessed, and target skills, which the examiner wants to assess (see Braden & Elliott, 2003). Changes in the assessment that address access skills, but leave target skills intact, are recommended. However, final accommodation decisions must adapt general guidelines to meet the examinee's unique characteristics. General recommendations cannot be applied across subtests (e.g., extra time on the Matrix Reasoning subtest is valid, but extra time on Processing Speed subtests is invalid) nor examinees (e.g., some examinees need extra time to organize motor responses, whereas others might experience increased anxiety and fatigue).

STEP 6: CONSIDER THE VALIDITY OF THE ASSESSMENT

Examinee behavior that is unusual or unexpected may suggest invalid results. Examiners must always consider whether they developed adequate rapport with the examinee, that is, whether the examinee understood the test demands, exhibited appropriate effort on tasks, and the like. Although examinees who are hard-of-hearing or deaf are much like other examinees, examiners may not have sufficient experience with these populations to understand what is and is not normative behavior. Consultation with the interpreter (if one is used), the child's teacher and parents and individuals with expertise in deafness and hearing loss can help the examiner appropriately interpret behaviors to judge whether the assessment rapport was sufficient to produce valid results.

Additionally, examiners should review assessment results for unusual or unexpected outcomes. When comparing scores, differences should be statistically reliable and unusual (i.e., occur rarely). The WISC-IV administration and technical manuals provide substantial documentation and guidance in regard to how examiners should make these judgments. Unusual differences between scores do not, in and of themselves, invalidate a composite based on scores that are different. In other words, just because a score is lower than others is not evidence that the low score is invalid. Likewise, unusually high scores are not necessarily more or less valid than lower scores. However, examiners should consider whether unusual and reliable differences indicate a problem with test validity. If they decide that a previously unknown aspect of the examinee might interact with the assessment situation to produce an invalid score, they should *not* simply eliminate the score from a composite or substitute another subtest score when calculating the composite. Rather, the examiner should conduct additional assessment to evaluate the hypothesis that the score is not representative (see Flanagan & Ortiz, 2002). Unusual scores are not necessarily more or less valid than other scores, and post hoc hypotheses must always be evaluated for accuracy (Kamphaus, 2001).

STEP 7: INTERPRET SCORES

When examiners judge that test results are valid, they can then interpret examinee results in light of available theory and research and the unique circumstances of the examinee and assessment. The most common, and best validated, use of WISC-IV scores is rendering psychoeducational diagnoses. If the examiner decided to use the PRI as the best estimate of the examinee's general intellectual ability in Step 3, and found no reason to change this decision in steps 5 and 6, then the examiner should use the PRI to substitute for FSIQ in diagnoses of mental retardation and giftedness. Furthermore, WMI and PSI composites may be useful in identifying deficits in cognitive processes that may influence learning and behavior. Given past research, and the available research on the WISC-IV, examiners should generally interpret scores on these instruments as they would for other examinees.

Two important issues are unique to deaf and hard-of-hearing examinees and therefore merit further consideration. The first is interpretation of the Verbal Comprehension index (VCI). Except for examinees recently deafened, interpretation of the VCI must be tempered by the strong possibility that the examinee has not had adequate access to English, and therefore may score low not because of intellectual deficits, but because of experiential deficits. Therefore, VCIs should be characterized as indicators of incidental learning, which reflect multiple influences (e.g., intelligence, hearing loss, opportunities to learn in home and school settings).

The second issue is deciding whether the examinee's academic performance is consistent with estimates of the examinee's intellectual abilities.

This judgment is essential for identifying learning disabilities, because learning disability diagnoses currently imply or require evidence that academic progress is delayed relative to the level expected for the examinee's intelligence. Because hearing loss typically lowers academic achievement (and VCI) scores, examiners must adjust the examinee's academic achievement level to reflect expectations associated with other hard-of-hearing or deaf children. I recommend that examiners use age-based percentiles drawn from deaf norms on the Stanford Achievement Test—9th edition as general indicators of what is typical for deaf and hard-of-hearing children, rather than the results of individually administered tests of achievement. Although there are problems with this recommendation (i.e., the use of group-administered tests, reliance on ordinal percentiles rather than interval-level standard scores), use of other achievement measures is generally not helpful because there is no direct and meaningful way to determine whether a score is typical or atypical for deaf and hard-of-hearing children. This is one instance in which special (i.e., "deaf") norms are advantageous for diagnosis, as they help the examiner determine expected levels of achievement relative to other deaf and hard-of-hearing children (see Braden, Wollack, & Allen, 1995; cf Kishor, 1995a, 1995b, for a discussion of this issue). In instances in which the examinee has unexpectedly low achievement scores, even after adjusting for hearing loss and regression influences, examiners should explore whether these unexpectedly low scores may be due to a lack of appropriate instruction, a specific cognitive deficit that influences learning, or a related disability (e.g., language processing or attention deficit disorder). Although diagnosis of disabilities in addition to hearing loss is not necessary to justify additional educational services (i.e., educational placement and services are not disability-specific), it may be helpful to inform parents, educators, the examinee, and other stakeholders of issues that may influence academic, social, and vocational progress.

At this time, the use of WISC-IV subtest and composite scores for uses beyond diagnosis or suggesting possible related conditions is not justified by the available research. Lower scores on subtests included in or similar to the Working Memory and Processing Speed scales have been associated with learning problems in children who are deaf and hard-of-hearing, but correlation cannot imply causation. Lower scores may indicate less-developed cognitive processes, untreated or related conditions (e.g., attention deficit disorder), or a lack of learning opportunities (e.g., delayed exposure to writing, the alphabet, and numerals may influence performance on tests independent of cognitive abilities). Examiners should be cautious in interpreting low scores as evidence of deficits in psychological processes until and unless they can plausibly rule out other competing explanations, and provide evidence of deficits in addition to test scores. There is no evidence to justify specific educational or psychological interventions on the basis of WISC-IV profile analysis. Furthermore, the neuropsychological interpretations of test scores provided in WISC-IV materials should be cautiously applied to deaf and hard-of-hearing examinees, because experiential, auditory, and language differences may be more plausible explanations of outcomes than (unusual) neuropsychological processes. Examiners should consider consultation with experts familiar with the intellectual assessment of deaf and hard-of-hearing children before drawing strong conclusions regarding unusual score variations.

CONCLUSIONS

The Wechsler Scales have a long and well-researched tradition in the assessment of intelligence in deaf and hard-of-hearing children. Unfortunately, the WISC-IV has yet to be systematically studied to evaluate its performance with deaf and hard-of-hearing children. Given the stability and robustness of previous research results, it is likely that future research will support the recommendations and interpretations in this chapter. However, speculation is a poor substitute for data. Therefore, the recommendations and interpretations offered here are considered provisional until data are available to confirm them. Examiners must consult the available research subsequent to the publication of this chapter to judge for themselves the validity of the WISC-IV with deaf and hard-of-hearing children.

REFERENCES

Akamatsu, C. T., Musselman, C., & Zwiebel, A. (2000). Nature versus nurture in the development of cognition in deaf people. In P. E. Spencer, C. J. Erting, & M. Marschark (Eds.), *The deaf child in the family and at school: Essays in honor of Kathryn P. Meadow-Orlans* (pp. 255–274). Mahwah, NJ: Lawrence Erlbaum.

Alade, E. B. (1992). Determining intelligence quotients of Nigerian deaf children with the Wechsler Intelligence Scale for Children, Revised. *Early Child Development and Care, 80*, 103–107.

American Educational Research Association, American Psychological Association, & National Council on Measurement in Education. (1999). *Standards for educational and psychological testing* (3rd ed.). Washington, DC: American Educational Research Association.

American Psychological Association. (2002). *Ethnical principles of psychologists and code of conduct*. Washington, DC: Author. Available: *http://www.apa.org/ethics/*.

Anderson, R. J., & Sisco, F. H. (1977). Standardization of the WISC-R Performance Scale for deaf children. Series T, No. 1, Office of Demographic Studies, Gallaudet College. Available from ERIC Document No. ED150801. Washington, DC: Gallaudet College.

Braden, J. P. (1985a). The structure of nonverbal intelligence in deaf and hearing subjects. *American Annals of the Deaf, 131*, 496–501.

Braden, J. P. (1985b). WISC R deaf norms reconsidered. *Journal of School Psychology, 23*, 375 382.

Braden, J. P. (1987). An explanation of the superior Performance IQs of deaf children of deaf parents. *American Annals of the Deaf, 132*, 263–266.

Braden, J. P. (1990). Do deaf persons have a characteristic psychometric profile on the Wechsler Performance Scales? *Journal of Psychoeducational Assessment, 8,* 518–526.

Braden, J. P. (1994). *Deafness, deprivation, and IQ.* New York: Plenum.

Braden, J. P. (2000). Deafness and hearing loss. In A. E. Kazdin (Ed.), *Encyclopedia of psychology* (vol. 2) (pp. 441–444). Washington, DC/Oxford: American Psychological Association/Oxford University Press.

Braden, J. P. (2003). Accommodating clients with disabilities on the WAIS-III/WMS. In D. Saklofske & D. Tulsky (Eds.), *Use of the WAIS-III/WMS in clinical practice* (pp. 451–486). New York: Houghton Mifflin.

Braden, J. P. & Athanasiou, M. S. (in press). A comparative review of nonverbal measures of intelligence. In D. P. Flangan and P. A. Harrison (Eds.) *Contemporary intellectual assessment: Theories, tests, and issues* (2nd ed.). New York: Guilford.

Braden, J. P., & Elliott, S. N. (2003). Accommodations on the Stanford-Binet Intelligence Scales (5th ed.). In G. Roid, *Interpretive manual for the Stanford-Binet* (5th ed.). *Intelligence Scales* (pp. 135–143). Itasca, IL: Riverside.

Braden, J. P., Kostrubala, C., & Reed, J. (1994). Why do deaf children score differently on performance v. motor-reduced nonverbal intelligence tests? *Journal of Psychoeducational Assessment, 12,* 357–363.

Braden, J. P., & Hannah, J. M. (1998). Assessment of hearing impaired and deaf children with the WISC-III. In D. Saklofske & A. Prifiter (Eds.), *Use of the WISC-III in clinical practice* (pp. 175–201). Boston: Houghton Mifflin.

Braden, J. P., & Kratochwill, T. R. (1997). Treatment utility of assessment: Myths and realities. *School Psychology Review, 26*(3), 475–485.

Braden, J. P., Maller, S. J., & Paquin, M. M. (1993). The effects of residential versus day placement on the Performance IQs of children with hearing impairment. *Journal of Special Education, 26,* 423–433.

Braden, J. P., Wollack, J. A., & Allen, T. E. (1995). Reply to Kishor: Choosing the right metric. *Journal of Psychoeducational Assessment, 13*(3), 250–265

Brauer, B. A., Braden, J. P., Pollard, R. Q., & Hardy-Braz, S. T. (1998). Deaf and hard of hearing people. In J. Sandoval, C. L. Frisby, K. F. Geisinger, J. Dowd Scheuneman, & J. Ramos Grenier (Eds.), *Test interpretation and diversity: Achieving equity in assessment* (pp. 297–315). Washington, DC: American Psychological Association.

Carroll, J. B. (1993). *Human cognitive abilities: A survey of factor-analytic studies.* New York: Cambridge University Press.

Elliott. S. N., Braden, J. P., & White, J. L. (2001). *Assessing one and all: Educational accountability for students with disabilities.* Reston, VA: Council for Exceptional Children.

Flanagan, D. P., & Ortiz, S. O. (2002). Best practices in intellectual assessment: Future directions. In A. Thomas & J. P. Grimes (Eds.). *Best practices in school psychology* (4th ed.) (pp. 1351–1372). Bethesdsa, MD: National Association of School Psychologists.

Ford, L. & Braden, J. P. (1996, Aug.). Equitable psychological assessment for language-minority learners: Theory, research, and practice. Symposium presented at the Annual Meeting of the American Psychological Association, Toronto, Canada.

Freeman, S. T. (1989). Cultural and linguistic bias in mental health evaluations of deaf people. *Rehabilitation Psychology, 34*(1), 51–63.

Gallaudet Research Institute (2002). *2001–2002 regional and national survey.* Washington, DC: Author. Available: *http://gri.gallaudet.edu/Demographics/.*

Gustason, G., & Zawolkow, E. (1993). *Signing exact English.* Rossmoor, CA: Modern Signs Press.

Hardy-Braz, S., & Sattler, J. M. (2002). Hearing Impairments. In J. M. Sattler, *Assessment of children: Behavioral and clinical applications* (pp. 377–389). San Diego, CA: Author.

Hunt, H. L. (1998). Assessing intelligence in deaf children: Is the Verbal Scale of the WISC-III valid? *Dissertation Abstracts International, 59(1),* 456B.

Jenkinson, J. (1989). Use of the WISC-R Performance Scale with hearing-impaired children: A review. *Psychological Test Bulletin, 2*(1), 33-38.

Kamphaus, R. W. (2001). *Clinical assessment of child and adolescent intelligence.* Boston: Allyn & Bacon.

Kaufman, A. S., & Lichtenberger, E. O. (2000). *Essentials of WISC-III and WPPSI-R assessment.* New York: Wiley.

Kelly, M., & Braden, J. P. (1990). Criterion-related validity of the WISC-R Performance Scale with the Stanford Achievement Test-Hearing Impaired Edition. *Journal of School Psychology, 28,* 147–151.

Kishor, N. (1995a). Evaluating predictive validity: A rejoinder to Braden *et al.* (1995). *Journal of Psychoeducational Assessment, 13*(3), 266–270.

Kishor, N. (1995b). Evaluating predictive validity by using different scales of the Stanford Achievement Test for the Hearing Impaired. *Journal of Psychoeducational Assessment, 13*(3), 241–249.

Kluwin, T. N. (1994). Interpreting services for youngsters who are deaf in local public school programs. *Journal of the American Deafness and Rehabilitation Association, 28(2),* 21–29.

Kostrubala, C. E., & Braden, J. P. (1998). *Administration of the WAIS-III in American Sign Language* [videotape]. San Antonio, TX: The Psychological Corporation.

Leutzinger, M. R. (2002). Use of the WAIS-III performance scale with deaf adults. *Dissertation Abstracts International, 63*(2), 1036B.

Lichtenberger, E. O., & Kaufman, A. S. (2004). *Essentials of WPPSI-III assessment.* Hoboken, NJ: Wiley.

Liddell, S. K. (2003). *Grammar, gesture, and meaning in American Sign Language.* Cambridge: Cambridge University Press.

Maller, S. J. (1997). Deafness and WISC-III item difficulty: Invariance and fit. *Journal of School Psychology, 35(3),* 299–314.

Maller, S. J. (2003). Best practices in detecting bias in nonverbal tests. In R. S. McCallum (Ed.), *Handbook of nonverbal assessment* (pp. 23–62). New York: Kluwer/Plenum.

Maller, S. J., & Braden, J. P. (1993). The construct and criterion-related validity of the WISC-III with deaf adolescents. *Journal of Psychoeducational Assessment,* Monograph Series: WISC-III, 104–113.

Maller, S. J., & Ferron, J. (1997). WISC-III factor invariance across deaf and standardization samples. *Educational and Psychological Measurement, 57(6),* 987–994.

McCallum, R. S. (2003). (Ed.), *Handbook of nonverbal assessment.* New York: Kluwer/Plenum.

McCallum, R. S., Bracken, B. A., & Wasserman, J. D. (2001). *Essentials of nonverbal assessment.* New York: Wiley.

McGrew, K. S., & Flanagan, D. P. (1998). *The intelligence test desk reference (ITDR): Gf-Gc cross-battery assessment.* Boston: Allyn and Bacon.

Meng, X., & Gong, Y. (1995). A comparative study on intelligence between deaf and hearing children. *Chinese Journal of Clinical Psychology, 3(3),* 137–139, 146.

Messick, S. (1995). Validity of psychological assessment: Validation of inferences from persons' responses and performances as scientific inquiry into score meaning. *American Psychologist, 50(9),* 741–749.

Miller, M. S. (1984). *Experimental use of signed presentations of the Verbal Scale of the WISC-R with profoundly deaf children: A preliminary report of the sign selection process and experimental test procedures.* Paper presented at the International Symposium on Cognition, Education, and Deafness, Washington, DC (ERIC Document Reproduction Service No. ED 170 082).

Myers, R. R. (Ed.). (1995). *Standards of care for the delivery of mental health services to deaf and hard of hearing people.* Silver Spring: National Association of the Deaf. Available: *http://deafness.dfmc.org/resources/MHStandards/index_zips.htm.*

National Association of the Deaf. (2003). *NAD position statement on mental health services for people who are deaf and hard of hearing.* Silver Spring, MD: Author. Available: *http:// www.nad.org/infocenter/newsroom/positions/mentalhealth.html.*

National Center for Health and Statistics (1994). *National interview survey* (Series 10, No. 188). Washington, DC: Author.

Office of Civil Rights. (2000). *The use of tests as part of high-stakes decision-making for students: A resource guide for educators and policy makers.* Washington, DC: U.S. Department of Education (author). Available: *http://www.ed.gov/offices/OCR/archives/testing/index1.html.*

Phelps, L, & Ensor, A. (1987). The comparison of performance by sex of deaf children on the WISC-R. *Psychology in the Schools, 24(3),* 209–214.

Phelps, L., & Ensor, A. (1989). Gender differences on the WAIS-R Performance Scale with young deaf adults. *Journal of the American Deafness and Rehabilitation Association, 22*(3), 48–52.

Phillips, S. E. (1993). Testing condition accommodations for disabled students. *West's Education Law Quarterly, 2(2),* 366–389.

Phillips, S. E. (1996). Legal defensibility of standards: Issues and policy perspectives. *Educational Measurement: Issues and Practice, 15(2),* 5–19.

Registry of Interpreters for the Deaf. (2002). *Registry of Interpreters for the Deaf Membership Directory 2002.* Alexandria, VA: Author. Registry also available at *http://www.rid.org.*

Reschly, D. J., & Grimes, J. P. (2002). Best practices in intellectual assessment. In A. Thomas & J. P. Grimes (Eds.), *Best practices in school psychology* (4th ed.) (vol. 2) (pp. 1337–1350). Silver Spring, MD: National Association of School Psychologists.

Rush, P. (1989). WAIS-R Verbal and Performance profiles of adolescents referred for atypical learning styles. In D. S. Martin (Ed.), *International symposium on cognition, education, and deafness: Trends in research and instruction.* ERIC Document Reproduction Service ED313840. Washington, DC: Gallaudet University.

Saraev, S. Y., & Kozlov, V. P. (1991). Age-related dynamics of mental functions in 7-to-12 year old deaf children (based on psychological data). *Defektologiya, 1,* 43–48.

Sattler, J. M. (2002). *Assessment of children* (4th ed.). La Mesa, CA: Author.

Sattler, J. M., & Hardy-Braz, S. T. (2002). Hearing impairments. In J. M. Sattler (Ed.), *Assessment of children* (4th ed.) (pp. 377–389). La Mesa, CA: Jerome M. Sattler.

Schick, B., Williams, K., & Bolster, L. (1999). Skill levels of educational interpreters working in public schools. *Journal of Deaf Studies and Deaf Education, 4(2),* 144–155.

Slate, J. R., & Fawcett, J. (1995). Validity of the WISC-III for deaf and hard of hearing persons. *American Annals of the Deaf, 140(3),* 250–254.

Slate, J. R., & Fawcett, J. (1996). Gender differences in Wechsler Performance scores of school-age children who are deaf or hard of hearing. *American Annals of the Deaf, 141(1),* 19–23.

Spragins, A. B., & Blennerhasset, L. (1998). *Reviews of assessment instruments used with deaf and hard of hearing students 1998 update.* Washington, DC: Gallaudet Research Institute. Available: *http://gri.gallaudet.edu/~catraxle/reviews.html.*

Stewart, D. A., & Luetke-Stahlman, B. (1998). *The signing family: What every parent should know about sign communication.* Washington, DC: Gallaudet University Press.

Stewart, J. H. (1981). Wechsler Performance IQ Scores and social behaviors of hearing-impaired students. *Volta Review, 83(4),* 215–222.

Sullivan, P. M. (1982). Administration modifications on the WISC-R Performance Scale with different categories of deaf children. *American Annals of the Deaf, 127,* 780–788.

Sullivan, P. M., & Montoya, L. A. (1997). Factor analysis of the WISC-III with deaf and hard-of-hearing children. *Psychological Assessment, 9(3),* 317–312.

Sullivan, P. M., & Schulte, L. E. (1992). Factor analysis of WISC-R with deaf and hard-of-hearing children. *Psychological Assessment, 4(4),* 537–540.

Thurlow, M. L., Elliott, J. L., & Ysseldyke, J. E. (1998). *Testing students with disabilities: Practical strategies for complying with district and state requirements.* Thousand Oaks, CA: Corwin Press.

United States Department of Education (2002). *24th annual report to Congress on the implementation of the Individuals with Disabilities Education Act.* Washington, DC: Author. Available: *http://www.ed.gov/about/reports/annual/osep/2002/.*

Vernon, M., & Andrews, J. F. (1990). *The psychology of deafness: Understanding deaf and hard-of-hearing people.* New York: Longman.

Wechsler, D. (2003). *Wechsler Intelligence Scale for Children* (4th ed.) (pp. 12–18). San Antonio, TX: The Psychological Corporation.

Wilhoit, B. E., & McCallum, R. S. (2003). Cross-battery assessment of nonverbal cognitive ability. In R. S. McCallum (Ed.), *Handbook of nonverbal assessment* (pp. 63–86). New York: Kluwer/Plenum.

CASE STUDY ILLUSTRATION

This case study illustrates the application of recommended practices for the WISC-IV in the assessment of a deaf examinee. Assessment data were abbreviated to match format constraints in the chapter, but the gist of the case study illustrates key principles of the assessment (e.g., a priori selection of composites for interpretation, exploration, and accommodation of the examinee's communication primary modality). The psychologist conducting the assessment is fluent in ASL and sign pidgin, can hear normally, and holds a degree from Gallaudet University's School Psychology Program, which specializes in deafness. Therefore, the psychologist met the prerequisite for appropriate expertise to conduct the assessment. All names are fictitious, and the report combines elements from at least two different clients for confidentiality and pedagogical reasons.

PSYCHOLOGICAL CASE REPORT

Name: Rusty B.   **Gender**: Male

Test Date: 4 Oct., 2003   **Ethnicity**: European/white

Birth Date: 23 Nov., 1991   **School**: Anderson Elementary

Test Age: 11 years, 10 mo., 11 days   **Parents**: Daniel & Rachel B.

Reason for Assessment: Rusty was tested to determine whether cognitive delays might be contributing to his lack of progress in his current educational program.

Background: Rusty lives with his parents and younger sister (Misty), as he has done since birth. He was diagnosed with a profound, bilateral sensorineural hearing impairment at age 20 months, although his parents had suspected hearing loss much earlier. Rusty's nonlinguistic developmental milestones have been typical, but his language development has been delayed and slow, as is typical of children with his hearing loss.

Rusty's mother reported that he received a hearing aid and was enrolled in speech training immediately following diagnosis of his hearing impairment. Ms. B. has worked with speech therapists, educators, and Rusty to implement oral/aural speech training. However, she reports that Rusty has become increasingly frustrated with his hearing aid and his speech training, and occasionally refuses to wear his aid or work with her and others on speech training. She admitted that she occasionally uses home signs and writing to communicate with Rusty, although Rusty's teachers and speech therapist have warned her to use speech exclusively. She confided that she wondered whether Rusty would benefit from sign language instruction, despite the concerns of Rusty's teacher, and speculated that improved communication might reduce occasional episodes of frustration between Rusty and others (including family members and teachers).

Educational records and contact with Rusty's teachers indicated that Rusty and his mother have been actively and consistently involved in his schooling since Rusty was a toddler. Rusty gets along well with other children, and, except for occasional episodes when he resists wearing his hearing aids and participating in speech, is cooperative and motivated. However, previous educational tests suggest limited academic progress, and reports of Rusty's speech skills were mixed. Whereas teacher descriptions and other narrative reports suggested strong progress, Ms. B. reported that she could understand only some of his speech, and others (even in the family) had very little ability to understand his speech. Rusty's teacher also noted that Rusty generally spends less time learning subject matter domains (e.g., reading, writing, mathematics) than he does in oral/aural training.

Previous Assessment Data: The most recent data from Rusty's IEP show Stanford Achievement Test—9th Edition scores in the beginning first grade range for Reading, Mathematics, Language, and Science. These scores are extremely low (below the 5th percentile) relative to normal-hearing and hearing-impaired children of the same age. Previous test data and teacher records are consistent with these findings. Rusty had a psychoeducational assessment in April, 2001. Records indicate the psychologist administered the WISC-III via speech supplemented with gestures, but had some difficulties understanding Rusty's replies. Rusty's Verbal IQ was 62, his Performance IQ was 80, and his Full Scale IQ was 72. Given the limited communication, the psychologist was reluctant to accept the scores as valid indicators of Rusty's intellectual abilities.

Current Assessment Instruments and Procedures: I administered the Wechsler Intelligence Scale for Children—4th Ed. (WISC-IV), curriculum-based reading probes, and the Social Skills Rating Scale (given to parent and teacher) to survey intellectual, academic achievement, and social adjustment functions. Before the assessment, I decided to use the Perceptual Reasoning index to estimate Rusty's general intellectual ability, to use the Working Memory and Processing Speed indexes as indicators of psychological processes, and to consider his Verbal Comprehension index as an indicator of prior learning rather than intellectual ability. I also used observations, interviews, and record reviews to supplement data collection.

Behavioral Observations: Rusty greeted me with a smile, which quickly became an expression of shock as I spoke and signed to him. He looked about to see if others were watching, and hesitantly asked me in speech and sign "OK sign?" I nodded, and asked him if he would prefer to use sign, speech, or both. He signed "both," but relied on signs, using his voice only sporadically during the rest of the session. I asked him where he learned signs, and, after making me promise he would not be punished, he explained that he learned signs from his friends and that they used signs to communicate except when they were monitored by adults. His speech was unintelligible to me, and his sign proficiency, although better than his speech, was limited relative to peers who use sign at school and home. When we began testing, Rusty attended to my directions, quickly began items when I indicated he should do so, worked diligently, and indicated appropriate involvement with the test demands. I interpreted his behavior as indicative of good rapport, and I believe the scores obtained are valid.

Results: Rusty's WISC-IV scores suggest his intellectual ability is within the Average range. His Perceptual Reasoning index (PRI) of 96 exceeds 39% of normal-hearing children of the same age, and his true score is likely (95% chance) to fall between 90 and 103. Although his Processing Speed Index (84) is lower than his PRI, differences of this magnitude are common (i.e., more than 40% of the norm sample has a 12-point difference). In contrast, Rusty's Working Memory index (70) and his Verbal Comprehension index (66) are lower than his PRI, and these differences are uncommon, occurring in less than 10% of the population. Although subtest scores within each index varied somewhat, the variation was within the normative range, supporting the accuracy of the index values. After administration of the WISC-IV, I administered some additional items resembling Working Memory subtests, and prompted Rusty to use his fingers to form letters and digits as a means of improving his recall. His performance increased in accuracy and complexity.

Rusty's performance on curriculum-based measures of reading indicated Rusty had very limited vocabulary recognition. He applied phonetic word attack strategies to unfamiliar words, but these strategies were ineffective, as he often did not know the word he sounded out. However, he recognized some words when I signed them, indicating that his conceptual knowledge and sign vocabulary exceeded his ability to recognize words via speech and print. Social Skills Rating Scale (SSRS) results concurred with my observations and interview data in suggesting adequate social development, peer relationships, and adjustment.

Discussion: I interpret Rusty's results to indicate that his intellectual abilities do not inhibit his educational progress. Rusty's scores suggest adequate, and average, intellectual development relative to other children of the same age. He also exhibits appropriate social development and skills. However, Rusty clearly has deficits in some areas of performance. His academic achievement and speech development are severely delayed, and his sign language skills are somewhat below expected levels. Furthermore, test scores indicate that he has substantial knowledge deficits relative to similar peers, which I believe are primarily a function of prior learning opportunities (primarily due to his hearing loss, and secondarily due to a lack of instruction) rather than limited intellectual abilities. Although Rusty's Working Memory index is low, it improved markedly when I prompted him to use information management strategies that were manual (rather than oral/aural) in nature, leading me to suspect that working memory problems are more a function of learning and practice rather than deficits in a basic psychological process.

Recommendations:

1. Convene a meeting of Rusty's IEP team to consider changes in his educational placement and/or program. The available evidence suggests Rusty is not making appropriate progress given his intellectual and social abilities, and this lack of progress is not due to a lack of effort on the part of his teachers or parents, or limited cognitive abilities. Rather, oral/aural training does not appear to be meeting Rusty's academic and language development needs.

2. Before the IEP meeting, conduct a formal and thorough analysis of Rusty's signed language. Teachers at his current placement are apparently unaware of his signing skills, and because these appear to be better developed than his oral/aural skills, he may have stronger language skills than current estimates suggest. Rusty's signing skills may be an asset to consider when considering educational program changes.

3. Rusty should be involved in making decisions about the communication he uses at home and school. Current communication difficulties have caused conflict and frustration with his parents and teachers. As Rusty approaches adolescence, it is developmentally appropriate for him to assume greater control over his own life and learning, and it is likely that conflicts with authority will increase even when there are no barriers to communication. Taking steps now to improve communication may be helpful in facilitating Rusty's development and reducing conflict in the coming years.

Anne S. McVernon
Anne S. McVernon, PhD

12

CULTURAL CONSIDERATIONS IN THE USE OF THE WECHSLER INTELLIGENCE SCALE FOR CHILDREN—FOURTH EDITION (WISC-IV)

JOSETTE G. HARRIS

Departments of Psychiatry and Neurology
University of Colorado School of Medicine
Denver, Colorado

ANTOLIN M. LLORENTE

Department of Pediatrics
University of Maryland School of Medicine
Baltimore, Maryland

Topics concerned with cross-cultural assessment of cognition and intelligence were once primarily associated with research methodologies comparing groups of individuals residing within different countries. Over time, however, within an increasingly mobile world, and with sophistication in conceptualizing the facets of diversity existing within regional and national boundaries, cross-cultural topics are appropriately seen to additionally encompass "cultures" within broader cultures, such as a single country. In our efforts to understand the relationship between culture and certain psychological variables, such as intelligence, it is necessary to characterize those

WISC-IV Clinical Use and Interpretation:
Scientist-Practitioner Perspectives

cultures of study interest and to define the measurement of intelligence. Efforts to do so, however, sometimes oversimplify the constructs and obscure the interpretation of both group and individual performances.

The intellectual assessment of "minority" children is an example of such constructs of convenience. Describing children as "minority" says little about the cultural, linguistic, educational, and socioeconomic issues that may differentially impact these children and their performances on tests of intelligence. Further distinctions by racial or ethnic grouping may be similarly limited in value because of the heterogeneity within such groups. This chapter focuses on this topic of heterogeneity as a means to inform our thinking about individual and group differences in performance. While many of the issues described in this chapter, such as language proficiency, are applicable to individuals from a variety of backgrounds and ethnicities, we have chosen to focus primarily on the "Hispanic" population, because it represents a particularly large segment of the world's population; that is, there are numerous Spanish-speaking countries around the world, including the United States. Ultimately the goal of this chapter is to raise issues and examples that will foster individualized assessment practices with all school-children who are evaluated with the Wechsler Intelligence Scale for Children–Fourth Edition (WISC-IV) (Wechsler, 2003).

HETEROGENEITY IN ETHNIC MINORITY POPULATIONS

While an argument can be made that any ethnic group residing within a society or country may represent a heterogeneous group, the Hispanic population provides a particularly salient example. The term *Hispanic* represents diversity in all its splendor and complexity. It is a broad term, encompassing all Spanish-speaking peoples; it is intended to represent those of Latin American origin (i.e., Latinos), as well as other Spanish speakers (e.g., Spaniards) originating outside of Latin America. Hispanic individuals living within a given country share many societal institutional structures such as the political, economic, and general educational systems. Yet, groups of individuals representing different Hispanic cultures vary greatly with regard to country of origin, educational attainment, religion, use of language(s), and other important variables. The panethnic label *Hispanic* fails to capture these unique attributes, and in reality is a term of convenience with little descriptive specificity to any given Hispanic individual.

The term *Hispanic* has often been used as a racial category, creating significant confusion. Its distinction as a separate race stems from the blending of races in the history of some Hispanic peoples. The conquest of Mesoamerica by the Spaniards in the sixteenth century, for example, led to the intermingling of the European Spaniards with the indigenous Indians, producing offspring referred to as *mestizo* (mixed). Many Mexican-Americans (some favoring the additional distinction of "Chicanos" to represent certain political perspectives, as well as a shared ethnic identity) consider themselves to be descendents of this "new race" of mestizos that migrated northward to the United States. Similarly, the blending of the white and black, such as through the intermarriage of the Spaniards with the various African peoples, produced the "mulatto." The term *Hispanic* is, in fact, an umbrella term for a number of cultural and ethnic groupings. Hispanic individuals can claim any racial origin(s), as well as any ethnicity or culture. Table 12.1 presents the most recent census estimates for the U.S. Hispanic population, according to country of origin (United States Census Bureau, 2001a).

Even within a specific category, such as the largest group, Mexican, there are additional variables to consider. For example, the label Mexican encompasses both Mexican immigrants and US born descendents of Mexican ancestry. Those emigrating from Mexico may identify with any of at least 50 indigenous ethnic groups that reside in the home country (Vázquez, 1994), including Nahuas, Mayas, Zapotecas, Mixtecas, Otomíes, Tzeltales, Tzotziles, Totonacos, Mazatecos, Choses, Mazahuas, Huastecos, Chinantecos, and Purépechas. In addition to the traditional Spanish language, there are 27 distinct indigenous languages recognized by the Mexican government for the publication of the "Bill of Rights and Labor Responsibilities" (Carta de Derechos y Obligaciones Laborales), including Náhuatl, Maya, Mixteco,

TABLE 12.1   Census Estimates for the Hispanic Population Living in the United States According to Country of Origin[a]

Hispanic or Latino by Type	Number	Percent
Mexican	20,640,711	58.5
Puerto Rican	3,406,178	9.6
Central American	1,686,937	4.8
South American	1,353,562	3.8
Cuban	1,241,685	3.5
Dominican	764,945	2.2
Spaniard	100,135	0.3
All Other Hispanic or Latino (e.g., write in Hispanic or Latino)	6,111,665	17.3
Total	35,305,818	100

Source: The Hispanic Population 2000, U.S. Census Bureau, 2001.
[a]For the purpose of Census reporting, country of origin is defined by the origin of the head of household, the individual responsible for completing the Census.

Zapoteco, Tarhaumara, and Huichol (México, Gobierno de la República, 2004). There are reportedly in excess of 200 additional living languages spoken by indigenous peoples throughout Mexico (Grimes & Grimes, 2004). Hispanic children within the United States may consequently be of any race(s), any ethnicity or a combination of ethnicities (e.g., parents with Puerto Rican and Colombian nationalities), and may be monolingual Spanish speakers, monolingual English speakers, bilingual (e.g., Spanish-Mayan), or multilingual (e.g., Tarhaumara-Spanish-English), even if English is not yet a proficient language. At one end of the continuum Hispanic children may represent recently immigrated monolingual Spanish-speaking children, and at the other end of the continuum they may represent children whose ancestors have been living in the United States for multiple generations and whose parents may not share the same ethnicity (Hispanic or other), and may not even speak the Spanish language.

Similar diversity exists for other racial and ethnic groupings, such as black, African American, North American Native, Aboriginal, and Alaskan Native. In Canada, where English and French are predominantly spoken, approximately 32,000 individuals reported they could carry on a conversation in Inuktitut, the second most common Aboriginal language, according to reliable governmental surveys (Canadian Heritage, 2002). In fact, although rarely addressed, complex considerations of diversity exist even within the racial construct "white." A white child from a bayou in Louisiana who speaks "Cajun French" at home and English only in the context of school may share both similarities and differences with a white English-speaking child of another background elsewhere in the country. For individuals belonging to any of these groups, the assimilation of a specific language as primary or secondary varies according to such factors as age of language exposure and acquisition, degree of acculturation to "mainstream" society, regional location within a country, and support for maintenance of the native language and culture.

This discussion begins to provide a glimpse into the complexities of psychological assessment with diverse individuals. It underscores the need for appropriate psychological and cognitive instruments to assess such diverse populations, as well as the need for methods to understand individual performance and the meaning of both individual and group differences.

ETHNIC DIFFERENCES IN WECHSLER SCALE PERFORMANCE

The original Wechsler Intelligence Scale for Children (Wechsler, 1949) has undergone three revisions since its publication in 1949. The resulting publications are the WISC-R (Wechsler, 1974), the WISC-III (Wechsler, 1991), and the most recent, WISC-IV (Wechsler, 2003). These revisions have each reflected concomitant advances in theoretical models of intelligence, cognitive theory, information processing paradigms, test construction, and professional practice and assessment guidelines. For example, the most recent WISC-IV manual specifically addresses the application of the WISC-IV to diverse individuals, including English-language learners and recent immigrants, reflecting standards and guidelines developed by the American Educational Research Association (American Educational Research Association, American Psychological Association, & National Council on Measurement in Education, 1999) and by the American Psychological Association (APA 1990; 2002).

With each revision, however, a rather stable scientific finding persists concerning the lower performance, relative to nonminority examinees, of African American and Hispanic children in the standardization sample (see Chapter 1 this volume) (Kaufman & Doppelt, 1976; Prifitera, Weiss & Saklofske, 1998; Sattler, 1992; Weiss, Prifitera, & Roid, 1993). This disparity in cognitive performance is not unique to the WISC nor to the other Wechsler scales. There has been considerable scientific and public debate concerning the explanations for these findings (Hernstein & Murray, 1994; Neisser *et al.*, 1996), including for example, concerns that cognitive measures lack cultural equivalence and that there are inherent problems with bias in the measures (Helms, 1992). In evaluating the Wechsler scales for various types of bias, it has been noted that impressions of bias most often reflect personal reactions to test content, rather than specific findings resulting from bias analyses (Reynolds & Kaiser, 2003; Reynolds, 2000). However, these issues remain open to debate.

CONCEPTUAL EQUIVALENCE OF INTELLIGENCE AND WISC-IV MODERATOR VARIABLES

Differences exist in the conceptualization of intelligence by various theoreticians (Carroll, 1993; Cattell, 1971; Ceci, 1996; Gardner, 1983; Spearman, 1927; Sternberg *et al.*, 2000; Thurstone, 1938). Each model has implications for a specific culturally defined context or question. For example, what is the likelihood of academic success in a public school for an Aboriginal child of a given intellect living in Ontario, Canada? How is this different from the intelligence that describes the successful adaptation of a child to his community in Zambia? It is certainly not contested that intelligence can be represented differently within different cultures, but it can also be represented similarly when individuals share salient aspects of their cultural and educational backgrounds.

Studies concerning the cultural equivalence of the WISC in cross-national studies support the notion of universal cognitive processes across cultures (Georgas, Weiss, Van de Vijver, & Saklofske, 2003). There is remarkable consistency in the factor structure of the WISC, when adapted and translated into other languages in other countries (Georgas *et al.*, 2003). When mean score differences have been identified among cross-national samples, these findings have been thought to be attributable to education-related or economic factors (Georgas, Van de Vijver, Weiss, & Saklofske, 2003). Variations in IQ scores across countries have, for example, been found to be related to the pupil-teacher ratio for preprimary, primary, and secondary education and duration of each education level, according to these authors. These investigators also suggested that affluence-related factors, such as the physical quality of the child's living environment, may explain cross-cultural score differences, although education and affluence are also noted to be highly and positively correlated.

The factor structure for specific racial and ethnic groups within the United States (i.e., white, African American, and Hispanic) is also generally consistent, although there may be some differences in factor loadings in the lower age ranges within groups due to developmental differences in the acquisition of specific cognitive abilities, such as working memory skills (Wechsler, 2003). In score comparisons among ethnic groups within a given country, socioeconomic factors have been found to partially account for variability in performance (Prifitera *et al.*, 1998). In group comparisons of WISC-IV performance, the typical pattern of reduced performances in the Hispanic group emerges, with a difference of 10 points evident on the Full Scale IQ (FSIQ) and a similar depressed score exhibited on the Verbal Comprehension index (VCI) compared with white non-Hispanic children (Table 12.2). However, when subjects are matched on age, gender, region of the country, parental education level (a proxy for socioeconomic status (SES), and number of parents living in the household, differences are reduced with the largest differences of approximately 5 and 6 points found on FSIQ and VCI, respectively (Table 12.3) (Prifitera *et al.*) (see Chapter 1 this volume).

TABLE 12.2   Mean WISC-IV Scores of Hispanic and White Non-Hispanic Children from the Standardization Sample

IQ or Index Score	Hispanic	White Non-Hispanic
FSIQ	93.1	103.2
VCI	91.5	102.9
PRI	95.7	102.8
WMI	94.2	101.3
PSI	97.7	101.4

n = 2080
Source: Wechsler Intelligence Scale for Children-Fourth Edition, 2003. Reprinted with permission by Harcourt Assessment.

TABLE 12.3 Standardization Mean WISC-IV Scores of Hispanic and White Non-Hispanic Children Equated for Age, Gender, Number of Parents Living in the Household, Parental Education Level, and US Region

IQ or Index Score	Hispanic	White Non-Hispanic
FSIQ	95.2	100.0
VCI	93.7	99.7
PRI	97.7	100.3
WMI	95.7	98.7
PSI	97.9	99.6

$n = 161$

For some members of ethnic minority groups, the interplay of education and economics is particularly complex. While educational attainment to a large degree dictates and certainly facilitates income potential, it is also the case that socioeconomic advancement facilitates educational attainment. For example, immigrant high school graduates who do not have legal residency status but who wish to attend college, are ineligible for in-state tuition rates in most jurisdictions in the United States (National Conference of State Legislatures, 2003; 2004). Parental income of these children is often constrained by the lack of legal residency. Language constraints may further limit parental educational and income opportunities. Data on the number of undocumented students who graduate high school and are unable to enroll in college are not readily available. It is estimated, however, that there are 1.6 million children under the age of 18 years old living without legal residency status in the United States (Passel, Capps, & Fix, 2004). These circumstances certainly contribute to the low percentage of Hispanics graduating college in the United States. Table 12.4 presents the profile of educational attainment for Hispanics within the United States (US Census Bureau, 2003a). Across all Hispanic groups, 28.2% graduate high school. In contrast, in the white non-Hispanic population, 33.7% graduate high school, 27.3% achieve a minimum of a bachelor's degree, and 4.8% have attained less than 9 years of education. It is noteworthy that the dropout rate for Hispanic students for grades 10 through 12 in 2002 was 5.3% (male = 6.2%; female = 4.4%), higher than any other ethnic group (US Census Bureau, 2004) As course content demands increase in school, the need for linguistic competence increases. Those children who immigrate at later ages and who are denied support for their emerging second language skills are clearly most at risk to fail and to remove themselves from the school environment.

These realities conspire to depress the SES for the group of Hispanics as a whole. As a given minority group gains an economic foothold, educational and other opportunities tend to increase. For example, Portes and Rumbaut

TABLE 12.4   Educational Attainment of US Hispanics 25+ Years Old by Country of Origin

Educational attainment	Mexican	Central/South American	Puerto Rican	Cuban	Other Hispanic	Non-Hispanic
Less than 9th grade	31.7%	22.1%	16.7%	17.3%	14.6%	4.8%
9th to 12th grade (no diploma)	16.9%	13.3%	18.5%	9.0%	13.3%	8.3%
High school graduate	26.6%	29.5%	29.8%	33.3%	32.0%	33.7%
Some college/associate degree	17.7%	17.8%	22.1%	17.2%	25.4%	26.0%
Bachelor's degree	5.2%	11.7%	8.5%	13.9%	9.1%	18.1%
Advanced degree	1.8%	5.5%	4.4%	9.3%	5.6%	9.2%

Source: U.S. Census Bureau, Current Population Survey, March 2000. Educational Supplement, Internet Release date: June 18, 2003. US Hispanics include native and foreign born.

(1990) noted that Koreans surpassed other ethnic minority groups that have historically immigrated to the United States in their rapid rate of success, measured from an economic standpoint. The authors attributed part of this rapid rise to the group's higher average SES before immigrating to the United States, which serves to facilitate additional gains. However, with limitations in the accessibility of education and employment to some immigrant groups, it is obvious that the initial economic foothold may be very difficult if not impossible to achieve. While 17.1% of all children live below the poverty level in the United States, 30.4% of all Hispanic children live below the poverty level (US Census Bureau, 2003b), a testimony to this economic disparity and challenge.

There are significant implications of these disparities for normative studies. Test publishers typically stratify socioeconomic status (using parental education) within racial and ethnic groupings to reflect the characteristics of the country's population. When IQ scores are compared across ethnic groups, the overall reference group, which is overwhelmingly represented by the nonminority cases, will tend to have higher mean SES and parental education than the subgroups that are the focus of the comparison (Prifitera et al., 1998). The lower performances of individuals from ethnic minority groups reflects both the correlation between SES and IQ (Prifitera et al., 1998), as well as the composition of the normative sample.

IMMIGRATION PATTERNS AND THE REPRESENTATIVENESS OF NORMS

There are additional variables that impact the composition of a normative sample, with implications for group and individual comparisons of performance. Patterns of immigration to the United States are one such consideration and provide often overlooked data that should be considered in the norming process of psychoeducational and neuropsychological instruments (Llorente, Ponton, Tausig, & Satz, 1999; Llorente, Tausig, Perez, & Satz, 2000). Migration is not the result of chance processes (Hamilton & Chinchilla, 1990; US Immigration and Naturalization Service, 1991; Portes & Rumbaut, 1990; Portes and Borocsz, 1989). Rather, the nonrandom nature of migration is the result of selective factors associated with both the sending and host countries (Hamilton & Chinchilla, 1990; Portes and Rumbaut, 1990). For example, favorable U.S. policies toward specific countries have contributed to increased immigration of individuals from those countries. Those policies may be dictated by humanitarian concerns, manpower needs, or other international policies and political agendas.

The proportion of "Hispanic" immigrants from specific countries may vary substantially over time for different ethnic groups relative to their representation in the US population (Llorente et al., 1999). Migrations to the United States from some countries (e.g., Uruguay) have remained relatively constant and small in magnitude over time relative to migrations from other countries (e.g., Mexico), which have exhibited profound increases (Table 12.5). The US Department of Homeland Security (2003) reported that 20.5% of all legally admitted immigrants came from Mexico in 2000. Patterns of immigration have implications for the inclusion of specific Hispanic ethnicities in normative samples. For example, while Cubans represented 3.5% of the total US Hispanic population in 2002, a target of 9% Cuban children was established for the standardization of the WISC-IV Spanish (in press), in order to adequately represent Cubans in the standardization sample and to perform supplemental data analyses. Additional criteria for all examinees in the standardization sample included a limit of no more than five consecutive years attendance in a US school and the requirement that children speak and/or understand Spanish better than English or be adept in both languages. These criteria were established to target those children most likely to benefit from assessment in Spanish. Given that Cubans represent the smallest numbers immigrating in recent years, however, it was difficult to access Cuban children that met all the standardization requirements and the stratification of parental education. This strained the data collection process, although the target was eventually met.

Ultimately, while a normative reference group reflects overall population statistics, the norms may not reflect the specific demographic characteristics of an individual from a given ethnic group. Gravitations toward certain occupations vary for specific groups of immigrants (Llorente et al., 1999; Llorente et al., 2000). For example, recent data indicate that approximately 66.2% of Mexican immigrants have less than a high school education and are primarily employed in manual and unskilled labor (US Census Bureau,

2001b). Related to these occupational affiliations, Hispanic ethnic groups tend to differentially exhibit geographical affinity for certain areas within the United States. What this means, for example, is that there is a concentration of lower educated immigrants from Mexico in the Southwest and California, while segments of the East Coast and Florida may reflect a broader socio-economic spectrum of Cuban and Central and South American immigrants, who have migrated for both economic and humanitarian reasons. These geographical predilections may confound the acquisition of data utilized in establishing standardization norms. Further, the geographic concentrations of various ethnic groups have implications for the degree of assimilation of American culture and use of languages by its group members. So, for example, in Miami, Florida, it is quite possible to function well within the community as a monolingual Spanish speaker without the need to use English and possible to retain many of the traditions of the country of origin. Ultimately, these issues impact the utility of the norms used for interpretation of individual test performance and are variables that test users, regardless of purpose (research or clinical), should consider in evaluating the appropriateness of specific test norms.

As a case in point, Rey, Feldman, Rivas-Vasquez, Levin, and Benton (1999) found differences in psychological test performance among Cuban and Mexican normative groups living in Dade County, Florida. Close scrutiny of demographic variables associated with the two samples of Spanish speakers revealed that *selection biases* associated with lower levels of education in the Mexican group were responsible for the differences observed in test performance. The limited representation of Mexican nationality examinees in Dade County compared with Cuban examinees had limited the range of education of participants accessible to the researchers. When

TABLE 12.5 Immigration Trends for Fiscal Years 1995–2002

Region and country of birth	1995	1996	1997	1998	1999	2000	2001	2002
Mexico	89,932	163,572	146,865	131,575	147,573	173,919	206,426	219,380
South America	45,666	61,769	52,877	45,394	41,585	56,074	68,888	74,506
Central America	31,814	44,289	43,676	35,679	43,216	66,443	75,914	68,979
Cuba	17,937	26,466	33,587	17,375	14,132	20,831	27,703	28,272
Spain	1,321	1,659	1,241	1,043	874	1,264	1,726	1,376
Uruguay	414	540	429	368	271	430	545	549
Puerto Rico	1	2	1	2	3	3	4	2

Source: Statistical Yearbook of the Immigration and Naturalization Service, 2002.
Immigrants admitted by Region and Country of Birth Fiscal Years 1992–2002

Cuban and Mexican subjects were matched on age, gender, and education, the observed discrepancies in performance between the two groups of participants vanished.

Such results underscore the potential confounds associated with both traditional (education) and nontraditional (geographic locale) demographic characteristics. These variables must be carefully scrutinized to avoid the introduction of systematic error into the normative data acquisition and interpretation processes. Certainly, comparing the WISC-IV scores of a young Cuban immigrant to the general population of US schoolchildren will yield important information about the child's ability to "compete" among his or her broadly defined peer group. However, possessing additional knowledge about the US Cuban population, the specific child's background, parental education, and the representativeness of the reference group being used for comparison will enable the examiner to hone his or her interpretation of and inferences regarding test performance. Careful consideration of these factors by test users is necessary to avoid individual misdiagnosis, misattribution of differences in cognitive and neuropsychological performance among ethnic groups, and between nonminority and various ethnic groups.

Differences in immigration patterns for various Hispanic groups are not typically considered in sampling stratification, but should be addressed, particularly when large-scale and rapid changes have occurred in these patterns between test revisions. The child of migrant parents seeking economic opportunities in a new country likely differs substantially from the background of a child whose parents are escaping political persecution in another country. Clearly, all these factors have the potential to impact the acquisition of normative data and the inferences derived from the use of psychological instruments, including the WISC-IV. Other potential confounds, such as age of immigration, acculturation (Marin & Marin, 1991), and proficiency in a second language may be difficult to measure accurately but may synergistically interact with demographic variables known to influence test performance (c.f., Heaton, Grant, & Matthews, 1986).

LANGUAGE PROFICIENCY AND COGNITIVE PERFORMANCE

The relationship of language proficiency and bilingualism to cognitive performance has long been a sensitive topic but one that has direct bearing on the performance discrepancies observed for some ethnic minority (e.g., Hispanic) vs nonminority groups on the WISC-IV. Early studies concluded that bilingualism was a cognitive and academic learning liability. This was later identified as in part a reflection of flawed research methodologies, such as failure to control for socioeconomic and other confounding variables, the heterogeneity in the samples designated as "bilingual," and failure to measure abilities in both the stronger and the weaker languages (Hakuta, 1986; Hamers & Blanc, 1989; Romaine, 1995). The social and political context of bilingualism and acceptance of the acquisition of two languages is also a critical factor in the perceived advantages or disadvantages of speaking two languages. In other words, social expectations and support for bilingualism are essential to the acquisition and development of proficiency in a second language as much as other factors, such as individual differences in ability to learn a second language (Ardila, 1998, 2002; Centeno & Obler, 2001). Support may not exist until a language has been officially sanctioned by governmental policies (e.g., Canada's Official Language Act of 1968–1969 and similar European laws) (Centeno & Obler, 2001) or when the norm for bilingualism is otherwise ingrained in the societal and educational structure of a nation. Unfortunately, in the United States preserving the native language has always been viewed as incompatible with learning the English language and indeed bilingual education has a controversial and poorly understood history.

IMPLICATIONS OF LANGUAGE PROFICIENCY FOR WISC-IV PERFORMANCE

This discussion exposes a rather unique constellation of considerations in examinees who may fall anywhere along a continuum of limited English proficient on one extreme to balanced bilingual (i.e., equal proficiency in the two languages) on the other extreme. Children who make up a specific ethnic group or culture may vary considerably in their English-language proficiency. To place this in the proper context, 2000–2001 survey data of school-age children indicated that 18.4% of the population ages 5 to 17 years spoke a non-English language at home (U.S. Census Bureau, 2003c). Nationwide, in the 2000–2001 school year, it was estimated that more than 4.5 million English-language learners or limited English-proficient students were enrolled in public schools. In a survey conducted for this period, more than 400 languages spoken by English language learners (ELL) nationwide were identified, with the majority of ELL students speaking Spanish (79%) as their native language, followed by Vietnamese (2.0%), Hmong (1.6%), Cantonese (1.0%), Korean (1.0%), Haitian Creole (.9%), Arabic (.9%), and other (15.4) (Kindler, 2002). In some states, such as Colorado, the growth has been particularly evident, with the number of residents who speak a language other than English growing by 88.4% to 604,019 in 2000 alone (US Census Bureau, 2003d).

In developing norms for a measure such as the WISC or WAIS, it is common practice to exclude individuals from the standardization sample who are not proficient in the English language, although those who speak English as a second language may be included. These children indeed represent a proportion of US schoolchildren who are ELLs. Realistically, however, little is known about the language abilities of these learners and the degree to which they are bilingual. It is uncommon to find children screened or otherwise assessed to verify reported linguistic proficiency or competency before inclusion in standardization. Even in settings where children are assessed for their fluency or language competencies before testing, such as in clinical or school settings, there is little consistency in method, measure, or specific criteria for a determination of "fluent" or "proficient." Establishing proficiency in English presents considerable challenges, a problem encountered by all clinicians. Often examiners are dependent on the report of the child, parents, or teacher for an estimate of linguistic ability.

Those investigating second language acquisition have noted that academic English proficiency takes years longer to acquire than the simple ability to use English for social purposes, a fact that presents additional complexities. Cummins (1979; 1989) was one of the first to write of the dangers in interpreting control over the surface structures of a language as indicative of sufficiently developed academic language skills. He initially distinguished between "surface fluency" (basic interpersonal communication skills or BICS) and more cognitively and academically related aspects of language proficiency (CALP). In an effort to move away from the oversimplification of his theory into "communicative" vs "cognitive" proficiency, he later attempted to couch his theory in terms of contextualized language and decontextualized language experiences, and cognitive demand. He argued that in face-to-face verbal communication, the meaning of the communication is supported by contextual cues (e.g., facial expression, gestures, and intonation), where this is rarely the case in academic uses of a language (e.g., reading a text). He described intellectual test situations as context reduced, cognitively demanding circumstances, requiring significant language proficiency in excess of that utilized in basic social communication. In general, those tests that show fewer group differences may be less "culturally biased" in the sense that they are less cognitively demanding and more context independent, or embedded.

Cummins' (1981a, 1981b) work and that of others demonstrated that it is not until the later grades of elementary school that students acquiring English approach grade norms of native English speakers. In his studies in both the United States and Canada, he found that those arriving after the age of 6 years needed 5 to 7 years on average to approach grade norms in academic related aspects of English proficiency. These findings were echoed by Ramirez, Pasta, Yuen, Ramey, and Billings (1991), who studied three different bilingual programs (immersion strategy, early-exit, and late-exit), which varied only on the amount of L1 (first language) instruction. While after 2 years of education (K-1) students appeared to be doing equally well in the three programs, differences began to emerge by the end of grade 3. Students in the immersion programs who received no L1 instruction were declining in performance (normal curve equivalents, NCE). In early exit programs, where children received limited L1 support in grades K through 2, slight gains in NCEs relative to the norm in English reading and slight declines in English math were observed (Ramirez *et al.*, 1991). Most striking were the findings that students in the late exit programs who received L1 support for grades K through 6 were, by sixth grade, at the 51st NCE in English math and at the 45th NCE in English Reading. In a review of other studies of long-term language minority student data on academic achievement, Collier (1992) concluded that the investigations repeatedly demonstrated "... the greater the amount of L1 instructional support for language-minority students, combined with balanced L2 support, the higher they are able to achieve academically in L2 in each succeeding academic year, in comparison to matched groups being schooled monolingually in L2." (p. 205).

It seems logical, then, to conclude that children acquiring skills in English may not possess sufficient proficiency to effectively perform on the more demanding, context-reduced IQ tests. But what about examinees who appear to be fluent and proficient? A study of non-native English-speaking adults who participated in the WAIS-III standardization illustrates the concerns and challenges of determining when an examinee possesses sufficient proficiency for English language intellectual assessment.

A sample of 151 adult examinees was selected for study inclusion, all of whom reported that they were born outside of the United States. In addition, all individuals reported that they were fluent in English, a criterion corroborated by the standardization test examiner based on observation of the examinees' conversation before and during the testing session. The individuals represented 37 countries of origin, with Mexico and Cuba representing two thirds of the sample. Three variables, obtained from a demographic questionnaire completed by all study participants, served as proxies for acculturation: (1) a "language preference" variable, derived by weighting reported language preference for speaking, thinking, reading, and writing in English and in the additional spoken language; (2) a variable "U.S. experience," calculated by dividing the number of years residing in the United States by the total age of the examinee, and (3) a variable "U.S. education," calculated by dividing the number of years educated in the United States by the total number of years of education attained by the examinee. For additional detail, see Harris, Tulsky, and Schultheis (2003). The relationship of these variables to performance on the Wechsler Adult Intelligence Scale III and Wechsler Memory Scale III factor scores was analyzed. All of the variables were significant predictors of performance on the various factor scores, with the variable "language preference" predicting performance on the Verbal Comprehension, Perceptual Organization, Processing Speed, and Visual Memory (using the Visual Reproduction subtest) indices. While language preference is not synonymous with language proficiency, clearly the examinee's self-reported preferred language is a key variable for planning assessment strategies and for other decision making, such as inclusion in normative studies.

Children who are ELLs, even if well on their way to becoming expressive bilinguals, do not necessarily have the foundational skills for academic success in spite of possessing the necessary oral and auditory skills for social communicative competence. Furthermore, it has been noted that children who are ELLs have limited access to courses such as science and mathematics compared with other English-speaking students (Minicucci & Olsen, 1992) and may be placed into curricula that have less challenging course content (Oakes, 1990). What are the implications of this for demonstrating academic knowledge as assessed by standardized academic or intelligence tests? At least for some proportion of Hispanic children, they are lagging in learning as a function of their status as ELLs and the fact that they may not be learning the same academic content as their peers.

Presumably, an adequate level of linguistic competence and proficiency has been achieved by all the ELLs included in a standardization sample. As already noted, however, the degree of proficiency can vary widely among individuals with minority group status, which is not the case for the vast majority of nonminority white examinees. In a sample of standardization participants who agreed to complete the "WISC-IV Home Environment Questionnaire," 6% of children were identified as speaking a native language other than English. Of the Hispanic standardization participants who responded to the survey, 34% indicated that English was not the child's native language and nearly all endorsed Spanish as the native tongue. Within various ethnic groups represented in the standardization sample, not only is there heterogeneity of English receptive and expressive abilities, but the very concept of bilingualism signifies more than a simple characterization of two languages for these children.

To further examine the possible influence of English language acquisition on performance, we studied a group of WISC-IV standardization participants, matched on age, parental education level, and gender. However, the examinees selected for study differed along one important language variable, gleaned from a comprehensive Family Survey administered to WISC-IV examinees. One group, the white non-Hispanic sample was composed of monolingual English speakers. A second group of Hispanic children were selected who indicated that they spoke English as their native language. A third group of Hispanic children indicated that they spoke Spanish as their native language. Table 12.6 illustrates the impact of controlling for language when comparing index score performances across the three groups.

The "typical" finding of reduced performance, particularly in verbal indices, for Hispanic examinees is now evident only in the group of Hispanic children who speak Spanish as their native language. In fact, although the sample is small, the native English-speaking Hispanic children surpass the nonminority examinees in their Processing Speed index. Such findings are a powerful illustration of the impact of socioeconomic and linguistic variables

TABLE 12.6   Matched Sample Mean WISC-IV Scores of Spanish vs English-Speaking Hispanic and White Non-Hispanic English-Speaking Children (Equated for Age, Gender, and Parental Education Level)

IQ/Index Score	Hisp–Spanish	Hisp–English	Non-Hispanic White
FSIQ	93.00 (10.95)	96.58 (12.87)	94.12 (15.58)
VCI	92.31 (9.74)	96.19 (13.02)	94.31 (12.06)
PRI	94.50 (12.24)	97.92 (11.54)	96.69 (15.73)
WMI	93.65 (13.07)	96.27 (15.20)	97.42 (15.04)
PSI	98.31 (11.47)	98.27 (13.84)	91.58 (14.23)

n = 26

on performance. What initially appeared to be a large gap between Hispanic and non-Hispanic white students now appears to be a minimal difference. This finding is not to be construed in any way as indicative of liabilities associated with retaining the native language, but rather indicative of the challenges test developers and clinicians must address in determining when a suitable level of proficiency has been reached for testing in English. Indeed, scientifically rigorous studies of bilingualism conducted in the later half of the twentieth century in adults and children suggest that bilingualism is associated with a number of advantages in cognition (Galloway, 1982; Mohanty 1990; Ricciardelli, 1992a, 1992b; Bialystok, 1988; Bialystok & Cummins, 1991). These advantages may persist into adulthood and old age. A recent study concluded that the lifelong experience of managing two languages attenuates the typical age-related decline in the efficiency of inhibitory processing, and reduced "working memory costs" in bilingual adults (Bialystok, Craik, Klein, & Viswanathan, 2004).

CASE STUDY

The use of the WISC-IV is illustrated within the context of a neuro-psychological evaluation of a Hispanic child. The use of the WISC-IV in this context permits the elucidation of a broad array of issues, including the use of the WISC in a longitudinal assessment, and educational programming and rehabilitative recommendations.

BACKGROUND INFORMATION

In this case, the WISC-IV was administered to Jamie, a 12-year-old, right-handed, first-generation, bilingual (Spanish-English), Mexican-American male with a history of right temporal lobe astrocytoma, which was partially resected 26 months before assessment. He was referred by his neurooncologist to assess his current level of functioning, to identify areas of cognitive strengths and weaknesses, and to assist with therapeutic and educational programming.

Jamie experienced his first seizure approximately 33 months before the evaluation. The day before the seizure he had experienced a "funny taste" in his mouth, lip smacking, one episode of vomiting, mild disorientation, and gaze deviation to the left. He was taken to a local hospital where he had a computed tomography (CT) scan, followed by magnetic resonance imaging (MRI), which revealed a 1.5 × 1.5 cm right temporal lobe tumor. He was placed immediately on oxcarbazepine (Trileptal) with positive results. However, later that year, Jamie had another seizure and increasingly experienced episodes of vomiting. An MRI obtained at that time showed that his tumor had increased in size and involved the insula, external capsule, caudate, thalamus, subcallosum, anterior temporal lobe, and hippocampus. He then underwent surgery for resection of the tumor, followed by radiation and chemotherapy.

The mother reported that her pregnancy with Jamie was medically uneventful and he was born at 38 weeks of gestation. She received consistent prenatal care and denied the use of alcohol, controlled substances, or tobacco products during the pregnancy. Jamie reportedly weighed 8 pounds, 7 ounces at birth. He achieved all developmental milestones within normal limits. Jamie did not have any history of significant illnesses, or head injury with loss of consciousness. There is no reported family history of developmental delays, learning difficulties, or severe psychiatric illnesses.

Before entering school, Jamie was a monolingual Spanish speaker. He conversed with his parents and grandparents in Spanish, although his father was bilingual (Spanish-English). For 2 years on entering school, he received 4 hours of English as a second language (ESL) instruction per day with regular educational instruction in math. Although Jamie continued to speak primarily Spanish with his mother and grandparents, he spoke both Spanish and English with his father, and most of his peers were English speakers. His parents reported that he rapidly gained expressive language competencies in English, and at the time of assessment, they considered him to be bilingual.

Before his surgery, Jamie attended an eminent private middle school. He repeated the sixth grade as a result of school absences due to his illness, but his teachers indicated that his academic progress was not a "major" concern. Before his illness, he obtained excellent grades (A-Bs). Because of his medical condition, he received home schooling after his surgery and then returned to school. At the time of the evaluation he was unlabeled in a public school, receiving regular education services with after-school assistance and minor laboratory support, and receiving Bs in the sixth grade without any curriculum modifications (e.g., extra time on tests). Jamie reported that he has many friends (bilingual and monolingual English speakers) and he is involved in Boy Scouts. He presently sleeps well and his appetite is normal; however, he continues to occasionally experience mild nausea. Jamie reported that his mood is typically happy. His mother acknowledged that he is coping well with his medical condition and maintains a positive outlook.

PRIOR ASSESSMENTS

Jamie underwent two psychological evaluations before the current assessment. He was administered the WISC-III before his enrollment in a private middle school. That evaluation revealed an overall performance in the very superior range across all IQ and Index scores (IQ = 132–139). He was administered the WISC-III again 3 months after his surgery (approximately 3 years from the initial WISC III evaluation) where he obtained IQ and index scores in the low average range (80s), with the exception of Freedom from Distractibility and Processing Speed indices on which he obtained scores in the borderline (70s) and deficient (60s) range, respectively.

BEHAVIORAL OBSERVATIONS

For the current evaluation, Jamie was evaluated over two sessions. He was appropriately dressed and groomed during both assessment sessions. He demonstrated a broad range of affect. He interacted well with the examiners and rapport was easily established. He was mildly active and somewhat fidgety throughout the evaluation, although he responded well to redirection. He informed the examiner that he preferred English for "schoolwork and tests," but acknowledged that he spoke Spanish daily, particularly with his mother, and that he was comfortable with both languages. His speech was fluent and coherent in both languages. He appeared to put forth excellent effort on all tests administered, yielding valid results.

CURRENT ASSESSMENT

INTELLECT

A summary of test data is shown in Table 12.7. His scores, as assessed by the Wechsler Intelligence Scale for Children–Fourth Edition (WISC-IV), were within the low average to very superior range. Jamie obtained a Full Scale IQ score (FSIQ) of 121, which placed his performance within the superior range (92nd percentile). With 95% confidence his score would fall between 116 and 125. His Verbal Comprehension index score (VCI) of 136 fell in the very superior range (99th percentile) and his Perceptual Reasoning index (PRI) of 125 (95th percentile) fell in the superior range. In contrast, the Working Memory index score (107) (68th percentile) and Processing Speed index

TABLE 12.7   Case Study: Neuropsychological Test Scores

Wechsler Intelligence Scale for Children-Fourth Edition (WISC IV)

	Index and IQ Score
Verbal Comprehension Index (VCI)	136
Perceptual Reasoning Index (PRI)	125
Working Memory Index (WMI)	107
Processing Speed Index (PSI)	85
Full Scale Intelligence Quotient (FSIQ)	121 (116–125)

VCI	**Scaled Score**
Similarities	16
Vocabulary	17
Comprehension	15
PRI	
Block Design	16
Picture Concepts	15
Matrix Reasoning	11
WMI	
Digit Span	12
Letter-Number Sequence	11
PSI	
Coding	7
Symbol Search	8

California Verbal Learning Test-Children's Version (CVLT-C)

	Raw	T-Score
List A 1–5 Trials Free Recall	52	53
		Standard Score
List A Trial 1 Free Recall	6	−0.5
List A Trial 5 Free Recall	13	0.5
List B Free Recall	5	−0.5
List A Short Delay Free Recall	10	0.0
List A Short Delay Cued Recall	11	0.0
List A Long Delay Free Recall	11	0.0
List A Long Delay Cued Recall	12	0.5
Recognition Hits	14	0.0
Discriminability	97.78	0.5
False positives	0	−0.5

(*Continues*)

TABLE 12.7   (*Continued*)

Children's Memory Scale (CMS)

	Scaled Score
Faces-Immediate	3
Faces-Delayed	7
Stories-Immediate	11
Stories-Delayed	11
Stories-Recognition	11

Rey-Osterrieth Complex Figure Test (RCFT)

	Raw Score	Z-score	Percentile
Delay	14	−1.44	8
Copy	34	0.57	69

Wechsler Individual Achievement Test-Second Edition (WIAT-II)

	Standard Score
Word Reading	123
Numerical Operations	124
Spelling	115

Clinical Evaluation of Language Fundamentals—Fourth Edition (CELF-4)

	Standard Score
Concepts and Directions	13
Recalling Sentences	12

Boston Naming Test (BNT)

	Raw Score	Z-score
Total	55	1.63

Grooved Pegboard Test (GPT)

	Raw Score	Z-score
Dominant	62	0.66
Non-Dominant	117	−1.01

Finger Tapping Test (FTT)

	Raw Score	Z-score
Dominant	42.2	0.19
Non-Dominant	30.8	−1.13

Reitan-Kløve Sensory-Perceptual Examination

	Errors
Finger Recognition	0
Finger-Tip Number Writing	0

(*Continues*)

TABLE 12.7   *(Continued)*

Test of Visual-Perceptual Skills (nonmotor) (TVPS)

	Scaled Score
Visual Memory	14
Visual Sequential Memory	10

Developmental Test of Visual-Motor Integration (VMI)

	Standard Score
Total	128

Judgment of Line Orientation Test (JLO)

	Raw Score	Z-score
Total	28	0.87

Delis-Kaplan Executive Function System (D-KEFS)

	Scaled Score
Trails-scan	7
Trails-number	11
Trails-letter	13
Trails-switch	12
Trails-motor	13
Verbal fluency-letter	14
Verbal fluency-category	11
Verbal fluency-switch	15

Wisconsin Card Sorting Test (WCST)

	Raw Score	T-score
Total Error	15	61
% Error	18	59
Perseverative Responses	6	65
% Perseverative Responses	7	65
Perseverative Errors	6	65
% Perseverative Errors	7	64
Nonperseverative Errors	9	56
% Nonperseverative Errors	11	53
% Conceptual Level Responses	79	60
	Raw Score	Percentile
Categories Completed	6	>16
Trials to complete Ist Category	11	>16
Set Failure	0	>16
Learning to Learn	0	>16

(Continues)

TABLE 12.7   (*Continued*)

Behavior Rating Inventory of Executive Function (BRIEF)

(parent)	T-score
Inhibit	50
Shift	42
Emotional Control	48
Initiate	44
Working Memory	47
Plan/Organize	53
Organization of materials	55
Monitor	60
BRI	50
MI	52
GEC	51

Behavioral Assessment Scale for Children (BASC)

(parent)	T-score
Hyperactivity	46
Aggression	45
Conduct	47
Anxiety	56
Depression	50
Somatization	58
Atypicality	45
Withdrawal	51
Attention	43
Social Skills	57
Leadership	58
Externalizing Problems	45
Internalizing Problems	56
BSI	47
Adaptive	58

BASC (self)

	T-score
Attitude to School	52
Attitude to Teachers	40
Sensation Seeking	49
Atypicality	47
Locus of Control	56

(*Continues*)

TABLE 12.7   (*Continued*)

Somatization	65
Social Stress	52
Anxiety	57
Depression	49
Sense of Inadequacy	45
Parent Relations	57
Interpersonal Problems	51
Self-Esteem	46
Self-Reliance	52
School Maladjustment	46
Clinical Maladjustment	57
Personal adjustment	52
ESI	51
Children's Depression Inventory (CDI)	

	T-score
Total	52

score (85) (16th percentile) were in the average and low average range, respectively. The discrepancy between these two index scores and his Verbal Comprehension index score and Perceptual Reasoning index score was clinically significant. An examination of base rates indicated that such discrepancies occurred only in a small percentage of the children comprising the WISC-IV standardization sample. Thus, his verbal comprehension and perceptual reasoning skills appear to represent relative strengths when compared to his working memory, and to a greater extent, his processing speed. Clearly, he has made significant gains since his evaluation 3 months after the surgery, and a select number of his scores have either returned to or are near baseline levels when compared to his scores from the examination conducted before entering middle school. Although it is not possible to directly compare WISC-III and WISC-IV performances due to changes in the composition of the subtests, the WISC-IV scores appear to reflect improvements in function associated with resolution of Jamie's illness and any treatment side effects.

With regard to specific subtests, his scores varied from the very superior range on measures of word knowledge (Vocabulary), verbal abstraction (Similarities), and "conventional standards of behavior" (Comprehension) to the low average range on subtests assessing attention, speed of information processing, and visual-motor skills (e.g., Coding, Symbol Search). From a qualitative standpoint, his scores on the latter measures were observed to be the result of a slow processing posture without errors. All other subtests fell in the high average to average range.

Memory and Learning

Memory assessment consisted of measures of verbal and visual memory, evaluating both rote and contextual components of this domain. On a measure of rote verbal memory (California Verbal Learning Test–Children's Version; CVLT-C), Jamie was able to remember detailed new information even after a delay with interspersed distracting information. Repeated exposure to the information assisted his recall. His score on a test of contextual verbal memory (Children's Memory Scale, Stories; CMS), requiring recall and recognition of stories, revealed performance within normal limits on the immediate and delayed recall portions of the test. Recognition memory on this task also fell within normal limits. In contrast, his performance on measures of visual memory revealed moderate variability. For instance, his visual sequential memory and visual memory on the Test of Visual-Perceptual Skills (TVPS) fell in the average and above average range, respectively. However, he experienced much more difficulty while recalling a complex geometric figure (Rey-Osterrieth Complex Figure Test; RCFT) and remembering pictures of faces on the CMS (Faces) in which his scores fell in the borderline range of functioning. The latter performance appeared to be a problem with encoding as his delayed recall was better than immediate recall. The CMS and RCFT are different than the TVPS in that they require the individual to encode larger and more complex amounts of information before recalling the information. In addition, far more data organization is required in the two former procedures relative to the TVPS.

Language Functions

Jamie did not exhibit speech difficulties in any area of functioning informally assessed. Likewise, formal language assessment revealed normal functioning in receptive and expressive language skills. On a measure of emergent confrontational object naming (Boston Naming Test; BNT) he scored within normal limits (above average). Similarly, his scores on subtests assessing the ability to follow increasingly complex directions (Clinical Evaluation of Language Fundamentals—Fourth Edition; CELF-4, Concepts and Directions), sentence repetition (CELF-4, Recalling Sentences), and controlled word generation (Delis-Kaplan Executive Function System; DKEFS, Verbal Fluency) were all within normal limits.

Visual Processing and Visual-Motor Skills

On measures assessing visual processing and visual-motor skills, all scores fell within the expected range. He scored within the upper end of the average range on a measure assessing his ability to copy a complex geometric design (RCFT). On a simpler visual-motor task requiring that he copy geometric designs of increasing complexity, he scored in the superior range (Developmental Test of Visual-Motor Integration; VMI). He obtained a score within normal limits on a measure assessing visual processing without a motor component which required that he determine the angular distance between pairs of lines (Judgment of Line Orientation Test; JLO).

Sensory-Perceptual and Motor Skills

Bilateral sensory-perceptual and dominant (right) hand fine motor skills were within normal limits. An area where subtle weaknesses were found on the evaluation was fine motor speed in the nondominant (left) hand (Grooved Pegboard Test, GPT; Finger Tapping Test, FTT). On both fine motor measures administered, his scores fell within the borderline range with his nondominant hand. More important, a significant raw score lateralizing difference emerged between his dominant and nondominant hand.

Executive Skills

Procedures assessing executive functions (D-KEFS) revealed subtle weakness, but these were circumscribed to visual scanning difficulties, which may very well represent fluctuations in attention or test artifact. Inspection of the other test results in this domain revealed scores within the expected range. For example, Jamie was able to effectively develop and implement problem-solving strategies on the Wisconsin Card Sorting Test (WCST). He was also able to adequately plan, organize, and integrate complex visual information (RCFT, Copy). Evaluation of executive functioning skills in daily life based on parental report was measured using the Behavior Rating Inventory of Executive Function (BRIEF). No problems were identified with regard to behavioral regulation or metacognitive awareness.

Academic Achievement Screening

Academic achievement was briefly screened for reading, mathematics, and spelling skills using the Wechsler Individual Achievement Test—Second Edition (WIAT-II). His word reading and mathematical computational skills were in the superior range, whereas his spelling skills fell in the high-average range. His academic scores were commensurate with his chronological age, current grade placement, and overall intellectual scores. Close scrutiny of his Spelling score revealed that the majority of his difficulties were associated with simple misspellings, most likely the result of inattention. Screening in Spanish using the Woodcock-Johnson Pruebas de Aprovechamiento-Revisada revealed performance in the average range. These scores suggested proficiency in Spanish consistent with his spoken abilities and parental report regarding competency in the language.

Behavioral and Emotional Functioning

With regard to behavioral and emotional indicators, Jamie was asked to complete the Behavior Assessment System for Children-Self Report (BASC) to assess his coping, adjustment, and behavior. He produced a valid and consistent profile, with only mild elevation on the somatization scale, which is consistent with his medical presentation. His mother also completed the BASC and did not report any concerns or problems. On the Children's Depression Inventory (CDI), Jamie obtained a score well within normal limits.

Summary, Conclusions, and Recommendations

Jamie was diagnosed with a right temporal lobe anaplastic astrocytoma and underwent partial resection of the tumor with significant success. Jamie and his mother do not report acute changes in his behavior, cognition, or personality. He is repeating the sixth grade but does not receive formal (e.g., individualized education plan [IEP]) special education.

Results of the neuropsychological evaluation revealed that the majority of Jamie's cognitive skills fall in the average to superior range. The only relative weaknesses that were identified in the evaluation included difficulties related to remembering complex visual information, visual scanning, and fine motor speed in the nondominant (left) hand. These subtle inefficiencies or weaknesses are consistent with the typology and nature of his medical condition (excised tumor from the right temporal lobe). Aside from the possible effects of his current medication on memory functions, his relatively lower scores on indices of processing speed and working memory could be partially attributed to effects of his tumor, the subsequent chemotherapy and radiation therapy, and their impact on overall processing speed. A portion of his difficulties could be attributed to the impact of his tumor and subsequent treatment on centers and circuitry of the brain associated with memory and learning functions. A similar conclusion may be reached related to his circumscribed delays in fine motor skills of his nondominant (left) hand. Possible mild side effects of his antiseizure medication regimen may also partially explain his relative weaknesses in processing speed.

With regard to his emotional status, it appears that Jamie is coping adequately with his medical condition at the time of assessment. Both Jamie and his mother did not report any concerns related to depression, anxiety, or adjustment at that time.

His academic curriculum appears to be appropriate with accommodations, and he has been making suitable progress despite his complex medical and academic history and the rigorous nature of his educational programming in a highly demanding public school. However, given his medical condition and treatment, including radiation, chemotherapy, and the use of antiseizure medication, he is at risk for possible cognitive difficulties in the future, particularly as demands in school increase. Typically, the impact of radiation on cognitive functioning is not identified until 12 to 24 months after treatment. Therefore, it will be important to continue to monitor Jamie's academic progress, as well as cognitive and emotional functioning.

With regard to specific school recommendations, given the subtle and overt findings that emerged during the course of this evaluation, it is important to keep in mind several factors when working with Jamie, all of which were discussed with school officials. For instance, his relative weaknesses in information processing led to direct recommendations addressing structural classroom recommendations including seating arrangement (i.e., in front of the classroom next to his teacher), work environment (e.g., smaller work groups, smaller teacher-to-student ratio, use of a teacher's aid), and adjusting the quantity of work (e.g., use of criterion-based learning with reduction in quantity of work). School officials also were reminded of the importance of providing him with extra time (or untimed) to complete hands-on tasks or demanding academic tasks requiring significant sustained attention and fine motor skills, particularly if using his nondominant hand. It was also noted that visual information will need to be kept clear and organized so as to avoid a lot of visual scanning, which may be difficult for him. His score on the WISC IV, Working Memory index, in conjunction with his scores on other measures assessing this functional domain, also were used to underscore and buttress the importance of repetition of instructions to address his memory weaknesses. In this regard, it was recommended that new and unfamiliar materials, particularly those to be recalled at a later date, be repeatedly exposed to help the child better encode such information. It was also recommended that previous lessons be reviewed before exposing the child to new material. In addition, the use of memorization strategies, including verbal and visual mnemonics, were recommended for this child. Other school recommendations included requesting the school to label the child under the Other Health Impaired label as a result of his medical condition, which was accomplished through attendance at his IEP meeting. The results from the WISC-IV index scores were used in that meeting to substantiate claims that the child would benefit from programming accommodations as a result of his relative weaknesses in information processing speed and working memory. Ongoing involvement in structured age-appropriate social activities was noted to be important, including continued extracurricular activities in school and in the home.

CASE SUMMARY

This case underscores several important practice issues. First and foremost, the approach taken with this patient is consistent with ethical standards and practice guidelines set forth by the APA (APA, 1990; 2002) and the Standards for Educational and Psychological Testing (AERA et al., 1999). The language and choice of assessment measures were guided by both the examinee's language preference and the examinee's educational history as a non-native English speaker. Although this child is "Hispanic," he is unique with respect to acculturation, language, immigration, and socioeconomic status. In fact, he does not "fit" the panethnic "Hispanic" or the ethnocultural label "Mexican-American," illustrating the lack of specificity and inadequacy of such constructs. The child has maintained his native language and culture, but has also assimilated US culture. It appears that this child is truly bilingual beyond surface fluency. His competencies in both languages were observed, screened, and corroborated by his parents. While he may have been effectively assessed in either language, he is most appropriate for evaluation in English as a result of his formal educational experiences and bicultural background. Had there been concerns about either his established level of English proficiency or a possible language impairment, additional testing in Spanish (e.g., WISC-IV Spanish, CELF-3 Spanish) would be recommended. Because this child never immigrated, a number of potential acute or chronic stressors associated with the process of immigration that would be capable of influencing test performance are not applicable to this child (e.g., anxiety, depression, posttraumatic stress disorder). Clearly all these factors could have had significant implications for test selection and the validity of the inferences derived from the WISC-IV and other tests. Finally, the educational and socioeconomic background of the parents varies from average Census and other governmental survey statistics for individuals of Mexican origin. The standardization sample from the WISC-IV is appropriately representative of the child's current demographic background and is suitable for score interpretation.

CONCLUSION

When one considers the multitude of variables masked by ethnic umbrella terms, and particularly the variability of cultures and language competencies among diverse individuals, it is actually surprising that WISC score differences and discrepancies traditionally identified among and within groups are not more dramatic. Factor score differences in the WISC-IV between Hispanic and white non-Hispanic children were reduced to 6 points or less when subjects were matched on important demographic variables, including parental education, number of parents living in the home, and geographic residence. The remaining score differences disappeared when the native languages of children were controlled in our analyses.

Taking into consideration the issues addressed in this chapter, it is critical that examiners understand the background of the individual, and not simply rely on general group membership to determine test selection and interpretation practices (Harris, Echemendía, Ardila, & Rosselli, 2001). Practitioners must fully appreciate the composition of the normative sample used for comparison and appreciate the potential inherent limitations of the nomothetic approach for interpretation of individual performance. For those children who are relative newcomers to a country, such as those who have 5 years or less experience within the educational system of the new host country, there is a good likelihood that linguistic competencies necessary to optimally demonstrate intellectual abilities are not fully developed. In such cases, it may still be informative to assess the child in English with the caveat that the test may be measuring language skills as much as, or more so, than cognitive abilities, rendering the scores a crude approximation. True abilities may consequently be underestimated. For those children assessed in English, reevaluation should proceed on a more frequent basis to capture cognitive gains associated with the rapid development of English language competencies. Whenever possible, children should, at the very least, have the opportunity to respond to test stimuli in either the primary or secondary language, unless specific English-language abilities must be quantified and described. A translated and adapted version of the WISC-IV, for example the WISC-IV Spanish (2004) or another language adaptation of the earlier WISC-III (1991), may be a more suitable alternative in many cases where a child speaks English as a second language.

Even for standardization samples that include Hispanics or other ethnic groups representative of the US population, it is important to consider the proportion of cases within that sample. Because individuals who originate from Mexico account for 58.5% of the US Hispanic population, they likely represent the largest proportion of Hispanics in most standardization samples. Given the lower average educational attainment for individuals of Mexican nationality residing within the United States, the average obtained scores of "Hispanics" in a given normative sample may consequently be depressed. For tests that publish norms specific to ethnic groups or broad ethnodemographic (e.g., African American or Hispanic) adjustments, supplemental tables may be necessary to sufficiently understand the performance of a child from a specific background and to avoid errors in test interpretation.

The rich diversity of the highly mobile and migratory world of the twenty-first century is difficult to capture in psychological measures designed to assess the intellectual and cognitive abilities of individuals. Ethnic umbrella categories, such as "white" or "Hispanic" are typically used as a matter of convenience to organize test data both for test developers and test users. Unfortunately, these broad terms are often viewed as representing homogeneities and consistencies among individuals that will somehow ensure the integrity of data collection and score interpretation. Failure to appreciate the true variability within ethnic groupings may constrain not only the ability to appropriately select and utilize measures, but also interfere with the practitioner's own success in diagnostic decision making and the development of appropriate treatment interventions. For generations, the Wechsler scales and their adaptations have been reliable and valid tools for the assessment of intellectual abilities. Each revision has reflected the most current advances in cognitive and neuropsychological assessment and has validated its utility. The continued success of the WISC-IV with culturally diverse children will depend on the combined efforts of both its developers and users to incorporate the advances in society's own evolution to understand and embrace the diversity among the population of schoolchildren for whom the measure was developed.

ACKNOWLEDGMENTS

The authors extend their gratitude to Alejandrina Guzmán Bonilla, Susan Kongs, and Diana, Allensworth for their assistance with manuscript preparation and for their helpful comments on earlier drafts of this chapter. The authors also wish to thank Eric Rolfhus for assistance with data analyses.

REFERENCES

American Educational Research Association, American Psychological Association, & National Council on Measurement in Education. (1999). *The standards for educational and psychological testing.* Washington, DC: American Psychological Association.

American Psychological Association. (2002). Ethical principles of psychologists and code of conduct. *American Psychologist, 57,* 1060–1073.

American Psychological Association. (1990). *Guidelines for providers of services to ethnic, linguistic, and culturally diverse populations.* Washington, DC: American Psychological Association.

Ardila, A. (1998). Bilingualism: A neglected and chaotic area. *Aphasiology,12,* 131–134.

Ardila, A. (2002). Spanish-English bilingualism in the United States of America. In F. Fabbro (Ed.), *Advances of neurolinguistics of bilingualism. Essays in honor of Michael Paradis.* Udine (Italy): Forum. (pp. 49–67)

Bialystok, E. (1988). Levels of bilingualism and levels of linguistic awareness. *Developmental Psychology, 24,* 560–567.

Bialystok, E., & Cummins, J., (1991). Language, cognition, and education of bilingual children. In B. Ellen (Ed.), *Language processing in bilingual children* (pp. 222–232). Cambridge, UK: Cambridge University Press.

Bialystok, E., Craik, F. I. M., Klein, R., & Viswanathan, M. (2004). Bilingualism, aging, and cognitive control: Evidence from the Simon task. *Psychology and Aging, 19,* 290–303.

Canadian Heritage (2002). Canadian heritage: Annual report. Official languages 2000–2001. Ottawa: Public Works and Government Services.

Carroll, J. B. (1993). *Human cognitive abilities: A survey of factor-analytic studies.* Cambridge, MA: Cambridge University Press.

Cattell, R. B. (1971). *Abilities: Their structure, growth, and action.* Boston: Houghton Mifflin.

Ceci, S. J. (1996). *On intelligence* (expanded ed.). Cambridge, MA: Harvard University Press.

Centeno, J. G., & Obler, L. K. (2001). Principles of Bilingualism. In M. O. Pontón & J. León-Carrión, (Eds.), *Neuropsychology and the Hispanic patient: A clinical handbook.* (pp. 75–86). Mahwah, NJ: Lawrence Erlbaum Associates, Publishers.

Collier, V. P. (1992). A synthesis of studies examining long-term language minority student data on academic achievement. *Bilingual Education Research Journal 16(1/2),* 187–221.

Cummins, J. (1979). Linguistic interdependence and the educational development of bilingual children. *Review of Educational Research, 49(2),* 222–251.

Cummins, J. (1981a). Age on arrival and immigrant second language learning in Canada: A reassessment. *Applied Linguistics, 2(2),* 132–149.

Cummins, J. (1981b). The role of primary language development in promoting educational success for language minority students. In California State Department of Education, *Schooling and language minority students: A theoretical framework.* Los Angeles: Evaluation, Dissemination and Assessment Center.

Cummins, J. (1989). *Empowering language minority students.* Sacramento, CA: California Association for Bilingual Education.

Galloway, L. M. (1982). Bilingualism: Neuropsychological considerations. *Journal of Research and Development in Education, 15(3),* 12–28.

Gardner, H. (1983). *Frames of mind: The theory of multiple intelligences.* New York: Basic Books.

Georgas, J., Van de Vijver, F. J. R., Weiss, L. G., & Saklofske, D. H. (2003). A cross-cultural analysis of the WISC-III. In Georgas, J., Weiss, L. G., Van de Vijver, F. J. R., & Saklofske, D. H. (Eds.), *Culture and children's intelligence: Cross-cultural analysis of the WISC-III.* (pp. 277 –313). San Diego CA: Academic Press.

Georgas, J., Weiss, L. G., Van de Vijver, F. J. R., & Saklofske, D. H. (Eds.), (2003). *Culture and Children's Intelligence: Cross-cultural analysis of the WISC-III.* San Diego: Academic Press.

Grimes, B. F., & Grimes, J. E. (2004). *Ethnologue: Languages of the world* (14th ed.). Dallas, TX: SIL International.

Hakuta, K. (1986). *Mirror of language.* New York: Basic Books.

Hamers, J. F., & Blanc M. H. A. (1989). *Bilinguality and bilingualism.* Cambridge, England: Cambridge University Press.

Hamilton, N., & Chinchilla, N. S. (1990). Central American migration: A framework for analysis. *Latin American Research Review, 25,* 75–110.

Harris, J. G., Echemendía, R., Ardila, A., & Rosselli, M. (2001). Cross-cultural cognitive and neuropsychological assessment. In J. W. Andrews, H. Janzen, & D. Saklofske (Eds.), *Handbook of psychoeducational assessment: Ability, achievement, and behavior in Children.* San Diego: Academic Press.

Harris, J. G., Tulsky D. S., & Schultheis, M. T. (2003). Assessment of the non-native English speaker: Assimilating history and research findings to guide clinical practice. In D. S. Tulsky, D. H. Saklofske, G. J. Chelune, R. J. Heaton, R. J. Ivnik, R. Bornstein *et al.* (Eds.), *Clinical interpretation of the WAIS-III and WMS-III.* (pp. 343–390). San Diego: Academic Press.

Heaton, R. K., Grant, I., & Matthews, C. G. (1986). Differences in neuropsychological test performance associated with age, education, and sex. In I. Grant & K. M. Adams (Eds.), *Neuropsychological assessment of neuropsychiatric disorders* (pp. 100–120). New York: Oxford University Press.

Helms, J. (1992). Why is there no study of cultural equivalence in standardized cognitive ability testing? *American Psychologist, 47,* 1083–1101.

Hernstein, R. J., & Murray, C. (1994). *The bell curve: Intelligence and class structure in American life.* New York: Free Press.

Kaufman, A. S., & Doppelt, J. E. (1976). Analysis of WISC-R standardization data in terms of stratification variables. *Child Development, 74,* 165–171.

Kindler, A. (2002). *What are the most common language groups for LEP students?* Retrieved June 23, 2004 from http://www.ncela.gwu.edu/pubs/reports/state-data/2000/usa.pdf.

Llorente, A. M., Ponton, M. O., Taussig, I. M., & Satz, P. (1999). Patterns of American immigration and their influence on the acquisition of neuropsychological norms for Hispanics. *Archives of Clinical Neuropsychology, 14,* 603–614.

Llorente, A. M., Taussig, I. M., Perez, L., & Satz, P. (2000). Trends in American immigration: Influences on neuropsychological assessment and inferences with ethnic-minority populations. In E. Fletcher-Janzen, T. Strickland, & C. R. Reynolds (Eds.), *Handbook of cross-cultural neuropsychology* (pp. 345–359). New York: Kluwer Academic/Plenum Publishers.

Marin G., & Marin, B. V. (1991). *Research with Hispanic populations.* Newbury Park, CA: Sage.

México, Gobierno de La República. Carta de derechos y obligaciones laborales en lenguas indígenas. Retrieved June 20, 2004 from http://www.gob.mx/wb2/egobierno/egob_Derechos_y_Obligaciones_Laborales.

Minicucci, C., & Olsen, L. (1992, Spring). *Programs for secondary limited English proficient students: A California study.* (Occasional Papers in Bilingual Education, No. 5.) Washington, DC: National Clearinghouse for Bilingual Education.

Mohanty, A. K. (1990). Psychological consequences of mother-tongue maintenance and the language of literacy for linguistic minorities in India. *Psychology and Developing Societies, 2,* 31–51.

National Conference of State Legislatures (2004). In-state tuition and unauthorized immigrant students. Issued: April 29, 2003. Retrieved July 1, 2004 from http://www.ncsl.org/programs/immig/TuitionApril04.htm.

National Conference of State Legislatures (2003). Tuition and unauthorized immigrant students. Issued: August 14, 2003. Retrieved July 1, 2004 from http://www.ncsl.org/programs/immig/tuition 2003.htm.

Neisser, U., Boooo, G., Bouchard, T. J., Boykin, A. W., Brody, N., Ceci, S. J., Halpern, D. F., Loehlin, J. C., Perloff, R., Sternberg, R. J., & Urbina, S. (1996). Intelligence: Knowns and unknowns. *American Psychologist, 51,* 77–101.

Oakes, J. (1990). *Multiplying inequalities: The effects of race social class, and tracking on opportunities to learn mathematics and science.* Santa Monica, CA: RAND.

Passel, J. S., Capps, R., & Fix, M. (2004). Undocumented immigrants: Facts and figures. http://www.urban.org/UploadedPDF/1000587_undoc_immigrants_facts.pdf.

Portes, A., & Borocsz, J. (1989). Contemporary immigration: Theoretical perspectives on determinants and modes of incorporation. *International Migration Review, 23,* 606–630.

Portes, A., & Rumbaut, R. G. (1990). *Immigrant America: A portrait.* Los Angeles, University of California Press.

Prifitera, A., Weiss, L. G., & Saklofske, D. H. (1998). The WISC-III in context. In A. Prifitera, & D. H. Saklofske (Eds.), *WISC-III Clinical use and interpretation: Scientist-practitioner perspectives.* (pp. 1–38.) San Diego CA: Academic Press.

Ramírez, J., Pasta, D., Yuen, S., Ramey, D., & Billings, D. (1991). *Final report: longitudinal study of structured English immersion strategy, early-exit and late-exit bilingual education programs for language-minority children.* (Vols. I, II) (No. 300–87–0156). San Mateo, CA: Aguirre International.

Rey, G. J., Feldman, E., Rivas-Vasquez, R., Levin, B. E., Benton, A. (1999). Neuropsychological test development for Hispanics. *Archives of Clinical Neuropsychology, 14,* 593–601.

Reynolds, C. R. (2000). Methods for detecting and evaluating cultural bias in neuropsychological tests. In E. Fletcher-Janzen, T. Strickland, & C. R. Reynolds (Eds.), *Handbook of cross-cultural neuropsychology* (pp. 249–285). New York: Kluwer Academic/Plenum Publishers.

Reynolds, C. R. & Kaiser, S. M. (2003). Bias in the assessment of aptitude. In C. R. Reynolds & R. W. Kamphaus (Eds.), *Handbook of psychological and educational assessment of children* (2nd ed.). (pp. 519–562). New York: Wiley.

Ricciardelli, L. A. (1992a). Creativity and bilingualism. *Journal of Creative Behavior, 26,* 246–254.

Ricciardelli, L. A. (1992b). Bilingualism and cognitive development in relation to threshold theory. *Journal of Psycholinguistic Research, 21,* 301–316.

Romaine, S. (1995). *Bilingualism* (2nd ed.). Oxford, England: Blackwell.

Sattler, J. M. (1992). *Assessment of children* (Revised and updated, 3rd ed.). San Diego: Author.

Spearman, C. E. (1927). *The abilities of man.* New York: Macmillian.

Sternberg, R. J., Forsythe, G. B., Hedlund, J., Horvath, J., Snook, S., Williams, W. M., Wagner, R. K., & Grigorenko, E. L. (2000). *Practical intelligence in everyday life.* New York: Cambridge University Press.

Thurstone, L. L. (1938). *Primary mental abilities.* Chicago: University of Chicago Press.

United States Census Bureau (2004). Annual high school dropout rates by sex, race, grade, and Hispanic origin: October 1967 to 2002. Internet release date: January 9, 2004. Retrieved June 23, 2004, from http://www.census.gov/population/socdemo/school/tabA-4.pdf.

United States Census Bureau (2003a). Educational attainment of the population 25 years and over by age, sex, race, and Hispanic or Latino origin type: March 2000. Internet release date: June 18, 2003. Retrieved June 23, 2004, from http://www.census.gov/prod/2003pubs/c2kbr-24.pdf.

United States Census Bureau (2003b). Poverty status of the population in 1999 by sex, age, Hispanic orgin, and race: March 2000. Internet release date: June 18, 2003. Retrieved June 23, 2004, from http://www.census.gov/populations/socdemo/hispanic/ppl-171/tabl4-1.pdf.

United States Census Bureau (2003c). Language use, English ability, and linguistic isolation for the population 5 to 17 years by state: 2000. Internet release date: February 25, 2003. Retrieved June 23, 2004, from http://www/census.gov/population/cen2000/phc-t20/tab02.pdf.

United States Census Bureau (2003d). Language use and English speaking ability: 2000. Issued October, 2003. Retrieved October 9, 2003 from http://www.census.gov/prod/2003pubs/c2kbr-29.pdf.

United States Census Bureau (2001a). *The Hispanic population 2000.* Issued May 2001. Retrieved June 23, 2004, from http://www.census.gov/prod/2001 pubs/c2kbr01-3.pdf.

United States Census Bureau (2001b). Profile of foreign-born population in the United States: 2000. Issued December 2001. Retrieved July 8, 2004, from http://www.census.gov/prod/2002pubs/p23-206.pdf.

United States Department of Homeland Security. (2003). *2002 yearbook of immigration statistics.* (Formerly entitled Statistical Yearbook of the Immigration and Naturalization Service.) Washington, DC: U.S. Government Printing Office.

United States Immigration and Naturalization Service. (1991). *1990 statistical yearbook of the Immigration and Naturalization Service.* Washington, DC: U.S. Government Printing Office.

Vázquez, J. Z. (1994). *Una Historia de Mexico.* [A history of Mexico]. Mexico City: L Editorial Patria.

Weiss, L. G., Prifitera, A., & Roid, G. H. (1993). The WISC-III and fairness of predicting achievement across ethnic and gender groups. *Journal for Psychoeducational Assessment* monograph series, *Advances in psychological assessment: Wechsler Intelligence Scale for Children–Third Edition* (pp. 35–42).

Wechsler, D. (1949). *Manual for the Wechsler Intelligence Scale for Children.* New York: The Psychological Corporation.

Wechsler, D. (1974). *Manual for the Wechsler Intelligence Scale for Children-Revised.* San Antonio, TX: The Psychological Corporation.

Wechsler, D. (1991). *Manual for the Wechsler Intelligence Scale for Children-Third Edition.* San Antonio, TX: The Psychological Corporation.

Wechsler, D. (2003). *Manual for the Wechsler Intelligence Scale for Children-Fourth Edition.* San Antonio, TX: The Psychological Corporation.

Wechsler, D. (in press). *Manual for the Wechsler Intelligence Scale for Children: Fourth Edition Spanish.* San Antonio, TX: Harcourt.

13

THE WISC-IV AND NEUROPSYCHOLOGICAL ASSESSMENT

KEITH OWEN YEATES

Columbus Children's Research Institute
Department of Pediatrics, The Ohio State University
Columbus, Ohio

JACOBUS DONDERS

Mary Free Bed Rehabilitation Hospital
Grand Rapids, Michigan

Neuropsychological assessment of children is a complex process by which historical information, behavioral observations, and standardized psychological tests are used to make inferences about brain impairment and its implications for adaptive functioning in a developmental context (Yeates & Taylor, 2001). Intelligence tests have traditionally been a standard part of neuropsychological assessment, and surveys indicate that the Wechsler tests specifically are the most frequently used measures of intelligence among practicing neuropsychologists (Butler, Retzlaff, & Vanderploeg, 1991; Camara, Nathan, & Puente, 2000; Sullivan & Bowden, 1997).

Although intelligence tests were originally developed primarily to predict academic achievement, as opposed to brain function, they have long been used to assess cognitive dysfunction in individuals with brain injury and disease (Groth-Marnat, Gallagher, Hale, & Kaplan, 2000). Nevertheless, the use of intelligence tests in neuropsychological assessment is not without controversy. Indeed, some neuropsychologists have advocated the complete abandonment of intelligence tests (Lezak, 1995).

A balanced perspective on the use of intelligence tests in neuropsychological assessment acknowledges that they have both advantages and disadvantages (Baron, 2004). On one hand, intelligence tests are well-standardized measures that assess a broad range of cognitive skills. They typically have excellent psychometric properties, in terms of both reliability and validity, and are standardized using large normative samples (Sattler, 2001). The Wechsler series of intelligence tests in particular has been used extensively in research on the effects of brain damage or dysfunction, and has demonstrated both criterion and ecological validity. In other words, the Wechsler intelligence tests are sensitive to brain impairment as well as predictive of important functional outcomes (Groth-Marnat et al., 2000). Intelligence tests are also important from a practical perspective when used with children, because they are often necessary to justify recommendations for special education and other services in clinical practice.

On the other hand, intelligence tests were not developed to assess the distinct or unitary cognitive abilities that are of primary interest to neuropsychologists. As a consequence, despite their sensitivity to brain impairment in general, they often do not provide much insight into the specific nature of the underlying impairment. In other words, they are not always helpful in delineating the patterns of domain-specific strengths and weaknesses demonstrated by children with brain damage or dysfunction, and hence may not be especially useful for drawing specific inferences about brain function. Intelligence tests also do not assess the entire range of abilities that are relevant to predicting important functional outcomes, as reflected in the robust relationships between academic achievement and specific neuropsychological test performances, even after IQ is controlled statistically (Taylor, Fletcher, & Satz, 1982).

Our perspective is that intelligence tests are an important component of neuropsychological assessment, despite their limitations, in part because they are useful from a heuristic perspective for generating hypotheses about patterns of cognitive skills. Among neuropsychologists working with children, the Wechsler Intelligence Scale for Children (WISC) in its various iterations has been the most widely adopted intelligence test (Butler et al., 1991; Camara et al., 2000; Sullivan & Bowden, 1997). The WISC has evolved over time, and is now in its fourth generation. In the current chapter, we review the role of the Wechsler Intelligence Scale for Children-Fourth Edition (WISC-IV; Wechsler, 2003a) in neuropsychological assessment.

Because the WISC-IV is just recently published, and hence has not yet been the focus of published research, we begin by summarizing the neuropsychological research literature pertaining to the Wechsler Intelligence Scale for Children-Third Edition (WISC-III; Wechsler, 1991). We then describe the WISC-IV, focusing on changes in it compared to the WISC-III and their implications for neuropsychological assessment. Some validity data for the WISC-IV is then presented, based on a co-norming study involving the Children's Memory Scale (Cohen, 1997) and on a clinical study of children with traumatic brain injury (TBI) and a matched comparison group, both described in the WISC-IV Technical and Interpretive

Manual (Wechsler, 2003b). We conclude with the presentation of a case study illustrating the use of the WISC-IV in neuropsychological assessment.

THE WISC-III IN NEUROPSYCHOLOGICAL ASSESSMENT AND RESEARCH

Several interpretive methods have been applied to the WISC-III in the context of clinical neuropsychological assessment, as well as in applied research (Hynd, Cohen, Riccio, & Arceneaux, 1998). The most widespread ones have focused on discrepancies between IQ or subtest scores, but additional approaches have addressed the construct and criterion validity of the four factor index scores. We will address each of these methods, with specific reference to some of the most common conditions in which they have been investigated.

VIQ–PIQ PATTERNS

Historically, studies involving the WISC-III or its predecessors have reported only modest specificity in terms of the effect of unilateral cerebral lesions. Ballantyne, Scarvie, and Trauner (1994) reported that, in children who had suffered perinatal strokes, FSIQ was generally lower than expected, but VIQ and PIQ were similar in the group with left hemisphere strokes, whereas PIQ was more affected than VIQ in children with right hemisphere lesions. More recently, Hogan, Kirkham, and Isaacs (2000) concluded on the basis of a comprehensive literature review that, unlike with adults, unilateral strokes are not typically associated with marked VIQ–PIQ discrepancies in young children and that only a trend toward lateralizing profiles emerges in older children. Klein, Levin, Duchovny, and Llabre (2000) also did not find consistent effects of laterality on VIQ–PIQ discrepancies in children with cortical dysplasia and epilepsy. On the other hand, clearly lateralized lesions are much less common in children than in adults, and cognitive impairments after early unilateral lesions may also be affected by factors other than laterality, such as a history of seizures or time since injury (Vargha-Khadem, Isaacs, & Muter, 1994).

VIQ–PIQ discrepancies have also been investigated in nonfocal neurological disorders. Some authors have suggested that the direction of VIQ–PIQ discrepancies may change with age, such as after prenatal exposure to alcohol, due to the increasing emphasis on speed with advancing age on the WISC-III (Korkman, Kettunen, & Autti-Rämö, 2003). For other conditions, such as the syndrome of nonverbal learning disability, VIQ–PIQ discrepancies have been deemphasized as classification criteria in recent years (Pelletier, Ahmad, & Rourke, 2001). A pattern of relatively better VIQ than PIQ has been reported more consistently in studies of children with hydrocephalus (Donders, Canady, & Rourke, 1990; Wills, 1993; Brookshire *et al.*, 1995), and this pattern also has been found recently when utilizing the Verbal Comprehension and Perceptual Organization factor indexes of the WISC-III (Yeates, Loss, Colvin, & Enrile, 2003).

The WISC-IV no longer utilizes separate VIQ and PIQ scores, but instead emphasizes interpretation of four factor indexes, including Verbal Comprehension, Perceptual Reasoning, Working Memory, and Processing Speed, in addition to Full Scale IQ. Further research is needed to determine whether findings based on VIQ–PIQ scores generalize to those involving Verbal Comprehension and Perceptual Reasoning, although the respective indices are moderately to highly correlated.

SUBTEST PATTERNS

Considerable folklore exists among practitioners that cerebral dysfunction is associated with increased variability in performance within and between WISC-III subtests. In this context, the scatter and shape of the subtest profile should be distinguished. Scatter typically refers to the difference between the highest and the lowest subtest scaled scores, although it is sometimes defined as the degree to which subtest scaled scores diverge from the mean of the profile. Scatter also can be defined as a form of variability within a subtest (e.g., item scores of 0 interspersed with scores of 1 or 2). Shape, on the other hand, reflects where the high and low points in the profile occur. For example, a 6-point difference between Vocabulary and Similarities scaled scores would represent a different shape than a similar sized discrepancy between Vocabulary and Symbol Search scaled scores, even though the degree of scatter is identical.

Most of the existing research has focused on scatter rather than shape, and much of it has been conducted with children with learning disabilities. The consensus over the past decade clearly indicates that extensive interpretation of intrasubtest or intersubtest scatter on the WISC-III is a dubious enterprise, for which research provides little support in terms of either validity or utility (Dumont & Willis, 1995; Daley & Nagle, 1996; Greenway & Milne, 1999). For example, although some variability in subtest patterns has been noted in various clinical samples (Mayes, Calhoun, & Crowell, 1998; Prifitera & Dersch, 1993; Schwean & Saklofske, 1998), individual subtests have demonstrated insufficient predictive power in the identification and differentiation of children with attention deficit–hyperactivity disorder (ADHD) (Perugini, Harvey, Lovejoy, Sandstrom, & Webb, 2000; Assesmany, McIntosh, Phelps, & LeAdelle, 2001).

One major problem with the interpretation of WISC-III subtest scatter is that clinicians tend to underestimate its base rate (Schinka, Vanderploeg, & Curtiss, 1997). Even when a particularly marked degree of scatter can be classified as unusual in comparison to base rates, it should never be interpreted in isolation but considered within the context of a broader neuro-psychological evaluation (Schinka, Vanderploeg, & Greblo, 1998). Profile shape may contribute some amount of incremental diagnostic information, but it, too, is typically fairly limited (Pritchard, Livingston, Reynolds, & Moses, 2000; Watkins & Glutting, 2000).

FACTOR INDEX SCORES

A major innovation of the WISC-III, and now central to the WISC-IV and WAIS-III, was the introduction of factor index scores as an alternative approach to the interpretation of performance. The four-factor structure of Verbal Comprehension, Perceptual Organization, Freedom from Distractibility, and Processing Speed has been challenged by some authors (Kamphaus, Benson, Hutchinson, & Platt, 1994; see also Sattler & Saklofske, 2001), but on balance, most studies utilizing confirmatory factor analysis have supported it. Roid and Worrall (1997) replicated the four-factor structure in an independent normative sample. More recently, Georgas, Weiss, Van de Vijver, and Saklofske (2003) provided compelling results in support of the robustness of the factor structure in countries in North America, Europe, and Asia. In addition, support for the construct validity of this structure has also been reported in various clinical samples, including children with traumatic brain injury (Donders & Warschausky, 1996), a mixed sample with various special education needs (Konold, Kush, & Canivez, 1997), and psychiatric inpatients (Tupa, Wright, & Fristad, 1997). More recent research has suggested that support for the construct validity of Verbal Comprehension, Perceptual Organization, and Processing Speed appears to be relatively stronger than that for Freedom from Distractibility (Watkins & Kush, 2002).

Within the context of a neuropsychological evaluation, criterion validity is another important consideration. Substantial research has addressed this, particularly with regard to the newer factor index scores, Freedom from Distractibility (FFD) index and Processing Speed index (PSI). With regard to FFD, the findings have been somewhat disappointing. Reinecke, Beebe, and Stein (1999) reported that the majority of their 200 participants with ADHD did not show a relative weakness on FFD compared with the other factor index scores and that FFD scores were not correlated with an independent measure of sustained attention. Furthermore, Doyle, Biederman, Seidman, Weber, and Faraone (2000) found only moderate positive predictive power and poor negative predictive power for FFD in the differentiation of 113 participants with ADHD from 103 normal control subjects. On the other hand, FFD was not designed to be diagnostic of ADHD or necessarily to measure attention. Indeed, FFD may have less to do with inattention or distractibility than with working memory, as reflected in correlations with measures of sentence recall and repetition of hand movements (Riccio,

Cohen, Hall, & Ross, 1997). Based on this research, FFD has been restructured considerably and renamed Working Memory on the WISC–IV (see later).

The findings have been more encouraging with regard to PSI in children with cerebral dysfunction. Several studies have found fairly strong relationships between injury severity and performance on PSI in children with TBI (Donders, 1997; Tremont, Mittenberg, & Miller, 1999). In addition, PSI appears to be a mediating variable with regard to other abilities (e.g., memory efficiency) in such children (Donders & Woodward, 2003). On the other hand, PSI scores do not appear to be particularly helpful in the diagnosis of ADHD (Riccio *et al.*, 1997).

ABILITY AND ACHIEVEMENT

The co-norming of the WISC-III with the Wechsler Individual Achievement Test (WIAT; Wechsler, 1992) also offered the opportunity to make predictions about expected academic achievement and to consider the magnitude and the base rate of discrepancies between the two. The WISC-IV has also been linked with the revision of the WIAT, the WIAT-II (Wechsler, 2002). However, caution has been expressed about conducting multivariate comparisons (i.e., comparing FSIQ to several WIAT composite scores as opposed to only one), because 17% of the WISC-III and WIAT linking sample displayed at least one significant discrepancy, raising concerns about possible false positive results in clinical practice (Glutting, McDermott, Prifitera, & McGrath, 1994). Furthermore, significant reservations have been expressed about the validity of the IQ–achievement discrepancy concept in the diagnosis of learning disabilities (Fletcher *et al.*, 2002; Sternberg & Grigorenko, 2002). Concerns arise from statistical considerations, such as the unreliability of difference scores, and from the fact that discrepancies of similar magnitude do not necessarily mean the same thing along the IQ spectrum. In addition, a substantial overlap exists in cognitive test scores between low-achieving children who do and do not display IQ–achievement discrepancies. Thus, classifications of learning disability on the basis of discrepancy with FSIQ appear to have limited validity.

CHANGES IN THE WISC-IV

The WISC-IV embodies a number of changes compared to the WISC-III, as described in the Technical and Interpretive Manual (Wechsler, 2003b). We will not describe all of the changes here, but focus on those with the most import for neuropsychological assessment. One of the most notable set of changes in the WISC-IV involves the elimination of certain subtests and addition of others. The Picture Arrangement, Object Assembly, and Mazes subtests from the WISC-III have been eliminated. New subtests on the WISC-IV include Word Reasoning, Matrix Reasoning, Picture Concepts, Letter-Number Sequencing, and Cancellation.

The structure of the test also has been altered. The four factor indexes have been retained, but Verbal Comprehension index (VCI) is now defined by three core subtests rather than four, because Information has been made a supplemental subtest. The Perceptual Organization index (POI) has been renamed the Perceptual Reasoning index (PRI), because the three core subtests that now define it—Block Design, Matrix Reasoning, and Picture Concepts—are thought to place a greater emphasis on fluid reasoning and less emphasis on visuospatial skills. The elimination of Object Assembly and assignment of Picture Completion as a supplemental subtest is consistent with this goal. The FFD has been renamed the Working Memory index (WMI) to better reflect the nature of its constituent subtests and is now defined by Digit Span and Letter-Number Sequencing, with Arithmetic as a supplemental subtest. Finally, the PSI has a new supplemental subtest, Cancellation.

The composite scores generated by the WISC-IV also have been altered. The traditional Verbal and Performance IQ scores are no longer computed. Instead, a Full Scale IQ is computed based on equal weighting of all 10 core subtests. The Full Scale IQ is supplemented by the four index scores. The elimination of VIQ and PIQ scores reflects a greater emphasis on the factor structure of the WISC-IV and its consistency with theories of intelligence (Wechsler, 2003b).

IMPLICATIONS FOR NEUROPSYCHOLOGICAL ASSESSMENT

The substantive changes that have been incorporated in the WISC-IV have potentially significant implications for neuropsychological assessment. The interpretation of the VCI is unlikely to be significantly different because its constituent subtests have not changed. In contrast, the PRI and WMI have been changed substantially as compared to, respectively, the WISC-III POI and FFD. Two subtests (as opposed to one) from both WMI and PSI now contribute to FSIQ, which makes it less dependent on the traditional verbal and nonverbal components.

PERCEPTUAL REASONING

As a result of the changes described previously, the WISC-IV PRI may not be as strongly correlated with other measures of visual-perceptual and constructional skills as was the POI on the WISC-III. Although Block Design remains one of the core subtests of the PRI, and is a traditional measure of constructional skills, the two new core subtests, Matrix Reasoning and Picture Concepts, are less clearly measures of visuospatial skills. Indeed, they were added to make the PRI more of a measure of fluid reasoning, a construct that does not map cleanly onto traditional ability domains in neuropsychology. Notably, the correlation between the PRI and POI was the lowest among the four sets of paired index scores in a study involving administration of both the WISC-III and WISC-IV to a sample of 244 children ages 6 to 16, as presented in the Technical and Interpretive Manual (Wechsler, 2003b).

The sensitivity of the PRI to brain impairment is also uncertain, but may be less than that of the POI or PIQ from the WISC-III. The roles of speeded performance and motor skills have been substantially reduced on the PRI as compared to the POI. Bonuses for speed of performance are given only on Block Design, which also is the only subtest to require manipulation of objects. Additionally, an alternative scoring procedure is available to generate a standard score on Block Design that does not include time bonuses, as are tables to determine the base rates of differences between the untimed score and the usual score in the standardization sample. Because deficits in processing speed and motor skills are very common among children with brain impairment, these changes may make the PRI less likely to be sensitive to neurological deficits.

In addition, recent evidence suggests that matrix reasoning tests are not especially sensitive to acute brain impairment in adults (Donders, Tulsky, & Zhu, 2001). The sensitivity of the Picture Concepts subtest to brain impairment is a question for future research. Although the task uses pictorial stimuli rather than printed words, it is analogous to the Verbal Concept Attainment Test (Bornstein, 1982, 1983), which has demonstrated sensitivity to brain damage in adults, and specifically to focal frontal lesions (Bornstein & Leason, 1985). However, a similar relationship may not necessarily hold in children. Interestingly, children with TBI displayed deficits on the PRI in the clinical validity study presented in the WISC-IV Technical and Interpretive Manual (Wechsler, 2003b), but differences among its constituent subtests were significant only for the Block Design and Picture Completion subtests, and not for Picture Concepts or Matrix Reasoning.

WORKING MEMORY

The WMI has been restructured by making the Arithmetic subtest supplemental and adding the Letter-Number Sequencing subtest. The WMI is now likely to be a purer measure of working memory, because it is no longer confounded by arithmetic skills. In addition, the Arithmetic subtest itself was altered to reduce the demands for mathematical knowledge and to increase working memory demands. The standard score for the Digit Span subtest that is used in the calculation of the WMI continues to be based on both forward and backward trials, although standard scores can now be computed separately for the different types of trials and tables are available to determine the base rates of differences in the standardization sample. Notably, in the clinical validity studies presented in the Technical and Interpretive Manual (Wechsler, 2003b), deficits on WMI were identified among groups of children with reading disorders, language disorders, and ADHD, but not among children with TBI. A closer examination in the latter sample, though, reveals that deficits were significant on Letter-Number Sequencing and Arithmetic, but not on Digit Span, in part because simple forward span remained relatively intact.

PROCESSING SPEED

The PSI is likely to remain the composite measure from the WISC-IV that is most sensitive to acute brain impairment, just as it was on the WISC-III (Donders, 1997; Tremont *et al.*, 1999), because of the ubiquity of processing speed deficits among children with acute brain insults. In the clinical validity studies presented in the Technical and Interpretive Manual (Wechsler, 2003b), children with TBI displayed their most pronounced deficits on the PSI. The core subtests composing the PSI have not been altered, but the addition of Cancellation as a supplemental subtest may prove helpful to neuropsychologists, who have used similar tasks for many years to measure constructs including focused attention, spatial neglect, and processing speed (Baron, 2004; Geldmacher, 1996; Halligan, Marshall, & Wade, 1989). In factor analytic studies presented in the Technical and Interpretive Manual (Wechsler, 2003b), the Cancellation subtest actually loads somewhat higher on the PSI than does Coding, and neuropsychologists may want to consider substituting it for Coding, especially if they wish to remove the confounding demand for graphomotor control on Coding. The Cancellation subtest has an alternative scoring system that allows for a comparison of performance on the structured and random arrays in terms of base rates in the standardization sample. Poor performance on random vs structured array potentially may be sensitive to planning skills, as suggested by the finding that children with ADHD displayed deficits on the random but not structured array in the clinical validity study presented in the Technical and Interpretive Manual (Wechsler, 2003b).

VALIDITY OF THE WISC-IV

Because the WISC-IV has only recently been published, studies of its validity are limited to those presented in the Technical and Interpretive Manual (Wechsler, 2003b). For neuropsychologists, two of the validity studies may be of particular interest. These involve the joint administration of the WISC-IV with, respectively, the Children's Memory Scale (CMS; Cohen, 1997) and the Delis–Kaplan Executive Function System (D-KEFS; Delis, Kaplan, & Kramer, 2001).

WISC–IV AND CMS

The first validity study we discuss involved the administration of the WISC-IV and CMS to a sample of 126 normal children ranging in age from 6 to 16 years (m = 11.28, SD = 3.00). The Technical and Interpretive Manual presents the correlations between the four index scores and FSIQ from the WISC-IV and the primary composite scores from the CMS. To supplement the zero-order correlations, we conducted multiple regression analyses using the four WISC-IV indices as predictors of the major CMS composites (Table 13.1). Taken together, several findings are of interest for neuropsychologists:

1. The correlations between the WISC-IV and CMS scores are significant, but not of such magnitude to suggest that they are measuring the same constructs.

2. With the exception of the PSI, the WISC-IV indices consistently display lower correlations with the Visual Immediate and Delayed composites from the CMS than with the Verbal Immediate and Delayed composites. The four WISC-IV indices explain about 33% to 37% of the variance in the CMS verbal composites as compared to about 10% to 14% in the CMS visual composites (Table 13.1). Thus, the WISC-IV overlaps more with verbal than visual memory tasks.

TABLE 13.1   Regression Analyses Predicting CMS Composite Scores from Four WISC-IV Index Scores

| WISC-IV Index | CMS Composite | | | | | | | |
	Visual Immediate	Visual Delayed	Verbal Immediate	Verbal Delayed	General Memory	Attention/ Concentration	Learning	Delayed Recognition
VCI	−0.05	−0.02	*0.37*	*0.35*	*0.24*	0.11	0.17	*0.40*
PRI	0.15	0.22	0.03	0.08	0.14	*0.17*	0.10	0.01
WMI	*0.30*	0.16	*0.28*	*0.21*	*0.30*	*0.55*	*0.36*	0.11
PSI	0.03	0.02	−0.01	0.14	0.06	0.09	−0.01	0.02
Total R^2	.14	.10	.33	.37	.35	.57	.27	.23

Note. Values listed for each WISC-IV index are standardized beta weights for prediction of the CMS composite score. Significant values ($p < .05$ for t test) are italicized. All total R^2 are significant ($p < .05$).
VCI = Verbal Comprehension index; PRI = Perceptual Reasoning index; WMI = Working Memory index; PSI = Processing Speed index.

3. Both the PRI and WMI correlate more strongly with the Visual Immediate and Delayed composites than do the VCI and PSI. As Table 13.1 shows, only the WMI accounted for unique variance in the visual memory composites. Thus, the visual memory composites appear to tap working memory more than verbal comprehension, perceptual reasoning, or processing speed.

4. Conversely, the VCI and WMI are correlated somewhat more strongly with the Verbal Immediate and Delayed composites than are the PRI and PSI. Multiple regression analyses showed that the VCI and WMI accounted for unique variance in the verbal composites, but the PRI and PSI did not (Table 13.1). The findings reflect modest domain specificity in terms of the distinction between verbal and visual/nonverbal skills.

5. The PSI has lower correlations with the CMS than any of the other WISC-IV indices, and did not account for unique variance in any of the CMS composites. The PSI seems to be tapping a cognitive dimension largely unrelated to memory.

6. All WISC-IV indices are significantly correlated with the Attention/Concentration composite from the CMS, but the largest correlation is with the WMI. The latter correlation is not surprising, given the identical content of two of the component subtests (i.e., Digit Span for WMI, Numbers for the CMS Attention/Concentration composite). The significant correlations with the other WISC-IV indices may reflect the strong relationship that has been posited between working memory and other cognitive abilities (Fry & Hale, 1996; Swanson, 1996).

We also examined the correlations between the WISC-IV indices and the specific subtests that comprise the CMS. Three findings emerged that help to qualify the results obtained using the CMS composites:

1. The Faces subtest was not significantly correlated with any of the WISC-IV indices, and the four WISC-IV indices did not account for significant variance in the Faces subtest in multiple regression analyses. Thus, the Faces measure appears to be measuring something distinct from the cognitive abilities tapped by the WISC-IV.

2. The Dot Locations subtest was significantly correlated with all of the WISC-IV indices except the PSI. In multiple regression analyses, the WMI and PRI accounted for unique variance in performance on Dot Locations, but the VCI and PSI did not. Therefore, the Dot Locations subtest appears to require working memory and perceptual reasoning skills.

3. The Numbers subtest was most strongly correlated with the WMI, which is to be expected given their overlapping content. More surprising, however, were the significant correlations between the CMS Sequences subtest and all WISC-IV indices. In multiple regression analyses, all four WISC-IV indices contributed unique variance to Sequences. Performance on the Sequences subtest appears to depend on a wide variety of cognitive skills, and probably not simply on attention.

In summary, the WISC-IV and CMS appear to assess related but distinct abilities. Processing speed appears to have little to do with memory functioning, at least as assessed by the CMS in neurologically normal children. In contrast, verbal knowledge, perceptual reasoning, and working memory are all related to memory performance in such children. The patterns of correlations suggest a modest amount of domain specificity, particularly for verbal measures on the two tests. Whether the same relationships exist in clinical samples with brain impairment needs to be addressed in future research.

WISC-IV AND D-KEFS

We also wanted to investigate the validity of the WISC-IV compared to other neuropsychological tests in children with brain impairment. As part of its clinical validation, the WISC-IV was given to a group of children with TBI. A total of 36 of these children were also administered the D–KEFS, a group of tasks designed to evaluate executive skills. The vast majority of the injuries sustained by the children were of moderate severity, with no prolonged coma but with intracranial lesions noted on neuroimaging. The average age of these children was 13.55 years (SD = 2.53). Their average WISC-IV index scores are presented in Figure 13.1. Inspection of the figure suggests a relative weakness on PSI, consistent with previous research with the WISC-III (Donders, 1997; Tremont et al., 1999).

We were particularly interested in the relations between the new WISC-IV subtests (i.e., Picture Concepts, Letter-Number Sequencing, Matrix Reasoning, Cancellation, and Word Reasoning) and performance on the D-KEFS. Table 13.2 presents the correlations between the new subtests from the WISC-IV and the various tasks from the D-KEFS. Given the large number of possible comparisons, we focus our analysis of the results on correlations that are statistically significant at $p < .01$. Several results are notable:

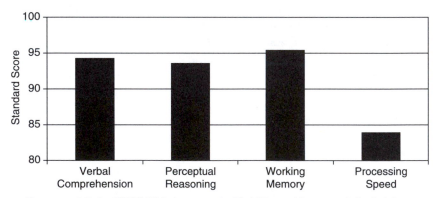

FIGURE 13.1   WISC-IV Index scores in 36 children with traumatic brain injury.

TABLE 13.2   Correlations between WISC-IV and Delis–Kaplan Executive Function System (D-KEFS) Scaled Scores in 36 Children with Traumatic Brain Injury

D-KEFS subtest	WISC-IV subtest				
	Picture Concepts	Letter–Number Sequencing	Matrix Reasoning	Cancellation	Word Reasoning
Trail Making[a]	.23	.21	.32	*.40*	.34
Verbal Fluency[b]	.38	*.48*	.36	*.44*	*.53*
Design Fluency[c]	*.41*	.22	.23	.37	.35
Color-Word[d]	−.04	.28	.27	−.03	.25
Sorting[e]	*.42*	*.53*	.30	.21	*.52*
Tower[f]	.05	*.42*	.13	−.13	*.42*

Note. Statistically significant ($p < .01$) correlations are italicized.
[a]Number-Letter Sequencing, total time.
[b]Category Switching, total accuracy.
[c]Combined filled and empty dots, total correct.
[d]Inhibition, total time.
[e]Confirmed correct sorts.
[f]Total Achievement.

1. Word Reasoning and Letter-Number Sequencing show strong correlations with both a verbal fluency task and with tasks that assess concept formation and planning. Results suggest that, in children with TBI, these WISC-IV subtests tap into higher-level cognitive skills that are not mediated exclusively by language abilities. Thus, Word Reasoning may be measuring abilities other than the crystallized intelligence usually presumed to be underlying VCI, and Letter-Number Sequencing may tap a broader range of executive functions, as opposed to only working memory. Conversely, working memory appears to be a component ability tapped by the Verbal Fluency, Sorting, and Tower subtests on the D-KEFS.

2. Of the two new PRI subtests, only Picture Concepts shows a clear association with D-KEFS tasks, correlating significantly with tasks involving perceptual fluency and concept formation skills. In fact, Matrix Reasoning does not demonstrate statistically significant ($p < .01$) correlations with any D-KEFS subtests, raising concerns about the validity of this WISC-IV subtest in children with TBI.

3. Cancellation demonstrates consistent covariance with a variety of tasks that emphasize speed of performance, both with and without motor demands. This finding provides support for the construct validity of this WISC-IV subtest in the evaluation of children with TBI.

Of course, these interpretations are provisional, because they are based on a fairly small sample and limited to children with TBI. The validity of the WISC-IV needs to be explored more carefully in larger studies with various clinical samples. However, the current findings suggest promise for the potential information that the WISC-IV can provide in the context of a broader neuropsychological evaluation.

CASE STUDY

The following case example is presented to illustrate the potential role of the WISC-IV in clinical neuropsychological assessment. The case information is provided with informed parental consent and child assent, but some of the identifying characteristics have been altered to protect confidentiality.

Jane was a 15-year-old, right-handed White girl who sustained a severe TBI as the passenger in a motor vehicle crash. Neuroimaging revealed a right-frontal subdural hematoma and a left-temporal contusion. She did not respond to verbal commands until 3 days after injury. Review of her school records suggested that she had been a good student before injury, with a cumulative grade point average of 3.58. Prior developmental, medical, and psychosocial histories were entirely unremarkable.

Jane was seen for neuropsychological evaluation 10 weeks after injury. Some of the results from the assessment are presented in Table 13.3, with the complete WISC-IV subtest scores presented for illustrative purposes in Figure 13.2. To assist with interpretation of Table 13.3, all scores have been converted to standard scores (M = 100, SD = 15). Higher scores reflect better performance on the WISC-IV, the California Verbal Learning Test-Children's Version (CVLT-C; Delis, Kramer, Kaplan, & Ober, 1994), and the Wisconsin Card Sorting Test (WCST; Heaton, Chelune, Talley, Kay, & Curtiss, 1993), whereas lower scores indicate better functioning on the Behavior Rating Inventory of Executive Function (BRIEF; Gioia, Isquith, Guy, & Kenworthy, 2000).

The findings on the WISC-IV revealed high–average scores on VCI and PRI, consistent with her estimated premorbid functioning. However, notable relative weaknesses were apparent on WMI and, to a lesser extent, PSI. WMI in particular was statistically significantly lower than VCI, and the base rate of a discrepancy of that magnitude is less than 1% in the standardization sample, suggesting the difference was unusually large. Inspection of the component WMI subtests suggested relatively greatest difficulty with the Backward trial of Digit Span and with Letter-Number Sequencing. This WISC-IV profile raised the possibility that Jane might have particular difficulty with auditory working memory, or more specifically the efficient processing of detailed novel verbal information "in her head."

TABLE 13.3 Psychometric Findings (in Standard Scores) in a Girl with Traumatic Brain Injury

WISC-IV[a]	
Verbal Comprehension	119
Perceptual Reasoning	112
Working Memory	83
Processing Speed	100
CVLT–C[a]	
List A, trial 1	85
List A, trial 5	85
Long delay free recall	100
WCST[a]	
Perseverative errors	120
Nonperseverative errors	110
BRIEF[b]	
Behavioral Regulation	88
Metacognition	115

Note: WISC-IV = Wechsler Intelligence Scale for Children-Fourth Edition; CVLT-C = California Verbal Learning Test-Children's Version; WCST = Wisconsin Card Sorting Test; BRIEF = Behavioral Rating Inventory of Executive Function.
[a]Higher scores reflect better performance.
[b]Higher scores reflect worse performance.

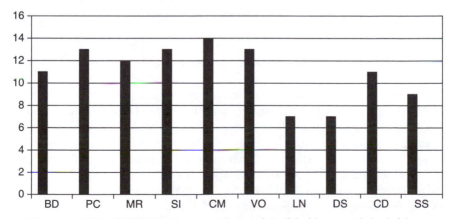

FIGURE 13.2 WISC-IV Subtest scaled scores in a girl with traumatic brain injury.

Inspection of some of the other neuropsychological test results confirmed the initial impression of a working memory problem. Jane had difficulty learning an orally presented shopping list (CVLT–C). After only one presentation of the list, her performance was one standard deviation below the mean (A1), which was much lower than her high–average verbal ability, as reflected in the VCI, but consistent with her WMI. Even with repeated exposure to the list, Jane was not able to increase her recall to within normal limits (A5). However, she was able to retain the information that she had learned; after a 20-minute delay during which she performed other activities, she recalled the same number of items as she had after five learning trials, resulting in an average standardized score for delayed recall. This pattern of results suggested that her problem had indeed been with working memory and not with consolidation or retrieval of information. In contrast, Jane successfully completed all six categories on a task requiring learning and problem solving with tangible materials under an interactive format without significant demands on working memory (WCST).

The impression of a working memory deficit was also noted by Jane's mother as reflected in her responses to a standardized rating scale about her daughter's every-day executive skills (BRIEF). Although the mother did not endorse any concerns about behavioral regulation, she did describe her child as having difficulties with metacognitive abilities, such as keeping her attention focused, grasping the gist of new information immediately, and showing sufficient independent initiative. These findings were quite compatible with the neuropsychological test results.

This case study suggests that the WISC-IV has potential for yielding important information as part of a broader neuropsychological evaluation. Of course, findings from the WISC-IV should never be interpreted in isolation. As the case illustrates, congruence between an unusual WISC-IV index score pattern on the one hand, and specific neuropsychological test results and standardized parent inventories on the other, is what is likely to allow clinicians to come to the most accurate diagnosis.

CONCLUSION

The Wechsler intelligence tests have long played an important role in child neuropsychological assessment, and the WISC-IV, as the most recent iteration, will almost certainly continue to do so. The WISC-IV incorporates several major changes that are likely to affect test interpretation, and additional research is needed to further clarify the implications of the changes for neuropsychological assessment. We cannot simply assume that the existing literature on the WISC-III and its predecessors is applicable to the WISC-IV. However, we believe that the WISC-IV will remain a useful tool for child neuropsychologists. Within the context of a broader neuropsychological assessment, the WISC-IV can provide assistance in assessing cognitive abilities, generating hypotheses regarding strengths and weaknesses, and guiding recommendations for services.

In the evaluation of children with known or suspected brain impairment, clinicians must consider the pattern of the index scores, as opposed to relying exclusively on the FSIQ, given the differential sensitivity of the various indexes to cerebral compromise. In this context, clear consideration must also be given to the base rate of any discrepancies between scores, because profiles vary substantially in the standardization sample. Although preliminary data presented in the WISC-IV manual and expanded upon here suggest that decrements on PSI will likely be relatively common in children with cerebral impairment, more studies are needed to determine the actual positive and negative predictive power of such decrements in samples with different base rates of the condition in question. Similarly, more research is needed about the degree to which the WMI will be an improvement in terms of construct and criterion validity as compared to the WISC-III FDI in the assessment of conditions like ADHD.

REFERENCES

Assesmany, A., McIntosh, D. E., Phelps, L., & Rizza, M. G. (2001). Discriminant validity of the WISC-III with children classified as ADHD. *Journal of Psychoeducational Assessment, 19,* 137–147.

Ballantyne, A. O., Scarvie, K. M., & Trauner, D. A. (1994). Verbal and Performance IQ patterns in children after perinatal stroke. *Developmental Neuropsychology, 10,* 39–50.

Baron, I. S. (2004). *Neuropsychological evaluation of the child.* New York: Oxford University Press.

Bornstein, R. A. (1982). A factor analytic study of the Verbal Concept Attainment Test. *Journal of Clinical Neuropsychology, 4,* 43–50.

Bornstein, R. A. (1983). Verbal Concept Attainment Test: Cross-validation and validation of a booklet form. *Journal of Clinical Psychology, 39,* 743–745.

Bornstein, R. A., & Leason, M. (1985). Effects of localized lesions on the Verbal Concept Attainment Test. *Journal of Clinical and Experimental Neuropsychology, 7,* 421–429.

Brookshire, B. L., Fletcher, J. M., Bohan, T. P., Landry, S. H., Davidson, K. C., & Francis, D. J. (1995). Verbal and nonverbal skill discrepancies in children with hydrocephalus: A five-year longitudinal follow-up. *Journal of Pediatric Psychology, 20,* 785–800.

Butler, M., Retzlaff, P. D., & Vanderploeg, R. (1991). Neuropsychological test usage. *Professional Psychology: Research & Practice, 22,* 510–512.

Camara, W. J., Nathan, J. S., & Puente, A. E. (2000). Psychological test usage: Implications in professional psychology. *Professional Psychology: Research & Practice, 31,* 141–154.

Cohen, M. J. (1997). *Children's Memory Scale manual.* San Antonio, TX: Psychological Corporation.

Daley, C. E., & Nagle, R. J. (1996). Relevance of WISC–III indicators for assessment of children with learning disabilities. *Journal of Psychoeducational Assessment, 14,* 320–333.

Delis, D. C., Kaplan, E., & Kramer, J. H. (2001). *Delis-Kaplan Executive Function System.* San Antonio, TX: The Psychological Corporation.

Delis, D. C., Kramer, J. H., Kaplan, E., & Ober, B. A. (1994). *California Verbal Learning Test-Children's Version*. San Antonio, TX: The Psychological Corporation.

Donders, J. (1997). Sensitivity of the WISC–III to injury severity in children with traumatic head injury. *Assessment, 4*, 107–109.

Donders, J., Canaday, A. I., & Rourke, B. P. (1990). Psychometric intelligence after infantile hydrocephalus: A critical review and reinterpretation. *Child's Nervous System, 6*, 148–154.

Donders, J., & Warschausky, S. (1996). A structural equation analysis of the WISC–III in children with traumatic head injury. *Child Neuropsychology, 2*, 185–192.

Donders, J., & Woodward, H. R. (2003). Gender as a moderator of memory after traumatic brain injury in children. *Journal of Head Trauma Rehabilitation, 18*, 106–115.

Donders, J., Tulsky, D. S., & Zhu, J. (2001). Criterion validity of new WAIS–III subtest scores after traumatic brain injury. *Journal of the International Neuropsychological Society, 7*, 892–898.

Doyle, A. E., Biederman, J., Seidman, L. J., Weber, W., & Faraone, S. V. (2000). Diagnostic efficiency of neuropsychological test scores for discriminating boys with and without attention-deficit/hyperactivity disorder. *Journal of Consulting and Clinical Psychology, 68*, 477–488.

Dumont, R., & Willis, J. O. (1995). Intrasubtest scatter on the WISC–III for various clinical samples vs. the standardization sample: An examination of WISC folklore. *Journal of Psychoeducational Assessment, 13*, 271–285.

Fletcher, J. M., Foorman, B. R., Boudousquie, A., Barnes, M. A., Schatschneider, C., & Francis, D. J. (2002). Assessment of reading and learning disabilities: A research-based intervention-oriented approach. *Journal of School Psychology, 40*, 27–63.

Fry, A. F., & Hale, S. (1996). Processing speed, working memory, and fluid intelligence: Evidence for a developmental cascade. *Psychological Science, 7*, 237–241.

Geldmacher, D. S. (1996). Effects of stimulus number and target-to-distractor ratio on the performance of random array letter cancellation tasks. *Brain and Cognition, 32*, 405–415.

Georgas, J., Weiss, J. G., Van de Vijver, F. J. R., & Saklofske, D. H. (2003). *Culture and children's intelligence: Cross-cultural analysis of the WISC–III*. San Diego, CA: Academic Press.

Gioia, G. A., Isquith, P. K., Guy, S. C., & Kenworthy, L. (2000). *Behavior Rating Inventory of Executive Function*. Odessa, FL: Psychological Assessment Resources.

Glutting, J. J., McDermott, P. A., Prifitera, A., & McGrath, E. A. (1994). Core profile types for the WISC–III and WIAT: Their development and application in identifying multivariate IQ-achievement discrepancies. *School Psychology Review, 23*, 619–639.

Greenway, P., & Milne, L. (1999). Relationship between psychopathology, learning disabilities, or both and WISC–III subtest scatter in adolescents. *Psychology in the Schools, 36*, 103–108.

Groth-Marnat, G., Gallagher, R. E., Hale, J. B., & Kaplan, E. (2000). The Wechsler intelligence scales. In G. Groth-Marnat (Ed.), *Neuropsychological assessment in clinical practice: A guide to test interpretation and integration* (pp. 129–194). New York: John Wiley and Sons.

Halligan, P. W., Marshall, J. C., & Wade, D. T. (1989). Visuospatial neglect: Underlying factors and test sensitivity. *Lancet, October 14*, 908–911.

Heaton, R. K., Chelune, G. J., Talley, J. L., Kay, G. G., & Curtiss, G. (1993). *Wisconsin Card Sorting Test Manual: Revised and Expanded*. Odessa, FL: Psychological Assessment Resources.

Hogan, A. M., Kirkham, F. J., & Isaacs, E. B. (2000). Intelligence after stroke in childhood: Review of the literature and suggestions for future research. *Journal of Child Neurology, 15*, 325–332.

Hynd, G. W., Cohen, M. J., Riccio, R. A., & Arceneaux, J. M. (1998). Neuropsychological basis of intelligence and the WISC-III. In A. Prifitera & D. Saklofske (Eds.), *WISC-III clinical use and interpretation: Scientist-practitioner perspectives* (pp. 203–226). San Diego, CA: Academic Press.

Kamphaus, R. W., Benson, J., Hutchinson, S., & Platt, L. O. (1994). Identification of factor models for the WISC–III. *Educational and Psychological Measurement, 54*, 174–186.

Klein, B., Levin, B. E., Duchovny, M. S., & Llabre, M. M. (2000). Cognitive outcome of children with epilepsy and malformations of cortical development. *Neurology, 55*, 230–235.

Konold, T. R., Kush, J. C., & Canivez, G. L. (1997). Factor replication of the WISC–III in three independent samples of children receiving special education. *Journal of Psychoeducational Assessment, 15*, 123–157.

Korkman, M., Kettunen, S., & Autti-Rämö, I. (2003). Neurocognitive impairment in early adolescence following prenatal alcohol exposure of varying duration. *Child Neuropsychology, 9*, 117–128.

Lezak, M. D. (1995). *Neuropsychological assessment* (3rd ed.). New York: Oxford University Press.

Mayes, S. D., Calhoun, S. L., & Crowell, E. W. (1998). WISC-III Freedom from Distractibility as a measure of attention in children with and without attention deficit disorder. *Journal of Attention Disorders, 2*, 217–227.

Pelletier, P. M., Ahmad, S. A., & Rourke, B. P. (2001). Classification rules for basic phonological processing disabilities and nonverbal learning disabilities: Formulation and external validity. *Child Neuropsychology, 7*, 84–98.

Perugini, E. M., Harvey, E. A., Lovejoy, D. W., Sandstrom, K., & Webb, A. H. (2000). The predictive power of combined neuropsychological measures for attention-deficit/hyperactivity disorder in children. *Child Neuropsychology, 6*, 101–114.

Prifitera, A., & Dersch, J. (1993). Base rates of WISC-III diagnostic subtest patterns among normal, learning-disabled, and ADHD samples. In B. A. Bracken (Ed.), *Journal of Psychoeducational Assessment Monograph Series, Advances in Psychoeducational Assessment: Wechsler Intelligence Scale for Children* (3rd ed.). (pp. 43–55). Germantown, TN: Psychoeducational Corporation.

Pritchard, D. A., Livingston, R. B., Reynolds, C. R., & Moses, J. A. (2000). Modal profiles for the WISC–III. *School Psychology Quarterly, 15*, 400–418.

Reinecke, M. A., Beebe, D. W., & Stein, M. A. (1999). The third factor of the WISC–III: It's (probably) not freedom from distractibility. *Journal of the American Academy of Child and Adolescent Psychiatry, 38*, 322–328.

Riccio, C. A., Cohen, M. J., Hall, J., & Ross, C. M. (1997). The third and fourth factors of the WISC–III: What they don't measure. *Journal of Psychoeducational Assessment, 15*, 27–39.

Roid, G. H., & Worrall, W. (1997). Replication of the Wechsler Intelligence Scale for Children-Third Edition four-factor model in the Canadian normative sample. *Psychological Assessment, 9*, 512–515.

Sattler, J. M., Ed. (2001). *Assessment of children: Cognitive applications* (4th ed.). San Diego, CA: Author.

Sattler, J. M., & Saklofske, D. H. (2001). Wechsler Intelligence Scale for Children-III (WISC-III): Description. In J. M. Sattler (Ed.), *Assessment of children: Cognitive applications* (4th ed.) (pp. 220–265). San Diego, CA: Author.

Schinka, J. A., Vanderploeg, R. D., & Curtiss, G. (1997). WISC–III subtest scatter as a function of highest subtest scaled score. *Psychological Assessment, 9*, 83–88.

Schinka, J. A., Vanderploeg, R. D., & Greblo, P. (1998). Frequency of WISC–III and WAIS–R pairwise subtest differences. *Psychological Assessment, 10*, 171–175.

Schwean, V. L., & Saklofske, D. H. (1998). WISC-III assessment of children with Attention Deficit / Hyperactivity Disorder. In A. Prifitera & D. H. Saklofske (Eds.), *WISC-III clinical use and interpretation: Scientist-practitioner perspectives* (pp. 91–118). San Diego, CA: Academic Press.

Sternberg, R. J., & Grigorenko, E. L. (2002). Difference scores in the identification of children with learning disabilities: It's time to use a different method. *Journal of School Psychology, 40*, 65–83.

Sullivan, K., & Bowden, S. C. (1997). Which tests do neuropsychologists use? *Journal of Clinical Psychology, 53,* 657–661.

Swanson, H. L. (1996). Individual and age-related differences in children's working memory. *Memory & Cognition, 24,* 70–82.

Taylor, H. G., Fletcher, J. M., & Satz, P. (1982). Component processes in reading disabilities: Neuropsychological investigation of distinct reading subskill deficits. In R. N. Malatesha & P. G. Aaron (Eds.), *Reading disorders: Varieties and treatments.* New York: Academic Press.

Tremont, G., Mittenberg, W., & Miller, L. J. (1999). Acute intellectual effects of pediatric head trauma. *Child Neuropsychology, 5,* 104–114.

Tupa, D. J., Wright, M. O., & Fristad, M. A. (1997). Confirmatory factor analysis of the WISC–III with child psychiatric inpatients. *Psychological Assessment, 9,* 302–306.

Vargha-Khadem, F., Isaacs, E., & Muter, V. (1994). A review of cognitive outcome after unilateral lesions sustained during childhood. *Journal of Child Neurology, 9(suppl),* 2S67–2S73.

Watkins, M. W., & Glutting, J. J. (2000). Incremental validity of WISC–III profile elevation, scatter, and shape information for predicting reading and math achievement. *Psychological Assessment, 12,* 402–408.

Watkins, M. W., & Kush, J. C. (2002). Confirmatory factor analysis of the WISC–III for students with learning disabilities. *Journal of Psychoeducational Assessment, 20,* 4–19.

Wechsler, D. (1991). *Wechsler Intelligence Scale for Children* (3rd ed.). San Antonio, TX: Psychological Corporation.

Wechsler, D. (1992). *Wechsler Individual Achievement Test.* San Antonio, TX: Psychological Corporation.

Wechsler, D. (2002). *Wechsler Individual Achievement Test* (2nd ed.). San Antonio, TX: Psychological Corporation.

Wechsler, D. (2003a). *WISC-IV administration and scoring manual.* San Antonio, TX: Psychological Corporation.

Wechsler, D. (2003b). *WISC-IV technical and interpretive manual.* San Antonio, TX: Psychological Corporation.

Wills, K. E. (1993). Neuropsychological functioning in children with spina bifida and/or hydrocephalus. *Journal of Clinical Child Psychology, 22,* 247–265.

Yeates, K. O., Loss, N., Colvin, A. N., & Enrile, B. G. (2003). Do children with myelomeningocele and hydrocephalus display nonverbal learning disabilities? An empirical approach to classification. *Journal of the International Neuropsychological Society, 9,* 653–662.

Yeates, K. O., & Taylor, H. G. (2001). Neuropsychological assessment of children. In J. J. W. Andrews, D. H. Saklofske, & H. L. Janzen (Eds.), *Handbook of psychoeducational assessment: Ability, achievement, and behavior in children* (pp. 415–450). New York: Academic Press.

14

ASSESSMENT OF TEST BEHAVIORS WITH THE WISC-IV

THOMAS OAKLAND

Department of Foundations Education
University of Florida
Gainesville, Florida

JOSEPH GLUTTING

School of Education
University of Delaware
Newark, Delaware

MARLEY W. WATKINS

Educational Psychology
Pennsylvania State University
University Park, Pennsylvania

THE TESTING PROCESS

Psychoeducational testing is a process in which skilled examiners carefully observe the actual performance of persons under standardized conditions.* The process incorporates elements of both science and art and draws on informal and formal assessment methods. From science we obtain rules that govern the collection, recording, and interpretation of data so as to

*As a matter of convenience, the terms children and child will be used in this chapter to refer to all age ranges covered by the WISC-IV.
Note: This chapter is adapted from "Assessment of Test Behaviors with the WISC-III," which appeared in the previous edition of this book.

establish standardized methods that guide the use of a test in every setting in which it is applied. Alternatively, examiners' artistic qualities come from their extended experience in administering tests and working in other ways with children, youth, and adults. This artistic and/or clinical aspect of assessment is especially important when working with individuals whose dispositions make them difficult to test. No set of rules can govern the manner in which a test always is administered. As every clinician knows, children differ in their personal needs and test-related qualities. In addition, testing conditions vary from setting to setting.

Two examples are provided. Christine willingly comes with the examiner. They develop rapport easily. She is eager to help the examiner set up the testing room, listens attentively to directions, endeavors to do her best, and sustains a high level of interest and motivation throughout the examination. In contrast, David accompanies the examiner to the testing room only after considerable encouragement, seems distracted and inattentive, is uncooperative, and displays low levels of interest and motivation. The needs and test-related behaviors of Christine and David differ considerably. Keen observation skills are needed to assist in guiding the test's administration, in interpreting results from cognitive (i.e., intelligence and achievement) measures, and in deciding whether the test results are valid.

The two examples illustrate the importance of observing behaviors peripheral to scorable test responses. Examiners traditionally have relied on informal methods (e.g., observations, interviews) almost exclusively to better understand conditions that impact the test's administration and children's test behaviors. However, their use of formal observational methods, including instruments designed specifically for this purpose, is increasing.

This chapter reviews qualities that may impact a child's test performance and discusses in detail those qualities found through research to have a measurable influence on the performance. Discussion focuses on individually administered measures of cognitive abilities. Possible benefits in using test-behavior information are identified. Several measures currently used to record children's test performance also are discussed. The most widely used standardized measure of test performance, the *Guide to the Assessment of Test Session Behavior* (GATSB) (Glutting & Oakland, 1993), is described in some detail.

EXAMINER'S OBSERVATIONS ARE CRITICAL TO TEST USE

An examiner's observations are critical to all features of test use. Their observations enable them to accurately record children's responses to test items. Moreover, information obtained through observations enables examiners to better understand the manner in which children arrive at their answers and to identify cognitive and other personal strengths and weaknesses, thus facilitating test interpretations. Their observations also enable examiners to describe children's spontaneous behaviors while being tested, including their interpersonal and learning styles and other qualities that may directly or indirectly impact test performance. This information enables examiners to make needed modifications in the manner in which the test session is orchestrated, to construct systematic records of children's behaviors, to compare their observations with reports from others who know the child, to assist in interpreting the test results, and to draw comparisons between the child being tested and others who are similar in terms of salient qualities. Thus, the employment of observational methods is critical to the assessment process (Sattler, 1988, 2001).

SEVEN IMPORTANT QUALITIES THAT MAY IMPACT TEST PERFORMANCE

Professionals prepared to systematically observe behavior are keenly alert to various qualities important to the assessment process. Children's responses to a test's questions constitute the most central and important behaviors to which examiners should attend. For example, when administering the WISC-IV (Wechsler, 2003), examiners diligently observe and record a child's response to each test item.

In addition, examiners observe various other qualities that fall just beyond this central focus, ones that may facilitate or adversely impact children's test behaviors and thus their ability to demonstrate their best performance. The following seven qualities fall within this second important focus: conditions within the testing room, language qualities, physical and motor qualities, rapport, personal readiness, motivation, and temperament. In addition, some test behaviors are associated with specific handicapping conditions. An examiner's knowledge of these qualities can greatly enhance the evaluation process.

Until recently, these seven qualities were assessed informally by the examiner who kept a watchful eye out for conditions that might impede test performance or jeopardize test validity. The somewhat recent development of standardized measures to assist in the assessment of test behaviors has aided the examiner, especially in the assessment of qualities related to rapport, personal readiness, motivation, temperament, and special conditions associated with some handicapping conditions. As will be noted, measures of test-taking behavior are intended to utilize and supplant and not substitute for well-honed observations skills.

TESTING ROOM CONDITIONS

Examiners are responsible for ensuring that the testing room provides a comfortable and distraction-free testing environment. Furniture should be of appropriate height and comfortable to the children. Their attention and concentration should not be attenuated by auditory and visual distractions. Young children, children with moderate to severe handicapping conditions, and those for whom testing is a new experience often need additional time to become oriented to the testing room. Examiners must remain alert to signs that children are uncomfortable or distracted and, when present, work to alleviate problems. Examiners must ensure that physical conditions enhance the assessment process by creating conditions that are relatively standard from test to test, ones that enable the examinee to feel comfortable and relaxed, encourage suitable test-taking behaviors, and promote valid testing.

LANGUAGE QUALITIES

Language qualities also figure importantly. Most measures of cognitive abilities rely on language to form a bridge between the examiner and examinee, enabling them to communicate. Although the WISC-IV is not intended to assess language directly, the quality and nature of children's language can facilitate or impede test use. Language qualities include both receptive (i.e., listening comprehension and reading) and expressive (oral expression and writing) skills and abilities together with pragmatic (i.e., functional) language features. Language also may reflect dialect differences, including the use of non-standard English. In addition, some children have little to no knowledge of English.

Examiners typically rely on informal observations and information from interviews together with prior test data when forming judgments of children's language abilities. More formal assessment of language is warranted when language deficits and differences are apparent. In addition, modifications in test use may be needed when using them with children who exhibit deficits or differences in one or more of these language areas. Modifications will be needed when using tests with children not fluent in English. The examiner's keen attention to children's language-related test behaviors together with information provided by other sources enable them to conduct their work in a more effective and efficient fashion.

PHYSICAL AND MOTOR QUALITIES

Children's physical and motor qualities also may impact test performance. Information on general health conditions (e.g., respiratory problems, cardiovascular conditions, chronic or acute diseases and illnesses) and muscle control should be acquired from a parent or other informed adult. Gross muscle control can impact the assessment of adaptive behaviors. Fine muscle control is important to writing and other physical manipulations important to finger dexterity. Control of muscles in the oral cavity is prerequisite to comprehensible speech. Examiners must remain alert to physical and motor qualities that may adversely impact children's test performance.

RAPPORT

Rapport refers to the nature of the interpersonal relationships between the child and examiner. Good rapport is characterized by harmony, conformity, and cooperation. The child should feel comfortable with the examiner and the examination process. The examiner's behaviors are intended to promote trust and faith, qualities that are enhanced by taking time to talk with the child before beginning the test, encouraging the child to be of assistance (thereby promoting cooperation), smiling frequently, using the child's name liberally, and reinforcing the child's efforts (e.g., "I really like the way you are working hard.").

The manner in which the test is introduced also is intended to facilitate rapport. The following introduction may be used to introduce the WISC-IV and other measures of cognitive abilities: "I will be giving you a test that most people enjoy. Some of the questions will be easy and others will be hard. I do not expect you to answer every question. However, I do want you to do your very best. Do you have any questions before we begin?"

PERSONAL READINESS

Personal readiness refers to physical and psychological qualities prerequisite to valid testing. Children must have the physical stamina needed to complete the examination. In addition, alertness, attention, and concentration also are prerequisite to valid testing. Various psychological qualities also contribute to readiness: self-confidence, willingness to leave one's teacher or parent with an examiner who often is unknown to the child, and lack of shyness. Nutritional and sleep conditions also contribute to readiness. Information as to whether the child has had adequate food, drink, and sleep should be acquired before the test.

MOTIVATION

Motivation refers to a child's willingness to engage in the testing activity and to sustain such engagement over a period of time. Motivation often is enhanced by providing suitable physical conditions for test-taking, building and maintaining rapport, and ensuring personal readiness. In addition, motivation is enhanced when activities are thought to be neither too easy nor too hard yet somewhat challenging. Motivation also is enhanced by novelty, changing the nature of the tasks (as occurs when administering different WISC-IV subtests), and by taking periodic breaks.

TEMPERAMENT

Children's temperament also may impact their test performance. Children who display strong preferences for extroversion or introversion styles, practical or imaginative styles, thinking or feeling styles, and organized or flexible styles (Oakland, Glutting, & Horton, 1996) are likely to display different behaviors while taking tests. Some examples follow.

Children who are strongly extroverted generally prefer to express their ideas verbally. Moreover, their ideas often become better known to them after they hear themselves express their thoughts. In contrast, those who are strongly introverted generally prefer to express their ideas after they have time to reflect on the question or in writing.

Children who express strong practical preferences often are very attentive to details and can memorize well. In contrast, those who express strong preferences for imaginative styles are less attentive to detail, more interested in theories, and are more inclined to have problems memorizing specific facts and figures.

Children who are inclined toward thinking preferences generally enjoy competitive activities and displaying their knowledge. In contrast, those who express strong preferences for feeling are most inclined to disdain competition and favor cooperation and to rely on personalized standards when evaluating others. Furthermore, emotions seemingly have an impact on self-regulations important to taking tests (Schutz & Davis, 2000).

Children who prefer organized styles like their lives to be well organized, problems resolved, and things settled as quickly as possible. They often appreciate the structure tests provide. In contrast, those with flexible styles are more inclined to postpone decisions, generally prefer fewer rules and regulations, and enjoy situations that are not highly organized. They may find the rules governing testing to be too confining.

Examiners often observe these and other temperament-related behaviors while testing children and youth. These qualities may impact children's test performance styles. Examiners are encouraged to administer a measure of temperament to children and youth (e.g., Oakland, Glutting, & Horton, 1996) so as to better understand their preferred styles and the impact these styles may have on their test and school performance.

MODERATE TO SEVERE HANDICAPPING CONDITIONS

Various alterations often are needed when testing children who evidence moderate to severe handicapping conditions (e.g., children with visual or auditory handicaps, mental retardation, cerebral palsy, autism, emotional difficulties). The nature of the needed alterations depends on the child's age, the nature and severity of the child's handicapping condition, and prior testing experiences. The use of testing accommodations for persons with disabilities is common (Pitoniak & Royer, 2001).

Popular textbooks on intelligence testing discuss these issues in considerable detail (Gregory, 1992; Kamphaus, 2001; Kaufman, 1994; Palmer, 1983; Sattler, 1988, 2001). Thus, with the exception of referencing research on test-taking behaviors of children with attention deficit disorders, test-taking behaviors associated with each handicapping condition are not discussed here. Nevertheless, examiners must remain attentive to the special needs of children with handicapping conditions and strive to make modifications in the testing process while maintaining standardized methods. Considerable ingenuity and experience may be required when testing children with severe and multiple disorders.

BACKGROUND INFORMATION AND PERSONAL QUALITIES

Some qualities identified previously (e.g., medical, motor, food, sleep, acuity, and language status) can be considered background variables (Bracken, 1991). Information on them should be acquired before tests are administered. This information may assist the examiner in planning for the evaluation, in preventing the occurrence of problems, and addressing them should they occur.

Other qualities consist of ethnographically relevant expressions of personal qualities that can be observed only during testing. These include rapport and children's readiness for testing, their personality, and motivation. Although scales designed to assess test-taking qualities may include information on background variables, personal qualities displayed during testing always should be the main focus.

DISTINGUISH BETWEEN COLLECTING AND EVALUATING TEST BEHAVIOR

Distinctions should be drawn between the process of collecting and evaluating test behaviors. When collecting this information, examiners focus on qualities thought to facilitate and impede the administration of standardized tests. Examiners using informal or formal methods to collect test-behavior data enjoy similar degrees of flexibility when selecting the behaviors on which they focus. However, those using formal measures to assess test-taking behaviors should include behaviors identified by research as being important. Those using informal methods are neither guided by this knowledge nor governed by this constraint.

THREE STANDARDS FOR EVALUATING INFORMATION

When evaluating information on children's test-session behaviors, examiners must decide the standard to use in judging whether the behaviors are suitable. Three standards may be used. Examiners may evaluate a child's test-taking behaviors in reference to their notions of perfection, potential, or from normative standards.

Perfection. Perfection refers to whether the child's test behaviors were impeccable and unblemished, conditions that rarely occur. In addition, few examiners would agree on the exact qualities that constitute a perfect administration or be able to judge them reliably.

Potential. Potential refers to whether the test behaviors were as good as can be expected, given the conditions found among the seven previously described qualities that may impact test performance. This standard also is difficult to form and thus to use knowledgeably and reliably.

Normative standards. Normative standards are derived from data acquired from nationally standardized, normed, and well-validated measures designed specifically to assess test-taking behaviors. The use of this standard does not preclude consideration of the other two.

Examiners who rely only on informal evaluation methods also must rely on standards of perfection and potential. Those who use formal (i.e., standardized and structured) evaluation methods have the added advantage of using normative standards when age-appropriate norms are available for the structured rating scale they are using.

All examiners do and should use observational methods to describe the seven previously identified test-related behaviors. Examiners differ in how they use this observational information in an evaluative format to form judgments about the suitability of a child's test-taking behaviors and the resulting validity of the test data.

SOME BENEFITS OF USING INFORMAL PROCESSES

Some benefits may occur from using informal processes to evaluate test behaviors. The primary advantage in using informal processes over standardized and structured measures to evaluate test-taking behavior may lie in their flexibility. They allow examiners to tailor their observations in light of each child's qualities. For example, the test-taking behaviors most likely to impact the performance of children who are visually impaired will differ somewhat from those who are autistic. However, this flexibility is available when both informal and formal evaluation procedures are used.

Some examiners have years of experience testing children with specific types of disabilities (e.g., autism, visual handicaps) and thus are able to judge whether a child's behaviors are similar to others who display the disability. Nationally standardized scales designed to assist in evaluating test-taking behaviors do not provide norms for the various handicapping conditions.

Moreover, examiners often resist change and tend to follow traditions. They often continue to use a battery of measures they were taught in graduate school. Standardized measures of test-taking behaviors are relatively new. Thus, many examiners were not introduced to them during their graduate training. In addition, some examiners dislike the need to purchase test-taking scales as well as the structure they provide. Thus, their widespread use will require both time and knowledge of their benefits.

SOME DISADVANTAGES TO USING INFORMAL PROCESSES

Informal methods to evaluate test behaviors have a number of disadvantages. Eight are identified here.

QUALITIES OBSERVED MAY BE IRRELEVANT

Examiners differ in the test-taking qualities they believe are most important. Their clinical preparation on this topic often is very uneven. Some receive excellent coursework and supervision while others labor under inadequate instructional systems that reflect diminished resources for expensive clinical graduate programs. As can be expected, examiners differ in their knowledge as to what test behaviors are most important to record and how to evaluate this information. Items on standardized measures help overcome some of these differences in preparation by enabling examiners to focus on important test-taking behaviors.

QUALITIES ARE UNSUPPORTED BY RESEARCH

Examiner's information about test behaviors rarely is based on solid research. Information on informal methods generally is embedded within extensive discussions of test-taking behaviors (cf. Bracken, 1991; Culbertson & Willis, 1993; Gregory, 1992; Kamphaus & Reynolds, 1987). Despite the volumes written on this topic (Culbertson & Willis, 1993; Epps, 1988; Gregory, 1992; Jensen, 1980; Kamphaus & Reynolds, 1987; Kaufman, 1990; Kaufman, 1994; Palmer, 1983; Reynolds & Kamphaus, 1990a, 1990b; Salvia & Ysseldyke, 1988; Sattler, 1988, 2001; Simeonsson, 1996), the amount of research in well-respected publications on test-taking behaviors is meager and can be carried easily by a 3-year-old child. Thus, our scientific knowledge as to the qualities that constitute test-taking behaviors is inadequate. In addition, reliance on informal methods to evaluate test behaviors has contributed to this deficit. The availability of standardized measures of test-taking abilities is likely to lead to more research on this important topic and thus improved literature on this important component of assessment.

QUALITIES EMANATE FROM FOLKLORE

Related to the first two points, informal methods are difficult to replicate and often breed folklore (i.e., opinions that over time take the form of widely held established fact). The use of informal methods to clinically assess test-taking skills has contributed to folklore about various test-related issues. For example, examiners often believe that behaviors people evidence while taking a test (e.g., shyness) express personal traits they are likely to display in their everyday life. As we will see later, there is little evidence for this widely held belief. The continued overreliance on informal methods prevents the validation of this and other clinical folklore.

OBSERVATIONS ARE UNSTRUCTURED

Informal methods lack standardized methodology to record and score important test-taking behaviors. Methods to record and evaluate test behaviors differ from examiner to examiner as well as within an examiner. These conditions jeopardize the reliable and valid collection of information and thus attenuate their use.

EXAMINERS ARE LESS CREDIBLE

Examiners who use informal measures are less able to justify their conclusions. They increasingly are being required to justify their findings to colleagues, while testifying, and in other legal and professional settings. They are likely to be asked to justify the validity of their test results and often face challenging questions as to the nature of the test conditions and the examinee's behaviors. Failure to record these qualities at the time of test administration jeopardizes their ability to successfully face cross-examination. Reliance on informal methods also may further jeopardize their testimony.

AGE-RELATED DIFFERENCES MAY BE OVERLOOKED

Examiners may be insensitive to important age-related differences. Children display different test behaviors at different ages (Glutting & Oakland, 1993). In general, test behaviors improve with age. Examiners who rely on informal methods to evaluate test-taking behaviors may be unaware of subtle but important age-related differences.

NORMS ARE LACKING

Clearly, the greatest limitation in using informal measures lies in their lack of a normative basis for comparisons. The availability of properly stratified norms is consistent with commonly accepted standards (i.e., *Standards for Educational and Psychological Testing*, American Educational Research Association *et al.*, 1999) for test use as well as the expectations of those who receive clinical services. Thus, attempts to evaluate test behaviors without the use of norms invite error and should be avoided when possible.

FAILURE TO CO-NORM OBSERVATION SYSTEM WITH STANDARDIZED TESTS

The co-norming of two or more tests is becoming more common. This process enables examiners to better utilize information from the tests through their knowledge of relationships between them. The process also enables testing companies to economize when standardizing tests. One measure of test-taking ability, the *Guide to the Assessment of Test Session Behavior* (GATSB; Glutting & Oakland, 1993) has been co-normed with both the *Wechsler Intelligence Scale for Children III* (Wechsler, 1991) and the *Wechsler Individual Achievement Test* (WIAT; Wechsler, 1992), thus providing direct normative links with two widely used measures. Before discussing the GATSB, other formal measures designed to assess test-taking qualities are identified.

OTHER FORMAL MEASURES OF TEST-TAKING BEHAVIOR

Many older clinicians were introduced to the importance of test behaviors by Caldwell (1951), who provided an integrated view of test session behavior. Caldwell also introduced the *Test Behavior Observation Guide* (Caldwell, 1951), one of the first formal (i.e., structured) measures of test-related qualities. It contains 19 items that identify preexisting background characteristics as well as 15 items that focus on observable test behaviors.

A number of standardized measures of intelligence include a structured test-behavior scale. Some examples are provided here.

The *Stanford-Binet Observation Schedule* (Terman & Merrill, 1960; Thorndike, Hagen, & Sattler, 1986) appeared as part of the test's record booklet beginning with the 1960 edition and continuing through to its most recent version. Rational analysis was used in selecting the items that assess five domains: attention, reaction during test performance, emotional independence, problem-solving behavior, and independence of examiner support. Despite its availability and widespread visibility, evidence as to the scale's reliability and validity may be found in only one study (Glutting & McDermott, 1988).

The *Stanford Binet Intelligence Scale Fifth Edition* (Roid, 2003) protocol provides for the recording of eight test behaviors (e.g., adequacy of English usage, motor abilities, vision, health, and general testing conditions).

The WISC-IV protocol provides for the recording of seven test behaviors: language, physical appearance, acuity problems, unusual behaviors, attention and concentration, attitudes toward testing, and affect/mood. The first four focus on more general qualities while the last three focus on those identified through research on the GATSB as being important.

The *Leiter International Performance Scale-Revised* (Roid & Miller, 2000) provides one of the more complete scales for recoding test-related behaviors. Its 49 items assess the following eight qualities: attention, organization/ impulse control, activity level, sociability, energy and feelings, self-regulation, anxiety, and sensory reactivity. The items were selected, in part, to assess qualities displayed by children who exhibit some common psychological and social problems.

The *Kaufman Integrated Interpretive System Checklist for Behaviors Observed During Administration of WISC-III Subtests* (Kaufman, Kaufman, Dougherty, & Tuttle, 1994) was developed to measure behaviors specific to individual subtests from the WISC-III. Example items include these: "Has difficulty understanding the long verbal directions to nonverbal tasks such as Picture Arrangement and Coding" and "Was distracted when trying to repeat digits forwards and backwards or solve oral arithmetic items."

The *Woodcock-Johnson Tests of Cognitive Abilities* (Woodcock, McGrew, & Mather, 2001) protocol also provides for the recording of seven test behaviors: conversational proficiency, cooperation, activity, attention and concentration, self-confidence, care in responding, and responses to difficult tasks (Schrank & Read, 2002).

Additional methods that assess test-taking behaviors are not a part of existing tests and thus may be used with most measures of cognitive abilities. The *Behavior and Attitude Checklist* (Sattler, 2001) contains 41 items covering 12 domains. The domains with the largest number of items include work habits, attitudes toward test situation, and expressive language. The *Test Behavior Checklist* (Aylward & MacGruder, 1986) contains 18 items, 3 of which focus on preexisting conditions and 15 on test-related behaviors.

DEFICIENCIES IN THESE FORMAL SCALES

The structured nature of each of the foregoing scales makes them somewhat useful in codifying children's test behaviors. Nevertheless, a number of qualities limit their utility. Threats to the interpretability of data from these and other tests of test-taking occur as a result of construct irrelevant variance. For example, they include domains and behaviors thought to be important to the assessment of test-taking behaviors. However, empirical support for including them is lacking. Additionally, these tests generally display construct underrepresentation. That is, domains relevant to the assessment of test-taking behaviors may not be included on the test. Thus, the tests cited previously generally do not meet the two standards of construct relevance and construct representation.

Sound observations consider relevant and verifiable aspects of child functioning, including normal development (Glutting, 1986; McDermott, 1986; McDermott & Watkins, 1985). Most items on these structured test-behavior scales overlook normal adjustment (Glutting & Oakland, 1993). Instead, they largely are limited to evaluating pathological symptoms and negative behaviors.

A potentially more serious problem relates to the identification of integral dimensions (i.e., scales) underlying item sets. The majority of structured, test-behavior instruments are composed of undifferentiated lists of symptoms, or rationally derived symptom "domains." These test-behavior measures do not present empirical evidence in support of either a single unifying construct or for their separate domains.

Perhaps their greatest deficiency is the absence of norms, information needed when evaluating how one child's behaviors compare to those of others. As a result, examiners are left to their own resources in determining when a given child's test behavior is normal or exceptional.

EMPIRICAL RESEARCH ON CHILDREN'S TEST BEHAVIORS

The validity of test observations rarely has been studied. Thus, until recently, clinicians had to rely on professional experience and wise judgments when evaluating test-taking behaviors. Conditions changed during the 1980s as researchers began to initiate a series of investigations designed to better understand the construct and criterion-related validity of test observations.

CONSTRUCT VALIDITY

A synthesis of research on test-behavior studies (Glutting, Youngstrom, Oakland, & Watkins, 1996) identified only two studies that examined the construct validity of children's test behaviors (Glutting & McDermott, 1988; Glutting, Oakland, & McDermott, 1989). Each study reported the results of factor-analyzed data from existing formal scales of children's test behavior to determine the psychometric properties of these instruments and simultaneously to identify the number and nature of integral domains (i.e., scales) underlying children's test behaviors.

Our initial investigation (Glutting & McDermott, 1988) examined the *Stanford-Binet Observation Schedule* (Terman & Merrill, 1960; Thorndike *et al.*, 1986). A factor analysis of the *Stanford-Binet Observation Schedule* yielded two dimensions that accounted for 54% of the variance. The larger of the two factors was identified as *Avoidance* and the smaller domain was identified as *Inattentiveness*.

The factor structure and reliability of *Test Behavior Observation Guide*-related test observation data obtained from children between the ages of 7 and 14 years (Glutting *et al.*, 1989) yielded a three-factor model that explained 58% of the total item variance. Respectively, the names and ordering of the factors were as follows: *Inattentiveness*, *Avoidance*, and *Uncooperative Mood*. Internal consistency estimates, based on Cronbach's (1951) formula for coefficient alpha, were .88, .77, and .72, respectively.

Results across these two factor–analytic studies showed that empirically derived domains of children's test behaviors possessed only modest relationships with rationally derived domains (Glutting & McDermott, 1988; Glutting *et al.*, 1989). More important, empirically derived domains were fewer in number and had demonstrated reliability. Thus, the findings served to demonstrate that structured symptom lists and scales developed through the rational analysis of children's test behaviors are likely to be unproductive for most referrals that examiners encounter and generally should not be used for these purposes.

CRITERION-RELATED VALIDITY

Criterion-related validity, when applied to test observations, focuses on relationships between children's test-session behavior and their scores on formal tests (e.g., cognitive abilities) or behaviors observed in other contexts. *Intrasession validity*, a term we coined, refers to the strength of association between measures of test-session behaviors and test scores from measures of cognitive abilities (cf. Glutting & McDermott, 1988; Glutting *et al.*, 1989). Thus, intrasession validity examines the potential impact of test behaviors on children's formal scores on the WISC-III and WIAT as well as other individually administered measures of cognitive abilities and indicates the extent to which scores from these measures can be considered to be accurate.

The construct of ecological validity draws attention to the importance of examining the generalizability of test behaviors to diverse settings (cf. Neisser, 1991). We developed the term *exosession validity*, similar in meaning to the constructs of external validity or generalizability, to describe the degree of accuracy of using children's test-taking behaviors to predict their behavior in other situations (Glutting *et al.*, 1989).

Our synthesis of previous test-behavior research (Glutting *et al.*, 1996) found six studies on the topic of intrasession validity. The sources yielded a total of 33 correlation coefficients. An averaged coefficient was calculated according to the meta-analysis procedures recommended by Hunter, Schmidt, and Jackson (1982) and Rosenthal (1991). The overall relationship was $-.34$ between children's test behaviors and IQs obtained during the same test session. Thus, test-taking behaviors can impact test performance.

Four studies (Glutting *et al.*, 1996) discussed exosession validity, producing 26 correlations. The average correlation was .18 between children's test behaviors and their conduct in other contexts (e.g., their classroom or community). Thus, these results indicate test-taking behaviors have little relationship with children's test behaviors in their classrooms and communities.

The pattern shows modest but meaningful levels of intrasession validity (average $r = -.34$). Moreover, the magnitude of intrasession validity is higher than that found for exosession validity (average $r = .18$). The findings of high intrasession validity provide important evidence that clinicians are able to utilize test observations to form judgments of children's test behaviors that are both reliable and valid. These findings also provide a foundation for establishing a formal measure of test-taking behaviors that, after norming, would enable examiners to more accurately acquire and interpret test observations. When used jointly with measures of cognitive abilities, information from a measure of test-taking behaviors then could be used to help validate scores obtained from measures of cognitive abilities and to form inferences regarding children's test-taking qualities.

The evidence of limited exosession validity was not surprising. Behaviors that occur in natural settings are best understood by acquiring information from multiple sources and using multiple assessment methods that assess multiple traits displayed over time. Examiners should not expect to be able to describe complex peripheral behaviors only from observing a person in controlled testing situations. Evidence of limited exosession validity does not diminish the value of test observations. Instead, clinicians are encouraged to refrain from drawing conclusions as to the generalizability of test observations to conditions outside the immediate test situation. This inference is consistent with other information regarding the situational specificity of children's behavior. A meta-analysis of behavioral data (Achenbach, McConaughty, & Howell, 1987) demonstrated that much of the behavior observed by parents at home and teachers in school is contextually dependent and specific to the situation in which it occurs.

TEST BEHAVIOR OBSERVATION FORM: AN EMPIRICALLY DERIVED AND NORMED SCALE

The *Test Behavior Observation Form* (TOF) (McConaughy & Achenbach, 2004) is designed to assess behavioral and emotional problems in children, ages 2 to 18 years, based on their test-session behaviors. Behaviors assessed include withdrawn/depression, language/thought problems, anxiety, oppositional disorders, as well as inattentiveness and hyperactivity. The authors suggest the TOF data can be compared with profiles derived from the authors' other behavioral measures (e.g., Child Behavior Checklist).

THE GUIDE TO THE ASSESSMENT
OF TEST SESSION BEHAVIOR FOR THE
WISC-III AND WIAT

The *Guide to the Assessment of Test Session Behavior for the WISC-III and WIAT* (GATSB) (Glutting & Oakland, 1993) was constructed to overcome the shortcomings of other measures of children's test behaviors. The GATSB is a structured 29-item behavior-rating instrument designed to evaluate the test-session behavior of children quickly and reliably when administering measures of cognitive abilities. The instrument is brief and requires less than 5 minutes to complete, including scoring. Examiners rate GATSB items immediately after testing. As a result, the process of rating does not interfere with the recording of children's performance on the standardized test that is being administered, and the behavioral data are recorded while still easily recalled.

Children's behaviors are rated using a three-point scale (i.e., 2, 1, or 0) in reference to *usually applies*, s*omewhat applies*, and *doesn't apply*. Higher raw scores denote inappropriate behavior. Raw scores are summed and converted to standard T scores (M = 50, SD = 10) according to three factor-based scales (Avoidance, Uncooperative Mood, Inattentiveness). In addition, a Total Score is obtained. The Total Score is a combination of scores from the GATSB's three other scales and also is expressed as a standard T score.

ITEMS

Example items are presented from the three factor-based scales. The examples make clear that the GATSB does not overlook normal adjustment; its items depict both appropriate and inappropriate behavior.

Avoidance
  "Shows marked interest in test activities"
  "Hesitates when giving answers"
Uncooperative Mood
  "Performance deteriorates toward end of testing"
  "Asks how soon testing will finish"
Inattentiveness
  "Listens attentively to directions and test items"
  "Attempts to answer before questions are completed"

NORMS

The GATSB was designed for use with children ages 6 years 0 months through 16 years 11 months. It was co-normed with both the WISC-III and the WIAT. Thus, unlike all previous measures for evaluating children's test behaviors, the GATSB alone was co-normed with tests of intelligence and achievement. As previously noted, norms are essential in determining when children's test behaviors are sufficiently aberrant, compared to others of similar age and experience, to affect the validity of test scores.

Each of the GATSB's two standardization samples (one each for the WISC-III and for the WIAT) included 640 children. The samples were stratified on the basis of the 1988 U.S. census data according to age, race-ethnicity, gender, and parent education. Furthermore, the samples were selected to ensure that children's overall intellectual abilities (M WISC-III FSIQ $\cong$ 100, SD $\cong$ 15) and their achievement levels (M WIAT Total Battery Composite $\cong$ 100, SD $\cong$ 15) matched those of the general population. Thus, ratings on the GATSB are typical of distributional means, standard deviations, kurtosis, and skewness found in measures of children's intellectual ability and achievement.

AGE-BASED STANDARD SCORES

An analysis of variance was conducted using the factor-based raw scores from the two standardization samples to determine whether norms could be collapsed over years or should be provided for each year for which the GATSB was designed. Results showed some age differences in test-related qualities, warranting the need for separate norms for three age groups: 6 to 8 years, 9 to 12 years, and 13 through 16 years. Consequently, norms for the GATSB respect age-related differences that occur in children's test behaviors.

RELIABILITY

Internal consistency reliability estimates for the GATSB are high. Alpha coefficients were calculated separately for the three age groups. Results showed an averaged coefficient of .92 for the Total Score and coefficients between .84 and .88 for the three factor-based scales. Stability estimates (M interval $\cong$ 1 day) also are high. Results across the three age levels show an averaged .87 for the Total Score and .71 to .77 for the three factor-based scales.

CONSTRUCT VALIDITY

The GATSB was not developed using rational analysis. Instead, its scales were assembled according to the substantive or construct approach to test development (cf. Cronbach & Meehl, 1955). Thus, both theoretical and empirical issues were considered. Factor analytic findings from our earlier studies indicated that test behaviors do not form a single unitary construct and instead are governed by as many as three underlying dimensions: avoidance, uncooperative mood, and inattentiveness (Glutting & McDermott, 1988; Glutting et al., 1989). These findings served as the theoretical underpinning of the GATSB.

Both items and factor analyses were used with the WISC-III/GATSB standardization data ($N = 640$) to develop a final scale composed of 29 items. Initial items in the pool ($n = 102$) were deleted when they showed no appreciable loading on the three hypothesized factors and when an item loaded appreciably on a factor contrary to theory. Thus, retained items were required to show structural relationships (i.e., factor loadings) paralleling theoretical relationships postulated for children's test behaviors. In turn, this methodology increased the probability that GATSB items would contribute to important underlying behavioral constructs evident during testing.

Principal components analysis and principle axis factor analysis (using both orthogonal and oblique rotations) yielded three dimensions for the standardization sample: Avoidance, Uncooperative Mood, and Inattentiveness. These dimensions are theoretically congruent, align with findings from previous studies of children's test behaviors, and are similar to established dimensions for evaluating children's adjustment and well-being in other contexts (cf. Achenbach & Edlebrock, 1983; Quay, 1986).

THREE SECONDARY FACTORS

Avoidance

The first pattern found in the GATSB is directly related to task aversion and fearfulness. Therefore, the term *Avoidance* was selected to refer to these qualities. Strong conceptual links exist between this factor and a major constellation of behaviors children display both in home and school environments. The factor is similar to one labeled Anxiety Withdrawal by Quay (1986) and Internalizing by Achenbach and Edelbrock (1983). Eleven items load on the Avoidance domain. This factor captures the lion's share of the total variance (49%) and suggests that children's task engagement and/or avoidance are likely to have the largest impact on their obtained intelligence and achievement test scores.

Uncooperative Mood

The second GATSB factor, Uncooperative Mood, consists of eight items. It accounts for 11% of the total item variance on the GATSB and reflects children's improper initial adjustment, lack of cooperation, and/or need for praise and encouragement during the examination session. Thus, the second factor appears to measure behaviors more specific to test sessions than the first factor.

Inattentiveness

The third and smallest factor, Inattentiveness, consists of 10 items and accounts for about 8% of the total variance. This factor is characterized by inadequate impulse control and attending behaviors. It, like the Avoidance factor, is associated with other overarching dimensions of child behavior. In the contexts of home and school, this factor is similar to one labeled Conduct Disorder by Quay (1986) and Externalizing by Achenbach and Edelbrock (1983).

CRITERION-RELATED VALIDITY

A substantial number of criterion-related validity studies are presented in the GATSB manual, including bivariate correlation analyses, canonical correlation analyses, and discriminant function analyses. However, other studies were needed. Since the publication of GATSB, researchers have used it to investigate whether children's test behaviors are affected by criterion-related bias (Glutting, Oakland, & Konold, 1994), item bias (Nandakumar, Glutting, & Oakland, 1993), and factor bias (Konold, Glutting, Oakland, & O'Donnell, 1995). The criterion-related validity of the GATSB also has been examined for children with attention deficit–hyperactivity disorders (Glutting, Robins, & deLancy, 1997), and for samples of both normal and referred children (Glutting *et al.*, 1996).

Findings from the previously cited investigations strongly attest to the GATSB's validity for use with children who differ by age, gender, race, and ethnicity. The correlation between the GATSB Total Score and the WISC-III Full Scale IQ for children generally is substantial: –.36. This correlation is –.28 for Anglos, –.37 for African-Americans, and –.55 for Hispanics. Thus, for children generally, approximately 13% of the variance associated with Full Scale scores may be attributable to their test-taking behaviors. The amount of variances attributable to test-taking behaviors is 14% for African-American children and 30% for Hispanic children. Among the three factors, Avoidance accounts for the plurality of the variance.

The correlation between the GATSB Total Score and the WIAT Total Composite score again is substantial: –.38. Thus, approximately 14% of the variance associated with the measurement of achievement may be attributable to their test-taking behaviors. Correlations between the GATSB Total Score and the four WIAT Composites scores are similar.

Perhaps the most interesting finding from these studies is that children with inappropriate test behaviors, as measured by the GATSB, obtain WISC-III Full Scale IQs anywhere from 7 to 10 points lower than children with more suitable test behaviors. Effect sizes this large (more than half of a standard deviation) represent a substantial difference in IQs and testifies to the importance of observing peripheral test behaviors as a means of validating the integrity of formal scores obtained on standardized tests of intelligence and achievement.

RECENT CRITERION-RELATED FINDINGS

The intrasession and exosession validity of the GATSB was reexamined using new data. Data were obtained in 1995 and 2003 on 224 children and adolescents (67% males) who ranged in age from 6 years, 0 months through 16 years, 11 months (M = 10.7 years, SD = 2.5 years). Participants were public school students from 34 school districts.

The sample was heterogeneous with respect to race and ethnicity. Although 27% attended regular education, the majority were eligible for special education: 48% were identified as having a learning disability, 11% with mental retardation, 8% with a serious emotional disturbance, 2% with an attention deficit disorder, and the remaining 5% with other impairments. Examiner characteristics were recorded as well (N = 34). Postgraduate experience among the 34 examiners ranged from 7 to 21 years (M = 12.7 years, SD = 7.1 years).

Standardized scales were used as validity criteria. Intrasession validity was assessed through WISC-III Full Scale IQs (FSIQ), Verbal Scale IQs (VIQ), and Performance Scale IQs (PIQ). Exosession validity (i.e., the generalizability of observations from the test session to other settings) was evaluated through teacher ratings on the *Adjustment Scales for Children and Adolescents* (ASCA; McDermott, Marston, & Stott, 1993). The ASCA has six core scales: Attention Deficit–Hyperactivity, Solitary Aggressive (Provocative), Solitary Aggressive (Impulsive), Oppositional Defiant, Diffident, and Avoidant. The ASCA also yields two overall dimensions: Overreactivity (obtained by adding item scores from the first four core scales) and Underreactivity (based on item scores from the last two core scales). All eight ASCA scores were used as criteria.

Table 14.1 shows statistics for the GATSB predictors and criteria. Means for the GATSB predictors were near their population expectancy. Alternatively, means for the WISC-III criteria were below their population averages, while means for the Overreactivity, Attention Deficit–Hyperactivity, and Oppositional Defiant were elevated (i.e., suggesting more problem behaviors). These departures were anticipated given that the majority of the sample was eligible for special education services. The departures also are comparable to levels reported for a referral cohort during an earlier investigation of the GATSB (Glutting *et al.*, 1996).

Correlations between the GATSB Total Score and FSIQs, VIQs, and PIQs are similar and significant ($p < .001$): $-.29$, $-.26$, and $-.29$, respectively (Table 14.2). Scores from the GATSB's Avoidance scale are more predictive than those from the Inattentiveness and Uncooperative Mood scales. The correlations between the GATSB Total Score and IQs are somewhat lower than that found when norming the GATSB (i.e., the correlation between the GATSB Total Score and the WISC-III Full Scale IQ was $-.36$). The somewhat lower correlations may be due to this sample being smaller and unrepresentative of children nationally.

Whether test-taking behaviors impact intelligence test scores constitutes the more practical and important question. This question was examined by dividing children according to whether they exhibited compliant or non-

TABLE 14.1   Distributional Statistics of GATSB Predictors and IQ, Achievement, and Behavioral Criteria

	M	SD
GATSB Predictor		
Total Score	52.0	8.5
Avoidance	52.8	9.8
Inattentiveness	51.0	8.5
Uncooperative Mood	50.5	7.4
WISC-III Criteria		
Full Scale IQ	86.1	18.3
Verbal Scale IQ	84.8	18.1
Performance Scale IQ	90.0	18.2
ASCA Criteria		
Underreactivity	52.7	12.2
Overreactivity	57.8	12.6
Avoidant	52.0	12.9
Diffident	50.6	12.9
Solitary Aggressive–Provocative	53.5	13.8
Solitary Aggressive–Impulsive	53.8	13.1
Attention Deficit–Hyperactivity	56.8	12.4
Oppositional Defiant	55.6	16.3

Note: $N = 224$.

TABLE 14.2   Correlations of GATSB Predictors and WISC-III Criteria

	GATSB Predictor			
	Total Score	Avoidance	Inattentiveness	Uncooperative Mood
WISC-III Criteria				
FSIQ	$-.29^a$	$-.41^a$	$-.10$	$-.13^b$
VIQ	$-.26^a$	$-.37^a$	$-.08$	$-.12$
PIQ	$-.29^a$	$-.41^a$	$-.09$	$-.12$

Note: FSIQ = Full Scale IQ, VIQ = Verbal Scale IQ, PIQ = Performance Scale IQ, $N = 224$.
[a] $p < .001$.
[b] $p < .05$.

compliant test behaviors during administrations of the WISC-III (Table 14.3). The former group had GATSB Total Scores in the average range (i.e., T scores < 59), while the latter group had GATSB Total Scores 1 standard deviation or more above the mean (i.e., T scores > 60). In contrast to children with compliant test behaviors, those who did not demonstrate compliance averaged 8.6 points lower FSIQs, 7.2 points lower VIQs, and 9.5 points lower PIQs. Thus, children with compliant test behavior obtain FSIQs, VIQs, and PIQs 0.5 to .66 of a standard deviation higher than children with less suitable test behaviors.

These data confirm that children's test-taking behaviors are meaningfully related to the magnitude of their measured intelligence. Current findings generally are consistent with earlier findings and support the conclusion that test observations are modestly yet meaningfully related to children's IQs.

The GATSB and ASCA evaluate similar constructs albeit displayed in different contexts. The GATSB assesses behaviors displayed in the context of testing while the ASCA assesses behaviors displayed in the context of school. Construct validity is suggested when an appropriate pattern of convergent and divergent associations is found between similar tests (Campbell, 1960; Thorndike, 1982). Higher correlations were expected between identical or convergent scales from the two tests (e.g., GATSB Avoidance and ASCA Avoidance) and lower correlations were expected between divergent scales (e.g., GATSB Avoidance and ASCA Attention Deficit–Hyperactivity). As expected, the anticipated convergent associations were collectively higher than divergent associations and support inferences of the GATSB's construct validity (Table 14.4). Thus, behaviors observed in test sessions are more related to behaviors in the same than in other contexts.

The averaged coefficient between the GATSB and ASCA provides evidence of the degree test behaviors are generalizable across contexts to situations important to child adjustment, namely their behavior in school.

TABLE 14.3　Differences in WISC-III Scores for Children Showing Compliant and Noncompliant Test Behaviors

Variable	Group	Mean	t-value	p
FSIQ	Compliant (n = 182)	87.7	2.81	.005
	Noncompliant (n = 42)	79.1		
VIQ	Compliant (n = 182)	86.2	2.35	.02
	Noncompliant (n = 42)	79.0		
PIQ	Compliant (n = 182)	91.7	3.09	.002
	Noncompliant (n = 42)	82.2		

Note: FSIQ = Full Scale IQ, VIQ = Verbal Scale IQ, PIQ = Performance Scale IQ, N = 224.

TABLE 14.4   Correlations of GATSB Predictors and ASCA

| ASCA Criteria | GATSB Predictor | | | |
	Total Score	Avoidance	Inattentiveness	Uncooperative Mood
Underreactivity	.24[a]	.38[a]	.07	.04
Overreactivity	.18[b]	.07	.22[b]	.18[b]
Avoidant	.17[c]	.23[a]	.10	.03
Diffident	.12	.28[a]	−.04	−.01
Solitary Aggressive–Provocative	.15[c]	.09	.19[b]	.15[c]
Solitary Aggressive–Impulsive	.21[a]	.09	.29[a]	.21[a]
Attention Deficit–Hyperactivity	.18[b]	.05	.23[a]	.21[a]
Oppositional Defiant	.07	.08	.09	.01

Note: $N = 224$.
[a] $p < .001$.***
[b] $p < .01$.
[c] $p < .05$.

The averaged coefficient among correlations between the GATSB and ASCA is low ($r = .14$) and lower than the average correlations between GATSB Total Score and FS, V, and P IQs ($r = .28$). Furthermore, the averaged exosession validity coefficient of .14 suggests that up to 98% of the variation in test behaviors is unaccounted by in-school behaviors measured by the ASCA.

The belief that behaviors psychologists observe while testing may not generalize well to behaviors reported by teachers and parents also is supported by finding for 122 children ages 6 through 16 referred for a psychological evaluation (Daleiden, Brabman, & Benton, 2002). The GATSB correlated moderately with the WISC-III and Woodcock-Johnson Psychoeducational Battery—Revised and the Wide Range Assessment of Memory and Learning and correlated considerably lower with reports from parents and teachers on the Child Behavior Checklist. The conclusion that most of the variation in test behaviors may be specific to the context in which they occur seems reasonable. However, clinicians are advised to confer with teachers, parents, and other significant sources to determine the generalizability of findings from measures of test-taking abilities to broader contexts on a case-by-case basis. Moreover, knowledge of behaviors displayed at school and home is essential when interpreting GATSB data.

POSSIBLE USES OF TEST BEHAVIOR INFORMATION

Accomplished examiners typically rely heavily on their observations to assist them in various components of the assessment process. As previously noted, this information assists them in understanding the processes used by children in arriving at their responses, in screening important qualities not measured directly by the test, in discussing the child's qualities intelligibly in conferences with parents and teachers, and in making needed modifications in how the test is administered. Knowledge of test behaviors also enables examiners to decide whether the test results accurately reflect the child's cognitive abilities.

A RETURN TO TWO-TEST PERFORMANCE STANDARDS

One of two standards typically is used when evaluating whether the test data are considered to be valid: *optimal* and *typical* performance. Examiners often differ in their views as to which should be used.

OPTIMAL PERFORMANCE

Examiners favoring optimal performance strive to create conditions that facilitate the examinee's highest performance (for tests of ability) or most representative performance (for tests of personality and social skills) as the standard for test performance. Test behaviors that negatively influence test performance and thus attenuate or in other ways distort scores are thought to be inappropriate. Those who employ optimal performance standards generally believe test scores from examinees who display unmotivated, uncooperative, and inattentive test behaviors are invalid and thus should be discarded.

TYPICAL PERFORMANCE

Examiners favoring typical performance standards also are likely to interpret these test behaviors as being inappropriate and negatively influencing test performance. However, when assessing children whose unsuitable test-session behaviors are similar to those displayed at home and school, those using typical performance standards are likely to interpret aberrant test-taking behaviors as reflecting broader personal traits and thus will accept the test results as being valid, given their belief that the deleterious behaviors observed during the test also are likely to negatively influence the examinee's general behaviors. Thus, the results from cognitive tests are thought to reflect real-life conditions and are valid. In contrast, those who adhere to an optimal performance standard are more inclined to reject the data as being invalid.

A CASE STUDY

The following case study, taken from the GATSB manual, demonstrates how the GATSB data may be used to facilitate the assessment of cognitive abilities.

Anne, a 13-year-old middle-school student, was seen for testing and a clinical interview on one occasion, from 8:30 to 11:45 AM. She was suitably dressed and groomed, wearing tennis shoes, modest jewelry, and a matching skirt and blouse. Her short hair was clean and informally styled. Anne is of average height and somewhat overweight. School records indicate normal visual and auditory acuity, and her primary and only language is English. School attendance is regular. Anne indicated an absence of medical problems; moreover, no problems were apparent in her fine- and gross-motor coordination skills and in her linguistic proficiency. Anne had been informed about and was fully oriented to the testing; however, she expressed concern about being tested. As indicated in the following GATSB results, her test-taking behaviors, assessed after administration of the WISC were problematic.

	T Scores	Confidence Interval Magnitude (68% Level)	Cumulative Percentile Rank
Total Score	74	± 2.83	96.8
Avoidance Scale	76	± 3.74	97.4
Inattentiveness Scale	84	± 4.80	98.7
Uncooperative Mood Scale	59	± 3.46	85.8

Anne's Total Score T score of 74 reflects an atypical pattern of test session behavior. This atypical pattern is also reflected in the highly elevated scores on the Avoidance (T score = 76) and Inattentiveness (T score = 84) scales. The highly elevated Avoidance score reflects Anne's inability to remember test directions, her lack of eye contact with the examiner, her frequent requests to take a break, and a deterioration in performance during the last three WISC subtests that was a result of her withdrawal.

Anne's highly elevated score on the Inattentiveness scale reflects her difficulty in completing work within time limits and her failure to attend to test directions. It also reflects her increasing restlessness during the test session and the deterioration in her efforts toward the end of the session.

Discussions with Anne's English teacher and counselor after the testing confirmed the presence of the inappropriate behaviors in class. Thus, there is

some indication that the behaviors observed during the WISC-III administration are transituational. The examiner conducting this evaluation uses
optimal performance as a standard. Consequently, Anne's WISC results are
not reported. The examiner will confer with Anne's parents and Anne to
discuss the extent to which these and similar behaviors may be displayed at
home. After these conferences the examiner will work with Anne to minimize
any adverse effects avoidance and inattentive behaviors have on a second
administration of the WISC.

CONCLUSION

Progress is being made in our ability to carefully observe and understand
the relevance of test-taking behaviors of children and youth. Research
during the last two decades has helped define the nature of important test-
taking behaviors, to measure them reliably, and to understand their degree
of impact on measures of cognitive abilities. Most recently developed individually administered tests of cognitive abilities include methods to assess
test-taking abilities—albeit using methods that lack norms and demonstrated empirical validity. Continued progress in improving the use of
these observational abilities requires added emphasis in two areas: instruction and research.

In reference to instruction, most clinicians have little formal study on
issues important to observing, recording, and interpreting test-taking behaviors. As a result, clinicians generally rely on time-honored but untested
informal methods when recording and interpreting test-taking behaviors.
Our profession now has available a new and growing body of information
that leads to the conclusion that the use of standardized and norm-
referenced measures of test-taking behaviors can significantly enhance
assessment. Professors teaching assessment courses should include this content when preparing student clinicians. Established professionals should
become acquainted with this content in other ways.

Research on test-taking behaviors began about 20 years ago and thus is in
its infancy. Additional research is needed to help verify the full range of
behaviors that may characterize test-taking behaviors, to fully define this
construct, and to continue investigations as to possible demographic differences in these qualities. Relationships between measures of test-taking behaviors (e.g., the GATSB) and performance on measures other than the WISC
and WIAT are greatly needed. We concur with the Kaufmans (1994) that
information from the GATSB may be relevant to the understanding of a wide
range of measures. These may include the *Clinical Evaluation of Language
Functions-Third Edition* (Semel, Wiig, & Secord 1995), *Differential Abilities
Scale* (Elliott, 1995), *Kaufman Assessment Battery for Children* (Kaufman &
Kaufman, 1985), *Stanford-Binet Intelligence Scale: Fifth Edition* (Roid, 2003),

Woodcock-Johnson Tests of Cognitive Abilities (Woodcock, McGrew, & Mather, 2001), and various other individually administered measures. In addition, the assets and limitations of test behaviors to our understanding of noncognitive qualities (e.g., personality and temperament) deserve further study.

REFERENCES

Achenbach, T. M., & Edelbrock, C. (1983). *Manual for the child behavior profile.* Burlington, CT: University of Vermont, Department of Psychiatry.

Achenbach, T. M., McConaughty, S. H., & Howell, C. T. (1987). Child/adolescent behavioral and emotional problems: Implications of cross-informant correlations for situational specificity. *Psychological Bulletin, 101,* 213-232.

American Educational Research Association (1999). *Standards for education and psychological testing.* Washington, DC: Author.

Aylward, G. P., & MacGruder, R. W. (1986). *Test behavior checklist.* Brandon, VT: Clinical Psychology Publishing.

Bracken, B. A. (1991). The clinical observation of preschool assessment behavior. In B. A. Bracken (Ed.), *The psychoeducational assessment of preschool children* (2nd. ed.) (pp. 40-52). Boston: Allyn and Bacon.

Caldwell, B. M. (1951). Test behavior observation guide. In R. Watson, *The clinical method in psychology* (pp. 67-71). New York: Harper & Brothers.

Campbell, D. T. (1960). Recommendation for APA test standards regarding construct, trait, or discriminant validity. *American Psychologist, 15,* 546-555.

Cronbach, L. J. (1951). Coefficient alpha and the internal structure of tests. *Psychometrika, 16,* 297-334.

Cronbach, L. J., & Meehl, P. E. (1955). Construct validity in psychological tests. *Psychological Bulletin, 52,* 281-302.

Culbertson, J., & Willis, D. (Eds.) (1993). *Testing young children* (pp. 41, 101-127, 319, 326, 353, 356, & 358). Austin, TX: Pro-ed.

Daleiden, E., Drabman, R. S., & Benton, J. (2002). The guide to the assessment of test session behavior: Validity in relation to cognitive testing and parent-reported behavior problems in a clinical sample. *Journal of Clinical Child Psychology, 31,* 263-271.

Elliott, C. (1995). *Differential abilities scale.* San Antonio, TX: The Psychological Corporation.

Epps, S. (1988). Best practices in behavioral observations. In A. Thomas & J. Grimes (Eds.), *Best practices in school psychology* (pp. 95-112). Washington, DC: National Association of School Psychologists.

Glutting, J. J. (1986). The McDermott Multidimensional Assessment of Children: Applications to the classification of childhood exceptionality. *Journal of Learning Disabilities, 19,* 331-335.

Glutting, J. J., & McDermott, P. A. (1988). Generality of test session observations to kindergartners' classroom behavior. *Journal of Abnormal Child Psychology, 16,* 527-537.

Glutting, J. J., & Oakland, T. (1993). *GATSB: Guide to the Assessment of Test Session Behavior for the WISC-III and WIAT.* San Antonio, TX: The Psychological Corporation.

Glutting, J. J., Oakland, T., & Konold, T. R. (1994). Criterion-related bias with the Guide to the Assessment of Test-Session Behavior for the WISC-III and WIAT: Possible race, gender, and SES effects. *Journal of School Psychology, 32,* 355-369.

Glutting, J. J., Oakland, T., & McDermott, P. A. (1989). Observing child behavior during testing: Constructs, validity, and situational generality. *Journal of School Psychology, 27,* 155-164.

Glutting, J. J., Robins, P. M., & de Lancey, E. (1997). Validity of test observations for children with attention-deficit/hyperactivity disorder. *Journal of School Psychology, 35*, 391-401.

Glutting, J. J., Youngstrom, E. A., Oakland, T., & Watkins, M. W. (1996). Situational specificity of generality of test behaviors for samples of normal and referred children. *School Psychology Review, 25,* 64-107.

Gregory, R. (1992). *Psychological testing* (pp. 37, 58, 64, 66, 342, 515, 519, & 615-618) Boston: Allyn and Bacon.

Hunter, J. E., Schmidt, F. L., & Jackson, G. B. (1982). *Meta-analysis: Cumulating research findings across studies.* Beverly Hills, CA: Sage.

Jensen, R. (1980). *Bias in mental testing* (pp. 269, 284-285, 589-590, & 615-618) New York. The Free Press.

Kamphaus, R. W. (2001). *Clinical assessment of child and adolescent intelligence.* Boston: Allyn and Bacon.

Kamphaus, R., & Reynolds, C. (1987). *Clinical and research applications of the K-ABC* (pp. 74, 120, & 124). Circle Pines, Minnesota. American Guidance Service.

Kaufman, A. A. (1990). *Assessing adolescent and adult intelligence* (pp. 360, 362, & 367). Boston: Allyn and Bacon.

Kaufman, A. S. (1994). *Intelligent testing with the WISC-III.* New York: John Wiley & Sons, Inc. (pp. 9 & 91).

Kaufman, A. S., Kaufman, N. L., Dougherty, E. H., & Tuttle, K. S. C. (1994). *Kaufman Integrated Interpretive System Checklist for Behaviors Observed During Administration of WISC-III Subtests.* Odessa, FL: Psychological Assessment Resources.

Kaufman, A., & Kaufman, N. (1985). *Kaufman Assessment Battery for Children.* Circle Pines, MN: American Guidance Services

Kaufman, N., & Kaufman, A. (1993). GATSB: Guide to the Assessment of Test Session Behavior for the WISC-III and the WIAT. *Journal of Psychoeducational Assessment, 13,* 318-325.

Konold, T. R., Glutting, J. J., Oakland, T., & O'Donnell, L. (1995). Congruence of test-behavior dimensions among child groups varying in gender, race-ethnicity, and SES. *Journal of Psychoeducational Assessment, 13,* 111-119.

McConaughy, S., & Achenbach, T. (2004). Test Behavior Observation Form. http://www.aseba.org/products/TOF.htm.

McDermott, P. A. (1986). The observation and classification of exceptional child behavior. In R. T. Brown & C. R. Reynolds (Eds.), *Psychological perspectives on childhood exceptionality: A handbook* (pp. 136-180). New York: Wiley Interscience.

McDermott, P. A., Marston, N. C., & Stott, D. H. (1993). Adjustment scales for children and adolescents. Philadelphia: Edumetric and Clinical Science.

McDermott, P. A., & Watkins, M. A. (1985). *Microcomputer systems manual for McDermott Multidimensional Assessment of Children.* New York: The Psychological Corporation.

Nandakumar, R., Glutting, J. J., & Oakland, T. (1993). Mantel-Haenszel methodology for detecting item bias: An introduction and example using the Guide to the Assessment of Test Session Behavior. *Journal of Psychoeducational Assessment, 11,* 108-119.

Neisser, U. (1991). A case for misplaced nostalgia. *American Psychologist, 46,* 34-36.

Oakland, T., Glutting, J. J., & Horton, C. B. (1996). *Student Styles Questionnaire: Star qualities in learning, relating, and working.* San Antonio, TX: The Psychological Corporation.

Palmer, J. (1983). *The psychological assessment of children.* (pp. 177-186, 214-245, 262, & 500-514). New York: John Wiley & Sons, Inc.

Pitoniak, M. J., & Royer, J. M. (2001). Testing accommodations for examinees with disabilities: A review of psychometric, legal, and social policy issues. *Review of Educational Research, 71,* 53-104.

Quay, H. C. (1986). Classification. In H. C. Quay & J. S. Werry (Eds.), *Psychopathological disorders of childhood* (3rd ed.) (pp. 1-34). New York: Wiley.

Reynolds, C. R., & Kamphaus, R. (Eds.) (1990a). *Handbook of psychological and educational assessment of children: Personality, behavior, and context.* New York: Guilford Press.

Reynolds, C. R., & Kamphaus, R. (Eds.) (1990b). *Handbook of psychological and educational assessment of children: Intelligence and Achievement* (pp. 160-161). New York: Guilford Press.

Roid, G. H., & Miller, L. (2000). Leiter International Performance Scale Revised. (Leiter R). Lutz, FL: Psychological Assessment Resources

Roid, G. H. (2003). *Stanford-Binet Intelligence Scales* (ed. 5). Itasca, IL: Riverside Publishing.

Rosenthal, R. (1991). *Meta-analytic procedures for social research.* Newbury Park, CA: Sage.

Salvia, J., & Ysseldyke, J. (1988). *Assessment* (pp. 15, 119). Boston: Houghton Mifflin Company. Sattler, J. M. (1988). *Assessment of children* (pp. 86, 89-91, 93, 95, 97, 99, 105-106, 472-530, 581, 618, & 625). San Diego, CA: Jerome M. Sattler, Publisher.

Sattler, J. M. (2001). *Assessment of children: Cognitive applications.* San Diego, CA: Jerome M. Sattler, Publisher.

Schrank, F. A., & Read, B.G. (2002). Test session observations and qualitative analysis of performance on the WJ III. Unpublished document: authors.

Schutz, P. A., & Davis, H. (2000). Emotions and self-regulation during test taking. *Educational Psychologist, 35,* 243-256.

Semel, E., Wiig, E., & Secord, H (1995). *Clinical Evaluation of Language Functions-Third Edition.* San Antonio, TX: The Psychological Corporation.

Simeonsson, R. (1996). *Psychological and developmental assessment of children* (pp. 32, 39, 42, 88, 257, & 313). Newton, MA: Allyn and Bacon, Inc.

Terman, L. M., & Merrill, M. A. (1960). *Stanford-Binet Intelligence Scale: Manual for the third revision. Form L-M.* Boston: Houghton Mifflin.

Thorndike, R. L. (1982). *Applied psychometrics.* Boston: Houghton Mifflin.

Thorndike, R. L, Hagen, E. P., & Sattler, J. M. (1986). *Guide for administering and scoring the Stanford-Binet Intelligence Scale: Fourth Edition.* Chicago: Riverside.

Wechsler, D. (1992). *Wechsler Individual Achievement Test.* San Antonio, TX: The Psychological Corporation.

Wechsler, D. (1991). *Wechsler Intelligence Scale for Children: Third edition.* San Antonio, TX: The Psychological Corporation.

Wechsler, D. (2003). *Wechsler Intelligence Scale for Children: Fourth edition.* San Antonio, TX: The Psychological Corporation.

Woodcock, R. W., McGrew, K. S., & Mather, N. (2001). *Woodcock-Johnson Tests of Cognitive Abilities.* Itasca, IL: Riverside Publishing.

AUTHOR INDEX

References in *italics* denote main citation(s).

Fry, A. F., 86, *88*, 424, *432*
Fry, E., 221, *231*
Fuchs, D., 335, *348*
Fulbright, R. K., 13, *31*, 193, 228, *232*
Fuller, F., 157, *183*, 196, *230*
Fuller, S., 207, *230*

G
Gagné, F., 282, *297*
Gaither, R. A., 85, *89*
Gallagher, J. J., 305, *330*
Gallagher, R. E., 415–416, *432*
Galloway, L. M., 396, *411*
Gardner, H., 282, *297*, 385, *411*
Garfinkel, B., 237, *274*
Garwan, C., 153, *185*, 208, *233*
Gathercole, S., 207, *229*
Gayan, J., 153, *184*
Geisinger, K. F., *373*
Geldmacher, D. S., 423, *432*
Genshaft, J. L., *30*, *149*
Georgas, J., 7, 21, *29*, 34, 60, *62*, 306, *329*,
    385–386, *411*, 419, *432*
German, D. J., 339–340, *348*
Geurts, H., *278*
Gilberg, C., 246, *276*
Gioia, G. A., 428, *432*
Glutting, J. J., 16, *30*, 317–318, *329–330*,
    419–420, *432*, *434*, 436, 439–440,
    444–445, 447–448, 450–451, 453–454,
    461–462
Godfrey, H. P. D., *63*, 66
Gold, J. M., 306, *329*
Goldberg, M. C., 246, *275*
Goldstein, H. S., 248, *272*
Goldstein, S., *276*
Gong, Y., 358, *374*
Goodyer, I. M., *280*
Gore, J. C., 13, *31*, 193, 228, *232*
Gorsuch, R. L., 7, *31*, 43, *64*, 306, *330*
Gottfredson, L. S., 38, *62*, 104
Graf, P., *232*
Graham, S., 157, 165, *183–184*, *230*
Grainger, J., 250, *277*
Grant, I., 391, *411*
Greblo, P., 419, *433*
Green, P., 193, *232*
Greenawalt, C. G., 286, *298*
Greenblatt, E., 190, *231*
Greenhill, L., 237, *274*
Greenway, P., 418, *432*
Gregory, R., 440, 443, *462*

Grice, J. W., 7, *29*, 306, *329*
Gridley, B. E., 48, *62*
Grigorenko, E. L., 385, *413*, 420, *433*
Grimes, B. F., 384, *411*
Grimes, J. E., 384, *411*
Grimes, J. P., 362, *373*, *375*
Grossman, H. J., 303, *329*
Groth-Marnat, G., 15, *31*, 415–416, *432*
Guevremont, D. C., *270*
Gundelfinger, R., *279*
Gunter, T., 207, *231*
Gureasko, M., 259, *269*
Gureasko-Moore, D. P., 259, *269*
Gurland, S. T., 284, *298*
Gustason, G., 353, *373*
Gutierrez, J. E., 248, *277*
Gutkin, T. B., *30*
Guy, S. C., 428, *432*

H
Hagelthorn, K. M., *275*
Hagen, E. P., 195, *233*, 247, *279*, 286,
    297–298, 445, 447, *463*
Haith, M. M., 85, *88*, 193, *232*
Hakuta, K., 392, *411*
Hale, G. A., *272*
Hale, J. B., 12, 16, 23, *29*, 85, *88–89*, 206, *231*,
    415–416, *432*
Hale, R. L., *329*
Hale, S., 424, *432*
Hall, J., 419, *433*
Hallahan, D., 151, *184–185*
Halligan, P. W., 423, *432*
Halpern, D. F., 21, 24, *30*, 37, *63*, 385, *412*
Hamers, J. F., 392, *411*
Hamilton, N., 389, *411*
Hammeke, T., 207, *230*
Handler, M. W., 258, 260, *273*
Hannah, J. M., 357, *373*
Hardy-Braz, S. T., 356–357, 363, 369, *373*,
    375
Hargung, C. M., *273*
Harrington, R. G., 284, *297*
Harris, J. G., 22, *29*, 36, 59, *62*, 394, 408, *411*
Harris, K., *230*
Harris, L., 333–334, 336, *348*
Harris, S. M., 237, *275*
Harrison, P. L., *30*, 47, *62*, *149*, 284–285, 291,
    297, 304, 313, *329*
Hart, E. L., 237, *274*
Hart, T., 151, *183*, 190, 228, *230*
Hartdagen, S., 237, *274*

Subject Index